SEVENTH EDITION

A
WORLD OF
IDEAS

ESSENTIAL READINGS
FOR
COLLEGE WRITERS

LEE A. JACOBUS

University of Connecticut

BEDFORD/ST. MARTINS
Boston ◆ *New York*

For Bedford/St. Martin's

Developmental Editor: Gregory S. Johnson
Senior Production Editor: Michael Weber
Production Supervisor: Christopher Logan Gross
Senior Marketing Manager: Rachel Falk
Art Direction and Cover Design: Lucy Krikorian
Text Design: Anna Palchik
Copy Editor: Virginia Rubens
Photo Research: Linda Finigan
Cover Art: © Frank L. Edwards / SPL / Photonica
Composition: Macmillan India Inc.
Printing and Binding: Haddon Craftsmen,
    an R.R. Donnelley & Sons Company

President: Joan E. Feinberg
Editorial Director: Denise B. Wydra
Editor in Chief: Nancy Perry
Director of Marketing: Karen Melton Soeltz
Director of Editing, Design, and Production: Marcia Cohen
Managing Editor: Erica T. Appel

Library of Congress Control Number: 2005922466

For information, write: Bedford/St. Martin's, 75 Arlington Street, Boston, MA 02116   (617-399-4000)

ISBN: 0-312-43444-8
EAN: 978-0-312-43444-1

Acknowledgments

PREFACE

Among the pleasures of editing *A World of Ideas* are the discussions I have had over the years with students and teachers who have used the book in their writing classes. Recently, a student wrote to tell me that the book meant a great deal to her and that her experience with it impelled her to wonder what originally inspired me to assemble the first edition. I explained that my teaching of first-year writing has always inclined toward ideas that serious writers and thinkers have explored and contemplated throughout the ages; early on, I could not find a composition reader that introduced students to the important thinkers whose writing I believe should be basic to everyone's education. As a result of that need, *A World of Ideas* took shape and has continued to grow and develop through seven editions, attracting a wide audience of teachers and students who value the thought-provoking ideas that affect the way we interpret the world.

In preparing the seventh edition of *A World of Ideas*, I have benefited, as usual, from the suggestions of hundreds of users of earlier editions. The primary concern of both teachers and students is that the book remain centered on the tradition of important ideas and on the writers whose work has had a lasting influence on society. To that end, I have chosen writers whose ideas are central to our most important and lasting concerns. A new edition offers the opportunity to reevaluate old choices and make new ones that expand and deepen what has always been the fundamental purpose of this composition reader: to provide college students in first-year writing courses with a representative sampling of important ideas examined by men and women who have shaped the way we think today.

The selections in this volume are of the highest quality. Each was chosen because it clarifies important ideas and can sustain discussion and stimulate good writing. Unlike most composition readers, *A World of Ideas* presents substantial excerpts from the work of each of its authors. The selections are presented as they originally appeared; only rarely are they edited and marked with ellipses. They average fifteen pages in length, and their arguments are presented completely as the authors wrote them. Developing a serious idea in writing takes time and a willingness to experiment. Most students are willing to read deeply into the work of important thinkers to grasp their ideas better because the knowledge yielded by the effort is so vast and rewarding.

A Text for Readers and Writers

Because students perceive writers such as Plato and Thoreau as serious and important, they take the writing course more seriously: they learn to read more attentively, think more critically, and write more effectively. But more important, this may be a student's only opportunity to encounter the thinkers whose ideas have shaped civilization. No other composition reader offers such a comparable collection of important readings along with the supportive apparatus students need to understand, analyze, and respond to them.

Classic Readings. *A World of Ideas* draws its forty-six selections from the writing of some of the world's most important thinkers. Those writers with selections that remain from the sixth edition are Lao-tzu, Niccolò Machiavelli, Jean-Jacques Rousseau, Thomas Jefferson, Henry David Thoreau, Elizabeth Cady Stanton, Martin Luther King Jr., Frederick Douglass, Adam Smith, Karl Marx, John Kenneth Galbraith, Robert B. Reich, Plato, Carl Jung, Howard Gardner, Francis Bacon, Charles Darwin, Stephen J. Gould, Michio Kaku, St. Matthew, Mary Wollstonecraft, Virginia Woolf, Simone de Beauvoir, and Carol Gilligan.

A Focus on Eight Great Ideas. *A World of Ideas'* unique structure highlights seminal ideas as developed by great thinkers throughout history and facilitates cross-disciplinary comparisons. Each of the eight parts of the book focuses on one great idea — government, justice, education, wealth and poverty, mind, nature, ethics and morality, and feminism. Part introductions ground students in the history of each idea and connect the philosophies of individual writers.

"Evaluating Ideas: An Introduction to Critical Reading." This introduction demonstrates a range of methods students can adopt to participate in a meaningful dialogue with each selection. This dialogue — an active, questioning approach to texts and ideas — is one

of the keys to critical reading. In the introduction, a portion of Machiavelli's "The Qualities of the Prince" is presented in annotated form, and the annotations are discussed for their usefulness in understanding this essay and in helping students develop their own annotations while reading the other essays in the book. The introduction encourages students to mark what they think are the most interesting and important ideas in an essay and highlight or underline all sentences that they might want to quote in an essay of their own.

Selection Headnotes. Each selection is preceded by a detailed headnote on the author's life and work and by comments about the primary ideas presented in the reading. The most interesting rhetorical aspects of the selection are identified and discussed to help students see how rhetorical techniques can achieve specific effects.

Prereading Questions. To emphasize critical thinking, reading, and writing, prereading questions precede every selection. The content of the selections is challenging, and these prereading questions can help students in first-year writing courses overcome minor difficulties in understanding the author's meaning. These brief questions are designed to help students focus on central issues during their first reading of each selection.

Extensive Apparatus. At the end of each selection is a group of discussion questions designed for use inside or outside the classroom. "Questions for Critical Reading" focus on key issues and ideas and can be used to stimulate general class discussion and critical thinking. "Suggestions for Writing" help students practice some of the rhetorical strategies employed by the author of a given selection. These suggestions ask for personal responses, as well as complete essays that involve research. A number of these assignments, labeled "Connections," promote critical reading by requiring students to connect particular passages in a selection with a selection by another writer, either in the same part of the book or in another part. The variety of connections is intriguing — Lao-tzu with Machiavelli, Rawls with Rousseau, Freire with Arendt, Smith with Jefferson, Klein with de Beauvoir and Gilligan, Carson with Darwin, the Dalai Lama with Nietzsche, hooks with Wollstonecraft and Woolf, and many more.

"Writing about Ideas: An Introduction to Rhetoric." This appendix explains how a reader can make annotations while reading critically and then use those annotations to write effectively in response to the ideas presented in any selection in the book. The appendix relies on the annotations of the Machiavelli selection illustrated in "Evaluating

Ideas: An Introduction to Critical reading." A sample student essay on Machiavelli, using all the techniques taught in the context of reading and writing, gives students a model for writing their own material. In addition, this section helps students understand how they can apply some of the basic rhetorical principles discussed throughout the book.

Instructor's Resource Manual.   I have prepared an extensive manual, *Resources for Teaching A WORLD OF IDEAS*, that contains further background on the selections, examples from my own classroom responses to the selections, and more suggestions for classroom discussion and student writing assignments. Sentence outlines for the selections—which have been carefully prepared by Michael Hennessy, Carol Verberg, Ellen Troutman, and Ellen Darion—can be photocopied or downloaded from the book's companion Web site, bedfordstmartins.com/worldofideas, and given to students. The idea for these sentence outlines came from the phrase outlines that Darwin created to precede each chapter of *On the Origin of Species*. These outlines may be used to discuss the more difficult selections and to provide additional guidance for students. At the end of the manual, brief bibliographies are provided for all forty-six authors. These bibliographies may be photocopied or downloaded and distributed to students who wish to explore the primary selections in greater depth.

New in the Seventh Edition

The seventh edition offers a number of new features to help students engage and interact with the texts as they learn to analyze ideas and develop their own thoughts in writing.

New Essential Readings.   The selections in *A World of Ideas* explore the key ideas that have defined the human experience and shaped civilization. Of the forty-six selections (one more than in the sixth edition), twenty-two are new to the seventh edition, including ones by new authors Stephen L. Carter, Marcus Tullius Cicero, John Rawls, Martha C. Nussbaum, Michel Eyquem de Montaigne, Ralph Waldo Emerson, Maria Montessori, John Dewey, Paulo Freire, John Maynard Keynes, René Descartes, Melanie Klein, Iris Murdoch, and the Dalai Lama. Some of the authors and works in the sixth edition now appear with new selections: Hannah Arendt, Sigmund Freud, Rachel Carson, the Torah, Aristotle, the Koran, Friedrich Nietzsche, and bell hooks.

Two New Foundational Ideas.   The selections in the new parts on "Education" and on "Ethics and Morality" cover considerable historical periods and attitudes toward their subjects. The material in these two new sections has affected every one of us in profound ways. The "Education" part includes some of the most important names not only among professional educators but also among significant thinkers such as Michel Eyquem de Montaigne and Frederick Douglass. These selections contemplate what it means to educate and be educated in theory and in practice. The "Ethics and Morality" part introduces major religious writings as well as important philosophers, ancient and modern. These selections illustrate the shaping of ethics and morality across time and cultures.

New Ways into the World of Ideas.   In addition to the new selections and new part on "Education" and on "Ethics and Morality," the seventh edition includes more help for students to connect to the thinkers' ideas and participate in conversations about ideas across time.

- *Introductory quotations* Each part introduction now features a series of quotations by influential figures who helped shape modern thought—in the "Justice" part, for example, Hammurabi, Aeschylus, Anselm of Canterbury, Voltaire, Frederick Douglass, and Michel Foucault. These quotations help prepare students to engage the ideas in the texts that follow. The quotations are brief but significant in that they place the parts' selections in the context of a continuing dialogue across the ages.

- *"Seeing Connections" questions* To help students sharpen their textual *and* visual analysis skills, one selection per part is accompanied by a photograph and a "Seeing Connections" question. The "Seeing Connections" questions ask students to explore the relationships between the images and the ideas, as well as the contrasts of the images with the authors' portraits. "Seeing Connections" photographs and questions appear after the selections from Thomas Jefferson, Martin Luther King Jr., Frederick Douglass, Charles Darwin, Karl Marx, the Torah, and Virginia Woolf.

- *New author portraits* Replacing the previous editions' line drawings of the authors are photographs and reproductions from works of art, adding an engaging new visual dimension to the book. For some time, instructors have been asking me to remove the line drawings, and I feel that the new photographs and images make the authors and their ideas more real—and relevant—for students.

- *New companion Web site* A fully revised and expanded companion Web site, bedfordstmartins.com/worldofideas, provides students with a wealth of opportunities for exploring the world of ideas. At the site, students will find links to full-text documents of historical and philosophical interest, historical information and timelines, and more information on each selection's author and his or her ideas. The site also features Bedford/St. Martin's resources for conducting research and writing a research paper, evaluating and citing sources, and avoiding plagiarism.

Acknowledgments

I am grateful to a number of people who made important suggestions for earlier editions, among them Shoshana Milgram Knapp of Virginia Polytechnic and State University and Michael Hennessy of Texas State University–San Marcos. I also remain grateful to Michael Bybee of Saint John's College in Santa Fe for suggesting many fascinating pieces by Eastern thinkers, all of which he has taught to his own students. Thanks to him, this edition includes Lao-tzu.

Like its predecessors, the seventh edition is indebted to a great many creative people at Bedford/St. Martin's, whose support is invaluable. I want to thank Charles Christensen, former president, whose concern for the excellence of this book and whose close attention to detail are truly admirable. I appreciate as always the advice of Joan E. Feinberg, president, and Denise Wydra, editorial director, whose suggestions were timely and excellent. Nancy Perry, editor in chief, New York; Karen Henry, editor in chief, Boston; and Steve Scipione, executive editor, offered many useful ideas and suggestions as well, especially in the early stages of development, and kept their sharp eyes on the project throughout. My editor, Greg Johnson, has been a reliable judge of material, especially through the process of considering many selections that do not appear in these pages. He has helped me stabilize the material and achieve the kind of coherence and completeness that only good editors can provide. I found both his help and his friendship invaluable. Michael Weber, senior project editor, also helped with innumerable important details and suggestions. Virginia Rubens, copyeditor, improved the prose and watched out for inconsistencies. Thanks also to several staff members and researchers: Diane Kraut cleared text permissions, Lucy Krikorian designed the cover and new author portrait pages, Donna Dennison found the cover art, and Linda Finigan secured all the new photographs. In earlier editions, I had help from Sarah Cornog, Rosemary Winfield, Michelle Clark, Professor Mary

W. Cornog, Ellen Kuhl, Mark Reimold, Andrea Goldman, Beth Castrodale, Jonathan Burns, Mary Beth McNulty, Beth Chapman, and Mika De Roo; I feel I had a personal relationship with each of them. I also want to thank the students—quite a few of them—who wrote me directly about their experiences in reading the first six editions. I have attended carefully to what they told me, and I am warmed by their high regard for the material in this book.

Earlier editions named hundreds of users of this book who sent their comments and encouragement. I would like to take this opportunity to thank them again. In addition, the following professors were generous with criticism, praise, and detailed recommendations for the seventh edition: Kristine Anderson, Riverside Community College; Helen Becker, Shepherd College; Katrina Blasingame, Southern Illinois University–Carbondale; Sharon Campbell, Colorado State University–Pueblo; Michael Cissell, Wichita State University; Roberta Costa, Gwynedd-Mercy College; Veronica Doerr, Community College of Allegheny County–Allegheny; Laurel Eason, Catawba College; David Elias, Eastern Kentucky University; John Frederick, Santa Monica College; Lesley Gale, Cosumnes River College; Gwen Gresham, North Arkansas College; Brett Griffiths-Holloway, Southern Illinois University–Murphysboro; Ann Hall, Ohio Dominican College; Leone Hankey, California State University–Los Angeles; Margaret Harbers, Nashville State Community College; James Hawthorne, Colorado State University–Pueblo; Gregg Hecimovich, Eastern Illinois University; Michael Hennessy, Texas State University–San Marcos; Catherine Houghton, Point Park College; James Kenkel, Eastern Kentucky University; Walter Kokernot, Ohio Dominican College; Kay Kolb, University of Texas–Permian Basin; Doug Mitchell, University of Mobile; Dan Mittag, University of Rochester; Barbara Mueller, Ceritos College; Lyndall Nairn, Lynchburg College; Lindee Ownes, University of Central Florida; Witt Salley, North Arkansas College; Annabel Servat, Southeastern Louisiana University; William Sheidley, Colorado State University–Pueblo; Misty Standage, Southern Illinois University–Murphysboro; Sarah Tebbe, Southern Illinois University–Murphysboro; Sarah Tsiang, Eastern Kentucky University; and Beth Wheeler, Lorain County Community College.

I want to mention particularly the experiences I had visiting Professor Elizabeth Deis and the faculty and students of Hampden-Sydney College in connection with their writing and humanities programs. Professors James Kenkel and Charlie Sweet were gracious in welcoming me to Eastern Kentucky University for workshops and classes using *A World of Ideas*. These were delightful and fruitful experiences that helped me shape this edition of the book. I am grateful to all who took part in these workshops.

TO THE STUDENT

When the first edition of *A World of Ideas* was published, the notion that students in first-year composition courses should be able to read and write about challenging works by great thinkers was a radical one. In fact, no other composition reader at the time included selections from such important thinkers as Hannah Arendt, Marcus Tullius Cicero, John Dewey, Karl Marx, Plato, Charles Darwin, St. Matthew, or bell hooks. I had expected a moderate response from a small number of people. Instead, teachers and students alike sent me a swarm of mail commending the book for the challenge it provided and the insights they gained.

One of the first letters I received was from a young woman who had read the book after she graduated from college. She said she had heard of the thinkers included in *A World of Ideas* but in her college career had never read any of their works. Reading them now, she said, was long overdue. Another student wrote me an elaborate letter in which he demonstrated that every one of the selections in the book had been used as the basis of a *Star Trek* episode. He sagely connected every selection to a specific episode and convinced me that whoever was writing *Star Trek* had read some of the world's most important thinkers. Other students have written to tell me that they found themselves using the material in this book in other courses, such as psychology, philosophy, literature, and history, among others. In many cases, these students were the only ones among their peers who had read the key authors in their discipline.

Most of the time you will have to read the selections in *A World of Ideas* more than once. Works by influential thinkers, such as Jean-Jacques Rousseau, John Rawls, Paulo Freire, Adam Smith, Sigmund Freud, Francis Bacon, Iris Murdoch, and Simone de Beauvoir, can be very challenging. But do not let the challenge discourage you. In "Evaluating Ideas: An Introduction to Critical Reading," I suggest methods for annotating and questioning texts that are designed to help you keep track of what you read and to help you master the material. In addition, each selection is accompanied by a headnote on the author's life and work, comments about the primary ideas presented in the selection, and a host of questions to help you overcome minor difficulties in understanding the author's meaning. Some students have written to tell me that their first reading of the book was off-putting, but most of them have written later to tell me how they eventually overcame their initial fear that the selections would be too difficult for them. Ultimately, these students agreed with me that this material is important enough to merit their absolute attention.

The purpose of *A World of Ideas* is to help you learn to write better by giving you something really significant to think and write about. The selections not only are avenues into some of the most serious thought on their subjects but also are stimulating enough to sustain close analysis and to produce many good ideas for writing. For example, when you think about ethical behavior, it helps to know where our sense of ethics comes from. Early selections in the "Ethics and Morality" part—from the Torah, Aristotle, St. Matthew, and the Koran—have important things to say on the matter of ethics and have been instrumental in shaping the concept of ethics and morality across time and cultures. Later selections in the part—from Friedrich Nietzsche, Iris Murdoch, and the Dalai Lama—amplify and respond to the earlier ideas and add interesting new perspectives to the conversation. When you write, you add your own voice to the conversation. By commenting on the selections, expressing and arguing a position, and pointing out contradictions or contrasts among texts, you are participating in the world of ideas.

Keep in mind that I prepared *A World of Ideas* for my own students, most of whom work their way through college and do not take the idea of an education lightly. For that reason, I felt I owed them the opportunity to encounter the very best minds I could put them in touch with. Anything less seemed to me to be a missed opportunity. I hope you, like so many other writing students, find this book both educational and inspiring.

CONTENTS

PART ONE

GOVERNMENT

– 13 –

PART TWO

JUSTICE

– 113 –

PART THREE

EDUCATION

– 225 –

PART FOUR

WEALTH AND POVERTY

– 335 –

PART FIVE

MIND

– 437 –

universe but that cannot be seen or touched: dark matter. Eminent physicist Kaku explains the history of the theory of dark matter and reveals the difficulties modern physicists face in describing how the universe works.

PART EIGHT

FEMINISM

– 739 –

EVALUATING IDEAS
An Introduction to Critical Reading

The selections in this book demand a careful and attentive reading. The authors, whose works have changed the way we view our world, our institutions, and ourselves, make every effort to communicate their views with clarity and style. But their views are complex and subtle, and we must train ourselves to read them sensitively, responsively, and critically. Critical reading is basic for approaching the essays in this book. Indeed, it is fundamental for approaching any reading material that deserves serious attention.

Reading critically means reading actively: questioning the premises of the argument, speculating on the ways in which evidence is used, comparing the statements of one writer with those of another, and holding an inner dialogue with the author. These skills differ from the passive reception we employ when we watch television or read lightweight materials. Being an active, participating reader makes it possible for us to derive the most from good books.

Critical reading involves most of the following processes:

- *Prereading*   Developing a sense of what the piece is about and what its general purposes seem to be.

- *Annotating*   Using a pencil or a pen to mark those passages that seem important enough to return to later. Annotations establish a dialogue between you and the author.

- *Questioning*   Raising issues that you feel need to be taken into consideration. These may be issues that you believe the author has treated either well or badly and that you feel are important. Questioning can be part of the annotation process.

- *Reviewing*   Rereading your annotations and underlinings in order to grasp the entire "picture" of what you've just read. Sometimes

1

writing a summary of the piece as you review makes the meaning even clearer.

* *Forming your own ideas*   Reviewing what you have read, evaluating the way that the writer presents the issues, and developing
your own views on the issues. This is the final step.

THE PROCESS OF CRITICAL READING

Prereading

Before you read a particular selection, you may find it useful
to turn to the beginning of the part in which it appears. There you
will find an introduction discussing the broader issues and questions central to all the selections in the part. This may help you to
focus your thoughts and formulate your opinions as you read the
essays themselves.

Begin any selection in this book by reading its headnote. Each
headnote supplies historical background on the writer, sets the intellectual stage for the ideas discussed in the essay, and comments on the
writer's main points. The second part of each headnote introduces the
main rhetorical or stylistic methods that the writer uses to communicate his/her thoughts. In the process of reading the headnote, you will
develop an overview that helps prepare you for reading the essay.

This kind of preparation is typical of critical reading. It makes the
task of reading more delightful, more useful, and much easier. A review of the headnote to Niccolò Machiavelli and part of his essay "The
Qualities of the Prince" will illustrate the usefulness of such preparation. This essay appears in Part One—Government—so the content
can already be expected to be concerned with styles of government.
The introduction to Machiavelli provides the following points, each
followed here by the number of the paragraph in which it appears:

Machiavelli was an Italian aristocrat in Renaissance Italy. (1)

Machiavelli describes the qualities necessary for a prince—that
is, any ruler—to maintain power. (2)

A weak Italy was prey to the much stronger France and Spain at
this time. (2)

Machiavelli recommends securing power by whatever means
necessary and maintaining it. (3)

His concern for moralizing or acting out of high moral principle
is not great. (3)

He supports questionable means of becoming and remaining prince. (3)

Machiavelli does not fret over the means used to achieve his ends and sometimes advocates repression, imprisonment, and torture. (3)

Machiavelli has been said to have a cynical view of human nature. (4)

His rhetorical method is to discuss both sides of an issue: cruelty and mercy, liberality and stinginess. (8)

He uses aphorisms to persuade the reader that he is saying something wise and true. (9)

With these observations in mind, the reader knows that the selection that follows will be concerned with governance in Renaissance Italy. The question of ends versus means is central to Machiavelli's discussion, and he does not idealize people and their general goodness. Yet because of Machiavelli's rhetorical methods, particularly his use of aphorism,[1] the reader can expect that Machiavelli's argument will be exceptionally persuasive.

Thus, as a critical reader, you will be well advised to keep track of these basic statements from the headnote. You need not accept all of them, but you should certainly be alert to the issues that will probably be central to your experience of the essay. Remember: it is just as reasonable to question the headnote as it is to question the essay itself.

Before reading the essay in detail, you might develop an overview of its meaning by scanning it quickly. In the case of "The Qualities of the Prince," note the subheadings, such as "On Those Things for Which Men, and Particularly Princes, Are Praised or Blamed." Checking each of the subheadings before you read the entire piece might provide you with a map or guide to the essay.

Each passage is preceded by two or three prereading questions. These are designed to help you keep two or three points in mind as you read. Each of these questions focuses your attention on an important idea or interpretation in the passage. For Machiavelli the questions are:

1. Why does Machiavelli praise skill in warfare in his opening pages? How does that skill aid a prince?
2. Is it better for a prince to be loved or to be feared?

---

[1] **aphorism** A short, pithy statement of truth.

In each case a key element in Machiavelli's argument is the center of each question. By watching for the answer to these questions you will find yourself focusing on some of the most important aspects of the passage.

Annotating and Questioning

As you read a text, your annotations establish a dialogue between you and the author. You can underline or highlight important statements that you feel help clarify the author's position. They may be statements to which you will want to refer later. Think of them as serving one overriding purpose: to make it possible for you to review the piece and understand its key points without having to reread it entirely.

Your dialogue with the author will be most visible in the margins of the essay, which is one reason the margins in this book are so generous. Take issue with key points or note your assent — the more you annotate, the more you free your imagination to develop your own ideas. My own methods involve notating both agreement and disagreement. I annotate thoroughly, so that after a quick second glance I know what the author is saying as well as what I thought of the essay when I read it closely. My annotations help me keep the major points fresh in my mind.

Annotation keeps track both of what the author says and of what our responses are. No one can reduce annotation to a formula — we all do it differently — but it is not a passive act. Reading with a pencil or a pen in hand should become second nature. Without annotations, you often have to reread entire sections of an essay to remember an argument that once was clear and understandable but after time has become part of the fabric of the prose and thus "invisible." Annotation is the conquest of the invisible; it provides a quick view of the main points.

When you annotate,

- Read with a pen or a pencil.
- Underline key sentences — for example, definitions and statements of purpose.
- Underline key words that appear often.
- Note the topic of paragraphs in the margins.
- Ask questions in the margins.
- Make notes in the margins to remind yourself to develop ideas later.

- Mark passages you might want to quote later.
- Keep track of points with which you disagree.

Some sample annotations follow, again from the second essay in the book, Niccolò Machiavelli's "The Qualities of the Prince." A sixteenth-century text in translation, *The Prince* is challenging to work with. My annotations appear in the form of underlinings and marginal comments and questions. Only the first few paragraphs appear here, but the entire essay is annotated in my copy of the book.

A Prince's Duty Concerning Military Matters

A prince, therefore, must not have any other object nor any other thought, nor must he take anything as his profession but war, its institutions, and its discipline; because that is the only profession which befits one who commands; and it is of such importance that not only does it maintain those who were born princes, but many times it enables men of private station to rise to that position; and, on the other hand, it is evident that when princes have given more thought to personal luxuries than to arms, they have lost their state. And the first way to lose it is to neglect this art; and the way to acquire it is to be well versed in this art.

The prince's profession should be war.

Examples

Francesco Sforza became Duke of Milan from being a private citizen because he was armed; his sons, since they avoided the inconveniences of arms, became private citizens after having been dukes. For, among the other bad effects it causes, being disarmed makes you despised; this is one of those infamies a prince should guard himself against, as will be treated below: for between an armed and an unarmed man there is no comparison whatsoever, and it is not reasonable for an armed man to obey an unarmed man willingly, nor that an unarmed man should be safe among armed servants; since, when the former is suspicious and the latter are contemptuous, it is impossible for them to work well together. And therefore, a prince who does not understand military matters, besides the other misfortunes already noted, cannot be esteemed by his own soldiers, nor can he trust them.

Being disarmed makes you despised. Is this true?

Training:
action/mind

He must, therefore, never raise his thought from this exercise of war, and in peacetime he must train himself more than in time of war; this can be done in two ways: one by <u>action, the other by the mind</u>. And as far as actions are concerned, besides <u>keeping his soldiers well disciplined and trained,</u> he must always be out hunting, and must <u>accustom his body to hardships</u> in this manner; and he must

Knowledge of
terrain

also learn the nature of the terrain, and know how mountains slope, how valleys open, how plains lie, and understand the nature of rivers and swamps; and he should devote much attention to such activ-

Two benefits

ities. <u>Such knowledge is useful in two ways:</u> first, one learns to know one's own country and can better understand how to defend it; second, with the knowledge and experience of the terrain, one can easily comprehend the characteristics of any other terrain that it is necessary to explore for the first time; for the hills, valleys, plains, rivers, and swamps of Tuscany, for instance, have certain similarities to those of other provinces; so that by knowing the lay of the land in one province one can easily understand it in others. And a prince who lacks this ability lacks the most important quality in a leader; because this skill teaches you to find the enemy, choose a campsite, lead troops, organize them for battle, and besiege towns to your own advantage.

[There follow the examples of Philopoemon, who was always observing terrain for its military usefulness, and a recommendation that princes read histories and learn from them. Three paragraphs are omitted.]

On Those Things for Which Men, and Particularly Princes, Are Praised or Blamed

Now there remains to be examined what should be the <u>methods and procedures of a prince</u> in dealing with his subjects and friends. And because I know that many have written about this, I am afraid that by writing about it again I shall be thought of as presumptuous, since in discussing this material I depart radically from the procedures of others. But since my intention is to write something useful for anyone who understands it, it seemed more suitable to me to search after the effectual truth of the matter rather than its imagined one. And many writers have imagined for themselves republics and principalities that have never been seen nor known to exist in reality; for there is such a gap between how one lives and how one ought to live that anyone who abandons what is done for what ought to be done learns his ruin rather than his preservation: for a man who wishes to make a vocation of being good at all times will come to ruin among so many who are not good. Hence it is necessary for a prince who wishes to maintain his position to learn how not to be good, and to use this knowledge or not to use it according to necessity.

Those who are good at all times come to ruin among those who are not good.

Prince must learn how not to be good.

Leaving aside, therefore, the imagined things concerning a prince, and taking into account those that are true, I say that all men, when they are spoken of, and particularly princes, since they are placed on a higher level, are judged by some of these qualities which bring them either blame or praise. And this is why one is considered generous, another miserly (to use a Tuscan word, since "avaricious" in our language is still used to mean one who wishes to acquire by means of theft; we call "miserly" one who excessively avoids using what he has); one is considered a giver, the other rapacious; one cruel, another merciful; one treacherous, another faithful; one effeminate and cowardly, another bold and courageous; one humane, another haughty; one lascivious, another chaste; one trustworthy, another cunning; one harsh, another lenient; one serious, another frivolous; one religious, another unbelieving; and the like. And I know that everyone will admit that it would be a very praiseworthy thing to find in a prince, of the qualities mentioned above, those that are held to be good, but since it is neither possible to have them nor to observe them all completely, because human nature does not permit it, a prince must be prudent enough to know how to escape the bad reputation of those vices that would lose the state

Note the prince's reputation.

Prince must avoid reputation for the worst vices.

*Some vices
may be needed
to hold the
state. True?*

*Some virtues
may end in
destruction.*

for him, and must protect himself from those that
will not lose it for him, if this is possible; but if
he cannot, he need not concern himself unduly if he
ignores these less serious vices. And, moreover, he
need not worry about incurring the bad reputation
of those vices without which it would be difficult to
hold his state; since, carefully taking everything into
account, one will discover that something which
appears to be a virtue, if pursued, will end in his
destruction; while some other thing which seems to
be a vice, if pursued, will result in his safety and his
well-being.

Reviewing

The process of review, which takes place after a careful reading, is
much more useful if you have annotated and underlined the text well.
To a large extent, the review process can be devoted to accounting for
the primary ideas that have been uncovered by your annotations and
underlinings. For example, reviewing the Machiavelli annotations
shows that the following ideas are crucial to Machiavelli's thinking:

- The prince's profession should be war, so the most successful
  princes are probably experienced in the military.
- If they do not pay attention to military matters, princes will lose
  their power.
- Being disarmed makes the prince despised.
- The prince should be in constant training.
- The prince needs a sound knowledge of terrain.
- Machiavelli says he tells us what is true, not what ought to be true.
- Those who are always good will come to ruin among those who
  are not good.
- To remain in power, the prince must learn how not to be good.
- The prince should avoid the worst vices in order not to harm
  his reputation.
- To maintain power, some vices may be necessary.
- Some virtues may end in destruction.

Putting Machiavelli's ideas in this raw form does an injustice to
his skill as a writer, but annotation is designed to result in such summary statements. We can see that there are some constant themes,

such as the insistence that the prince be a military person. As the headnote tells us, in Machiavelli's day Italy was a group of rival city-states, and France, a larger, united nation, was invading these states one by one. Machiavelli dreamed that one powerful prince, such as his favorite, Cesare Borgia, could fight the French and save Italy. He emphasized the importance of the military because he lived in an age in which war was a constant threat.

Machiavelli anticipates the complaints of pacifists—those who argue against war—by telling us that those who remain unarmed are despised. To demonstrate his point, he gives us examples of those who lost their positions as princes because they avoided being armed. He clearly expects these examples to be persuasive.

A second important theme pervading Machiavelli's essay is his view on moral behavior. For Machiavelli, being in power is much more important than being virtuous. He is quick to admit that vice is not desirable and that the worst vices will harm the prince's reputation. But he also says that the prince need not worry about the "less serious" vices. Moreover, the prince need not worry about incurring a bad reputation by practicing vices that are necessary if he wishes to hold his state. In the same spirit, Machiavelli tells us that there are some virtues that might lead to the destruction of the prince.

Forming Your Own Ideas

One of the most important reasons for reading the texts in this book critically is to enable you to develop your own positions on issues that these writers raise. Identifying and clarifying the main ideas is only the first step; the next step in critical reading is evaluating those ideas.

For example, you might ask whether Machiavelli's ideas have any relevance for today. After all, he wrote nearly five hundred years ago and times have changed. You might feel that Machiavelli was relevant strictly during the Italian Renaissance or, alternatively, that his principles are timeless and have something to teach every age. For most people, Machiavelli is a political philosopher whose views are useful anytime and anywhere.

If you agree with the majority, then you may want to examine Machiavelli's ideas to see whether you can accept them. Consider just two of those ideas and their implications:

- Should rulers always be members of the military? Should they always be armed? Should the ruler of a nation first demonstrate competence as a military leader?

- Should rulers ignore virtue and practice vice when it is conve- nient?

In his commentary on government, Lao-tzu offers different ad- vice from Machiavelli because his assumptions are that the ruler ought to respect the rights of individuals. For Lao-tzu the waging of war is an annoying, essentially wasteful activity. Machiavelli, on the other hand, never questions the usefulness of war: to him, it is basic to government. As a critical reader, you can take issue with such an assumption, and in doing so you will deepen your understanding of Machiavelli.

If we were to follow Machiavelli's advice, then we would choose American presidents on the basis of whether or not they had been good military leaders. Among those we would not have chosen might be Thomas Jefferson, Abraham Lincoln, and Franklin Delano Roose- velt. Those who were high-ranking military men include George Washington, Ulysses S. Grant, and Dwight D. Eisenhower. If you fol- lowed Machiavelli's rhetorical technique of using examples to convince your audience, you could choose from either group to prove your case.

Of course, there are examples from other nations. It has been common since the 1930s to see certain leaders dressed in their mili- tary uniforms: Benito Mussolini (Italy), Adolf Hitler (Germany), Joseph Stalin (the Soviet Union), Idi Amin (Uganda), Muammar al-Qaddafi (Libya), Saddam Hussein (Iraq). These are all tyrants who tormented their citizens and their neighbors. That gives us something to think about. Should a president dress in full military regalia all the time? Is that a good image for the ruler of a free nation to project?

Do you want a ruler, then, who is usually virtuous but embraces vice when it is necessary? This is a very difficult question to answer. President Richard Nixon tried to hide the Watergate break-in scandal, President Ronald Reagan did not reveal the details of the Iran-Contra scandal, and President Bill Clinton lied about his relations with Mon- ica Lewinsky. Yet all these presidents are noted for important achieve- ments while in office. How might Machiavelli have handled these problems differently? How much truthfulness do we expect from our presidents? How much do we deserve?

These are only a few of the questions that are raised by my an- notations in the few pages from Machiavelli examined here. Many other issues could be uncovered by these annotations, and many more from subsequent pages of the essay. Critical reading can be a powerful means by which to open what you read to discovery and discussion.

Once you begin a line of questioning, the ways in which you think about a passage begin expanding. You find yourself with more ideas of your own that have grown in response to those you have been reading about. Reading critically, in other words, gives you an enormous return on your investment of time. If you have the chance to investigate your responses to the assumptions and underlying premises of passages such as Machiavelli's, you will be able to refine your thinking even further. For example, if you agree with Machiavelli that rulers should be successful military leaders for whom small vices may be useful at times, and you find yourself in a position to argue with someone who feels Machiavelli is mistaken in this view, then you will have a good opportunity to evaluate the soundness of your thinking. You will have a chance to see your own assumptions and arguments tested.

In many ways, this entire book is about such opportunities. The essays that follow offer you powerful ideas from great thinkers. They invite you to participate in their thoughts, exercise your own knowledge and assumptions, and arrive at your own conclusions. Basically, that is the meaning of education.

PART ONE

GOVERNMENT

Lao-tzu
Niccolò Machiavelli
Jean-Jacques Rousseau
Thomas Jefferson
Hannah Arendt
Stephen L. Carter

INTRODUCTION

He who exercises government by means of his virtue may be
compared to the north polar star, which keeps its place and all
the stars turn towards it.

–CONFUCIUS (551–479 B.C.)

When a government becomes powerful it is destructive,
extravagant and violent; it is an usurer which takes bread from
innocent mouths and deprives honorable men of their
substance, for votes with which to perpetuate itself.

–MARCUS TULLIUS CICERO (106–43 B.C.)

All the ills of mankind, all the tragic misfortunes that fill the
history books, all the political blunders, all the failures of the
great leaders have arisen merely from a lack of skill at dancing.

–MOLIÈRE (1622–1673)

Society in every state is a blessing, but Government, even in its
best state, is but a necessary evil; in its worst state, an intolerable
one.

–THOMAS PAINE (1737–1809)

No government can be long secure without formidable
opposition.

–BENJAMIN DISRAELI (1804–1881)

A government is the most dangerous threat to man's rights: it
holds a legal monopoly on the use of physical force against
legally disarmed victims.

–AYN RAND (1902–1982)

At the core of any idea of government is the belief that individuals need an organized allocation of authority to protect their well-being. However, throughout history the form of that allocation of authority has undergone profound shifts, and each successive type of government has inspired debates and defenses. The first civilizations in Mesopotamia and Egypt (4000–3000 B.C.) were theocracies ruled by a high priest. Gradually these political systems evolved into monarchies in which a king whose role was separate from that of the religious leaders held power. During the sixth century B.C. the Greek city-state Athens developed the first democratic system wherein male citizens (but not women or slaves) could elect a body of leaders. As these forms of government developed, so too did the concept of government as the center of law and administration. However, governments and ideas of governments (actual or ideal) have not followed a straight path. History has witnessed constant

14

oscillations between various forms and functions of government, from tyrannies to republics. In turn, these governments and their relation to the individual citizen have been the focus of many great thinkers.

In this section, the thinkers represented have concentrated on both the role and form of government. Lao-tzu reflects on the ruler who would, by careful management, maintain a happy citizenry. Machiavelli places the survival of the prince above all other considerations of government and, unlike Lao-tzu, ignores the concerns and rights of the individual. For Machiavelli, power is the issue, and maintaining it is the sign of good government. Rousseau's emphasis on the social contract focuses on the theory that citizens voluntarily submit to governance in the hope of gaining greater personal freedom.

Whereas governing well concerns most of these thinkers, the forms of government concern others. Thomas Jefferson struggled with the monarchical form of government, as did Rousseau before him, and envisioned a republic that would serve the people. Kings were a threatened species in eighteenth-century Europe, and with Jefferson's aid, they became extinct in the United States. Hannah Arendt was convinced that the totalitarian governments of the twentieth century needed concentration camps in order to practice total domination.

Lao-tzu, whose writings provide the basis for Taoism, one of three major Chinese religions, was interested primarily in political systems. His work, the *Tao-te Ching*, has been translated loosely as "The Way of Power." One thing that becomes clear from reading his work—especially the selections presented here—is his concern for the well-being of the people in any government. He does not recommend specific forms of government (monarchic, representative, democratic) or advocate election versus the hereditary transfer of power. But he does make it clear that the success of the existing forms of government (in his era, monarchic) depends on good relations between the leader and the people. He refers to the chief of state as Master or Sage, implying that one obligation of the governor is to be wise. One expression of that wisdom is the willingness to permit things to take their natural course. His view is that the less the Master needs to do—or perhaps the less government needs to intervene—the happier the people will be.

Niccolò Machiavelli was a pragmatic man of the Renaissance in Italy. As a theoretician and as a member of the political court, he understood government from the inside and carefully examined its philosophy. Because his writings stress the importance of gaining and holding power at any cost, Machiavelli's name has become synonymous with political cunning. However, a careful reading of his work as a reflection of the instability of his time shows that his advice to wield power ruthlessly derived largely from his fear that a weak prince would lose the city-state of Florence to France or to another powerful, plundering nation. His commitment to a powerful prince is based on his view that in the long run strength will guarantee the peace and happiness of the citizen for whom independence is otherwise irrelevant. Therefore, Machiavelli generally ignores questions concerning the comfort and rights of the individual.

In contrast, Jean-Jacques Rousseau is continually concerned with the basic questions of personal freedom and liberty. A fundamental principle in "The Origin of Civil Society" is that the individual's agreement with the state is designed to increase the individual's freedoms, not to diminish them. Rousseau makes this assertion while at the same time admitting that the individual forfeits certain rights to the body politic in order to gain overall freedom. Moreover, Rousseau describes civil society as a body politic that expects its rulers—including the monarch—to behave in a way designed to benefit the people. Such a view in eighteenth-century France was revolutionary. The ruling classes at that time treated the people with great contempt, and the monarch rarely gave any thought to the well-being of the common people. Rousseau's advocacy of a republican form of government in which the monarch served the people was a radical view and would find its ultimate expression decades later in the French Revolution.

Thomas Jefferson's views were also radical for his time. Armed with the philosophy of Rousseau and others, his Declaration of Independence advocates the eradication of the monarch entirely. Not everyone in the colonies agreed with this view. Indeed, his political opponents, such as Alexander Hamilton and Aaron Burr, were far from certain such a view was correct. In fact, some efforts were made to install George Washington as king (he refused). In the Declaration of Independence, Jefferson reflects Rousseau's philosophy by emphasizing the right of the individual to "life, liberty, and the pursuit of happiness" and the obligation of government to serve the people by protecting those rights.

The issues of freedom, justice, and individual rights were all virtually irrelevant in the totalitarian regimes that served as the focus of Hannah Arendt's work. Arendt argued that the fascist states, especially Nazi Germany, and the communist states, especially the Soviet Union, represented a form of government in which individual rights were sacrificed for the good of "the state." In "Total Domination," Arendt argues that the power of totalitarian states depends on the use of terror to enforce the state's ideology. The result is a form of government that eclipses the tyrannical extremes Rousseau and Jefferson sought to eradicate and exceeds even Machiavelli's imaginings of absolute power.

Stephen L. Carter addresses the relationship of government to religion from the point of view of a lawyer committed to the preservation of religious freedom. He reviews some of the contemporary concerns that inform the debates regarding prayer in public schools and federal funding of religious organizations that perform public service. One important point he makes toward the beginning of his essay is that the First Amendment's separation of church and state was designed by the country's founders as a means of protecting religion from the state, not the state from religion. From this basic premise, Carter argues a powerful case.

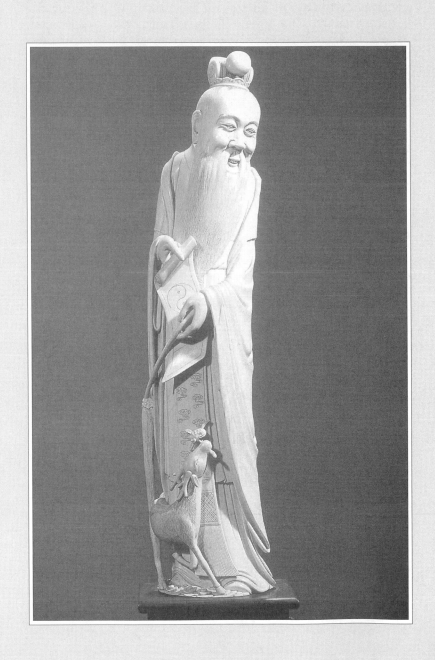

LAO-TZU
Thoughts from the Tao-te Ching

THE AUTHOR of the *Tao-te Ching* (in English often pronounced "dow deh jing") is unknown, although the earliest texts ascribe the work to Lao-tzu (sixth century B.C.), whose name can be translated as "Old Master." However, nothing can be said with certainty about Lao-tzu (lou′ dzu′) as a historical figure. One tradition holds that he was named Li Erh and born in the state of Ch'u in China at a time that would have made him a slightly older contemporary of Confucius (551–479 B.C.). Lao-tzu was said to have worked in the court of the Chou dynasty for most of his life. When he decided to leave the court to pursue a life of contemplation, the keeper of the gate urged him to write down his thoughts before he went into a self-imposed exile. Legend has it that he wrote the *Tao-te Ching* and then left the state of Ch'u, never to be seen again.

Lao-tzu's writings offered a basis for Taoism, a religion officially founded by Chang Tao-ling in about A.D. 150. However, the *Tao-te Ching* is a philosophical document as much about good government as it is about moral behavior. The term *Tao* cannot be easily understood or easily translated. In one sense it means "the way," but it also means "the method," as in "the way to enlightenment" or "the way to live." Some of the chapters of the *Tao-te Ching* imply that the Tao is the allness of the universe, the ultimate reality of existence, and perhaps even a synonym for God. The text is marked by numerous complex ambiguities and paradoxes. It constantly urges us to look beyond ourselves, beyond our circumstances, and become one with the Tao—even though it cannot tell us what the Tao is.

The *Tao-te Ching* has often been called a feminine treatise because it emphasizes the creative forces of the universe and frequently

From *Tao-te Ching*. Translated by Stephen Mitchell.

employs the imagery and metaphor of the womb—for example, "The Tao is called the Great Mother." The translator, Stephen Mitchell, translates some of the pronouns associated with the Master as "she," with the explanation that Chinese has no equivalent for the male- and female-gendered pronouns and that "of all the great world religions the teaching of Lao-tzu is by far the most female."

The teachings of Lao-tzu are the opposite of the materialist quest for power, dominance, authority, and wealth. Lao-tzu takes the view that possessions and wealth are leaden weights of the soul, that they are meaningless and trivial, and that the truly free and enlightened person will regard them as evil. Because of his antimaterialist view, his recommendations may seem ironic or unclear, especially when he urges politicians to adopt a practice of judicious inaction. Lao-tzu's advice to politicians is not to do nothing but to intercede only when it is a necessity and then only inconspicuously. Above all, Lao-tzu counsels avoiding useless activity: "the Master / acts without doing anything / and teaches without saying anything." Such a statement is difficult for modern westerners to comprehend, although it points to the concept of enlightenment, a state of spiritual peace and fulfillment that is central to the *Tao-te Ching.*

Lao-tzu's political philosophy minimizes the power of the state—especially the power of the state to oppress the people. Lao-tzu takes the question of the freedom of the individual into account by asserting that the wise leader will provide the people with what they need but not annoy them with promises of what they do not need. Lao-tzu argues that by keeping people unaware that they are being governed, the leader allows the people to achieve good things for themselves. As he writes, "If you want to be a great leader, / you must learn to follow the Tao. / Stop trying to control. / Let go of fixed plans and concepts, / and the world will govern itself" (Verse 57); or in contrast, "If a country is governed with repression, / the people are depressed and crafty" (Verse 58).

To our modern ears this advice may or may not sound sensible. For those who feel government can solve the problems of the people, it will seem strange and unwise. For those who believe that the less government the better, the advice will sound sane and powerful.

The Rhetoric of the *Tao-te Ching*

Traditionally, Lao-tzu is said to have written the *Tao-te Ching* as a guide for the ruling sage to follow. In other words, it is a handbook for politicians. It emphasizes the virtues that the ruler must possess, and in this sense the *Tao-te Ching* invites comparison with Machiavelli's efforts to instruct his ruler.

The visual form of the text is poetry, although the text is not metrical or image-laden. Instead of thoroughly developing his ideas, Lao-tzu uses a traditional Chinese form that resembles the aphorism, a compressed statement weighty with meaning. Virtually every statement requires thought and reflection. Thus, the act of reading becomes an act of cooperation with the text.

One way of reading the text is to explore the varieties of interpretation it will sustain. The act of analysis requires patience and willingness to examine a statement to see what lies beneath the surface. Take, for example, one of the opening statements:

> The Master leads
> by emptying people's minds
> and filling their cores,
> by weakening their ambition
> and toughening their resolve.
> He helps people lose everything
> they know, everything they desire,
> and creates confusion
> in those who think that they know.

This passage supports a number of readings. One centers on the question of the people's desire. "Emptying people's minds" implies eliminating desires that lead the people to steal or compete for power. "Weakening their ambition" implies helping people direct their powers toward the attainable and useful. Such a text is at odds with Western views that support advertisements for expensive computers, DVD players, luxury cars, and other items that generate ambition and desire in the people.

In part because the text resembles poetry, it needs to be read with attention to innuendo, subtle interpretation, and possible hidden meanings. One of the rhetorical virtues of paradox is that it forces the reader to consider several sides of an issue. The resulting confusion yields a wider range of possibilities than would arise from a self-evident statement. Through these complicated messages, Lao-tzu felt he was contributing to the spiritual enlightenment of the ruling sage, although he had no immediate hope that his message would be put into action. A modern state might have a difficult time following Lao-tzu's philosophy, but many individuals have tried to attain peace and contentment by leading lives according to its principles.

PREREADING QUESTIONS:
WHAT TO READ FOR

The following prereading questions may help you anticipate key issues in the discussion of Lao-tzu's "Thoughts from the *Tao-te Ching.*" Keeping them in mind during your first reading of the selection should help focus your attention.

- What is the Master's attitude toward action?

- The Tao is "the way"—how are we to understand its meaning? What does it mean to be in harmony with the Tao?

- According to Lao-tzu, why is moderation important in government?

Thoughts from the Tao-te Ching

3

If you overesteem great men,   1
people become powerless.
If you overvalue possessions,
people begin to steal.

The Master leads   2
by emptying people's minds
and filling their cores,
by weakening their ambition
and toughening their resolve.
He helps people lose everything
they know, everything they desire,
and creates confusion
in those who think that they know.

Practice not-doing,   3
and everything will fall into place.

17

When the Master governs, the people   4
are hardly aware that he exists.
Next best is a leader who is loved.
Next, one who is feared.
The worst is one who is despised.

If you don't trust the people,   5
you make them untrustworthy.

The Master doesn't talk, he acts.   6
When his work is done,
the people say, "Amazing:
we did it, all by ourselves!"

18

When the great Tao is forgotten,   7
goodness and piety appear.
When the body's intelligence declines,
cleverness and knowledge step forth.
When there is no peace in the family,
filial piety begins.
When the country falls into chaos,
patriotism is born.

19

Throw away holiness and wisdom,   8
and people will be a hundred times happier.
Throw away morality and justice,
and people will do the right thing.
Throw away industry and profit,
and there won't be any thieves.

If these three aren't enough,   9
just stay at the center of the circle
and let all things take their course.

26

The heavy is the root of the light.   10
The unmoved is the source of all movement.

Thus the Master travels all day   11
without leaving home.
However splendid the views,
she stays serenely in herself.

Why should the lord of the country   12
flit about like a fool?
If you let yourself be blown to and fro,

you lose touch with your root.
If you let restlessness move you,
you lose touch with who you are.

29

Do you want to improve the world?   13
I don't think it can be done.

The world is sacred.   14
It can't be improved.
If you tamper with it, you'll ruin it.
If you treat it like an object, you'll lose it.

There is a time for being ahead,   15
a time for being behind;
a time for being in motion,
a time for being at rest;
a time for being vigorous,
a time for being exhausted;
a time for being safe,
a time for being in danger.

The Master sees things as they are,   16
without trying to control them.
She lets them go their own way,
and resides at the center of the circle.

30

Whoever relies on the Tao in governing men   17
doesn't try to force issues
or defeat enemies by force of arms.
For every force there is a counterforce.
Violence, even well intentioned,
always rebounds upon oneself.

The Master does his job   18
and then stops.
He understands that the universe
is forever out of control,
and that trying to dominate events
goes against the current of the Tao.
Because he believes in himself,
he doesn't try to convince others.

Because he is content with himself,
he doesn't need others' approval.
Because he accepts himself,
the whole world accepts him.

31

Weapons are the tools of violence;   19
all decent men detest them.

Weapons are the tools of fear;   20
a decent man will avoid them
except in the direst necessity
and, if compelled, will use them
only with the utmost restraint.
Peace is his highest value.
If the peace has been shattered,
how can he be content?
His enemies are not demons,
but human beings like himself.
He doesn't wish them personal harm.
Nor does he rejoice in victory.
How could he rejoice in victory
and delight in the slaughter of men?

He enters a battle gravely,   21
with sorrow and with great compassion,
as if he were attending a funeral.

37

The Tao never does anything,   22
yet through it all things are done.

If powerful men and women   23
could center themselves in it,
the whole world would be transformed
by itself, in its natural rhythms.
People would be content
with their simple, everyday lives,
in harmony, and free of desire.

When there is no desire,   24
all things are at peace.

38

The Master doesn't try to be powerful;   25
thus he is truly powerful.
The ordinary man keeps reaching for power;
thus he never has enough.

The Master does nothing,   26
yet he leaves nothing undone.
The ordinary man is always doing things,
yet many more are left to be done.

The kind man does something,   27
yet something remains undone.
The just man does something,
and leaves many things to be done.
The moral man does something,
and when no one responds
he rolls up his sleeves and uses force.

When the Tao is lost, there is goodness.   28
When goodness is lost, there is morality.
When morality is lost, there is ritual.
Ritual is the husk of true faith,
the beginning of chaos.

Therefore the Master concerns himself   29
with the depths and not the surface,
with the fruit and not the flower.
He has no will of his own.
He dwells in reality,
and lets all illusions go.

46

When a country is in harmony with the Tao,   30
the factories make trucks and tractors.
When a country goes counter to the Tao,
warheads are stockpiled outside the cities.

There is no greater illusion than fear,   31
no greater wrong than preparing to defend yourself,
no greater misfortune than having an enemy.

Whoever can see through all fear   32
will always be safe.

53

The great Way is easy,   33
yet people prefer the side paths.
Be aware when things are out of balance.
Stay centered within the Tao.

When rich speculators prosper   34
while farmers lose their land;
when government officials spend money
on weapons instead of cures;
when the upper class is extravagant and irresponsible
while the poor have nowhere to turn—
all this is robbery and chaos.
It is not in keeping with the Tao.

57

If you want to be a great leader,   35
you must learn to follow the Tao.
Stop trying to control.
Let go of fixed plans and concepts,
and the world will govern itself.

The more prohibitions you have,   36
the less virtuous people will be.
The more weapons you have,
the less secure people will be.
The more subsidies you have,
the less self-reliant people will be.

Therefore the Master says: 37
I let go of the law,
and people become honest.
I let go of economics,
and people become prosperous.
I let go of religion,
and people become serene.
I let go of all desire for the common good,
and the good becomes common as grass.

58

If a country is governed with tolerance,   38
the people are comfortable and honest.
If a country is governed with repression,
the people are depressed and crafty.

When the will to power is in charge,   39
the higher the ideals, the lower the results.
Try to make people happy,
and you lay the groundwork for misery.
Try to make people moral,
and you lay the groundwork for vice.

Thus the Master is content   40
to serve as an example
and not to impose her will.
She is pointed, but doesn't pierce.
Straightforward, but supple.
Radiant, but easy on the eyes.

59

For governing a country well   41
there is nothing better than moderation.

The mark of a moderate man   42
is freedom from his own ideas.
Tolerant like the sky,
all-pervading like sunlight,
firm like a mountain,
supple like a tree in the wind,
he has no destination in view
and makes use of anything
life happens to bring his way.

Nothing is impossible for him.   43
Because he has let go,
he can care for the people's welfare
as a mother cares for her child.

60

Governing a large country   44
is like frying a small fish.
You spoil it with too much poking.

Center your country in the Tao   45
and evil will have no power.
Not that it isn't there,
but you'll be able to step out of its way.

Give evil nothing to oppose   46
and it will disappear by itself.

61

When a country obtains great power,   47
it becomes like the sea:
all streams run downward into it.
The more powerful it grows,
the greater the need for humility.
Humility means trusting the Tao,
thus never needing to be defensive.

A great nation is like a great man: 48
When he makes a mistake, he realizes it.
Having realized it, he admits it.
Having admitted it, he corrects it.
He considers those who point out his faults
as his most benevolent teachers.
He thinks of his enemy
as the shadow that he himself casts.

If a nation is centered in the Tao,   49
if it nourishes its own people
and doesn't meddle in the affairs of others,
it will be a light to all nations in the world.

65

The ancient Masters   50
didn't try to educate the people,
but kindly taught them to not-know.

When they think that they know the answers,   51
people are difficult to guide.
When they know that they don't know,
people can find their own way.

If you want to learn how to govern,   52
avoid being clever or rich.
The simplest pattern is the clearest.
Content with an ordinary life,
you can show all people the way
back to their own true nature.

66

All streams flow to the sea   53
because it is lower than they are.
Humility gives it its power.

If you want to govern the people,   54
you must place yourself below them.
If you want to lead the people,
you must learn how to follow them.

The Master is above the people,   55
and no one feels oppressed.
She goes ahead of the people,
and no one feels manipulated.
The whole world is grateful to her.
Because she competes with no one,
no one can compete with her.

67

Some say that my teaching is nonsense.   56
Others call it lofty but impractical.
But to those who have looked inside themselves,
this nonsense makes perfect sense.
And to those who put it into practice,
this loftiness has roots that go deep.

I have just three things to teach: 57
simplicity, patience, compassion.
These three are your greatest treasures.
Simple in actions and in thoughts,
you return to the source of being.
Patient with both friends and enemies,
you accord with the way things are.
Compassionate toward yourself,
you reconcile all beings in the world.

75

When taxes are too high,   58
people go hungry.
When the government is too intrusive,
people lose their spirit.

Act for the people's benefit.   59
Trust them; leave them alone.

80

If a country is governed wisely,   60
its inhabitants will be content.
They enjoy the labor of their hands
and don't waste time inventing
labor-saving machines.
Since they dearly love their homes,
they aren't interested in travel.
There may be a few wagons and boats,
but these don't go anywhere.
There may be an arsenal of weapons,
but nobody ever uses them.
People enjoy their food,
take pleasure in being with their families,
spend weekends working in their gardens,
delight in the doings of the neighborhood.
And even though the next country is so close
that people can hear its roosters crowing and its dogs barking,
they are content to die of old age
without ever having gone to see it.

QUESTIONS FOR CRITICAL READING

1. According to Lao-tzu, what must the ruler provide the people with if they are to be happy? See especially Verse 66.
2. To what extent does Lao-tzu concern himself with individual happiness?
3. How would you describe Lao-tzu's attitude toward the people?
4. Why does Lao-tzu think the world cannot be improved? See Verse 29.
5. Which statements made in this selection do you feel support a materialist view of experience? Can they be reconciled with Lao-tzu's overall thinking in the selection?
6. What are the limits and benefits of the expression: "Practice not-doing, / and everything will fall into place"? See Verse 3.
7. To what extent is Lao-tzu in favor of military action? What seem to be his views about the military? See Verse 31.
8. The term *Master* is used frequently in the selection. What can you tell about the character of the Master?

SUGGESTIONS FOR WRITING

1. The term *the Tao* is used often in this selection. Write a short essay that
   defines what Lao-tzu seems to mean by the term. If you were a politician and had the responsibility of governing a state, how would you
   follow the Tao as it is implied in Lao-tzu's statements? Is the Tao re-
   strictive? Difficult? Open to interpretation? How well do you think it
   would work?

2. Write a brief essay that examines the following statements from the
   perspective of a young person today:

   > The more prohibitions you have,
   > the less virtuous people will be.
   > The more weapons you have,
   > the less secure people will be.
   > The more subsidies you have,
   > the less self-reliant people will be. (Verse 57)

   To what extent do you agree with these statements, and to what extent
   do you feel they are statements that have a political importance? Do
   people in the United States seem to agree with these views, or do they
   disagree? What are the most visible political consequences of our nation's position regarding these ideas?

3. Some people have asserted that the American political system benefits
   the people most when the following views of Lao-tzu are carefully applied:

   > Therefore the Master says:
   > I let go of the law,
   > and people become honest.
   > I let go of economics,
   > and people become prosperous.
   > I let go of religion,
   > and people become serene.
   > I let go of all desire for the common good,
   > and the good becomes common as grass. (Verse 57)

   In a brief essay, decide to what extent American leaders follow these
   precepts. Whether you feel they do or not, do you think that they
   should follow these precepts? What are the likely results of their being
   put into practice?

4. Some of the statements Lao-tzu makes are so packed with meaning that
   it would take pages to explore them. One example is "When they think
   that they know the answers, / people are difficult to guide." Take this
   statement as the basis of a short essay and, in reference to a personal experience, explain the significance of this statement.

5. What does Lao-tzu imply about the obligation of the state to the individual it governs, and about the obligation of the individual to the
   state? Is one much more important than the other? Using the texts in
   this selection, establish what you feel is the optimum balance in the relationship between the two.

6. **CONNECTIONS**　Compare Lao-tzu's view of government with that of Machiavelli in the next selection. Consider what seem to be the ultimate purposes of government, what seem to be the obligations of the leader to the people being led, and what seems to be the main work of the state. What comparisons can you make between Lao-tzu's Master and Machiavelli's prince?

NICCOLÒ MACHIAVELLI
The Qualities of the Prince

NICCOLÒ MACHIAVELLI (1469–1527) was an aristocrat whose fortunes wavered according to the shifts in power in Florence. Renaissance Italy was a collection of powerful city-states, which were sometimes volatile and unstable. When Florence's famed Medici princes were returned to power in 1512 after eighteen years of banishment, Machiavelli did not fare well. He was suspected of crimes against the state and imprisoned. Even though he was not guilty, he had to learn to support himself as a writer instead of continuing his career in civil service.

His works often contrast two forces: luck (one's fortune) and character (one's virtues). His own character outlasted his bad luck in regard to the Medicis, and he was returned to a position of responsibility. *The Prince* (1513), his most celebrated work, was a general treatise on the qualities the prince (that is, ruler) must have to maintain his power. In a more particular way, it was directed at the Medicis to encourage them to save Italy from the predatory incursions of France and Spain, whose troops were nibbling at the crumbling Italian principalities and who would, in time, control much of Italy.

The chapters presented here contain the core of the philosophy for which Machiavelli became famous. His instructions to the prince are curiously devoid of any high-sounding moralizing or any encouragement to be good as a matter of principle. Instead, Machiavelli recommends a very practical course of action for the prince: secure power by direct and effective means. It may be that Machiavelli fully expects that the prince will use his power for good ends—certainly he does not recommend tyranny. But he also supports using questionable means to achieve the final end of becoming

---

From *The Prince*. Translated by Peter Bondanella and Mark Musa.

and remaining the prince. Although Machiavelli recognizes that
there is often a conflict between the ends and the means used to
achieve them, he does not fret over the possible problems that may
accompany the use of "unpleasant" means, such as punishment of
upstarts, or the use of repression, imprisonment, and torture.

Through the years Machiavelli's view of human nature has
come under criticism for its cynicism. For instance, he suggests
that a morally good person would not remain long in any high office because that person would have to compete with the mass of
people, who, he says, are basically bad. Machiavelli constantly tells
us that he is describing the world as it really is, not as it should be.
Perhaps Machiavelli is correct, but people have long condemned
the way he approves of cunning, deceit, and outright lying as
means of staying in power.

The contrast between Machiavelli's writings and Lao-tzu's opinions in the *Tao-te Ching* is instructive. Lao-tzu's advice issues from a
detached view of a universal ruler; Machiavelli's advice is very personal, embodying a set of directives for a specific prince. Machiavelli
expounds upon a litany of actions that must be taken; Lao-tzu, on
the other hand, advises that judicious inaction will produce the
best results.

Machiavelli's Rhetoric

Machiavelli's approach is less poetic and more pragmatic than
Lao-tzu's. Whereas Lao-tzu's tone is almost biblical, Machiavelli's
is that of a how-to book, relevant to a particular time and a particular place. Yet, like Lao-tzu, Machiavelli is brief and to the point.
Each segment of the discussion is terse and economical.

Machiavelli announces his primary point clearly, refers to historical precedents to support his point, and then explains why his
position is the best one by appealing to both common sense and
historical experience. When he suspects the reader will not share
his view wholeheartedly, he suggests an alternate argument and then
explains why it is wrong. This is a very forceful way of presenting
one's views. It gives the appearance of fairness and thoroughness—
and, as we learn from reading Machiavelli, he is very much concerned with appearances. His method also gives his work fullness,
a quality that makes us forget how brief it really is.

Another of his rhetorical methods is to discuss opposite pair-
ings, including both sides of an issue. From the first he explores a
number of oppositions—the art of war and the art of life, liberality
and stinginess, cruelty and clemency, the fox and the lion. The

method may seem simple, but it is important because it employs two of the basic techniques of rhetoric—comparison and contrast.

The aphorism is another of Machiavelli's rhetorical weapons. An aphorism is a saying—a concise statement of a principle—that has been accepted as true. Familiar examples are "A penny saved is a penny earned" and "There is no fool like an old fool." Machiavelli tells us: "A man who wishes to make a vocation of being good at all times will come to ruin among so many who are not good."

Such definite statements have several important qualities. One is that they are pithy: they seem to say a great deal in a few words. Another is that they appear to contain a great deal of wisdom, in part because they are delivered with such certainty, and in part because they have the ring of other aphorisms that we accept as true. Because they sound like aphorisms, they gain a claim to (unsubstantiated) truth, and we tend to accept them much more readily than perhaps we should. This may be why the speeches of contemporary politicians (modern versions of the prince) are often sprinkled with such expressions and illustrates why Machiavelli's rhetorical technique is still reliable, still effective, and still worth studying.

PREREADING QUESTIONS: WHAT TO READ FOR

The following prereading questions may help you anticipate key issues in the discussion of Niccolò Machiavelli's "The Qualities of the Prince." Keeping them in mind during your first reading of the selection should help focus your attention.

- Why does Machiavelli praise skill in warfare in his opening pages? How does that skill aid a prince?

- Is it better for a prince to be loved or to be feared?

The Qualities of the Prince

A Prince's Duty Concerning Military Matters

A prince, therefore, must not have any other object nor any other thought, nor must he take anything as his profession but war, its institutions, and its discipline; because that is the only profession

which befits one who commands; and it is of such importance that
not only does it maintain those who were born princes, but many
times it enables men of private station to rise to that position; and,
on the other hand, it is evident that when princes have given more
thought to personal luxuries than to arms, they have lost their state.
And the first way to lose it is to neglect this art; and the way to acquire it is to be well versed in this art.

Francesco Sforza[1] became Duke of Milan from being a private   2
citizen because he was armed; his sons, since they avoided the
inconveniences of arms, became private citizens after having been
dukes. For, among the other bad effects it causes, being disarmed
makes you despised; this is one of those infamies a prince should
guard himself against, as will be treated below: for between an
armed and an unarmed man there is no comparison whatsoever,
and it is not reasonable for an armed man to obey an unarmed man
willingly, nor that an unarmed man should be safe among armed
servants; since, when the former is suspicious and the latter are contemptuous, it is impossible for them to work well together. And
therefore, a prince who does not understand military matters, besides the other misfortunes already noted, cannot be esteemed by
his own soldiers, nor can he trust them.

He must, therefore, never raise his thought from this exercise of   3
war, and in peacetime he must train himself more than in time of
war; this can be done in two ways: one by action, the other by the
mind. And as far as actions are concerned, besides keeping his soldiers well disciplined and trained, he must always be out hunting,
and must accustom his body to hardships in this manner; and he
must also learn the nature of the terrain, and know how mountains
slope, how valleys open, how plains lie, and understand the nature
of rivers and swamps; and he should devote much attention to such
activities. Such knowledge is useful in two ways: first, one learns to
know one's own country and can better understand how to defend
it; second, with the knowledge and experience of the terrain, one
can easily comprehend the characteristics of any other terrain that it
is necessary to explore for the first time; for the hills, valleys, plains,
rivers, and swamps of Tuscany,[2] for instance, have certain similarities to those of other provinces; so that by knowing the lay of the
land in one province one can easily understand it in others. And
a prince who lacks this ability lacks the most important quality in a

---

[1] **Francesco Sforza (1401–1466)** Became duke of Milan in 1450. He was,
like most of Machiavelli's examples, a skilled diplomat and soldier. His court was a
model of Renaissance scholarship and achievement.

[2] **Tuscany** Florence is in the region of Italy known as Tuscany.

leader; because this skill teaches you to find the enemy, choose a campsite, lead troops, organize them for battle, and besiege towns to your own advantage.

Philopoemon, Prince of the Achaeans,[3] among the other praises   4 given to him by writers, is praised because in peacetime he thought of nothing except the means of waging war; and when he was out in the country with his friends, he often stopped and reasoned with them: "If the enemy were on that hilltop and we were here with our army, which of the two of us would have the advantage? How could we attack them without breaking formation? If we wanted to retreat, how could we do this? If they were to retreat, how could we pursue them?" And he proposed to them, as they rode along, all the contingencies that can occur in an army; he heard their opinions, expressed his own, and backed it up with arguments; so that, because of these continuous deliberations, when leading his troops no unforeseen incident could arise for which he did not have the remedy.

But as for the exercise of the mind, the prince must read histo-   5 ries and in them study the deeds of great men; he must see how they conducted themselves in wars; he must examine the reasons for their victories and for their defeats in order to avoid the latter and to imitate the former; and above all else he must do as some distinguished man before him has done, who elected to imitate someone who had been praised and honored before him, and always keep in mind his deeds and actions; just as it is reported that Alexander the Great imitated Achilles; Caesar, Alexander; Scipio, Cyrus.[4] And anyone who reads the life of Cyrus written by Xenophon then realizes how important in the life of Scipio that imitation was to his glory and how much, in purity, goodness, humanity, and generosity, Scipio conformed to those characteristics of Cyrus that Xenophon had written about.

Such methods as these a wise prince must follow, and never in   6 peaceful times must he be idle; but he must turn them diligently to

---

[3] **Philopoemon (252?–182 B.C.), Prince of the Achaeans** Philopoemon, from the city-state of Megalopolis, was a Greek general noted for skillful diplomacy. He led the Achaeans, a group of Greek states that formed the Achaean League, in several important expeditions, notably against Sparta. His cruelty in putting down a Spartan uprising caused him to be reprimanded by his superiors.

[4] **Cyrus (585?–529? B.C.)** Cyrus II (the Great), Persian emperor. Cyrus and the other figures featured in this sentence—Alexander the Great (356–323 B.C.); Achilles, hero of Homer's *Iliad;* Julius Caesar (100?–44 B.C.); and Scipio Africanus (236–184/3 B.C.), legendary Roman general—are all examples of politicians who were also great military geniuses. Xenophon (431–350? B.C.) was one of the earliest Greek historians; he chronicled the lives and military exploits of Cyrus and his son-in-law Darius.

his advantage in order to be able to profit from them in times of adversity, so that, when Fortune changes, she will find him prepared to withstand such times.

On Those Things for Which Men, and Particularly Princes, Are Praised or Blamed

Now there remains to be examined what should be the methods   7
and procedures of a prince in dealing with his subjects and friends.
And because I know that many have written about this, I am afraid
that by writing about it again I shall be thought of as presumptuous,
since in discussing this material I depart radically from the procedures of others. But since my intention is to write something useful
for anyone who understands it, it seemed more suitable to me to
search after the effectual truth of the matter rather than its imagined
one. And many writers have imagined for themselves republics and
principalities that have never been seen nor known to exist in reality; for there is such a gap between how one lives and how one
ought to live that anyone who abandons what is done for what
ought to be done learns his ruin rather than his preservation: for a
man who wishes to make a vocation of being good at all times will
come to ruin among so many who are not good. Hence it is necessary for a prince who wishes to maintain his position to learn how
not to be good, and to use this knowledge or not to use it according
to necessity.

Leaving aside, therefore, the imagined things concerning a   8
prince, and taking into account those that are true, I say that all men,
when they are spoken of, and particularly princes, since they are
placed on a higher level, are judged by some of these qualities which
bring them either blame or praise. And this is why one is considered
generous, another miserly (to use a Tuscan word, since "avaricious"
in our language is still used to mean one who wishes to acquire by
means of theft; we call "miserly" one who excessively avoids using
what he has); one is considered a giver, the other rapacious; one
cruel, another merciful; one treacherous, another faithful; one effeminate and cowardly, another bold and courageous; one humane,
another haughty; one lascivious, another chaste; one trustworthy, another cunning; one harsh, another lenient; one serious, another frivolous; one religious, another unbelieving; and the like. And I know
that everyone will admit that it would be a very praiseworthy thing
to find in a prince, of the qualities mentioned above, those that are
held to be good, but since it is neither possible to have them nor to
observe them all completely, because human nature does not permit

it, a prince must be prudent enough to know how to escape the bad reputation of those vices that would lose the state for him, and must protect himself from those that will not lose it for him, if this is possible; but if he cannot, he need not concern himself unduly if he ignores these less serious vices. And, moreover, he need not worry about incurring the bad reputation of those vices without which it would be difficult to hold his state; since, carefully taking everything into account, one will discover that something which appears to be a virtue, if pursued, will end in his destruction; while some other thing which seems to be a vice, if pursued, will result in his safety and his well-being.

On Generosity and Miserliness

Beginning, therefore, with the first of the above-mentioned 9 qualities, I say that it would be good to be considered generous; nevertheless, generosity used in such a manner as to give you a reputation for it will harm you; because if it is employed virtuously and as one should employ it, it will not be recognized and you will not avoid the reproach of its opposite. And so, if a prince wants to maintain his reputation for generosity among men, it is necessary for him not to neglect any possible means of lavish display; in so doing such a prince will always use up all his resources and he will be obliged, eventually, if he wishes to maintain his reputation for generosity, to burden the people with excessive taxes and to do everything possible to raise funds. This will begin to make him hateful to his subjects, and, becoming impoverished, he will not be much esteemed by anyone; so that, as a consequence of his generosity, having offended many and rewarded few, he will feel the effects of any slight unrest and will be ruined at the first sign of danger; recognizing this and wishing to alter his policies, he immediately runs the risk of being reproached as a miser.

A prince, therefore, unable to use this virtue of generosity in a 10 manner which will not harm himself if he is known for it, should, if he is wise, not worry about being called a miser; for with time he will come to be considered more generous once it is evident that, as a result of his parsimony, his income is sufficient, he can defend himself from anyone who makes war against him, and he can undertake enterprises without overburdening his people, so that he comes to be generous with all those from whom he takes nothing, who are countless, and miserly with all those to whom he gives nothing, who are few. In our times we have not seen great deeds accomplished except by those who were considered miserly; all others were done away with. Pope Julius II,[5] although he made use of his reputation for generosity in order to gain the papacy, then decided not to maintain it in order to be able to wage war; the present King of France[6] has waged many wars without imposing extra taxes on his subjects, only because his habitual parsimony has provided for the additional expenditures; the present King of Spain,[7] if he had been considered generous, would not have engaged in nor won so many campaigns.

Therefore, in order not to have to rob his subjects, to be able to   11
defend himself, not to become poor and contemptible, and not to be forced to become rapacious, a prince must consider it of little importance if he incurs the name of miser, for this is one of those vices that permits him to rule. And if someone were to say: Caesar with his generosity came to rule the empire, and many others, because they were generous and known to be so, achieved very high positions; I reply: you are either already a prince or you are on the way to becoming one; in the first instance such generosity is damaging; in the second it is very necessary to be thought generous. And Caesar was one of those who wanted to gain the principality of Rome; but if, after obtaining this, he had lived and had not moderated his expenditures, he would have destroyed that empire. And if someone were to reply: there have existed many princes who have accomplished great deeds with their armies who have been reputed to be generous; I answer you: a prince either spends his own money and that of his subjects or that of others; in the first case he must be economical; in the second he must not restrain any part of his generosity. And for that prince who goes out with his soldiers and lives by looting, sacking, and ransoms, who controls the property of others, such generosity is necessary; otherwise he would not be followed by his troops. And with what does not belong to you or to your subjects you can be a more liberal giver, as were Cyrus, Caesar, and Alexander; for spending the wealth of others does not lessen your reputation but adds to it; only the spending of your own is what harms you. And there is nothing that uses itself up faster than generosity, for as you employ it you lose the means of employing it, and you become either poor or despised or, in order to escape

---

[5] **Pope Julius II (1443–1513)** Giuliano della Rovere, pope from 1503 to 1513. Like many of the popes of the day, Julius II was also a diplomat and a general.

[6] **present King of France** Louis XII (1462–1515). He entered Italy on a successful military campaign in 1494.

[7] **present King of Spain** Ferdinand V (1452–1516). A studied politician; he and Queen Isabella (1451–1504) financed Christopher Columbus's voyage to the New World in 1492.

poverty, rapacious and hated. And above all other things a prince must guard himself against being despised and hated; and generosity leads you to both one and the other. So it is wiser to live with the reputation of a miser, which produces reproach without hatred, than to be forced to incur the reputation of rapacity, which produces reproach along with hatred, because you want to be considered as generous.

On Cruelty and Mercy and Whether It Is Better to Be Loved than to Be Feared or the Contrary

Proceeding to the other qualities mentioned above, I say that every 12
prince must desire to be considered merciful and not cruel; nevertheless, he must take care not to misuse this mercy. Cesare Borgia[8] was considered cruel; nonetheless, his cruelty had brought order to Romagna,[9] united it, restored it to peace and obedience. If we examine this carefully, we shall see that he was more merciful than the Florentine people, who, in order to avoid being considered cruel, allowed the destruction of Pistoia.[10] Therefore, a prince must not worry about the reproach of cruelty when it is a matter of keeping his subjects united and loyal; for with a very few examples of cruelty he will be more compassionate than those who, out of excessive mercy, permit disorders to continue, from which arise murders and plundering; for these usually harm the community at large, while the executions that come from the prince harm one individual in particular. And the new prince, above all other princes, cannot escape the reputation of being called cruel, since new states are full of dangers. And Virgil, through Dido, states: "My difficult condition and the newness of my rule make me act in such a manner, and to set guards over my land on all sides."[11]

Nevertheless, a prince must be cautious in believing and in act- 13
ing, nor should he be afraid of his own shadow; and he should proceed in such a manner, tempered by prudence and humanity, so

---

[8] **Cesare Borgia (1476–1507)** He was known for his brutality and lack of scruples, not to mention his exceptionally good luck. He was a firm ruler, son of Pope Alexander VI.

[9] **Romagna** Region northeast of Tuscany; includes the towns of Bologna, Ferrara, Ravenna, and Rimini. Borgia united it as his base of power in 1501.

[10] **Pistoia** (also known as Pistoria) A town near Florence, disturbed in 1501 by a civil war that could have been averted by strong repressive measures.

[11] The quotation is from the *Aeneid* (II. 563–564), the greatest Latin epic poem, written by Virgil (70–19 B.C.). Dido, a woman general, ruled Carthage.

that too much trust may not render him imprudent nor too much distrust render him intolerable.

From this arises an argument: whether it is better to be loved than to be feared, or the contrary. I reply that one should like to be both one and the other; but since it is difficult to join them together, it is much safer to be feared than to be loved when one of the two must be lacking. For one can generally say this about men: that they are ungrateful, fickle, simulators and deceivers, avoiders of danger, greedy for gain; and while you work for their good they are completely yours, offering you their blood, their property, their lives, and their sons, as I said earlier, when danger is far away; but when it comes nearer to you they turn away. And that prince who bases his power entirely on their words, finding himself stripped of other preparations, comes to ruin; for friendships that are acquired by a price and not by greatness and nobility of character are purchased but are not owned, and at the proper moment they cannot be spent. And men are less hesitant about harming someone who makes himself loved than one who makes himself feared because love is held together by a chain of obligation which, since men are a sorry lot, is broken on every occasion in which their own self-interest is concerned; but fear is held together by a dread of punishment which will never abandon you. 14

A prince must nevertheless make himself feared in such a manner that he will avoid hatred, even if he does not acquire love; since to be feared and not to be hated can very well be combined; and this will always be so when he keeps his hands off the property and the women of his citizens and his subjects. And if he must take someone's life, he should do so when there is proper justification and manifest cause; but, above all, he should avoid the property of others; for men forget more quickly the death of their father than the loss of their patrimony. Moreover, the reasons for seizing their property are never lacking; and he who begins to live by stealing always finds a reason for taking what belongs to others; on the contrary, reasons for taking a life are rarer and disappear sooner. 15

But when the prince is with his armies and has under his command a multitude of troops, then it is absolutely necessary that he not worry about being considered cruel; for without that reputation he will never keep an army united or prepared for any combat. Among the praiseworthy deeds of Hannibal[12] is counted this: that, 16

---

[12] **Hannibal (247–183 B.C.)** An amazingly inventive military tactician who led the Carthaginian armies against Rome for more than fifteen years. He crossed the Alps from Gaul (France) in order to surprise Rome. He was noted for use of the ambush and for "inhuman cruelty."

having a very large army, made up of all kinds of men, which he commanded in foreign lands, there never arose the slightest dissention, neither among themselves nor against their prince, both during his good and his bad fortune. This could not have arisen from anything other than his inhuman cruelty, which, along with his many other abilities, made him always respected and terrifying in the eyes of his soldiers; and without that, to attain the same effect, his other abilities would not have sufficed. And the writers of history, having considered this matter very little, on the one hand admire these deeds of his and on the other condemn the main cause of them.

And that it be true that his other abilities would not have been 17 sufficient can be seen from the example of Scipio, a most extraordinary man not only in his time but in all recorded history, whose armies in Spain rebelled against him; this came about from nothing other than his excessive compassion, which gave to his soldiers more liberty than military discipline allowed. For this he was censured in the senate by Fabius Maximus,[13] who called him the corruptor of the Roman militia. The Locrians,[14] having been ruined by one of Scipio's officers, were not avenged by him, nor was the arrogance of that officer corrected, all because of his tolerant nature; so that someone in the senate who tried to apologize for him said that there were many men who knew how not to err better than they knew how to correct errors. Such a nature would have, in time, damaged Scipio's fame and glory if he had maintained it during the empire; but, living under the control of the senate, this harmful characteristic of his not only concealed itself but brought him fame.

I conclude, therefore, returning to the problem of being feared 18 and loved, that since men love at their own pleasure and fear at the pleasure of the prince, a wise prince should build his foundation upon that which belongs to him, not upon that which belongs to others: he must strive only to avoid hatred, as has been said.

How a Prince Should Keep His Word

How praiseworthy it is for a prince to keep his word and to live 19 by integrity and not by deceit everyone knows; nevertheless, one sees from the experience of our times that the princes who have accomplished great deeds are those who have cared little for keeping

---

[13] **Fabius Maximus (?–203 B.C.)** Roman general who fought Hannibal. He was jealous of the younger Roman general Scipio.

[14] **Locrians** Inhabitants of Locri, an Italian town settled by the Greeks in c. 680 B.C.

their promises and who have known how to manipulate the minds of men by shrewdness; and in the end they have surpassed those who laid their foundations upon honesty.

You must, therefore, know that there are two means of fighting: 20 one according to the laws, the other with force; the first way is proper to man, the second to beasts; but because the first, in many cases, is not sufficient, it becomes necessary to have recourse to the second. Therefore, a prince must know how to use wisely the natures of the beast and the man. This policy was taught to princes allegorically by the ancient writers, who described how Achilles and many other ancient princes were given to Chiron[15] the Centaur to be raised and taught under his discipline. This can only mean that, having a half-beast and half-man as a teacher, a prince must know how to employ the nature of the one and the other; and the one without the other cannot endure.

Since, then, a prince must know how to make good use of the 21 nature of the beast, he should choose from among the beasts the fox and the lion; for the lion cannot defend itself from traps and the fox cannot protect itself from wolves. It is therefore necessary to be a fox in order to recognize the traps and a lion in order to frighten the wolves. Those who play only the part of the lion do not understand matters. A wise ruler, therefore, cannot and should not keep his word when such an observance of faith would be to his disadvantage and when the reasons which made him promise are removed. And if men were all good, this rule would not be good; but since men are a sorry lot and will not keep their promises to you, you likewise need not keep yours to them. A prince never lacks legitimate reasons to break his promises. Of this one could cite an endless number of modern examples to show how many pacts, how many promises have been made null and void because of the infidelity of princes; and he who has known best how to use the fox has come to a better end. But it is necessary to know how to disguise this nature well and to be a great hypocrite and a liar: and men are so simpleminded and so controlled by their present necessities that one who deceives will always find another who will allow himself to be deceived.

I do not wish to remain silent about one of these recent in- 22 stances. Alexander VI[16] did nothing else, he thought about nothing else, except to deceive men, and he always found the occasion to do

---

[15] **Chiron** A mythical figure, a centaur (half man, half horse). Unlike most centaurs, he was wise and benevolent; he was also a legendary physician.

[16] **Alexander VI (1431–1503)** Roderigo Borgia, pope from 1492 to 1503. He was Cesare Borgia's father and a corrupt but immensely powerful pope.

this. And there never was a man who had more forcefulness in his oaths, who affirmed a thing with more promises, and who honored his word less; nevertheless, his tricks always succeeded perfectly since he was well acquainted with this aspect of the world.

Therefore, it is not necessary for a prince to have all of the above-   23
mentioned qualities, but it is very necessary for him to appear to have them. Furthermore, I shall be so bold as to assert this: that having them and practicing them at all times is harmful; and appearing to have them is useful; for instance, to seem merciful, faithful, humane, forth-right, religious, and to be so; but his mind should be disposed in such a way that should it become necessary not to be so, he will be able and know how to change to the contrary. And it is essential to understand this: that a prince, and especially a new prince, cannot observe all those things by which men are considered good, for in order to maintain the state he is often obliged to act against his promise, against charity, against humanity, and against religion. And therefore, it is necessary that he have a mind ready to turn itself according to the way the winds of Fortune and the changeability of affairs require him; and, as I said above, as long as it is possible, he should not stray from the good, but he should know how to enter into evil when necessity commands.

A prince, therefore, must be very careful never to let anything   24
slip from his lips which is not full of the five qualities mentioned above: he should appear, upon seeing and hearing him, to be all mercy, all faithfulness, all integrity, all kindness, all religion. And there is nothing more necessary than to seem to possess this last quality. And men in general judge more by their eyes than their hands; for everyone can see but few can feel. Everyone sees what you seem to be, few perceive what you are, and those few do not dare to contradict the opinion of the many who have the majesty of the state to defend them; and in the actions of all men, and espe-cially of princes, where there is no impartial arbiter, one must con-sider the final result.[17] Let a prince therefore act to seize and to maintain the state; his methods will always be judged honorable and will be praised by all; for ordinary people are always deceived by ap-pearances and by the outcome of a thing; and in the world there is nothing but ordinary people; and there is no room for the few, while the many have a place to lean on. A certain prince[18] of the present day, whom I shall refrain from naming, preaches nothing but peace and faith, and to both one and the other he is entirely opposed; and

---

[17] The Italian original, *si guarda al fine*, has often been mistranslated as "the ends justify the means," something Machiavelli never wrote. [Translators' note]

[18] **A certain prince** Probably King Ferdinand V of Spain (1452–1516).

both, if he had put them into practice, would have cost him many times over either his reputation or his state.

On Avoiding Being Despised and Hated

But since, concerning the qualities mentioned above, I have 25 spoken about the most important, I should like to discuss the others briefly in this general manner: that the prince, as was noted above, should think about avoiding those things which make him hated and despised; and when he has avoided this, he will have carried out his duties and will find no danger whatsoever in other vices. As I have said, what makes him hated above all else is being rapacious and a usurper of the property and the women of his subjects; he must refrain from this; and in most cases, so long as you do not deprive them of either their property or their honor, the majority of men live happily; and you have only to deal with the ambition of a few, who can be restrained without difficulty and by many means. What makes him despised is being considered changeable, frivolous, effeminate, cowardly, irresolute; from these qualities a prince must guard himself as if from a reef, and he must strive to make everyone recognize in his actions greatness, spirit, dignity, and strength; and concerning the private affairs of his subjects, he must insist that his decision be irrevocable; and he should maintain himself in such a way that no man could imagine that he can deceive or cheat him.

That prince who projects such an opinion of himself is greatly 26 esteemed; and it is difficult to conspire against a man with such a reputation and difficult to attack him, provided that he is understood to be of great merit and revered by his subjects. For a prince must have two fears: one, internal, concerning his subjects; the other, external, concerning foreign powers. From the latter he can defend himself by his good troops and friends; and he will always have good friends if he has good troops; and internal affairs will always be stable when external affairs are stable, provided that they are not already disturbed by a conspiracy; and even if external conditions change, if he is properly organized and lives as I have said and does not lose control of himself, he will always be able to withstand every attack, just as I said that Nabis the Spartan[19] did. But concerning his subjects, when external affairs do not change, he has to fear that they may conspire secretly: the prince secures himself

---

[19]**Nabis the Spartan** Tyrant of Sparta from 207 to 192 B.C., routed by Philopoemon and the Achaean League.

from this by avoiding being hated or despised and by keeping the people satisfied with him; this is a necessary matter, as was treated above at length. And one of the most powerful remedies a prince has against conspiracies is not to be hated by the masses; for a man who plans a conspiracy always believes that he will satisfy the people by killing the prince; but when he thinks he might anger them, he cannot work up the courage to undertake such a deed; for the problems on the side of the conspirators are countless. And experience demonstrates that conspiracies have been many but few have been concluded successfully; for anyone who conspires cannot be alone, nor can he find companions except from amongst those whom he believes to be dissatisfied; and as soon as you have uncovered your intent to one dissatisfied man, you give him the means to make himself happy, since he can have everything he desires by uncovering the plot; so much is this so that, seeing a sure gain on the one hand and one doubtful and full of danger on the other, if he is to maintain faith with you he has to be either an unusually good friend or a completely determined enemy of the prince. And to treat the matter briefly, I say that on the part of the conspirator there is nothing but fear, jealousy, and the thought of punishment that terrifies him; but on the part of the prince there is the majesty of the principality, the laws, the defenses of friends and the state to protect him; so that, with the good will of the people added to all these things, it is impossible for anyone to be so rash as to plot against him. For, where usually a conspirator has to be afraid before he executes his evil deed, in this case he must be afraid, having the people as an enemy, even after the crime is performed, nor can he hope to find any refuge because of this.

One could cite countless examples on this subject; but I want to satisfy myself with only one which occurred during the time of our fathers. Messer Annibale Bentivoglio, prince of Bologna and grandfather of the present Messer Annibale, was murdered by the Canneschi[20] family, who conspired against him; he left behind no heir except Messer Giovanni,[21] then only a baby. As soon as this murder occurred, the people rose up and killed all the Canneschi. This came about because of the good will that the house of the Bentivoglio enjoyed in those days; this good will was so great that with Annibale dead, and there being no one of that family left in the city who could rule Bologna, the Bolognese people, having heard that in Florence there was one of the Bentivoglio blood who was believed until

---

[20] **Canneschi** Prominent family in Bologna.
[21] **Giovanni Bentivoglio (1443–1508)** Former tyrant of Bologna. In sequence he was a conspirator against, then a conspirator with, Cesare Borgia.

that time to be the son of a blacksmith, went to Florence to find
him, and they gave him the control of that city; it was ruled by him
until Messer Giovanni became of age to rule.

I conclude, therefore, that a prince must be little concerned   28
with conspiracies when the people are well disposed toward him;
but when the populace is hostile and regards him with hatred, he
must fear everything and everyone. And well-organized states and
wise princes have, with great diligence, taken care not to anger the
nobles and to satisfy the common people and keep them contented;
for this is one of the most important concerns that a prince has.

QUESTIONS FOR CRITICAL READING

1. The usual criticism of Machiavelli is that he advises his prince to be
   unscrupulous. Find examples for and against this claim.
2. Why do you agree or disagree with Machiavelli when he asserts that
   the great majority of people are not good? Does our government assume that to be true too?
3. Politicians—especially heads of state—are the contemporary counterparts of the prince. To what extent should successful heads of modern
   states show skill in war? Is modern war similar to wars in Machiavelli's
   era? If so, in what ways?
4. Clarify the advice Machiavelli gives concerning liberality and stinginess. Is this still good advice?
5. Are modern politicians likely to succeed by following all or most of
   Machiavelli's recommendations? Why or why not?

SUGGESTIONS FOR WRITING

1. In speaking of the prince's military duties, Machiavelli says that "being
   disarmed makes you despised." Choose an example or instance to
   strengthen your argument for or against this position. Is it possible that
   in modern society being defenseless is an advantage?
2. Find evidence within this excerpt to demonstrate that Machiavelli's attitude toward human nature is accurate. Remember that the usual criticism of Machiavelli is that he is cynical—that he thinks the worst of
   people rather than the best. Find quotations from the excerpt that support either or both of these views; then use them as the basis for an
   essay analyzing Machiavelli's views on human nature.
3. By referring to current events and leaders—either local, national, or
   international—decide whether Machiavelli's advice to the prince is useful to the modern politician. Consider whether the advice is completely
   useless or completely reliable, or whether its value depends on specific

conditions. First state the advice, then show how it applies (or does not apply) to specific politicians, and finally critique its general effectiveness.

4. Probably the chief ethical issue raised by *The Prince* is the question of whether the desired ends justify the means used to achieve them. Write an essay in which you take a stand on this question. Begin by defining the issue: What does the concept "the ends justify the means" actually mean? What difficulties may arise when unworthy means are used to achieve worthy ends? Analyze Machiavelli's references to circumstances in which questionable means were (or should have been) used to achieve worthy ends. Use historical or personal examples to give your argument substance.

5. **CONNECTIONS**   One of Machiavelli's most controversial statements is: "A man who wishes to make a vocation of being good at all times will come to ruin among so many who are not good." How would Lao-tzu respond to this statement? How does the American political environment in the current decade support this statement? Under what conditions would such a statement become irrelevant?

6. **CONNECTIONS**   For some commentators, the prince that Machiavelli describes resembles the kind of ruler Hannah Arendt deplores in her essay "Total Domination." Examine Machiavelli's views in terms of how his principles would result in a form of government similar to that which Arendt describes. Is terror a legitimate weapon for Machiavelli's prince? How would Machiavelli rationalize the prince's use of terror, should it become necessary?

JEAN-JACQUES ROUSSEAU
The Origin of Civil Society

JEAN-JACQUES ROUSSEAU (1712–1778) was the son of Suzanne Bernard and Isaac Rousseau, a watchmaker in Geneva, Switzerland. Shortly after his birth, Rousseau's mother died, and a rash duel forced his father from Geneva. Rousseau was then apprenticed at age thirteen to an engraver, a master who treated him badly. He soon ran away from his master and found a home with a Catholic noblewoman who at first raised him as her son and then, when he was twenty, took him as her lover. In the process Rousseau converted from Calvinist Protestantism to Roman Catholicism. Eventually, he left Switzerland for Paris, where he won an important essay contest and became celebrated in society.

Over the course of his lifetime, Rousseau produced a wide variety of literary and musical works, including a novel, *Emile* (1762), an opera, *The Village Soothsayer* (1752), and an autobiography, *The Confessions* (published posthumously in 1789). *The Social Contract* (1762) was part of a never-completed longer work on political systems. In many ways Rousseau wrote in reaction to political thinkers such as Hugo Grotius and Thomas Hobbes, to whom he responds in the following selection. He contended that the Dutch philosopher and legal expert Grotius unquestioningly accepted the power of the aristocracy. He felt Grotius paid too much attention to what was rather than what ought to be. On the other hand, Hobbes, the English political philosopher, asserted that people had a choice of being free or being ruled. In other words, those who were members of civil society chose to give up their freedom and submit to the monarch's rule. Either they relinquished their freedom, or they removed themselves from civil society to live a brutish existence.

From *Social Contract: Essays by Locke, Hume, and Rousseau.* Translated by Gerald Hopkins.

Rousseau argued against Grotius by examining the way things ought to be. He argued against Hobbes by asserting that both the body politic and the monarch were sovereign and that when people created a civil society they surrendered their freedom to themselves as a group. If one person acted as sovereign or lawgiver, then that lawgiver had the responsibility of acting in accord with the will of the people. In a sense, this view parallels some of the views of Lao-tzu in the *Tao-te Ching*.

Popularly referred to as a defender of republicanism, Rousseau looked to the Republic of Geneva, his birthplace, as a model of government. He also idealized the generally democratic government of smaller Swiss cantons, such as Neuchatel, which used a form of town meeting where people gathered face to face to settle important issues. Ironically, Geneva put out a warrant for his arrest upon the publication of *The Social Contract* because although it praised Geneva's republicanism, it also condemned societies that depended on rule by a limited aristocracy. Unfortunately for Rousseau, at that time Geneva was governed by a small number of aristocratic families. Rousseau was deprived of his citizenship and could not return to his native home.

Similarly, Rousseau's controversial views were not easily received by those in power in France. After the publication of *Emile* offended the French Parliament, Rousseau was forced to abandon his comfortable rustic circumstances—living on country estates provided by patrons from the court—and spend the rest of his life in financial uncertainty. Ironically, in 1789, a decade after his death, Rousseau's philosophy was adopted by supporters of the French Revolution in their bloody revolt against the aristocracy.

Rousseau's Rhetoric

Rousseau's method is in many ways antagonistic: he establishes the views of other thinkers, counters them, and then offers his own ideas. An early example appears in the opening of paragraph 8: "Grotius denies that political power is ever exercised in the interests of the governed, and quotes the institution of slavery in support of his contention. His invariable method of arguing is to derive Right from Fact." Among other things, Rousseau expects his readers to know who Grotius was and what he said. He also expects his readers to agree that Grotius derives "Right from Fact" by understanding that the fact of monarchy justifies it as being right. As Rousseau tells us, that kind of circular reasoning is especially kind to tyrants, because it justifies them by their existence.

Rousseau uses analysis and examination of detail as his main rhetorical approaches. Whether he examines the ideas of others or presents ideas of his own, he is careful to examine the bases of the argument and to follow the arguments to their conclusions. He does this very thoroughly in his section "Of Slavery," in which he demonstrates that slavery is unacceptable no matter which of the current arguments are used to support it, including the widely held view that it was justifiable to enslave captured soldiers on the grounds that they owed their lives to their captors.

Rousseau also makes careful use of aphorism and analogy. His opening statement, "Man is born free, and everywhere he is in chains," is an aphorism that has been often quoted. It is a powerful and perplexing statement. How do people who are born free lose their freedom? Is it taken from them, or do they willingly surrender it? Rousseau spends considerable time examining this point.

The use of analogy is probably most striking in his comparison of government with the family. The force of the analogy reminds us that the members of a family are to be looked after by the family. As he tells us beginning in paragraph 5, the family is the only natural form of society. But instead of stopping there, he goes on to say that children are bound to the father only as long as they need him. Once they are able to be independent, they dissolve the natural bond and "return to a condition of equal independence." This analogy differs from the existing popular view that the monarch was like the father in a family and the people like his children; in fact, the analogy works against the legitimacy of the traditional monarchy as it was known in eighteenth-century France.

Rousseau also refers to other writers, using a rhetorical device known as *testimony:* he paraphrases the views of other authorities and moves on to promote his own. But in referring to other writers, Rousseau is unusually clever. For example, in paragraph 10 he begins with the analogy of the shepherd as the ruler in this fashion: "Just as the shepherd is superior in kind to his sheep, so, too, the shepherds of men, or, in other words, their rulers, are superior in kind to their peoples. This, according to Philo, was the argument advanced by Caligula, the Emperor, who drew from the analogy the perfectly true conclusion that either Kings are Gods or their subjects brute beasts." Caligula was a madman and an emperor guilty of enormous cruelty; from his point of view it may have seemed true that kings were gods. But Rousseau, in citing this questionable authority, disputes the validity of the analogy.

He argues as well against the view that might makes right in "Of the Right of the Strongest." The value of the social contract, he explains, is to produce a society that is not governed by the mightiest and most ruthless and that permits those who are not mighty to live peacefully and unmolested. Thus, those who participate in the social contract give up certain freedoms but gain many more—among them the freedom not to be dominated by physical brutality.

Rousseau concentrates on the question of man in nature, or natural society. His view is that natural society is dominated by the strongest individuals but that at some point natural society breaks down. Thus, in order to guarantee the rights of those who are not the strongest, the political order must change. "Some form of association" is developed "for the protection of the person and property of each constituent member." By surrendering some freedom to the group as a whole—to "the general will"—the individuals in the group can expect to prosper more widely and to live more happily. According to Rousseau, the establishment of a social contract ensures the stability of this form of civil society.

PREREADING QUESTIONS:
WHAT TO READ FOR

The following prereading questions may help you anticipate key issues in the discussion of Jean-Jacques Rousseau's "The Origin of Civil Society." Keeping them in mind as you read should help focus your attention.

- When Rousseau says, "Man is born free, and everywhere he is in chains," does he seem to be referring literally to slaves in chains, or more figuratively to people in general?

- How convincing is Rousseau when he claims that the oldest form of government is the family?

- The "Social Contract" is one of Rousseau's chief ideas. What does it seem to mean?

The Origin of Civil Society

Note

It is my wish to inquire whether it be possible, within the civil order, to 1
discover a legitimate and stable basis of Government. This I shall do by considering human beings as they are and laws as they might be. I shall attempt, throughout my investigations, to maintain a constant connection between

what right permits and interest demands, in order that no separation may be made between justice and utility. I intend to begin without first proving the importance of my subject. Am I, it will be asked, either prince or legislator that I take it upon me to write of politics? My answer is—No; and it is for that very reason that I have chosen politics as the matter of my book. Were I either the one or the other I should not waste my time in laying down what has to be done. I should do it, or else hold my peace.

I was born into a free state and am a member of its sovereign body. 2
My influence on public affairs may be small, but because I have a right to exercise my vote, it is my duty to learn their nature, and it has been for me a matter of constant delight, while meditating on problems of Government in general, to find ever fresh reasons for regarding with true affection the way in which these things are ordered in my native land.

The Subject of the First Book

Man is born free, and everywhere he is in chains. Many a man be- 3
lieves himself to be the master of others who is, no less than they, a slave. How did this change take place? I do not know. What can make it legitimate? To this question I hope to be able to furnish an answer.

Were I considering only force and the effects of force, I should 4
say: "So long as a People is constrained to obey, and does, in fact, obey, it does well. So soon as it can shake off its yoke, and succeeds in doing so, it does better. The fact that it has recovered its liberty by virtue of that same right by which it was stolen, means either that it is entitled to resume it, or that its theft by others was, in the first place, without justification." But the social order is a sacred right which serves as a foundation for all other rights. This right, however, since it comes not by nature, must have been built upon conventions. To discover what these conventions are is the matter of our inquiry. But, before proceeding further, I must establish the truth of what I have so far advanced.

Of Primitive Societies

The oldest form of society—and the only natural one—is the 5
family. Children remain bound to their father for only just so long as they feel the need of him for their self-preservation. Once that need ceases the natural bond is dissolved. From then on, the children, freed from the obedience which they formerly owed, and the father, cleared of his debt of responsibility to them, return to a condition of equal independence. If the bond remain operative it is no longer

something imposed by nature, but has become a matter of deliberate choice. The family is a family still, but by reason of convention only.

This shared liberty is a consequence of man's nature. Its first law 6
is that of self-preservation: its first concern is for what it owes itself. As soon as a man attains the age of reason he becomes his own master, because he alone can judge of what will best assure his continued existence.

We may, therefore, if we will, regard the family as the basic model 7
of all political associations. The ruler is the father writ large: the people are, by analogy, his children, and all, ruler and people alike, alienate their freedom only so far as it is to their advantage to do so. The only difference is that, whereas in the family the father's love for his children is sufficient reward to him for the care he has lavished on them, in the State, the pleasure of commanding others takes its place, since the ruler is not in a relation of love to his people.

Grotius[1] denies that political power is ever exercised in the in- 8
terests of the governed, and quotes the institution of slavery in support of his contention. His invariable method of arguing is to derive Right from Fact. It might be possible to adopt a more logical system of reasoning, but none which would be more favorable to tyrants.

According to Grotius, therefore, it is doubtful whether the term 9
"human race" belongs to only a few hundred men, or whether those few hundred men belong to the human race. From the evidence of his book it seems clear that he holds by the first of these alternatives, and on this point Hobbes[2] is in agreement with him. If this is so, then humanity is divided into herds of livestock, each with its "guardian" who watches over his charges only that he may ultimately devour them.

Just as the shepherd is superior in kind to his sheep, so, too, the 10
shepherds of men, or, in other words, their rulers, are superior in kind to their peoples. This, according to Philo,[3] was the argument advanced by Caligula,[4] the Emperor, who drew from the analogy the

---

[1] **Hugo Grotius (1583–1645)** A Dutch lawyer who spent some time in exile in Paris. His fame as a child prodigy was considerable; his book on the laws of war (*De jure belli ac Pacis*) was widely known in Europe.

[2] **Thomas Hobbes (1588–1679)** An Englishman known as a materialist philosopher who did not credit divine influence in politics. He became famous for *Leviathan*, a study of politics that treated the state as if it were a monster (leviathan) with a life of its own.

[3] **Philo (13? B.C.–A.D. 47?)** A Jew who absorbed Greek culture and who wrote widely on many subjects. His studies on Mosaic law were considered important.

[4] **Caligula (A.D. 12–41)** Roman emperor of uncertain sanity. He loved his sister Drusilla so much that he had her deified when she died. A military commander, he was assassinated by an officer.

perfectly true conclusion that either Kings are Gods or their subjects brute beasts.

The reasoning of Caligula, of Hobbes, and of Grotius is funda- 11 mentally the same. Far earlier, Aristotle,[5] too, had maintained that men are not by nature equal, but that some are born to be slaves, others to be masters.

Aristotle was right: but he mistook the effect for the cause. 12 Nothing is more certain than that a man born into a condition of slavery is a slave by nature. A slave in fetters loses everything—even the desire to be freed from them. He grows to love his slavery, as the companions of Ulysses grew to love their state of brutish transformation.[6]

If some men are by nature slaves, the reason is that they have 13 been made slaves *against* nature. Force made the first slaves: cowardice has perpetuated the species.

I have made no mention of King Adam or of the Emperor Noah, 14 the father of three great Monarchs[7] who divided up the universe between them, as did the children of Saturn,[8] whom some have been tempted to identify with them. I trust that I may be given credit for my moderation, since, being descended in a direct line from one of these Princes, and quite possibly belonging to the elder branch, I may, for all I know, were my claims supported in law, be even now the legitimate Sovereign of the Human Race.[9] However that may be, all will concur in the view that Adam was King of the World, as was Robinson Crusoe of his island, only so long as he was its only inhabitant, and the great advantage of empire held on such terms was that the Monarch, firmly seated on his throne, had no need to fear rebellions, conspiracy, or war.

---

[5] **Aristotle (384–322 B.C.)** A student of Plato; his philosophical method became the dominant intellectual force in Western thought.

[6] **state of brutish transformation** This sentence refers to the Circe episode in Homer's *Odyssey* (X, XII). Circe was a sorceress who, by means of drugs, enchanted men and turned them into swine. Ulysses (Latin name of Odysseus), king of Ithaca, is the central figure of the *Odyssey*.

[7] **the father of three great Monarchs** Adam in the Bible (Genesis 4:1–25) fathered Cain, Abel, Enoch, and Seth. Noah's sons, Shem, Ham, and Japheth, repopulated the world after the Flood (Genesis 6:9–9:19).

[8] **children of Saturn** Saturn is a mythic god associated with the golden age of Rome and with the Greek god Cronus. It is probably the children of Cronus—Zeus, Poseidon, Hades, Demeter, and Hera—referred to here, because the Roman god Saturn had only one son, Picus.

[9] **Sovereign of the Human Race** Rousseau is being ironic; like the rest of us, he is descended from Adam (according to the Bible).

Of the Right of the Strongest

However strong a man, he is never strong enough to remain   15
master always, unless he transform his Might into Right, and Obedience into Duty. Hence we have come to speak of the Right of the
Strongest, a right which, seemingly assumed in irony, has, in fact, become established in principle. But the meaning of the phrase has
never been adequately explained. Strength is a physical attribute, and
I fail to see how any moral sanction can attach to its effects. To yield
to the strong is an act of necessity, not of will. At most it is the result
of a dictate of prudence. How, then, can it become a duty?

Let us assume for a moment that some such Right does really exist.   16
The only deduction from this premise is inexplicable gibberish. For to
admit that Might makes Right is to reverse the process of effect and
cause. The mighty man who defeats his rival becomes heir to his Right.
So soon as we can disobey with impunity, disobedience becomes legitimate. And, since the Mightiest is always right, it merely remains for us
to become possessed of Might. But what validity can there be in a Right
which ceases to exist when Might changes hands? If a man be constrained by Might to obey, what need has he to obey by Duty? And if
he is not constrained to obey, there is no further obligation on him to
do so. It follows, therefore, that the word Right adds nothing to the
idea of Might. It becomes, in this connection, completely meaningless.

Obey the Powers that be. If that means Yield to Force, the precept   17
is admirable but redundant. My reply to those who advance it is that
no case will ever be found of its violation. All power comes from God.
Certainly, but so do all ailments. Are we to conclude from such an argument that we are never to call in the doctor? If I am waylaid by a
footpad at the corner of a wood, I am constrained by force to give him
my purse. But if I can manage to keep it from him, is it my duty to
hand it over? His pistol is also a symbol of Power. It must, then, be admitted that Might does not create Right, and that no man is under an
obligation to obey any but the legitimate powers of the State. And so I
continually come back to the question I first asked.

Of Slavery

Since no man has natural authority over his fellows, and since   18
Might can produce no Right, the only foundation left for legitimate
authority in human societies is Agreement.

If a private citizen, says Grotius, can alienate his liberty and   19
make himself another man's slave, why should not a whole people do
the same, and subject themselves to the will of a King? The argument
contains a number of ambiguous words which stand in need of

explanation. But let us confine our attention to one only—*alienate*. To alienate means to give or to sell. Now a man who becomes the slave of another does not give himself. He sells himself in return for bare subsistence, if for nothing more. But why should a whole people sell themselves? So far from furnishing subsistence to his subjects, a King draws his own from them, and from them alone. According to Rabelais,[10] it takes a lot to keep a King. Do we, then, maintain that a subject surrenders his person on condition that his property be taken too? It is difficult to see what he will have left.

It will be said that the despot guarantees civil peace to his sub-   20
jects. So be it. But how are they the gainers if the wars to which his ambition may expose them, his insatiable greed, and the vexatious demands of his Ministers cause them more loss than would any outbreak of internal dissension? How do they benefit if that very condition of civil peace be one of the causes of their wretchedness? One can live peacefully enough in a dungeon, but such peace will hardly, of itself, ensure one's happiness. The Greeks imprisoned in the cave of Cyclops[11] lived peacefully while awaiting their turn to be devoured.

To say that a man gives himself for nothing is to commit oneself   21
to an absurd and inconceivable statement. Such an act of surrender is illegitimate, null, and void by the mere fact that he who makes it is not in his right mind. To say the same thing of a whole People is tantamount to admitting that the People in question are a nation of imbeciles. Imbecility does not produce Right.

Even if a man can alienate himself, he cannot alienate his chil-   22
dren. They are born free, their liberty belongs to them, and no one but themselves has a right to dispose of it. Before they have attained the age of reason their father may make, on their behalf, certain rules with a view to ensuring their preservation and well-being. But any such limitation of their freedom of choice must be regarded as neither irrevocable nor unconditional, for to alienate another's liberty is contrary to the natural order, and is an abuse of the father's rights. It follows that an arbitrary government can be legitimate only on condition that each successive generation of subjects is free either to accept or to reject it, and if this is so, then the government will no longer be arbitrary.

When a man renounces his liberty he renounces his essential   23
manhood, his rights, and even his duty as a human being. There is no compensation possible for such complete renunciation. It is incompatible with man's nature, and to deprive him of his free will is to deprive his actions of all moral sanction. The convention, in short, which sets

---

[10] **François Rabelais (c. 1494–1553)** French writer, author of *Gargantua* and *Pantagruel*, satires on politics and religion.

[11] **cave of Cyclops** The cyclops is a one-eyed giant cannibal whose cave is the scene of one of Odysseus's triumphs in Homer's *Odyssey* (IX).

up on one side an absolute authority, and on the other an obligation to obey without question, is vain and meaningless. Is it not obvious that where we can demand everything we owe nothing? Where there is no mutual obligation, no interchange of duties, it must, surely, be clear that the actions of the commanded cease to have any moral value? For how can it be maintained that my slave has any "right" against me when everything that he has is my property? His right being *my* right, it is absurd to speak of it as ever operating to my disadvantage.

Grotius, and those who think like him, have found in the fact of war another justification for the so-called "right" of slavery. They argue that since the victor has a *right* to kill his defeated enemy, the latter may, if he so wish, ransom his life at the expense of his liberty, and that this compact is the more legitimate in that it benefits both parties. 24

But it is evident that this alleged *right* of a man to kill his enemies is not in any way a derivative of the state of war, if only because men, in their primitive condition of independence, are not bound to one another by any relationship sufficiently stable to produce a state either of war or of peace. They are not *naturally* enemies. It is the link between *things* rather than between *men* that constitutes war, and since a state of war cannot originate in simple personal relations, but only in relations between things, private hostility between man and man cannot obtain either in a state of nature where there is no generally accepted system of private property, or in a state of society where law is the supreme authority. 25

Single combats, duels, personal encounters are incidents which do not constitute a "state" of anything. As to those private wars which were authorized by the Ordinances of King Louis IX[12] and suspended by the Peace of God, they were merely an abuse of Feudalism — that most absurd of all systems of government, so contrary was it to the principles of Natural Right and of all good polity. 26

War, therefore, is something that occurs not between man and man, but between States. The individuals who become involved in it are enemies only by accident. They fight not as men or even as citizens, but as soldiers: not as members of this or that national group, but as its defenders. A State can have as its enemies only other States, not men at all, seeing that there can be no true relationship between things of a different nature. 27

This principle is in harmony with that of all periods, and with the constant practice of every civilized society. A declaration of war is a warning, not so much to Governments as to their subjects. The 28

---

[12] **King Louis IX (1214–1270)** King of France, also called St. Louis. He was looked upon as an ideal monarch.

foreigner—whether king, private person, or nation as a whole—who steals, murders, or holds in durance the subjects of another country without first declaring war on that country's Prince, acts not as an enemy but as a brigand. Even when war has been joined, the just Prince, though he may seize all public property in enemy territory, yet respects the property and possessions of individuals, and, in so doing, shows his concern for those rights on which his own laws are based. The object of war being the destruction of the enemy State, a commander has a perfect right to kill its defenders so long as their arms are in their hands: but once they have laid them down and have submitted, they cease to be enemies, or instruments employed by an enemy, and revert to the condition of men, pure and simple, over whose lives no one can any longer exercise a rightful claim. Sometimes it is possible to destroy a State without killing any of its subjects, and nothing in war can be claimed as a right save what may be necessary for the accomplishment of the victor's end. These principles are not those of Grotius, nor are they based on the authority of poets, but derive from the Nature of Things, and are founded upon Reason.

The Right of Conquest finds its sole sanction in the Law of the 29 Strongest. If war does not give to the victor the right to massacre his defeated enemies, he cannot base upon a nonexistent right any claim to the further one of enslaving them. We have the right to kill our enemies only when we cannot enslave them. It follows, therefore, that the right to enslave cannot be deduced from the right to kill, and that we are guilty of enforcing an iniquitous exchange if we make a vanquished foeman purchase with his liberty that life over which we have no right. Is it not obvious that once we begin basing the right of life and death on the right to enslave, and the right to enslave on the right of life and death, we are caught in a vicious circle? Even if we assume the existence of this terrible right to kill all and sundry, I still maintain that a man enslaved, or a People conquered, in war is under no obligation to obey beyond the point at which force ceases to be operative. If the victor spares the life of his defeated opponent in return for an equivalent, he cannot be said to have shown him mercy. In either case he destroys him, but in the latter case he derives value from his act, while in the former he gains nothing. His authority, however, rests on no basis but that of force. There is still a state of war between the two men, and it conditions the whole relationship in which they stand to one another. The enjoyment of the Rights of War presupposes that there has been no treaty of Peace. Conqueror and conquered have, to be sure, entered into a compact, but such a compact, far from liquidating the state of war, assumes its continuance.

Thus, in whatever way we look at the matter, the "Right" to en- 30 slave has no existence, not only because it is without legal validity, but because the very term is absurd and meaningless. The words *Slavery* and *Right* are contradictory and mutually exclusive. Whether we be considering the relation of one man to another man, or of an individual to a whole People, it is equally idiotic to say—"You and I have made a compact which represents nothing but loss to you and gain to me. I shall observe it so long as it pleases me to do so—and so shall you, until I cease to find it convenient."

That We Must Always Go Back to an Original Compact

Even were I to grant all that I have so far refuted, the champions   31 of despotism would not be one whit the better off. There will always be a vast difference between subduing a mob and governing a social group. No matter how many isolated individuals may submit to the enforced control of a single conqueror, the resulting relationship will ever be that of Master and Slave, never of People and Ruler. The body of men so controlled may be an agglomeration; it is not an association. It implies neither public welfare nor a body politic. An individual may conquer half the world, but he is still only an individual. His interests, wholly different from those of his subjects, are private to himself. When he dies his empire is left scattered and disintegrated. He is like an oak which crumbles and collapses in ashes so soon as the fire consumes it.

"A People," says Grotius, "may give themselves to a king." His ar-   32 gument implies that the said People were already a People before this act of surrender. The very act of gift was that of a political group and presupposed deliberation. Before, therefore, we consider the act by which a People chooses their king, it were well if we considered the act by which a People is constituted as such. For it necessarily precedes the other, and is the true foundation on which all Societies rest.

Had there been no original compact, why, unless the choice   33 were unanimous, should the minority ever have agreed to accept the decision of the majority? What right have the hundred who desire a master to vote for the ten who do not? The institution of the franchise is, in itself, a form of compact, and assumes that, at least once in its operation, complete unanimity existed.

Of the Social Pact

I assume, for the sake of argument, that a point was reached in   34 the history of mankind when the obstacles to continuing in a state of Nature were stronger than the forces which each individual could employ to the end of continuing in it. The original state of Nature, therefore, could no longer endure, and the human race would have perished had it not changed its manner of existence.

Now, since men can by no means engender new powers, but 35 can only unite and control those of which they are already possessed, there is no way in which they can maintain themselves save by coming together and pooling their strength in a way that will enable them to withstand any resistance exerted upon them from without. They must develop some sort of central direction and learn to act in concert.

Such a concentration of powers can be brought about only as 36 the consequence of an agreement reached between individuals. But the self-preservation of each single man derives primarily from his own strength and from his own freedom. How, then, can he limit these without, at the same time, doing himself an injury and neglecting that care which it is his duty to devote to his own concerns? This difficulty, in so far as it is relevant to my subject, can be expressed as follows:

"Some form of association must be found as a result of which 37 the whole strength of the community will be enlisted for the protection of the person and property of each constituent member, in such a way that each, when united to his fellows, renders obedience to his own will, and remains as free as he was before." That is the basic problem of which the Social Contract provides the solution.

The clauses of this Contract are determined by the Act of Asso- 38 ciation in such a way that the least modification must render them null and void. Even though they may never have been formally enunciated, they must be everywhere the same, and everywhere tacitly admitted and recognized. So completely must this be the case that, should the social compact be violated, each associated individual would at once resume all the rights which once were his, and regain his natural liberty, by the mere fact of losing the agreed liberty for which he renounced it.

It must be clearly understood that the clauses in question can be 39 reduced, in the last analysis, to one only, to wit, the complete alienation by each associate member to the community of *all his rights*. For, in the first place, since each has made surrender of himself without reservation, the resultant conditions are the same for all: and, because they are the same for all, it is in the interest of none to make them onerous to his fellows.

Furthermore, this alienation having been made unreservedly, 40 the union of individuals is as perfect as it well can be, none of the associated members having any claim against the community. For should there be any rights left to individuals, and no common authority be empowered to pronounce as between them and the public, then each, being in some things his own judge, would soon claim to be so in all. Were that so, a state of Nature would still remain in being, the conditions of association becoming either despotic or ineffective.

In short, whoso gives himself to all gives himself to none. And, 41 since there is no member of the social group over whom we do not acquire precisely the same rights as those over ourselves which we have surrendered to him, it follows that we gain the exact equivalent of what we lose, as well as an added power to conserve what we already have.

If, then, we take from the social pact everything which is not es- 42 sential to it, we shall find it to be reduced to the following terms: "each of us contributes to the group his person and the powers which he wields as a person under the supreme direction of the general will, and we receive into the body politic each individual as forming an indivisible part of the whole."

As soon as the act of association becomes a reality, it substitutes 43 for the person of each of the contracting parties a moral and collective body made up of as many members as the constituting assembly has votes, which body receives from this very act of constitution its unity, its dispersed *self*, and its will. The public person thus formed by the union of individuals was known in the old days as a *City*, but now as the *Republic* or *Body Politic*. This, when it fulfills a passive role, is known by its members as *The State*, when an active one, as *The Sovereign People*, and, in contrast to other similar bodies, as a *Power*. In respect of the constituent associates, it enjoys the collective name of *The People*, the individuals who compose it being known as *Citizens* in so far as they share in the sovereign authority, as *Subjects* in so far as they owe obedience to the laws of the State. But these different terms frequently overlap, and are used indiscriminately one for the other. It is enough that we should realize the difference between them when they are employed in a precise sense.

Of the Sovereign

It is clear from the above formula that the act of association im- 44 plies a mutual undertaking between the body politic and its constituent members. Each individual comprising the former contracts, so to speak, with himself and has a twofold function. As a member of the sovereign people he owes a duty to each of his neighbors, and, as a Citizen, to the sovereign people as a whole. But we cannot here apply that maxim of Civil Law according to which no man can be held to an undertaking entered into with himself, because there is a great difference between a man's duty to himself and to a whole of which he forms a part.

Here it should be pointed out that a public decision which can 45 enjoin obedience on all subjects to their Sovereign, by reason of the double aspect under which each is seen, cannot, on the contrary, bind the sovereign in his dealings with himself. Consequently, it is against the nature of the body politic that the sovereign should impose upon himself a law which he cannot infringe. For, since he can regard himself under one aspect only, he is in the position of an individual entering into a contract with himself. Whence it follows that there is not, nor can be, any fundamental law which is obligatory for the whole body of the People, not even the social contract itself. This does not mean that the body politic is unable to enter into engagements with some other Power, provided always that such engagements do not derogate from the nature of the Contract; for the relation of the body politic to a foreign Power is that of a simple individual.

But the body politic, or Sovereign, in that it derives its being 46 simply and solely from the sanctity of the said Contract, can never bind itself, even in its relations with a foreign Power, by any decision which might derogate from the validity of the original act. It may not, for instance, alienate any portion of itself, nor make submission to any other sovereign. To violate the act by reason of which it exists would be tantamount to destroying itself, and that which is nothing can produce nothing.

As soon as a mob has become united into a body politic, any at- 47 tack upon one of its members is an attack upon itself. Still more important is the fact that, should any offense be committed against the body politic as a whole, the effect must be felt by each of its members. Both duty and interest, therefore, oblige the two contracting parties to render one another mutual assistance. The same individuals should seek to unite under this double aspect all the advantages which flow from it.

Now, the Sovereign People, having no existence, outside that of 48 the individuals who compose it, has, and can have, no interest at variance with theirs. Consequently, the sovereign power need give no guarantee to its subjects, since it is impossible that the body should wish to injure all its members, nor, as we shall see later, can it injure any single individual. The Sovereign, by merely existing, is always what it should be.

But the same does not hold true of the relation of subject to sov- 49 ereign. In spite of common interest, there can be no guarantee that the subject will observe his duty to the sovereign unless means are found to ensure his loyalty.

Each individual, indeed, may, as a man, exercise a will at vari-   50
ance with, or different from, that general will to which, as citizen, he contributes. His personal interest may dictate a line of action quite other than that demanded by the interest of all. The fact that his own existence as an individual has an absolute value, and that he is, by nature, an independent being, may lead him to conclude that what he owes to the common cause is something that he renders of his own free will; and he may decide that by leaving the debt unpaid he does less harm to his fellows than he would to himself should he make the necessary surrender. Regarding the moral entity constitut-ing the State as a rational abstraction because it is not a man, he might enjoy his rights as a citizen without, at the same time, fulfill-ing his duties as a subject, and the resultant injustice might grow until it brought ruin upon the whole body politic.

In order, then, that the social compact may not be but a vain   51
formula, it must contain, though unexpressed, the single undertak-ing which can alone give force to the whole, namely, that whoever shall refuse to obey the general will must be constrained by the whole body of his fellow citizens to do so: which is no more than to say that it may be necessary to compel a man to be free — freedom being that condition which, by giving each citizen to his country, guarantees him from all personal dependence and is the foundation upon which the whole political machine rests, and supplies the power which works it. Only the recognition by the individual of the rights of the community can give legal force to undertakings entered into between citizens, which, otherwise, would become absurd, tyrannical, and exposed to vast abuses.

Of the Civil State

The passage from the state of nature to the civil state produces a   52
truly remarkable change in the individual. It substitutes justice for in-stinct in his behavior, and gives to his actions a moral basis which formerly was lacking. Only when the voice of duty replaces physical impulse and when right replaces the cravings of appetite does the man who, till then, was concerned solely with himself, realize that he is under compulsion to obey quite different principles, and that he must now consult his reason and not merely respond to the prompt-ings of desire. Although he may find himself deprived of many ad-vantages which were his in a state of nature, he will recognize that he

has gained others which are of far greater value. By dint of being exercised, his faculties will develop, his ideas take on a wider scope, his sentiments become ennobled, and his whole soul be so elevated, that, but for the fact that misuse of the new conditions still, at times, degrades him to a point below that from which he has emerged, he would unceasingly bless the day which freed him forever from his ancient state, and turned him from a limited and stupid animal into an intelligent being and a Man.

Let us reduce all this to terms which can be easily compared. 53 What a man loses as a result of the Social Contract is his natural liberty and his unqualified right to lay hands on all that tempts him, provided only that he can compass its possession. What he gains is civil liberty and the ownership of what belongs to him. That we may labor under no illusion concerning these compensations, it is well that we distinguish between natural liberty which the individual enjoys so long as he is strong enough to maintain it, and civil liberty which is curtailed by the general will. Between possessions which derive from physical strength and the right of the first-comer, and ownership which can be based only on a positive title.

To the benefits conferred by the status of citizenship might be 54 added that of Moral Freedom, which alone makes a man his own master. For to be subject to appetite is to be a slave, while to obey the laws laid down by society is to be free. But I have already said enough on this point, and am not concerned here with the philosophical meaning of the word *liberty*.

Of Real Property

Each individual member of the Community gives himself to it at 55 the moment of its formation. What he gives is the whole man as he then is, with all his qualities of strength and power, and everything of which he stands possessed. Not that, as a result of this act of gift, such possessions, by changing hands and becoming the property of the Sovereign, change their nature. Just as the resources of strength upon which the City can draw are incomparably greater than those at the disposition of any single individual, so, too, is public possession when backed by a greater power. It is made more irrevocable, though not, so far, at least, as regards foreigners, more legitimate. For the State, by reason of the Social Contract which, within it, is the basis of all Rights, is the master of all its members' goods, though, in its dealings with other Powers, it is so only by virtue of its rights as

first occupier, which come to it from the individuals who make
it up.

The Right of "first occupancy," though more real than the "Right   56
of the strongest," becomes a genuine right only after the right of
property has been established. All men have a natural right to what
is necessary to them. But the positive act which establishes a man's
claim to any particular item of property limits him to that and excludes him from all others. His share having been determined, he
must confine himself to that, and no longer has any claim on the
property of the community. That is why the right of "first occupancy," however weak it be in a state of nature, is guaranteed to
every man enjoying the status of citizen. In so far as he benefits from
this right, he withholds his claim, not so much from what is another's, as from what is not specifically his.

In order that the right of "first occupancy" may be legalized, the   57
following conditions must be present. (1) There must be no one already living on the land in question. (2) A man must occupy only so
much of it as is necessary for his subsistence. (3) He must take possession of it, not by empty ceremony, but by virtue of his intention
to work and to cultivate it, for that, in the absence of legal title,
alone constitutes a claim which will be respected by others.

In effect, by according the right of "first occupancy" to a man's   58
needs and to his will to work, are we not stretching it as far as it will
go? Should not some limits be set to this right? Has a man only to set
foot on land belonging to the community to justify his claim to be its
master? Just because he is strong enough, at one particular moment,
to keep others off, can he demand that they shall never return? How
can a man or a People take possession of vast territories, thereby excluding the rest of the world from their enjoyment, save by an act of
criminal usurpation, since, as the result of such an act, the rest of
humanity is deprived of the amenities of dwelling and subsistence
which nature has provided for their common enjoyment? When
Nuñez Balboa,[13] landing upon a strip of coast, claimed the Southern
Sea and the whole of South America as the property of the crown of
Castille, was he thereby justified in dispossessing its former inhabitants, and in excluding from it all the other princes of the earth?
Grant that, and there will be no end to such vain ceremonies. It
would be open to His Catholic Majesty[14] to claim from his Council

---

[13] **Nuñez Balboa (1475–1519)** Spanish explorer who discovered the Pacific
Ocean.
[14] **His Catholic Majesty** A reference to the king of Spain, probably Ferdinand
II of Aragon (1452–1516).

Chamber possession of the whole Universe, only excepting those portions of it already in the ownership of other princes.

One can understand how the lands of individuals, separate but 59 contiguous, become public territory, and how the right of sovereignty, extending from men to the land they occupy, becomes at one real and personal—a fact which makes their owners more than ever dependent, and turns their very strength into a guarantee of their fidelity. This is an advantage which does not seem to have been considered by the monarchs of the ancient world, who, claiming to be no more than kings of the Persians, the Scythians, the Macedonians, seem to have regarded themselves rather as the rulers of men than as the masters of countries. Those of our day are cleverer, for they style themselves kings of France, of Spain, of England, and so forth. Thus, by controlling the land, they can be very sure of controlling its inhabitants.

The strange thing about this act of alienation is that, far from 60 depriving its members of their property by accepting its surrender, the Community actually establishes their claim to its legitimate ownership, and changes what was formerly mere usurpation into a right, by virtue of which they may enjoy possession. As owners they are Trustees for the Commonwealth. Their rights are respected by their fellow citizens and are maintained by the united strength of the community against any outside attack. From ceding their property to the State—and thus, to themselves—they derive nothing but advantage, since they have, so to speak, acquired all that they have surrendered. This paradox is easily explained once we realize the distinction between the rights exercised by the Sovereign and by the Owner over the same piece of property, as will be seen later.

It may so happen that a number of men begin to group them- 61 selves into a community before ever they own property at all, and that only later, when they have got possession of land sufficient to maintain them all, do they either enjoy it in common or parcel it between themselves in equal lots or in accordance with such scale of proportion as may be established by the sovereign. However this acquisition be made, the right exercised by each individual over his own particular share must always be subordinated to the overriding claim of the Community as such. Otherwise there would be no strength in the social bond, nor any real power in the exercise of sovereignty.

I will conclude this chapter, and the present Book, with a re- 62 mark which should serve as basis for every social system: that, so far from destroying natural equality, the primitive compact substitutes for it a moral and legal equality which compensates for all those physical inequalities from which men suffer. However unequal they may be in bodily strength or in intellectual gifts, they become equal in the eyes of the law, and as a result of the compact into which they have entered.

QUESTIONS FOR CRITICAL READING

1. Examine Rousseau's analogy of the family as the oldest and only natural form of government. Do you agree that the analogy is useful and that its contentions are true? Which aspects of this natural form of government do not work to help us understand the basis of government?
2. Rousseau seems to accept the family as a patriarchal structure. How would his views change if he accepted it as a matriarchal structure? How would they change if he regarded each member of the family as absolutely equal in authority from birth?
3. What does it mean to reason from what is fact instead of from what is morally right?
4. What features of Rousseau's social contract are like those of a legal contract? How does a person contract to be part of society?
5. What distinctions can be made among natural, moral, and legal equality? Which kind of equality is most important to a social system?

SUGGESTIONS FOR WRITING

1. When Rousseau wrote, "Man is born free, and everywhere he is in chains," the institution of slavery was widely practiced and justified by many authorities. Today slavery has been generally abolished. How is this statement relevant to people's condition in society now? What are some ways in which people relinquish their independence or freedom?
2. Clarify the difference between your duty to yourself and your duty to society (your social structure—personal, local, national). Establish your duties in relation to each structure. How can these duties conflict with one another? How does the individual resolve the conflicts?
3. Do you agree with Rousseau when he says, "All men have a natural right to what is necessary to them"? What is necessary to all people, and in what sense do they have a right to what is necessary? Who should provide those necessities? Should necessities be provided for everyone or only for people who are unable to provide for themselves? If society will not provide these necessities, does the individual have the right to break the social contract by means of revolution?
4. What seems to be Rousseau's opinion regarding private property or the ownership of property? Beginning with paragraph 59, Rousseau distinguishes between monarchs with sovereignty over people and those with sovereignty over a region, such as France, Italy, or another country.

What is Rousseau's view of the property that constitutes a state and who actually owns it? He mentions that the rights of individual owners must give way to the rights of the community in general. What is your response to this view?

5. Rousseau makes an important distinction between natural liberty and civil liberty. People in a state of nature enjoy natural liberty, and when they bind themselves together into a body politic, they enjoy civil liberty. What are the differences? Define each kind of liberty as carefully as you can, and take a stand on whether you feel civil liberty or natural liberty is superior. How is the conflict between the two forms of liberty felt today?

6. **CONNECTIONS** Rousseau's thinking emphasizes the role played by the common people in any civil society. How does that emphasis compare with Machiavelli's thinking? Consider the attitudes each writer has toward the essential goodness of people and the essential responsibilities of the monarch or government leader. In what ways is Rousseau closer in thinking to Lao-tzu than to Machiavelli?

THOMAS JEFFERSON
The Declaration of Independence

THOMAS JEFFERSON (1743–1826) authored one of the most memorable statements in American history: the Declaration of Independence. He composed the work in 1776 under the watchful eyes of Benjamin Franklin, John Adams, and the rest of the Continental Congress, which spent two and a half days going over every word. Although the substance of the document was developed in committee, Jefferson, because of the grace of his writing style, was selected to craft the actual wording.

Jefferson rose to eminence in a time of great political upheaval. By the time he took a seat in the Virginia legislature in 1769, the colony was already on the course toward revolution. His pamphlet "A Summary View of the Rights of British America" (1774) brought him to the attention of those who were agitating for independence and established him as an ardent republican and revolutionary. In 1779 he was elected governor of Virginia. After the Revolutionary War he moved into the national political arena as the first secretary of state (1790–1793). He then served as John Adams's vice president (1797–1801) and was himself elected president in 1800. Perhaps one of his greatest achievements during his two terms (1801–1809) in office was his negotiation of the Louisiana Purchase, in which the United States acquired 820,000 square miles of land west of the Mississippi from France for about $15 million.

One of the fundamental paradoxes of Jefferson's personal and political life has been his attitude toward slavery. Like most wealthy Virginians, Jefferson owned slaves. However, in 1784 he tried to abolish slavery in the western territories that were being added to the United States. His "Report on Government for the Western Territory" failed by one vote. Historians have pointed out that Jefferson probably had an affair with Sally Hemmings, a mixed-race slave, and fathered children with her.

However unclear his personal convictions, many of Jefferson's accomplishments, which extend from politics to agriculture and mechanical invention, still stand. One of the most versatile Americans of any generation, he wrote a book, *Notes on Virginia* (1782); designed and built Monticello, his famous homestead in Virginia; and in large part founded and designed the University of Virginia (1819).

Despite their revolutionary nature, the ideas Jefferson expressed in the Declaration of Independence were not entirely original. Rousseau's republican philosophies greatly influenced the work. When Jefferson states in the second paragraph that "all men are created equal, that they are endowed by their Creator with certain unalienable rights," he reflects Rousseau's emphasis on the political equality of men and on protecting certain fundamental rights (see Rousseau beginning with paragraph 39, p. 65). Jefferson also wrote that "Governments are instituted among Men, deriving their just powers from the consent of the governed." This is one of Rousseau's primary points, although it was Jefferson who immortalized it in these words.

Jefferson's Rhetoric

Jefferson's techniques include the use of the periodic sentence, which was especially typical of the age. The first sentence of the Declaration of Independence is periodic—that is, it is long and carefully balanced, and the main point comes at the end. Such sentences are not popular today, although an occasional periodic sentence can still be powerful in contemporary prose. Jefferson's first sentence says (in paraphrase): *When one nation must sever its relations with a parent nation . . . and stand as an independent nation itself . . . the causes ought to be explained.* Moreover, the main body of the Declaration of Independence lists the "causes" that lead to the final and most important element of the sentence. Causal analysis was a method associated with legal thought and reflects Jefferson's training in eighteenth-century legal analysis. One understood things best when one understood their causes.

The periodic sentence demands certain qualities of balance and parallelism that all good writers should heed. The first sentence in paragraph 2 demonstrates both qualities. The balance is achieved by making each part of the sentence roughly the same length. The parallelism is achieved by linking words in deliberate repetition for effect (they are in italicized type in the following analysis). Note how the "truths" mentioned in the first clause are enumerated in the succession of noun clauses beginning with "that"; "Rights" are enumerated in the final clause:

> We hold these truths to be self-evident,
>> *that* all men are created equal,
>> *that* they are endowed by their Creator with certain inalienable Rights,
>> *that* among these are Life, Liberty and the pursuit of Happiness.

Parallelism is one of the greatest stylistic techniques available to a writer sensitive to rhetoric. It is a natural technique: many untrained writers and speakers develop it on their own. The periodicity of the sentences and the balance of their parallelism suggest thoughtfulness, wisdom, and control.

Parallelism creates a natural link to the useful device of enumeration, or listing. Many writers using this technique establish their purpose from the outset — "I wish to address three important issues . . ." — and then number them: "First, I want to say . . . Second . . . ," and so on. Jefferson devotes paragraphs 3 through 29 to enumerating the "causes" he mentions in paragraph 1. Each one constitutes a separate paragraph; thus, each has separate weight and importance. Each begins with "He" or "For" and is therefore in parallel structure. The technique of repetition of the same words at the beginning of successive lines is called *anaphora*. Jefferson's use of anaphora here is one of the best known and most effective in all literature. The "He" referred to is Britain's King George III (1738–1820), who is never mentioned by name. Congress is opposed not to a personality but to the sovereign of a nation that is oppressing the United States and a tyrant who is not dignified by being named. The "For" introduces grievous acts the king has given his assent to; these are offenses against the colonies.

However, Jefferson does not develop the causes in detail. We do not have specific information about what trade was cut off by the British, what taxes were imposed without consent, or how King George waged war or abdicated government in the colonies. Presumably, Jefferson's audience knew the details and was led by the twenty-seven paragraphs to observe how numerous the causes were. And all are serious; any one alone was enough cause for revolution. The effect of Jefferson's enumeration is to illustrate the patience of the colonies up to this point and to tell the world that the colonies have finally lost patience on account of the reasons listed. The Declaration of Independence projects the careful meditations and decisions of exceptionally calm, patient, and reasonable people.

PREREADING QUESTIONS: WHAT TO READ FOR

The following prereading questions may help you anticipate key issues in the discussion of Thomas Jefferson's Declaration of Independence. Keeping them in mind during your first reading of the selection should help focus your attention.

- Under what conditions may a people alter or abolish their government?
- Why does Jefferson consider King George a tyrant?

The Declaration of Independence

In Congress, July 4, 1776

The Unanimous Declaration of the Thirteen United States of America

When in the Course of human events, it becomes necessary for   1
one people to dissolve the political bands which have connected them with another, and to assume among the Powers of the earth, the separate and equal station to which the Laws of Nature and of Nature's God entitle them, a decent respect to the opinions of mankind requires that they should declare the causes which impel them to the separation.

We hold these truths to be self-evident, that all men are created   2
equal, that they are endowed by their Creator with certain inalienable Rights, that among these are Life, Liberty and the pursuit of Happiness. That to secure these rights, Governments are instituted among Men, deriving their just powers from the consent of the governed. That whenever any Form of Government becomes destructive of these ends, it is the Right of the People to alter or to abolish it, and to institute new Government, laying its foundation on such principles and organizing its powers in such form, as to them shall seem most likely to effect their Safety and Happiness. Prudence, indeed, will dictate that Governments long established should not be changed for light and transient causes; and accordingly all experience hath shown, that mankind are more disposed to suffer, while evils are sufferable, than to right themselves by abolishing the forms to which they are accustomed. But when a long train of abuses and usurpations, pursuing

invariably the same Object evinces a design to reduce them under absolute Despotism, it is their right, it is their duty, to throw off such Government, and to provide new Guards for their future security.— Such has been the patient sufferance of these Colonies; and such is now the necessity which constrains them to alter their former Systems of Government. The history of the present King of Great Britain is a history of repeated injuries and usurpations, all having in direct object the establishment of an absolute Tyranny over these States. To prove this, let Facts be submitted to a candid world.

He has refused his Assent to Laws, the most wholesome and   3
necessary for the public good.

He has forbidden his Governors to pass Laws of immediate and   4
pressing importance, unless suspended in their operation till his Assent should be obtained; and when so suspended, he has utterly neglected to attend to them.

He has refused to pass other laws for the accommodation of   5
large districts of people, unless those people would relinquish the right of Representation in the Legislature, a right inestimable to them and formidable to tyrants only.

He has called together legislative bodies at places unusual, un-   6
comfortable, and distant from the depository of their Public Records, for the sole purpose of fatiguing them into compliance with his measures.

He has dissolved Representative Houses repeatedly, for oppos-   7
ing with manly firmness his invasions on the rights of the people.

He has refused for a long time, after such dissolutions, to cause   8
others to be elected; whereby the Legislative Powers, incapable of Annihilation, have returned to the People at large for their exercise; the State remaining in the mean time exposed to all the dangers of invasion from without, and convulsions within.

He has endeavoured to prevent the population of these States;[1]   9
for that purpose obstructing the Laws for Naturalization of Foreigners; refusing to pass others to encourage their migration hither, and raising the conditions of new Appropriations of Lands.

He has obstructed the Administration of Justice, by refusing his   10
Assent to Laws for establishing Judiciary Powers.

He has made Judges dependent on his Will alone, for the tenure   11
of their offices, and the amount and payment of their salaries.

He has erected a multitude of New Offices, and sent hither   12
swarms of Officers to harass our People, and eat out their substance.

---

[1] **prevent the population of these States** This meant limiting migration to the Colonies, thus controlling their growth.

He has kept among us, in times of peace, Standing Armies with- 13
out the Consent of our legislature.

He has affected to render the Military independent of and supe- 14
rior to the Civil Power.

He has combined with others to subject us to a jurisdiction for- 15
eign to our constitution, and unacknowledged by our laws; giving
his Assent to their acts of pretended Legislation:

For quartering large bodies of armed troops among us: 16

For protecting them, by a mock Trial, from Punishment for any 17
Murders which they should commit on the Inhabitants of these
States:

For cutting off our Trade with all parts of the world: 18

For imposing taxes on us without our Consent: 19

For depriving us in many cases, of the benefits of Trial by Jury: 20

For transporting us beyond Seas to be tried for pretended of- 21
fences:

For abolishing the free System of English Laws in a neighbour- 22
ing Province, establishing therein an Arbitrary government, and enlarging its Boundaries so as to render it at once an example and fit
instrument for introducing the same absolute rule into these
Colonies:

For taking away our Charters, abolishing our most valuable 23
Laws, and altering fundamentally the Forms of our Governments:

For suspending our own Legislatures, and declaring themselves 24
invested with Power to legislate for us in all cases whatsoever.

He has abdicated Government here, by declaring us out of his 25
Protection and waging War against us.

He has plundered our seas, ravaged our Coasts, burnt our 26
towns, and destroyed the lives of our people.

He is at this time transporting large armies of foreign mercenar- 27
ies to compleat the works of death, desolation and tyranny, already
begun with circumstances of Cruelty & perfidy scarcely paralleled in
the most barbarous ages, and totally unworthy the Head of a civilized nation.

He has constrained our fellow Citizens taken Captive on the 28
high Seas to bear Arms against their Country, to become the executioners of their friends and Brethren, or to fall themselves by their
Hands.

He has excited domestic insurrections amongst us, and has en- 29
deavoured to bring on the inhabitants of our frontiers, the merciless
Indian Savages, whose known rule of warfare, is an undistinguished
destruction of all ages, sexes and conditions.

In every stage of these Oppressions We have Petitioned for Re- 30
dress in the most humble terms: Our repeated Petitions have been

answered only by repeated injury. A Prince, whose character is thus marked by every act which may define a Tyrant, is unfit to be the ruler of a free People.

Nor have We been wanting in attention to our British brethren. 31 We have warned them from time to time of attempts by their legislature to extend an unwarrantable jurisdiction over us. We have reminded them of the circumstances of our emigration and settlement here. We have appealed to their native justice and magnanimity, and we have conjured them by the ties of our common kindred to disavow these usurpations, which, would inevitably interrupt our connections and correspondence. They too have been deaf to the voice of justice and of consanguinity. We must, therefore, acquiesce in the necessity, which denounces our Separation, and hold them, as we hold the rest of mankind, Enemies in War, in Peace Friends.

We, therefore, the Representatives of the United States of Amer- 32 ica, in General Congress, Assembled, appealing to the Supreme Judge of the world for the rectitude of our intentions, do, in the Name, and by Authority of the good People of these Colonies, solemnly publish and declare, That these United Colonies are, and of Right ought to be Free and Independent States, that they are Absolved from all Allegiance to the British Crown, and that all political connection between them and the State of Great Britain, is and ought to be totally dissolved; and that as Free and Independent States, they have full Power to levy War, conclude Peace, contract Alliances, establish Commerce, and to do all other Acts and Things which Independent States may of right do. And for the support of this Declaration, with a firm reliance on the Protection of Divine Providence, we mutually pledge to each other our Lives, our Fortunes and our sacred Honor.

QUESTIONS FOR CRITICAL READING

1. What laws of nature does Jefferson refer to in paragraph 1?
2. What do you think Jefferson feels is the function of government (para. 2)?
3. What does Jefferson say about women? Is there any way you can determine his views from reading this document? Does he appear to favor a patriarchal system?
4. Find at least one use of parallel structure in the Declaration (see p. 77 in the section on Jefferson's rhetoric for a description of parallelism). What key terms are repeated in identical or equivalent constructions, and to what effect?
5. Which causes listed in paragraphs 3 through 29 are the most serious? Are any trivial? Which ones are serious enough to cause a revolution?

6. What do you consider to be the most graceful sentence in the entire Declaration? Where is it placed in the Declaration? What purpose does it serve there?
7. In what ways does the king's desire for stable government interfere with Jefferson's sense of his own independence?

SUGGESTIONS FOR WRITING

1. Jefferson defines the inalienable rights of a citizen as "Life, Liberty and the pursuit of Happiness." Do you think these are indeed inalienable rights? Answer this question by including some sentences that use parallel structure and repeat key terms in similar constructions. Be certain that you define each of these rights both for yourself and for our time.
2. Write an essay discussing what you feel the function of government should be. Include at least three periodic sentences (underline them). You may first want to establish Jefferson's view of government and then compare or contrast it with your own.
3. Jefferson envisioned a government that allowed its citizens to exercise their rights to life, liberty, and the pursuit of happiness. Has Jefferson's revolutionary vision been achieved in America? Begin with a definition of these three key terms: "life," "liberty," and "the pursuit of happiness." Then, for each term use examples—drawn from current events, your own experience, American history—to take a clear and well-argued stand on whether the nation has achieved Jefferson's goal.
4. Slavery was legal in America in 1776, and Jefferson reluctantly owned slaves. He never presented his plan for gradual emancipation of the slaves to Congress because he realized that Congress would never approve it. But Jefferson and Franklin did finance a plan to buy slaves and return them to Africa, where in 1821 returning slaves founded the nation of Liberia. Agree or disagree with the following statement and defend your position: the ownership of slaves by the people who wrote the Declaration of Independence invalidates it. You may wish to read the relevant chapters on Jefferson and slavery in Merrill D. Peterson's *Thomas Jefferson and the New Nation* (1970).
5. What kind of government does Jefferson seem to prefer? In what ways would his government differ from that of the king he is reacting against? Is he talking about an entirely different system or about the same system but with a different kind of "prince" at the head? How would Jefferson protect the individual against the whim of the state, while also protecting the state against the whim of the individual?
6. **CONNECTIONS** Write an essay in which you examine the ways in which Jefferson agrees or disagrees with Lao-tzu's conception of human nature and of government. How does Jefferson share Lao-tzu's commitment to judicious inactivity? What evidence is there that the king subscribes to it? Describe the similarities and differences between Jefferson's views and those of Lao-tzu.

7. **CONNECTIONS** What principles does Jefferson share with Jean-Jacques Rousseau? Compare the fundamental demands of the Declaration of Independence with Rousseau's conceptions of liberty and independence. How would Rousseau have reacted to this Declaration?

8. **SEEING CONNECTIONS** In 1862 the United States issued its first $2 notes, which featured a portrait of Alexander Hamilton (1755–1804), the country's first secretary of the treasury. Thomas Jefferson's portrait replaced Hamilton's in 1869, and in 1976, to commemorate the U.S. bicentennial, the reverse of the $2 bill was redesigned to feature John Trumbull's painting *The Signing of the Declaration of Independence.* The $2 bill has remained unchanged since then and is still in circulation.

   In paragraph 2 of the Declaration of Independence, Jefferson states that "all men are created equal, that they are endowed by their Creator with certain inalienable Rights, that among these are Life, Liberty and the pursuit of Happiness." How essential is money for an individual to realize the rights Jefferson enumerates? In paragraphs 18 and 19, Jefferson addresses the issues of Great Britain's interference with the American colonies' trade with other countries and its unfair taxation. What importance do you think the signers of the Declaration placed on economic independence?

HANNAH ARENDT
Total Domination

HANNAH ARENDT (1906–1975) was born and educated in
Germany, earning her doctorate from the University of Heidelberg
when she was twenty-two years old. She left Germany for Paris after
Hitler came to power in 1933 and early in the development of Nazi
ideology. In New York City she worked with Jewish relief groups
and in 1940 married Heinrich Bluecher, a professor of philosophy.
Arendt joined the faculty of the University of Chicago in 1963 and
then taught as a visiting professor at a number of universities, eventually settling at the New School for Social Research in New York.

The Origins of Totalitarianism, from which this selection is excerpted, was first published in 1951 and solidified Arendt's reputation as an important political philosopher. She began work on the
book in 1945, after Nazism was defeated in Europe, and finished
most of it by 1949, during the period of growing tension between
the United States and the Soviet Union that began the Cold War.
Much of the book analyzes the politics of ideology in fascist and
communist countries. Arendt went on to write a number of other
influential works, such as *The Human Condition* (1958) and *Crises
of the Republic* (1972), both of which address the problems she saw
connected with a decline in moral values in modern society. One of
her most controversial books, *Eichmann in Jerusalem* (1963), examined Adolf Eichmann, head of the Gestapo's Jewish section, who
was tried and executed in Jerusalem. She observed that the nature
of Eichmann's evil was essentially banal — that his crime involved
going along with orders without taking the time to assess them
critically. Her last work, *The Life of the Mind,* was not completed,
although two of its planned three volumes were published posthumously in 1978.

From *The Origins of Totalitarianism.*

"Total Domination" is part of one of the last chapters in *The Origins of Totalitarianism*. The first part of the book sets forth a brief history of modern anti-Semitism because the rise of totalitarianism in Germany was based in large part on Hitler's belief that the Aryan race was biologically and morally more evolved than all other races. In this selection Hannah Arendt shows how the totalitarian state derives its power from propagating a set of ideas, or ideology, such as the view that one race is superior to all others. Once that premise is accepted, she demonstrates, then any and all atrocities against people of other races can be permitted and promoted.

In two instances, describing the ideology of German fascism and the ideology of Soviet communism, Arendt demonstrates the ways in which the uncritical acceptance of an ideology provides the core of power for totalitarian states. In the case of Germany, racism led to the theory that if some races are inferior and debased then they must be destroyed for the good of humanity—a theory that was put into brutal practice by the Nazis. Arendt shows how this view derives from a misunderstanding of Darwin's theories of the survival of the fittest (see Darwin's "Natural Selection," p. 559). In the case of the Soviet Union, totalitarianism depended on the "scientific" theory of history put forth by Karl Marx (see Marx's "Communist Manifesto," p. 353) that insisted on class struggle and the need of the most "progressive class" to destroy the less progressive classes. Marx was referred to as the "Darwin of history" in part because his views reflected the same scientific logic as Darwin's theories of biology. According to Arendt, both the Nazi and communist totalitarian regimes claimed those laws of biology or history as the justification for their own brutal acts of terror.

Arendt's Rhetoric

Arendt is a careful rhetorician. She works in a logical fashion to analyze basic principles to see how they control the outcome of events. In this case, the outcome is the totalitarian institution of the concentration camp in which human dignity is destroyed. For the totalitarian government, the terror and torment of concentration camps demonstrate "that everything is possible" (para. 1), even though it might seem impossible to reduce a person to a thing. Total domination, as she states, is designed to reduce the diversity and complexity of humanity to a single reaction to terror and pain.

Interestingly, Arendt can find no economic virtue in maintaining huge numbers of people in concentration camps. Occasionally in the Soviet Union, inmates' labor was of value, but some 60 percent or more of the inmates died under the harsh labor conditions. In Nazi Germany the work done in the concentration camps was of such poor quality that it usually had to be done again. Further, during World War II, German resources that might have been used to fight the war were diverted to the concentration camps, which functioned as extermination centers even while Germany reeled under potential defeat. In other words, the concentration camps were self-defeating in every important way except that they demonstrated to a populace that total domination was possible.

One important rhetorical principle at work in this essay is the essential definition of total domination by the process of describing the circumstances of the concentration camps as well as the rationale for their construction. The Nazis knew, and Hitler had already trumpeted the news to the world in his book *Mein Kampf* (My Struggle), that if a lie was big enough, large numbers of people would believe it even if it stood against common sense. "The Big Lie" has become a common principle of modern political science. Likewise, if the enormity of the crime is great enough, it is not likely that people will believe it actually occurred. Therefore, it should not have been a surprise that the few people who had escaped the camps before the war were not believed. They told their stories, but even future victims of the camps refused to believe they existed. Western governments thought the accounts of the concentration camps were monstrous exaggerations.

Throughout the book from which this passage comes, Arendt insists that the essence of totalitarianism is terror and that without it the totalitarian state collapses. The concentration camps are the "laboratories" in which absolute terror dominates and that represent total domination. Individual liberty and freedom are erased by the terror of total domination, and in this sense the values that Rousseau and Jefferson argue for are irrelevant. In some states, such as the one Machiavelli imagined, terror might be useful for controlling the opposition, but in the totalitarian state it controls everyone. As Arendt states, "a victory of the concentration-camp system would mean the same inexorable doom for human beings as the use of the hydrogen bomb would mean the doom of the human race" (para. 14).

PREREADING QUESTIONS:
WHAT TO READ FOR

The following prereading questions may help you anticipate key issues in the discussion of Hannah Arendt's "Total Domination." Keeping them in mind during your first reading of the selection should help focus your attention.

- What is the role of terror in the totalitarian state?
- Why is total domination necessary in a totalitarian state?
- What happens to human beings in concentration camps?

Total Domination

The concentration and extermination camps of totalitarian   1
regimes serve as the laboratories in which the fundamental belief of
totalitarianism that everything is possible is being verified. Compared
with this, all other experiments are secondary in importance—
including those in the field of medicine whose horrors are recorded
in detail in the trials against the physicians of the Third Reich—although it is characteristic that these laboratories were used for experiments of every kind.

Total domination, which strives to organize the infinite plural-   2
ity and differentiation of human beings as if all of humanity were
just one individual, is possible only if each and every person can be
reduced to a never-changing identity of reactions, so that each of
these bundles of reactions can be exchanged at random for any
other. The problem is to fabricate something that does not exist,
namely, a kind of human species resembling other animal species
whose only "freedom" would consist in "preserving the species."
Totalitarian domination attempts to achieve this goal both through
ideological indoctrination of the elite formations[1] and through absolute terror in the camps; and the atrocities for which the elite
formations are ruthlessly used become, as it were, the practical application of the ideological indoctrination—the testing ground in
which the latter must prove itself—while the appalling spectacle of
the camps themselves is supposed to furnish the "theoretical" verification of the ideology.

The camps are meant not only to exterminate people and de-   3
grade human beings, but also serve the ghastly experiment of eliminating, under scientifically controlled conditions, spontaneity itself
as an expression of human behavior and of transforming the human
personality into a mere thing, into something that even animals are

---

[1] **elite formations** By this term Arendt seems to mean the SS men and camp
guards.

not; for Pavlov's dog,[2] which, as we know, was trained to eat not when it was hungry but when a bell rang, was a perverted animal.

Under normal circumstances this can never be accomplished, be-   4
cause spontaneity can never be entirely eliminated insofar as it is connected not only with human freedom but with life itself, in the sense of simply keeping alive. It is only in the concentration camps that such an experiment is at all possible, and therefore they are not only *"la société la plus totalitaire encore réalisée"*[3] (David Rousset) but the guiding social ideal of total domination in general. Just as the stability of the totalitarian regime depends on the isolation of the fictitious world of the movement from the outside world, so the experiment of total domination in the concentration camps depends on sealing off the latter against the world of all others, the world of the living in general, even against the outside world of a country under totalitarian rule. This isolation explains the peculiar unreality and lack of credibility that characterize all reports from the concentration camps and constitute one of the main difficulties for the true understanding of totalitarian domination, which stands or falls with the existence of these concentration and extermination camps; for, unlikely as it may sound, these camps are the true central institution of totalitarian organizational power.

There are numerous reports by survivors. The more authentic they   5
are, the less they attempt to communicate things that evade human understanding and human experience—sufferings, that is, that transform men into "uncomplaining animals." None of these reports inspires those passions of outrage and sympathy through which men have always been mobilized for justice. On the contrary, anyone speaking or writing about concentration camps is still regarded as suspect; and if the speaker has resolutely returned to the world of the living, he himself is often assailed by doubts with regard to his own truthfulness, as though he had mistaken a nightmare for reality.

This doubt of people concerning themselves and the reality of   6
their own experience only reveals what the Nazis have always known: that men determined to commit crimes will find it expedient to organize them on the vastest, most improbable scale. Not only because this renders all punishments provided by the legal system

---

[2] **Pavlov's dog** Between 1898 and 1930 the Russian psychologist Ivan Petrovich Pavlov (1849–1936) trained a dog to associate the sound of a ringing bell with food. Eventually the dog's reflex was to salivate at the sound of the bell even when there was no food.

[3] **la société . . . réalisée** "The most totalitarian society yet achieved." David Rousset (1912–1997) survived the concentration camps and wrote *The Other Kingdom* (1947) about his experience.

inadequate and absurd; but because the very immensity of the crimes guarantees that the murderers who proclaim their innocence with all manner of lies will be more readily believed than the victims who tell the truth. The Nazis did not even consider it necessary to keep this discovery to themselves. Hitler circulated millions of copies of his book in which he stated that to be successful, a lie must be enormous—which did not prevent people from believing him as, similarly, the Nazis' proclamations, repeated *ad nauseam*,[4] that the Jews would be exterminated like bedbugs (*i.e.*, with poison gas), prevented anybody from *not* believing them.

There is a great temptation to explain away the intrinsically in-   7 credible by means of liberal rationalizations. In each one of us, there lurks such a liberal, wheedling us with the voice of common sense. The road to totalitarian domination leads through many intermediate stages for which we can find numerous analogies and precedents. The extraordinarily bloody terror during the initial stage of totalitarian rule serves indeed the exclusive purpose of defeating the opponent and rendering all further opposition impossible; but total terror is launched only after this initial stage has been overcome and the regime no longer has anything to fear from the opposition. In this context it has been frequently remarked that in such a case the means have become the end, but this is after all only an admission, in paradoxical disguise, that the category "the end justifies the means" no longer applies, that terror has lost its "purpose," that it is no longer the means to frighten people. Nor does the explanation suffice that the revolution, as in the case of the French Revolution, was devouring its own children, for the terror continues even after everybody who might be described as a child of the revolution in one capacity or another—the Russian factions, the power centers of party, the army, the bureaucracy—has long since been devoured. Many things that nowadays have become the specialty of totalitarian government are only too well known from the study of history. There have almost always been wars of aggression; the massacre of hostile populations after a victory went unchecked until the Romans mitigated it by introducing the *parcere subjectis*;[5] through centuries the extermination of native peoples went hand in hand with the colonization of the Americas, Australia and Africa; slavery is one of the oldest institutions of mankind and all empires of antiquity were based on the labor of state-owned slaves who erected their public buildings. Not even concentration camps are an invention of totalitarian movements. They emerge for the

---

[4]**Ad nauseam** To the point of sickness.
[5]***parcere subjectis*** A Roman policy of lenience and mercy toward those they defeated.

first time during the Boer War,[6] at the beginning of the century, and continued to be used in South Africa as well as India for "undesirable elements"; here, too, we first find the term "protective custody" which was later adopted by the Third Reich. These camps correspond in many respects to the concentration camps at the beginning of totalitarian rule; they were used for "suspects" whose offenses could not be proved and who could not be sentenced by ordinary process of law. All this clearly points to totalitarian methods of domination; all these are elements they utilize, develop and crystallize on the basis of the nihilistic principle that "everything is permitted," which they inherited and already take for granted. But wherever these new forms of domination assume their authentically totalitarian structure they transcend this principle, which is still tied to the utilitarian motives and self-interest of the rulers, and try their hand in a realm that up to now has been completely unknown to us: the realm where "everything is possible." And, characteristically enough, this is precisely the realm that cannot be limited by either utilitarian motives or self-interest, regardless of the latter's content.

What runs counter to common sense is not the nihilistic principle that "everything is permitted," which was already contained in the nineteenth-century utilitarian conception[7] of common sense. What common sense and "normal people" refuse to believe is that everything is possible. We attempt to understand elements in present or recollected experience that simply surpass our powers of understanding. We attempt to classify as criminal a thing which, as we all feel, no such category was ever intended to cover. What meaning has the concept of murder when we are confronted with the mass production of corpses? We attempt to understand the behavior of concentration-camp inmates and SS-men psychologically, when the very thing that must be realized is that the psyche *can* be destroyed even without the destruction of the physical man; that, indeed, psyche, character, and individuality seem under certain circumstances to express themselves only through the rapidity or slowness with which they disintegrate. The end result in any case is inanimate men, *i.e.*, men who can no longer be psychologically understood, whose return to the psychologically or otherwise intelligibly human world closely resembles the resurrection of Lazarus.[8] All

---

[6]**Boer War** South Africa (1899–1902). The British established concentration camps in which some forty thousand people died during the suppression of a revolution by Dutch and other settlers.

[7]**utilitarian conception** Utilitarianism, often known for its doctrine of the greatest good for the greatest number, was a nineteenth-century philosophy rooted in what people felt was essentially common sense.

[8]**Lazarus** From the Bible (John 11:18–48). Jesus, urged by Martha, resurrected Lazarus, who had been dead for four days.

statements of common sense, whether of a psychological or socio-
logical nature, serve only to encourage those who think it "superficial" to "dwell on horrors."

If it is true that the concentration camps are the most consequen-   9
tial institution of totalitarian rule, "dwelling on horrors" would seem
to be indispensable for the understanding of totalitarianism. But recollection can no more do this than can the uncommunicative eyewitness
report. In both these genres there is an inherent tendency to run away
from the experience; instinctively or rationally, both types of writer
are so much aware of the terrible abyss that separates the world of the
living from that of the living dead, that they cannot supply anything
more than a series of remembered occurrences that must seem just
as incredible to those who relate them as to their audience. Only the
fearful imagination of those who have been aroused by such reports
but have not actually been smitten in their own flesh, of those who
are consequently free from the bestial, desperate terror which, when
confronted by real, present horror, inexorably paralyzes everything
that is not mere reaction, can afford to keep thinking about horrors.
Such thoughts are useful only for the perception of political contexts
and the mobilization of political passions. A change of personality of
any sort whatever can no more be induced by thinking about horrors than by the real experience of horror. The reduction of a man to
a bundle of reactions separates him as radically as mental disease
from everything within him that is personality or character. When,
like Lazarus, he rises from the dead, he finds his personality or character unchanged, just as he had left it.

Just as the horror, or the dwelling on it, cannot affect a change of   10
character in him, cannot make men better or worse, thus it cannot become the basis of a political community or party in a narrower sense.
The attempts to build up a European elite with a program of intra-
European understanding based on the common European experience
of the concentration camps have foundered in much the same manner
as the attempts following the first World War to draw political conclusions from the international experience of the front generation.[9] In
both cases it turned out that the experiences themselves can communicate no more than nihilistic banalities. Political consequences such
as postwar pacifism, for example, derived from the general fear of war,
not from the experiences in war. Instead of producing a pacifism devoid of reality, the insight into the structure of modern wars, guided
and mobilized by fear, might have led to the realization that the only

---

[9] **the front generation** The generation that fought or experienced the fighting
in World War I (1914–1918).

standard for a necessary war is the fight against conditions under which people no longer wish to live—and our experiences with the tormenting hell of the totalitarian camps have enlightened us only too well about the possibility of such conditions. Thus the fear of concentration camps and the resulting insight into the nature of total domination might serve to invalidate all obsolete political differentiations from right to left and to introduce beside and above them the politically most important yardstick for judging events in our time, namely: whether they serve totalitarian domination or not.

In any event, the fearful imagination has the great advantage to   11 dissolve the sophistic-dialectical[10] interpretations of politics which are all based on the superstition that something good might result from evil. Such dialectical acrobatics had at least a semblance of justification so long as the worst that man could inflict upon man was murder. But, as we know today, murder is only a limited evil. The murderer who kills a man—a man who has to die anyway—still moves within the realm of life and death familiar to us; both have indeed a necessary connection on which the dialectic is founded, even if it is not always conscious of it. The murderer leaves a corpse behind and does not pretend that his victim has never existed; if he wipes out any traces, they are those of his own identity, and not the memory and grief of the persons who loved his victim; he destroys a life, but he does not destroy the fact of existence itself.

The Nazis, with the precision peculiar to them, used to register   12 their operations in the concentration camps under the heading "under cover of the night (*Nacht und Nebel*)." The radicalism of measures to treat people as if they had never existed and to make them disappear in the literal sense of the word is frequently not apparent at first glance, because both the German and the Russian system are not uniform but consist of a series of categories in which people are treated very differently. In the case of Germany, these different categories used to exist in the same camp, but without coming into contact with each other; frequently, the isolation between the categories was even stricter than the isolation from the outside world. Thus, out of racial considerations, Scandinavian nationals during the war were quite differently treated by the Germans than the members of other peoples, although the former were outspoken enemies of the Nazis. The latter in turn were divided into those whose "extermination" was immediately on the agenda, as in the case of the Jews, or

---

[10] **sophistic-dialectical** Arendt seems to be referring to Marxist communist views that pit two mighty historical forces—like good and evil—against one another. Her point is that such a dialectic is artificial and dangerous.

could be expected in the predictable future, as in the case of the Poles, Russians and Ukrainians, and into those who were not yet covered by instructions about such an over-all "final solution," as in the case of the French and Belgians. In Russia, on the other hand, we must distinguish three more or less independent systems. First, there are the authentic forced-labor groups that live in relative freedom and are sentenced for limited periods. Secondly, there are the concentration camps in which the human material is ruthlessly exploited and the mortality rate is extremely high, but which are essentially organized for labor purposes. And, thirdly, there are the annihilation camps in which the inmates are systematically wiped out through starvation and neglect.

The real horror of the concentration and extermination camps   13 lies in the fact that the inmates, even if they happen to keep alive, are more effectively cut off from the world of the living than if they had died, because terror enforces oblivion. Here, murder is as impersonal as the squashing of a gnat. Someone may die as the result of systematic torture or starvation, or because the camp is overcrowded and superfluous human material must be liquidated. Conversely, it may happen that due to a shortage of new human shipments the danger arises that the camps become depopulated and that the order is now given to reduce the death rate at any price. David Rousset called his report on the period in a German concentration camp "*Les Jours de Notre Mort*,"[11] and it is indeed as if there were a possibility to give permanence to the process of dying itself and to enforce a condition in which both death and life are obstructed equally effectively.

It is the appearance of some radical evil, previously unknown to   14 us, that puts an end to the notion of developments and transformations of qualities. Here, there are neither political nor historical nor simply moral standards but, at the most, the realization that something seems to be involved in modern politics that actually should never be involved in politics as we used to understand it, namely all or nothing—all, and that is an undetermined infinity of forms of human living-together, or nothing, for a victory of the concentration-camp system would mean the same inexorable doom for human beings as the use of the hydrogen bomb would mean the doom of the human race.

There are no parallels to the life in the concentration camps. Its   15 horror can never be fully embraced by the imagination for the very reason that it stands outside of life and death. It can never be fully reported for the very reason that the survivor returns to the world of

---

[11] **Les Jours . . . Mort** Literally, the days of our death.

the living, which makes it impossible for him to believe fully in his own past experiences. It is as though he had a story to tell of another planet, for the status of the inmates in the world of the living, where nobody is supposed to know if they are alive or dead, is such that it is as though they had never been born. Therefore all parallels create confusion and distract attention from what is essential. Forced labor in prisons and penal colonies, banishment, slavery, all seem for a moment to offer helpful comparisons, but on closer examination lead nowhere.

Forced labor as a punishment is limited as to time and intensity. 16 The convict retains his rights over his body; he is not absolutely tortured and he is not absolutely dominated. Banishment banishes only from one part of the world to another part of the world, also inhabited by human beings; it does not exclude from the human world altogether. Throughout history slavery has been an institution within a social order; slaves were not, like concentration-camp inmates, withdrawn from the sight and hence the protection of their fellowmen; as instruments of labor they had a definite price and as property a definite value. The concentration-camp inmate has no price, because he can always be replaced; nobody knows to whom he belongs, because he is never seen. From the point of view of normal society he is absolutely superfluous, although in times of acute labor shortage, as in Russia and in Germany during the war, he is used for work.

The concentration camp as an institution was not established 17 for the sake of any possible labor yield; the only permanent economic function of the camps has been the financing of their own supervisory apparatus; thus from the economic point of view the concentration camps exist mostly for their own sake. Any work that has been performed could have been done much better and more cheaply under different conditions. Especially Russia, whose concentration camps are mostly described as forced-labor camps because Soviet bureaucracy has chosen to dignify them with this name, reveals most clearly that forced labor is not the primary issue; forced labor is the normal condition of all Russian workers, who have no freedom of movement and can be arbitrarily drafted for work to any place at any time. The incredibility of the horrors is closely bound up with their economic uselessness. The Nazis carried this uselessness to the point of open anti-utility when in the midst of the war, despite the shortage of building material and rolling stock, they set up enormous, costly extermination factories and transported millions of people back and forth. In the eyes of a strictly utilitarian world the obvious contradiction between these acts and military expediency gave the whole enterprise an air of mad unreality.

This atmosphere of madness and unreality, created by an apparent lack of purpose, is the real iron curtain which hides all forms of concentration camps from the eyes of the world. Seen from outside, they and the things that happen in them can be described only in images drawn from a life after death, that is, a life removed from earthly purposes. Concentration camps can very aptly be divided into three types corresponding to three basic Western conceptions of a life after death: Hades, Purgatory, and Hell. To Hades correspond those relatively mild forms, once popular even in nontotalitarian countries, for getting undesirable elements of all sorts—refugees, stateless persons, the asocial and the unemployed—out of the way; as DP camps,[12] which are nothing other than camps for persons who have become superfluous and bothersome, they have survived the war. Purgatory is represented by the Soviet Union's labor camps, where neglect is combined with chaotic forced labor. Hell in the most literal sense was embodied by those types of camp perfected by the Nazis, in which the whole of life was thoroughly and systematically organized with a view to the greatest possible torment. 18

All three types have one thing in common: the human masses sealed off in them are treated as if they no longer existed, as if what happened to them were no longer of any interest to anybody, as if they were already dead and some evil spirit gone mad were amusing himself by stopping them for a while between life and death before admitting them to eternal peace. 19

---

[12] **DP camps** Displaced Persons camps. These camps were common in Europe after World War II.

QUESTIONS FOR CRITICAL READING

1. Why are concentrations camps described as "laboratories" for the totalitarian regime?
2. What is the importance of the concentration camps' goal of removing human spontaneity?
3. In what sense are the concentration camps "the true central institution of totalitarian organizational power" (para. 4)?
4. Arendt implies that the experience of the concentration camp has the effect of "a mental disease." Why would that be so?
5. How is murder different from the mass death that characterizes the concentration camps?
6. Why is the concentration camp "useful" to the totalitarian government?

SUGGESTIONS FOR WRITING

1. Examine the economic issues Arendt raises that are involved in the establishment and operation of concentration camps in a totalitarian state. Decide whether a totalitarian state, whose goal is to achieve total domination, would be able to derive economic advantage from concentration camps. Why would this be an important issue? If there were a considerable economic advantage to maintaining concentration camps, would that fact make them any less terrifying?

2. Arendt reflected the fears of her own time in this essay. For her the most terrifying and immediate totalitarian governments were those of Nazi Germany and the Soviet Union. What evidence do you see in our contemporary world that might suggest totalitarianism is not completely "dead"? Do you perceive any threatening totalitarian governments anywhere in the world today? How do they seem to function and to interact with other nations?

3. Should you establish that a government is functioning as a totalitarian state today, do you feel it is a moral imperative that you do everything possible to overthrow that state? Would it be ethical and moral to go to war against such a state even if it did not immediately threaten you? Would it be ethical and moral for you to turn your back on a totalitarian state and ignore its operation so that it could achieve the kind of total domination Arendt describes?

4. **CONNECTIONS** Which of the authors in this section on government would be most likely to find the nature of the totalitarian state absolutely unacceptable? Would that author have recommended war to overthrow that government? What convinces you that the author is willing to risk everything to destroy such a state? Does that author hold to an ideology that contrasts profoundly from the ideology of totalitarianism? If so, how would you describe it?

5. **CONNECTIONS** How would Machiavelli interpret Arendt's discussion of ends and means in paragraph 8? Would Machiavelli have recommended concentration camps to his Prince as a means of maintaining power? If a Prince believed that concentration camps would be the means by which a state could achieve stability and power, would he be right in assuming that the stability and power thus achieved were worthwhile ends? Do you think Machiavelli would have accepted a totalitarian Prince?

STEPHEN L. CARTER
The Separation of Church and State

STEPHEN L. CARTER (b. 1954) is William Nelson Cromwell Professor of Law at Yale Law School, specializing in constitutional law and contracts. He also maintains a deep concern for issues of law and religion. Carter writes a regular column for *Christianity Today*, a magazine of general interest to Christians and others. He is himself a member of a communion that is reputed to be the oldest predominantly black Episcopal church in the nation. As such, he has a personal stake in issues in which law and religion intersect. He is also a very prominent intellectual, with strong and measured opinions on major controversies in American life. His books treat specialized legal issues as well as general issues of morality and behavior. In addition, he has received recent attention as the author of the best-selling novel *The Emperor of Ocean Park* (2000).

Carter graduated from Stanford University and took his law degree from Yale University. After Yale, he clerked with a Washington, D.C., appeals court judge for a year, then clerked for Justice Thurgood Marshall of the U.S. Supreme Court. He later went into practice in Washington for a short time and then proceeded to a professorship at Yale Law School.

A book that catapulted Carter into the public's attention was *Reflections of an Affirmative Action Baby* (1991), in which he analyzed the complexities of affirmative action as well as its helpful and damaging results for young black people. He spoke out on the issue because he felt that even though black Americans might be stigmatized by affirmative action, they needed to support it.

His specialized books on law, *The Confirmation Mess: Cleaning Up the Federal Appointments Process* (1994) and *The Dissent of the*

From *The Culture of Disbelief: How American Law and Politics Trivialize Religious Devotion.*

Governed: A Meditation on Law, Religion, and Loyalty (1998), have been widely praised for their clarity and seriousness. They maintain a concern for the larger issues of government processes as they affect all citizens. In 1998 Carter also published *Civility: Manners, Morals, and the Etiquette of Democracy,* a strongly personal view of the need to struggle against the encroaching rudeness that threatens the civility of our society.

The book *The Culture of Disbelief: How American Law and Politics Trivialize Religious Devotion* (1993), from which the following selection comes, is a powerfully argued examination of religion and politics. With the emergence of religion and religious issues in modern politics, especially during election years, this book made an effort to clarify the state's obligations to citizens of various religious persuasions. What makes the book remarkable is that it is written by an expert in constitutional law who is also a practicing Christian with strong religious views. Balancing the responsibilities of religion and law is one of the book's primary goals.

Carter has further explored the subject of religion in politics in *God's Name in Vain: The Wrongs and Rights of Religion in Politics* (2000), which expands on the ideas of separation of church and state presented in the selection that follows.

Carter's Rhetoric

Carter is a prominent lawyer teaching at a prominent law school. Therefore, it is natural that he should use logical principles in maintaining his positions. Moreover, he makes reference to legal precedents much in the manner of a lawyer or judge considering the merits of a case. He also establishes early on the position that is the bedrock of his argument. To begin with, he addresses the First Amendment and points out that of its five clauses, the relation of religion to government comes first and may, therefore, be considered first in importance. The complete text of the First Amendment is as follows:

> Congress shall make no law respecting an establishment of religion, or prohibiting the free exercise thereof; or abridging the freedom of speech, or of the press; or the right of the people peaceably to assemble, and to petition the government for a redress of grievances.

Carter refers to the first of these clauses, "Congress shall make no law respecting an establishment of religion," as the "Establishment Clause"; the second, "prohibiting the free exercise thereof," as the "Free Exercise Clause." These are the bases of all arguments that proceed from the Bill of Rights in the Constitution. In essence, Carter's argument constitutes an analysis of that text. As a way of calling attention to his text as such, he establishes what he calls "The Separation Metaphor," which alerts us to the need to interpret the Constitution carefully, almost as if it were a literary document.

Prior to this discussion, his opening two paragraphs establish that the Constitution was designed to protect religion from the state, not the state from religion. Given that premise, much that has exercised politicians in recent decisions may seem less clear, less certain, and less desirable than it might otherwise appear to be.

After establishing basic principles, Carter uses the device of the anecdotal example in paragraph 4, in which he recounts the story of a minister whose drug rehabilitation program succeeded where others failed. The reason for the success was, the minister said, the effect of prayer. Despite the overwhelming success (as told to Carter) of this program, the minister could not secure state or federal funds to continue his work. Carter then examines the rationale behind the decision to withhold funds from the minister's drug-treatment program.

A brief examination of historical precedent follows in paragraphs 7 to 10, with more examples that demonstrate the difficulties faced in interpreting the First Amendment. In paragraph 10, Carter addresses the concept of metaphor, citing U.S. Supreme Court Justice Hugo Black's famous statement that, "[t]he First Amendment has erected a wall between church and state." Black's choice of metaphor was attacked by other lawyers; Carter emends it to suggest that the wall is acceptable as a metaphor, but it should "have a few doors in it." His point is simply that one cannot be absolute in reference to the First Amendment.

Subsequent paragraphs deal with the "*Lemon* test," a reference to a legal case, *Lemon v. Kurtzman*, in which the U.S. Supreme Court found that states could not fund religious schools even if they taught nonreligious subjects. But as Carter points out, even that legal precedent is interpreted in conflicting ways. In other words, there really is no established test of the Establishment Clause, so people must argue every case individually.

In paragraphs 14 and 15, Carter demonstrates how the U.S. Supreme Court has "missed the point" in a specific case. What he demonstrates in his analysis of the Court's ruling is that there are inconsistencies that the Court did not seem to take into account. In these paragraphs he introduces the concept of the motivation of people who might be seen as challenging the First Amendment. A religiously motivated "nuclear arms freeze," for example, might not get support from local or national government agencies because of the involvement of religion.

Carter raises an interesting point in the final paragraphs of the essay. The "fabric of our society" is a term the U.S. Supreme Court used to justify providing government funds for a Christmas display because the celebration of Christmas is part of the fabric of our society. Carter points out that this is an unreliable test because other things, such as more than two hundred years of slavery, were part of the fabric of our society as well, and they were undesirable and indeed illegal today.

In paragraph 23, following the evidence he has presented, Carter recapitulates the point that the Establishment Clause was designed to protect religion from the state, not the state from religion.

PREREADING QUESTIONS: WHAT TO READ FOR

The following prereading questions may help you anticipate key issues in your discussion of Stephen L. Carter's "The Separation of Church and State." Keeping them in mind during your first reading of the selection should help focus your attention.

- What is the Establishment Clause?
- Does the First Amendment protect religion from the state or the state from religion?
- What constitutes a test of the Establishment Clause?

The Separation of Church and State

By now, many a patient reader will be ready with another objection: it is all very well to talk about allowing the religious to enter the public square to participate in political debate alongside everybody else. But what about the Constitution? What about the separation of church and state? Don't we have long-standing constitutional and philosophical traditions that limit the influence of religious sectarianism on government policy?

The answer to the last question—as so often in the law—is "not exactly." The courts do indeed enforce a separation of church and state, and it is backed by some very impressive legal philosophy, but one must be careful not to misunderstand what the doctrine and the First Amendment that is said to embody it were designed to do. Simply put, the metaphorical separation of church and state originated in an effort to protect religion from the state, not the state from religion. The religion clauses of the First Amendment were crafted to permit maximum freedom to the religious. In modern, religiously pluralistic America, where, as we have seen, the religions play vital roles as independent sources of meaning for their adherents, this means that the government should neither force people into sectarian religious observances, such as classroom prayer in public schools, nor favor some religions over others, as by erecting a crèche paid for with public funds, nor punish people for their religiosity without a very strong reason other than prejudice. It does not mean, however, that people whose motivations are religious are banned from trying to influence government, nor that the government is banned from listening to them. Understanding this distinction is the key to preserving the necessary separation of church and state without resorting to a philosophical rhetoric that treats religion as an inferior way for citizens to come to public judgment.

The Separation Metaphor

Religion is the first subject of the First Amendment. The amendment begins with the Establishment Clause ("Congress shall make no law respecting an establishment of religion . . .") which is immediately followed by the Free Exercise Clause ("or prohibiting the free exercise thereof"). Although one might scarcely know it from the zeal with which the primacy of the other First Amendment freedoms (free press, free speech) is often asserted, those protections come *after* the clauses that were designed to secure religious liberty, which Thomas Jefferson called "the most inalienable and sacred of all human rights." What this means in practice, however, is often quite complicated.   3

Consider an example: at a dinner party in New York City a few years ago, I met a Christian minister who told me about a drug-rehabilitation program that he runs in the inner city. His claim—I cannot document it—was that his program had a success rate much higher than other programs. The secret, he insisted, was prayer. It was not just that he and his staff prayed for the drug abusers they were trying to help, he told me, although they naturally did that. But the reason for the program's success, he proclaimed, was that he and his staff taught those who came to them for assistance to pray as well; in other words, they converted their charges, if not to Christianity, then at least to religiosity. But this program, he went on with something close to   4 bitterness, could receive no state funding, because of its religious nature.

Well, all right. To decide that the program should not receive   5
any funds, despite the success of its approach, might seem to be a straightforward application of the doctrine holding that the Constitution sets up a wall of separation between church and state. After all, the program is frankly religious: it uses prayer, and even teaches prayer to its clients. What could be more threatening to the separation of church and state than to provide a government subsidy for it? The Supreme Court has said many times that the government may neither "advance" religion nor engage in an "excessive entanglement" with it. On its face, a program of drug-rehabilitation therapy that relies on teaching people to pray would seem to do both.

It is doubtless frustrating to believe deeply that one has a call from   6
God to do what one does, and then to discover that the secular society often will not support that work, no matter how important it is to the individual. Yet that frustration is itself a sign of the robustness of religious pluralism in America. For the most significant aspect of the separation of church and state is not, as some seem to think, the shielding of the secular world from too strong a religious influence; the principal task of the separation of church and state is to secure religious liberty.

The separation of church and state is one of the great gifts that   7
American political philosophy has presented to the world, and if it has few emulators, that is the world's loss. Culled from the writings of Roger Williams[1] and Thomas Jefferson, the concept of a "wall of separation" finds its constitutional moorings in the First Amendment's firm statement that the "Congress shall make no law respecting an establishment of religion." Although it begins with the word "Congress," the Establishment Clause for decades has been quite sensibly interpreted by the Supreme Court as applying to states as well as to the federal government.

For most of American history, the principal purpose of the Es-   8
tablishment Clause has been understood as the protection of the religious world against the secular government. A century ago, Philip Schaff[2] of Union Seminary in New York celebrated the clause as "the Magna Carta of religious freedom," representing as it did "the first example in history of a government deliberately depriving itself of all legislative control over religion." Note the wording: not religious control over government—government control over religion.

---

[1] **Roger Williams (1603–1683)** A staunch advocate of religious liberty, he founded Rhode Island in reaction to the dogmatic ways of Plymouth Colony.
[2] **Philip Schaff (1819–1893)** Swiss-American historian and theologian of considerable importance to nineteenth-century religious thought.

Certainly this voluntary surrender of control is an indispensable separation if the religions are to serve as the independent intermediary institutions that Tocqueville[3] envisioned.

Over the years, the Supreme Court has handed down any number of controversial decisions under the Establishment Clause, many of them landmarks of our democratic culture. The best known are the cases in which the Justices struck down the recital of organized prayer in the public school classrooms, decisions that for three decades have ranked (in surveys) as among the most unpopular in our history. But the decisions were plainly right, for if the state is able either to prescribe a prayer to begin the school day or to select a holy book from which a prayer must be taken, it is exercising control over the religious aspects of the life of its people—precisely what the religion clauses were written to forbid. But although the separation of church and state is essential to the success of a vibrant, pluralistic democracy, the doctrine does not entail all that is done in its name. I have already mentioned the school district in Colorado that thought it the better part of valor to forbid a teacher to add books on Christianity to a classroom library that already included works on other religions. The town of Hamden, Connecticut, where I live, briefly ruled that a church group could not rent an empty schoolhouse for Sunday services. (Cooler heads in the end prevailed.) These rulings were both defended as required by the separation of church and state; so is the intermittent litigation to strike the legend IN GOD WE TRUST from America's coins or the phrase "under God" from the Pledge of Allegiance, an effort, if successful, that would wipe away even the civil religion. In short, it is not hard to understand the frequent complaints that the secular world acts as though the constitutional command is that the nation and its people must keep religion under wraps.

Proponents of the hostility thesis believe that the Supreme Court bears a heavy burden of responsibility for what they see as the disfavored position of religion in America. Justice Hugo Black,[4] in *Everson v. Board of Education* (1947), often is said to have started the ball rolling when he wrote these words: "The First Amendment has erected a wall between church and state. That wall must be kept high and impregnable. We could not approve the slightest breach." A year later, Justice Stanley Reed[5] warned that "a rule of law should

---

[3] **Alexis de Tocqueville (1805–1859)** French writer and traveler, famous for the still important book *Democracy in America* (vol. 1, 1835; vol. 2, 1840).

[4] **Hugo Black (1886–1971)** Justice of the U.S. Supreme Court influential in school desegregation. He demanded the admission of James Meredith to the University of Mississippi, the first African American to study there.

[5] **Stanley Reed (1884–1980)** Justice appointed to the Supreme Court in 1938.

not be drawn from a figure of speech." One critic wrote years later that Black had simply penned a few "lines of fiction." The critics are not quite right, but they are not quite wrong, either. There is nothing wrong with the metaphor of a wall of separation. The trouble is that in order to make the Founders' vision compatible with the structure and needs of modern society, the wall has to have a few doors in it.

Souring on *Lemon*

The embarrassing truth is that the Establishment Clause has no 11
theory; that is, the Supreme Court has not really offered guidance on how to tell when the clause is violated. Since 1971, the Justices have relied on the "*Lemon* test," so named because it was framed (quite awkwardly, one is compelled to add) in the Court's 1971 decision in *Lemon v. Kurtzman*. The case is so often cited that legal scholars tend to forget what it involved: a state program to reimburse all private schools, including religious schools, for expenses of textbooks, materials, and, in part, salaries used to teach nonreligious subjects. The Court held the program unconstitutional and, in so doing, enunciated the *Lemon* test—a lemon indeed, for it has proved well nigh impossible to apply. In order to pass Establishment Clause muster, the Justices wrote, the statute in question must meet three criteria: "First, the statute must have a secular legislative purpose; second, its principal or primary effect must be one that neither advances nor inhibits religion; finally, the statute must not foster 'an excessive entanglement with religion.'"

Thus conceived, the clause exists less for the benefit of religious 12
autonomy than for the benefit of secular politics; that is, to borrow from the test itself, the Establishment Clause was written to further "a secular legislative purpose," trying to erect around the political process a wall almost impossible to take seriously. It is perhaps needless to add that *Lemon* left the critics in their glory. Did the legislation enacted at the behest of the religiously motivated civil rights movement have a secular purpose? If granting tax relief to parents whose children attend parochial schools advances religion by making the schools cheaper, does refusing to grant them inhibit religion by making the schools more expensive? If competing factions within the same church both seek control of the same church building, does judicial resolution represent an excessive entanglement?

When it promulgates complex multipart tests for constitu- 13
tional violations, the Supreme Court is almost always luckless, but the *Lemon* test has been extraordinarily unhelpful to the lower courts. Indeed, the courts have reached results that are all over the

map—sometimes quite literally, for one of the more interesting cases involved a rather bland "Motorists' Prayer" to God for safety that North Carolina printed on its official state maps. A federal court, missing the significance of America's civil religion, held the practice to be a violation of the Establishment Clause. Another federal court ruled that the clause prohibits religious groups from petitioning the Congress for special laws (available to all other groups) in order to secure copyrights when they are unable to meet the statutory criteria. The list goes on and on—but *Lemon* remains.

The Supreme Court itself has not fared much better than the lower courts in applying its test. The *Lemon* framework might not work too badly, could the courts but take the requirement of a "secular legislative purpose" to mean, as one scholar has proposed, any "political purpose"—that is, any goal the state legitimately is able to pursue. Recently, however, the courts have seemed to fumble this point, confusing the political purpose for which the statute is enacted with the religious sensibilities of legislators or their constituents.

A majority of the Supreme Court missed this point in *Edwards v. Aguillard* (1987), with the suggestion that a law requiring schools to teach scientific creationism is unconstitutional because most of its supporters were religiously motivated—a suggestion that would also render unconstitutional the religiously motivated teaching of evolution, or, for that matter, a religiously motivated nuclear arms freeze. A similar suggestion has been made by some pro-choice scholars who have argued that pro-life legislation violates the Establishment Clause because of the religious motivation of many supporters. For the religiously devout citizen, faith may be so intertwined with personality that it is impossible to tell when one is acting, or not acting, from religious motive—and this is certainly true for legislators, unless we dismiss as hypocritical cynics the entire Congress of the United States, where over 90 percent of the members say that they consult their religious beliefs before voting on important matters. Indeed, by some estimates, an absolute majority of the laws now on the books were motivated, at least in part, by religiously based moral judgments. That is why inquiring into *why* legislators have voted as they have, rather than *what* their legislation does, is almost always a mistake. "That values happen to be religious," New York's Governor Mario Cuomo[6] has warned, "does not deny them acceptability" as part of "the consensus view" needed to support public policy. The result in *Edwards* is probably correct, but

14

15

---

[6] **Mario Cuomo (b. 1932)** Former governor of New York, sometimes described as the "conscience of the Democratic Party."

not because of the Court's discussion of what was in the minds of the supporters of the statute.

The idea that religious motivation renders a statute suspect was   16
never anything but a tortured and unsatisfactory reading of the clause. As one scholar has put the matter, there is good reason to think that "what the religion clauses of the first amendment were designed to do was not to remove religious values from the arena of public debate, but to keep them there." The Establishment Clause by its terms forbids the imposition of religious belief by the state, not statements of religious belief in the course of public dialogue. The distinction is one of more than semantic significance.

Consider the call by Reinhold Niebuhr[7] and others back in the   17
1920s for the "Christianization" of American industry. Their use of the word "Christianization" did not mean the imposition of ritual and doctrine; it meant, rather, the transformation of industry into a new form that would accord with a principle of respect for the human spirit that Niebuhr and the rest found lacking in industrial organizations of the day. Critics called it socialism, or perhaps communism. But whatever it was, religious faith was plainly at its heart.

Niebuhr struck a chord, not only with any number of left-   18
leaning Protestants, but also with a good number of socialists, many of them Jews, and with other reformers of no religious persuasion. (A well-known support group was Atheists for Niebuhr.) Suppose the response had been greater, that public support had burgeoned; suppose that legislatures had begun enacting programs that matched the socialist spirit of Christianization. This reform legislation would be purely secular in operation and could certainly be justified in secular terms. But under an establishment clause that is read to equate *acting* out of religious motivation with *imposing* religious belief, the programs might be unconstitutional, because both those who proposed them and many of those who voted for them would have done so out of religious conviction.

That should be a deeply troubling result. A rule holding that the   19
religious convictions of the proponents are enough to render a statute constitutionally suspect represents a sweeping rejection of the deepest beliefs of millions of Americans, who are being told, in effect, that their views do not matter. In a nation that prides itself on cherishing religious freedom, it would be something of a puzzle to conclude that the Establishment Clause means that a Communist or a Republican may try to have his or her world view reflected in the nation's law,

---

[7]**Reinhold Niebuhr (1892–1971)** A prominent Protestant theologian who often wrote about social issues.

but a religionist cannot. Although some critics fear we are already at that point, the truth is that we have a good long way to go; but we are heading in the wrong direction in our jurisprudence, and if the courts continue to read *Lemon* as they have, the Establishment Clause might well end up not antiestablishment but antireligion.

Recognizing this danger, the Justices, and the scholars who sup- 20 port their Establishment Clause jurisprudence, have simply ignored the rules of *Lemon v. Kurtzman* when applying them might prove too disruptive. In particular, they have tried to tiptoe around many widely accepted practices that seem to run afoul of *Lemon*. But squaring *Lemon's* rules with the accepted usages of the society's civil religion often requires some fancy footwork. How, for example, does one justify the expenditure of government funds to provide armed forces chaplains, which looks like government sponsorship of religion? Answers one observer: "This is not so much 'setting up a church' as providing access to churches already existing for those removed by government action from their normal communities." Okay, but how to explain the use of public funds during the Christmas season to build and maintain a crèche, which celebrates the nativity of Jesus Christ? The Court itself tackled that one: "The display engenders a friendly community spirit of good will in keeping with the season" and any advancement of particular religions "is indirect, remote and incidental." Oh, really? Well, what about the offering of prayers at the opening of legislative sessions? The Justices had an answer for that one too: "In light of the unambiguous and unbroken history of more than 200 years, there can be no doubt that the practice of opening legislative sessions with prayer has become part of the fabric of our society."

Part of the fabric of our society—it is easy to see why the Court is 21 reluctant to hold that the fabric of society includes some threads of unconstitutionality, but it is difficult to imagine how that can be the right test. Racial segregation was once part of the fabric of our society; so was prohibiting the women's vote, and corrupt patronage politics in the big cities. The idea, for example, that a crèche does not advance religion is ridiculous; the point of the crèche is to celebrate the birth of the Lord. So if the Court is willing to ignore *Lemon* and hold that government funds can pay for one, it is simply not doing its job. If the Justices dare not even follow their own rules, it may be time to find a new way to look at these problems. Yet the Supreme Court, although hinting around the edges, has not yet decided to make a full retreat.

Part of the problem is figuring out where the Justices can possi- 22 bly retreat to. For even if the Court's *Lemon* test is insupportable, it is far from clear what should be put in its place. On this point, not surprisingly, there is a considerable scholarly battle, in which it is healthiest to be a spectator. Michael McConnell[8] has proposed a standard based on coercion of belief, which he has labeled the "lost element" of Establishment Clause jurisprudence. Douglas Laycock[9] has shot back that this test would leave the Establishment Clause void of content. Justice Sandra Day O'Connor[10] has proposed a test asking whether the government is endorsing religious belief or not. Mark Tushnet[11] has answered that Christian judges in a Christian-dominated society are not in the best position to tell whether a message of endorsement is being sent. Steven D. Smith,[12] distinguishing between religious individuals and their organizations, has suggested prohibiting only concerted action by state and religious institutions. Kathleen Sullivan[13] has taken the opposite position, proposing to use the clause to guarantee a secular public order. And one could go on this way at some considerable length.

Constitutional provisions all too rarely, alas, have easily dis-   23 cernible meanings, and there are elements of truth in all these readings of the Establishment Clause. Yet what is most vital, in coming to a sensible understanding of the clause, is to avoid the ahistorical conclusion that its principal purpose is to protect the secular from the religious, an approach that, perhaps inevitably, carries us down the road toward a new establishment, the establishment of religion as a hobby, trivial and unimportant for serious people, not to be mentioned in serious discourse. And nothing could be further from the constitutional, historical, or philosophical truth.

---

[8]**Michael W. McConnell** Presidential Professor of Law at the University of Utah, and Judge, Tenth U.S. Circuit Court of Appeals.

[9]**Douglas Laycock** Alice McKean Young Regents Professor of Law at the University of Texas.

[10]**Sandra Day O'Connor (b. 1930)** Appointed first female Justice of the U.S. Supreme Court in 1981.

[11]**Mark Tushnet** Carmack Waterhouse Professor of Constitutional Law at Georgetown University.

[12]**Steven D. Smith** Professor at the University of San Diego School of Law, specializing in law and religion.

[13]**Kathleen Sullivan** Professor at Stanford Law School, specializing in constitutional law.

QUESTIONS FOR CRITICAL READING

1. Why is the separation of church and state described as "metaphorical"?
2. Does the fact that religion comes first in the First Amendment imply that it is first in importance?

3. Why was the Christian minister unable to secure public funds to support his project?
4. Why does Carter describe the separation of church and state as "one of the great gifts that American political philosophy has presented to the world" (para. 7)?
5. Who struck down the recitation of prayers in public schools? Why?
6. What is the significance of the problems involved in the "*Lemon* test"?
7. What problems are raised by the Supreme Court's ruling in *Edwards v. Aguillard*?
8. How have jurists justified the support of army chaplains with public funds?
9. What is the meaning of the term "part of the fabric of our society" (para. 20), as used by the Supreme Court?

SUGGESTIONS FOR WRITING

1. In paragraph 7, Carter implies the Constitution does not make it clear whether the Establishment Clause should be administered by the federal government or by individual state governments. Which do you think should be the case? How might different states interpret the Establishment Clause? Why do you think there would be a difference among states at all on this account? How do you suppose Plymouth Colony, which existed 150 years before the Constitution, would have interpreted the Establishment Clause?
2. Take a position on the introduction of prayer in the public schools. Argue a case that either defends or attacks it. Consider Carter's concerns for the "*Lemon* test" and consider the ways in which the Supreme Court has interpreted cases in the light of what it calls the "fabric of our society."
3. Why, in a nation whose citizens are preponderantly religious, should there be any question at all about the support of Christmas displays on public land or Bible reading in public schools? In a democracy, shouldn't the will of the majority rule? Why should people whose beliefs differ from those of the majority have their views taken into consideration? Take a position on this issue and argue it carefully.
4. Carter refers to theologian Reinhold Niebuhr's campaign to "Christianize" American industry. What did Niebuhr mean? Describe, in as much detail as you can, how a typical American business might follow Niebuhr's request. What would it do differently? For example, would job outsourcing continue to be a desirable practice if Niebuhr's program went into effect?
5. Should private religious schools receive support from local and state governments in the teaching of nonreligious subjects? Should public school students who wish to study in private religious schools receive the same financial support they would get in the public schools? If it cost $7,500 a year to educate a student in a public school, would it be

desirable to give that student, say, $5,000 toward his or her private school tuition? Why or why not? Consider the way in which Carter argues his case and try to emulate his methods of analysis.

6. **CONNECTIONS**   How would Thomas Jefferson have reacted to our current refusal to permit prayer and Bible reading in public schools? Examine the Declaration of Independence and "The Separation of Church and State" carefully to see if you can interpret Jefferson in terms of Carter.

7. **CONNECTIONS**   Read Henry David Thoreau's "Civil Disobedience" (p. 133). If Thoreau were a student in public school today, how would he react to the prohibition of prayer? Where would Thoreau stand on the issue of separation of church and state? Would his views have been similar to Thomas Jefferson's? To Carter's? Explain.

8. **CONNECTIONS**   What aspects of Carter's argument would have made most sense to Lao-Tzu? What aspects would be least acceptable? What would have been Lao-Tzu's position on prayer in public schools or the use of public funds for the support of religious celebrations? Would Lao-Tzu have supported the Establishment Clause if it had existed in his time and culture?

PART TWO

JUSTICE

Marcus Tullius Cicero
Henry David Thoreau
Elizabeth Cady Stanton
Martin Luther King Jr.
John Rawls
Martha C. Nussbaum

INTRODUCTION

> If any one steal the property of a temple or of the court, he shall
> be put to death, and also the one who receives the stolen thing
> from him shall be put to death.
> > —HAMMURABI (1792–1750 B.C.)

> Justice turns the scale, bringing to some learning through
> suffering.
> > —AESCHYLUS (525–456 B.C.)

> Spare me through your mercy, do not punish me through your
> justice.
> > —ANSELM OF CANTERBURY (1033–1109)

> The sentiment of justice is so natural, and so universally acquired
> by all mankind, that it seems to be independent of all law, all
> party, all religion.
> > —VOLTAIRE (1694–1778)

> Where justice is denied, where poverty is enforced, where
> ignorance prevails, and where any one class is made to feel that
> society is in an organized conspiracy to oppress, rob, and degrade
> them, neither persons nor property will be safe.
> > —FREDERICK DOUGLASS (1817–1895)

> Justice must always question itself, just as society can exist only
> by means of the work it does on itself and on its institutions.
> > —MICHEL FOUCAULT (1926–1984)

Ideas of justice have revolved historically around several closely related concepts: moral righteousness, equity of treatment, and reciprocity of action. Justice is an element of interpersonal relations, but philosophers usually link it to the individual's relationship to the state. In the Western tradition, the Greek philosopher Plato (428–347 B.C.) was the first to frame the concept of justice in terms of the health of the state. In his work *The Republic* he defined justice both as an overarching ideal and as a practical necessity for the functioning of a harmonious society. In his view, justice was served when each stratum of society (philosopher-rulers, soldiers, and artisans and workers) operated within its own sphere of action and did not interfere with others.

Like Plato, the Greek philosopher Aristotle (384–322 B.C.) viewed the general concept of justice as an important eternal quality that the individual should strive to uphold. He defined general justice as the overarching goal of moral righteousness that ensures a good society, legislative justice as the duty of the individual to comply with the laws of the society (civic virtue), and particular justice as the duty of the judge to redress inequalities in personal transactions. In turn each of these forms of justice works to maintain the overarching ideals of political and economic justice and thus protect the society from collapse. Ironically, although political justice centers on the concept of freedom and liberty, in Aristotle's time warring states enslaved defeated warriors and their families. Aristotle justified this practice by asserting that basic inequalities between people rendered some people natural slaves.

In later centuries, philosophers such as Thomas Hobbes (English, 1588–1679) drew on Aristotle's theories of natural justice — the justice found in a state of nature where the strong always impose their will on the weak. However, Hobbes found that because people actually live in communities with a political structure that leads them to suffer or commit injustices, the concept of justice becomes essentially moral. Hobbes wrestled with the moral parameters of justice and finally concluded that it is impossible to form a universal concept of justice and that justice is whatever laws are most useful and expedient for society.

This tension between justice as a moral ideal and its manifestation in society as practical law has been a hallmark of its evolution as an idea. Indeed, as the writers in this section so eloquently reveal, the laws that are meant to ensure justice within a society often enforce deep injustices. All the authors in this section investigate the relationship between the individual (or group of individuals) and society in an attempt to come to an understanding of how laws contribute to just ends and the promotion of equality, or how they enforce unequal treatment. Some of these authors respond to the laws that have affected them directly, while others respond to concepts that they feel should be in place in order to guarantee justice to all people.

Cicero presents a dialogue with a character, Philus, whose assignment is to create an argument in favor of injustice. As a great rhetorician and orator, Cicero plays an interesting game in asking someone whose personal views are strongly in favor of justice to argue against it. The procedure is interesting for us because we can see more clearly the virtue of justice by examining in detail the arguments against it. Philus does a creditable job by relying on arguments already developed by another philosopher, Carneades. His appeal is to the strength of the state and the need for the individual to yield to collective values. The result is an argument for injustice that is dangerous because we might be convinced by it.

The question of how the individual should react in the face of unjust laws is taken up by Henry David Thoreau. He refused to pay taxes that would be used in a war against Mexico that he felt was dishonorable, realized that he would have to pay a penalty for his views, and was willing to do so. Thoreau makes a special plea to conscience as a way of dealing with injustice by requiring the individual to place conscience first and law second. His "Civil Disobedience" reminds us that we are the citizens of the nation and that we ought to make our own will known. Thoreau stresses that there is a price for doing what is right, but that all honest citizens must pay it.

Elizabeth Cady Stanton relies on the rhetorical device of parody in her Declaration of Sentiments and Resolutions. Modeled directly on Thomas Jefferson's Declaration of Independence, Stanton's appeal serves as a reminder that Jefferson spoke only of men's independence, not that of women. Her demands are no less reasonable than Jefferson's, and it is a source of embarrassment to her that she has to redress such an omission after so much time has elapsed since Jefferson's Declaration was adopted.

Like Thoreau, Martin Luther King Jr. was also imprisoned for breaking a law his conscience deemed unjust. In his struggle against the Jim Crow laws enforcing segregation in the South, King acted on his belief that the individual can and should fight laws that treat members of society unjustly. King's *Letter from Birmingham Jail* provides a masterful and moving definition of what makes laws just or unjust. Furthermore, King develops the concept of nonviolent demonstration as a method by which the individual can protest unjust laws.

The modern thinker who has had the largest impact on discussion of the idea of justice is John Rawls. In his book *Theory of Justice*, he examines the ideas of Plato and Aristotle and defends the rights of the individual against the demands of the state in insisting on justice as fairness. In this selection from the book, which includes the main idea of his theory of justice, Rawls takes a view that differs from those of many practical thinkers. He feels that any just society will provide certain "Primary Goods," such as freedom, equality, and opportunity, to every citizen. He also feels that the justice of any law ought to be measured by its effect on the least advantaged citizens rather than the greatest number of citizens. His view is radical, and his argument in favor of it is carefully couched.

Martha C. Nussbaum, also one of the most prominent of modern legal scholars, builds on Rawls's ideas of "Primary Goods" and expands them into what she calls human functional capabilities. Her argument is that justice depends on a society providing the individual with the capabilities to enjoy life, health, freedom, human dignity, and so forth, all of which contribute, she argues, to helping an individual live a truly human life. Nussbaum's background involves work with underdeveloped nations, and her resultant point of view naturally takes into account various cultural attitudes that may be difficult for others to understand. Her argument attempts to find the cultural universals that will constitute a basis for justice in all societies.

The writers in this section discuss justice and injustice as it is both conceived and experienced by individuals. They consider the needs of the state and the rights of the individual while they also probe the underlying concepts of justice in any society. Some writers are theoretical in their views, while others write about practical matters of justice as these affect people in their everyday lives. For us, the arguments these writers develop should help us understand the complexities of the idea of justice. There is no simple way to define justice, despite the fact that we ordinarily know injustice when we see it.

MARCUS TULLIUS CICERO
The Defense of Injustice

MARCUS TULLIUS CICERO (106–43 B.C.) lived in Rome during some of the empire's most turbulent times. He was a great writer and a legendary orator. His works, with some exceptions, have survived to modern times and are often cited by rhetoricians — those who study the art of persuasion and fine writing. His letters are collected in four volumes; his books include *De Amicitiae* (On Friendship), *De Officiis* (On Duty), *De Oratore* (The Orator), *De Senectute* (On Old Age), *Tusculan Disputations, On the Nature of the Gods,* and many more influential texts, including some interesting poetry.

These books were written in a characteristic style that has been described as Ciceronian, a reference to his fullness of expression, his sometimes decorative language, and his rhythmic flow. His elegance inspired many imitators, including some modern writers who read him only in translation. His reliance on dialogue in his serious works connects him with Plato, whose dialogues were well known in Rome. Often, Cicero included philosophical ideas taken from his reading of Plato and Aristotle, whom he may have read in Greek.

Cicero was not just a philosopher. He was a lawyer and a politician as well as one of the most eloquent of Romans during a period when political debate was conducted at a very high level in the Roman Senate. He was a fierce republican and wrote *On the Republic* to help foster ideas that would help maintain the Republic at a time when civil wars were threatening it. Cicero was close to Julius Caesar, who was victorious in a struggle against Pompey and others and became the equivalent of a dictator in Rome. Cicero urged Caesar to honor the republican ideals that he felt represented the highest values of justice of any government in Rome. He

From *On Government*. Translated by Michael Grant.

also realized that he might be in danger if Caesar were out of office. Cicero had spoken against Marc Antony, who came into a position of influence when Caesar was assassinated in 44 B.C. Cicero was not in the senate when Caesar was murdered, nor did he have any connections with Brutus and the conspirators, and for a short while he stayed away from Rome.

Eventually Marc Antony joined in a new triumvirate with Octavian, Caesar's adopted son. Cicero had been guilty of speaking about Octavian in such a way as to seem disloyal and perhaps dangerous. Despite the fact that Cicero supported Octavian, and that Octavian tried to protect him against his enemies, Cicero was marked as dangerous by Marc Antony because he had condemned Marc Antony's policies in his collection of political criticism called *Philippics*. Because his arguments against the triumvirate were so powerful, Cicero was captured and killed on December 7, 43 B.C. His head and hands were brought to Octavian in Rome as a symbolic gesture.

Cicero's Rhetoric

The selection that follows is from pieces he wrote on the nature of the state. It begins with a dialogue between two powerful speakers. Laelius challenges Philus to argue against justice and in praise of injustice. This is a typical approach among master rhetoricians, whose skills often permit them to argue either side of an issue with equal deftness. For many people this skill invalidates rhetoric because they see the disputants as having no fundamental interests to defend, instead behaving like lawyers who are willing to argue a case that they know is not worthy to be argued. However, in this situation Cicero is clever. He realizes that in the hands of a skillful rhetorician, the case against justice will do a great deal to reveal the qualities of justice that make it most valuable to society. Philus is chosen to make this argument in part because he has a reputation for being impeccably honest, is profoundly committed to justice, and is the last person one would connect with a speech against justice. Cicero tells us as much in an effort to convince us that Philus is playing the role of devil's advocate for injustice.

In a way perhaps designed to protect his own reputation, Philus tells us that he will argue by using the words and arguments of another important rhetorician, Carneades (c. 213–128 B.C.), who had a reputation for ridiculing "the best causes." Carneades was a skeptic philosopher who enjoyed dismantling what appeared to be the most secure arguments just to demonstrate that there was nothing one could absolutely believe without examination. Cicero hopes that, as powerful as Philus's speech may be, we will not accept his views as desirable. However, Philus makes such a remarkable case for injustice that, if we are not careful, we may end up accepting it.

Philus begins by reminding Laelius and us that justice is rare and valuable, "far more valuable than all the gold in the world" (para. 4). Once that is said, he launches into his argument for injustice by commenting on those people who have praised it and wondering whether there could be such a thing as natural justice. He reasons that justice must be unnatural and a creation of government because, unlike things in nature, it is not "the same thing to all human beings" (para. 6). In paragraph 7 he surveys different societies and points out the diversity of ideas on important subjects. Since there is no universal view of justice, it must be constructed by each government independently.

In paragraph 10 Philus tells us that justice has been interpreted differently over the ages. Justice is not one static thing; it changes over time and in different places because it is not—like trees, rocks, and colors—a natural thing that is perceptible to everyone. Justice may mean obeying the laws, but which laws should a person obey? If laws came from God or from nature they would be easy to follow. Philus says, "laws are *not* imposed on us by nature—or by our innate sense of justice. They are imposed by the fear of being penalized. In other words, human beings are not just, by nature, at all" (para. 12).

Some lines or pages are lost between paragraphs 13 and 14, and when Philus returns to his speech he begins describing the action of governments, comparing government by men "exploiting their wealth or noble birth" with government by "the people." He condemns the latter as a government in chaos, and in his analysis he arrives at the compromise Scipio recommends: a government with a single leader, but with the council of the nobles and with the voice of the people in evidence. This structure would balance the powers of three important groups and possibly produce justice.

In paragraph 16 Philus begins to offer us some frightening alternatives:

1. We can perform injustice and not suffer it ourselves;
2. We can both perform it and suffer it; or,
3. We can neither perform it nor suffer it.

He evaluates the choices and says the best one is to perform injustice and get away with it without suffering it ourselves. In paragraph 17 he slyly reveals that the current policy of Rome, and by implication all empires, is to conquer lands and take them from other people. If justice were the uppermost concern, Rome would be merciful to all people, but if that were true Rome would lose its empire.

Philus contrasts what he calls wisdom with justice. Everyday wisdom says that the empire must be preserved. But justice says that merciful behavior is right and all other behavior is wrong. Justice says people should not be conquered against their will; wisdom says that the empire cannot grow and be great unless weak people are conquered by the strong. In paragraph 19, Philus begins to examine the choices of an individual, and in paragraph 20 he unleashes his most powerful argument against justice. He offers a hypothetical argument: "Let us imagine that there are two men, one a paragon of virtue, fairness, justice and honesty, and the other an outrageous ruffian." He asks: Which would we rather be, a good man who has been blinded, ruined, expelled and beggared, or a bad man who receives all the world's blessings? Philus knows which we would choose.

Then, by process of analogy, he likens the condition of the individual to the condition of the state. "No country would not rather be an unjust master than a just slave" (para. 21). Unfortunately, much of Philus's speech is lost at this point, and Laelius ends the "experiment" by making some profound and direct statements that are designed to counter Philus's argument.

In paragraph 22 Laelius begins by talking about "true law," something Philus implied did not exist. Laelius defends the concept of a natural law that conforms to reason and is the same for everyone. "To invalidate this law is sinful," he says. He goes on to say in the next and final paragraph that "[t]here will not be one law at Rome, and another at Athens," by which he means that laws should be consistent from state to state. "Instead there will be one single, everlasting, immutable law, which applies to all nations and all times. The maker, and umpire, and proposer of this law will be God, the single master and ruler of us all."

PREREADING QUESTIONS: WHAT TO READ FOR

The following prereading questions may help you anticipate key issues in the discussion of Marcus Tullius Cicero's "The Defense of Injustice." Keeping them in mind during your first reading of the selection should help focus your attention.

- Why does Philus point out the differences in the ways people in other nations practice their religions?

- Which arguments for injustice are most persuasive?
- Which virtues of justice seem most important in light of Philus's argument?

The Defense of Injustice

LAELIUS: For the purposes of argument, see if you can offer a defence 1
of injustice!

PHILUS: What a fine cause you have handed over to me — to speak in 2
favour of evil!

LAELIUS: Yes, I can see what you have reason to fear. You are afraid 3
that, if you repeat the customary arguments against justice, you
might be supposed also to approve of them. Yet you yourself, I must
point out, stand for old-fashioned integrity and honour to an almost
unparalleled degree! And your habit of arguing on the other side — on
the grounds that you find it the easiest way to arrive at the truth — is
something with which we are quite familiar.

PHILUS: All right, then. In order to humour you, I will smear myself 4
with dirt, quite deliberately. For that is what people who are looking
for gold always feel that they have to do. So we who are looking for justice, which is far more valuable than all the gold in the world, surely
ought to do the same, without shrinking from any hardship whatever.

But I only wish that since I am now going to make use of what 5
someone else has said, I could also use his own language! The man I
am referring to is Carneades.[1] For he, with his gift for sophistical
disputation, was quite accustomed to making the best causes sound
ridiculous! And so, after reviewing the arguments of Plato and Aristotle in favour of justice — a subject on which the latter filled four
large books[2] — what Carneades then proceeded to do was to refute
them! From Chrysippus[3] I did not expect anything substantial or
impressive. He uses his own peculiar method of argument, analysing
everything from a purely verbal rather than a factual point of view.

These heroes acted correctly in exalting the virtue of justice, in dis- 6
repair as it was. For justice, when it exists, is the most generous and
liberal of all virtues, loving itself less than it loves all the people in the

---

[1] **Carneades (c. 213–128 B.C.)** North African skeptic philosopher known for
his teaching and public arguments. Known to the modern world through Cicero and
other writers.

[2] The four-book commentary on justice no longer exists.

[3] **Chrysippus (c. 280–207 B.C.)** A prominent Stoic philosopher.

world, and living for the benefit of others rather than of itself. In seating it, therefore, upon that heavenly throne, not far from wisdom itself, those philosophers were perfectly right. But one more thing has to be pointed out. They did not, evidently, lack the desire to exalt justice. For, if they had, what would have been their reason and purpose for writing at all? Nor did they lack the ability to do so, in which, indeed, they surpassed everyone else. Yet their enthusiasm and eloquence alike were undermined by a certain weakness. For the justice into which we are inquiring is not just something that naturally exists, but a quality that is created by those who are occupied in government. It cannot be merely natural, because if it was, justice and injustice would be the same thing to all human beings, like heat and cold, or bitter and sweet.

But that is not the case; on the contrary, beliefs on the subject 7 vary enormously. If, for example, one could climb into Pacuvius's "chariot of winged snakes"[4] and drop in on many diverse nations and have a good look at them, one would find, first of all, that in Egypt, that most unchanging country of all in which the written records of the events of a vast series of centuries are preserved, a bull is considered a god—which the Egyptians call Apis. And numerous other monsters and animals of every kind are ranked among divinities and regarded as holy. That, to us, appears thoroughly alien. Here in Rome, on the other hand, as in Greece, splendid shrines can be seen, adorned with statues of deities in human form.

Yet the Persians have always considered that to be a blasphemous 8 custom. Indeed, Xerxes I is said to have commanded that the temples of Athens should be burnt down, for this sole reason, that he considered it blasphemous to keep the gods shut up within walls, when they belong to the entire world. Indeed subsequently Philip II of Macedonia, who planned to attack the Persians, and Alexander III the Great,[5] who actually did so, quoted as their pretext their determination to avenge the Greek temples—which the Greeks had decided that they must never rebuild, so that later generations would always have before their eyes this visible memorial of Persian sacrilege.

Furthermore, a considerable number of peoples, unlike ourselves, 9 have believed that the practice of human sacrifice is pious and thoroughly pleasing to the immortal gods. They include the Taurians on the coast of the Euxine Sea, King Busiris of Egypt,[6] and the Gauls and the Carthaginians. Indeed, people's life-styles are sometimes so

---

[4] **Pacuvius (c. 220–130 B.C.)** Cicero's favorite tragic poet. His work is quoted frequently in Cicero's works, but Pacuvius's plays exist only in fragments today.

[5] **Philip . . . Great** Philip II and Alexander the Great were rulers of Greece in the fourth century B.C., and Xerxes I was ruler of Persia in the fifth century B.C.

[6] **Busiris** Legendary Egyptian king.

divergent that the Cretans and Aetolians consider banditry respectable. As for the Spartans, they declared, habitually, that any territory whatever that they could touch with their spears belonged to themselves! And the Athenians, too, swore oaths, in public, pronouncing that every piece of ground that produced olives or grain was their own property. The Gauls, however, consider it degrading to grow grain by manual labour. For that reason they take up arms so that they can go and reap other people's fields. But consider the customs that we—who are, of course, the most just of men!—habitually follow. What we do is to tell the Gauls across the Alps that they must not plant olives and vines, because we want to increase the value of our own. That, you might say, is prudent; "just" is not the word you could apply to it. One can see, from this example, that what is sensible is not always truly wise. Consider Lycurgus.[7] He invented a series of admirably wise and sensible laws. Yet he felt able to insist, all the same, that the lands of the rich should be cultivated by the poor as if they were slaves.

Moreover, if I wanted to describe the differing ideas of justice, 10 and the divergent institutions and customs and ways of life, that have prevailed, not only in various nations of the world, but even in this single city of our own, I could show you, also, that they have not remained the same, but have been changed in a thousand different ways. Take for example Manius Manilius here, our interpreter of the law. The advice that he generally gave you about women's legacies and inheritance when he was a young man, before the Voconian Law was passed, was not at all the same advice as he would give you now.[8] (Yet that law, I might add, was passed for the benefit of males, and is very unfair to women. For why should a woman not have money of her own? And why should a Vestal Virgin be permitted to have an heir, when her mother cannot? Nor can I see why, if a limit had to be set to the amount of property a woman could possess, the daughter of Publius Licinius Crassus Dives Mucianus,[9] provided that she were her father's only child, should be authorized by law to own a hundred million *sesterces*, while three million is more than my own daughter is entitled to own.)[10] . . .

So laws, then, can vary considerably, and can be changed. If they 11 had all come from God, that would not be so. For, in that case, the

---

[7] **Lycurgus** Possibly legendary, Lycurgus was known as a lawgiver and founder of the Spartan constitution.

[8] **Voconian law** A law enacted in 169 B.C. that prevented women from receiving inheritances. Cicero in *On Old Age* reports that he once spoke in favor of the law.

[9] **Mucianus (180–130 B.C.)** Roman politician.

[10] Several lines are missing from the original manuscript.

same laws would be applicable to all, and, besides, a man would not be bound by one law at one time of his life and by another later on. But what I ask, therefore, is this. Let us accept that it is the duty of a just and good man to obey the laws. But *which* laws is he to obey? All the different laws that exist?

There are difficulties here. Inconsistency, between laws, ought   12
to be impermissible, since it is contrary to what nature demands. But the point is that laws are *not* imposed on us by nature—or by our innate sense of justice. They are imposed by the fear of being penalized. In other words, human beings are not just, by nature, at all.

Let us reject, moreover, the argument that, although laws vary,   13
good men naturally follow the true, authentic path of justice, and not merely what is thought to be just. That argument maintains that what a good and just man does is to give everyone his due. (One problem which arises in this connection is what, if anything, we are to grant *dumb animals* as their due. Men of far from mediocre calibre, indeed men of powerful learning such as Pythagoras and Empedocles,[11] insist that identical standards of justice apply to all living creatures, and declare that inexorable penalties await those who ill-treat animals. To do them harm, in other words, seems to them to be criminal.)[12]

PHILUS: Anyone who has the power of life and death over a people is   14
a despot—though they prefer to be known as kings, following the example of Jupiter the Best.

When however, instead, a group of men seize the state by ex-   15
ploiting their wealth or noble birth or some other resource, that is a political upheaval, though they call themselves conservatives. If, on the other hand, the people gain the supremacy, and the whole government is conducted according to their wishes, a state of affairs has arisen which is hailed as liberty, but is, in fact, chaos. But when there is a situation of mutual fear, with one person or one class fearing another, then because nobody has sufficient confidence in his own strength a kind of bargain is struck between the ordinary people and the men who are powerful. The result, in that case, is the mixed form of constitution which Scipio[13] recommends. Which means that weakness, not nature or good intention, is the mother of justice.

For we have to choose one of three things. We can perform   16
injustice and not suffer it. Or we can both perform and suffer it. Or

---

[11] **Pythagoras (582–507 B.C.) . . . Empedocles (493–433 B.C.)** Influential Greek philosophers whose works were well known to Cicero.

[12] At this point some of the original manuscript is lost.

[13] **Scipio (185–129 B.C.)** Roman general.

we can neither perform it nor suffer it. The most fortunate choice is the first, to perform injustice, if you can get away with it. The second best is neither to perform it nor suffer it. And the worst is to engage in an everlasting turmoil consisting of both performing it and suffering it.

Wisdom, as commonly understood, prompts us to increase our resources, to multiply our riches, to enlarge our frontiers. For the essential significance, surely, of those eulogistic words inscribed upon the monuments of our greatest generals, "he extended the boundaries of the empire," is that he had extended them by taking territory from someone else. That, then, is the teaching of "wisdom," that we should rule over as many subjects as possible, indulge in pleasures, hold on to power, be rulers and masters. But justice, on the other hand, demands that we should be merciful to all men, act in the interests of the entire human race, give everyone what they are entitled to, and never tamper with religious property or what belongs to the community or to private persons.

If you follow the dictates of what we call wisdom, then, you acquire wealth, power, resources, lofty status, military commands and positions of supreme authority, whether you are a state or a private person. What we, however, are at present considering is the former of these two categories, the state, and so what is done by states assumes priority for our present purpose. True, the same standards of justice apply to states and individuals alike, but the former are what we now have to consider. In particular, not to mention other nations, it is clear enough that our own Roman people, whose history Scipio traced from its beginnings in yesterday's discussion, and whose empire is now world-wide, grew from the smallest to the greatest dimensions by wisdom, and not by justice.

When, however, one sets justice against wisdom in the way I have attempted to do here, the contrast is sometimes blurred by arguments that complicate the issue. The men who put these arguments forward understand very well how to argue; and their reasoning on the subject carries all the more impressive weight because, in the course of their investigation into how to find the good man (a man who himself should be open and frank), they, like him, refrain from using underhand, crafty or dishonest methods of argument. What these philosophers do, then, is take a closer look at the "wise" man, and put forward the view that he is good not because goodness or justice automatically, or in themselves, offer him satisfaction, but, on the contrary, because a good man's life is free of fear, worry, anxiety and peril, whereas bad men always have something to feel uneasy about, and the prospects of trials and penalties are never out of their sight. No benefit or reward gained by injustice, these thinkers add,

17

18

19

is substantial enough to counterbalance perpetual fear, or the never-ending thought that some punishment or other is not far away.[14] . . .

Let us imagine that there are two men, one a paragon of virtue,   20
fairness, justice and honesty, and the other an outrageous ruffian. And
let us suppose that their country is so misguided that it believes that
the good man is an evil, villainous criminal, and that the bad man, on
the other hand, is a model of honourable propriety. Then let us go
on to suppose that, since this is the unanimous opinion, the good
man is attacked, seized, imprisoned, blinded, convicted, chained,
branded, expelled and beggared, so that everyone feels, quite rightly,
that he is the most wretched man alive. Whereas the bad man, on the
other hand, is praised, courted and loved by one and all. Every kind
of public office and military command is showered upon him, as well
as riches and wealth from every quarter. To sum up, then, he will
have the universal reputation of being the best man in the world, who
deserves everything good that fortune can give him. Now, I ask you,
who could be so mad as to doubt which of the two men he would
prefer to be?

The same applies to states, just as much as to individuals. No   21
country would not rather be an unjust master than a just slave. I
shall not range far ahead for the example I am going to quote. While
I was consul, and you were on my council, the question of the treaty
with Numantia came up before me. Everyone knew that treaties had
been made already, by Quintus Pompeius and then by Gaius Hostilius Mancinus.[15] Mancinus, a good man, went so far as to favour the
bill which I myself had proposed in accordance with a senatorial decree, even though he was to be the sufferer. Pompeius, on the other
hand, fought back strongly against an equally critical resolution directed against himself. If you are looking for self-denial, honour and
integrity, those are the qualities that Mancinus displayed. But if you
want rationality, good sense and prudence, Pompeius wins.[16] . . .

LAELIUS: True law is in keeping with the dictates both of reason and   22
of nature. It applies universally to everyone. It is unchanging and
eternal. Its commands are summons to duty, and its prohibitions
declare that nothing wrongful must be done. As far as good men are
concerned, both its commands and its prohibitions are effective;
though neither have any effect on men who are bad. To attempt to

---

[14] Some of the original manuscript is lost here.

[15] **Quintus Pompeius . . . Gaius Hostilius Mancinus** Roman consuls in 141
and 137 B.C.

[16] Much of Carneades' argument (which Philus relies upon) is missing here.

invalidate this law is sinful. Nor is it possible to repeal any part of it, much less to abolish it altogether. From its obligations neither Senate nor people can release us. And to explain or interpret it we need no one outside our own selves.

There will not be one law at Rome, and another at Athens. There will not be different laws now and in the future. Instead there will be one single, everlasting, immutable law, which applies to all nations and all times. The maker, and umpire, and proposer of this law will be God, the single master and ruler of us all. If a man fails to obey God, then he will be in flight from his own self, repudiating his own human nature. As a consequence, even if he escapes the normal punishment for wrongdoing, he will suffer the penalties of the gravest possible sort.

QUESTIONS FOR CRITICAL READING

1. Why does Laelius choose Philus to argue against justice?
2. Does arguing against a positive value help our understanding of that value's importance?
3. What is Philus's reputation and how does it affect his argument?
4. How do ideas of justice differ in the different lands Philus mentions?
5. On which side of this argument is Cicero himself?
6. To what extent is Philus a feminist?
7. Which of Laelius's statements in the final paragraphs of the selection seem weakest to you?
8. What are the strengths of Laelius's argument at the end of the selection?

SUGGESTIONS FOR WRITING

1. In paragraph 13 Philus reminds us that Pythagoras and Empedocles both insisted that "identical standards of justice apply to all living creatures." Do you feel that the question of justice applies to our treatment of animals? How would one construct an argument that took one side or the other of this argument? Is anyone making this argument in public today?
2. Philus says you can't have one law that everyone will obey. Make an argument in favor of maintaining one law for all people in all nations. Remember that different societies treat women in vastly different ways and, in effect, have one law for men and another for women. Some societies still tolerate slavery, and at one time slavery was maintained by law in many nations of the world. In Cicero's time the citizens of any defeated nation could expect to become slaves. Slavery had been legal in the ancient world of both Rome and Greece.

3. In paragraph 15, Philus says that "weakness, not nature or good inten-
    tion, is the mother of justice." Do you agree? Does our desire for justice
    arise from a sense of our own weakness? What differences may exist
    between the strong and the weak in terms of their attitude toward jus-
    tice? Who needs justice more?

4. Philus mentions natural law or natural justice several times. He argues
    against there being any such law or justice. Develop an argument that
    defends the concept of natural law. What, for instance, might people
    living outside society in a natural setting hope for in terms of justice?
    What might their concept of justice be? How necessary would justice
    be in a state of nature?

5. Clarify what Philus means by the term "wisdom," which he introduces
    in paragraph 18. How do you understand his use of the term and how
    appropriate is the word "wisdom" for the ideas he describes? Would
    most people today regard the behavior he sketches out as an example
    of wisdom? Is it wisdom for you? What moral or ethical problems arise
    from Philus's concept of wisdom?

6. Philus asks you to make a choice between being one of two different
    men. He describes them in detail in paragraph 20. Which one would
    you rather be? Defend your choice by reference to your best under-
    standing of justice. Would it be just for you to behave as you would,
    given the choices Philus gives you?

7. Philus gives us three choices in regard to injustice: 1. We can perform
    injustice and not suffer it ourselves; 2. We can both perform it and suf-
    fer it; or 3. We can neither perform it nor suffer it. He says the best
    choice is clearly the first. Do you think that is true? Do you think he
    feels it is true? Argue a case that supports one of these three choices,
    but that at the same time condemns the other two.

8. Aristotle warns us that it is dangerous to argue from analogy. But
    Philus makes his strongest points at the end of his argument when he
    compares the individual in paragraph 20 with the entire state in para-
    graph 21. How strong is his argument in the last paragraphs of his pre-
    sentation? Basically, he tells us that strength creates its own justice and
    that the weak must go along with the strong. Is this what you under-
    stand as justice?

9. **CONNECTIONS**   Compare Philus's views of what justice is and how
    wisdom works in a political environment with the views of Henry
    David Thoreau in his "Civil Disobedience." How do their views on jus-
    tice differ and how do their views on just laws differ?

HENRY DAVID THOREAU
Civil Disobedience

HENRY DAVID THOREAU (1817–1862) began keeping a journal when he graduated from Harvard in 1837. The journal was preserved and published, and it shows us the seriousness, determination, and elevation of moral values characteristic of all his work. He is best known for *Walden* (1854), a record of his departure from the warm congeniality of Concord, Massachusetts, and the home of his close friend Ralph Waldo Emerson (1803–1882), for the comparative "wilds" of Walden Pond, where he built a cabin, planted a garden, and lived simply. In *Walden* Thoreau describes the deadening influence of ownership and extols the vitality and spiritual uplift that come from living close to nature. He also argues that civilization's comforts sometimes rob a person of independence, integrity, and even conscience.

Thoreau and Emerson were prominent among the group of writers and thinkers who were referred to as the Transcendentalists. They believed in something that transcended the limits of sensory experience—in other words, something that transcended materialism. Their philosophy was based on the works of Immanuel Kant (1724–1804), the German idealist philosopher; Samuel Taylor Coleridge (1772–1834), the English poet; and Johann Wolfgang von Goethe (1749–1832), the German dramatist and thinker. These writers praised human intuition and the capacity to see beyond the limits of common experience.

The Transcendentalists' philosophical idealism carried over into the social concerns of the day, expressing itself in works such as *Walden* and "Civil Disobedience," which was published with the title "Resistance to Civil Government" in 1849, a year after the publication of *The Communist Manifesto*. Although Thoreau all but denies his idealism in "Civil Disobedience," it is obvious that after spending a night in the Concord jail, he realizes he cannot quietly accept his government's behavior in regard to slavery. He begins

133

to feel that it is not only appropriate but imperative to disobey unjust laws.

In Thoreau's time the most flagrantly unjust laws were those that supported slavery. The Transcendentalists strongly opposed slavery and spoke out against it. Abolitionists in Massachusetts harbored escaped slaves and helped them move to Canada and freedom. The Fugitive Slave Act, enacted in 1850, the year after "Civil Disobedience" was published, made Thoreau a criminal because he refused to comply with Massachusetts civil authorities when in 1851 they began returning escaped slaves to the South as the law required.

"Civil Disobedience" was much more influential in the twentieth century than it was in the nineteenth. Mohandas Gandhi (1869–1948) claimed that while he was editor of an Indian newspaper in South Africa, it helped to inspire his theories of nonviolent resistance. Gandhi eventually implemented these theories against the British empire and helped win independence for India. In the 1960s, Martin Luther King Jr. applied the same theories in the fight for racial equality in the United States. Thoreau's essay once again found widespread adherents among the many young men who resisted being drafted into the military to fight in Vietnam because they believed that the war was unjust.

"Civil Disobedience" was written after the Walden experience (which began on July 4, 1845, and ended on September 6, 1847). Thoreau quietly returned to Emerson's home and "civilization." His refusal in 1846 to pay the Massachusetts poll tax—a "per head" tax imposed on all citizens to help support what he considered an unjust war against Mexico—landed him in the Concord jail. He spent just one day and one night there—his aunt paid the tax for him—but the experience was so extraordinary that he began examining it in his journal.

Thoreau's Rhetoric

Thoreau maintained his journal throughout his life and eventually became convinced that writing was one of the few professions by which he could earn a living. He made more money, however, from lecturing on the lyceum circuit. The lyceum, a New England institution, was a town adult education program, featuring important speakers such as the very successful Emerson and foreign lecturers. Admission fees were very reasonable, and in the absence of other popular entertainment, the lyceum was a popular proving ground for speakers interested in promoting their ideas.

"Civil Disobedience" was first outlined in rough-hewn form in the journal, where the main ideas appear and where experiments in phrasing began. (Thoreau was a constant reviser.) Then in February 1848, Thoreau delivered a lecture on "Civil Disobedience" at the Concord Lyceum urging people of conscience to actively resist a government that acted badly. Finally, the piece was prepared for publication in *Aesthetic Papers*, an intellectual journal edited by Elizabeth Peabody (1804–1894), the sister-in-law of another important New England writer, Nathaniel Hawthorne (1804–1864). There it was refined again, and certain important details were added.

"Civil Disobedience" bears many of the hallmarks of the spoken lecture. For one thing, it is written in the first person and addresses an audience that Thoreau expects will share many of his sentiments but certainly not all his conclusions. His message is to some extent anarchistic, virtually denying an unjust government any authority or respect.

Modern political conservatives generally take his opening quote — "That government is best which governs least" — as a rallying cry against governmental interference in everyday affairs. Such conservatives usually propose reducing government interference by reducing the government's capacity to tax wealth for unpopular causes. In fact, what Thoreau opposes is simply any government that is not totally just, totally moral, and totally respectful of the individual.

The easiness of the pace of the essay also derives from its original form as a speech. Even such locutions as "But to speak practically and as a citizen" (para. 3) connect the essay with its origins. Although Thoreau was not an overwhelming orator — he was short and somewhat homely, an unprepossessing figure — he ensured that his writing achieved what some speakers might have accomplished by means of gesture and theatrics.

Thoreau's language is marked by clarity. He speaks directly to every issue, stating his own position and recommending the position he feels his audience, as reasonable and moral people, should accept. One impressive achievement in this selection is Thoreau's capacity to shape memorable, virtually aphoristic statements that remain "quotable" generations later, beginning with his own quotation from the words of John L. O'Sullivan: "That government is best which governs least." Thoreau calls it a motto, as if it belonged on the great seal of a government or on a coin. It contains an interesting and impressive rhetorical flourish — the device of repeating "govern" and the near rhyme of "best" with "least."

His most memorable statements show considerable attention to the rhetorical qualities of balance, repetition, and pattern. "The only obligation which I have a right to assume is to do at any time what I think right" (para. 4) uses the word *right* in two senses: first, as a matter of personal volition; second, as a matter of moral rectitude. One's right, in other words, becomes the opportunity to do right. "For it matters not how small the beginning may seem to be: what is once well done is done forever" (para. 21) also relies on repetition for its effect and balances the concept of a beginning with its capacity to reach out into the future. The use of the rhetorical device of *chiasmus*, a criss-cross relationship between key words, marks "Under a government which imprisons any unjustly, the true place for a just man is also a prison" (para. 22). Here is the pattern:

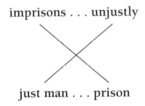

imprisons . . . unjustly

just man . . . prison

Such attention to phrasing is typical of speakers whose expressions must catch and retain the attention of listeners. Audiences do not have the advantage of referring to a text, so the words they hear must be forceful.

Thoreau relies also on analogy—comparing men with machines, people with plants, even the citizen with states considering secession from the Union. His analogies are effective and thus worth examining in some detail. He draws on the analysis of circumstance throughout the essay, carefully examining government actions to determine their qualities and their results. His questions include comments on politics (para. 1), on the Bible (para. 23), on Confucius (para. 24), and finally on his contemporary, Daniel Webster (1782–1852) (para. 42), demonstrating a wide range of influences but avoiding the pedantic tone that can come from using quotations too liberally or from citing obscure sources. This essay is simple, direct, and uncluttered. Its enduring influence is in part due to the clarity and grace that characterize Thoreau's writing at its best. Its power derives from Thoreau's demand that citizens act on the basis of conscience.

PREREADING QUESTIONS: WHAT TO READ FOR

The following prereading questions may help you anticipate key issues in the discussion of Henry David Thoreau's "Civil Disobedience." Keeping them in mind during your first reading of the selection should help focus your attention.

- What kind of government does Thoreau feel would be most just?

- What is the individual's responsibility regarding supporting the government when it is wrong?

- How does Thoreau deal with unjust laws?

Civil Disobedience

I heartily accept the motto—"That government is best which governs least,"[1] and I should like to see it acted up to more rapidly and systematically. Carried out, it finally amounts to this, which also I believe—"That government is best which governs not at all"; and when men are prepared for it, that will be the kind of government which they will have. Government is at best but an expedient; but most governments are usually, and all governments are sometimes, inexpedient. The objections which have been brought against a standing army, and they are many and weighty, and deserve to prevail, may also at last be brought against a standing government. The standing army is only an arm of the standing government. The government itself, which is only the mode which the people have chosen to execute their will, is equally liable to be abused and perverted before the people can act through it. Witness the present Mexican war,[2] the work of comparatively a few individuals using the standing government as their tool; for in the outset the people would not have consented to this measure.

---

[1] "**. . . governs least**" John L. O'Sullivan (1813–1895) wrote in the *United States Magazine and Democratic Review* (1837) that "all government is evil, and the parents of evil. . . . The best government is that which governs least." Thomas Jefferson wrote, "That government is best which governs the least, because its people discipline themselves." Both comments echo the *Tao-te Ching*.

[2] **the present Mexican war (1846–1848)** The war was extremely unpopular in New England because it was an act of a bullying government anxious to grab land from a weaker nation. The United States had annexed Texas in 1845, precipitating a retaliation from Mexico.

This American government — what is it but a tradition, a recent   2
one, endeavoring to transmit itself unimpaired to posterity but each
instant losing some of its integrity? It has not the vitality and force of
a single living man; for a single man can bend it to his will. It is a
sort of wooden gun to the people themselves. But it is not the less
necessary for this; for the people must have some complicated machinery or other, and hear its din, to satisfy that idea of government
which they have. Governments show thus how successfully men can
be imposed on, even impose on themselves, for their own advantage. It is excellent, we must all allow. Yet this government never of
itself furthered any enterprise but by the alacrity with which it got
out of its way. *It* does not keep the country free. *It* does not settle the
West. *It* does not educate. The character inherent in the American
people has done all that has been accomplished; and it would have
done somewhat more if the government had not sometimes got in
its way. For government is an expedient by which men would fain
succeed in letting one another alone; and, as has been said, when it
is most expedient the governed are most let alone by it. Trade and
commerce, if they were not made of India-rubber, would never
manage to bounce over the obstacles which legislators are continually putting in their way; and, if one were to judge these men wholly
by the effects of their actions and not partly by their intentions, they
would deserve to be classed and punished with those mischievous
persons who put obstructions on the railroads.

But to speak practically and as a citizen, unlike those who call   3
themselves no-government men, I ask for, not at once no government, but *at once* a better government. Let every man make known
what kind of government would command his respect, and that will
be one step toward obtaining it.

After all, the practical reason why, when the power is once in   4
the hands of the people, a majority are permitted, and for a long period continue, to rule is not because they are most likely to be in the
right, nor because this seems fairest to the minority but because they
are physically the strongest. But a government in which the majority
rule in all cases cannot be based on justice, even as far as men understand it. Can there not be a government in which majorities do
not virtually decide right and wrong but conscience? — in which
majorities decide only those questions to which the rule of expediency is applicable? Must the citizen ever for a moment, or in the
least degree, resign his conscience to the legislator? Why has every
man a conscience then? I think that we should be men first and subjects afterward. It is not desirable to cultivate a respect for the law,
so much as for the right. The only obligation which I have a right to
assume is to do at any time what I think right. It is truly enough said

that a corporation has no conscience; but a corporation of conscientious men is a corporation *with* a conscience. Law never made men a whit more just; and, by means of their respect for it, even the well-disposed are daily made the agents of injustice. A common and natural result of an undue respect for law is that you may see a file of soldiers, colonel, captain, corporal, privates, powder-monkeys,[3] and all, marching in admirable order over hill and dale to the wars, against their wills, ay, against their common sense and consciences, which makes it very steep marching indeed and produces a palpitation of the heart. They have no doubt that it is a damnable business in which they are concerned; they are all peaceably inclined. Now, what are they? Men at all? or small movable forts and magazines at the service of some unscrupulous man in power? Visit the Navy-Yard,[4] and behold a marine, such a man as an American government can make, or such as it can make a man with its black arts—a mere shadow and reminiscence of humanity, a man laid out alive and standing, and already, as one may say, buried under arms with funeral accompaniments, though it may be—

> Not a drum was heard, not a funeral note,
> As his corse to the rampart we hurried;
> Not a soldier discharged his farewell shot
> O'er the grave where our hero we buried.[5]

The mass of men serve the state thus, not as men mainly, but as machines, with their bodies. They are the standing army, and the militia, jailers, constables, posse comitatus,[6] &c. In most cases there is no free exercise whatever of the judgment or of the moral sense; but they put themselves on a level with wood and earth and stones; and wooden men can perhaps be manufactured that will serve the purpose as well. Such command no more respect than men of straw or a lump of dirt. They have the same sort of worth only as horses and dogs. Yet such as these even are commonly esteemed good citizens. Others—as most legislators, politicians, lawyers, ministers, and office-holders—serve the state chiefly with their heads; and, as they rarely make any moral distinctions, they are as likely to serve the Devil, without *intending* it, as God. A very few, as heroes, patriots, martyrs, reformers in the great sense, and *men*, serve the state with

5

---

[3] **powder-monkeys** The boys who delivered gunpowder to cannons.

[4] **Navy-Yard** This is apparently the U.S. naval yard at Boston.

[5] These lines are from "Burial of Sir John Moore at Corunna" (1817) by the Irish poet Charles Wolfe (1791–1823).

[6] **posse comitatus** Literally, the power of the county; the term means a law-enforcement group made up of ordinary citizens.

their consciences also and so necessarily resist it for the most part;
and they are commonly treated as enemies by it. A wise man will
only be useful as a man and will not submit to be "clay" and "stop a
hole to keep the wind away," but leave that office to his dust at least:

> I am too high-born to be propertied,
> To be a secondary at control,
> Or useful serving-man and instrument
> To any sovereign state throughout the world.[7]

He who gives himself entirely to his fellow-men appears to them   6
useless and selfish; but he who gives himself partially to them is pronounced a benefactor and philanthropist.

How does it become a man to behave toward this American   7
government today? I answer, that he cannot without disgrace be associated with it. I cannot for an instant recognize that political organization as *my* government which is the *slave's* government also.

All men recognize the right of revolution; that is, the right to   8
refuse allegiance to, and to resist the government when its tyranny
or its inefficiency are great and unendurable. But almost all say that
such is not the case now. But such was the case, they think, in the
Revolution of '75. If one were to tell me that this was a bad government because it taxed certain foreign commodities brought to its
ports, it is most probable that I should not make an ado about it, for
I can do without them. All machines have their friction; and possibly this does enough good to counterbalance the evil. At any rate, it
is a great evil to make a stir about it. But when the friction comes to
have its machine, and oppression and robbery are organized, I say
let us not have such a machine any longer. In other words, when a
sixth of the population of a nation which has undertaken to be the
refuge of liberty are slaves, and a whole country is unjustly overrun
and conquered by a foreign army and subjected to military law, I
think that it is not too soon for honest men to rebel and revolutionize. What makes this duty the more urgent is the fact that the country so overrun is not our own, but ours is the invading army.

Paley,[8] a common authority with many on moral questions, in his   9
chapter on the "Duty of Submission to Civil Government," resolves all

---

[7] **"clay," "stop a hole . . . wind away," I am too high-born . . .** These
lines are from Shakespeare; the first is from *Hamlet*, V.i.226–227. The verse is from
King John, V.ii.79–82.

[8] **William Paley (1743–1805)** An English theologian who lectured widely on
moral philosophy. Paley is famous for *A View of the Evidences of Christianity* (1794).
"Duty of Submission to Civil Government Explained" is Chapter 3 of Book 6 of *The
Principles of Moral and Political Philosophy* (1785).

civil obligation into expediency; and he proceeds to say, "that so long as the interest of the whole society requires it, that is, so long as the established government cannot be resisted or charged without public inconveniency, it is the will of God that the established government be obeyed, and no longer. . . . This principle being admitted, the justice of every particular case of resistance is reduced to a computation of the quantity of the danger and grievance on the one side, and of the probability and expense of redressing it on the other." Of this, he says, every man shall judge for himself. But Paley appears never to have contemplated those cases to which the rule of expediency does not apply, in which a people, as well as an individual, must do justice, cost what it may. If I have unjustly wrested a plank from a drowning man, I must restore it to him though I drown myself. This, according to Paley, would be inconvenient. But he that would save his life, in such a case, shall lose it. This people must cease to hold slaves and to make war on Mexico, though it cost them their existence as a people.

In their practice, nations agree with Paley; but does anyone think   10
that Massachusetts does exactly what is right at the present crisis?

> A drab of state, a cloth-o'-silver slut,
> To have her train borne up, and her soul trail in the dirt.[9]

Practically speaking, the opponents to a reform in Massachusetts are not a hundred thousand politicians at the South but a hundred thousand merchants and farmers here, who are more interested in commerce and agriculture than they are in humanity, and are not prepared to do justice to the slave and to Mexico, cost what it may. I quarrel not with far-off foes but with those who, near at home, co-operate with, and do the bidding of, those far away, and without whom the latter would be harmless. We are accustomed to say that the mass of men are unprepared; but improvement is slow because the few are not materially wiser or better than the many. It is not so important that many should be as good as you as that there be some absolute goodness somewhere; for that will leaven the whole lump. There are thousands who are in opinion opposed to slavery and to the war who yet in effect do nothing to put an end to them; who, esteeming themselves children of Washington and Franklin, sit down with their hands in their pockets and say that they know not what to do, and do nothing; who even postpone the question of freedom to the

---

[9]**A drab . . .**   From Cyril Tourneur (1575?–1626), *Revenger's Tragedy* (1607), IV.iv.70–72. "Drab" is an obsolete term for a prostitute. Thoreau quotes the lines to imply that Massachusetts is a "painted lady" with a defiled soul.

question of free trade, and quietly read the prices-current along with
the latest advices from Mexico after dinner and, it may be, fall asleep
over them both. What is the price-current of an honest man and patriot today? They hesitate and they regret and sometimes they petition; but they do nothing in earnest and with effect. They will wait,
well disposed, for others to remedy the evil, that they may no longer
have it to regret. At most, they give only a cheap vote, and a feeble
countenance and God-speed, to the right, as it goes by them. There
are nine hundred and ninety-nine patrons of virtue to one virtuous
man. But it is easier to deal with the real possessor of a thing than
with the temporary guardian of it.

All voting is a sort of gaming, like checkers or backgammon,   11
with a slight moral tinge to it, a playing with right and wrong, with
moral questions; and betting naturally accompanies it. The character
of the voters is not staked. I cast my vote, perchance, as I think
right; but I am not vitally concerned that that right should prevail. I
am willing to leave it to the majority. Its obligation, therefore, never
exceeds that of expediency. Even voting *for the right* is *doing* nothing
for it. It is only expressing to men feebly your desire that it should
prevail. A wise man will not leave the right to the mercy of chance,
nor wish it to prevail through the power of the majority. There is
but little virtue in the action of masses of men. When the majority
shall at length vote for the abolition of slavery, it will be because
they are indifferent to slavery, or because there is but little slavery
left to be abolished by their vote. *They* will then be the only slaves.
Only *his* vote can hasten the abolition of slavery who asserts his own
freedom by his vote.

I hear of a convention to be held at Baltimore,[10] or elsewhere,   12
for the selection of a candidate for the Presidency, made up chiefly
of editors, and men who are politicians by profession; but I think,
what is it to any independent, intelligent, and respectable man what
decision they may come to? Shall we not have the advantage of his
wisdom and honesty nevertheless? Can we not count upon some independent votes? Are there not many individuals in the country
who do not attend conventions? But no: I find that the responsible
man, so called, has immediately drifted from his position, and de-
spairs of his country when his country has more reason to despair of
him. He forthwith adopts one of the candidates thus selected as the
only *available* one, thus proving that he is himself *available* for any
purposes of the demagogue. His vote is of no more worth than that of

---

[10]**Baltimore** In 1848 the political environment was particularly intense; it was
a seedbed for theoreticians of the Confederacy, which was only beginning to be contemplated seriously.

any unprincipled foreigner or hireling native who may have been bought. O for a man who is a *man* and, as my neighbor says has a bone in his back which you cannot pass your hand through! Our statistics are at fault: the population has been returned too large. How many *men* are there to a square thousand miles in this country? Hardly one. Does not America offer any inducement for men to settle here? The American has dwindled into an Odd Fellow[11]—one who may be known by the development of his organ of gregariousness and a manifest lack of intellect and cheerful self-reliance; whose first and chief concern, on coming into the world, is to see that the Almshouses are in good repair; and, before yet he has lawfully donned the virile garb, to collect a fund for the support of the widows and orphans that may be; who, in short, ventures to live only by the aid of the Mutual Insurance Company, which has promised to bury him decently.

It is not a man's duty, as a matter of course, to devote himself to   13
the eradication of any, even the most enormous wrong; he may still properly have other concerns to engage him; but it is his duty, at least, to wash his hands of it and, if he gives it no thought longer, not to give it practically his support. If I devote myself to other pursuits and contemplations, I must first see, at least, that I do not pursue them sitting upon another man's shoulders. I must get off him first, that he may pursue his contemplations too. See what gross inconsistency is tolerated. I have heard some of my townsmen say, "I should like to have them order me out to help put down an insurrection of the slaves, or to march to Mexico—see if I would go"; and yet these very men have each directly by their allegiance and so indirectly, at least, by their money, furnished a substitute. The soldier is applauded who refuses to serve in an unjust war by those who do not refuse to sustain the unjust government which makes the war; is applauded by those whose own act and authority he disregards and sets at naught; as if the State were penitent to that degree that it hired one to scourge it while it sinned, but not to that degree that it left off sinning for a moment. Thus, under the name of Order and Civil Government, we are all made at last to pay homage to and support our own meanness. After the first blush of sin comes its indifference; and from immoral it becomes, as it were, *un*moral, and not quite unnecessary to that life which we have made.

The broadest and most prevalent error requires the most disin-   14
terested virtue to sustain it. The slight reproach to which the virtue

------

[11] **Odd Fellow** The Independent Order of Odd Fellows, a fraternal and benevolent secret society, founded in England in the eighteenth century and first established in the United States in 1819 in Baltimore.

of patriotism is commonly liable, the noble are most likely to incur. Those who, while they disapprove of the character and measures of a government, yield to it their allegiance and support, are undoubtedly its most conscientious supporters, and so frequently the most serious obstacles to reform. Some are petitioning the State to dissolve the Union, to disregard the requisitions of the President. Why do they not dissolve it themselves—the union between themselves and the State—and refuse to pay their quota into its treasury? Do not they stand in the same relation to the State that the State does to the Union? And have not the same reasons prevented the State from resisting the Union which have prevented them from resisting the State?

How can a man be satisfied to entertain an opinion merely, and   15 enjoy *it*? Is there any enjoyment in it if his opinion is that he is aggrieved? If you are cheated out of a single dollar by your neighbor, you do not rest satisfied with knowing that you are cheated, or with saying that you are cheated, or even with petitioning him to pay you your due; but you take effectual steps at once to obtain the full amount and see that you are never cheated again. Action from principle, the perception and the performance of right, changes things and relations; it is essentially revolutionary and does not consist wholly with anything which was. It not only divides states and churches, it divides families; ay, it divides the *individual*, separating the diabolical in him from the divine.

Unjust laws exist: shall we be content to obey them, or shall we   16 endeavor to amend them and obey them until we have succeeded, or shall we transgress them at once? Men generally, under such a government as this, think that they ought to wait until they have persuaded the majority to alter them. They think that if they should resist the remedy would be worse than the evil. *It* makes it worse. Why is it not more apt to anticipate and provide for reform? Why does it not cherish its wise minority? Why does it cry and resist before it is hurt? Why does it not encourage its citizens to be on the alert to point out its faults and *do* better than it would have them? Why does it always crucify Christ and excommunicate Copernicus and Luther[12] and pronounce Washington and Franklin rebels?

One would think that a deliberate and practical denial of its au-   17 thority was the only offence never contemplated by government; else why has it not assigned its definite, its suitable and proportionate

---

[12] **Nicolaus Copernicus (1473–1543) and Martin Luther (1483–1546)** Copernicus revolutionized astronomy and the way humankind perceives the universe; Luther was a religious revolutionary who began the Reformation and created the first Protestant faith.

penalty? If a man who has no property refuses but once to earn nine shillings for the State, he is put in prison for a period unlimited by any law that I know, and determined only by the discretion of those who placed him there; but if he should steal ninety times nine shillings from the State, he is soon permitted to go at large again.

If the injustice is part of the necessary friction of the machine of government, let it go, let it go: perchance it will wear smooth — certainly the machine will wear out. If the injustice has a spring or a pulley or a rope or a crank exclusively for itself, then perhaps you may consider whether the remedy will not be worse than the evil; but if it is of such a nature that it requires you to be the agent of injustice to another, then I say break the law. Let your life be a counter friction to stop the machine. What I have to do is to see, at any rate, that I do not lend myself to the wrong which I condemn. 18

As for adopting the ways which the State has provided for remedying the evil, I know not of such ways. They take too much time, and a man's life will be gone. I have other affairs to attend to. I came into this world, not chiefly to make this a good place to live in, but to live in it, be it good or bad. A man has not everything to do, but something; and because he cannot do *everything*, it is not necessary that he should do *something* wrong. It is not my business to be petitioning the Governor or the Legislature any more than it is theirs to petition me; and if they should not hear my petition what should I do then? But in this case the State has provided no way: its very Constitution is the evil. This may seem to be harsh and stubborn and unconciliatory; but it is to treat with the utmost kindness and consideration the only spirit that can appreciate or deserves it. So is all change for the better, like birth and death, which convulse the body. 19

I do not hesitate to say that those who call themselves Abolitionists should at once effectually withdraw their support, both in person and property, from the government of Massachusetts, and not wait till they constitute a majority of one before they suffer the right to prevail through them. I think that it is enough if they have God on their side, without waiting for that other one. Moreover, any man more right than his neighbors constitutes a majority of one already. 20

I meet this American government or its representative, the State government, directly and face to face once a year — no more — in the person of its tax-gatherer; this is the only mode in which a man situated as I am necessarily meets it; and it then says distinctly, Recognize me; and the simplest, the most effectual and, in the present posture of affairs, the indispensablest mode of treating with it on this head, of expressing your little satisfaction with and love for it, is to deny it then. My civil neighbor, the tax-gatherer, is the very man 21

I have to deal with—for it is, after all, with men and not with parchment that I quarrel—and he has voluntarily chosen to be an agent of the government. How shall he ever know well what he is and does as an officer of the government, or as a man, until he is obliged to consider whether he shall treat me, his neighbor, for whom he has respect, as a neighbor and well-disposed man, or as a maniac and disturber of the peace, and see if he can get over this obstruction to his neighborliness without a ruder and more impetuous thought or speech corresponding with his action. I know this well, that if one thousand, if one hundred, if ten men whom I could name—if ten *honest* men only—ay, if *one* HONEST man in this State of Massachusetts, *ceasing to hold slaves*, were actually to withdraw from this copartnership and be locked up in the county jail therefor, it would be the abolition of slavery in America. For it matters not how small the beginning may seem to be: what is once well done is done forever. But we love better to talk about it: that we say is our mission. Reform keeps many scores of newspapers in its service but not one man. If my esteemed neighbor,[13] the State's ambassador, who will devote his days to the settlement of the question of human rights in the Council Chamber, instead of being threatened with the prisons of Carolina, were to sit down the prisoner of Massachusetts, that State which is so anxious to foist the sin of slavery upon her sister—though at present she can discover only an act of inhospitality to be the ground of a quarrel with her—the Legislature would not wholly waive the subject the following winter.

Under a government which imprisons any unjustly, the true place   22
for a just man is also a prison. The proper place today, the only place which Massachusetts has provided for her freer and less desponding spirits is in her prisons, to be put out and locked out of the State by her own act, as they have already put themselves out by their principles. It is there that the fugitive slave and the Mexican prisoner on parole and the Indian come to plead the wrongs of his race should find them; on that separate but more free and honorable ground where the State places those who are not *with* her but *against* her—the only house in a slave State in which a free man can abide with honor. If any think that their influence would be lost there, and their voices no longer afflict the ear of the State, that they would not be as an enemy within its walls, they do not know by how much truth is stronger than

---

[13] **esteemed neighbor** Thoreau refers to Samuel Hoar (1778–1856), a Massachusetts congressman, who went to South Carolina to protest that state's practice of seizing black seamen from Massachusetts ships and enslaving them. South Carolina threatened Hoar and drove him out of the state. He did not secure the justice he demanded.

error, nor how much more eloquently and effectively he can combat injustice who has experienced a little in his own person. Cast your whole vote, not a strip of paper merely, but your whole influence. A minority is powerless while it conforms to the majority; it is not even a minority then; but it is irresistible when it clogs by its whole weight. If the alternative is to keep all just men in prison or give up war and slavery, the State will not hesitate which to choose. If a thousand men were not to pay their tax-bills this year, that would not be a violent bloody measure, as it would be to pay them, and enable the State to commit violence and shed innocent blood. This is, in fact, the definition of a peaceable revolution, if any such is possible. If the tax-gatherer or any other public officer asks me, as one has done, "But what shall I do?" my answer is, "If you really wish to do anything, resign your office." When the subject has refused allegiance and the officer has resigned his office, then the revolution is accomplished. But even suppose blood should flow. Is there not a sort of blood shed when the conscience is wounded? Through this wound a man's real manhood and immortality flow out, and he bleeds to an everlasting death. I see this blood flowing now.

I have contemplated the imprisonment of the offender rather than the seizure of his goods—though both will serve the same purpose—because they who assert the purest right, and consequently are most dangerous to a corrupt State, commonly have not spent much time in accumulating property. To such the State renders comparatively small service, and a slight tax is wont to appear exorbitant, particularly if they are obliged to earn it by special labor with their hands. If there were one who lived wholly without the use of money, the State itself would hesitate to demand it of him. But the rich man—not to make any invidious comparison—is always sold to the institution which makes him rich. Absolutely speaking, the more money, the less virtue; for money comes between a man and his objects and obtains them for him; and it was certainly no great virtue to obtain it. It puts to rest many questions which he would otherwise be taxed to answer; while the only new question which it puts is the hard but superfluous one, how to spend it. Thus his moral ground is taken from under his feet. The opportunities of living are diminished in proportion as what are called the "means" are increased. The best thing a man can do for his culture when he is rich is to endeavor to carry out those schemes which he entertained when he was poor. Christ answered the Herodians[14] according to their condition. "Show

23

---

[14] **Herodians** Followers of King Herod who were opposed to Jesus Christ (see Matthew 22:16).

me the tribute-money," said he—and one took a penny out of his pocket—if you use money which has the image of Caesar on it, and which he has made current and valuable, that is, if *you are men of the State* and gladly enjoy the advantages of Caesar's government, then pay him back some of his own when he demands it; "Render therefore to Caesar that which is Caesar's, and to God those things which are God's"—leaving them no wiser than before as to which was which; for they did not wish to know.

When I converse with the freest of my neighbors, I perceive that   24
whatever they may say about the magnitude and seriousness of the question, and their regard for the public tranquillity, the long and the short of the matter is that they cannot spare the protection of the existing government, and they dread the consequences to their property and families of disobedience to it. For my own part, I should not like to think that I ever rely on the protection of the State. But if I deny the authority of the State when it presents its tax-bill, it will soon take and waste all my property and so harass me and my children without end. This is hard. This makes it impossible for a man to live honestly, and at the same time comfortably, in outward respects. It will not be worth the while to accumulate property; that would be sure to go again. You must hire or squat somewhere and raise but a small crop and eat that soon. You must live within yourself and depend upon yourself always tucked up and ready for a start, and not have many affairs. A man may grow rich in Turkey even, if he will be in all respects a good subject of the Turkish government. Confucius[15] said: "If a state is governed by the principles of reason, poverty and misery are subjects of shame; if a state is not governed by the principles of reason, riches and honors are the subjects of shame." No; until I want the protection of Massachusetts to be extended to me in some distant Southern port, where my liberty is endangered, or until I am bent solely on building up an estate at home by peaceful enterprise, I can afford to refuse allegiance to Massachusetts and her right to my property and life. It costs me less in every sense to incur the penalty of disobedience to the State than it would to obey. I should feel as if I were worth less in that case.

Some years ago the State met me in behalf of the Church and com-   25
manded me to pay a certain sum toward the support of a clergyman whose preaching my father attended, but never I myself. "Pay," it said, "or be locked up in the jail." I declined to pay. But, unfortunately,

---

[15] **Confucius (551–479 B.C.)** The most important Chinese religious leader. His *Analects* (collection) treated not only religious but moral and political matters as well.

another man saw fit to pay it. I did not see why the schoolmaster should be taxed to support the priest, and not the priest the schoolmaster; for I was not the State's schoolmaster, but I supported myself by voluntary subscription. I did not see why the lyceum should not present its tax-bill and have the State to back its demand, as well as the Church. However, at the request of the selectmen, I condescended to make some such statement as this in writing: — "Know all men by these presents, that I, Henry Thoreau, do not wish to be regarded as a member of any incorporated society which I have not joined." This I gave to the town clerk; and he has it. The State, having thus learned that I did not wish to be regarded as a member of that church, has never made a like demand on me since; though it said that it must adhere to its original presumption that time. If I had known how to name them, I should then have signed off in detail from all the societies which I never signed on to; but I did not know where to find a complete list.

I have paid no poll-tax[16] for six years. I was put into a jail once   26 on this account, for one night; and, as I stood considering the walls of solid stone, two or three feet thick, the door of wood and iron, a foot thick, and the iron grating which strained the light, I could not help being struck with the foolishness of that institution which treated me as if I were mere flesh and blood and bones, to be locked up. I wondered that it should have concluded at length that this was the best use it could put me to and had never thought to avail itself of my services in some way. I saw that if there was a wall of stone between me and my townsmen, there was a still more difficult one to climb or break through before they could get to be as free as I was. I did not for a moment feel confined, and the walls seemed a great waste of stone and mortar. I felt as if I alone of all my townsmen had paid my tax. They plainly did not know how to treat me but behaved like persons who are underbred. In every threat and in every compliment there was a blunder; for they thought that my chief desire was to stand the other side of that stone wall. I could not but smile to see how industriously they locked the door on my meditations, which followed them out again without let or hindrance, and *they* were really all that was dangerous. As they could not reach me, they had resolved to punish my body; just as boys, if they cannot come at some person against whom they have a spite, will abuse his dog. I saw that the State was half-witted, that it was timid as a lone woman with her silver spoons, and that it did not

---

[16] **poll-tax** A tax levied on every citizen living in a given area; *poll* means "head," so it is a tax per head. The tax Thoreau refers to, about $2, was used to support the Mexican War.

know its friends from its foes, and I lost all my remaining respect for it and pitied it.

Thus the State never intentionally confronts a man's sense, intel- 27
lectual or moral, but only his body, his senses. It is not armed with superior wit or honesty but with superior physical strength. I was not
born to be forced. I will breathe after my own fashion. Let us see who
is the strongest. What force has a multitude? They only can force me
who obey a higher law than I. They force me to become like themselves. I do not hear of *men* being *forced* to live this way or that by
masses of men. What sort of life were that to live? When I meet a government which says to me, "Your money or your life," why should I
be in haste to give it my money? It may be in a great strait and not
know what to do: I cannot help that. It must help itself; do as I do. It is
not worth the while to snivel about it. I am not responsible for the successful working of the machinery of society. I am not the son of the engineer. I perceive that, when an acorn and a chestnut fall side by side,
the one does not remain inert to make way for the other, but both obey
their own laws and spring and grow and flourish as best they can till
one, perchance, overshadows and destroys the other. If a plant cannot
live according to its nature, it dies; and so a man.

The night in prison was novel and interesting enough. The prison- 28
ers in their shirt-sleeves were enjoying a chat and the evening air in the
doorway when I entered. But the jailer said, "Come, boys, it is time to
lock up"; and so they dispersed, and I heard the sound of their steps
returning into the hollow apartments. My room-mate was introduced
to me by the jailer as "a first-rate fellow and a clever man." When the
door was locked, he showed me where to hang my hat and how he
managed matters there. The rooms were whitewashed once a month;
and this one, at least, was the whitest, most simply furnished, and
probably the neatest apartment in the town. He naturally wanted to
know where I came from and what brought me there; and when I had
told him, I asked him in my turn how he came there, presuming him
to be an honest man, of course; and, as the world goes, I believe he
was. "Why," said he, "they accuse me of burning a barn; but I never
did it." As near as I could discover, he had probably gone to bed in a
barn when drunk and smoked his pipe there; and so a barn burnt. He
had the reputation of being a clever man, had been there some three
months waiting for his trial to come on, and would have to wait as
much longer; but he was quite domesticated and contented, since he
got his board for nothing and thought that he was well treated.

He occupied one window, and I the other; and I saw that if one 29
stayed there long, his principal business would be to look out the window. I had soon read all the tracts that were left there and examined

where former prisoners had broken out and where a grate had been sawed off and heard the history of the various occupants of that room; for I found that even here there was a history and a gossip which never circulated beyond the walls of the jail. Probably this is the only house in the town where verses are composed, which afterward printed in a circular form but not published. I was shown quite a long list of verses which were composed by some young men who had been detected in an attempt to escape, who avenged themselves by signing them.

I pumped my fellow-prisoner as dry as I could, for fear I should 30 never see him again; but at length he showed me which was my bed and left me to blow out the lamp.

It was like travelling into a far country, such as I had never 31 expected to behold, to lie there for one night. It seemed to me that I never had heard the town-clock strike before, nor the evening sounds of the village; for we slept with the windows open, which were inside the grating. It was to see my native village in the light of the Middle Ages, and our Concord was turned into a Rhine stream, and visions of knights and castles passed before me. They were the voices of old burghers that I heard in the streets. I was an involuntary spectator and auditor of whatever was done and said in the kitchen of the adjacent village-inn—a wholly new and rare experience to me. It was a closer view of my native town. I was fairly inside of it. I never had seen its institutions before. This is one of its peculiar institutions; for it is a shire town.[17] I began to comprehend what its inhabitants were about.

In the morning our breakfasts were put through the hole in the 32 door, in small oblong-square tin pans, made to fit, and holding a pint of chocolate, with brown bread and an iron spoon. When they called for the vessels again, I was green enough to return what bread I had left; but my comrade seized it and said that I should lay that up for lunch or dinner. Soon after he was let out to work at haying in a neighboring field, whither he went every day, and would not be back till noon; so he bade me good-day, saying that he doubted if he should see me again.

When I came out of prison—for someone interfered and paid 33 that tax—I did not perceive that great changes had taken place on the common, such as he observed who went in a youth and emerged a tottering and gray-headed man; and yet a change had to my eyes come over the scene—the town and State and country—greater than any that mere time could effect. I saw yet more distinctly the State in

---

[17]**shire town** A county seat, which means the town had a court, county offices, and jails.

which I lived. I saw to what extent the people among whom I lived could be trusted as good neighbors and friends; that their friendship was for summer weather only; that they did not greatly propose to do right; that they were a distinct race from me by their prejudices and superstitions, as the Chinamen and Malays are; that, in their sacrifices to humanity, they ran no risks, not even to their property; that, after all, they were not so noble but they treated the thief as he had treated them and hoped, by a certain outward observance and a few prayers, and by walking in a particular straight though useless path from time to time, to save their souls. This may be to judge my neighbors harshly; for I believe that many of them are not aware that they have such an institution as the jail in their village.

It was formerly the custom in our village, when a poor debtor   34
came out of jail, for his acquaintances to salute him, looking through their fingers, which were crossed to represent the grating of a jail window, "How do ye do?" My neighbors did not thus salute me but first looked at me and then at one another as if I had returned from a long journey. I was put into jail as I was going to the shoemaker's to get a shoe which was mended. When I was let out the next morning I proceeded to finish my errand, and having put on my mended shoe, joined a huckleberry party who were impatient to put themselves under my conduct; and in half an hour—for the horse was soon tackled—was in the midst of a huckleberry field on one of our highest hills two miles off, and then the State was nowhere to be seen.

This is the whole history of "My Prisons."   35

I have never declined paying the highway tax, because I am as   36
desirous of being a good neighbor as I am of being a bad subject; and as for supporting schools I am doing my part to educate my fellow countrymen now. It is for no particular item in the tax-bill that I refuse to pay it. I simply wish to refuse allegiance to the State, to withdraw and stand aloof from it effectually. I do not care to trace the course of my dollar, if I could, till it buys a man or a musket to shoot one with—the dollar is innocent—but I am concerned to trace the effects of my allegiance. In fact, I quietly declare war with the State, after my fashion, though I will still make what use and get what advantage of her I can, as is usual in such cases.

If others pay the tax which is demanded of me from a sympathy   37
with the State, they do but what they have already done in their own case, or rather they abet injustice to a greater extent than the State requires. If they pay the tax from a mistaken interest in the individual taxed, to save his property, or prevent his going to jail, it is because they have not considered wisely how far they let their private feelings interfere with the public good.

This, then, is my position at present. But one cannot be too much   38
on his guard in such a case, lest his action be biassed by obstinacy or
an undue regard for the opinions of men. Let him see that he does
only what belongs to himself and to the hour.

I think sometimes, Why, this people mean well; they are only   39
ignorant; they would do better if they knew how: why give your
neighbors this pain to treat you as they are not inclined to? But I
think again, this is no reason why I should do as they do or permit
others to suffer much greater pain of a different kind. Again, I sometimes say to myself, When many millions of men, without heat,
without ill will, without personal feeling of any kind, demand of you
a few shillings only, without the possibility, such is their constitution, of retracting or altering their present demand, and without the
possibility, on your side, of appeal to any other millions, why expose yourself to this overwhelming brute force? You do not resist
cold and hunger, the winds and the waves, thus obstinately; you
quietly submit to a thousand similar necessities. You do not put your
head into the fire. But just in proportion as I regard this as not wholly
a brute force but partly a human force, and consider that I have relations to those millions as to so many millions of men, and not of
mere brute or inanimate things, I see that appeal is possible, first
and instantaneously, from them to the Maker of them, and secondly,
from them to themselves. But if I put my head deliberately into the
fire, there is no appeal to fire or to the Maker of fire, and I have only
myself to blame. If I could convince myself that I have any right to
be satisfied with men as they are, and to treat them accordingly, and
not according, in some respects, to my requisitions and expectations
of what they and I ought to be, then, like a good Mussulman[18] and
fatalist, I should endeavor to be satisfied with things as they are and
say it is the will of God. And, above all, there is this difference between resisting this and a purely brute or natural force, that I can resist this with some effect; but I cannot expect, like Orpheus,[19] to
change the nature of the rocks and trees and beasts.

I do not wish to quarrel with any man or nation. I do not wish to   40
split hairs, to make fine distinctions, or set myself up as better than
my neighbors. I seek rather, I may say, even an excuse for conform-
ing to the laws of the land. I am but too ready to conform to them.
Indeed, I have reason to suspect myself on this head; and each year,
as the tax-gatherer comes round, I find myself disposed to review the

---

[18] **Mussulman** Muslim; a follower of the religion of Islam.
[19] **Orpheus** In Greek mythology Orpheus was a poet whose songs were so
plaintive that they affected animals, trees, and even stones.

acts and position of the general and State governments, and the spirit of the people, to discover a pretext for conformity.

> We must affect our country as our parents;
> And if at any time we alienate
> Our love or industry from doing it honor,
> We must respect effects and teach the soul
> Matter of conscience and religion,
> And not desire of rule or benefit.[20]

I believe that the State will soon be able to take all my work of this sort out of my hands, and then I shall be no better a patriot than my fellow-countrymen. Seen from a lower point of view, the Constitution, with all its faults, is very good; the law and the courts are very respectable; even this State and this American government are, in many respects, very admirable and rare things, to be thankful for, such as a great many have described them; but seen from a point of view a little higher, they are what I have described them; seen from a higher still, and the highest, who shall say what they are, or that they are worth looking at or thinking of at all?

However, the government does not concern me much, and I   41 shall bestow the fewest possible thoughts on it. It is not many moments that I live under a government, even in this world. If a man is thought-free, fancy-free, imagination-free, that which *is not* never for a long time appearing *to be* to him, unwise rulers or reformers cannot fatally interrupt him.

I know that most men think differently from myself; but those   42 whose lives are by profession devoted to the study of these or kindred subjects content me as little as any. Statesmen and legislators, standing so completely within the institution, never distinctly and nakedly behold it. They speak of moving society but have no restingplace without it. They may be men of a certain experience and discrimination and have no doubt invented ingenious and even useful systems, for which we sincerely thank them; but all their wit and usefulness lie within certain not very wide limits. They are wont to forget that the world is not governed by policy and expediency. Webster[21] never goes behind government and so cannot speak with

---

[20]**We must affect . . .** From George Peele (1556–1596), *The Battle of Alcazar* (acted 1588–1589, printed 1594), II.ii. Thoreau added these lines in a later printing of the essay. They emphasize the fact that one is disobedient to the state as one is to a parent — with love and affection and from a cause of conscience. Disobedience is not taken lightly.

[21]**Daniel Webster (1782–1852)** One of the most brilliant orators of his time. He was secretary of state from 1841 to 1843, which is why Thoreau thinks he cannot be a satisfactory critic of government.

authority about it. His words are wisdom to those legislators who contemplate no essential reform in the existing government; but for thinkers, and those who legislate for all time, he never once glances at the subject. I know of those whose serene and wise speculations on this theme would soon reveal the limits of his mind's range and hospitality. Yet, compared with the cheap professions of most reformers, and the still cheaper wisdom and eloquence of politicians in general, his are almost the only sensible and valuable words, and we thank Heaven for him. Comparatively, he is always strong, original, and, above all, practical. Still his quality is not wisdom but prudence. The lawyer's truth is not Truth but consistency, or a consistent expediency. Truth is always in harmony with herself and is not concerned chiefly to reveal the justice that may consist with wrong-doing. He well deserves to be called, as he has been called, the Defender of the Constitution. There are really no blows to be given by him but defensive ones. He is not a leader but a follower. His leaders are the men of '87.[22] "I have never made an effort," he says, "and never propose to make an effort; I have never countenanced an effort, and never mean to countenance an effort, to disturb the arrangement as originally made, by which the various States came into the Union." Still thinking of the sanction which the Constitution gives to slavery, he says, "Because it was a part of the original compact—let it stand." Notwithstanding his special acuteness and ability, he is unable to take a fact out of its merely political relations and behold it as it lies absolutely to be disposed of by the intellect—what, for instance, it behooves a man to do here in America today with regard to slavery but ventures, or is driven, to make some such desperate answer as the following, while professing to speak absolutely, and as a private man—from which what new and singular code of social duties might be inferred? "The manner," says he, "in which the governments of those States where slavery exists are to regulate it, is for their own consideration, under their responsibility to their constituents, to the general laws of propriety, humanity, and justice, and to God. Associations formed elsewhere, springing from a feeling of humanity, or any other cause, have nothing whatever to do with it. They have never received any encouragement from me, and they never will."[23]

They who know of no purer sources of truth, who have traced   43 up its stream no higher, stand, and wisely stand, by the Bible and the Constitution, and drink at it there with reverence and humility;

---

[22] **men of '87** The men who framed the Constitution in 1787.
[23] These extracts have been inserted since the Lecture was read. [Thoreau's note]

but they who behold where it comes trickling into this lake or that pool gird up their loins once more and continue their pilgrimage toward its fountain-head.

No man with a genius for legislation has appeared in America. 44 They are rare in the history of the world. There are orators, politicians, and eloquent men by the thousand; but the speaker has not yet opened his mouth to speak who is capable of settling the much-vexed questions of the day. We love eloquence for its own sake and not for any truth which it may utter or any heroism it may inspire. Our legislators have not yet learned the comparative value of free-trade and of freedom, of union, and of rectitude, to a nation. They have no genius or talent for comparatively humble questions of taxation and finance, commerce and manufacturers and agriculture. If we were left solely to the wordy wit of legislators in Congress for our guidance, uncorrected by the seasonable experience and the effectual complaints of the people, America would not long retain her rank among the nations. For eighteen hundred years, though perchance I have no right to say it, the New Testament has been written; yet where is the legislator who has wisdom and practical talent enough to avail himself of the light which it sheds on the science of legislation?

The authority of government, even such as I am willing to sub- 45 mit to—for I will cheerfully obey those who know and can do better than I, and in many things even those who neither know nor can do so well—is still an impure one: to be strictly just, it must have the sanction and consent of the governed. It can have no pure right over my person and property but what I concede to it. The progress from an absolute to a limited monarchy, from a limited monarchy to a democracy, is a progress toward a true respect for the individual. Even the Chinese philosopher[24] was wise enough to regard the individual as the basis of the empire. Is a democracy such as we know it the last improvement possible in government? Is it not possible to take a step further towards recognizing and organizing the rights of man? There will never be a really free and enlightened State until the State comes to recognize the individual as a higher and independent power, from which all its own power and authority are derived, and treats him accordingly. I please myself with imagining a State at last which can afford to be just to all men and to treat the individual with respect as a neighbor; which even would not think it inconsistent with its own repose if a few were to live aloof from it, not meddling with it, nor embraced by it, who fulfilled all the duties of neighbors

---

[24] **Chinese philosopher** Thoreau probably means Confucius.

and fellow-men. A State which bore this kind of fruit and suffered it to drop off as fast as it ripened would prepare the way for a still more perfect and glorious State, which also I have imagined but not yet anywhere seen.

QUESTIONS FOR CRITICAL READING

1. How would you characterize the tone of Thoreau's address? Is he chastising his audience? Is he praising it? What opinion do you think he has of his audience?
2. Explain what Thoreau means when he says, "But a government in which the majority rule in all cases cannot be based on justice, even as far as men understand it" (para. 4).
3. How is injustice "part of the necessary friction of the machine of government" (para. 18)?
4. Why does Thoreau provide us with "the whole history of 'My Prisons'" (paras. 28–35)? Describe what being in jail taught Thoreau. Why do you think Thoreau reacted so strongly to being in a local jail for a single day?
5. Choose an example of Thoreau's use of irony, and comment on its effectiveness. (One example appears in para. 25.)
6. How might Thoreau view the responsibility of the majority to a minority within the sphere of government?
7. How clear are Thoreau's concepts of justice? On what are they based?
8. Is it possible that when Thoreau mentions "the Chinese philosopher" (para. 45) he means Lao-tzu? Would Lao-tzu agree that the individual is "the basis of the empire"?

SUGGESTIONS FOR WRITING

1. Thoreau insists, "Law never made men a whit more just" (para. 4). He introduces the concept of conscience as a monitor of law and government. Explain his views on conscience and the conscientious person. How can conscience help create justice? Why is it sometimes difficult for law to create justice?
2. Do you agree with Thoreau when he says, "All voting is a sort of gaming" (para. 11)? Examine his attitude toward elections and the relationship of elections to the kind of justice one can expect from a government.
3. Answer Thoreau's question: "Unjust laws exist: shall we be content to obey them, or shall we endeavor to amend them and obey them until we have succeeded, or shall we transgress them at once?" (para. 16). Thoreau reminds us that the law has been created by the majority and to disobey would put him in a minority—a "wise minority." Why should the wise minority have the right to disobey laws created by the majority?

4. In what ways was the United States government of Thoreau's time built on the individual or on the individual's best interests? In what way is our current government based on the individual's best interests? How can satisfying the individual's best interests be reconciled with satisfying the community's interest? Which would produce more justice?

5. Examine quotations from Thoreau that focus on justice for the individual, and write an essay that establishes the values of the government Thoreau describes. How might that government see its obligations to the governed? How would it treat matters of justice and moral issues? Describe Thoreau's view of the American government of his time in enough detail to give a clear sense of the essay to someone who has not read it.

6. Reread Thoreau's question in item 3 above. Answer it in an essay that focuses on issues that are significant to you. Be as practical and cautious as you feel you should be, and provide your own answer—not the one you feel Thoreau might have given. Then describe the forms that Thoreau's disobedience would be likely to take. What probably would be the limits of his actions?

7. **CONNECTIONS** Thoreau admits (para. 41) that he is not very concerned with government because he does not have to pay much attention to it. His life goes on regardless of government. He also says that "[t]he authority of government . . . is still an impure one: to be strictly just, it must have the sanction and consent of the governed" (para. 45). How would Thomas Jefferson have reacted to Thoreau's attitudes toward government? Would he have agreed with Thoreau's view that it is essentially unimportant to the individual? Does Thoreau derive from Jefferson his view that the success of a government depends on the sanction of the governed? Or did Jefferson have a different idea about the relationship between the government and the governed?

8. **CONNECTIONS** Thoreau was especially sympathetic to the plight of African American slaves and would likely have shared the views of Martin Luther King Jr. What advice might Thoreau have given King? Write an essay that applies the basic ideas of "Civil Disobedience" to the circumstances in which King found himself.

ELIZABETH CADY STANTON
Declaration of Sentiments and Resolutions

ELIZABETH CADY STANTON (1815–1902) was exceptionally intelligent, and because her lawyer father was willing to indulge her gifts, she was provided the best education a woman in her time in America could expect. Born and raised in Johnstown, New York, she was one of six children, five girls and one boy, Eleazar, in whom all the hopes of the family rested. When Eleazar died after graduating from college, Elizabeth strove to replace him in the admiration of her father. She studied Greek so successfully that she was admitted as the only young woman in the local secondary school, where she demonstrated her abilities—which on the whole were superior to those of the boys with whom she studied.

Nonetheless, she did not win the esteem she hoped for. Her father, although he loved and cared for her, continually told her he wished she had been born a boy. In Johnstown, as elsewhere, women had few rights and rather low expectations. The question of education was a case in point: it was a profound exception for Elizabeth Cady to go to school with boys or even to study what they studied. She had no hopes of following in their paths because all the professions they aimed for were closed to women. This fact was painfully brought home to her when she finished secondary school. All the boys she studied with went on to Union College in Schenectady, but she was barred from attending the all-male institution. Instead, she attended the much inferior Troy Female Seminary, run by a pioneer of American education, Emma Willard (1787–1870).

Troy was as good a school as any woman in America could attend; yet it emphasized a great many traditional womanly pursuits

From the *History of Woman Suffrage*.

as well as the principles of Calvinism, which Elizabeth Cady came to believe were at the root of the problem women had in American society. In the 1830s women did not have the vote; if they were married, they could not own property; and they could not sue for divorce no matter how ugly their marital situation. A husband expected a dowry from his wife, and he could spend it exactly as he wished: on gambling, carousing, or speculating. Not until 1848, the year of the Seneca Falls Convention, did New York pass laws to change this situation.

Elizabeth Cady married when she was twenty-four years old. Her husband, Henry Stanton, was a prominent abolitionist and journalist. He had little money, and the match was not entirely blessed by Elizabeth's father. In characteristic fashion she had the word *obey* struck from the marriage vows; thus she had trouble finding a preacher who would adhere to her wishes. And, preferring never to be known as Mrs. Stanton, she was always addressed as Elizabeth Cady Stanton.

Early on, the couple settled in Boston, where Elizabeth found considerable intellectual companionship and stimulation. Good servants made her household tasks minimal. But soon Henry Stanton's health demanded that they move to Seneca Falls, New York, where there were few servants of any caliber, and where there were few people of intellectual independence to stimulate her. Her lot in life became much like that of any housewife, and she could not abide it.

After a discussion at tea with a number of like-minded women, she proposed a woman's convention to discuss their situation. On July 14, 1848 (a year celebrated for revolutions in every major capital of Europe), the following notice appeared in the *Seneca County Courier*, a semiweekly journal:

SENECA FALLS CONVENTION

WOMAN'S RIGHTS CONVENTION. — A Convention to discuss the social, civil, and religious condition and rights of woman, will be held in the Wesleyan Chapel, at Seneca Falls, N.Y., on Wednesday and Thursday, the 19th and 20th of July, current; commencing at 10 o'clock A.M. During the first day the meeting will be exclusively for women, who are earnestly invited to attend. The public generally are invited to be present on the second day, when Lucretia Mott, of Philadelphia, and other ladies and gentlemen, will address the convention.

On the appointed day, less than a week after the notice, carriages and other vehicles tied up the streets around the Wesleyan Chapel with a large number of interested people. The first shock was that the chapel was locked, and the first order of business was for a man to climb through an open window to unlock the doors. The chapel was filled immediately, but not only with women. Many men were present, including Frederick Douglass, and the women decided that because they were already there, the men could stay.

The convention was a significant success, establishing a pattern that has been repeated frequently since. Elizabeth Cady Stanton, in her Declaration, figured as a radical in the assembly, proposing unheard-of reforms such as granting women the vote, which most of the moderates in the assembly could not agree on. For a while the assembly wished to omit the question of the vote, but Stanton by presenting it as her first statement in the Declaration, made it clear that without the right to vote on legislation and legislators, women would never be able to change the status quo. Eventually, with the help of Douglass and others, the convention accepted her position, and the women's movement in America was under way.

Stanton's Rhetoric

Because the Seneca Falls Declaration is modeled directly on Jefferson's Declaration of Independence, we cannot get a good idea of Stanton's rhetorical gifts. However, by relying on Jefferson, she exercised a powerful wit (for which her other writing is well known) by reminding her audience that when the Declaration of Independence was uttered, no thought was given to half its potential audience—women. Thus, the Seneca Falls Declaration is a parody, and it is especially effective in the way it parodies its model so closely.

The same periodic sentences, parallelism, and balance are used and largely to the same effect. She employed the same profusion of one-paragraph utterances and exactly the same opening for each of them. Stanton played a marvelous trick, however. In place of the tyrannical foreign King George—Jefferson's "He"—she has put the tyrant man. Because of the power of her model, her Declaration gathers strength and ironically undercuts the model.

The most interesting aspect of Stanton's rhetorical structure has to do with the order in which she includes the abuses and wrongs that she asks to be made right. She begins with the vote, just as Jefferson began with the law. Both are essential to the entire argument, and both are the key to change. Whereas Jefferson demands an entirely new government, Elizabeth Cady Stanton ends by demanding the "equal participation" of women with men in the government they have already won.

PREREADING QUESTIONS:
WHAT TO READ FOR

The following prereading questions may help you anticipate key issues in the discussion of Elizabeth Cady Stanton's Declaration of Sentiments and Resolutions. Keeping them in mind during your first reading of the selection should help focus your attention.

- What power has man had over women, according to Stanton?
- What is Stanton's attitude toward just and unjust laws?

Declaration of Sentiments and Resolutions

Adopted by the Seneca Falls Convention, July 19–20, 1848

When, in the course of human events, it becomes necessary for   1
one portion of the family of man to assume among the people of the
earth a position different from that which they have hitherto occupied, but one to which the laws of nature and of nature's God entitle
them, a decent respect to the opinions of mankind requires that they
should declare the causes that impel them to such a course.

We hold these truths to be self-evident: that all men and women   2
are created equal; that they are endowed by their Creator with certain
inalienable rights; that among these are life, liberty, and the pursuit
of happiness; that to secure these rights governments are instituted,
deriving their just powers from the consent of the governed. Whenever any form of government becomes destructive of these ends, it is
the right of those who suffer from it to refuse allegiance to it, and to
insist upon the institution of a new government, laying its foundation
on such principles, and organizing its powers in such form, as to
them shall seem most likely to effect their safety and happiness. Prudence, indeed, will dictate that governments long established should
not be changed for light and transient causes; and accordingly all experience hath shown that mankind are more disposed to suffer, while
evils are sufferable, than to right themselves by abolishing the forms
to which they were accustomed. But when a long train of abuses and
unsurpations, pursuing invariably the same object, evinces a design
to reduce them under absolute despotism, it is their duty to throw off

such government, and to provide new guards for their future security. Such has been the patient sufferance of the women under this government, and such is now the necessity which constrains them to demand the equal station to which they are entitled.

The history of mankind is a history of repeated injuries and 3 usurpations on the part of man toward woman, having in direct object the establishment of an absolute tyranny over her. To prove this, let facts be submitted to a candid world.

He has never permitted her to exercise her inalienable right to 4 the elective franchise.

He has compelled her to submit to laws, in the formation of 5 which she had no voice.

He has withheld from her rights which are given to the most ig- 6 norant and degraded men — both natives and foreigners.

Having deprived her of this first right of a citizen, the elective 7 franchise, thereby leaving her without representation in the halls of legislation, he has oppressed her on all sides.

He has made her, if married, in the eye of the law, civilly dead. 8

He has taken from her all right in property, even to the wages 9 she earns.

He has made her, morally, an irresponsible being, as she can com- 10 mit many crimes with impunity, provided they be done in the presence of her husband. In the covenant of marriage, she is compelled to promise obedience to her husband, he becoming to all intents and purposes, her master — the law giving him power to deprive her of her liberty, and to administer chastisement.

He has so framed the laws of divorce, as to what shall be the 11 proper causes, and in case of separation, to whom the guardianship of the children shall be given, as to be wholly regardless of the happiness of women — the law, in all cases, going upon a false supposition of the supremacy of man, and giving all power into his hands.

After depriving her of all rights as a married woman, if single, 12 and the owner of property, he has taxed her to support a government which recognizes her only when her property can be made profitable to it.

He has monopolized nearly all the profitable employments, and 13 from those she is permitted to follow, she receives but a scanty remuneration. He closes against her all the avenues to wealth and distinction which he considers most honorable to himself. As a teacher of theology, medicine, or law, she is not known.

He has denied her the facilities for obtaining a thorough educa- 14 tion, at colleges being closed against her.

He allows her in Church, as well as State, but a subordinate posi- 15 tion, claiming Apostolic authority for her exclusion from the ministry, and, with some exceptions, from any public participation in the affairs of the Church.

He has created a false public sentiment by giving to the world a   16
different code of morals for men and women, by which moral delinquencies which exclude women from society, are not only tolerated, but deemed of little account in man.

He has usurped the prerogative of Jehovah himself, claiming it   17
as his right to assign for her a sphere of action, when that belongs to her conscience and to her God.

He has endeavored, in every way that he could, to destroy her   18
confidence in her own powers, to lessen her self-respect, and to make her willing to lead a dependent and abject life.

Now, in view of this entire disfranchisement of one-half the people   19
of this country, their social and religious degradation—in view of the unjust laws above mentioned, and because women do feel themselves aggrieved, oppressed, and fraudulently deprived of their most sacred rights, we insist that they have immediate admission to all the rights and privileges which belong to them as citizens of the United States.

In entering upon the great work before us, we anticipate no   20
small amount of misconception, misrepresentation, and ridicule; but we shall use every instrumentality within our power to effect our object. We shall employ agents, circulate tracts, petition the State and National legislatures, and endeavor to enlist the pulpit and the press in our behalf. We hope this Convention will be followed by a series of Conventions embracing every part of the country.

[The following resolutions were discussed by Lucretia Mott,   21
Thomas and Mary Ann McClintock, Amy Post, Catharine A. F. Stebbins, and others, and were adopted:]

WHEREAS, The great precept of nature is conceded to be, that "man   22
shall pursue his own true and substantial happiness." Blackstone[1] in his Commentaries remarks, that this law of Nature being coeval[2] with mankind, and dictated by God himself, is of course superior in obligation to any other. It is binding over all the globe, in all countries and at all times; no human laws are of any validity if contrary to this, and such of them as are valid, derive all their force, and all their validity, and all their authority, mediately and immediately, from this original; therefore,

---

[1] **Sir William Blackstone (1723–1780)** The most influential of English scholars of the law. His *Commentaries of the Laws of England* (4 vols., 1765–1769) form the basis of the study of law in England.
[2] **being coeval** Existing simultaneously.

Resolved, That such laws as conflict, in any way, with the true 23 and substantial happiness of woman, are contrary to the great precept of nature and of no validity, for this is "superior in obligation to any other."

Resolved, That all laws which prevent woman from occupying 24 such a station in society as her conscience shall dictate, or which place her in a position inferior to that of man, are contrary to the great precept of nature, and therefore of no force or authority.

Resolved, That woman is man's equal—was intended to be so 25 by the Creator, and the highest good of the race demands that she should be recognized as such.

Resolved, That the women of this country ought to be enlight- 26 ened in regard to the laws under which they live, that they may no longer publish their degradation by declaring themselves satisfied with their present position, nor their ignorance, by asserting that they have all the rights they want.

Resolved, That inasmuch as man, while claiming for himself in- 27 tellectual superiority, does accord to woman moral superiority, it is pre-eminently his duty to encourage her to speak and teach, as she has an opportunity, in all religious assemblies.

Resolved, That the same amount of virtue, delicacy, and refine- 28 ment of behavior that is required of woman in the social state, should also be required of man, and the same transgressions should be visited with equal severity on both man and woman.

Resolved, That the objection of indelicacy and impropriety, which 29 is so often brought against woman when she addresses a public audience, comes with a very ill-grace from those who encourage, by their attendance, her appearance on the stage, in the concert, or in feats of the circus.

Resolved, That woman has too long rested satisfied in the circum- 30 scribed limits which corrupt customs and a perverted application of the Scriptures have marked out for her, and that it is time she should move in the enlarged sphere which her great Creator has assigned her.

Resolved, That it is the duty of the women of this country to se- 31 cure to themselves their sacred right to the elective franchise.

Resolved, That the equality of human rights results necessarily 32 from the fact of the identity of the race in capabilities and responsibilities.

Resolved, therefore, That, being invested by the Creator with the 33 same capabilities, and the same consciousness of responsibility for their exercise, it is demonstrably the right and duty of woman, equally with man, to promote every righteous cause by every righteous means; and especially in regard to the great subjects of morals and religion, it is self-evidently her right to participate with her brother

in teaching them, both in private and in public, by writing and by
speaking, by any instrumentalities proper to be used, and in any assemblies proper to be held; and this being a self-evident truth growing out of the divinely implanted principles of human nature, any
custom or authority adverse to it, whether modern or wearing the
hoary sanction of antiquity, is to be regarded as a self-evident falsehood, and at war with mankind.

[At the last session Lucretia Mott[3] offered and spoke to the fol-   34
lowing resolution:]

Resolved, That the speedy success of our cause depends upon   35
the zealous and untiring efforts of both men and women, for the
overthrow of the monopoly of the pulpit, and for the securing to
woman an equal participation with men in the various trades, professions, and commerce.

---

[3]**Lucretia Mott (1793–1880)** One of the founders of the 1848 convention at
which these resolutions were presented. She was one of the earliest and most important of the feminists who struggled to proclaim their rights. She was also a prominent abolitionist.

QUESTIONS FOR CRITICAL READING

1. Stanton begins her Declaration with a diatribe against the government.
   To what extent is the government responsible for the wrongs she complains about?
2. Exactly what is Stanton complaining about? What are the wrongs that
   have been done? Do they seem important to you?
3. How much of the effect of the selection depends upon the parody of
   the Declaration of Independence?
4. Which of the individual declarations is the most important? Which is
   the least important?
5. Are any of the declarations serious enough to warrant starting a revolution?
6. Why do you think the suggestion that women deserve the vote was so
   hard to put across at the convention?

SUGGESTIONS FOR WRITING

1. Make a careful comparison between the Declaration and Jefferson's
   Declaration of Independence. What are the similarities? What are the

differences? Why would Stanton's Declaration be particularly more distinguished because it is a parody of such a document? What weaknesses might be implied because of the close resemblance?

2. Write an essay that is essentially a declaration in the same style Stanton uses. Choose a cause carefully and follow the same pattern that Stanton does in the selection. Establish the appropriate relationship between government and the cause you are interested in defending or promoting.

3. To what extent is it useful to petition a government to redress the centuries of wrongs done to women? Is it the government's fault that women were treated so badly? Is the government able to have a significant effect on helping to change the unpleasant circumstances of women? Is it appropriate or inappropriate for Stanton to attack government in her search for equality?

4. The Declaration of Independence was aimed at justifying a war. Is the question of war anywhere implied in Stanton's address? If war is not the question, what is? Is there any substitute for war in Stanton's essay?

5. Read down the list of declarations and resolutions that Stanton enumerates. Have all of these issues been dealt with in our times? Would such a declaration as this still be appropriate, or has the women's movement accomplished all its goals?

6. Examine the issues treated in paragraph 16, concerning "a different code of morals" for men and women. Explain exactly what Stanton meant by that expression, and consider how different things are today from what they were in Stanton's day.

7. **CONNECTIONS** To what extent do you think Henry David Thoreau would have agreed with Elizabeth Cady Stanton? What aspects of her Declaration would he have found most useful for his own position? Would he have urged women to practice civil disobedience on behalf of women's rights, or would he have accepted the general point of view of his time and concerned himself only with the independence of men?

MARTIN LUTHER KING JR.
Letter from Birmingham Jail

MARTIN LUTHER KING JR. (1929–1968) was the most influential civil rights leader in America for a period of more than fifteen years. He was an ordained minister with a doctorate in theology from Boston University. He worked primarily in the South, where he labored steadily to overthrow laws that promoted segregation and to increase the number of black voters registered in southern communities.

From 1958 to 1968 demonstrations and actions opened up opportunities for African Americans who in the South hitherto had been prohibited from sitting in certain sections of buses, using facilities such as water fountains in bus stations, and sitting at luncheon counters with whites. Such laws — unjust and insulting, not to mention unconstitutional — were not challenged by local authorities. Martin Luther King Jr., who became famous for supporting a program to integrate buses in Montgomery, Alabama, was asked by the Southern Christian Leadership Conference (SCLC) to assist in the fight for civil rights in Birmingham, Alabama, where an SCLC meeting was to be held.

King was arrested as the result of a program of sit-ins at luncheon counters and wrote the letter printed here to a group of clergymen who had criticized his position. King had been arrested before and would be arrested again — resembling Thoreau somewhat in his attitude toward laws that did not conform to moral justice.

King, like Thoreau, was willing to suffer for his views, especially when he found himself faced with punitive laws denying civil rights to all citizens. His is a classic case in which the officers of the government pled that they were dedicated to maintaining a stable civil society, even as they restricted King's individual rights. In 1963, many of the good people to whom King addressed this letter firmly believed that peace and order might be threatened by granting African Americans the true independence and freedom that

171

King insisted were their rights and indeed were guaranteed under the Constitution. This is why King's letter objects to an injustice that was rampant in Frederick Douglass's time but inexcusable in the time of John F. Kennedy.

Eventually the causes King promoted were victorious. His efforts helped change attitudes in the South and spur legislation that has benefited all Americans. His views concerning nonviolence spread throughout the world, and by the early 1960s he had become famous as a man who stood for human rights and human dignity virtually everywhere. He won the Nobel Peace Prize in 1964.

Although King himself was nonviolent, his program left both him and his followers open to the threat of violence. The sit-ins and voter registration programs spurred countless bombings, threats, and murders by members of the white community. King's life was often threatened, his home bombed, his followers harassed. He was assassinated at the Lorraine Motel in Memphis, Tennessee, on April 4, 1968. But before he died he saw—largely through his own efforts, influence, and example—the face of America change.

King's Rhetoric

The most obvious rhetorical tradition King assumes in this important work is that of the books of the Bible that were originally letters, such as Paul's Epistle to the Ephesians and his several letters to the Corinthians. Many of Paul's letters were written while he was in prison in Rome, and he established a moral position that could inspire the citizens who received the letters. At the same time Paul carried out the most important work of the early Christian church—spreading the word of Jesus to those who wished to be Christians but who needed clarification and encouragement.

It is not clear that the clergymen who received King's letter fully appreciated the rhetorical tradition he drew upon—but they were men who preached from the Bible and certainly should have understood it. The text itself alludes to the mission of Paul and to his communications to his people. King works with this rhetorical tradition not only because it is effective but because it resonates with the deepest aspect of his calling—spreading the gospel of Christ. Brotherhood and justice were his message.

King's tone is one of utmost patience with his critics. He seems bent on winning them over to his point of view, just as he seems confident that—because they are, like him, clergymen—their goodwill should help them see the justice of his views.

His method is that of careful reasoning, focusing on the substance of their criticism, particularly on their complaints that his actions were "unwise and untimely" (para. 1). King takes each of those charges in turn, carefully analyzes it against his position, and then follows with the clearest possible statement of his own views and why he feels they are worth adhering to. The "Letter from Birmingham Jail" is a model of close and reasonable analysis of a very complex situation. It succeeds largely because it remains concrete, treating one issue after another carefully, refusing to be caught up in passion or posturing. Above all, King remains grounded in logic, convinced that his arguments will in turn convince his audience.

PREREADING QUESTIONS:
WHAT TO READ FOR

The following prereading questions may help you anticipate key issues in the discussion of Martin Luther King's "Letter from Birmingham Jail." Keeping them in mind during your first reading of the selection should help focus your attention.

- What kind of injustice did Martin Luther King find in Birmingham?

- Why was Martin Luther King disappointed in the white churches?

Letter from Birmingham Jail

April 16, 1963

MY DEAR FELLOW CLERGYMEN:[1]

While confined here in the Birmingham city jail, I came across   1
your recent statement calling my present activities "unwise and untimely." Seldom do I pause to answer criticism of my work and ideas. It

---

[1] This response to a published statement by eight fellow clergymen from Alabama (Bishop C. C. J. Carpenter, Bishop Joseph A. Durick, Rabbi Hilton L. Grafman, Bishop Paul Hardin, Bishop Holan B. Harmon, the Reverend George M. Murray, the Reverend Edward V. Ramage, and the Reverend Earl Stallings) was composed under somewhat constricting circumstances. Begun on the margins of the newspaper in which the statement appeared while I was in jail, the letter was continued on scraps of writing paper supplied by a friendly Negro trusty, and concluded on a pad my attorneys were eventually permitted to leave me. Although the text remains in substance unaltered, I have indulged in the author's prerogative of polishing it for publication. [King's note]

I sought to answer all the criticisms that cross my desk, my secretaries would have little time for anything other than such correspondence in the course of the day, and I would have no time for constructive work. But since I feel that you are men of genuine good will and that your criticisms are sincerely set forth, I want to try to answer your statement in what I hope will be patient and reasonable terms.

I think I should indicate why I am here in Birmingham, since   2
you have been influenced by the view which argues against "out-siders coming in." I have the honor of serving as president of the Southern Christian Leadership Conference, an organization operat-ing in every southern state, with headquarters in Atlanta, Georgia. We have some eighty-five affiliated organizations across the South, and one of them is the Alabama Christian Movement for Human Rights. Frequently we share staff, educational, and financial re-sources with our affiliates. Several months ago the affiliate here in Birmingham asked us to be on call to engage in a nonviolent direct-action program if such were deemed necessary. We readily con-sented, and when the hour came we lived up to our promise. So I, along with several members of my staff, am here because I was in-vited here. I am here because I have organizational ties here.

But more basically, I am in Birmingham because injustice is here.   3
Just as the prophets of the eighth century B.C. left their villages and car-ried their "thus saith the Lord" far beyond the boundaries of their home towns, and just as the Apostle Paul left his village of Tarsus[2] and carried the gospel of Jesus Christ to the far corners of the Greco-Roman world, so am I compelled to carry the gospel of freedom beyond my own home town. Like Paul, I must constantly respond to the Mace-donian call for aid.[3]

Moreover, I am cognizant of the interrelatedness of all commu-   4
nities and states. I cannot sit idly by in Atlanta and not be concerned about what happens in Birmingham. Injustice anywhere is a threat to justice everywhere. We are caught in an inescapable network of mutuality, tied in a single garment of destiny. Whatever affects one directly, affects all indirectly. Never again can we afford to live with the narrow, provincial, "outside agitator" idea. Anyone who lives in-side the United States can never be considered an outsider anywhere within its bounds.

---

[2] **village of Tarsus** Birthplace of St. Paul (?–A.D. 67), in Asia Minor, present-day Turkey, close to Syria.
    [3] **the Macedonian call for aid** The citizens of Philippi, in Macedonia (northern Greece), were among the staunchest Christians. Paul went to their aid frequently; he also had to resolve occasional bitter disputes within the Christian community there (see Philippians 2:2–14).

You deplore the demonstrations taking place in Birmingham. 5
But your statement, I am sorry to say, fails to express a similar concern for the conditions that brought about the demonstrations. I am
sure that none of you would want to rest content with the superficial
kind of social analysis that deals merely with effects and does not
grapple with underlying causes. It is unfortunate that demonstrations are taking place in Birmingham, but it is even more unfortunate that the city's white power structure left the Negro community
with no alternative.

In any nonviolent campaign there are four basic steps: collec- 6
tion of the facts to determine whether injustices exist; negotiation;
self-purification; and direct action. We have gone through all these
steps in Birmingham. There can be no gainsaying the fact that racial
injustice engulfs this community. Birmingham is probably the most
thoroughly segregated city in the United States. Its ugly record of
brutality is widely known. Negroes have experienced grossly unjust
treatment in the courts. There have been more unsolved bombings
of Negro homes and churches in Birmingham than in any other city
in the nation. These are the hard brutal facts of the case. On the
basis of these conditions, Negro leaders sought to negotiate with the
city fathers. But the latter consistently refused to engage in good-
faith negotiation.

Then, last September, came the opportunity to talk with leaders 7
of Birmingham's economic community. In the course of the negotiations, certain promises were made by the merchants—for example,
to remove the stores' humiliating racial signs. On the basis of these
promises, the Reverend Fred Shuttlesworth and the leaders of the Alabama Christian Movement for Human Rights agreed to a morato-
rium on all demonstrations. As the weeks and months went by, we
realized that we were the victims of a broken promise. A few signs,
briefly removed, returned; the others remained.

As in so many past experiences, our hopes had been blasted, 8
and the shadow of deep disappointment settled upon us. We had
no alternative except to prepare for direct action, whereby we
would present our very bodies as a means of laying our case before
the conscience of the local and the national community. Mindful of
the difficulties involved, we decided to undertake a process of self-
purification. We began a series of workshops on nonviolence, and
we repeatedly asked ourselves: "Are you able to accept blows without retaliating?" "Are you able to endure the ordeal of jail?" We decided to schedule our direct-action program for the Easter season,
realizing that except for Christmas, this is the main shopping period
of the year. Knowing that a strong economic-withdrawal program
would be the by-product of direct action, we felt that this would be

the best time to bring pressure to bear on the merchants for the needed change.

Then it occurred to us that Birmingham's mayoral election was   9 coming up in March, and we speedily decided to postpone action until after election day. When we discovered that the Commissioner of Public Safety, Eugene "Bull" Connor, had piled up enough votes to be in the run-off, we decided again to postpone action until the day after the run-off so that the demonstrations could not be used to cloud the issues. Like many others, we waited to see Mr. Connor defeated, and to this end we endured postponement after postponement. Having aided in this community need, we felt that our direct-action program could be delayed no longer.

You may well ask, "Why direct action? Why sit-ins, marches, 10 and so forth? Isn't negotiation a better path?" You are quite right in calling for negotiation. Indeed, this is the very purpose of direct action. Nonviolent direct action seeks to create such a crisis and foster such a tension that a community which has constantly refused to negotiate is forced to confront the issue. It seeks so to dramatize the issue that it can no longer be ignored. My citing the creation of tension as part of the work of the nonviolent resister may sound rather shocking. But I must confess that I am not afraid of the word "tension." I have earnestly opposed violent tension, but there is a type of constructive, nonviolent tension which is necessary for growth. Just as Socrates[4] felt that it was necessary to create a tension in the mind so that individuals could rise from the bondage of myths and half truths to the unfettered realm of creative analysis and objective appraisal, so must we see the need for nonviolent gadflies to create the kind of tension in society that will help men rise from the dark depths of prejudice and racism to the majestic heights of understanding and brotherhood.

The purpose of our direct-action program is to create a situation 11 so crisis-packed that it will inevitably open the door to negotiation. I therefore concur with you in your call for negotiation. Too long has our beloved Southland been bogged down in a tragic effort to live in monologue rather than dialogue.

One of the basic points in your statement is that the action that I 12 and my associates have taken in Birmingham is untimely. Some have asked: "Why didn't you give the new city administration time to act?"

---

[4] **Socrates (470?–399 B.C.)** The "tension in the mind" King refers to is created by the question-answer technique known as the Socratic method. By posing questions at the beginning of the paragraph, King shows his willingness to share Socrates' rhetorical techniques. Socrates was imprisoned and killed for his civil disobedience (see paras. 21 and 25). He was the greatest of the Greek philosophers.

The only answer that I can give to this query is that the new Birmingham administration must be prodded about as much as the outgoing one, before it will act. We are sadly mistaken if we feel that the election of Albert Boutwell as mayor will bring the millennium[5] to Birmingham. While Mr. Boutwell is a much more gentle person than Mr. Connor, they are both segregationists, dedicated to maintenance of the status quo. I have hoped that Mr. Boutwell will be reasonable enough to see the futility of massive resistance to desegregation. But he will not see this without pressure from devotees of civil rights. My friends, I must say to you that we have not made a single gain in civil rights without determined legal and nonviolent pressure. Lamentably, it is an historical fact that privileged groups seldom give up their privileges voluntarily. Individuals may see the moral light and voluntarily give up their unjust posture; but, as Reinhold Niebuhr[6] has reminded us, groups tend to be more immoral than individuals.

We know through painful experience that freedom is never voluntarily given by the oppressor; it must be demanded by the oppressed. Frankly, I have yet to engage in a direct-action campaign that was "well timed" in the view of those who have not suffered unduly from the disease of segregation. For years now I have heard the word "Wait!" It rings in the ear of every Negro with piercing familiarity. This "Wait" has almost always meant "Never." We must come to see, with one of our distinguished jurists, that "justice too long delayed is justice denied."[7]   13

We have waited for more than 340 years for our constitutional and God-given rights. The nations of Asia and Africa are moving with jet-like speed toward gaining political independence, but we still creep at horse-and-buggy pace toward gaining a cup of coffee at a lunch counter. Perhaps it is easy for those who have never felt the stinging darts of segregation to say, "Wait." But when you have seen vicious mobs lynch your mothers and fathers at will and drown your sisters and brothers at whim; when you have seen hate-filled policemen curse, kick, and even kill your black brothers and sisters; when   14

---

[5] **the millennium** A reference to Revelation 20, according to which the second coming of Christ will be followed by one thousand years of peace, when the devil will be incapacitated. After this will come a final battle between good and evil, followed by the Last Judgment.

[6] **Reinhold Niebuhr (1892–1971)** Protestant American philosopher who urged church members to put their beliefs into action against social injustice. He urged Protestantism to develop and practice a code of social ethics and wrote in *Moral Man and Immoral Society* (1932) of the point King mentions here.

[7] **"justice too long delayed is justice denied"** Chief Justice Earl Warren's expression in 1954 was adapted from English writer Walter Savage Landor's phrase "Justice delayed is justice denied."

you see the vast majority of your twenty million Negro brothers smothering in an airtight cage of poverty in the midst of an affluent society; when you suddenly find your tongue twisted and your speech stammering as you seek to explain to your six-year-old daughter why she can't go to the public amusement park that has just been advertised on television, and see tears welling up in her eyes when she is told that Funtown is closed to colored children, and see ominous clouds of inferiority beginning to form in her little mental sky, and see her beginning to distort her personality by developing an unconscious bitterness toward white people; when you have to concoct an answer for a five-year-old son who is asking, "Daddy, why do white people treat colored people so mean?"; when you take a cross-country drive and find it necessary to sleep night after night in the uncomfortable corners of your automobile because no motel will accept you; when you are humiliated day in and day out by nagging signs reading "white" and "colored"; when your first name becomes "nigger," your middle name becomes "boy" (however old you are) and your last name becomes "John," and your wife and mother are never given the respected title "Mrs."; when you are harried by day and haunted by night by the fact that you are a Negro, living constantly at tiptoe stance, never quite knowing what to expect next, and are plagued with inner fears and outer resentments; when you are forever fighting a degenerating sense of "nobodiness"—then you will understand why we find it difficult to wait. There comes a time when the cup of endurance runs over, and men are no longer willing to be plunged into the abyss of despair. I hope, sirs, you can understand our legitimate and unavoidable impatience.

You express a great deal of anxiety over our willingness to break 15 laws. This is certainly a legitimate concern. Since we so diligently urge people to obey the Supreme Court's decision of 1954 outlawing segregation in the public schools, at first glance it may seem rather paradoxical for us consciously to break laws. One may well ask: "How can you advocate breaking some laws and obeying others?" The answer lies in the fact that there are two types of laws: just and unjust. I would be the first to advocate obeying just laws. One has not only a legal but a moral responsibility to obey just laws. Conversely, one has a moral responsibility to disobey unjust laws. I would agree with St. Augustine[8] that "an unjust law is no law at all."

Now, what is the difference between the two? How does one de- 16 termine whether a law is just or unjust? A just law is a manmade

---

[8] **St. Augustine (354–430)** Early bishop of the Christian Church who deeply influenced the spirit of Christianity for many centuries.

code that squares with the moral law or the law of God. An unjust law is a code that is out of harmony with the moral law. To put it in the terms of St. Thomas Aquinas:[9] An unjust law is a human law that is not rooted in eternal law and natural law. Any law that uplifts human personality is just. Any law that degrades human personality is unjust. All segregation statutes are unjust because segregation distorts the soul and damages the personality. It gives the segregator a false sense of superiority and the segregated a false sense of inferiority. Segregation, to use the terminology of the Jewish philosopher Martin Buber,[10] substitutes an "I-it" relationship for an "I-thou" relationship and ends up relegating persons to the status of things. Hence segregation is not only politically, economically, and sociologically unsound, it is morally wrong and sinful. Paul Tillich[11] has said that sin is separation. Is not segregation an existential expression of man's tragic separation, his awful estrangement, his terrible sinfulness? Thus it is that I can urge men to obey the 1954 decision of the Supreme Court, for it is morally right; and I can urge them to disobey segregation ordinances, for they are morally wrong.

Let us consider a more concrete example of just and unjust laws. An unjust law is a code that a numerical or power majority group compels a minority group to obey but does not make binding on itself. This is *difference* made legal. By the same token, a just law is a code that a majority compels a minority to follow and that it is willing to follow itself. This is *sameness* made legal.   17

Let me give another explanation. A law is unjust if it is inflicted on a minority that, as a result of being denied the right to vote, had no part in enacting or devising the law. Who can say that the legislature of Alabama which set up that state's segregation laws was democratically elected? Throughout Alabama all sorts of devious methods are used to prevent Negroes from becoming registered voters, and there are some counties in which, even though Negroes constitute a majority of the population, not a single Negro is registered. Can any   18

---

[9] **St. Thomas Aquinas (1225–1274)** The greatest of the medieval Christian philosophers and one of the greatest church authorities.

[10] **Martin Buber (1878–1965)** Jewish theologian. *I and Thou* (1923) is his most famous book.

[11] **Paul Tillich (1886–1965)** An important twentieth-century Protestant theologian who held that Christianity was reasonable and effective in modern life. Tillich saw sin as an expression of man's separation from God, from himself, and from his fellow man. King sees the separation of the races as a further manifestation of man's sinfulness. Tillich, who was driven out of Germany by the Nazis, stresses the need for activism and the importance of action in determining moral vitality, just as King does.

law enacted under such circumstances be considered democratically structured?

Sometimes a law is just on its face and unjust in its application. For instance, I have been arrested on a charge of parading without a permit. Now, there is nothing wrong in having an ordinance which requires a permit for a parade. But such an ordinance becomes unjust when it is used to maintain segregation and to deny citizens the First Amendment privilege of peaceful assembly and protest. 19

I hope you are able to see the distinction I am trying to point out. In no sense do I advocate evading or defying the law, as would the rabid segregationist. That would lead to anarchy. One who breaks an unjust law must do so openly, lovingly, and with a willingness to accept the penalty. I submit that an individual who breaks a law that conscience tells him is unjust, and who willingly accepts the penalty of imprisonment in order to arouse the conscience of the community over its injustice, is in reality expressing the highest respect for law. 20

Of course, there is nothing new about this kind of civil disobedience. It was evidenced subliminally in the refusal of Shadrach, Meshach, and Abednego to obey the laws of Nebuchadnezzar,[12] on the ground that a higher moral law was at stake. It was practiced superbly by the early Christians, who were willing to face hungry lions and the excruciating pain of chopping blocks rather than submit to certain unjust laws of the Roman Empire. To a degree, academic freedom is a reality today because Socrates practiced civil disobedience. In our own nation, the Boston Tea Party represented a massive act of civil disobedience. 21

We should never forget that everything Adolf Hitler did in Germany was "legal" and everything the Hungarian freedom fighters[13] did in Hungary was "illegal." It was "illegal" to aid and comfort a Jew in Hitler's Germany. Even so, I am sure that, had I lived in Germany at the time, I would have aided and comforted my Jewish brothers. If today I lived in a Communist country where certain principles dear to the Christian faith are suppressed, I would openly advocate disobeying that country's antireligious laws. 22

I must make two honest confessions to you, my Christian and Jewish brothers. First, I must confess that over the past few years I 23

---

[12] **Nebuchadnezzar (c. 630–562 B.C.)** Chaldean king who twice attacked Jerusalem. He ordered Shadrach, Meshach, and Abednego to worship a golden image. They refused, were cast into a roaring furnace, and were saved by God (see Daniel 1:7–3:30).

[13] **Hungarian freedom fighters** The Hungarians rose in revolt against Soviet rule in 1956. Soviet forces put down the uprising with great force, which shocked the world. Many freedom fighters died, and many others escaped to the West.

have been gravely disappointed with the white moderate. I have almost reached the regrettable conclusion that the Negro's great stumbling block in his stride toward freedom is not the White Citizen's Counciler[14] or the Ku Klux Klanner, but the white moderate, who is more devoted to "order" than to justice; who prefers a negative peace which is the absence of tension to a positive peace which is the presence of justice; who constantly says, "I agree with you in the goal you seek, but I cannot agree with your methods of direct action"; who paternalistically believes he can set the timetable for another man's freedom; who lives by a mythical concept of time and who constantly advises the Negro to wait for a "more convenient season." Shallow understanding from people of good will is more frustrating than absolute misunderstanding from people of ill will. Lukewarm acceptance is much more bewildering than outright rejection.

I had hoped that the white moderate would understand that law 24
and order exist for the purpose of establishing justice and that when they fail in this purpose they become the dangerously structured dams that block the flow of social progress. I had hoped that the white moderate would understand that the present tension in the South is a necessary phase of the transition from an obnoxious negative peace, in which the Negro passively accepted his unjust plight, to a substantive and positive peace, in which all men will respect the dignity and worth of human personality. Actually, we who engage in nonviolent direct action are not the creators of tension. We merely bring to the surface the hidden tension that is already alive. We bring it out in the open, where it can be seen and dealt with. Like a boil that can never be cured so long as it is covered up but must be opened with all its ugliness to the natural medicines of air and light, injustice must be exposed, with all the tension its exposure creates, to the light of human conscience and the air of national opinion, before it can be cured.

In your statement you assert that our actions, even though 25
peaceful, must be condemned because they precipitate violence. But is this a logical assertion? Isn't this like condemning a robbed man because his possession of money precipitated the evil act of robbery? Isn't this like condemning Socrates because his unswerving commitment to truth and his philosophical inquiries precipitated the act by the misguided populace in which they made him drink hemlock?

---

[14]**White Citizen's Counciler** White Citizen's Councils organized in southern states in 1954 to fight school desegregation as ordered by the Supreme Court in May 1954. The councils were not as secret or violent as the Klan; they were also ineffective.

Isn't this like condemning Jesus because his unique God-consciousness and never-ceasing devotion to God's will precipitated the evil act of crucifixion? We must come to see that, as the federal courts have consistently affirmed, it is wrong to urge an individual to cease his efforts to gain his basic constitutional rights because the quest may precipitate violence. Society must protect the robbed and punish the robber.

I had also hoped that the white moderate would reject the myth   26 concerning time in relation to the struggle for freedom. I have just received a letter from a white brother in Texas. He writes: "All Christians know that the colored people will receive equal rights eventually, but it is possible that you are in too great a religious hurry. It has taken Christianity almost two thousand years to accomplish what it has. The teachings of Christ take time to come to earth." Such an attitude stems from a tragic misconception of time, from the strangely irrational notion that there is something in the very flow of time that will inevitably cure all ills. Actually, time itself is neutral; it can be used either destructively or constructively. More and more I feel that the people of ill will have used time much more effectively than have the people of good will. We will have to repent in this generation not merely for the hateful words and actions of the bad people, but for the appalling silence of the good people. Human progress never rolls in on wheels of inevitability; it comes through the tireless efforts of men willing to be co-workers with God, and without this hard work, time itself becomes an ally of the forces of social stagnation. We must use time creatively, in the knowledge that the time is always ripe to do right. Now is the time to make real the promise of democracy and transform our pending national elegy into a creative psalm of brotherhood. Now is the time to lift our national policy from the quicksand of racial injustice to the solid rock of human dignity.

You speak of our activity in Birmingham as extreme. At first I   27 was rather disappointed that fellow clergymen would see my nonviolent efforts as those of an extremist. I began thinking about the fact that I stand in the middle of two opposing forces in the Negro community. One is a force of complacency, made up in part of Negroes who, as a result of long years of oppression, are so drained of self-respect and a sense of "somebodiness" that they have adjusted to segregation; and in part of a few middle-class Negroes who, because of a degree of academic and economic security and because in some ways they profit by segregation, have become insensitive to the problems of the masses. The other force is one of bitterness and hatred, and it comes perilously close to advocating violence. It is expressed in the various black nationalist groups that are springing up across the nation, the largest and best known being Elijah Muhammad's Muslim movement.[15] Nourished by the Negro's frustration over the continued existence of racial discrimination, this movement is made up of people who have lost faith in America, who have absolutely repudiated Christianity, and who have concluded that the white man is an incorrigible "devil."

I have tried to stand between these two forces, saying that we need emulate neither the "do-nothingism" of the complacent nor the hatred and despair of the black nationalist. For there is the more excellent way of love and nonviolent protest. I am grateful to God that, through the influence of the Negro church, the way of nonviolence became an integral part of our struggle.   28

If this philosophy had not emerged, by now many streets of the South would, I am convinced, be flowing with blood. And I am further convinced that if our white brothers dismiss as "rabble-rousers" and "outside agitators" those of us who employ nonviolent direct action, and if they refuse to support our nonviolent efforts, millions of Negroes will, out of frustration and despair, seek solace and security in black nationalist ideologies—a development that would inevitably lead to a frightening racial nightmare.[16]   29

Oppressed people cannot remain oppressed forever. The yearning for freedom eventually manifests itself, and that is what has happened to the American Negro. Something within has reminded him of his birthright of freedom, and something without has reminded him that it can be gained. Consciously or unconsciously, he has been caught up by the *Zeitgeist*,[17] and with his black brothers of Africa and his brown and yellow brothers of Asia, South America, and the Caribbean, the United States Negro is moving with a sense of great urgency toward the promised land of racial justice. If one recognizes this vital urge that has engulfed the Negro community, one should readily understand why public demonstrations are taking place. The Negro has many pent-up resentments and latent frustrations, and he must release them. So let him march; let him make prayer pilgrimages to   30

---

[15] **Elijah Muhammad's Muslim movement** The Black Muslim movement, which began in the 1920s but flourished in the 1960s under its leader, Elijah Muhammad (1897–1975). Among notable figures who became Black Muslims were the poet Imamu Amiri Baraka (b. 1934), the world champion prizefighter Muhammad Ali (b. 1942), and the controversial reformer and religious leader Malcolm X (1925–1965). King saw their rejection of white society (and consequently brotherhood) as a threat.

[16] **a frightening racial nightmare** The black uprisings of the 1960s in all major American cities, and the conditions that led to them, were indeed a racial nightmare. King's prophecy was quick to come true.

[17] ***Zeitgeist*** German word for the intellectual, moral, and cultural spirit of the times.

the city hall; let him go on freedom rides[18]—and try to understand why he must do so. If his repressed emotions are not released in nonviolent ways, they will seek expression through violence; this is not a threat but a fact of history. So I have not said to my people, "Get rid of your discontent." Rather, I have tried to say that this normal and healthy discontent can be channeled into the creative outlet of nonviolent direct action. And now this approach is being termed extremist.

But though I was initially disappointed at being categorized as an   31
extremist, as I continued to think about the matter I gradually gained a measure of satisfaction from the label. Was not Jesus an extremist for love: "Love your enemies, bless them that curse you, do good to them that hate you, and pray for them which despitefully use you, and persecute you." Was not Amos an extremist for justice: "Let justice roll down like waters and righteousness like an ever-flowing stream." Was not Paul an extremist for the Christian gospel: "I bear in my body the marks of the Lord Jesus." Was not Martin Luther an extremist: "Here I stand; I cannot do otherwise, so help me God." And John Bunyan: "I will stay in jail to the end of my days before I make a butchery of my conscience." And Abraham Lincoln: "This nation cannot survive half slave and half free." And Thomas Jefferson: "We hold these truths to be self-evident, that all men are created equal . . ."[19] So the question is not whether we will be extremists, but what kind of extremists we will be. Will we be extremists for hate or for love? Will we be extremists for the preservation of injustice or for the extension of justice? In that dramatic scene on Calvary's hill three men were crucified. We must never forget that all three were crucified for the same crime—the crime of extremism. Two were extremists for immorality, and thus fell below their environment. The other, Jesus Christ, was an extremist for love, truth, and goodness, and thereby rose above his environment. Perhaps the South, the nation, and the world are in dire need of creative extremists.

---

[18] **freedom rides** In 1961 the Congress of Racial Equality (CORE) organized rides of whites and blacks to test segregation in southern buses and bus terminals with interstate passengers. More than 600 federal marshals were needed to protect the riders, most of whom were arrested.

[19] **Amos, Old Testament prophet (eighth century B.C.); Paul (?–A.D. 67); Martin Luther (1483–1546); John Bunyan (1628–1688); Abraham Lincoln (1809–1865); and Thomas Jefferson (1743–1826)** These figures are all noted for religious, moral, or political innovations that changed the world. Amos was a prophet who favored social justice; Paul argued against Roman law; Luther began the Reformation of the Christian Church; Bunyan was imprisoned for preaching the gospel according to his own understanding; Lincoln freed America's slaves; Jefferson drafted the Declaration of Independence.

I had hoped that the white moderate would see this need. Per- 32
haps I was too optimistic; perhaps I expected too much. I suppose I
should have realized that few members of the oppressor race can understand the deep groans and passionate yearnings of the oppressed
race, and still fewer have the vision to see that injustice must be
rooted out by strong, persistent, and determined action. I am thankful, however, that some of our white brothers in the South have
grasped the meaning of this social revolution and committed themselves to it. They are still all too few in quantity, but they are big in
quality. Some—such as Ralph McGill, Lillian Smith, Harry Golden,
James McBride Dabbs, Ann Braden, and Sarah Patton Boyle—have
written about our struggle[20] in eloquent and prophetic terms. Others
have marched with us down nameless streets of the South. They have
languished in filthy, roach-infested jails, suffering the abuse and brutality of policemen who view them as "dirty nigger-lovers." Unlike so
many of their moderate brothers and sisters, they have recognized the
urgency of the moment and sensed the need for powerful "action" an-
tidotes to combat the disease of segregation.

Let me take note of my other major disappointment. I have been 33
so greatly disappointed with the white church and its leadership. Of
course, there are some notable exceptions. I am not unmindful of the
fact that each of you has taken some significant stands on this issue. I
commend you, Reverend Stallings, for your Christian stand on this
past Sunday, in welcoming Negroes to your worship service on a
nonsegregated basis. I commend the Catholic leaders of this state for
integrating Spring Hill College several years ago.

But despite these notable exceptions, I must honestly reiterate 34
that I have been disappointed with the church. I do not say this as
one of those negative critics who can always find something wrong
with the church. I say this as a minister of the gospel, who loves the
church; who was nurtured in its bosom; who has been sustained by
its spiritual blessings and who will remain true to it as long as the
cord of life shall lengthen.

When I was suddenly catapulted into the leadership of the bus 35
protest in Montgomery, Alabama, a few years ago, I felt we would be
supported by the white church. I felt that the white ministers,
priests, and rabbis of the South would be among our strongest allies.
Instead, some have been outright opponents, refusing to understand

---

[20]**written about our struggle** These are all prominent southern writers who
expressed their feelings regarding segregation in the South. Some of them, like Smith
and Golden, wrote very popular books with a wide influence. Some, like McGill and
Smith, were severely rebuked by white southerners.

the freedom movement and misrepresenting its leaders; all too many others have been more cautious than courageous and have remained silent behind the anesthetizing security of stained-glass windows.

In spite of my shattered dreams, I came to Birmingham with the   36 hope that the white religious leadership of this community would see the justice of our cause and, with deep moral concern, would serve as the channel through which our just grievances could reach the power structure. I had hoped that each of you would understand. But again I have been disappointed. . . .

There was a time when the church was very powerful—in the   37 time when the early Christians rejoiced at being deemed worthy to suffer for what they believed. In those days the church was not merely a thermometer that recorded the ideas and principles of popular opinion; it was a thermostat that transformed the mores of society. Whenever the early Christians entered a town, the people in power became disturbed and immediately sought to convict the Christians for being "disturbers of the peace" and "outside agitators." But the Christians pressed on, in the conviction that they were "a colony of heaven," called to obey God rather than man. Small in number, they were big in commitment. They were too God-intoxicated to be "astronomically intimidated." By their effort and example they brought an end to such ancient evils as infanticide and gladiatorial contests.

Things are different now. So often the contemporary church is a   38 weak, ineffectual voice with an uncertain sound. So often it is an archdefender of the status quo. Far from being disturbed by the presence of the church, the powerful structure of the average community is consoled by the church's silent—and often even vocal— sanction of things as they are.

But the judgment of God is upon the church as never before. If   39 today's church does not recapture the sacrificial spirit of the early church, it will lose its authenticity, forfeit the loyalty of millions, and be dismissed as an irrelevant social club with no meaning for the twentieth century. Every day I meet young people whose disappointment with the church has turned into outright disgust.

Perhaps I have once again been too optimistic. Is organized reli-   40 gion too inextricably bound to the status quo to save our nation and the world? Perhaps I must turn my faith to the inner spiritual church, the church within the church, as the true *ekklesia*[21] and the

---

[21] **ekklesia** Greek word for "church" meaning not just the institution but the spirit of the church.

hope of the world. But again I am thankful to God that some noble souls from the ranks of organized religion have broken loose from the paralyzing chains of conformity and joined us as active partners in the struggle for freedom. They have left their secure congregations and walked the streets of Albany, Georgia, with us. They have gone down the highways of the South on torturous rides for freedom. Yes, they have gone to jail with us. Some have been dismissed from their churches, have lost the support of their bishops and fellow ministers. But they have acted in the faith that right defeated is stronger than evil triumphant. Their witness has been the spiritual salt that has preserved the true meaning of the gospel in these troubled times. They have carved a tunnel of hope through the dark mountain of disappointment.

I hope the church as a whole will meet the challenge of this decisive hour. But even if the church does not come to the aid of justice, I have no despair about the future. I have no fear about the outcome of our struggle in Birmingham, even if our motives are at present misunderstood. We will reach the goal of freedom in Birmingham and all over the nation, because the goal of America is freedom. Abused and scorned though we may be, our destiny is tied up with America's destiny. Before the pilgrims landed at Plymouth, we were here. Before the pen of Jefferson etched the majestic words of the Declaration of Independence across the pages of history, we were here. For more than two centuries our forebears labored in this country without wages; they made cotton king; they built the homes of their masters while suffering gross injustice and shameful humiliation—and yet out of a bottomless vitality they continued to thrive and develop. If the inexpressible cruelties of slavery could not stop us, the opposition we now face will surely fail. We will win our freedom because the sacred heritage of our nation and the eternal will of God are embodied in our echoing demands.

Before closing I feel impelled to mention one other point in your statement that has troubled me profoundly. You warmly commended the Birmingham police force for keeping "order" and "preventing violence." I doubt that you would have so warmly commended the police force if you had seen its dogs sinking their teeth into unarmed, nonviolent Negroes. I doubt that you would so quickly commend the policemen if you were to observe their ugly and inhumane treatment of Negroes here in the city jail; if you were to watch them push and curse old Negro women and young Negro girls; if you were to see them slap and kick old Negro men and young boys; if you were to observe them, as they did on two occasions, refuse to give us food because we wanted to sing our grace together. I cannot join you in your praise of the Birmingham police department.

It is true that the police have exercised a degree of discipline in   43
handling the demonstrators. In this sense they have conducted themselves rather "nonviolently" in public. But for what purpose? To preserve the evil system of segregation. Over the past few years I have
consistently preached that nonviolence demands that the means
we use must be as pure as the ends we seek. I have tried to make clear
that it is wrong to use immoral means to attain moral ends. But now I
must affirm that it is just as wrong, or perhaps even more so, to use
moral means to preserve immoral ends. Perhaps Mr. Connor and his
policemen have been rather nonviolent in public, as was Chief
Pritchett in Albany, Georgia, but they have used the moral means of
nonviolence to maintain the immoral end of racial injustice. As T. S.
Eliot[22] has said, "The last temptation is the greatest treason: To do
the right deed for the wrong reason."

I wish you had commended the Negro sit-inners and demonstra-   44
tors of Birmingham for their sublime courage, their willingness to suffer, and their amazing discipline in the midst of great provocation.
One day the South will recognize its real heroes. They will be the
James Merediths,[23] with the noble sense of purpose that enables them
to face jeering and hostile mobs, and with the agonizing loneliness
that characterizes the life of the pioneer. They will be old, oppressed,
battered Negro women, symbolized in a seventy-two-year-old woman
in Montgomery, Alabama, who rose up with a sense of dignity and
with her people decided not to ride segregated buses, and who responded with ungrammatical profundity to one who inquired about
her weariness: "My feets is tired, but my soul is at rest." They will be
the young high school and college students, the young ministers of
the gospel and a host of their elders, courageously and nonviolently
sitting in at lunch counters and willingly going to jail for conscience's
sake. One day the South will know that when these disinherited children of God sat down at lunch counters, they were in reality standing
up for what is best in the American dream and for the most sacred values in our Judaeo-Christian heritage, thereby bringing our nation

---

[22] **Thomas Stearns Eliot (1888–1965)** Renowned as one of the twentieth
century's major poets, Eliot was born in the United States but in 1927 became a
British subject and a member of the Church of England. Many of his poems focused
on religious and moral themes. These lines are from Eliot's play *Murder in the Cathe-
dral*, about Saint Thomas à Becket (1118–1170), the archbishop of Canterbury, who
was martyred for his opposition to King Henry II.

[23] **the James Merediths** James Meredith (b. 1933) was the first black to become a student at the University of Mississippi. His attempt to register for classes in
1962 created the first important confrontation between federal and state authorities,
when Governor Ross Barnett personally blocked Meredith's entry to the university.
Meredith graduated in 1963 and went on to study law at Columbia University.

back to those great wells of democracy which were dug deep by the founding fathers in their formulation of the Constitution and the Declaration of Independence.

Never before have I written so long a letter. I'm afraid it is much   45
too long to take your precious time. I can assure you that it would have been much shorter if I had been writing from a comfortable desk, but what else can one do when he is alone in a narrow jail cell, other than write long letters, think long thoughts, and pray long prayers?

If I have said anything in this letter that overstates the truth and   46
indicates an unreasonable impatience, I beg you to forgive me. If I have said anything that understates the truth and indicates my having a patience that allows me to settle for anything less than brotherhood, I beg God to forgive me.

I hope this letter finds you strong in the faith. I also hope that cir-   47
cumstances will soon make it possible for me to meet each of you, not as an integrationist or a civil rights leader but as a fellow clergyman and a Christian brother. Let us all hope that the dark clouds of racial prejudice will soon pass away and the deep fog of misunderstanding will be lifted from our fear-drenched communities, and in some not too distant tomorrow the radiant stars of love and brotherhood will shine over our great nation with all their scintillating beauty.

> Yours in the cause of
> Peace and Brotherhood,
> MARTIN LUTHER KING, JR.

QUESTIONS FOR CRITICAL READING

1. Define "nonviolent direct action" (para. 2). In what areas of human experience is it best implemented? Is politics its best area of application? What are the four steps in a nonviolent campaign?
2. Do you agree that "law and order exist for the purpose of establishing justice" (para. 24)? Why? Describe how law and order either do or do not establish justice in your community. Compare notes with your peers.
3. King describes an unjust law as "a code that a numerical or power majority group compels a minority group to obey but does not make binding on itself" (para. 17). Devise one or two other definitions of an unjust law. What unjust laws currently on the books do you disagree with?
4. What do you think is the best-written paragraph in the essay? Why?
5. King cites "tension" in paragraph 10 and elsewhere as a beneficial force. Do you agree? What kind of tension does he mean?
6. In what ways was King an extremist (paras. 30–31)?

7. In his letter, to what extent does King consider the needs of women? Would he feel that issues of women's rights are unrelated to issues of racial equality?

8. According to King, how should a government function in relation to the needs of the individual? Does he feel, like Thoreau's "Chinese philosopher," that the empire is built on the individual?

SUGGESTIONS FOR WRITING

1. Write a brief letter protesting an injustice that you feel may not be entirely understood by people you respect. Clarify the nature of the injustice, the reasons that people hold an unjust view, and the reasons your views should be accepted. Consult King's letter, and use his techniques.

2. In paragraph 43, King says, "I have consistently preached that nonviolence demands that the means we use must be as pure as the ends we seek." What does he mean by this? Define the ends he seeks and the means he approves. Do you agree with him on this point? If you have read the selection from Machiavelli, contrast their respective views. Which view seems more reasonable to you?

3. The first part of the letter defends King's journey to Birmingham as a Christian to help his fellows gain justice. He challenges the view that he is an outsider, using such expressions as "network of mutuality" and "garment of destiny" (para. 4). How effective is his argument? Examine the letter for other expressions that justify King's intervention on behalf of his brothers and sisters. Using his logic, describe other social areas where you might be justified in acting on your own views on behalf of humanity. Do you expect your endeavors would be welcomed? Are there any areas where you think it would be wrong to intervene?

4. In paragraphs 15–22, King discusses two kinds of laws—those that are morally right and those that are morally wrong. Which laws did King regard as morally right? Which laws did he consider morally wrong? Analyze one or two current laws that you feel are morally wrong. Be sure to be fair in describing the laws and establishing their nature. Then explain why you feel they are morally wrong. Would you feel justified in breaking these laws? Would you feel prepared, as King was, to pay the penalties demanded of one who breaks the law?

5. Compare King's letter with sections of Paul's letters to the faithful in the New Testament. Either choose a single letter, such as the Epistle to the Romans, or select passages from Romans, the two letters to the Corinthians, the Galatians, the Ephesians, the Thessalonians, or the Philippians. How did Paul and King agree and disagree about brotherly love, the mission of Christ, the mission of the church, concern for the law, and the duties of the faithful? Inventory the New Testament letters and King's letter carefully for concrete evidence of similar or contrary positions.

6. **SEEING CONNECTIONS**   Martin Luther King Jr. wrote "Letter from Birmingham Jail" on April 16, 1963, while awaiting trial for contempt

charges stemming from staging a march in Birmingham, Alabama, without a permit and in violation of a court injunction. King and others were convicted of the charges. They appealed their case to the U.S. Supreme Court, which found that "no man can be judge in his own case . . . however righteous his motives" (*Walker v. Birmingham*) and let the convictions stand. Wyatt Tee Walker (b. 1929), King's codefendant and friend, took the following photograph in October 1967 at the Jefferson County Courthouse in Birmingham as the two men served out their four-day sentences for contempt of court.

How does this photograph compare with the portrait of King on p. 170? How would you describe the mood of this scene? What do King's

facial expression and posture reveal about his reaction to being imprisoned? How effective is this photograph in establishing King's reputation as a leader of the civil rights movement?

7. **CONNECTIONS**   To what extent do Martin Luther King Jr.'s views about government coincide with those of Lao-tzu? Is there a legitimate comparison to be made between King's policy of nonviolent resistance and Lao-tzu's judicious inactivity? To what extent would King have agreed with Lao-tzu's views? Would Lao-tzu have supported King's position in his letter, or would he have interpreted events differently?

8. **CONNECTIONS**   King cites conscience as a guide to obeying just laws and defying unjust laws. How close is his position to that of Thoreau? Do you think that King had read Thoreau's "Civil Disobedience" as an important document regarding justice and injustice? Compare and contrast the positions of these two writers.

JOHN RAWLS
A Theory of Justice

JOHN RAWLS (1921–2002) was widely considered one of the most distinguished moral philosophers of the second half of the twentieth century. He was educated at Princeton University and served in the 32nd Infantry Division in New Guinea and the Philippines from 1943 to 1946. After returning to Princeton for his doctorate, he taught at Cornell, Oxford, Massachusetts Institute of Technology, and finally Harvard University, where he was Conant University Professor, the highest-level professorship at the university.

Rawls began to work out the ideas that eventually formed his most important book, *A Theory of Justice* (1971), in the 1950s, both in his earliest articles and in his notes for his lectures and teaching. He spent more than ten years refining his thinking on the subject, and in the process began to attract the attention of other thinkers concerned with problems of justice and equality. Much to his surprise, *A Theory of Justice* became a best-seller, and it has affected the discourse in justice and politics so widely that contemporary scholars cannot discuss these issues without paying homage to Rawls's work. In essence, he changed the direction of thought away from the Utilitarian — a system of justice that benefits the greatest number with the greatest good — to a system of justice based on fairness, in which any social action must be measured by its effect on the least advantaged people in the society. Rawls argued that if a social action were to harm an individual, that action should be avoided.

In *A Theory of Justice*, Rawls develops two basic ideas: the "original position" and the "veil of ignorance." In what is called a thought experiment similar to Plato's Allegory of the Cave, Rawls proposes a version of a social contract much like Rousseau's. However, the

---

From *A Theory of Justice*.

principles are different. In the "original position" concept, Rawls proposes an original starting point for a society in which the designers of the society make certain assumptions about the "Primary Goods"—freedom, equality, opportunity, wealth, powers, and income—that each person in the society must have. The planners of the society, much like Jefferson and those who constructed our Constitution, were to take into consideration all the desirable qualities important to a rational society. Then, to make things more interesting and fair, Rawls devised the concept of the "veil of ignorance" in which the planners and the members of the society made their decisions about the Primary Goods without knowing where they themselves would actually fall in the society in terms of their sex, race, birth, or talent. If they were kept ignorant of those facts, Rawls believed, their decisions would not be biased by personal circumstances. Rawls assumed that every individual was directed by self-interest first, so the "veil of ignorance" would prevent the creation of a social structure that would benefit only those who were deciding how justice would be allocated.

Above all, Rawls believed that justice must be fair and that the rights of the individual should never be sacrificed for the greater good of society. Personal freedom insofar as it did not impinge on the freedom of others was one of his most sacred values. Underlying all these ideas is the insistence that people are equal and should be treated equally.

One of Rawls's most controversial ideas is often referred to as the "difference principle." Rawls felt that any inequality produced by a social structure must be measured by its effect on the least advantaged people in the society. For instance, a tax structure that produced inequality of wealth in a community must be measured by its harmful or beneficial effect on those who are least wealthy, and not on the middle class or those with the most advantages. This position has been attacked in part because it seems to penalize those who have the talent to create wealth for themselves. Rawls responds by suggesting that the society he envisions can accept a certain amount of inequality of distribution of wealth, as long as it does not upset the equilibrium of the society. Exactly how this position is worked out in practice is not clear, but on a theoretical level it seems to suggest that a certain amount of unequal distribution of Primary Goods could result in an internal revolution, thus destroying the equilibrium of the society as a result of a perceived injustice. Justice cannot be fair if only a certain group has most of the wealth, opportunities, power, or income. Such a situation constitutes a loss of equilibrium.

Rawls's Rhetoric

Rawls is not considered a stylish writer; his purpose is not to convince us by means of a poetic or graceful style, but to present the basic ingredients of an argument. His approach is methodical in the sense that he begins with principles that are carefully defined, then moves on to show us how these principles would be applied and in what conditions they would be appropriate. In other words, this is a method that demands careful attention from the first sentences onward because everything flows from those early statements.

He begins by alluding to related theories, such as Jean-Jacques Rousseau's social contract, which suggests that people in a society agree to an unspoken contract that binds them to accept the conditions of the society or else leave. But Rawls ignores the bases of the contracts proposed by Rousseau and others, and by contrast alludes to principles that "free and rational persons concerned to further their own interests would accept in an initial position of equality as defining the fundamental terms of their association" (para. 1). Rawls ends his first paragraph with a statement of purpose and definition: "This way of regarding the principles of justice I shall call justice as fairness." This principle is fundamental to his argument.

Rawls develops the concept of the "original position" in the third paragraph: "This original position . . . is understood as a purely hypothetical situation characterized so as to lead to a certain conception of justice." Whereas Rousseau refers to a "state of nature" that may have existed in which people bound themselves to a society, Rawls attempts to formulate an ideal or hypothetical situation that conforms with views that he feels may guarantee fairness.

The fourth paragraph examines the idea that justice should guarantee fairness to everyone in the society. Rawls considers the nature of cooperation that naturally pertains to a social order in which people voluntarily and rationally decide to join. In paragraph 5 he addresses the question of interest, a term he uses to clarify the position of individuals in a just society. When he states that individuals are "rational and mutually disinterested" (para. 5), he means that individuals make decisions based on their own concerns, not those of others. A disinterested decision could only be made by someone who does not benefit from the outcome.

Rawls reminds us that those who are designing the social order from the original position must decide what "conception of justice as fairness" (para. 6) they will choose. To be sure, this is a difficult concept. The framers of the U.S. Constitution faced a similar prospect, and despite their concern with equality and fairness, they ignored the conditions of the least advantaged in their society: slaves. In the sixth paragraph Rawls mentions the principle of utility, which means the Utilitarian view that the best society provides the greatest good to the greatest number of people. In that view, the Constitution achieved a Utilitarian end, but that does not satisfy Rawls because it ignores the rights of the least advantaged.

The seventh paragraph establishes the bedrock principles by which Rawls expects justice to be established. The planners of the society must assign "rights and duties" in an equal fashion. Economic inequities can be tolerated only if they benefit the least advantaged members of society. This is a difficult provision to implement—but not to implement it would mean failure to achieve a justice of fairness, which is the demand Rawls makes in his opening pages.

Several of the latter paragraphs examine what Rawls calls "the merit of the contract terminology" (para. 10) so that we will have as firm an understanding of the idea of the social contract as we can. This discussion reminds us that when members of a society agree to join a community, those members are expected to abide by an implied contract of behavior.

Rawls does not, in this introductory segment to *A Theory of Justice*, propose concrete judgments as to how justice as fairness would be established. In later sections of his book he undertakes the examination of certain aspects of a social order in which justice as fairness functions. Yet, throughout his book, his principles remain those of the philosopher, essentially abstract and ideal. Nonetheless, his ideas, like those of Plato in his *Republic*, have implications for any society that expects its members to respect those who administer justice, for when justice cannot be achieved in a society, dire consequences ensue.

PREREADING QUESTIONS: WHAT TO READ FOR

The following prereading questions may help you anticipate key issues in the discussion of John Rawls's "A Theory of Justice." Keeping them in mind during your first reading of the selection should help focus your attention.

- How does Rawls articulate his idea of "justice as fairness"?
- What are the "primary goods" that people in a society need?
- What is Rawls's attitude toward the least advantaged people in society?

A Theory of Justice

My aim is to present a conception of justice which generalizes and carries to a higher level of abstraction the familiar theory of the social contract as found, say, in Locke, Rousseau, and Kant.[1] In order to do this we are not to think of the original contract as one to enter a particular society or to set up a particular form of government. Rather, the guiding idea is that the principles of justice for the basic structure of society are the object of the original agreement. They are the principles that free and rational persons concerned to further their own interests would accept in an initial position of equality as defining the fundamental terms of their association. These principles are to regulate all further agreements; they specify the kinds of social cooperation that can be entered into and the forms of government that can be established. This way of regarding the principles of justice I shall call justice as fairness.

Thus we are to imagine that those who engage in social cooperation choose together, in one joint act, the principles which are to assign basic rights and duties and to determine the division of social benefits. Men are to decide in advance how they are to regulate their claims against one another and what is to be the foundation charter of their society. Just as each person must decide by rational reflection what constitutes his good, that is, the system of ends which it is rational for him to pursue, so a group of persons must decide once and for all what is to count among them as just and unjust. The choice which rational men would make in this hypothetical situation of equal liberty, assuming for the present that this choice problem has a solution, determines the principles of justice.

In justice as fairness the original position of equality corresponds to the state of nature in the traditional theory of the social contract. This original position is not, of course, thought of as an actual historical state of affairs, much less as a primitive condition of culture. It is understood as a purely hypothetical situation characterized so as to

---

[1] As the text suggests, I shall regard Locke's *Second Treatise of Government*, Rousseau's *The Social Contract*, and Kant's ethical works beginning with *The Foundations of the Metaphysics of Morals* as definitive of the contract tradition. For all of its greatness, Hobbes's *Leviathan* raises special problems. A general historical survey is provided by J. W. Gough, *The Social Contract*, 2nd ed. (Clarendon Press: Oxford, 1957), and Otto Gierke, *Natural Law and the Theory of Society*, trans. with an introduction by Ernest Barker (Cambridge University Press: Cambridge, 1934). A presentation of the contract view as primarily an ethical theory is to be found in G. R. Grice, *The Grounds of Moral Judgment* (Cambridge University Press: Cambridge, 1967). [Rawls's note]

lead to a certain conception of justice.[2] Among the essential features
of this situation is that no one knows his place in society, his class
position or social status, nor does any one know his fortune in the
distribution of natural assets and abilities, his intelligence, strength,
and the like. I shall even assume that the parties do not know their
conceptions of the good or their special psychological propensities.
The principles of justice are chosen behind a veil of ignorance. This
ensures that no one is advantaged or disadvantaged in the choice of
principles by the outcome of natural chance or the contingency of
social circumstances. Since all are similarly situated and no one is
able to design principles to favor his particular condition, the principles of justice are the result of a fair agreement or bargain. For given
the circumstances of the original position, the symmetry of everyone's relations to each other, this initial situation is fair between individuals as moral persons, that is, as rational beings with their own
ends and capable, I shall assume, of a sense of justice. The original
position is, one might say, the appropriate initial status quo, and thus
the fundamental agreements reached in it are fair. This explains the
propriety of the name "justice as fairness": it conveys the idea that the
principles of justice are agreed to in an initial situation that is fair.
The name does not mean that the concepts of justice and fairness
are the same, any more than the phrase "poetry as metaphor" means
that the concepts of poetry and metaphor are the same.

Justice as fairness begins, as I have said, with one of the most   4
general of all choices which persons might make together, namely
with the choice of the first principles of a conception of justice which
is to regulate all subsequent criticism and reform of institutions.
Then, having chosen a conception of justice, we can suppose that
they are to choose a constitution and a legislature to enact laws, and
so on, all in accordance with the principles of justice initially agreed
upon. Our social situation is just if it is such that by this sequence of
hypothetical agreements we would have contracted into the general
system of rules which defines it. Moreover, assuming that the original
position does determine a set of principles (that is, that a particular
conception of justice would be chosen), it will then be true that

---

[2] Kant is clear that the original agreement is hypothetical. See *The Metaphysics of
Morals*, pt. I (*Rechtslehre*), especially §§ 47, 52; and pt. II of the essay "Concerning
the Common Saying: This May Be True in Theory but It Does Not Apply in Practice," in *Kant's Political Writings*, ed. Hans Reiss and trans. H. B. Nisbet (Cambridge
University Press: Cambridge, 1970), 73–87. See Georges Vlachos, *La Pensée politique
de Kant* (Presses Universitaires de France: Paris, 1962), 326–35; and J. G. Murphy,
Kant: The Philosophy of Right (Macmillan: London, 1970), 109–12, 133–6, for a further discussion. [Rawls's note]

whenever social institutions satisfy these principles those engaged in them can say to one another that they are cooperating on terms to which they would agree if they were free and equal persons whose relations with respect to one another were fair. They could all view their arrangements as meeting the stipulations which they would acknowledge in an initial situation that embodies widely accepted and reasonable constraints on the choice of principles. The general recognition of this fact would provide the basis for a public acceptance of the corresponding principles of justice. No society can, of course, be a scheme of cooperation which men enter voluntarily in a literal sense; each person finds himself placed at birth in some particular position in some particular society, and the nature of this position materially affects his life prospects. Yet a society satisfying the principles of justice as fairness comes as close as a society can to being a voluntary scheme, for it meets the principles which free and equal persons would assent to under circumstances that are fair. In this sense its members are autonomous and the obligations they recognize self-imposed.

One feature of justice as fairness is to think of the parties in the   5
initial situation as rational and mutually disinterested. This does not mean that the parties are egoists, that is, individuals with only certain kinds of interests, say in wealth, prestige, and domination. But they are conceived as not taking an interest in one another's interests. They are to presume that even their spiritual aims may be opposed, in the way that the aims of those of different religions may be opposed. Moreover, the concept of rationality must be interpreted as far as possible in the narrow sense, standard in economic theory, of taking the most effective means to given ends. I shall modify this concept to some extent, but one must try to avoid introducing into it any controversial ethical elements. The initial situation must be characterized by stipulations that are widely accepted.

In working out the conception of justice as fairness one main   6
task clearly is to determine which principles of justice would be chosen in the original position. To do this we must describe this situation in some detail and formulate with care the problem of choice which it presents. . . . It may be observed, however, that once the principles of justice are thought of as arising from an original agreement in a situation of equality, it is an open question whether the principle of utility would be acknowledged. Offhand it hardly seems likely that persons who view themselves as equals, entitled to press their claims upon one another, would agree to a principle which may require lesser life prospects for some simply for the sake of a greater sum of advantages enjoyed by others. Since each desires to protect his interests, his capacity to advance his conception of the good, no one has a reason to acquiesce in an enduring loss for himself in order to bring

about a greater net balance of satisfaction. In the absence of strong
and lasting benevolent impulses, a rational man would not accept a
basic structure merely because it maximized the algebraic sum of
advantages irrespective of its permanent effects on his own basic
rights and interests. Thus it seems that the principle of utility is incompatible with the conception of social cooperation among equals
for mutual advantage. It appears to be inconsistent with the idea of
reciprocity implicit in the notion of a well-ordered society. Or, at
any rate, so I shall argue.

I shall maintain instead that the persons in the initial situation   7
would choose two rather different principles: the first requires equality in the assignment of basic rights and duties, while the second
holds that social and economic inequalities, for example inequalities
of wealth and authority, are just only if they result in compensating
benefits for everyone, and in particular for the least advantaged members of society. These principles rule out justifying institutions on the
grounds that the hardships of some are offset by a greater good in the
aggregate. It may be expedient but it is not just that some should
have less in order that others may prosper. But there is no injustice in
the greater benefits earned by a few provided that the situation of
persons not so fortunate is thereby improved. The intuitive idea is
that since everyone's well-being depends upon a scheme of cooperation without which no one could have a satisfactory life, the division of
advantages should be such as to draw forth the willing cooperation of
everyone taking part in it, including those less well situated. Yet this
can be expected only if reasonable terms are proposed. The two principles mentioned seem to be a fair agreement on the basis of which
those better endowed, or more fortunate in their social position, neither of which we can be said to deserve, could expect the willing
cooperation of others when some workable scheme is a necessary
condition of the welfare of all.[3] Once we decide to look for a conception of justice that nullifies the accidents of natural endowment and
the contingencies of social circumstance as counters in quest for political and economic advantage, we are led to these principles. They
express the result of leaving aside those aspects of the social world
that seem arbitrary from a moral point of view.

The problem of the choice of principles, however, is extremely   8
difficult. I do not expect the answer I shall suggest to be convincing
to everyone. It is, therefore, worth noting from the outset that justice
as fairness, like other contract views, consists of two parts: (1) an

---

[3] For the formulation of this intuitive idea I am indebted to Allan Gibbard.
[Rawls's note]

interpretation of the initial situation and of the problem of choice posed there, and (2) a set of principles which, it is argued, would be agreed to. One may accept the first part of the theory (or some variant thereof), but not the other, and conversely. The concept of the initial contractual situation may seem reasonable although the particular principles proposed are rejected. To be sure, I want to maintain that the most appropriate conception of this situation does lead to principles of justice contrary to utilitarianism and perfectionism, and therefore that the contract doctrine provides an alternative to these views. Still, one may dispute this contention even though one grants that the contractarian method is a useful way of studying ethical theories and of setting forth their underlying assumptions.

Justice as fairness is an example of what I have called a contract theory. Now there may be an objection to the term "contract" and related expressions, but I think it will serve reasonably well. Many words have misleading connotations which at first are likely to confuse. The terms "utility" and "utilitarianism" are surely no exception. They too have unfortunate suggestions which hostile critics have been willing to exploit; yet they are clear enough for those prepared to study utilitarian doctrine. The same should be true of the term "contract" applied to moral theories. As I have mentioned, to understand it one has to keep in mind that it implies a certain level of abstraction. In particular, the content of the relevant agreement is not to enter a given society or to adopt a given form of government, but to accept certain moral principles. Moreover, the undertakings referred to are purely hypothetical: a contract view holds that certain principles would be accepted in a well-defined initial situation.

The merit of the contract terminology is that it conveys the idea that principles of justice may be conceived as principles that would be chosen by rational persons, and that in this way conceptions of justice may be explained and justified. The theory of justice is a part, perhaps the most significant part, of the theory of rational choice. Furthermore, principles of justice deal with conflicting claims upon the advantages won by social cooperation; they apply to the relations among several persons or groups. The word "contract" suggests this plurality as well as the condition that the appropriate division of advantages must be in accordance with principles acceptable to all parties. The condition of publicity for principles of justice is also connoted by the contract phraseology. Thus, if these principles are the outcome of an agreement, citizens have a knowledge of the principles that others follow. It is characteristic of contract theories to stress the public nature of political principles. Finally there is the long tradition of the contract doctrine. Expressing the tie with this line of thought helps to define ideas and accords with natural piety. There are then several advantages in the use of the term "contract." With due precautions taken, it should not be misleading.

A final remark. Justice as fairness is not a complete contract the-   11
ory. For it is clear that the contractarian idea can be extended to the choice of more or less an entire ethical system, that is, to a system including principles for all the virtues and not only for justice. Now for the most part I shall consider only principles of justice and others closely related to them; I make no attempt to discuss the virtues in a systematic way. Obviously if justice as fairness succeeds reasonably well, a next step would be to study the more general view suggested by the name "rightness as fairness." But even this wider theory fails to embrace all moral relationships, since it would seem to include only our relations with other persons and to leave out of account how we are to conduct ourselves toward animals and the rest of nature. I do not contend that the contract notion offers a way to approach these questions which are certainly of the first importance; and I shall have to put them aside. We must recognize the limited scope of justice as fairness and of the general type of view that it exemplifies. How far its conclusions must be revised once these other matters are understood cannot be decided in advance.

QUESTIONS FOR CRITICAL READING

1. What is the "original position"? Why do you think Rawls named it so?
2. What personal qualities will people who are planning society in the original position need to have?
3. Rawls says the planners must be disinterested, or totally objective. How does the "veil of ignorance" help them achieve the desired level of objectivity?
4. Why is justice as fairness a desirable goal in society?
5. At the end of paragraph 3 Rawls states that justice and fairness are not the same thing. How does his example of distinguishing between poetry and metaphor explain his position?
6. Rawls states: "In justice as fairness the original position of equality corresponds to the state of nature in the traditional theory of the social contract" (para. 3). What does he mean by this, and what do the terms "state of nature" and "original position" mean to you?
7. One of the qualifications for people planning justice as fairness is that they be "rational and mutually disinterested." Why are these important qualities? How is justice as fairness harmed if the planners are not rational or if they operate only from self-interest?
8. In paragraph 6 Rawls suggests that rational planners would not conceive of a society that gave fewer opportunities to some people for the

sake of giving many more to others. Do you agree? Do you think our society operates on this rational principle?

9. What for you is the most important decision a society can make to help guarantee a justice of fairness?

SUGGESTIONS FOR WRITING

1. Keeping in mind that this selection is theoretical in nature and not a practical description of how justice should be applied in a society, offer a critique of the social order Rawls describes in which some people with the ability to make lots of money may have to share a great deal of it with others who make less. What is Rawls's position on such a situation? What is yours? How can you guarantee justice in a society that permits a small number of people to be extremely wealthy while many are relatively poor?

2. Rawls believes that justice must be fair. Do you feel that the system of justice under which we live is fair? Do you think that our system of justice is based on a workable conception of what fairness should be? Do you think justice should be fair? What prevents it from being so?

3. If you were one of the people given the job of designing a "conception of justice" for a society in which you would choose to live, what would you expect of that society in terms of fairness and justice? Can you possibly construct an ideal society without factoring in your own special circumstances, such as your gender, race, ethnicity, social status, level of privilege, or level of education? Rawls wants to factor those issues out of the process. Can you do that? Can anyone? If not, can any system of justice be fair?

4. The Utilitarian position emphasizes a form of justice in which the greatest good for the greatest number of people dictates social decisions. Since the nineteenth century, this view, sometimes called the principle of utility, has been fairly dominant in Western democracies. However, Rawls condemns this view because it does not improve the condition of the least advantaged members of society. In fact, it may even harm such people. What is your position on Rawls's rejection of utility? How carefully must a society that values justice work to prevent enacting laws that might make worse the lives of the least advantaged?

5. One of the most important of the "Primary Goods" Rawls considers is equality. Construct an essay in which you define what you think social equality means, taking into consideration such individual differences as genetic makeup, health, intelligence, and physical attributes. How should differences in gender, sexual orientation, or physical prowess be considered in any society that values equality? Why is equality a desirable goal? How can it be achieved?

6. Many religions have taken considered positions on questions of equality. For example, in some synagogues and mosques, men and women

cannot worship together. Some religions hold that women are inferior by nature and therefore must be ruled entirely by their husbands or fathers. A religion may forbid women to work outside the home or discourage educating children of either sex beyond grade school. How should a society that values equality and religious freedom resolve conflicts when such fundamental beliefs intersect and clash?

7. **CONNECTIONS**   Thomas Jefferson was in a position similar to those figures Rawls imagines planning a social order based on justice as fairness. What elements of the Declaration of Independence seem to aim toward goals Rawls would find acceptable? Do you feel Jefferson would have shared Rawls's views about trying to avoid any social decisions that might harm the least advantaged citizen? Would Jefferson have had the most advantaged people in society make sacrifices in order to avoid harming the least advantaged? Would you?

8. **CONNECTIONS**   Rawls suggests that what he describes is not really a total contract theory. Turn to Jean-Jacques Rousseau's "The Origin of Civil Society" and try to see how close these two writers are in their view of how a society forms itself and what kind of implicit contract people make with each other when they decide to create and maintain a social order. How concerned is Rousseau with the concept of justice? How much do Rousseau and Rawls have in common regarding their sense of what society should be like?

MARTHA C. NUSSBAUM
The Central Human Functional
Capabilities

MARTHA C. NUSSBAUM (b. 1947) is Ernst Freund Distinguished Service Professor of Law and Ethics at the University of Chicago, with appointments in the Philosophy Department and Divinity School. She is known for her work in philosophy and literature and for crossing disciplinary boundaries in an effort to examine principles of justice and the nature of law. She has taught at many universities, including Brown and Oxford, and is distinguished by having been awarded twenty-two honorary degrees.

She has a special interest in classical literature and has commented on Cicero, among others. Among her publications are several important books. *The Fragility of Goodness: Luck and Ethics in Greek Tragedy and Philosophy* (1986) draws on all the major works of the important Greek playwrights and philosophers. *Cultivating Humanity: A Classical Defense of Reform in Liberal Education* (1997) is a defense of using classical texts in a liberal education, with the purpose of educating people to become "citizens of the world." Among her other books are *Love's Knowledge: Essays on Philosophy and Literature* (1990) and two collections of lectures: *Poetic Justice: The Literary Imagination and Public Life* (1995) and *The Therapy of Desire: Theory and Practice in Hellenistic Ethics* (1994).

Sex and Social Justice (1999), in which the following selection appears, concerns the unequal treatment of women and gays. In her statements of intention in the book, she insists on an international attitude toward the problems of justice toward these groups. One word that constantly recurs in her writing is "equality," echoing Thomas Jefferson.

From *Sex and Social Justice.*

In the selection, Nussbaum focuses on a novel concept of capability. She sees justice as expressed not necessarily in what a person actually does as much as in what a person should be capable of doing. She takes a position that echoes John Rawls's concept of the "Primary Goods" that should be guaranteed to individuals in a just society, but she sees many other kinds of "goods" and expresses them in terms of capability. Nussbaum argues, for instance, that all people should be guaranteed the capability of getting an education, having enough to eat, having decent housing, having good health. If a person chooses not to get an education, or to fast rather than eat, or to live out of doors, or to avoid vaccinations, Nussbaum can tolerate those choices, behaviors, and cultural differences. How people choose to act is one thing, but the opportunity—or capability—to act represents a type of justice Nussbaum wishes to guarantee.

Nussbaum's Rhetoric

This selection is part of the opening chapter of her book. It is also part of an argument that began by considering non-Western societies' treatment, by tradition and by religion, of women. Nussbaum had begun with the example of a widowed Indian woman who by tradition could not leave her home to work and therefore feared she and her children would starve to death. This was an extreme example of the different ways in which a society structures itself in relation to custom, but it raised the question of whether there were universal values that all societies should aspire to. For example, female genital mutilation has been practiced in a number of societies for hundreds of years (or more). Such mutilation makes it impossible for a woman to enjoy sexual intercourse. Westerners who condemn this practice are accused of being imperial for imposing their values on non-Western societies. In her essay, Nussbaum looks for ways in which basic "capabilities" can be imagined for all people in all societies, with the understanding that choices made within societies will sometimes ignore the capabilities that any society should provide individuals.

The argument is subtle in many ways. Nussbaum is aware that most arguments of this type are normative in nature: they decide what is normal or desirable and argue that point. Her view is that people will approach many complex issues in different ways and should be permitted to do as they wish, just so long as they have the capability of doing otherwise.

Preliminary to her detailed discussion, Nussbaum begins by trying to establish what we mean when we say that someone is human. This seems simple enough, but she knows that people can live frighteningly animal-like existences, barely surviving, while we all wish for ourselves a life that is filled with potential and opportunity to live much more fully. Nussbaum also writes in reference to a quotation from the legal theorist Catharine MacKinnon, who has said, "Being a woman is not yet a way of being a human being." To emphasize that point, Nussbaum used this expression as an epigraph to her book *Sex and Social Justice*.

Nussbaum's argument has two parts. The first part defines the capabilities that she sees as essential for a person to live a truly human life. She uses the rhetorical device of enumeration, with ten items defining the "Central Human Functional Capabilities," which are related to John Rawls's "Primary Goods": freedom, equality, opportunity, wealth, powers, and income. His list is general, while Nussbaum's is more detailed and descriptive. As she states, her list isolates "some functions that seem central in defining the very presence of a human life" (para. 5), although she wishes to insist on moving beyond a merely functioning to a fully functioning human life. The distinction between capability and functioning is important in that Nussbaum presumes that once the capability to achieve something is available, the individual will turn that capability into a functional reality. In other words, it is not enough just to have the right to vote, but it is important to make a clear choice to vote (or not). One functions when one expresses a choice through behavior.

As Nussbaum explains at the end of paragraph 5, her purpose is to "introduce this as a list of capabilities rather than of actual functionings, because I shall argue that capability, not actual functioning, should be the goal of public policy." She explains not what people ought to do, but the range of freedom they should have in their choices.

In the second part of her argument, Nussbaum analyzes the ideas that underlie her concept of "Capability as Goal." But she also sees that it is possible to measure governments in terms of their making capabilities available to their citizens. As she states, "The question that should be asked when assessing quality of life in a country—and of course this is a central part of assessing the quality of its political arrangements—is, How well have the people of the country been enabled to perform the central human functions?" (para. 18). For Nussbaum, the degree to which justice is available in a society correlates with the ability of people to "perform the central human functions" enumerated in her list.

But in this second part of the argument, Nussbaum also makes a considerable effort to accommodate the various cultural differences that naturally affect people in many regions of the world. She is trying to avoid simply imposing her values on other people, a practice that she has seen as common in imperial governments' dealings with less industrialized populations. She wishes to argue for women's equality and human rights, but she wishes to do so without denying people's right to behave as they see fit.

In paragraph 20 Nussbaum addresses the distinction between functioning and capability. The way in which they differ is in the fact that when an imperial power tells a culture how it ought to function, it is imposing its values on that culture. However, when anyone insists that the capabilities to function in one of several ways must exist for people to live a truly human life, then it is up to the individual who possesses these capabilities to function as he or she chooses. Thus, one sees that Nussbaum's views are similar to some of John Rawls's, especially in terms of her agreement that it is the individual in a society, not the collective, that must be protected and preserved if true justice is to prevail.

In paragraph 22, Nussbaum enumerates the three kinds of capabilities. First are "basic capabilities," which enable most individuals to develop fully as human beings. Second are "internal capabilities," which are the capabilities that the grown individual will have in order to actually function in relation to a capability. For example, as Nussbaum mentions, a woman who has undergone genital mutilation would not have the internal capability for achieving sexual gratification. Another example would be the capacity to speak, which would usually be needed in order to enjoy the capability of freedom of speech. Third are what Nussbaum calls "combined capabilities," which are the combination of all basic and internal capabilities with a political and social environment that encourages those capabilities to become potential functionings. At this point, Nussbaum moves deeply into the political issues that impinge on the concept of justice as it applies to the individual.

PREREADING QUESTIONS: WHAT TO READ FOR

The following prereading questions may help you anticipate key issues in the discussion of Martha Nussbaum's "The Central Human Capabilities." Keeping them in mind during your first reading of the selection should help focus your attention.

- What are the central human capabilities?
- What is the difference between capability and functioning?
- How does the possession of the basic human capabilities represent social justice?

The Central Human Capabilities

The list of basic capabilities is generated by asking a question   1
that from the start is evaluative: What activities characteristically
performed by human beings are so central that they seem definitive
of a life that is truly human? In other words, what are the functions
without which (meaning, without the availability of which) we
would regard a life as not, or not fully, human? We can get at this
question better if we approach it via two somewhat more concrete
questions that we often really ask ourselves. First is a question
about personal continuity. We ask ourselves which changes or
transitions are compatible with the continued existence of that
being as a member of the human kind and which are not. Some
functions can fail to be present without threatening our sense that
we still have a human being on our hands; the absence of others
seems to signal the end of a human life. This question is asked regularly, when we attempt to make medical definitions of death in a
situation in which some of the functions of life persist, or to decide,
for others or (thinking ahead) for ourselves, whether a certain level
of illness or impairment means the end of the life of the being in
question.

The other question is a question about kind inclusion. We rec-   2
ognize other humans as human across many differences of time and
place, of custom and appearance. We often tell ourselves stories, on
the other hand, about anthropomorphic creatures who do not get
classified as human, on account of some feature of their form of life
and functioning. On what do we base these inclusions and exclu-
sions? In short, what do we believe must be there, if we are going to
acknowledge that a given life is human? The answer to these questions points us to a subset of common or characteristic human functions, informing us that these are likely to have a special importance
for everything else we choose and do.

Note that the procedure through which this account of the   3
human is derived is neither ahistorical nor a priori.[1] It is the attempt
to summarize empirical findings of a broad and ongoing cross-
cultural inquiry. As such, it is both open-ended and humble; it can
always be contested and remade. Nor does it claim to read facts of
"human nature" from biological observation; it takes biology into
account as a relatively constant element in human experience. It is

---

[1] **neither ahistorical nor a priori** The procedure is not ignorant of historical
issues, nor does it consider ideas decided in advance (*a priori* means beforehand).

because the account is evaluative from the start that it is called a conception of the good.

It should also be stressed that, like John Rawls's account of primary goods in *A Theory of Justice*,[2] this list of good functions, which is in some ways more comprehensive than his own list, is proposed as the object of a specifically political consensus. The political is not understood exactly as Rawls understands it because the nation state is not assumed to be the basic unit, and the account is meant to have broad applicablity to cross-cultural deliberations. This means, given the current state of world politics, that many of the obligations to promote the adequate distribution of these goods must rest with individuals rather than with any political institution, and in that way its role becomes difficult to distinguish from the role of other norms and goals of the individual. Nonetheless, the point of the list is the same as that of Rawlsian primary goods: to put forward something that people from many different traditions, with many different fuller conceptions of the good, can agree on, as the necessary basis for pursuing their good life. That is why the list is deliberately rather general. Each of its components can be more concretely specified in accordance with one's origins, religious beliefs, or tastes. In that sense, the consensus that it hopes to evoke has many of the features of the "overlapping consensus" described by Rawls.

Having isolated some functions that seem central in defining 5 the very presence of a human life, we do not rest content with mere bare humanness. We want to specify a life in which fully human functioning, or a kind of basic human flourishing, will be available. For we do not want politics to take mere survival as its goal; we want to describe a life in which the dignity of the human being is not violated by hunger or fear or the absence of opportunity. (The idea is very much Marx's idea, when he used an Aristotelian notion of functioning to describe the difference between a merely animal use of one's faculties and a "truly human use.") The following list of central human functional capabilities is an attempt to specify this basic notion of the good: All citizens should have these capabilities, whatever else they have and pursue. I introduce this as a list of capabilities rather than of actual functionings, because I shall argue that capability, not actual functioning, should be the goal of public policy.

---

[2] *A Theory of Justice*   A reference to John Rawls's book, from which the previous selection comes.

Central Human Functional Capabilities

1. *Life.* Being able to live to the end of a human life of normal   6
   length; not dying prematurely or before one's life is so reduced
   as to be not worth living
2. *Bodily health and integrity.* Being able to have good health, in-   7
   cluding reproductive health; being adequately nourished; being
   able to have adequate shelter
3. *Bodily integrity.* Being able to move freely from place to place;   8
   being able to be secure against violent assault, including sexual
   assault, marital rape, and domestic violence; having opportunities for sexual satisfaction and for choice in matters of reproduction
4. *Senses, imagination, thought.* Being able to use the senses; being   9
   able to imagine, to think, and to reason—and to do these
   things in a "truly human" way, a way informed and cultivated
   by an adequate education, including, but by no means limited
   to, literacy and basic mathematical and scientific training; being
   able to use imagination and thought in connection with experiencing and producing expressive works and events of one's own
   choice (religious, literary, musical, etc.); being able to use one's
   mind in ways protected by guarantees of freedom of expression
   with respect to both political and artistic speech and freedom of
   religious exercise; being able to have pleasurable experiences
   and to avoid nonbeneficial pain
5. *Emotions.* Being able to have attachments to things and persons   10
   outside ourselves; being able to love those who love and care for
   us; being able to grieve at their absence; in general, being able to
   love, to grieve, to experience longing, gratitude, and justified
   anger; not having one's emotional developing blighted by fear
   or anxiety. (Supporting this capability means supporting forms
   of human association that can be shown to be crucial in their
   development.)
6. *Practical reason.* Being able to form a conception of the good and   11
   to engage in critical reflection about the planning of one's own
   life. (This entails protection for the liberty of conscience.)
7. *Affiliation.* (a) Being able to live for and in relation to others, to   12
   recognize and show concern for other human beings, to engage
   in various forms of social interaction; being able to imagine the
   situation of another and to have compassion for that situation;
   having the capability for both justice and friendship. (Protecting this capability means, once again, protecting institutions
   that constitute such forms of affiliation, and also protecting

the freedoms of assembly and political speech.) (b) Having
the social bases of self-respect and nonhumiliation; being
able to be treated as a dignified being whose worth is equal
to that of others. (This entails provisions of nondiscrimi-
nation.)

8. *Other species.* Being able to live with concern for and in relation   13
   to animals, plants, and the world of nature

9. *Play.* Being able to laugh, to play, to enjoy recreational activ-   14
   ities

10. *Control over one's environment.* (a) *Political:* being able to partici-   15
    pate effectively in political choices that govern one's life; having
    the rights of political participation, free speech, and freedom of
    association (b) *Material:* being able to hold property (both
    land and movable goods); having the right to seek employment
    on an equal basis with others; having the freedom from unwar-
    ranted search and seizure. In work, being able to work as a
    human being, exercising practical reason and entering into
    meaningful relationships of mutual recognition with other
    workers.

The "capabilities approach," as I conceive it, claims that a life   16
that lacks any one of these capabilities, no matter what else it has,
will fall short of being a good human life. Thus it would be reasonable to take these things as a focus for concern, in assessing the
quality of life in a country and asking about the role of public policy
in meeting human needs. The list is certainly general—and this is
deliberate, to leave room for plural specification and also for further
negotiation. But like (and as a reasonable basis for) a set of constitutional guarantees, it offers real guidance to policymakers, and far
more accurate guidance than that offered by the focus on utility, or
even on resources.

The list is, emphatically, a list of separate components. We can-   17
not satisfy the need for one of them by giving a larger amount of another one. All are of central importance and all are distinct in quality.
This limits the trade-offs that it will be reasonable to make and thus
limits the applicability of quantitative cost-benefit analysis. At the
same time, the items on the list are related to one another in many
complex ways. Employment rights, for example, support health, and
also freedom from domestic violence, by giving women a better
bargaining position in the family. The liberties of speech and association turn up at several distinct points on the list, showing their
fundamental role with respect to several distinct areas of human
functioning.

Capability as Goal

The basic claim I wish to make — concurring with Amartya   18
Sen[3] — is that the central goal of public planning should be the
capabilities of citizens to perform various important functions. The
question that should be asked when assessing quality of life in a
country — and of course this is a central part of assessing the quality
of its political arrangements — is, How well have the people of the
country been enabled to perform the central human functions? And,
have they been put in a position of mere human subsistence with respect to the functions, or have they been enabled to live well? Politics, we argue (here concurring with Rawls), should focus on getting
as many people as possible into a state of capability to function, with
respect to the interlocking set of capabilities enumerated by that list.
Naturally, the determination of whether certain individuals and
groups are across the threshold is only as precise a matter as the determination of the threshold. I have left things deliberately somewhat open-ended at this point, in keeping with the procedures of
the *Human Development Report*,[4] believing that the best way to work
toward a more precise determination, at present, is to focus on comparative information and to allow citizens to judge for themselves
whether their policymakers have done as well as they should have.
Again, we will have to answer various questions about the costs we
are willing to pay to get all citizens above the threshold, as opposed
to leaving a small number below and allowing the rest a considerably above-threshold life quality. It seems likely, at any rate, that
moving all citizens above a basic threshold of capability should be
taken as a central social goal. When citizens are across the threshold,
societies are to a great extent free to choose the other goals they wish
to pursue. Some inequalities, however, will themselves count as capability failures. For example, inequalities based on hierarchies of
gender or race will themselves be inadmissible on the grounds that
they undermine self-respect and emotional development.

The basic intuition from which the capability approach starts,   19
in the political arena, is that human capabilities exert a moral claim
that they should be developed. Human beings are creatures such that,
provided with the right educational and material support, they can
become fully capable of the major human functions. That is, they are

---

[3]**Amartya Sen (b. 1933)** Indian-born Nobel Prize–winning economist is master at Trinity College, Cambridge, and author of books on economic inequality.

[4]**The Human Development Report** (Oxford U.P., 2003) monitors worldwide
issues related to health, education, and personal freedoms.

creatures with certain lower-level capabilities (which I call "basic capabilities") to perform the functions in question. When these capabilities are deprived of the nourishment that would transform them into the high-level capabilities that figure on my list, they are fruitless, cut off, in some way but a shadow of themselves. They are like actors who never get to go on the stage, or a person who sleeps all through life, or a musical score that is never performed. Their very being makes forward reference to functioning. Thus, if functioning never arrives on the scene they are hardly even what they are. This may sound like a metaphysical idea, and in a sense it is (in that it is an idea discussed in Aristotle's *Metaphysics*). But that does not mean it is not a basic and pervasive empirical idea, an idea that underwrites many of our daily practices and judgments in many times and places. Just as we hold that a child who dies before getting to maturity has died especially tragically—for her activities of growth and preparation for adult activity now have lost their point—so too with capability and functioning more generally: We believe that certain basic and central human endowments have a claim to be assisted in developing, and exert that claim on others, and especially, as Aristotle saw, on government. Without some such notion of the basic worth of human capacities, we have a hard time arguing for women's equality and for basic human rights. . . . If women were really just trees or turtles or filing cabinets, the fact that their current status in many parts of the world is not a fully human one would not be, as it is, a problem of justice. In thinking of political planning we begin, then, from a notion of the basic capabilities and their worth, thinking of them as claims to a chance for functioning, which give rise to correlated political duties.

I have spoken both of functioning and of capability. How are they related? Getting clear about this is crucial in defining the relation of the capabilities approach to liberalism. For if we were to take functioning itself as the goal of public policy, the liberal would rightly judge that we were precluding many choices that citizens may make in accordance with their own conceptions of the good. A deeply religious person may prefer not to be well nourished but to engage in strenuous fasting. Whether for religious or for other reasons, a person may prefer a celibate life to one containing sexual expression. A person may prefer to work with an intense dedication that precludes recreation and play. Am I saying that these are not fully human or flourishing lives? Does the approach instruct governments to nudge or push people into functioning of the requisite sort, no matter what they prefer?

Here we must answer: No, capability, not functioning, is the political goal. This is so because of the very great importance the approach attaches to practical reason, as a good that both suffuses all the other functions, making them human rather than animal, and figures, itself, as a central function on the list. It is perfectly true that functionings, not simply capabilities, are what render a life fully human: If there were no functioning of any kind in a life, we could hardly applaud it, no matter what opportunities it contained. Nonetheless, for political purposes it is appropriate for us to shoot for capabilities, and those alone. Citizens must be left free to determine their course after that. The person with plenty of food may always choose to fast, but there is a great difference between fasting and starving, and it is this difference we wish to capture. Again, the person who has normal opportunities for sexual satisfaction can always choose a life of celibacy, and we say nothing against this. What we do speak against, for example, is the practice of female genital mutilation, which deprives individuals of the opportunity to choose sexual functioning (and indeed, the opportunity to choose celibacy as well). A person who has opportunities for play can always choose a workaholic life; again, there is a great difference between that chosen life and a life constrained by insufficient maximum-hour protections and/or the "double day" that makes women in many parts of the world unable to play.

The issue will be clearer if we recall that there are three different types of capabilities that figure in the analysis. First, there are *basic capabilities*: the innate equipment of individuals that is the necessary basis for developing the more advanced capability. Most infants have from birth the basic capability for practical reason and imagination, though they cannot exercise such functions without a lot more development and education. Second, there are *internal capabilities*: states of the person herself that are, as far as the person herself is concerned, sufficient conditions for the exercise of the requisite functions. A woman who has not suffered genital mutilation has the internal capability for sexual pleasure; most adult human beings everywhere have the internal capability to use speech and thought in accordance with their own conscience. Finally, there are *combined capabilities*, which we define as internal capabilities *combined with* suitable external conditions for the exercise of the function. A woman who is not mutilated but is secluded and forbidden to leave the house has internal but not combined capabilities for sexual expression (and work and political participation). Citizens of repressive nondemocratic regimes have the internal but not the combined capability to exercise thought and speech in accordance with their conscience. The aim of public policy is the production of *combined capabilities*. This means promoting the states of the person by providing the necessary education and care; it also means preparing the environment so that it is favorable for the exercise of practical reason and the other major functions.

This clarifies the position. The approach does not say that pub- 23
lic policy should rest content with *internal capabilities* but remain indifferent to the struggles of individuals who have to try to exercise
these in a hostile environment. In that sense, it is highly attentive to
the goal of functioning, and instructs governments to keep it always
in view. On the other hand, we are not pushing individuals into the
function: Once the stage is fully set, the choice is up to them.

The approach is therefore very close to Rawls's approach using 24
the notion of primary goods. We can see the list of capabilities as like
a long list of opportunities for life functioning, such that it is always
rational to want them whatever else one wants. If one ends up having
a plan of life that does not make use of all of them, one has hardly
been harmed by having the chance to choose a life that does. (Indeed,
in the cases of fasting and celibacy it is the very availability of the alternative course that gives the choice its moral value.) The primary difference between this capabilities list and Rawls's list of primary goods
is its length and definiteness, and in particular its determination to
place on the list the social basis of several goods that Rawls has called
"natural goods," such as "health and vigor, intelligence and imagination." Since Rawls has been willing to put the social basis of self-
respect on his list, it is not at all clear why he has not made the same
move with imagination and health. Rawls's evident concern is that no
society can guarantee health to its individuals—in that sense, saying
that our goal is full combined capability may appear unreasonably
idealistic. Some of the capabilities (e.g., some of the political liberties)
can be fully guaranteed by society, but many others involve an element of chance and cannot be so guaranteed. We respond to this by
saying that the list is an enumeration of political *goals* that should be
useful as a benchmark for aspiration and comparison. Even though
individuals with adequate health support often fall ill, it still makes
sense to compare societies by asking about actual health capabilities,
because we assume that the comparison will reflect the different in-
puts of human planning and can be adjusted to take account of more
and less favorable natural situations.

Earlier versions of the list appeared to diverge from the ap- 25
proach of Rawlsian liberalism by not giving as central a place as
Rawls does to the traditional political rights and liberties—although
the need to incorporate them was stressed from the start. This version
of the list corrects that defect of emphasis. These political liberties
have a central importance in making well-being human. A society
that aims at well-being while overriding these has delivered to its
members a merely animal level of satisfaction. As Amartya Sen has
recently written, "Political rights are important not only for the fulfillment of needs, they are crucial also for the formulation of needs.

And this idea relates, in the end, to the respect that we owe each other as fellow human beings." This idea has recently been echoed by Rawls: Primary goods specify what citizens' needs are from the point of view of political justice.

The capability view justifies its elaborate list by pointing out that   26 choice is not pure spontaneity, flourishing independently of material and social conditions. If one cares about people's powers to choose a conception of the good, then one must care about the rest of the form of life that supports those powers, including its material conditions. Thus the approach claims that its more comprehensive concern with flourishing is perfectly consistent with the impetus behind the Rawlsian project, which has always insisted that we are not to rest content with merely formal equal liberty and opportunity but must pursue their fully equal worth by ensuring that unfavorable economic and social circumstances do not prevent people from availing themselves of liberties and opportunities that are formally open to them.

The guiding thought behind this Aristotelian enterprise is, at   27 its heart, a profoundly liberal idea, and one that lies at the heart of Rawls's project as well: the idea of the citizen as a free and dignified human being, a maker of choices. Politics has an urgent role to play here, getting citizens the tools they need, both to choose at all and to have a realistic option of exercising the most valuable functions. The choice of whether and how to use the tools, however, is left up to them, in the conviction that this is an essential aspect of respect for their freedom. They are seen not as passive recipients of social planning but as dignified beings who shape their own lives.

QUESTIONS FOR CRITICAL READING

1. Why is the possession of the functional capabilities Nussbaum describes a question of justice?
2. Choose one of the capabilities and explain why its denial would constitute an act of injustice.
3. What, according to Nussbaum, does it mean to be "fully human"?
4. Is it possible to think of other people as less than human? Under what circumstances?
5. Nussbaum sees her list of capabilities as having political implications. How is that true?
6. Do the concerns for other species (capability 8) have a significant element of justice in them? Are animals entitled to justice?
7. To what extent is personal dignity related to justice?
8. How can government help provide the capabilities Nussbaum enumerates? How can it help translate the capabilities into functionings?

SUGGESTIONS FOR WRITING

1. Consider alternative answers to Nussbaum's opening question: "What activities characteristically performed by human beings are so central that they seem definitive of a life that is truly human?" Take into account the activities you accept as essential to your way of life and write about why they should be included in Nussbaum's list. Which of the activities most important to you would make you feel most unhappy if you were denied it?

2. Examine Nussbaum's list of capabilities. How does the withholding or supplying of these capabilities represent a just or unjust act? Do you feel, for example, that it is unjust to withhold education from citizens? Why?

3. In paragraph 5 Nussbaum states, "I introduce this as a list of capabilities rather than of actual functionings, because I shall argue that capability, not actual functioning, should be the goal of public policy." What public policies in your own experience seem most to take into account the capabilities that Nussbaum lists? How aware do you think politicians in your region are to the issues that concern Nussbaum? Analyze recent political decisions that you feel may increase or decrease the opportunities for justice for the individual.

4. The tenth item on Nussbaum's list is "Control over one's environment." Examine your own environment and describe the ways in which your control or lack of control affects your capabilities to function in your environment. What are your political freedoms and how do they express themselves in terms of increasing your sense of personal justice? What are your material freedoms and how important are they to providing you with a sense of justice? Examine these issues with examples and with analysis. Decide how much justice you enjoy in your present environment.

5. In paragraph 18, Nussbaum states that "the central goal of public planning should be the *capabilities* of citizens to perform various important functions." Do you feel this statement is true and desirable and that it would result in justice to the individual? If so, how is this possible? If you disagree with the statement, explain your own position. What goal of public planning do you feel should be central instead of this one?

6. As Nussbaum tells us in paragraph 19, countries in some parts of the world do not feel that the inability to live a fully human life is "a problem of justice." Explain why such countries may not feel that justice is involved, or may not feel that the failure to live a fully human life is the result of injustice. What is the connection between justice and political decisions that inhibit human capabilities?

7. **CONNECTIONS** To what extent do the central human capabilities that Nussbaum describes coincide with the basic rights that Thomas Jefferson insists Americans must have in his Declaration of Independence? Does Jefferson have as strong a focus on the concepts of equality and justice as Nussbaum? If Nussbaum were to write the Declaration of Independence, what might she do differently?

8. **CONNECTIONS**   Martha Nussbaum is a close student of both Cicero and John Rawls. What similarities and differences do you see among these three writers' beliefs about justice? What political behaviors do they value? How do Nussbaum's functional capabilities relate to the Rawlsian concept of justice as fairness? How does Philus's argument (in Cicero) for injustice contrast with Nussbaum's position on justice? Does she offer persuasive counterarguments?

PART THREE

EDUCATION

Michel Eyquem de Montaigne
Ralph Waldo Emerson
Frederick Douglass
Maria Montessori
John Dewey
Paulo Freire

INTRODUCTION

Knowledge without education is but armed injustice.
—HORACE (65–8 B.C.)

The ink of the scholar is more sacred than the blood of the martyr.
—MUHAMMAD (570–632)

You cannot teach a man anything; you can only help him to find it within himself.
—GALILEO GALILEI (1564–1642)

There is less flogging in our great schools than formerly—but then less is learned there; so what the boys get at one end they lose at the other.
—SAMUEL JOHNSON (1709–1784)

In large states public education will always be mediocre, for the same reason that in large kitchens the cooking is usually bad.
—FRIEDRICH NIETZSCHE (1844–1900)

Education makes machines which act like men and produces men who act like machines.
—ERICH FROMM (1900–1980)

In classical times, when education was largely conducted at home or in schools that served the privileged few, education was rarely a matter of general philosophical discussion. In ancient Rome the schools taught Greek literature and modeled themselves on Greek schools. In Arab societies the traditions of the Platonic Greek academies were maintained until late in the Renaissance, and as a result Europe rediscovered the great Greek texts of Plato and Aristotle that those societies had preserved. However, in all these cases education was reserved for the privileged classes. The average person learned what was needed on the job and often could not read or write.

Among the early writings on the subject is John Milton's *Of Education* (1644), written as a public letter to Samuel Hartlib, who had written on education after having been influenced by Johann Comenius, a religious reformer in Europe. Milton was himself a schoolmaster for a few years, primarily teaching his sister's children. One of his famous statements concerns the learning of Latin and Greek, which was expected of all schoolchildren: "We do amiss to spend seven or eight years merely in scraping together so much miserable Latin and Greek as might be learned otherwise easily and delightfully in one year." Milton may have been a good teacher, but it is clear that he was working with a very select kind of student.

However, things were changing in the seventeenth century. For example, in America the Puritans declared in 1642 that every boy who did not train for a trade must go to school. The tradition of public schooling began in 1635 in Massachusetts and spread to the rest of the nation. The first schools were grammar schools in which Latin was usually emphasized. Most of these schools were for boys only; girls went to private "dame" schools conducted by women in their own homes. Public high schools were not created in the United States until 1821. On the other hand, a grammar school education was quite extensive and would in some cases prepare students for college study. The earliest college was Harvard, founded in 1639. Harvard's initial purpose was to train ministers for the church, but it rapidly expanded to include more secular studies.

Universal education was the law in the United States in the early part of the nineteenth century, and other nations soon followed, with modifications. Theoreticians of education developed a number of views on how to educate the masses. The selections that comprise this part of the book represent an international group of well-known educators and writers, all of whom had a personal stake in the success or failure of education in their time. They also understood the political implications of widespread free public education.

Michel Eyquem de Montaigne, a prominent gentleman of Renaissance France, addressed his essay "Of the Education of Children" to a countess pregnant with her first child. His advice concerns the education of an aristocrat, but his ideas applied to all young children who would have the opportunity for an education in his day. His views, surprisingly modern, include the warning that students should not take everything on authority but should be curious and skeptical about what they read and learn until their own experiences confirm the truth. Montaigne is as worried about the character of the child as about the child's learning, and he states in several ways that he is interested in producing a virtuous and well-rounded child rather than a merely bookish individual.

Ralph Waldo Emerson was a teacher for a short time, but eventually became famous as a speaker and essayist. He is still widely read and valued for his observations on important ideas of his own time. His speech "On Education," a favorite of his, was delivered many times at commencement ceremonies. It was not published until after his death. Emerson includes a great deal of simple wisdom in this speech, as in his statement, "The secret of a good Education lies in respecting the pupil." He was also a champion of nature in the classroom, by which he meant that one must pay attention to human nature and the natural desire of students to learn and teachers to teach. His advice, while general and applicable to several levels of education, is still valid and important in today's schools.

While not a teacher or formally a student, Frederick Douglass writes in his autobiography about his early education, focusing essentially on the acts of reading and writing. Douglass was a slave in the American South until he escaped and established himself as one of the most eloquent speakers against slavery in the country. When he was a child, his owner's wife, a northern woman who did not understand the rationale of the slaveholder's fear of slaves learning to read, gave him instruction in his alphabet and some preliminary reading. When her husband learned of what she was doing he put a stop to it instantly, but Douglass describes how he used other children to help him learn how to read. Douglass is a gifted writer and must have been an impressive speaker. His experiences help us understand some of the theoretical views of later educators in part because he achieved so much against such incredible odds.

One of the most influential of educators, Maria Montessori devoted her life to the education of young children, with an emphasis on the preschool child. She was a physician, anthropologist, professor, and sociologist. Her great experiment in education took place in the worst slum of Rome at the turn of the twentieth century. While the slum was being torn down and rebuilt with clean modern buildings, she was given the opportunity to build a school that would accommodate the neighborhood's youngest children. Again, against great odds, Montessori used what she called "scientific pedagogy" to help students find themselves and make discoveries about the world in an environment designed for learning. The results of her experiment were far more impressive than anyone could have expected. In this slum school she had three- and four-year-old children learning to read and write. She had them excited by opportunities to learn about science and mathematics. Her Montessori Method was introduced in a number of Italian cities, and eventually Montessori traveled the world training teachers to use her methods and establish Montessori schools. They still exist today, and their principles are based on the successes that Montessori achieved beginning in 1906.

The most influential American educator of the twentieth century was John Dewey, a philosopher who had many skills and many interests. He began his career as a philosopher writing about philosophers, but he moved into the field of pedagogy and quickly joined one of the early schools of education at Columbia University, where he became world famous. Dewey's focus in the selection included here is on thought and thinking in education. This subject may seem self-evident, but Dewey's emphasis is on critical thinking—the kind of thinking a skeptical and inquiring student would develop if given the opportunity. Dewey wanted students to be involved in activities that were interesting and educational and to have the opportunity to test their conclusions and validate their insights.

Paulo Freire of Brazil built on the works of both Montessori and Dewey in his very influential selection "The Banking Concept of Education." Freire uses a subtle analogy based on the metaphor of banking. He sees the traditional teacher as the depositor, depositing knowledge into the head of the student, who in this model is essentially an empty vessel. Such education depends on rote memorization of facts and concepts, but it does not lend itself to questioning or analysis. Moreover, it is abstract and remote from experience. For Freire, this method is useless in part because the knowledge that is being imparted is not relevant to the student. It is prepackaged in a curriculum that does not take the student's nature into account. Like Montessori, Freire was given an opportunity to develop a literacy program. His program was devoted not to children, but to adult peasants in Brazil, whom he considered part of an oppressed class. By understanding his students' world, Freire was able to teach them the basics and to give them hope for changing their lives.

Most of these commentators on education are concerned with the student and the environment in which the learning process takes place. They are almost uniform in their concern for the natural process of learning that characterizes all young people. Respecting that process, they believe, is a key to intelligent educational practices.

MICHEL EYQUEM DE MONTAIGNE
Of the Education of Children

MICHEL EYQUEM DE MONTAIGNE (1533–1592) was born
into a wealthy Catholic family near Bordeaux, France. Throughout his
life, Montaigne maintained a commitment to the Catholic faith, despite the fact that during his lifetime terrible wars between Catholics
and Protestants raged in Europe. In terms of religion, Montaigne was
a moderate and argued for tolerance.

Montaigne's father, a soldier, survived the religious wars, and
when he returned home he brought with him advanced ideas about
education. Some of those ideas are expressed in the following essay.
Montaigne's father was elected mayor of Bordeaux and set an
example for his son by working in public service. In 1581, Montaigne himself was elected mayor of Bordeaux and served for four
years. Before he retired to write, Montaigne had a long career in
government.

As a child, Montaigne's tutor and servants spoke to him only in
Latin, which became his native language for his first six years. Early
on he read Virgil and Ovid as well as other classical authors. Since
Latin was the second language of educated Europeans and the language of many of the most important books he would read, he was
at an early advantage in school. He went to Guyenne College in
Bordeaux—essentially a grammar school—at age six, and then later
to Toulouse to study law. He became a lawyer attached to the Bordeaux Parlement, but he spent some of his time in Paris. He developed one of the most important friendships of his life in Bordeaux
with Etienne de La Boétie (1530–1563), a writer who inspired one of
Montaigne's greatest essays, "Of Friendship." In 1571, three years
after his father's death and his inheritance of the estate of Montaigne,
he retired to pursue a life of thought and reflection.

From *The Complete Works*. Translated by Donald M. Frame.

Retirement produced a touch of melancholy, so he began a project that he thought of as a personal self-examination. He had St. Augustine's *Confessions* as an inspiration, but what he produced had no previous model. His *Essays*, as they came to be known, were original in form and have spawned innumerable imitations. But for Montaigne, the essays were not studies of things outside himself, but rather studies of his own nature and his own concerns. He said of himself that he was not looking outside, but inside — that the true subject of his essays was his inner life.

His first volume of twenty-one essays was produced in 1575, followed by two volumes of essays in 1580. Subsequent essays and revisions of earlier ones appeared until his death in 1592. His subjects are diverse: "Of Sadness," "Whether the Governor of a Besieged Place Should Go Out to Parley," "Of Idleness," "Of Liars," "Of Constancy," "Of Cannibals," "Of Drunkenness," "Of Vanity," "Of Experience," "Of the Punishment of Cowardice," and many more. Because of his early publication of "Apology for Raymond Sebond," in which he discusses the myriad ways in which people worship God, he gained a reputation for being a skeptic — one who is much quicker to doubt than to believe. As a skeptic, Montaigne found it easy to be tolerant of the behavior and beliefs of others — he felt he had no grounds for thinking that the way he did things was so correct that all others must follow his precepts. He felt, for example, that Stoic philosophies, which insisted that everything was the result of the divine will and that there was little people could do beyond enduring life as it was, were too limiting and did not respect the complexities of human difference.

Montaigne's Rhetoric

Montaigne was a lawyer, which meant that he was well educated and trained in argumentation. He studied logic and rhetoric and knew how to tailor a piece of writing to any audience. In "Of the Education of Children" his primary audience is Countess Diane de la Foix, pregnant with her first child, but the essay is also a self-reflective meditation on Montaigne himself as a student. As his editions became well known and he gained a very large audience, he began a pattern of incessantly revising and rethinking his work. Nonetheless, the hallmark of most of his essays is a relaxed form that meanders from one thought to the next, developing through the association of ideas. In a sense, the essays give insight into the associative nature of his mind. He responds to what he observes and writes what he thinks at a given moment. The result is writing that does not seem dogmatic or rigid, but flexible, cordial, and inviting.

Among the special rhetorical qualities of his writing is his tendency to produce pithy sentences that become epigrams—for example, "Only the fools are certain and assured" (para. 8), "He who follows another follows nothing" (para. 8), and "Let him be taught not so much the histories as how to judge them" (para. 21). In addition, he quotes classical writers such as Dante, Cicero, Horace, Propertius, and many others in support of his own views.

Montaigne is often praised for his ability to conjure up intense imagery. In this essay, his gift for metaphor is striking. Early on, he compares the progress of a child in school to the gait of a horse when he says of the tutor: "It is good that he should have his pupil trot before him, to judge the child's pace" (para. 4). Later, when speaking of how one makes use of wide reading of Plato and others, he uses the metaphor of bees: "The bees plunder the flowers here and there, but afterward they make of them honey, which is all theirs" (para. 8). Like bees, children should read widely and then, rather than adopt one or another position taken from a book, make the ideas thus gathered their own. As Montaigne implies, this will come from judging well and avoiding dogmatic acceptance.

One of the unusual rhetorical techniques he uses is personification. Late in the essay, he personifies Virtue as a woman: "Virtue's tool is moderation, not strength. Socrates, her prime favorite, deliberately gives up his strength, to slip into the naturalness and ease of her gait. She is the nursing mother of human pleasures" (para. 26).

Montaigne also reveals that he has a sense of humor. In paragraph 26 he suggests that if the tutor has a dull child who wants to play instead of learn, "I see no other remedy than for his tutor to strangle him early, if there are no witnesses, or apprentice him to a pastry cook in some good town."

Throughout the essay, Montaigne recommends some very interesting principles of education. The most important is that the tutor is not to fill the student's head with useless information, especially the kind of information that is to be memorized and recited. As he states, "To know by heart is not to know" (para. 11). What the student must aim for is judgment and understanding, which involves being skeptical enough to ask questions rather than to accept authorities—even Aristotle—without complete and independent examination.

PREREADING QUESTIONS:
WHAT TO READ FOR

The following prereading questions may help you anticipate key issues in the discussion of Michel Eyquem de Montaigne's "Of the Education of Children." Keeping them in mind during your first reading of the selection should help focus your attention.

- What should be the student's attitude toward authority?
- Which are the best writers for the student to read?
- How should the tutor behave toward his student?

Of the Education of Children

Madame, learning is a great ornament and a wonderfully ser- 1
viceable tool, notably for people raised to such a degree of fortune as you are. In truth, it does not receive its proper use in mean and lowborn hands. It is much prouder to lend its resources to conducting a war, governing a people, or gaining the friendship of a prince or a foreign nation, than to constructing a dialectical argument, pleading an appeal, or prescribing a mass of pills. Thus, Madame, because I think you will not forget this element in the education of your children, you who have tasted its sweetness and who are of a literary race (for we still have the writings of those ancient counts of Foix[1] from whom his lordship the count your husband and yourself are descended; and François, Monsieur de Candale, your uncle, every day brings forth others, which will extend for many centuries the knowledge of this quality in your family), I want to tell you a single fancy of mine on this subject, which is contrary to common usage; it is all that I can contribute to your service in this matter.

The task of the tutor that you will give your son, upon whose 2
choice depends the whole success of his education, has many other important parts, but I do not touch upon them, since I cannot offer anything worth while concerning them; and in this matter on which I venture to give him advice, he will take it only as far as it seems good to him. For a child of noble family who seeks learning not for gain (for such an abject goal is unworthy of the graces and favor of

---

[1] **Foix** A castle in Southern France. Montaigne addressed his essay to Countess Diane de la Foix while she was pregnant with her first child.

the Muses, and besides it looks to others and depends on them), or so much for external advantages as for his own, and to enrich and furnish himself inwardly, since I would rather make of him an able man than a learned man, I would also urge that care be taken to choose a guide with a well-made rather than a well-filled head; that both these qualities should be required of him, but more particularly character and understanding than learning; and that he should go about his job in a novel way.

Our tutors never stop bawling into our ears, as though they 3 were pouring water into a funnel; and our task is only to repeat what has been told us. I should like the tutor to correct this practice, and right from the start, according to the capacity of the mind he has in hand, to begin putting it through its paces, making it taste things, choose them, and discern them by itself; sometimes clearing the way for him, sometimes letting him clear his own way. I don't want him to think and talk alone, I want him to listen to his pupil speaking in his turn. Socrates, and later Arcesilaus,[2] first had their disciples speak, and then they spoke to them. *The authority of those who teach is often an obstacle to those who want to learn* [Cicero].

It is good that he should have his pupil trot before him, to judge 4 the child's pace and how much he must stoop to match his strength. For lack of this proportion we spoil everything; and to be able to hit it right and to go along in it evenly is one of the hardest tasks that I know; it is the achievement of a lofty and very strong soul to know how to come down to a childish gait and guide it. I walk more firmly and surely uphill than down.

If, as is our custom, the teachers undertake to regulate many 5 minds of such different capacities and forms with the same lesson and a similar measure of guidance, it is no wonder if in a whole race of children they find barely two or three who reap any proper fruit from their teaching.

Let him be asked for an account not merely of the words of his 6 lesson, but of its sense and substance, and let him judge the profit he has made by the testimony not of his memory, but of his life. Let him be made to show what he has just learned in a hundred aspects, and apply it to as many different subjects, to see if he has yet properly grasped it and made it his own, planning his progress according to the pedagogical method of Plato. It is a sign of rawness and indigestion to disgorge food just as we swallowed it. The stomach has not done its work if it has not changed the condition and form of what has been given it to cook.

---

[2] **Arcesilaus (315–240 B.C.)** Sixth director of Plato's Academy.

Our mind moves only on faith, being bound and constrained to 7
the whim of others' fancies, a slave and a captive under the authority
of their teaching. We have been so well accustomed to leading
strings that we have no free motion left; our vigor and liberty are extinct. *They never become their own guardians* [Seneca]. I had a private
talk with a man at Pisa, a good man, but such an Aristotelian that the
most sweeping of his dogmas is that the touchstone and measure of
all solid speculations and of all truth is conformity with the teaching
of Aristotle; that outside of this there is nothing but chimeras and
inanity; that Aristotle saw everything and said everything. This
proposition, having been interpreted a little too broadly and unfairly, put him once, and kept him long, in great danger of the In-
quisition at Rome.

Let the tutor make his charge pass everything through a sieve 8
and lodge nothing in his head on mere authority and trust: let not
Aristotle's principles be principles to him any more than those of the
Stoics or Epicureans. Let this variety of ideas be set before him; he
will choose if he can; if not, he will remain in doubt. Only the fools
are certain and assured.

> For doubting pleases me no less than knowing.
> —DANTE

For if he embraces Xenophon's[3] and Plato's opinions by his own
reasoning, they will no longer be theirs, they will be his. He who
follows another follows nothing. He finds nothing; indeed he seeks
nothing. *We are not under a king; let each one claim his own freedom*
[Seneca]. Let him know that he knows, at least. He must imbibe
their ways of thinking, not learn their precepts. And let him boldly
forget, if he wants, where he got them, but let him know how to
make them his own. Truth and reason are common to everyone,
and no more belong to the man who first spoke them than to the
man who says them later. It is no more according to Plato than according to me, since he and I understand and see it in the same
way. The bees plunder the flowers here and there, but afterward
they make of them honey, which is all theirs; it is no longer thyme
or marjoram. Even so with the pieces borrowed from others; he will
transform and blend them to make a work that is all his own, to wit,
his judgment. His education, work, and study aim only at forming
this.

Let him hide all the help he has had, and show only what he has 9
made of it. The pillagers, the borrowers, parade their buildings, their

---

[3] **Xenophon (430–355 B.C.)** His great book *Anabasis* is on the Persian wars.

purchases, not what they get from others. You do not see the gratu-
ities of a member of a Parlement, you see the alliances he has gained
and honors for his children. No one makes public his receipts;
everyone makes public his acquisitions.

The gain from our study is to have become better and wiser by it.   10

It is the understanding, Epicharmus[4] used to say, that sees and   11
hears; it is the understanding that makes profit of everything, that
arranges everything, that acts, dominates, and reigns; all other
things are blind, deaf, and soulless. Truly we make it servile and
cowardly, by leaving it no freedom to do anything by itself. Who
ever asked his pupil what he thinks of rhetoric or grammar, or of
such-and-such a saying of Cicero? They slap them into our memory
with all their feathers on, like oracles in which the letters and sylla-
bles are the substance of the matter. To know by heart is not to
know; it is to retain what we have given our memory to keep. What
we know rightly we dispose of, without looking at the model, without turning our eyes toward our book. Sad competence, a purely
bookish competence! I intend it to serve as decoration, not as foundation, according to the opinion of Plato, who says that steadfastness,
faith, and sincerity are the real philosophy, and the other sciences
which aim at other things are only powder and rouge.

I wish Paluel or Pompey,[5] those fine dancers of my time, could   12
teach us capers just by performing them before us and without moving us from our seats, as those people want to train our understanding without setting it in motion; or that we could be taught to
handle a horse, or a pike, or a lute, or our voice, without practicing
at it, as those people want to teach us to judge well and to speak
well, without having us practice either speaking or judging.

Now, for this apprenticeship, everything that comes to our eyes   13
is book enough: a page's prank, a servant's blunder, a remark at
table, are so many new materials.

For this reason, mixing with men is wonderfully useful, and vis-   14
iting foreign countries, not merely to bring back, in the manner of
our French noblemen, knowledge of the measurements of the Santa
Rotonda, or of the richness of Signora Livia's[6] drawers, or, like some
others, how much longer or wider Nero's[7] face is in some old ruin
there than on some similar medallion; but to bring back knowledge
of the characters and ways of those nations, and to rub and polish

---

[4] **Epicharmus (540–450 B.C.)** A Greek poet.

[5] Ludovico Palvalli and Pompeo Diobono, two famous Milanese dancing masters at the French court.

[6] Probably a Roman dancer of Montaigne's time.

[7] **Nero (A.D. 37–68)** One of Rome's most notorious emperors.

our brains by contact with those of others. I should like the tutor to start taking him abroad at a tender age, and first, to kill two birds with one stone, in those neighboring nations where the language is farthest from our own and where the tongue cannot be bent to it unless you train it early.

Likewise it is an opinion accepted by all, that it is not right to   15
bring up a child in the lap of his parents. This natural love makes them too tender and lax, even the wisest of them. They are capable neither of chastising his faults nor of seeing him brought up roughly, as he should be, and hazardously. They could not endure his returning sweating and dusty from his exercise, drinking hot, drinking cold, or see him on a skittish horse, or up against a tough fencer, foil in hand, or with his first harquebus.[8] For there is no help for it: if you want to make a man of him, unquestionably you must not spare him in his youth, and must often clash with the rules of medicine:

> Let him live beneath the open sky
> And dangerously.
>   –HORACE

It is not enough to toughen his soul; we must also toughen his   16
muscles. The soul is too hard pressed unless it is seconded, and has too great a task doing two jobs alone. I know how much mine labors in company with a body so tender and so sensitive, which leans so hard upon it. And I often perceive in my reading that in their writings my masters give weight, as examples of great spirit and stoutheartedness, to acts that are likely to owe more to thickness of skin and toughness of bones. I have seen men, women, and children naturally so constituted that a beating is less to them than a flick of the finger to me; who move neither tongue nor eyebrow at the blows they receive. When athletes imitate philosophers in endurance, their strength is that of sinews rather than of heart.

Now practice at enduring work is practice at enduring pain: 17
Work hardens one against pain [Cicero]. The boy must be broken in to the pain and harshness of exercises, to build him up against the pain and harshness of dislocation, colic, cauterization, and the dungeon, and torture. For he may yet be a prey to the last two, which threaten the good as well as the bad in a time like this. We have proof of this right now. Whoever fights the laws threatens even the best of men with the scourge and the noose.

And besides, the authority of the tutor, which should be sover-   18
eign over the pupil, is interrupted and hampered by the presence of

---

[8] **harquebus** A gun.

the parents. Add the fact that the respect the whole household pays the boy, and the consciousness of the power and greatness of his house, are in my opinion no slight drawbacks at that age.

In this school of dealing with men I have often noticed this flaw, 19 that instead of gaining knowledge of others we strive only to give knowledge of ourselves, and take more pains to peddle our wares than to get new ones. Silence and modesty are very good qualities for social intercourse. This boy will be trained to be sparing and thrifty with his ability when he has acquired it; not to take exception to the stupid things and wild tales that will be told in his presence, for it is uncivil and annoying to hit at everything that is not to our taste. Let him be content with correcting himself, and not seem to reproach others for everything that he refuses to do, or set himself up against common practices. *A man may be wise without ostentation, without arousing envy* [Seneca]. Let him shun these domineering and uncivil airs, and this childish ambition to try to seem more clever by being different and to gain reputation by finding fault and being original. As it is becoming only to great poets to indulge in poetic license, so it is tolerable only for great and illustrious souls to take unusual liberties. *If Socrates and Aristippus have done something contrary to the rules of behavior and custom, let him not think that he has a right to do the same; for they have gained that privilege by great and divine merits* [Cicero]. . . .

Put into his head an honest curiosity to inquire into all things; 20 whatever is unusual around him he will see: a building, a fountain, a man, the field of an ancient battle, the place where Caesar or Charlemagne passed:

> Which land is parched with heat, which numb with frost,
> What wind drives sails to the Italian coast
> —PROPERTIUS

He will inquire into the conduct, the resources, and the alliances of this prince and that. These are things very pleasant to learn and very useful to know.

In this association with men I mean to include, and foremost, 21 those who live only in the memory of books. He will associate, by means of histories, with those great souls of the best ages. It is a vain study, if you will; but also, if you will, it is a study of inestimable value, and the only study, as Plato tells us, in which the Lacedaemonians[9] had kept a stake for themselves. What profit will he not gain in this field by reading the *Lives* of our Plutarch?[10] But let my guide remember

---

[9] **Lacedaemonians** Spartans, the chief rivals of Athenians.
[10] **Plutarch (A.D. 46?–120)** Author of *Parallel Lives*, biographies of Greek and Roman dignitaries.

the object of his task, and let him not impress on his pupil so much the date of the destruction of Carthage as the characters of Hannibal and Scipio,[11] nor so much where Marcellus died as why his death there showed him unworthy of his duty. Let him be taught not so much the histories as how to judge them. That, in my opinion, is of all matters the one to which we apply our minds in the most varying degree. I have read in Livy[12] a hundred things that another man has not read in him. Plutarch has read in him a hundred besides the ones I could read, and perhaps besides what the author had put in. For some it is a purely grammatical study; for others, the skeleton of philosophy, in which the most abstruse parts of our nature are penetrated.

There are in Plutarch many extensive discussions, well worth   22 knowing, for in my judgment he is the master workman in that field; but there are a thousand that he has only just touched on; he merely points out with his finger where we are to go, if we like, and some-times is content to make only a stab at the heart of a subject. We must snatch these bits out of there and display them properly. Just as that remark of his, that the inhabitants of Asia served one single man because they could not pronounce one single syllable, which is "No," may have given the matter and the impulsion to La Boétie[13] for his *Voluntary Servitude*. Just to see him pick out a trivial action in a man's life, or a word which seems unimportant: that is a treatise in itself. It is a pity that men of understanding are so fond of brevity; doubtless their reputation gains by it, but we lose by it. Plutarch would rather we praised him for his judgment than for his knowledge; he would rather leave us wanting more of him than satiated. He knew that even of good things one may say too much, and that Alexandridas justly reproached the man who was talking sensibly but too long to the Ephors: "O stranger, you say what you should, but otherwise than you should." Those who have a thin body fill it out with padding; those who have slim substance swell it out with words.

Wonderful brilliance may be gained for human judgment by get-   23 ting to know men. We are all huddled and concentrated in ourselves, and our vision is reduced to the length of our nose. Socrates was asked where he was from. He replied not "Athens," but "The world." He, whose imagination was fuller and more extensive, embraced the universe as his city, and distributed his knowledge, his company, and his affections to all mankind, unlike us who look only at what is un-derfoot. When the vines freeze in my village, my priest infers that the

---

[11] **Hannibal (247–182 B.C.)** was a Carthaginian general who attacked Rome. **Scipio (237–183 B.C.)** was the general who defeated him.
[12] **Livy (64 B.C.–A.D. 17)** Great Roman historian.
[13] **Etienne de La Boétie (1530–1563)** Montaigne's closest friend.

wrath of God is upon the human race, and judges that the cannibals already have the pip. Seeing our civil wars, who does not cry out that this mechanism is being turned topsy-turvy and that the judgment day has us by the throat, without reflecting that many worse things have happened, and that ten thousand parts of the world, to our one, are meanwhile having a gay time? Myself, considering their licentiousness and impunity, I am amazed to see our wars so gentle and mild. When the hail comes down on a man's head, it seems to him that the whole hemisphere is in tempest and storm. And a Savoyard said that if that fool of a French king had known how to play his cards right, he would have had it in him to become chief steward to the duke of Savoy. His imagination conceived no higher dignity than that of his master. We are all unconsciously in this error, an error of great consequence and harm. But whoever considers as in a painting the great picture of our mother Nature in her full majesty; whoever reads such universal and constant variety in her face; whoever finds himself there, and not merely himself, but a whole kingdom, as a dot made with a very fine brush; that man alone estimates things according to their true proportions. . . .

After the tutor has told his pupil what will help make him wiser 24
and better, he will explain to him the meaning of logic, physics, geometry, rhetoric; and the science he chooses, now that his judgment is already formed, he will soon master. His lesson will be now in talk, now in a book; now his tutor will give him straight from the author some passage that is suitable to this purpose in his education, now he will give him the marrow and the substance predigested. And if the tutor himself is not familiar enough with books to find all the fine passages that are in them for his purpose, some man of letters may be associated with him, who as each need arises shall supply him with the material he requires, which he may then sort out and dispense to his nursling. And who can doubt that this kind of teaching is easier and more natural than that of Gaza?[14] There we find thorny and unpleasant precepts and empty and fleshless words that you cannot get a hold on, nothing that rouses your mind. Here the mind finds something to bite and feed on. The fruit of it is incomparably greater, and also it will be sooner ripe. . . .

My tutor, who knows he must fill his pupil's mind as much, or 25
more, with affection as with reverence for virtue, will be able to tell him that the poets agree with the common view, and to set his finger on the fact that the gods make men sweat harder in the approaches

---

[14] A fifteenth-century translator of Aristotle and author of a Greek grammar. [Translator's note]

to the chambers of Venus than of Pallas.[15] And when he begins to feel his oats, and the choice is offered him between Bradamante and Angelica as a mistress to be enjoyed — a natural, active, spirited, manly but not mannish beauty, next to a soft, affected, delicate, artificial beauty; one disguised as a boy, wearing a shining helmet, the other dressed as a girl, wearing a headdress of pearls — the tutor will think his pupil manly even in love if he chooses quite differently from that effeminate shepherd of Phrygia.[16]

He will teach him this new lesson, that the value and height of true virtue lies in the ease, utility, and pleasure of its practice, which is so far from being difficult that children can master it as well as men, the simple as well as the subtle. Virtue's tool is moderation, not strength. Socrates, her prime favorite, deliberately gives up his strength, to slip into the naturalness and ease of her gait. She is the nursing mother of human pleasures. By making them just, she makes them sure and pure. By moderating them, she keeps them in breath and appetite. By withdrawing the ones she refuses, she makes us keener for the ones she allows us; and she allows us abundantly all those that nature wills, even to satiety, in maternal fashion, if not to the point of lassitude (unless perchance we want to say that the regimen that stops the drinker short of drunkenness, the eater short of indigestion, the lecher short of baldness, is an enemy of our pleasures). If she lacks the fortune of ordinary men, she rises above it or does without it, and makes herself a different sort of fortune that is all her own, and no longer fluctuating and unsteady. She knows how to be rich and powerful and learned, and lie on perfumed mattresses. She loves life, she loves beauty and glory and health. But her own particular task is to know how to enjoy those blessings with temperance, and to lose them with fortitude: a task far more noble than harsh, without which the course of any life is denatured, turbulent, and deformed, and fit to be associated with those dangers, those brambles, and those monsters. [26]

If this pupil happens to be of such an odd disposition that he would rather listen to some idle story than to the account of a fine voyage or a wise conversation when he hears one; if, at the sound of the drum that calls the youthful ardor of his companions to arms, he turns aside to another that invites him to the tricks of the jugglers; if, [27]

---

[15] **Pallas** Venus was the goddess of love and Pallas was Pallas Athene, the owl-eyed goddess of war.

[16] Paris, whose award of the golden apple, the prize of beauty, to Aphrodite instead of Hera or Athene led to the Trojan War. Bradamante and Angelica are two heroines of Ariosto's *Orlando Furioso*. [Translator's note]

by his own preference, he does not find it more pleasant and sweet to return dusty and victorious from a combat than from tennis or a ball with the prize for that exercise, I see no other remedy than for his tutor to strangle him early, if there are no witnesses, or apprentice him to a pastry cook in some good town, even though he were the son of a duke; in accordance with Plato's precept that children should be placed not according to the faculties of their father, but according to the faculties of their soul.

Since it is philosophy that teaches us to live, and since there is a   28
lesson in it for childhood as well as for the other ages, why is it not imparted to children?

> He still is yielding clay; now, now, ere he congeal,
> Tirelessly we must shape him on the potter's wheel.
> —PERSIUS

QUESTIONS FOR CRITICAL READING

1. What are Montaigne's assumptions about the social class of the student?
2. How is the tutor to help shape the character of the student?
3. What does Montaigne think about a tutor's demand that children repeat what they are told?
4. Should the child be silent in the presence of the tutor?
5. What are Montaigne's views about the capacity of individual students to learn? What is the tutor's responsibility to the individual?
6. What are Montaigne's attitudes toward accepting the views of authorities? When, if ever, can those views be accepted?
7. Of what use is travel to the student?
8. Why should parents be somewhere else when the student is with the tutor?

SUGGESTIONS FOR WRITING

1. Throughout the essay, Montaigne insists that the tutor help the child make his learning his own. He writes, "let him judge the profit he has made by the testimony not of his memory, but of his life" (para. 6). What does Montaigne mean by making learning "his own"? How do you make your own learning your own?
2. In paragraph 5 Montaigne complains that when "teachers undertake to regulate many minds of such different capacities and forms with the same lesson," only a few students will get much out of it. In other words, Montaigne recommends that different students receive different "lessons." To what extent has your own experience confirmed or denied

this observation? Compare your experiences in large classes with experiences either in small classes or tutorials. How does your capacity for learning alter depending on the size of your class?

3. In paragraph 8 Montaigne discourses on the metaphor of the bees, who sample many flowers and make their honey from a unique mixture of pollen. Here he recommends that students read widely, collect many ideas, and then make those ideas their own. How can this be done? What is your own experience in gathering evidence and opinions and drawing your own conclusions? Give a clear example in which you have researched and developed your own views.

4. Montaigne recommends that children be removed from their parents when in school, as he was. Review his arguments in paragraph 15 and take a stand on this issue. As much as possible, model your response on Montaigne's essay. Make an effort to use metaphor where appropriate to bolster your argument.

5. In paragraph 16 Montaigne addresses the physical training of the child. He insists that physical training enables the child to face the trials of Renaissance life. What kinds of physical trials do you think the modern student would likely face later in life? Use as many examples of current physical threats as possible, and suggest ways in which physical training may help the student later in life.

6. Write your own essay titled "Of the Education of Children." Be sure to use some of Montaigne's techniques: use of metaphor and vivid imagery, quotations from important writers, and details concerning the point of instruction. What would you recommend, beginning with grade school, as the best way to educate children? What are your educational ideals and what would you recommend as the best setting and structure for a good education?

7. **CONNECTIONS** Compare Montaigne's views on education with those of Ralph Waldo Emerson. These men are three centuries removed from one another and come from societies that have totally different attitudes toward social class. What links Montaigne and Emerson in their common goal for the education of the young? What separates them? Compare them point by point. Examine, too, their respective rhetorical approaches to their subject. What are the principal ways in which their writing differs?

8. **CONNECTIONS** Would John Dewey or Paolo Freire agree with Montaigne's views about the education of children? Consider Montaigne's attitudes toward accepting authority, making one's learning one's own, the usefulness of travel, the separation of the child from home, and any other important issues you feel these writers either agree or disagree about.

RALPH WALDO EMERSON
On Education

RALPH WALDO EMERSON (1803–1882) was among the fore-
most American intellectuals of the nineteenth century. His father, a
Unitarian minister, settled the family in Concord, Massachusetts,
where Emerson lived virtually all his life. When his father died,
Emerson was seven years old, and his mother was essentially destitute. She worked at various jobs to keep the family together, but
there were nights when they did not have enough to eat. Emerson's
maiden aunt, Mary Moody Emerson, was a highly intelligent woman
and was responsible, in part, for Emerson's earliest education.

Despite having little or no money, Emerson went to Boston
Latin School, then enrolled in Harvard at age fourteen. After gradua-
tion he taught briefly at an uncle's school, then opened his own
school for girls, which he operated for about four years. Eventually
he realized that teaching was not the right vocation for him, and he
decided to become a minister. He went to Harvard Divinity School
but found he had difficulty accepting the religious dogma at the
heart of the program. He continued to have a problem with religious
strictures, and even though he became a popular Unitarian minister
in Boston, he eventually gave up his career in the church.

What he decided to do instead was to become a lecturer
and public speaker. In the years before and after the Civil War
(1861–1865), many speakers toured the United States almost the
way popular entertainers do today. Emerson was a popular intellectual whose style of delivery and quality of thought engaged New
Englanders for decades. He was known in Europe as well, where he
visited thinkers and absorbed ideas from the new wave of Romantic
philosophy that emanated primarily from Germany. He thought of
himself as an Idealist, although he was involved with a group of
intellectuals who described themselves as Transcendentalists.

From *The Complete Works of Ralph Waldo Emerson*.

Transcendentalism was not a systematic philosophy, but a way of approaching life by emphasizing the human soul, the soul's connection with nature, and the elevation of the spirit over materialism. Considering that the United States was enjoying a tremendous wave of materialist expansion during his lifetime, his views were what we would today call countercultural. His first book, *Nature* (1836), was a short tribute to his love of nature, especially his love of the woods around Concord. Some commentators hold that most of his later beliefs are either expressed or hinted at in this volume. Emerson praised freedom, intuition, respect for conscience, spontaneity, and personal responsibility, among other values. For Emerson, to praise something as "natural" was high praise indeed.

Like his neighbor Henry David Thoreau, Emerson campaigned against slavery and, during the Civil War, lobbied Washington to emancipate the slaves. He was a lifelong abolitionist and, again like Thoreau, refused to recognize laws that he felt went against nature. For instance, when Congress passed the Fugitive Slave Act, which would force him to turn in any escaped slave that he found, he declared that he would disobey the law.

Emerson produced a large body of work. His journal, begun when he was a student at Harvard, was later published. His two volumes of *Essays* (1841 and 1844) were and are widely read and studied. His essays "Self-Reliance," "The Over-Soul," and "The American Scholar" are among the most important American literary documents of the nineteenth century. His two volumes of poetry, *Poems* (1847) and *May–Day* (1867), include several memorable poems, such as "Hamatreya," that reveal the influence of eastern religious thought and the character of his idealism. Other books include *Representative Men* (1850)—short biographies of men such as Shakespeare, Goethe, and Napoleon; and *The Conduct of Life* (1860), which examines the way in which he himself lived while recognizing his limitations and his personal gifts.

Emerson's Rhetoric

"On Education" was originally a commencement address given to graduating classes, and Emerson delivered it often during the 1860s. It was not published until after his death—in part, probably, because it would not be useful to him as a speech if it were widely available in print. And because it is a speech, Emerson must be a bit more direct in his presentation than he might be in a closely argued essay in which he could depend on the reader's close attention to detail. As a result, it is among Emerson's more approachable essays.

The selection that follows is the second part of Emerson's speech. The first part begins with a discussion of the experiment in education that marked the United States: the provision of a free public education for every child. Emerson felt this to be an idealistic venture, but he welcomed it, although he also saw that it created profound problems. For Emerson, educating the masses meant slighting the individual. Emerson worried that an individual's genius, or special gifts, would be ignored in such a system. In the second part of his speech, he begins to be more specific about his concerns and recommendations for education. He may have intended to address young teachers, because he pauses occasionally to make suggestions for classroom decorum. He refers to students constantly as boys or men, but this does not mean he ignores education for women. He was, after all, the proprietor of a school dedicated to the training of women, and he was also a feminist. However, at the time Emerson wrote this speech, only men went on to university. As much as he is an idealist, he is also realistic.

Emerson begins by praising imagination and suggesting that whatever the content of the classroom, there ought to be room for good novels and good poetry. In Emerson's time the power of poetry was considerable, and he names a number of important poets whom he feels students ought to know primarily as a stimulus to their imagination, which he felt was important to develop.

Emerson states that "the secret of Education lies in respecting the pupil" (para. 2). He implies that every pupil will have a special ability, a special character, a special curiosity, and that teachers must do what they can to respect this individuality. He also realizes that while it is important to retain the student's natural abilities, the teacher's responsibility is to "stop off his uproar," which is to say, be sure to maintain peace in the classroom and not let the students run wild.

In paragraph 4, Emerson emphasizes the "two capital facts, Genius and Drill." Both are part of good education. Find the genius of the student, but engage him in the kind of drill that excites. Otherwise, the basics of mathematics and science, two of Emerson's pleasures, will not be learned. His advice to children is find a subject that inspires them and then follow it until it is mastered.

In paragraph 5, Emerson uses the rhetorical device of example. He points to the explorer Sir Charles Fellowes (1799–1860), who became curious about the carvings on ancient stone that he found in Turkey, in a region called Lycia. Because he was excited by his discoveries, he learned new languages and read history in order to

make better sense out of what he had found. The result of this enthusiasm was the discovery of the capital city, Xanthus, of an ancient settlement. In his expeditions he discovered several more
cities and sent various ancient stone structures back to England.

One of Emerson's techniques, repetition (or drill), is plain in
the central paragraphs of his speech when he praises nature for
providing all that is necessary for good learning and good instruction. As he states in paragraph 9, the process begins at the mother's
knee, with the child excited to learn and the adult just as excited to
teach. The process of education, he reminds us in several ways, is
essentially natural, and if what is natural in students is respected,
then education will take place naturally.

In paragraphs 9–12, Emerson points to several problems with
education as it currently exists. He complains that in most classrooms there are few geniuses and many who "are more sensual than
intellectual" (para. 11). What happens in a large classroom is that
the instruction is geared to the lowest common denominator, and
hence the individual is sometimes ignored or made dull. Unfortunately, that situation can produce a discouraged teacher, one who
may become "military" and more a disciplinarian than a teacher. In
Emerson's day, corporal punishment was the norm in most schools.
Students could be hit with a pandy bat for not knowing their lessons
or for causing a disturbance.

Emerson's ultimate remedy, also "drilled" into his speech, is
patience. Things in nature take more time than some of us are willing to give. But at the end of his speech, Emerson characteristically
reverts to nature and reminds us that things take their own time
and that the essence of good teaching is to be patient. The same
may be said of good learning.

PREREADING QUESTIONS:
WHAT TO READ FOR

The following prereading questions may help you anticipate key issues
in the discussion of Ralph Waldo Emerson's "On Education." Keeping them
in mind during your first reading of the selection should help focus your
attention.

- What does Emerson mean when he states that "the secret of Education
  lies in respecting the pupil" (para. 2)?

- What role does nature have in education?

- What does Emerson mean by Genius and Drill?

On Education

There comes the period of the imagination to each, a later youth; 1
the power of beauty, the power of books, of poetry. Culture makes
his books realities to him, their characters more brilliant, more effective on his mind, than his actual mates. Do not spare to put novels
into the hands of young people as an occasional holiday and experiment; but, above all, good poetry in all kinds, epic, tragedy, lyric. If
we can touch the imagination, we serve them, they will never forget
it. Let him read *Tom Brown at Rugby*, read *Tom Brown at Oxford*, —
better yet, read *Hodson's Life*[1] — Hodson who took prisoner the King
of Delhi. They teach the same truth — a trust, against all appearances,
against all privations, in your own worth, and not in tricks, plotting,
or patronage.

I believe that our own experience instructs us that the secret 2
of Education lies in respecting the pupil. It is not for you to choose
what he shall know, what he shall do. It is chosen and fore-
ordained, and he only holds the key to his own secret. By your tam-
pering and thwarting and too much governing he may be hindered
from his end and kept out of his own. Respect the child. Wait and
see the new product of Nature. Nature loves analogies, but not repetitions. Respect the child. Be not too much his parent. Trespass not
on his solitude.

But I hear the outcry which replies to this suggestion — Would 3
you verily throw up the reins of public and private discipline;
would you leave the young child to the mad career of his own passions and whimsies, and call this anarchy a respect for the child's nature? I answer — Respect the child, respect him to the end, but also
respect yourself. Be the companion of his thought, the friend of his
friendship, the lover of his virtue — but no kinsman of his sin. Let
him find you so true to yourself that you are the irreconcilable hater
of his vice and the imperturbable slighter of his trifling.

The two points in a boy's training are, to keep his *naturel*[2] and 4
train off all but that — to keep his *naturel*, but stop off his uproar,
fooling and horseplay — keep his nature and arm it with knowledge
in the very direction in which it points. Here are the two capital
facts, Genius and Drill. The first is the inspiration in the well-born
healthy child, the new perception he has of nature. Somewhat he

---

[1] Thomas Hughes wrote the *Tom Brown's Schooldays* books (1865) detailing his
schooling at Rugby, an English private school, and at Oxford University. W. S. R.
Hodson wrote *Twelve Years of a Soldier's Life in India* (1860). They remained popular
books well into the twentieth century.

[2] **naturel** By this Emerson means the basic nature of the student.

sees in forms or hears in music or apprehends in mathematics, or believes practicable in mechanics or possible in political society, which no one else sees or hears or believes. This is the perpetual romance of new life, the invasion of God into the old dead world, when he sends into quiet houses a young soul with a thought which is not met, looking for something which is not there, but which ought to be there: the thought is dim but it is sure, and he casts about restless for means and masters to verify it; he makes wild attempts to explain himself and invoke the aid and consent of the by-standers. Baffled for want of language and methods to convey his meaning, not yet clear to himself, he conceives that though not in this house or town, yet in some other house or town is the wise master who can put him in possession of the rules and instruments to execute his will. Happy this child with a bias, with a thought which entrances him, leads him, now into deserts now into cities, the fool of an idea. Let him follow it in good and in evil report, in good or bad company; it will justify itself; it will lead him at last into the illustrious society of the lovers of truth.

In London, in a private company, I became acquainted with a   5
gentleman, Sir Charles Fellowes, who, being at Xanthus, in the Aegean Sea, had seen a Turk point with his staff to some carved work on the corner of a stone almost buried in the soil. Fellowes scraped away the dirt, was struck with the beauty of the sculptured ornaments, and, looking about him, observed more blocks and fragments like this. He returned to the spot, procured laborers and uncovered many blocks. He went back to England, bought a Greek grammar and learned the language; he read history and studied ancient art to explain his stones; he interested Gibson[3] the sculptor; he invoked the assistance of the English Government; he called in the succor of Sir Humphry Davy[4] to analyze the pigments; of experts in coins, of scholars and connoisseurs; and at last in his third visit brought home to England such statues and marble reliefs and such careful plans that he was able to reconstruct, in the British Museum where it now stands, the perfect model of the Ionic trophy-monument, fifty years older than the Parthenon of Athens, and which had been destroyed by earthquakes, then by iconoclast Christians, then by savage Turks. But mark that in the task he had achieved an excellent education, and become associated with distinguished scholars

---

[3] **John Gibson (1790–1866)** Member of the Royal Academy and prominent Victorian sculptor who worked in marble. See "Emerson's Rhetoric" (pp. 248–250) for more information on Sir Charles Fellowes.

[4] **Sir Humphry Davy (1778–1829)** An important chemist capable of analyzing the pigments in question.

whom he had interested in his pursuit; in short, had formed a college for himself; the enthusiast had found the master, the masters, whom he sought. Always genius seeks genius, desires nothing so much as to be a pupil and to find those who can lend it aid to perfect itself.

Nor are the two elements, enthusiasm and drill, incompatible. 6 Accuracy is essential to beauty. The very definition of the intellect is Aristotle's: "that by which we know terms or boundaries." Give a boy accurate perceptions. Teach him the difference between the similar and the same. Make him call things by their right names. Pardon in him no blunder. Then he will give you solid satisfaction as long as he lives. It is better to teach the child arithmetic and Latin grammar than rhetoric or moral philosophy, because they require exactitude of performance; it is made certain that the lesson is mastered, and that power of performance is worth more than the knowledge. He can learn anything which is important to him now that the power to learn is secured: as mechanics say, when one has learned the use of tools, it is easy to work at a new craft.

Letter by letter, syllable by syllable, the child learns to read, and 7 in good time can convey to all the domestic circle the sense of Shakspeare [sic]. By many steps each just as short, the stammering boy and the hesitating collegian, in the school debate, in college clubs, in mock court, comes at last to full, secure, triumphant unfolding of his thought in the popular assembly, with a fullness of power that makes all the steps forgotten.

But this function of opening and feeding the human mind is not 8 to be fulfilled by any mechanical or military method; is not to be trusted to any skill less large than Nature itself. You must not neglect the form, but you must secure the essentials. It is curious how perverse and intermeddling we are, and what vast pains and cost we incur to do wrong. Whilst we all know in our own experience and apply natural methods in our own business—in education our common sense fails us, and we are continually trying costly machinery against nature, in patent schools and academies and in great colleges and universities.

The natural method forever confutes our experiments, and we 9 must still come back to it. The whole theory of the school is on the nurse's or mother's knee. The child is as hot to learn as the mother is to impart. There is mutual delight. The joy of our childhood in hearing beautiful stories from some skilful aunt who loves to tell them, must be repeated in youth. The boy wishes to learn to skate, to coast, to catch a fish in the brook, to hit a mark with a snowball or a stone; and a boy a little older is just as well pleased to teach him these sciences. Not less delightful is the mutual pleasure of teaching

and learning the secret of algebra, or of chemistry, or of good reading and good recitation of poetry or of prose, or of chosen facts in
history or in biography.

Nature provided for the communication of thought, by planting   10
with it in the receiving mind a fury to impart it. 'Tis so in every art,
in every science. One burns to tell the new fact, the other burns to
hear it. See how far a young doctor will ride or walk to witness a
new surgical operation. I have seen a carriage-maker's shop emptied
of all its workmen into the street, to scrutinize a new pattern from
New York. So in literature, the young man who has taste for poetry,
for fine images, for noble thoughts, is insatiable for this nourishment, and forgets all the world for the more learned friend — who
finds equal joy in dealing out his treasures.

Happy the natural college thus self-instituted around every nat-   11
ural teacher; the young men of Athens around Socrates; of Alexan-
dria around Plotinus; of Paris around Abelard; of Germany around
Fichte, or Niebuhr, or Goethe:[5] in short the natural sphere of every
leading mind. But the moment this is organized, difficulties begin.
The college was to be the nurse and home of genius; but, though
every young man is born with some determination in his nature,
and is a potential genius; is at last to be one; it is, in the most,
obstructed and delayed, and, whatever they may hereafter be, their
senses are now opened in advance of their minds. They are more
sensual than intellectual. Appetite and indolence they have, but no
enthusiasm. These come in numbers to the college: few geniuses:
and the teaching comes to be arranged for these many, and not for
those few. Hence the instruction seems to require skilful tutors, of
accurate and systematic mind, rather than ardent and inventive masters. Besides, the youth of genius are eccentric, won't drill, are irrita-
ble, uncertain, explosive, solitary, not men of the world, not good
for every-day association. You have to work for large classes instead
of individuals; you must lower your flag and reef your sails to wait
for the dull sailors; you grow departmental, routinary, military almost with your discipline and college police. But what doth such a
school to form a great and heroic character? What abiding Hope can
it inspire? What Reformer will it nurse? What poet will it breed to
sing to the human race? What discoverer of Nature's laws will it
prompt to enrich us by disclosing in the mind the statute which all

---

[5] **Socrates . . . Goethe** All these men were teachers who drew students to them.
Socrates (469–399 B.C.); **Plotinus (A.D. 205–270)**; **Peter Abelard (1079–1142)**;
Johann Gottlieb Fichte (1762–1814); **Barthold Georg Niebuhr (1776–1831)**;
Johann Wolfgang von Goethe (1749–1832) were all among the intellectual influ-
ences on Emerson and his time.

matter must obey? What fiery soul will it send out to warm a nation with his charity? What tranquil mind will it have fortified to walk with meekness in private and obscure duties, to wait and to suffer? Is it not manifest that our academic institutions should have a wider scope; that they should not be timid and keep the ruts of the last generation, but that wise men thinking for themselves and heartily seeking the good of mankind, and counting the cost of innovation, should dare to arouse the young to a just and heroic life; that the moral nature should be addressed in the school-room, and children should be treated as the high-born candidates of truth and virtue?

So to regard the young child, the young man, requires, no 12 doubt, rare patience: a patience that nothing but faith in the remedial forces of the soul can give. You see his sensualism; you see his want of those tastes and perceptions which make the power and safety of your character. Very likely. But he has something else. If he has his own vice, he has its correlative virtue. Every mind should be allowed to make its own statement in action, and its balance will appear. In these judgments one needs that foresight which was attributed to an eminent reformer, of whom it was said "his patience could see in the bud of the aloe the blossom at the end of a hundred years." Alas for the cripple Practice when it seeks to come up with the bird Theory, which flies before it. Try your design on the best school. The scholars are of all ages and temperaments and capacities. It is difficult to class them, some are too young, some are slow, some perverse. Each requires so much consideration, that the morning hope of the teacher, of a day of love and progress, is often closed at evening by despair. Each single case, the more it is considered, shows more to be done; and the strict conditions of the hours, on one side, and the number of tasks, on the other. Whatever becomes of our method, the conditions stand fast—six hours, and thirty, fifty, or a hundred and fifty pupils. Something must be done, and done speedily, and in this distress the wisest are tempted to adopt violent means, to proclaim martial law, corporal punishment, mechanical arrangement, bribes, spies, wrath, main strength and ignorance, in lieu of that wise genial providential influence they had hoped, and yet hope at some future day to adopt. Of course the devotion to details reacts injuriously on the teacher. He cannot indulge his genius, he cannot delight in personal relations with young friends, when his eye is always on the clock, and twenty classes are to be dealt with before the day is done. Besides, how can he please himself with genius, and foster modest virtue? A sure proportion of rogue and dunce finds its way into every school and requires a cruel share of time, and the gentle teacher, who wished to be a Providence to youth, is grown a martinet, sore with suspicions; knows as much

vice as the judge of a police court, and his love of learning is lost in
the routine of grammars and books of elements.

A rule is so easy that it does not need a man to apply it; an au-   13
tomaton, a machine, can be made to keep a school so. It facilitates
labor and thought so much that there is always the temptation in
large schools to omit the endless task of meeting the wants of each
single mind, and to govern by steam. But it is at frightful cost. Our
modes of Education aim to expedite, to save labor; to do for masses
what cannot be done for masses, what must be done reverently, one
by one: say rather, the whole world is needed for the tuition of each
pupil. The advantages of this system of emulation and display are so
prompt and obvious, it is such a time-saver, it is so energetic on
slow and on bad natures, and is of so easy application, needing no
sage or poet, but any tutor or schoolmaster in his first term can
apply it—that it is not strange that this calomel[6] of culture should
be a popular medicine. On the other hand, total abstinence from his
drug, and the adoption of simple discipline and the following of nature, involves at once immense claims on the time, the thoughts, on
the life of the teacher. It requires time, use, insight, event, all the
great lessons and assistances of God; and only to think of using it
implies character and profoundness; to enter on this course of discipline is to be good and great. It is precisely analogous to the difference between the use of corporal punishment and the methods of
love. It is so easy to bestow on a bad boy a blow, overpower him,
and get obedience without words, that in this world of hurry and
distraction, who can wait for the returns of reason and the conquest of self; in the uncertainty too whether that will ever come? And
yet the familiar observation of the universal compensations might
suggest the fear that so summary a stop of a bad humor was more
jeopardous than its continuance.

Now the correction of this quack practice is to import into Edu-   14
cation the wisdom of life. Leave this military hurry and adopt the
pace of Nature. Her secret is patience. Do you know how the naturalist learns all the secrets of the forest, of plants, of birds, of beasts,
of reptiles, of fishes, of the rivers and the sea? When he goes into the
woods the birds fly before him and he finds none; when he goes to
the river bank, the fish and the reptile swim away and leave him
alone. His secret is patience; he sits down, and sits still; he is a
statue; he is a log. These creatures have no value for their time, and
he must put as low a rate on his. By dint of obstinate sitting still,
reptile, fish, bird and beast, which all wish to return to their haunts,

---

[6] **calomel** A medicinal powder used to induce vomiting.

begin to return. He sits still; if they approach, he remains passive as the stone he sits upon. They lose their fear. They have curiosity too about him. By and by the curiosity masters the fear, and they come swimming, creeping and flying towards him; and as he is still immovable, they not only resume their haunts and their ordinary labors and manners, show themselves to him in their work-day trim, but also volunteer some degree of advances towards fellowship and good understanding with a biped who behaves so civilly and well. Can you not baffle the impatience and passion of the child by your tranquility? Can you not wait for him, as Nature and Providence do? Can you not keep for his mind and ways, for his secret, the same curiosity you give to the squirrel, snake, rabbit, and the sheldrake and the deer? He has a secret; wonderful methods in him; he is—every child—a new style of man; give him time and opportunity. Talk of Columbus and Newton![7] I tell you the child just born in yonder hovel is the beginning of a revolution as great as theirs. But you must have the believing and prophetic eye. Have the self-command you wish to inspire. Your teaching and discipline must have the reserve and taciturnity of Nature. Teach them to hold their tongues by holding your own. Say little; do not snarl; do not chide; but govern by the eye. See what they need, and that the right thing is done.

I confess myself utterly at a loss in suggesting particular reforms 15 in our ways of teaching. No discretion that can be lodged with a school-committee, with the overseers or visitors of an academy, of a college, can at all avail to reach these difficulties and perplexities, but they solve themselves when we leave institutions and address individuals. The will, the male power, organizes, imposes its own thought and wish on others, and makes that military eye which controls boys as it controls men; admirable in its results, a fortune to him who has it, and only dangerous when it leads the workman to overvalue and overuse it and precludes him from finer means. Sympathy, the female force—which they must use who have not the first—deficient in instant control and the breaking down of resistance, is more subtle and lasting and creative. I advise teachers to cherish mother-wit. I assume that you will keep the grammar, reading, writing and arithmetic in order; 'tis easy and of course you will. But smuggle in a little contraband wit, fancy, imagination, thought. If you have a taste which you have suppressed because it is not shared by those about you, tell them that. Set this law up, whatever becomes of the rules of the school: they must not whisper, much

---

[7] Two great discoverers: **Christopher Columbus (1451–1506)** discovered the New World, and **Isaac Newton (1642–1727)** discovered the laws of gravity.

less talk; but if one of the young people says a wise thing, greet it, and let all the children clap their hands. They shall have no book but school-books in the room; but if one has brought in a Plutarch or Shakspeare or Don Quixote or Goldsmith[8] or any other good book, and understands what he reads, put him at once at the head of the class. Nobody shall be disorderly, or leave his desk without permission, but if a boy runs from his bench, or a girl, because the fire falls, or to check some injury that a little dastard is inflicting behind his desk on some helpless sufferer, take away the medal from the head of the class and give it on the instant to the brave rescuer. If a child happens to show that he knows any fact about astronomy, or plants, or birds, or rocks, or history, that interests him and you, hush all the classes and encourage him to tell it so that all may hear. Then you have made your school-room like the world. Of course you will insist on modesty in the children, and respect to their teachers, but if the boy stops you in your speech, cries out that you are wrong and sets you right, hug him!

To whatsoever upright mind, to whatsoever beating heart I speak, 16 to you it is committed to educate men. By simple living, by an illimitable soul, you inspire, you correct, you instruct, you raise, you embellish all. By your own act you teach the beholder how to do the practicable. According to the depth from which you draw your life, such is the depth not only of your strenuous effort, but of your manners and presence.

The beautiful nature of the world has here blended your happi- 17 ness with your power. Work straight on in absolute duty, and you lend an arm and an encouragement to all the youth of the universe. Consent yourself to be an organ of your highest thought, and lo! suddenly you put all men in your debt, and are the fountain of an energy that goes pulsing on with waves of benefit to the borders of society, to the circumference of things.

---

[8] Four important writers of biography, drama, fiction, and poetry: **Plutarch (A.D. 46?–120)**, **William Shakespeare (1564–1616)**, **Mignel de Cervantes (1547–1616)**, **Oliver Goldsmith (1730–1774)**.

QUESTIONS FOR CRITICAL READING

1. Does the secret of education lie in respecting the pupil?
2. How does one keep a young student's *naturel*?
3. What is the significance of Emerson's example of Sir Charles Fellowes?
4. Are enthusiasm and drill incompatible in education?

5. How does a person's nature help in education?
6. What is Emerson's attitude toward rules?
7. How does Emerson regard mass education?
8. What does Emerson mean by referring to the need "to import into Education the wisdom of life" (para. 14)?

SUGGESTIONS FOR WRITING

1. Emerson offers us some examples of the natural way to education. What examples do you have of the natural development of a curiosity that resulted in what you would describe as a serious education? Do these examples derive from the interaction of student and pupil? What were the conditions that made these examples work best? In your essay, try to decide how valid Emerson's views on nature and education are for the example you choose.

2. To what extent has your education benefited from your natural desire to learn or a teacher's natural desire to teach? Think of a specific example from your own education and describe your experiences in detail.

3. Do you think Emerson is being unrealistic in suggesting that "every child" is "a new style of man" (para. 14)? His recommendation is that the teacher should "give [a student] time and opportunity" (para. 14) to reveal his inner self. How is this related to education? Has there been anything in your own experience that would lend credence to this observation? Do you feel that you yourself are a "new style of" person?

4. Emerson refers to two forces he feels should be at work in the classroom. He styles one as the male force, will; the second is the female force, sympathy. Study his analysis of these forces in paragraph 15 and decide whether these are really important to good education. Do you think Emerson's linking of these forces with the male and female genders is reasonable? Do you see evidence of these forces at work in your own education?

5. In paragraph 13, Emerson states, "Our modes of Education aim to expedite, to save labor; to do for masses what cannot be done for masses, what must be done reverently, one by one: say rather, the whole world is needed for the tuition of each pupil." What does he mean? Relying on what you know of education today, write an essay in which you either support or attack Emerson's statement.

6. "On Education" was written as a commencement address to graduating students, some of whom may have intended to teach. Write an essay of your own titled "On Education," which treats the subject in a way that would make sense for today's recent college graduates. What principles would you suggest for teachers? For students? Describe the kind of education you think you would be successful and meaningful to today's student.

7. Emerson seems to have been talking about the smaller academies that served the well-off when he was a young man. Do his views on

education have currency in relation to the large schools found today in most urban environments in the United States? How have students changed since Emerson's time? How have their educational opportunities changed? Could Emerson's views be effective in bringing about much-needed reform in U.S. public schools?

8. **CONNECTIONS** To what extent does the experience of Frederick Douglass, who was denied a school or classroom experience entirely, help to support Emerson's theories? Examine Douglass's experience in trying to learn to read and write, and compare it to the ideas recommended by Emerson. To what extent did nature and genius help Douglass?

9. **CONNECTIONS** What are the most important points of comparison and contrast between Emerson's view of education and Paolo Freire's? Do you feel that Emerson anticipates the views Friere condemns in his essay? Would Freire sympathize with Emerson's views, or would he see them as simply a variant of the views he attacks?

FREDERICK DOUGLASS
From *Narrative of the Life of Frederick Douglass, an American Slave*

FREDERICK DOUGLASS (1817–1895) was born into slavery
in Maryland; he died not only a free man but also a man who commanded the respect of his country, his government, and hosts of
supporters. Ironically, it was his owner's wife, Mrs. Hugh Auld, a
Northerner, who helped Douglass learn to read and write. Until her
husband forcefully convinced her that teaching slaves was "unlawful, as well as unsafe," Mrs. Auld taught Douglass enough so that
he could begin his own education—and escape to freedom. Mrs.
Auld eventually surpassed her husband in her vehement opposition
to having Douglass read, leading Douglass to conclude that slavery
had a negative effect on slave and slave holder alike: both suffered
the consequences of a political system that was inherently unjust.

The *Narrative* is filled with examples of the injustice of slavery. Douglass had little connection with his family. Separated from
his mother, Harriet Bailey, Douglass never knew who his father
was. In his *Narrative*, he records the beatings he witnessed as a
slave, the conditions under which he lived, and the struggles he felt
within himself to be a free man. Douglass himself survived brutal
beatings and torture by a professional slave "breaker."

The laws of the time codified the injustices that Douglass and
all American slaves suffered. The Fugitive Slave Act of 1793 tight-
ened the hold on all slaves who had gone north in search of freedom.
Federal marshals were enjoined to return slaves to their owners. The
Underground Railroad helped so many runaway slaves find their
way to Canada that a second Fugitive Slave Act was enacted in
1850 with stiff penalties for those who did not obey the law. In retaliation, many Northern states enacted personal freedom laws to
counter the Fugitive Slave Act. Eventually, these laws became central to the South's decision to secede. However, Douglass's fate,

when he eventually escaped in 1838 by impersonating an African American seaman (using his papers to board ship), was not secure. Abolitionists in New York helped him find work in shipyards in New Bedford, Massachusetts. He changed his name from Auld to Douglass to protect himself, and he began his career as an orator in 1841 at an antislavery meeting in Nantucket.

To avoid capture after publication of an early version of his autobiography, Douglass spent two years on a speaking tour of Great Britain and Ireland (1845–1847). He then returned to the United States, bought his freedom, and rose to national fame as the founder and editor of the *North Star*, an abolitionist paper published in Rochester, New York. One of his chief concerns was for the welfare of the slaves who had managed to secure their freedom. When the Civil War began, there were no plans to free the slaves, but Douglass managed to convince Lincoln that it would further the war effort to free them; in 1863 the president delivered the Emancipation Proclamation.

However, the years after the war and Lincoln's death were not good for freed slaves. Terrorist groups in both the North and the South worked to keep them from enjoying freedom, and training programs for former slaves that might have been effective were never fully instituted. During this time Douglass worked in various capacities for the government—as assistant secretary of the Santo Domingo Commission, as an official in Washington, D.C., and as U.S. minister to Haiti (1889–1891). He was the first African American to become a national figure and to have influence with the government.

Douglass's Rhetoric

Douglass was basically self-taught, but he knew enough to read the powerful writers of his day. He was a commanding speaker in an age in which eloquence was valued and speakers were rewarded handsomely. This excerpt from the *Narrative*—Chapters 6, 7, and 8—is notable for its clear and direct style. The use of the first-person narrative is as simple as one could wish, yet the feelings projected are sincere and moving.

Douglass's structure is the chronological narrative, relating events in the order in which they occurred. He begins his story at the point of meeting a new mistress, a woman from whom he expected harsh treatment. Because she was new to the concept of slavery, however, she behaved in ways that were unusual, and Douglass remarks on her initially kind attitude. Douglass does not interrupt himself with flashbacks or leaps forward in time but tells the story as it happened. At critical moments, he slows the narrative to describe people or incidents in unusual detail and lets the reader infer from these details the extent of the injustice he suffered.

By today's standards, Douglass's style may seem formal. His sentences are often longer than those of modern writers, although they are always carefully balanced and punctuated by briefer sentences. Despite his long paragraphs, heavy with example and description, after a century and a half his work remains immediate and moving. No modern reader will have difficulty responding to what Frederick Douglass has to say. His views on education are as accessible and as powerful now as when they were written.

PREREADING QUESTIONS: WHAT TO READ FOR

The following prereading questions may help you anticipate key issues in the discussion of the excerpt that follows from *Narrative of the Life of Frederick Douglass, an American Slave*. Keeping them in mind during your first reading of the selection should help focus your attention.

- How did Douglass learn to read and write?
- Why was it thought dangerous for a slave to learn to read and write?
- What was the effect on Douglass of his learning to read?

From *Narrative of the Life of Frederick Douglass, an American Slave*

My new mistress proved to be all she appeared when I first met   1
her at the door,—a woman of the kindest heart and finest feelings. She had never had a slave under her control previously to myself, and prior to her marriage she had been dependent upon her own industry for a living. She was by trade a weaver; and by constant application to her business, she had been in a good degree preserved from the blighting and dehumanizing effects of slavery. I was utterly astonished at her goodness. I scarcely knew how to behave towards her. She was entirely unlike any other white woman I had ever seen. I could not approach her as I was accustomed to approach other white

ladies. My early instruction was all out of place. The crouching ser-
vility, usually so acceptable a quality in a slave, did not answer when
manifested toward her. Her favor was not gained by it; she seemed
to be disturbed by it. She did not deem it impudent or unmannerly
for a slave to look her in the face. The meanest slave was put fully at
ease in her presence, and none left without feeling better for having
seen her. Her face was made of heavenly smiles, and her voice of
tranquil music.

But, alas! this kind heart had but a short time to remain such.   2
The fatal poison of irresponsible power was already in her hands,
and soon commenced its infernal work. That cheerful eye, under the
influence of slavery, soon became red with rage; that voice, made all
of sweet accord, changed to one of harsh and horrid discord; and
that angelic face gave place to that of a demon.

Very soon after I went to live with Mr. and Mrs. Auld, she very   3
kindly commenced to teach me the A, B, C. After I had learned this,
she assisted me in learning to spell words of three or four letters.
Just at this point of my progress, Mr. Auld found out what was
going on, and at once forbade Mrs. Auld to instruct me further,
telling her, among other things, that it was unlawful, as well as unsafe, to teach a slave to read. To use his own words, further, he said,
"If you give a nigger an inch, he will take an ell.[1] A nigger should
know nothing but to obey his master—to do as he is told to do.
Learning would *spoil* the best nigger in the world. Now," said he, "if
you teach that nigger (speaking of myself) how to read, there would
be no keeping him. It would forever unfit him to be a slave. He
would at once become unmanageable, and of no value to his master.
As to himself, it could do him no good, but a great deal of harm. It
would make him discontented and unhappy." These words sank
deep into my heart, stirred up sentiments within that lay slumber-
ing, and called into existence an entirely new train of thought. It was
a new and special revelation, explaining dark and mysterious things,
with which my youthful understanding had struggled, but struggled
in vain. I now understood what had been to me a most perplexing
difficulty—to wit, the white man's power to enslave the black man.
It was a grand achievement, and I prized it highly. From that moment, I understood the pathway from slavery to freedom. It was
just what I wanted, and I got it at a time when I the least expected it.
Whilst I was saddened by the thought of losing the aid of my kind
mistress, I was gladdened by the invaluable instruction which, by the
merest accident, I had gained from my master. Though conscious of

---

[1] **ell** A measure about a yard in length.

the difficulty of learning without a teacher, I set out with high hope, and a fixed purpose, at whatever cost of trouble, to learn how to read. The very decided manner with which he spoke, and strove to impress his wife with the evil consequences of giving me instruction, served to convince me that he was deeply sensible of the truths he was uttering. It gave me the best assurance that I might rely with the utmost confidence on the results which, he said, would flow from teaching me to read. What he most dreaded, that I most desired. What he most loved, that I most hated. That which to him was a great evil, to be carefully shunned, was to me a great good, to be diligently sought; and the argument which he so warmly urged, against my learning to read, only served to inspire me with a desire and determination to learn. In learning to read, I owe almost as much to the bitter opposition of my master, as to the kindly aid of my mistress. I acknowledge the benefit of both.

I had resided but a short time in Baltimore before I observed a   4 marked difference, in the treatment of slaves, from that which I had witnessed in the country. A city slave is almost a freeman, compared with a slave on the plantation. He is much better fed and clothed, and enjoys privileges altogether unknown to the slave on the plantation. There is a vestige of decency, a sense of shame, that does much to curb and check those outbreaks of atrocious cruelty so commonly enacted upon the plantation. He is a desperate slaveholder, who will shock the humanity of his nonslaveholding neighbors with the cries of his lacerated slave. Few are willing to incur the odium attaching to the reputation of being a cruel master; and above all things, they would not be known as not giving a slave enough to eat. Every city slaveholder is anxious to have it known of him, that he feeds his slaves well; and it is due to them to say, that most of them do give their slaves enough to eat. There are, however, some painful exceptions to this rule. Directly opposite to us, on Philpot Street, lived Mr. Thomas Hamilton. He owned two slaves. Their names were Henrietta and Mary. Henrietta was about twenty-two years of age, Mary was about fourteen; and of all the mangled and emaciated creatures I ever looked upon, these two were the most so. His heart must be harder than stone, that could look upon these unmoved. The head, neck, and shoulders of Mary were literally cut to pieces. I have frequently felt her head, and found it nearly covered with festering sores, caused by the lash of her cruel mistress. I do not know that her master ever whipped her, but I have been an eye-witness to the cruelty of Mrs. Hamilton. I used to be in Mr. Hamilton's house nearly every day. Mrs. Hamilton used to sit in a large chair in the middle of the room, with a heavy cowskin always by her side, and scarce an hour passed during the day but was marked by the blood of one of these slaves. The girls seldom passed her without her saying, "Move faster, you *black gip!*" at the same time giving them a blow with the cowskin over the head or shoulders, often drawing the blood. She would then say, "Take that, you *black gip!*"—continuing, "If you don't move faster, I'll move you!" Added to the cruel lashings to which these slaves were subjected, they were kept nearly half-starved. They seldom knew what it was to eat a full meal. I have seen Mary contending with the pigs for the offal thrown into the street. So much was Mary kicked and cut to pieces, that she was oftener called "*pecked*" than by her name.

I lived in Master Hugh's family about seven years. During this 5 time, I succeeded in learning to read and write. In accomplishing this, I was compelled to resort to various stratagems. I had no regular teacher. My mistress, who had kindly commenced to instruct me, had, in compliance with the advice and direction of her husband, not only ceased to instruct, but had set her face against my being instructed by any one else. It is due, however, to my mistress to say of her, that she did not adopt this course of treatment immediately. She at first lacked the depravity indispensable to shutting me up in mental darkness. It was at least necessary for her to have some training in the exercise of irresponsible power, to make her equal to the task of treating me as though I were a brute.

My mistress was, as I have said, a kind and tender-hearted 6 woman; and in the simplicity of her soul she commenced, when I first went to live with her, to treat me as she supposed one human being ought to treat another. In entering upon the duties of a slave-holder, she did not seem to perceive that I sustained to her the relation of a mere chattel, and that for her to treat me as a human being was not only wrong, but dangerously so. Slavery proved as injurious to her as it did to me. When I went there, she was a pious, warm, and tender-hearted woman. There was no sorrow or suffering for which she had not a tear. She had bread for the hungry, clothes for the naked, and comfort for every mourner that came within her reach. Slavery soon proved its ability to divest her of these heavenly qualities. Under its influence, the tender heart became stone, and the lamb-like disposition gave way to one of tiger-like fierceness. The first step in her downward course was in her ceasing to instruct me. She now commenced to practise her husband's precepts. She finally became even more violent in her opposition than her husband himself. She was not satisfied with simply doing as well as he had commanded; she seemed anxious to do better. Nothing seemed to make her more angry than to see me with a newspaper. She seemed to think that here lay the danger. I have had her rush at me with a face made all up of fury, and snatch from me a newspaper, in a manner that fully revealed her apprehension. She was an apt woman; and a little experience soon demonstrated, to her satisfaction, that education and slavery were incompatible with each other.

From this time I was most narrowly watched. If I was in a separate room any considerable length of time, I was sure to be suspected of having a book, and was at once called to give an account of myself. All this, however, was too late. The first step had been taken. Mistress, in teaching me the alphabet, had given me the *inch*, and no precaution could prevent me from taking the *ell*. 7

The plan which I adopted, and the one by which I was most successful, was that of making friends of all the little white boys whom I met in the street. As many of these as I could, I converted into teachers. With their kindly aid, obtained at different times and in different places, I finally succeeded in learning to read. When I was sent to errands, I always took my book with me, and by going one part of my errand quickly, I found time to get a lesson before my return. I used also to carry bread with me, enough of which was always in the house, and to which I was always welcome; for I was much better off in this regard than many of the poor white children in our neighborhood. This bread I used to bestow upon the hungry little urchins, who, in return, would give me that more valuable bread of knowledge. I am strongly tempted to give the names of two or three of those little boys, as a testimonial of the gratitude and affection I bear them; but prudence forbids;—not that it would injure me, but it might embarrass them; for it is almost an unpardonable offence to teach slaves to read in this Christian country. It is enough to say of the dear little fellows, that they lived on Philpot Street, very near Durgin and Bailey's ship-yard. I used to talk this matter of slavery over with them. I would sometimes say to them, I wished I could be as free as they would be when they got to be men. "You will be free as soon as you are twenty-one, *but I am a slave for life!* Have not I as good a right to be free as you have?" These words used to trouble them; they would express for me the liveliest sympathy, and console me with the hope that something would occur by which I might be free. 8

I was now about twelve years old, and the thought of being *a slave for life* began to bear heavily upon my heart. Just about this time, I got hold of a book entitled "The Columbian Orator." Every opportunity I got, I used to read this book. Among much of other interesting matter, I found in it a dialogue between a master and his slave. The slave was represented as having run away from his master three times. The dialogue represented the conversation which took place between them, when the slave was retaken the third time. In 9

this dialogue, the whole argument in behalf of slavery was brought
forward by the master, all of which was disposed of by the slave.
The slave was made to say some very smart as well as impressive
things in reply to his master—things which had the desired though
unexpected effect; for the conversation resulted in the voluntary
emancipation of the slave on the part of the master.

In the same book, I met with one of Sheridan's[2] mighty   10
speeches on and in behalf of Catholic emancipation. These were
choice documents to me. I read them over and over again with unabated interest. They gave tongue to interesting thoughts of my own
soul, which had frequently flashed through my mind, and died away
for want of utterance. The moral which I gained from the dialogue
was the power of truth over the conscience of even a slaveholder.
What I got from Sheridan was a bold denunciation of slavery, and a
powerful vindication of human rights. The reading of these documents enabled me to utter my thoughts, and to meet the arguments
brought forward to sustain slavery; but while they relieved me of
one difficulty, they brought on another even more painful than the
one of which I was relieved. The more I read, the more I was led to
abhor and detest my enslavers. I could regard them in no other light
than a band of successful robbers, who had left their homes, and
gone to Africa, and stolen us from our homes, and in a strange land
reduced us to slavery. I loathed them as being the meanest as well as
the most wicked of men. As I read and contemplated the subject,
behold! that very discontentment which Master Hugh had predicted
would follow my learning to read had already come, to torment
and sting my soul to unutterable anguish. As I writhed under it, I
would at times feel that learning to read had been a curse rather
than a blessing. It had given me a view of my wretched condition,
without the remedy. It opened my eyes to the horrible pit, but to no
ladder upon which to get out. In moments of agony, I envied my
fellow-slaves for their stupidity. I have often wished myself a beast. I
preferred the condition of the meanest reptile to my own. Any thing,
no matter what, to get rid of thinking! It was this everlasting thinking of my condition that tormented me. There was no getting rid of
it. It was pressed upon me by every object within sight or hearing,
animate or inanimate. The silver trump of freedom had roused my
soul to eternal wakefulness. Freedom now appeared, to disappear
no more forever. It was heard in every sound, and seen in every
thing. It was ever present to torment me with a sense of my wretched

---

[2] **Richard Brinsley Sheridan (1751–1816)** Irish dramatist and orator. However, Douglass really refers to a speech by Daniel O'Connell (1775–1847) in favor of
Irish Catholic emancipation.

condition. I saw nothing without seeing it, I heard nothing without hearing it, and felt nothing without feeling it. It looked from every star, it smiled in every calm, breathed in every wind, and moved in every storm.

I often found myself regretting my own existence, and wishing myself dead; and but for the hope of being free, I have no doubt but that I should have killed myself, or done something for which I should have been killed. While in this state of mind, I was eager to hear any one speak of slavery. I was a ready listener. Every little while, I could hear something about the abolitionists.[3] It was some time before I found what the word meant. It was always used in such connections as to make it an interesting word to me. If a slave ran away and succeeded in getting clear, or if a slave killed his master, set fire to a barn, or did any thing very wrong in the mind of a slaveholder, it was spoken of as the fruit of *abolition*. Hearing the word in this connection very often, I set about learning what it meant. The dictionary afforded me little or no help. I found it was "the act of abolishing"; but then I did not know what was to be abolished. Here I was perplexed. I did not dare to ask any one about its meaning, for I was satisfied that it was something they wanted me to know very little about. After a patient waiting, I got one of our city papers, containing an account of the number of petitions from the north, praying for the abolition of slavery in the District of Columbia, and of the slave trade between the States. From this time I understood the words *abolition* and *abolitionist*, and always drew near when that word was spoken, expecting to hear something of importance to myself and fellow-slaves. The light broke in upon me by degrees. I went one day down on the wharf of Mr. Waters; and seeing two Irishmen unloading a scow of stone, I went, unasked, and helped them. When we had finished, one of them came to me and asked me if I were a slave. I told him I was. He asked, "Are ye a slave for life?" I told him that I was. The good Irishman seemed to be deeply affected by the statement. He said to the other that it was a pity so fine a little fellow as myself should be a slave for life. He said it was a shame to hold me. They both advised me to run away to the north; that I should find friends there, and that I should be free. I pretended not to be interested in what they said, and treated them as if I did not understand them; for I feared they might be treacherous. White men have been known to encourage slaves to escape, and then, to get the reward, catch them and return them to their masters. I was afraid that these seemingly good men might use me so; but I nevertheless

[3] **abolitionists** Those who actively opposed slavery.

remembered their advice, and from that time I resolved to run away. I looked forward to a time at which it would be safe for me to escape. I was too young to think of doing so immediately; besides, I wished to learn how to write, as I might have occasion to write my own pass. I consoled myself with the hope that I should one day find a good chance. Meanwhile, I would learn to write.

The idea as to how I might learn to write was suggested to me by being in Durgin and Bailey's ship-yard, and frequently seeing the ship carpenters, after hewing, and getting a piece of timber ready for use, write on the timber the name of that part of the ship for which it was intended. When a piece of timber was intended for the larboard side, it would be marked thus—"L." When a piece was for the starboard side, it would be marked thus—"S." A piece for the larboard side forward, would be marked thus—"L.F." When a piece was for starboard side forward, it would be marked thus—"S.F." For larboard aft, it would be marked thus—"L.A." For starboard aft, it would be marked thus—"S.A." I soon learned the names of these letters, and for what they were intended when placed upon a piece of timber in the ship-yard. I immediately commenced copying them, and in a short time was able to make the four letters named. After that, when I met with any boy who I knew could write, I would tell him I could write as well as he. The next word would be, "I don't believe you. Let me see you try it." I would then make the letters which I had been so fortunate as to learn, and ask him to beat that. In this way I got a good many lessons in writing, which it is quite possible I should never have gotten in any other way. During this time, my copy-book was the board fence, brick wall, and pavement; my pen and ink was a lump of chalk. With these, I learned mainly how to write. I then commenced and continued copying the Italics in Webster's Spelling Book, until I could make them all without looking on the book. By this time, my little Master Thomas had gone to school, and learned how to write, and had written over a number of copy-books. These had been brought home, and shown to some of our near neighbors, and then laid aside. My mistress used to go to class meeting at the Wilk Street meeting-house every Monday afternoon, and leave me to take care of the house. When left thus, I used to spend the time in writing in the spaces left in Master Thomas's copy-book, copying what he had written. I continued to do this until I could write a hand very similar to that of Master Thomas. Thus, after a long, tedious effort for years, I finally succeeded in learning how to write. 12

In a very short time after I went to live at Baltimore, my old master's youngest son Richard died; and in about three years and six months after his death, my old master, Captain Anthony, died, leaving 13 only his son, Andrew, and daughter, Lucretia, to share his estate. He died while on a visit to see his daughter at Hillsborough. Cut off thus unexpectedly, he left no will as to the disposal of his property. It was therefore necessary to have a valuation of the property, that it might be equally divided between Mrs. Lucretia and Master Andrew. I was immediately sent for, to be valued with the other property. Here again my feelings rose up in detestation of slavery. I had now a new conception of my degraded condition. Prior to this, I had become, if not insensible to my lot, at least partly so. I left Baltimore with a young heart overborne with sadness, and a soul full of apprehension. I took passage with Captain Rowe, in the schooner Wild Cat, and, after a sail of about twenty-four hours, I found myself near the place of my birth. I had now been absent from it almost, if not quite, five years. I, however, remembered the place very well. I was only about five years old when I left it, to go and live with my old master on Colonel Lloyd's plantation; so that I was now between ten and eleven years old.

We were all ranked together at the valuation. Men and women, 14 old and young, married and single, were ranked with horses, sheep, and swine. There were horses and men, cattle and women, pigs and children, all holding the same rank in the scale of being, and were all subjected to the same narrow examination. Silvery-headed age and sprightly youth, maids and matrons, had to undergo the same indelicate inspection. At this moment, I saw more clearly than ever the brutalizing effects of slavery upon both slave and slave-holder.

After the valuation, then came the division. I have no language 15 to express the high excitement and deep anxiety which were felt among us poor slaves during this time. Our fate for life was now to be decided. We had no more voice in that decision than the brutes among whom we were ranked. A single word from the white men was enough—against all our wishes, prayers, and entreaties—to sunder forever the dearest friends, dearest kindred, and strongest ties known to human beings. In addition to the pain of separation, there was the horrid dread of falling into the hands of Master Andrew. He was known to us all as being a most cruel wretch,— a common drunkard, who had, by his reckless mismanagement and profligate dissipation, already wasted a large portion of his father's property. We all felt that we might as well be sold at once to the Georgia traders, as to pass into his hands; for we knew that that would be our inevitable condition,—a condition held by us all in the utmost horror and dread.

I suffered more anxiety than most of my fellow-slaves. I had 16 known what it was to be kindly treated; they had known nothing of the kind. They had seen little or nothing of the world. They were in very deed men and women of sorrow, and acquainted with grief. Their backs had been made familiar with the bloody lash, so that they had become callous; mine was yet tender; for while at Baltimore I got few whippings, and few slaves could boast of a kinder master and mistress than myself; and the thought of passing out of their hands into those of Master Andrew—a man who, but a few days before, to give me a sample of his bloody disposition, took my little brother by the throat, threw him on the ground, and with the heel of his boot stamped upon his head till the blood gushed from his nose and ears—was well calculated to make me anxious as to my fate. After he had committed this savage outrage upon my brother, he turned to me, and said that was the way he meant to serve me one of these days,—meaning, I suppose, when I came into his possession.

Thanks to a kind Providence, I fell to the portion of Mrs. Lucre- 17 tia, and was sent immediately back to Baltimore, to live again in the family of Master Hugh. Their joy at my return equalled their sorrow at my departure. It was a glad day to me. I had escaped a worse fate than lion's jaws. I was absent from Baltimore, for the purpose of valuation and division, just about one month, and it seemed to have been six.

Very soon after my return to Baltimore, my mistress, Lucretia, 18 died, leaving her husband and child, Amanda; and in a very short time after her death, Master Andrew died. Now all the property of my old master, slaves included, was in the hands of strangers,— strangers who had had nothing to do with accumulating it. Not a slave was left free. All remained slaves, from the youngest to the oldest. If any one thing in my experience, more than another, served to deepen my conviction of the infernal character of slavery, and to fill me with unutterable loathing of slaveholders, it was their base ingratitude to my poor old grandmother. She had served my old master faithfully from youth to old age. She had been the source of all his wealth; she had peopled his plantation with slaves; she had become a great grandmother in his service. She had rocked him in infancy, attended him in childhood, served him through life, and at his death wiped from his icy brow the cold death-sweat, and closed his eyes forever. She was nevertheless left a slave—a slave for life—a slave in the hands of strangers; and in their hands she saw her children, her grandchildren, and her great-grandchildren, divided, like so many sheep, without being gratified with the small privilege of a single word, as to their or her own destiny. And, to cap the climax of their base ingratitude and fiendish barbarity, my grandmother, who was now very old, having outlived my old master and all his children, having seen the beginning and end of all of them, and her present owners finding she was of but little value, her frame already racked with the pains of old age, and complete helplessness fast stealing over her once active limbs, they took her to the woods, built her a little hut, put up a little mud-chimney, and then made her welcome to the privilege of supporting herself there in perfect loneliness; thus virtually turning her out to die! If my poor old grandmother now lives, she lives to suffer in utter loneliness; she lives to remember and mourn over the loss of children, the loss of grandchildren, and the loss of great-grandchildren. They are, in the language of the slave's poet, Whittier,[4]—

> Gone, gone, sold and gone
> To the rice swamp dank and lone,
> Where the slave-whip ceaseless swings,
> Where the noisome insect stings,
> Where the fever-demon strews
> Poison with the falling dews,
> Where the sickly sunbeams glare
> Through the hot and misty air:—
>> Gone, gone, sold and gone
>> To the rice swamp dank and lone,
>> From Virginia hills and waters—
>> Woe is me, my stolen daughters!

The hearth is desolate. The children, the unconscious children, who once sang and danced in her presence, are gone. She gropes her way, in the darkness of age, for a drink of water. Instead of the voices of her children, she hears by day the moans of the dove, and by night the screams of the hideous owl. All is gloom. The grave is at the door. And now, when weighed down by the pains and aches of old age, when the head inclines to the feet, when the beginning and ending of human existence meet, and helpless infancy and painful old age combine together—at this time, this most needful time, the time for the exercise of that tenderness and affection which children only can exercise towards a declining parent—my poor old grandmother, the devoted mother of twelve children, is left all alone, in yonder little hut, before a few dim embers. She stands—she sits—she staggers—she falls—she groans—she dies— and there are none of her children or grandchildren present, to wipe   19

---

[4]**John Greenleaf Whittier (1807–1892)** New England abolitionist, journalist, and poet. The poem Douglass cites is "The Farewell" (1835).

from her wrinkled brow the cold sweat of death, or to place beneath the sod her fallen remains. Will not a righteous God visit for
these things?

In about two years after the death of Mrs. Lucretia, Master   20
Thomas married his second wife. Her name was Rowena Hamilton.
She was the eldest daughter of Mr. William Hamilton. Master now
lived in St. Michael's. Not long after his marriage, a misunderstanding took place between himself and Master Hugh; and as a means of
punishing his brother, he took me from him to live with himself at
St. Michael's. Here I underwent another most painful separation. It,
however, was not so severe as the one I dreaded at the division of
property; for, during this interval, a great change had taken place in
Master Hugh and his once kind and affectionate wife. The influence
of brandy upon him, and of slavery upon her, had effected a disastrous change in the characters of both; so that, as far as they were
concerned, I thought I had little to lose by the change. But it was not
to them that I was attached. It was to those little Baltimore boys that
I felt the strongest attachment. I had received many good lessons
from them, and was still receiving them, and the thought of leaving
them was painful indeed. I was leaving, too, without the hope of ever
being allowed to return. Master Thomas had said he would never let
me return again. The barrier betwixt himself and brother he considered impassable.

I then had to regret that I did not at least make the attempt to   21
carry out my resolution to run away; for the chances of success are
tenfold greater from the city than from the country.

I sailed from Baltimore for St. Michael's in the sloop Amanda,   22
Captain Edward Dodson. On my passage, I paid particular attention to the direction which the steamboats took to go to Philadelphia. I found, instead of going down, on reaching North Point
they went up the bay, in a north-easterly direction. I deemed
this knowledge of the utmost importance. My determination to run
away was again revived. I resolved to wait only so long as the offering of a favorable opportunity. When that came, I was determined
to be off.

QUESTIONS FOR CRITICAL READING

1. Douglass describes Mrs. Auld as possessing "the fatal poison of irresponsible power" (para. 2). What precisely does he mean by this?
2. How does the absence of justice undermine the force of law?

3. Why did the slaveholders believe learning to read would spoil a slave?
4. What were the results of Douglass's learning to read?
5. How did the slaveholders regard their slaves? What differences does Douglass describe in their behavior?

SUGGESTIONS FOR WRITING

1. Why would an oppressive society benefit from preventing its slaves from learning to read? What does reading have to do with their general education? Slave owners trained their slaves to perform complex tasks, such as farming, managing animals, working the fields. These are forms of education. Why would reading take on such importance in Douglass's life? Why is reading so important to education at any level?

2. The society in which Douglass lived was governed by laws established by officials who read the Bible and, whether they read them or not, benefited from the writings of Rousseau and Jefferson, among others. Why did they ignore the tenets of liberty and freedom as well as humanism and equality in their treatment of their slaves? In other words, why did their education fail slaveholders?

3. One of the defenses of slavery was that it was good for the slaves. Even some of the freed slaves told interviewers in the 1930s that things had been better for them under slavery than they were during the Depression. How would the lack of an education that included reading have affected a slave's judgment of his or her own well-being? How does a lack of education affect one's sense of self?

4. What kind of teacher was Mrs. Auld? What motivated her in trying to teach Douglass how to read? Why was her husband so annoyed at her and why did she change in her own attitude toward Douglass?

5. Judging from the quality of the prose of this selection, comment on what you feel were the strongest elements of Douglass's overall education. What evidence does he give of an advanced knowledge of politics, literature, science, mechanics, history, or social issues? How might he have acquired his knowledge? How subtle is his analysis of the situation he describes and considers important?

6. **CONNECTIONS** Examine the way in which Douglass taught himself to read and compare his process with the recommendations Emerson makes in "On Education," with a particular look at Emerson's constant advice to follow nature. How would you describe Douglass's nature as a young man? What kind of student was he? How did he make up for his lack of a formal education? What was the nature of his genius and how did it survive slavery?

7. **CONNECTIONS** How are the basic tenets of justice, as understood by Cicero, Thoreau, or Martin Luther King Jr., ignored in the world in which Douglass lived? When, if ever, was Douglass treated justly?

What is the result of the constant infliction of injustice on human beings, as revealed by Douglass? What was the effect of injustice on Douglass?

8. **SEEING CONNECTIONS**   Frederick Douglass, a former slave who taught himself to read and write, was among the most eloquent and committed speakers on civil rights in U.S. history. Douglass was also an adviser to President Abraham Lincoln (1809–1865) during the Civil War (1861–1865), an advocate for freed slaves after the war during the Reconstruction period, and an ambassador to Haiti from 1889 to 1891. The following photograph shows Douglass working at his desk in the library of his Washington, D.C., home.

In paragraph 7 Douglass states, "If I was in a separate room any considerable length of time, I was sure to be suspected of having a book, and was at once called to give an account of myself." Examine the photograph below closely. How does this scene compare with Douglass's description of his attempts to educate himself as a slave? What does this scene tell you about the role Douglass's education played in his life as a free man?

MARIA MONTESSORI
The Montessori Method

MARIA MONTESSORI (1870–1952) was born in Chiaravelle, Ancona, Italy. When she was twelve, her family moved to Rome so that she could receive a better education. At the age of fourteen, despite her father's misgivings and traditional views, Montessori enrolled in a technical college and studied engineering. Her interest in biology, however, led her to study medicine instead, and with Pope Leo XIII's help, Montessori was admitted to the University of Rome's medical school. In 1894 she graduated and became Italy's first female doctor, a feat that reinforced her commitment to women's rights.

Her appointment working with mentally challenged children in a hospital in Rome in 1897 catalyzed her interest in education. Montessori's work with these children convinced her that their problems were more connected with their education than with any perceived mental defects. She hypothesized that a change in education would make a large difference in the lives of these children, and she decided to devote her life to improving education for all children, not just those with mental handicaps.

In 1898 Montessori, unwed and devoutly Catholic, gave birth to a son, Mario. Guiseppe Montesano, the child's father, was a fellow educator who later became the director of an organization that trained Montessori-method teachers.

Montessori returned to the University of Rome in 1901 to study psychology and philosophy. When she completed her degree in 1904, she was made professor of anthropology, a position she held until 1906, when she began the experiment that altered her career forever. In 1907 she founded the *Casa dei Bambini* (Children's House) in one of Rome's worst slums. She helped design the building because she felt that the environment in which children studied

From *The Montessori Method*. Translated by Anne E. George.

should be conducive to their learning. In the beginning, her school was essentially a preschool daycare program. Her approach was based on her observations of how children naturally learn and teach each other. Her purpose was to avoid blunting children's natural impulse to learn what interests them.

Her methods differed in several ways from those then in use. She respected all her students, regardless of their background. She insisted on providing them with moveable child-sized furniture, and she maintained a quiet, clean, and safe environment at all times. Montessori's teaching methods showed results immediately. Although the children entered school as unruly as one might expect, it was not long before they began to reveal remarkable skills; in fact, some of the three- and four-year-olds had learned to read and were beginning to write. As Montessori observed elsewhere, "then we saw them 'absorb' far more than reading and writing . . . it was botany, zoology, mathematics, geography, and all with the same ease, spontaneously."

Montessori spent almost three decades helping to establish schools based on her education model in Europe and North America. Because of the rise of Mussolini and Italian fascism, she left Italy in 1934, but found herself in the midst of the Spanish Civil War in Barcelona. A British cruiser rescued her in 1936. She then went to Holland and opened a training center for her methods, which she had introduced in Amsterdam in 1929. She was in India in 1940 when that country entered World War II, and being Italian nationals, she and her son were interned as enemy aliens. After the war, she established Montessori schools in India and Sri Lanka. She died in Holland in 1952, still involved in her work.

The Montessori method is child-centered, aimed at letting the child determine solutions to the problems developed in the classroom. Montessori thought it important that a task involve the child's whole personality and that the teacher's role was to prepare the child to approach that task. For example, the senses had to be addressed, so there was a great deal of emphasis on seeing, hearing, and touching, which prepared children for intellectual processes that depend on those skills —as, for instance, reading depends on seeing. Parents were expected to be part of the process, and room was made for their visits to the school. Essentially, Montessori established an environment that freed children to learn spontaneously. Educators around the world still use the methods Montessori developed more than eighty years ago.

Montessori's Rhetoric

In the selection that follows, which is excerpted from the opening chapter of the book *The Montessori Method*, Montessori crafts a subtle argument for a new kind of "scientific pedagogy" (a scientific method of instruction) that emphasizes the freedom of the student. Montessori eventually moves to the adult life of people who have gone through traditional schools to point out that the restrictions they have in their daily office or work lives resemble the restrictions that characterized the environment in which they were taught as children. She argues in the early part of her discussion (para. 9) that stationary desks, benches, and chairs are proof that "the principle of slavery still pervades pedagogy."

Scientific approaches to teaching had been in vogue in the early years of the twentieth century, but they had been restricted to various quantifiable measures, such as the circumference of heads and upper bodies, general height and weight, or results of various psychological tests. These, Montessori argues, are scientifically irrelevant to the teaching of children. Her science depends on careful observation of the ways in which children pursue their own learning. Once those ways are understood, Montessori argues, better teaching and learning will result.

One of her rhetorical methods is comparison. She describes the zoologist who studies butterflies that have been killed and stuck on pins, "their outspread wings motionless" (para. 5). A teacher who behaves like the zoologist would teach in a school "where the children are repressed in the spontaneous expression of their personality till they are almost like dead beings. In such a school the children, like butterflies mounted on pins, are fastened each to his place, the desk, spreading the useless wings of barren and meaningless knowledge which they have acquired" (para. 6). In this paragraph she argues for life in the classroom and for freedom of the individual.

Montessori further develops her argument by referencing a concrete situation: the architecture of the classroom, with a close examination of the stationary desks and chairs. She spends quite a bit of time with this material (paras. 9–20) because she wants us to realize that people have thought out this unworkable system in a scientific fashion. She introduces a personal anecdote when she describes the woman who presented her with a brace or harness in which to place children in the classroom, thus absolutely immobilizing them in a manner similar to zoologists pinning butterflies. As she states, this approach perfects the "immobility" of the child and his or her repression.

The conflict between methods that produce "an instrument of slavery" in the classroom and the "movement of social liberation" that is growing throughout the modern world is central to much of the rest of her argument. Her example of the use of braces for spinal curvature is almost an absurd argument, but its absurdity makes all the more intense the insight Montessori has into educational practices that must be overturned. They look scientific, but they ignore the study of the child.

In paragraphs 37–40 Montessori addresses the inner spirit of the child. In this section, as in the opening paragraphs, some of her own religious views peek out in her emphasis on the freedom of the spirit. As she points out, the death of the spirit occurs in slavery, and her argument against slavery takes its shape in a reminder that "[a]ll forms of slavery tend little by little to weaken and disappear, even the sexual slavery of woman" (para. 28). Montessori ends her essay with an emphasis on the inner life of the child and a warning concerning criminality, which she considers a form of slavery. But criminals are a small portion of society and their punishment is exact. "The real punishment of normal man is the loss of the consciousness of that individual power and greatness which are the sources of his inner life" (para. 41). By respecting children, observing their natural behaviors, and permitting them to pursue tasks freely in an environment that is conducive to real learning, Montessori believes educators can bring out the best qualities in every individual.

PREREADING QUESTIONS:
WHAT TO READ FOR

The following prereading questions may help you anticipate key issues in the discussion of Maria Montessori's "The Montessori Method." Keeping them in mind during your first reading of the selection should help focus your attention.

- What is the basis of scientific pedagogy for Montessori?
- How does school furniture affect the education of the child?
- What effect does freedom have on the education of the child?

The Montessori Method

The interest in humanity to which we wish to educate the   1
teacher must be characterised by the intimate relationship between the observer and the individual to be observed; a relationship which does not exist between the student of zoology or botany and that form of nature which he studies. Man cannot love the insect or the

chemical reaction which he studies, without sacrificing a part of himself. This self-sacrifice seems to one who looks at it from the standpoint of the world, a veritable renunciation of life itself, almost a martyrdom.

But the love of man for man is a far more tender thing, and so   2
simple that it is universal. To love in this way is not the privilege of any especially prepared intellectual class, but lies within the reach of all men.

To give an idea of this second form of preparation, that of the   3
spirit, let us try to enter into the minds and hearts of those first followers of Christ Jesus as they heard Him speak of a Kingdom not of this world, greater far than any earthly kingdom, no matter how royally conceived. In their simplicity they asked of Him, "Master, tell us who shall be greatest in the Kingdom of Heaven?" To which Christ, caressing the head of a little child who, with reverent, wondering eyes, looked into His face, replied, "Whosoever shall become as one of these little ones, he shall be greatest in the Kingdom of Heaven." Now let us picture among those to whom these words were spoken, an ardent, worshipping soul, who takes them into his heart. With a mixture of respect and love, of sacred curiosity and of a desire to achieve this spiritual greatness, he sets himself to observe every manifestation of this little child. Even such an observer placed in a classroom filled with little children will not be the new educator whom we wish to form. But let us seek to implant in the soul the self-sacrificing spirit of the scientist with the reverent love of the disciple of Christ, and we shall have prepared the *spirit* of the teacher. From the child itself he will learn how to perfect himself as an educator.

Let us consider the attitude of the teacher in the light of   4
another example. Picture to yourself one of our botanists or zoologists experienced in the technique of observation and experimentation; one who has travelled in order to study "certain fungi" in their native environment. This scientist has made his observations in open country and, then, by the aid of his microscope and of all his laboratory appliances, has carried on the later research work in the most minute way possible. He is, in fact, a scientist who understands what it is to study nature, and who is conversant with all the means which modern experimental science offers for this study.

Now let us imagine such a man appointed, by reason of the   5
original work he has done, to a chair of science in some university, with the task before him of doing further original research work

with hymenoptera.[1] Let us suppose that, arrived at his post, he is shown a glass-covered case containing a number of beautiful butterflies, mounted by means of pins, their outspread wings motionless. The student will say that this is some child's play, not material for scientific study, that these specimens in the box are more fitly a part of the game which the little boys play, chasing butterflies and catching them in a net. With such material as this the experimental scientist can do nothing.

The situation would be very much the same if we should place a 6 teacher who, according to our conception of the term, is scientifically prepared, in one of the public schools where the children are repressed in the spontaneous expression of their personality till they are almost like dead beings. In such a school the children, like butterflies mounted on pins, are fastened each to his place, the desk, spreading the useless wings of barren and meaningless knowledge which they have acquired.

It is not enough, then, to prepare in our Masters the scientific 7 spirit. We must also make ready the *school* for their observation. The school must permit the *free, natural manifestations* of the *child* if in the school scientific pedagogy is to be born. This is the essential reform.

No one may affirm that such a principle already exists in peda- 8 gogy and in the school. It is true that some pedagogues, led by Rousseau,[2] have given voice to impracticable principles and vague aspirations for the liberty of the child, but the true concept of liberty is practically unknown to educators. They often have the same concept of liberty which animates a people in the hour of rebellion from slavery, or perhaps, the conception of *social liberty*, which although it is a more elevated idea is still invariably restricted. "Social liberty" signifies always one more round of Jacob's ladder. In other words it signifies a partial liberation, the liberation of a country, of a class, or of thought.

That concept of liberty which must inspire pedagogy is, instead, 9 universal. The biological sciences of the nineteenth century have shown it to us when they have offered us the means for studying life. If, therefore, the old-time pedagogy foresaw or vaguely expressed the principle of studying the pupil before educating him, and of leaving him free in his spontaneous manifestations, such an intuition, indefinite and barely expressed, was made possible of practical

---

[1] **hymenoptera** A class of insects including wasps, bees, and ants.
[2] **Jean-Jacques Rousseau (1712–1778)** Philosopher who wrote the novel *Emile or On Education*.

attainment only after the contribution of the experimental sciences during the last century. This is not a case for sophistry or discussion, it is enough that we state our point. He who would say that the principle of liberty informs the pedagogy of to-day, would make us smile as at a child who, before the box of mounted butterflies, should insist that they were alive and could fly. The principle of slavery still pervades pedagogy, and, therefore, the same principle pervades the school. I need only give one proof—the stationary desks and chairs. Here we have, for example, a striking evidence of the errors of the early materialistic scientific pedagogy which, with mistaken zeal and energy, carried the barren stones of science to the rebuilding of the crumbling walls of the school. The schools were at first furnished with the long, narrow benches upon which the children were crowded together. Then came science and perfected the bench. In this work much attention was paid to the recent contributions of anthropology. The age of the child and the length of his limbs were considered in placing the seat at the right height. The distance between the seat and the desk was calculated with infinite care, in order that the child's back should not become deformed, and, finally, the seats were separated and the width so closely calculated that the child could barely seat himself upon it, while to stretch himself by making any lateral movements was impossible. This was done in order that he might be separated from his neighbour. These desks are constructed in such a way as to render the child visible in all his immobility. One of the ends sought through this separation is the prevention of immoral acts in the schoolroom. What shall we say of such prudence in a state of society where it would be considered scandalous to give voice to principles of sex morality in education, for fear we might thus contaminate innocence? And, yet, here we have science lending itself to this hypocrisy, fabricating machines! Not only this; obliging science goes farther still, perfecting the benches in such a way as to permit to the greatest possible extent the immobility of the child, or, if you wish, to repress every movement of the child.

It is all so arranged that, when the child is well-fitted into his place, the desk and chair themselves force him to assume the position considered to be hygienically comfortable. The seat, the foot-rest, the desks are arranged in such a way that the child can never stand at his work. He is allotted only sufficient space for sitting in an erect position. It is in such ways that schoolroom desks and benches have advanced toward perfection. Every cult of the so-called scientific pedagogy has designed a model scientific desk. Not a few nations have become proud of their "national desk,"—and in the struggle of competition these various machines have been patented.

Undoubtedly there is much that is scientific underlying the con-   11
struction of these benches. Anthropology has been drawn upon in
the measuring of the body and the diagnosis of the age; physiology,
in the study of muscular movements; psychology, in regard to perversion of instincts; and, above all, hygiene, in the effort to prevent
curvature of the spine. These desks were indeed scientific, following
in their construction the anthropological study of the child. We have
here, as I have said, an example of the literal application of science
to the schools.

I believe that before very long we shall all be struck with great   12
surprise by this attitude. It will seem incomprehensible that the fundamental error of the desk should not have been revealed earlier
through the attention given to the study of infant hygiene, anthropology, and sociology, and through the general progress of thought.
The marvel is greater when we consider that during the past years
there has been stirring in almost every nation a movement toward the
protection of the child.

· I believe that it will not be many years before the public,   13
scarcely believing the descriptions of these scientific benches, will
come to touch with wondering hands the amazing seats that were
constructed for the purpose of preventing among our school children curvature of the spine!

The development of these scientific benches means that the   14
pupils were subjected to a régime, which, even though they were
born strong and straight, made it possible for them to become
humpbacked! The vertebral column, biologically the most primitive, fundamental, and oldest part of the skeleton, the most fixed
portion of our body, since the skeleton is the most solid portion of
the organism — the vertebral column, which resisted and was strong
through the desperate struggles of primitive man when he fought
against the desert-lion, when he conquered the mammoth, when he
quarried the solid rock and shaped the iron to his uses, bends, and
cannot resist, under the yoke of the school.

It is incomprehensible that so-called *science* should have worked   15
to perfect an instrument of slavery in the school without being enlightened by one ray from the movement of social liberation, growing and developing throughout the world. For the age of scientific
benches was also the age of the redemption of the working classes
from the yoke of unjust labor.

The tendency toward social liberty is most evident, and mani-   16
fests itself on every hand. The leaders of the people make it their slo-
gan, the labouring masses repeat the cry, scientific and socialistic
publications voice the same movement, our journals are full of it. The
underfed workman does not ask for a tonic, but for better economic

conditions which shall prevent malnutrition. The miner who, through the stooping position maintained during many hours of the day, is subject to inguinal rupture, does not ask for an abdominal support, but demands shorter hours and better working conditions, in order that he may be able to lead a healthy life like other men.

And when, during this same social epoch, we find that the children in our schoolrooms are working amid unhygienic conditions, so poorly adapted to normal development that even the skeleton becomes deformed, our response to this terrible revelation is an orthopedic bench. It is much as if we offered to the miner the abdominal brace, or arsenic to the underfed workman. 17

Some time ago a woman, believing me to be in sympathy with all scientific innovations concerning the school, showed me with evident satisfaction *a corset or brace for pupils.* She had invented this and felt that it would complete the work of the bench. 18

Surgery has still other means for the treatment of spinal curvature. I might mention orthopedic instruments, braces, and a method of periodically suspending the child, by the head or shoulders, in such a fashion that the weight of the body stretches and thus straightens the vertebral column. In the school, the orthopedic instrument in the shape of the desk is in great favour to-day; someone proposes the brace—one step farther and it will be suggested that we give the scholars a systematic course in the suspension method! 19

All this is the logical consequence of a material application of the methods of science to the decadent school. Evidently the rational method of combating spinal curvature in the pupils, is to change the form of their work—so that they shall no longer be obliged to remain for so many hours a day in a harmful position. It is a conquest of liberty which the school needs, not the mechanism of a bench. 20

Even were the stationary seat helpful to the child's body, it would still be a dangerous and unhygienic feature of the environment, through the difficulty of cleaning the room perfectly when the furniture cannot be moved. The foot-rests, which cannot be removed, accumulate the dirt carried in daily from the street by the many little feet. To-day there is a general transformation in the matter of house furnishings. They are made lighter and simpler so that they may be easily moved, dusted, and even washed. But the school seems blind to the transformation of the social environment. 21

It behooves us to think of what may happen to the *spirit* of the child who is condemned to grow in conditions so artificial that his very bones may become deformed. When we speak of the redemption of the workingman, it is always understood that beneath the 22 most apparent form of suffering, such as poverty of the blood, or ruptures, there exists that other wound from which the soul of the man who is subjected to any form of slavery must suffer. It is at this deeper wrong that we aim when we say that the workman must be redeemed through liberty. We know only too well that when a man's very blood has been consumed or his intestines wasted away through his work, his soul must have lain oppressed in darkness, rendered insensible, or, it may be, killed within him. The *moral* degradation of the slave is, above all things, the weight that opposes the progress of humanity— humanity striving to rise and held back by this great burden. The cry of redemption speaks far more clearly for the souls of men than for their bodies.

What shall we say then, when the question before us is that of   23
educating children?

We know only too well the sorry spectacle of the teacher who,   24
in the ordinary schoolroom, must pour certain cut and dried facts into the heads of the scholars. In order to succeed in this barren task, she finds it necessary to discipline her pupils into immobility and to force their attention. Prizes and punishments are every-ready and efficient aids to the master who must force into a given attitude of mind and body those who are condemned to be his listeners.

It is true that to-day it is deemed expedient to abolish official   25
whippings and habitual blows, just as the awarding of prizes has become less ceremonious. These partial reforms are another prop approved of by science, and offered to the support of the decadent school. Such prizes and punishments are, if I may be allowed the expression, the *bench* of the soul, the instrument of slavery for the spirit. Here, however, these are not applied to lessen deformities, but to provoke them. The prize and the punishment are incentives toward unnatural or forced effort, and, therefore we certainly cannot speak of the natural development of the child in connection with them. The jockey offers a piece of sugar to his horse before jumping into the saddle, the coachman beats his horse that he may respond to the signs given by the reins; and, yet, neither of these runs so superbly as the free horse of the plains.

And here, in the case of education, shall man place the yoke   26
upon man?

True, we say that social man is natural man yoked to society.   27
But if we give a comprehensive glance to the moral progress of society, we shall see that little by little, the yoke is being made easier, in other words, we shall see that nature, or life, moves gradually toward triumph. The yoke of the slave yields to that of the servant, and the yoke of the servant to that of the workman.

All forms of slavery tend little by little to weaken and disap-   28
pear, even the sexual slavery of woman. The history of civilisation
is a history of conquest and of liberation. We should ask in what
stage of civilisation we find ourselves and if, in truth, the good of
prizes and of punishments be necessary to our advancement. If we
have indeed gone beyond this point, then to apply such a form of
education would be to draw the new generation back to a lower
level, not to lead them into their true heritage of progress.

Something very like this condition of the school exists in society,   29
in the relation between the government and the great numbers of the
men employed in its administrative departments. These clerks work
day after day for the general national good, yet they do not feel or see
the advantage of their work in any immediate reward. That is, they do
not realise that the state carries on its great business through their
daily tasks, and that the whole nation is benefited by their work. For
them the immediate good is promotion, as passing to a higher class is
for the child in school. The man who loses sight of the really big aim
of his work is like a child who has been placed in a class below his
real standing: like a slave, he is cheated of something which is his
right. His dignity as a man is reduced to the limits of the dignity of a
machine which must be oiled if it is to be kept going, because it does
not have within itself the impulse of life. All those petty things such
as the desire for decorations or medals, are but artificial stimuli, light-
ening for the moment the dark, barren path in which he treads.

In the same way we give prizes to school children. And the fear   30
of not achieving promotion, withholds the clerk from running away,
and binds him to his monotonous work, even as the fear of not passing into the next class drives the pupil to his book. The reproof of
the superior is in every way similar to the scolding of the teacher. The
correction of badly executed clerical work is equivalent to the bad
mark placed by the teacher upon the scholar's poor composition.
The parallel is almost perfect.

But if the administrative departments are not carried on in a way   31
which would seem suitable to a nation's greatness; if corruption too
easily finds a place; it is the result of having extinguished the true
greatness of man in the mind of the employee, and of having
restricted his vision to those petty, immediate facts, which he has
come to look upon as prizes and punishments. The country stands,
because the rectitude of the greater number of its employees is such
that they resist the corruption of the prizes and punishments, and
follow an irresistible current of honesty. Even as life in the social
environment triumphs against every cause of poverty and death, and
proceeds to new conquests, so the instinct of liberty conquers all obstacles, going from victory to victory.

It is this personal and yet universal force of life, a force often la- 32
tent within the soul, that sends the world forward.

But he who accomplishes a truly human work, he who does 33
something really great and victorious, is never spurred to his task by
those trifling attractions called by the name of "prizes," nor by the
fear of those petty ills which we call "punishments." If in a war a
great army of giants should fight with no inspiration beyond the desire to win promotion, epaulets, or medals, or through fear of being
shot, if these men were to oppose a handful of pygmies who were
inflamed by love of country, the victory would go to the latter.
When real heroism has died within an army, prizes and punishments cannot do more than finish the work of deterioration, bringing in corruption and cowardice.

All human victories, all human progress, stand upon the inner 34
force.

Thus a young student may become a great doctor if he is 35
spurred to his study by an interest which makes medicine his real
vocation. But if he works in the hope of an inheritance, or of making
a desirable marriage, or if indeed he is inspired by any material advantage, he will never become a true master or a great doctor, and
the world will never make one step forward because of his work. He
to whom such stimuli are necessary, had far better never become a
physician. Everyone has a special tendency, a special vocation, modest, perhaps, but certainly useful. The system of prizes may turn an
individual aside from this vocation, may make him choose a false
road, for him a vain one, and forced to follow it, the natural activity
of a human being may be warped, lessened, even annihilated.

We repeat always that the world *progresses* and that we must urge 36
men forward to obtain progress. But progress comes from the *new
things that are born*, and these, not being foreseen, are not rewarded
with prizes: rather, they often carry the leader to martyrdom. God forbid that poems should ever be born of the desire to be crowned in the
Capitol! Such a vision need only come into the heart of the poet and
the muse will vanish. The poem must spring from the soul of the poet,
when he thinks neither of himself nor of the prize. And if he does win
the laurel, he will feel the vanity of such a prize. The true reward lies
in the revelation through the poem of his own triumphant inner force.

There does exist, however, an external prize for man; when, for 37
example, the orator sees the faces of his listeners change with the
emotions he has awakened, he experiences something so great that
it can only be likened to the intense joy with which one discovers
that he is loved. Our joy is to touch, and conquer souls, and this is
the one prize which can bring us a true compensation.

Sometimes there is given to us a moment when we fancy ourselves to be among the great ones of the world. These are moments of happiness given to man that he may continue his existence in peace. It may be through love attained or because of the gift of a son, through a glorious discovery or the publication of a book; in some such moment we feel that there exists no man who is above us. If, in such a moment, someone vested with authority comes forward to offer us a medal or a prize, he is the important destroyer of our real reward—"And who are you?" our vanished illusion shall cry, "Who are you that recalls me to the fact that I am not the first among men? Who stands so far above me that he may give me a prize?" The prize of such a man in such a moment can only be Divine.

As for punishments, the soul of the normal man grows perfect through expanding, and punishment as commonly understood is always a form of *repression*. It may bring results with those inferior natures who grow in evil, but these are very few, and social progress is not affected by them. The penal code threatens us with punishment if we are dishonest within the limits indicated by the laws. But we are not honest through fear of the laws; if we do not rob, if we do not kill, it is because we love peace, because the natural trend of our lives leads us forward, leading us ever farther and more definitely away from the peril of low and evil acts.

Without going into the ethical or metaphysical aspects of the question, we may safely affirm that the delinquent before he transgresses the law, has, *if he knows of the existence of a punishment*, felt the threatening weight of the criminal code upon him. He has defined it, or he has been lured into the crime, deluding himself with the idea that he would be able to avoid the punishment of the law. But there has occurred within his mind, a *struggle between the crime and the punishment*. Whether it be efficacious in hindering crime or not, this penal code is undoubtedly made for a very limited class of individuals; namely, criminals. The enormous majority of citizens are honest without any regard whatever to the threats of the law.

The real punishment of normal man is the loss of the consciousness of that individual power and greatness which are the sources of his inner life. Such a punishment often falls upon men in the fullness of success. A man whom we would consider crowned by happiness and fortune may be suffering from this form of punishment. Far too often man does not see the real punishment which threatens him.

And it is just here that education may help.

To-day we hold the pupils in school, restricted by those instruments so degrading to body and spirit, the desk—and material

38

39

40

41

42

43

prizes and punishments. Our aim in all this is to reduce them to the discipline of immobility and silence,—to lead them,—where? Far too often toward no definite end.

Often the education of children consists in pouring into their intel-   44
ligence the intellectual contents of school programmes. And often these programmes have been compiled in the official department of education, and their use is imposed by law upon the teacher and the child.

Ah, before such dense and wilful disregard of the life which is   45
growing within these children, we should hide our heads in shame and cover our guilty faces with our hands!

Sergi[3] says truly: "To-day an urgent need imposes itself upon so-   46
ciety: the reconstruction of methods in education and instruction, and he who fights for this cause, fights for human regeneration."

---

[3] **Giuseppe Sergi (1841–1936)** A professor of anthropology who worked with Montessori at the University of Rome.

QUESTIONS FOR CRITICAL READING

1. Why does Montessori emphasize love of the child in regard to scientific pedagogy?
2. What is the point of the reference to Jesus in paragraph 3?
3. How effective, in terms of argument, is the comparison of the pinned butterflies with the children penned in by their desks? Is the comparison valid?
4. Why is there so much emphasis on the example of the desks and chairs that have been scientifically provided for school children?
5. What does it mean to study the pupils before educating them?
6. Montessori says the principle of slavery still pervades pedagogy. Is that true even today?
7. Comment on Montessori's use of irony in paragraph 19.
8. How does Montessori connect the educational environment of the child with the working environment of the adult?

SUGGESTIONS FOR WRITING

1. In paragraph 3 Montessori asserts: "From the child itself he will learn how to perfect himself as an educator." In practical terms, how useful do you think this statement is in teaching preschool children? How valuable would it be in teaching children in the early grades? Is it less valuable or more valuable in teaching college students?

2. If you have had experience in a Montessori school, describe the ways in which learning occurred. Review your own experience and compare it with the principles that Montessori outlines in her selection. How many of her values were present in the school you attended? How effective was that early education for you? Did you feel that your inner spirit was developed as you learned?

3. Montessori states, "The school must permit the *free, natural manifestations* of the *child* if in the school scientific pedagogy is to be born" (para. 7). In terms of your experience, do you feel this statement is valid? How can scientific pedagogy be put into effect while also educating the child? What conditions need to be met?

4. Beginning in paragraph 24, Montessori writes extensively about school prizes and punishments. Examine her argument and either defend it on the basis of your observations, or attack it. Explain what the nature of her argument is and how it applies to the education of the child as Montessori understands it. What is your view on the usefulness of prizes and punishments in the education of children?

5. Montessori's great experiment took place in the San Lorenzo quarter of Rome, one of the toughest slums in the city. It was being rebuilt when Montessori got the opportunity to construct her "Children's House." Do some research on *Casa dei Bambini* and write an essay that clarifies exactly what she did there and what kind of results she eventually got. How successful was her experiment? What criticisms of the experiment seem valid to you?

6. Montessori states: "Everyone has a special tendency, a special vocation, modest, perhaps, but certainly useful" (para. 35). Explain what this statement means. Do you see evidence for Montessori's assertion in your friends? In yourself? Why is her statement important to consider in the education of a child? How has your education affected your sense of vocation?

7. **CONNECTIONS** Montessori and Emerson agree on several points. What are they? How complete is their agreement? What are the principal issues on which they seem either to disagree or ignore one another? Do you think it possible that Montessori read Emerson's essay on education and was influenced by it? What basic values most importantly connect their views on education?

8. **CONNECTIONS** To what extent is the "education" of Frederick Douglass evidence that Montessori's theories are sound? What does he do that validates her ideas concerning slavery and freedom? Consider Douglass's narrative of how he learned to read when he was a child. How were the conditions under which he learned similar to those Montessori describes?

JOHN DEWEY
Thinking in Education

JOHN DEWEY (1859–1952) was arguably the most influential voice in twentieth-century American education. He was born, raised, and educated in Vermont, having graduated from the University of Vermont at age nineteen. He went on to teach high school in Pennsylvania for two years, eventually moving on to graduate work at Johns Hopkins University. He studied philosophy, particularly the works of idealist German philosophers Immanuel Kant (1724–1804) and Georg Wilhelm Friedrich Hegel (1770–1831), both of whom felt that freedom was connected with reason, and that the end goal of history was to produce freedom. Dewey wrote a dissertation on the psychology of Kant; however, it has been lost.

Dewey was deeply interested in the connection between psychology and philosophy at a time when the discipline of philosophy was closely tied to principles of Christian theology. When he went to teach at the University of Michigan from 1884 to 1894 (with a year off teach at Minnesota), he was fortunate to have a department chair who valued Dewey's work in relation to what was then the study of modern German philosophers. Eventually, Dewey moved to the University of Chicago, which was only four years old and dedicated to graduate studies and serious original research. The new department Dewey joined combined studies of psychology, philosophy, and pedagogy. Eventually, Dewey managed to establish pedagogy as a separate department, making it one of the first schools of education.

Because of differences of opinion, Dewey left Chicago in 1904 and moved to Columbia University, with appointments in the department of philosophy and at Teachers College. He spent the rest of his professional career there. In these years his own philosophical views underwent a change. He embraced the then-modern

From *Democracy in Education*.

tenets of pragmatism, a philosophy that values ideas in terms of their usefulness and their ultimate effectiveness. Pragmatists emphasized the practical over the ideal. They placed a high value on experience as a way of knowing. Ideas were valued for what they actually effected in terms of behavior or change. In education the pragmatists were interested in results and in usefulness of instruction.

Dewey published more than forty books during his career. His first book was *Psychology* (1887). He also published *The School and Society* (1899), which revealed his lifelong interest in the social implications of educational programs. His *Ethical Principles Underlying Education* was published in 1908, and his enormously influential *Democracy and Education* (1916) developed some of his most important ideas about teaching and learning. In later books, such as *Human Nature and Conduct* (1922), *Experience and Nature* (1925), *Philosophy and Civilization* (1931), and *Freedom and Culture* (1939), Dewey continued to develop his ideas on issues of philosophic and social importance. All these books reveal the practical nature that was a hallmark of his most important work.

Dewey's Rhetoric

One of the first things one notices about "Thinking in Education" is that it is divided into sections announced with, first, an Arabic number 1, then by subsequent Roman numerals. Roman numeral I appears at paragraph 2; II at paragraph 9; III at paragraph 12; IV at paragraph 16. The final paragraph is a summary of all that precedes it, thus acting as a kind of review of what we just read.

Clearly, this indicates a pedagogic motive. Each basic issue is presented, defined, discussed, and analyzed to the extent necessary, and a conclusion is drawn. Considering the nature of this selection, one must conclude that the audience addressed is primarily the teacher. Given Dewey's concerns for the involvement of the student in an experiential activity that would result in ideas put into action, this structure, while clear and effective, would be less likely to appeal to a young student than to a more mature teacher or teacher-to-be.

In paragraph 1, Dewey explains that "thinking is the method of intelligent learning," which he realizes is a statement that might seem too obvious. But by thinking he means the process of dealing with experiential activities that deeply involve the student in such a way that the problems the student is to solve are really the student's and not just artificial problems set by the teacher. As he explains in paragraph 2, thinking must be connected with experience, with hands-on activity, an example of which is the activity of children making discoveries on their own with common materials such as blocks. He makes an important distinction between "genuine or simulated or mock problems" (para. 6) in the classroom.

Part of Dewey's rhetorical approach derives from the technique of dialectic, particularly as developed by one of his favorite philosophers, Hegel. Dialectic proceeds by opposing two concepts or truths and examining them to see which is preferable. As he sets genuine problems that truly involve students against simulated problems that are those only of the curriculum or the teacher, it is clear that he prefers problems that are "real" and produce enthusiasm in children. The dialectic is continued in terms of problems that relate to life experience and those that are limited to the classroom. As Dewey states, when the latter case is dominant, "A pupil has a problem, but it is the problem of meeting the peculiar requirements set by the teacher. His problem becomes that of finding out what the teacher wants" (para 8).

The four parts of the selection emphasize first experience, then data, then ideas, and finally the testing of ideas. Each section begins with an appropriate definition of terms, then proceeds to a discussion of the practical application of the terms, and then connects the subject of the section with the method of thinking that Dewey feels is the key to education. Dewey's ideas about thinking and education constitute a form of critical thinking if only because he is anxious to challenge pupils to examine their ideas critically. He condemns the classroom that makes pupils feel that the problems they are to solve are not connected to their experiences. Moreover, he hopes that ideas eventually will be translated into action in the life of the child.

He also has the rhetorical gift of making pithy statements that contain a great deal of meaning in a few words. For example, "The initial stage of that developing experience which is called thinking is *experience*" (para. 2). This innocent-sounding sentence contains much of his basic theory of education, which implies working from concrete experience toward ideas that can then be converted back into a new concrete experience. When speaking of a shared activity between teacher and pupil, he tells us: "In such shared activity, the teacher is a learner, and the learner is, without knowing it, a teacher" (para. 15). This judicious use of the rhetorical scheme called chiasmus is effective in part because Dewey uses very few such devices.

Dewey summarizes his material cogently in the final paragraph, thus tying all the elements of his argument together. The student must

a. be involved in an activity that's important on its own
b. be presented with a genuine problem to solve

c. be given information (data) that is necessary to solve the problem

d. develop reasonable solutions to the problem

e. be given the opportunity to test out his solutions in action.

Dewey was a careful thinker who could also communicate with a broad audience. He felt that in the interest of presenting important ideas, such as those in *Democracy and Education*, he would emphasize the organization and development of his ideas rather than aim for a smooth and poetic style. Dewey is pragmatic. He is simple and direct, although his ideas—especially for 1916—were radically different from those of most other educators.

PREREADING QUESTIONS: WHAT TO READ FOR

The following prereading questions may help you anticipate key issues in the discussion of John Dewey's "Thinking in Education." Keeping them in mind during your first reading of the selection should help focus your attention.

- What does Dewey seem to mean by the expression "thinking in education"?

- What conditions must exist for the student to use thinking in education?

- What seems to be the best process of education, according to Dewey?

Thinking in Education

1. The Essentials of Method

No one doubts, theoretically, the importance of fostering in   1
school good habits of thinking. But apart from the fact that the acknowledgement is not so great in practice as in theory, there is not adequate theoretical recognition that all which the school can or need do for pupils, so far as their *minds* are concerned (that is, leaving out certain specialized muscular abilities), is to develop their ability to think. The parceling out of instruction among various ends such as acquisition of skill (in reading, spelling, writing, drawing,

reciting); acquiring information (in history and geography), *and* training of thinking is a measure of the ineffective way in which we accomplish all three. Thinking which is not connected with increase of efficiency in action, and with learning more about ourselves and the world in which we live, has something the matter with it just as thought. And skill obtained apart from thinking is not connected with any sense of the purposes for which it is to be used. It consequently leaves a man at the mercy of his routine habits and of the authoritative control of others, who know what they are about and who are not especially scrupulous as to their means of achievement. And information severed from thoughtful action is dead, a mind-crushing load. Since it simulates knowledge and thereby develops the poison of conceit, it is a most powerful obstacle to further growth in the grace of intelligence. The sole direct path to enduring improvement in the methods of instruction and learning consists in centering upon the conditions which exact, promote, and test thinking. Thinking is the method of intelligent learning, of learning that employs and rewards mind. We speak, legitimately enough, about the method of thinking, but the important thing to bear in mind about method is that thinking is method, the method of intelligent experience in the course which it takes.

I.   The initial stage of that developing experience which is 2 called thinking is *experience*. This remark may sound like a silly truism. It ought to be one; but unfortunately it is not. On the contrary, thinking is often regarded both in philosophic theory and in educational practice as something cut off from experience, and capable of being cultivated in isolation. In fact, the inherent limitations of experience are often urged as the sufficient ground for attention to thinking. Experience is then thought to be confined to the senses and appetites; to a mere material world, while thinking proceeds from a higher faculty (of reason), and is occupied with spiritual or at least literary things. So, oftentimes, a sharp distinction is made between pure mathematics as a peculiarly fit subject matter of thought (since it has nothing to do with physical existences) and applied mathematics, which has utilitarian but not mental value.

Speaking generally, the fundamental fallacy in methods of in- 3 struction lies in supposing that experience on the part of pupils may be assumed. What is here insisted upon is the necessity of an actual empirical situation as the initiating phase of thought. Experience is here taken as previously defined: trying to do something and having the thing perceptibly do something to one in return. The fallacy consists in supposing that we can begin with ready-made subject matter of arithmetic, or geography, or whatever, irrespective of some direct personal experience of a situation. Even the kindergarten and

Montessori techniques are so anxious to get at intellectual distinctions, without "waste of time," that they tend to ignore—or reduce—the immediate crude handling of the familiar material of experience, and to introduce pupils at once to material which expresses the intellectual distinctions which adults have made. But the first stage of contact with any new material, at whatever age of maturity, must inevitably be of the trial and error sort. An individual must actually try, in play or work, to do something with material in carrying out his own impulsive activity, and then note the interaction of his energy and that of the material employed. This is what happens when a child at first begins to build with blocks, and it is equally what happens when a scientific man in his laboratory begins to experiment with unfamiliar objects.

Hence the first approach to any subject in school, if thought is to   4
be aroused and not words acquired, should be as unscholastic as possible. To realize what an experience or empirical situation, means, we have to call to mind the sort of situation that presents itself outside of school; the sort of occupations that interest and engage activity in ordinary life. And careful inspection of methods which are permanently successful in formal education, whether in arithmetic or learning to read, or studying geography, or learning physics or a foreign language, will reveal that they depend for their efficiency upon the fact that they go back to the type of the situation which causes reflection out of school in ordinary life. They give the pupils something to do, not something to learn; and the doing is of such a nature as to demand thinking, or the intentional noting of connections; learning naturally results.

That the situation should be of such a nature as to arouse think-   5
ing means of course that it should suggest something to do which is not either routine or capricious—something, in other words, presenting what is new (and hence uncertain or problematic) and yet sufficiently connected with existing habits to call out an effective response. An effective response means one which accomplishes a perceptible result, in distinction from a purely haphazard activity, where the consequences cannot be mentally connected with what is done. The most significant question which can be asked, accordingly, about any situation or experience proposed to induce learning is what quality of problem it involves.

At first thought, it might seem as if usual school methods mea-   6
sured well up to the standard here set. The giving of problems, the putting of questions, the assigning of tasks, the magnifying of difficulties, is a large part of school work. But it is indispensable to discriminate between genuine and simulated or mock problems. The following questions may aid in making such discrimination. (a) Is there anything but a problem? Does the question naturally suggest

itself within some situation or personal experience? Or is it an aloof thing, a problem only for the purposes of conveying instruction in some school topic? Is it the sort of trying that would arouse observation and engage experimentation outside of school? (b) Is it the pupil's own problem, or is it the teacher's or textbook's problem, made a problem for the pupil only because he cannot get the required mark or be promoted or win the teacher's approval, unless he deals with it? Obviously, these two questions overlap. They are two ways of getting at the same point: Is the experience a personal thing of such a nature as inherently to stimulate and direct observation of the connections involved, and to lead to inference and its testing? Or is it imposed from without, and is the pupil's problem simply to meet the external requirement?

Such questions may give us pause in deciding upon the extent to 7 which current practices are adapted to develop reflective habits. The physical equipment and arrangements of the average schoolroom are hostile to the existence of real situations of experience. What is there similar to the conditions of everyday life which will generate difficulties? Almost everything testifies to the great premium put upon listening, reading, and the reproduction of what is told and read. It is hardly possible to overstate the contrast between such conditions and the situations of active contact with things and persons in the home, on the playground, in fulfilling of ordinary responsibilities of life. Much of it is not even comparable with the questions which may arise in the mind of a boy or girl in conversing with others or in reading books outside of the school. No one has ever explained why children are so full of questions outside of the school (so that they pester grown-up persons if they get any encouragement), and the conspicuous absence of display of curiosity about the subject matter of school lessons. Reflection on this striking contrast will throw light upon the question of how far customary school conditions supply a context of experience in which problems naturally suggest themselves. No amount of improvement in the personal technique of the instructor will wholly remedy this state of things. There must be more actual material, more *stuff*, more appliances, and more opportunities for doing things, before the gap can be overcome. And where children are engaged in doing things and in discussing what arises in the course of their doing, it is found, even with comparatively indifferent modes of instruction, that children's inquiries are spontaneous and numerous, and the proposals of solution advanced, varied, and ingenious.

As a consequence of the absence of the materials and occupa- 8 tions which generate real problems, the pupil's problems are not his; or, rather, they are his *only as* a pupil, not as a human being.

Hence the lamentable waste in carrying over such expertness as is achieved in dealing with them to the affairs of life beyond the schoolroom. A pupil has a problem, but it is the problem of meeting the peculiar requirements set by the teacher. His problem becomes that of finding out what the teacher wants, what will satisfy the teacher in recitation and examination and outward deportment. Relationship to subject matter is no longer direct. The occasions and material of thought are not found in the arithmetic or the history or geography itself, but in skillfully adapting that material to the teacher's requirements. The pupil studies, but unconsciously to himself the objects of his study are the conventions and standards of the school system and school authority, not the nominal "studies." The thinking thus evoked is artificially one-sided at the best. At its worst, the problem of the pupil is not how to meet the requirements of school life, but how to *seem* to meet them — or, how to come near enough to meeting them to slide along without an undue amount of friction. The type of judgment formed by these devices is not a desirable addition to character. If these statements give too highly colored a picture of usual school methods, the exaggeration may at least serve to illustrate the point: the need of active pursuits, involving the use of material to accomplish purposes, if there are to be situations which normally generate problems occasioning thoughtful inquiry.

II.   There must be *data* at command to supply the considera- 9 tions required in dealing with the specific difficulty which has presented itself. Teachers following a "developing" method sometimes tell children to think things out for themselves as if they could spin them out of their own heads. The material of thinking is not thoughts, but actions, facts, events, and the relations of things. In other words, to think effectively one must have had, or now have, experiences which will furnish him resources for coping with the difficulty at hand. A difficulty is an indispensable stimulus to thinking, but not all difficulties call out thinking. Sometimes they overwhelm and submerge and discourage. The perplexing situation must be sufficiently like situations which have already been dealt with so that pupils will have some control of the meanings of handling it. A large part of the art of instruction lies in making the difficulty of new problems large enough to challenge thought, and small enough so that, in addition to the confusion naturally attending the novel elements, there shall be luminous familiar spots from which helpful suggestions may spring.

In one sense, it is a matter of indifference by what psychological 10 means the subject matter for reflection is provided. Memory, observation, reading, communication, are all avenues for supplying data.

The relative proportion to be obtained from each is a matter of the specific features of the particular problem in hand. It is foolish to insist upon observation of objects presented to the senses if the student is so familiar with the objects that he could just as well recall the facts independently. It is possible to induce undue and crippling dependence upon sense-presentations. No one can carry around with him a museum of all the things whose properties will assist the conduct of thought. A well-trained mind is one that has a maximum of resources behind it, so to speak, and that is accustomed to go over its past experiences to see what they yield. On the other hand, a quality or relation of even a familiar object may previously have been passed over, and be just the fact that is helpful in dealing with the question. In this case direct observation is called for. The same principle applies to the use to be made of observation on one hand and of reading and "telling" on the other. Direct observation is naturally more vivid and vital. But it has its limitations; and in any case it is a necessary part of education that one should acquire the ability to supplement the narrowness of his immediately personal experiences by utilizing the experiences of others. Excessive reliance upon others for data (whether got from reading or listening) is to be depreciated. Most objectionable of all is the probability that others, the book or the teacher, will supply solutions ready-made, instead of giving material that the student has to adapt and apply to the question in hand for himself.

There is no inconsistency in saying that in schools there is usu- 11 ally both too much and too little information supplied by others. The accumulation and acquisition of information for purposes of reproduction in recitation and examination is made too much of. "Knowledge," in the sense of information, means the working capital, the indispensable resources, of further inquiry; of finding out, or learning, more things. Frequently it is treated as an end itself, and then the goal becomes to heap it up and display it when called for. This static, cold-storage ideal of knowledge is inimical to educative development. It not only lets occasions for thinking go unused, but it swamps thinking. No one could construct a house on ground cluttered with miscellaneous junk. Pupils who have stored their "minds" with all kinds of material which they have never put to intellectual uses are sure to be hampered when they try to think. They have no practice in selecting what is appropriate, and no criterion to go by; everything is on the same dead static level. On the other hand, it is quite open to question whether, if information actually functioned in experience through use in application to the student's own purposes, there would not be need of more varied resources in books, pictures, and talks than are usually at command.

III.   The correlate in thinking of facts, data, knowledge already   12
acquired, is suggestions, inferences, conjectured meanings, suppositions, tentative explanations:—*ideas*, in short. Careful observation
and recollection determine what is given, what is already there, and
hence assured. They cannot furnish what is lacking. They define,
clarify, and locate the question; they cannot supply its answer. Projection, invention, ingenuity, devising come in for that purpose. The
data *arouse* suggestions, and only by reference to the specific data can
we pass upon the appropriateness of the suggestions. But the suggestions run beyond what is, as yet, actually *given* in experience. They
forecast possible results, things *to* do, not facts (things already done).
Inference is always an invasion of the unknown, a leap from the
known.

In this sense, a thought (what a thing suggests but is not as it is   13
presented) is creative,—an incursion into the novel. It involves some
inventiveness. What is suggested must, indeed, be familiar in *some*
context; the novelty, the inventive devising, clings to the new light in
which it is seen, the different use to which it is put. When Newton[1]
thought of his theory of gravitation, the creative aspect of his thought
was not found in its materials. They were familiar; many of them
commonplaces—sun, moon, planets, weight, distance, mass, square
of numbers. These were not original ideas; they were established facts.
His originality lay in the *use* to which these familiar acquaintances
were put by introduction into an unfamiliar context. The same is true
of every striking scientific discovery, every great invention, every admirable artistic production. Only silly folk identify creative originality
with the extraordinary and fanciful; others recognize that its measure
lies in putting everyday things to uses which had not occurred to
others. The operation is novel, not the materials out of which it is
constructed.

The educational conclusion which follows is that *all* thinking is   14
original in a projection of considerations which have not been previously apprehended. The child of three who discovers what can be
done with blocks, or of six who finds out what he can make by
putting five cents and five cents together, is really a discoverer, even
though everybody else in the world knows it. There is a genuine
increment of experience; not another item mechanically added on, but
enrichment by a new quality. The charm which the spontaneity of little children has for sympathetic observers is due to perception of this
intellectual originality. The joy which children themselves experience

---

[1]**Isaac Newton (1642–1727)** English scientist and mathematician who discovered the universal law of gravity and also invented calculus.

is the joy of intellectual constructiveness—of creativeness, if the word may be used without misunderstanding.

The educational moral I am chiefly concerned to draw is not, 15 however, that teachers would find their own work less of a grind and strain if school conditions favored learning in the sense of discovery and not in that of storing away what others pour into them; nor that it would be possible to give even children and youth the delights of personal intellectual productiveness—true and important as are these things. It is that no thought, no idea, can possibly be conveyed as an idea from one person to another. When it is told, it is, to the one to whom it is told, another given fact, not an idea. The communication may stimulate the other person to realize the question for himself and to think out a like idea, or it may smother his intellectual interest and suppress his dawning effort at thought. But what he *directly* gets cannot be an idea. Only by wrestling with the conditions of the problem at first hand, seeking and finding his own way out, does he think. When the parent or teacher has provided the conditions which stimulate thinking and has taken a sympathetic attitude toward the activities of the learner by entering into a common or conjoint experience, all has been done which a second party can do to instigate learning. The rest lies with the one directly concerned. If he cannot devise his own solution (not of course in isolation, but in correspondence with the teacher and other pupils) and find his own way out he will not learn, not even if he can recite some correct answer with one hundred per cent accuracy. We can and do supply ready-made "ideas" by the thousand; we do not usually take much pains to see that the one learning engages in significant situations where his own activities generate, support, and clinch ideas—that is, perceived meanings or connections. This does not mean that the teacher is to stand off and look on; the alternative to furnishing ready-made subject matter and listening to the accuracy with which it is reproduced is not quiescence, but participation, sharing, in an activity. In such shared activity, the teacher is a learner, and the learner is, without knowing it, a teacher—and upon the whole, the less consciousness there is, on either side, of either giving or receiving instruction, the better.

IV. Ideas, as we have seen, whether they be humble guesses or 16 dignified theories, are anticipations of possible solutions. They are anticipations of some continuity or connection of an activity and a consequence which has not as yet shown itself. They are therefore tested by the operation of acting upon them. They are to guide and organize further observations, recollections, and experiments. They are intermediate in learning, not final. All educational reformers, as we have had occasion to remark, are given to attacking the passivity of traditional education. They have opposed pouring in from without, and absorbing like a sponge; they have attacked drilling in material as into hard and resisting rock. But it is not easy to secure conditions which will make the getting of an idea identical with having an experience which widens and makes more precise our contact with the environment. Activity, even self-activity, is too easily thought of as something merely mental, cooped up within the head, or finding expression only through the vocal organs.

While the need of application of ideas gained in study is   17
acknowledged by all the more sucessful methods of instruction, the exercises in application are sometimes treated as devices for *fixing* what has already been learned and for getting greater practical skill in its manipulation. These results are genuine and not to be despised. But practice in applying what has been gained in study ought primarily to have an intellectual quality. As we have already seen, thoughts just as thoughts are incomplete. At best they are tentative; they are suggestions, indications. They are standpoints and methods for dealing with situations of experience. Till they are applied in these situations they lack full point and reality. Only application tests them, and only testing confers full meaning and a sense of their reality. Short of use made of them, they tend to segregate into a peculiar world of their own. It may be seriously questioned whether the philosophies which isolate mind and set it over against the world did not have their origin in the fact that the reflective or theoretical class of men elaborated a large stock of ideas which social conditions did not allow them to act upon and test. Consequently men were thrown back into their own thoughts as ends in themselves.

However this may be, there can be no doubt that a peculiar arti-   18
ficiality attaches to much of what is learned in schools. It can hardly be said that many students consciously think of the subject matter as unreal; but it assuredly does not possess for them the kind of reality which the subject matter of their vital experiences possesses. They learn not to expect that sort of reality of it; they become habituated to treating it as having reality for the purposes of recitations, lessons, and examinations. That it should remain inert for the experiences of daily life is more or less a matter of course. The bad effects are twofold. Ordinary experience does not receive the enrichment which it should; it is not fertilized by school learning. And the attitudes which spring from getting used to and accepting half-understood and ill-digested material weaken vigor and efficiency of thought.

If we have dwelt especially on the negative side, it is for the sake   19
of suggesting positive measures adapted to the effectual development of thought. Where schools are equipped with laboratories, shops,

and gardens, where dramatizations, plays, and games are freely used, opportunities exist for reproducing situations of life, and for acquiring and applying information and ideas in the carrying forward of progressive experiences. Ideas are not segregated, they do not form an isolated island. They animate and enrich the ordinary course of life. Information is vitalized by its function; by the place it occupies in direction of action.

The phrase "opportunities exist" is used purposely. They may not 20 be taken advantage of; it is possible to employ manual and constructive activities in a physical way, as means of getting just bodily skill; or they may be used almost exclusively for "utilitarian," *i.e.*, pecuniary, ends. But the disposition on the part of upholders of "cultural" education to assume that such activities are merely physical or professional in quality, is itself a product of the philosophies which isolate mind from direction of the course of experience and hence from action upon and with things. When the "mental" is regarded as a self-contained separate realm, a counterpart fate befalls bodily activity and movements. They are regarded as at the best mere external annexes to mind. They may be necessary for the satisfaction of bodily needs and the attainment of external decency and comfort, but they do not occupy a necessary place in mind nor enact an indispensable rôle in the completion of thought. Hence they have no place in a liberal education— *i.e.*, one which is concerned with the interests of intelligence. If they come in at all, it is as a concession to the material needs of the masses. That they should be allowed to invade the education of the élite is unspeakable. This conclusion follows irresistibly from the isolated conception of mind, but by the same logic it disappears when we perceive what mind really is—namely, the purposive and directive factor in the development of experience.

While it is desirable that all educational institutions should be 21 equipped so as to give students an opportunity for acquiring and testing ideas and information in active pursuits typifying important social situations, it will, doubtless, be a long time before all of them are thus furnished. But this state of affairs does not afford instructors an excuse for folding their hands and persisting in methods which segregate school knowledge. Every recitation in every subject gives an opportunity for establishing cross connections between the subject matter of the lesson and the wider and more direct experiences of everyday life. Classroom instruction falls into three kinds. The least desirable treats each lesson as an independent whole. It does not put upon the student the responsibility of finding points of contact between it and other lessons in the same subject, or other subjects of study. Wiser teachers see to it that the student is systematically led to utilize his earlier lessons to help understand the present one, and also to use the present to throw additional light upon what has already been acquired. Results are better, but school subject matter is still isolated. Save by accident, out-of-school experience is left in its crude and comparatively irreflective state. It is not subject to the refining and expanding influences of the more accurate and comprehensive material of direct instruction. The latter is not motivated and impregnated with a sense of reality by being intermingled with the realities of everyday life. The best type of teaching bears in mind the desirability of affecting this interconnection. It puts the student in the habitual attitude of finding points of contact and mutual bearings.

Summary

Processes of instruction are unified in the degree in which they   22
center in the production of good habits of thinking. While we may speak, without error, of the method of thought, the important thing is that thinking is the method of an educative experience. The essentials of method are therefore identical with the essentials of reflection. They are first that the pupil have a genuine situation of experience—that there be a continuous activity in which he is interested for its own sake; secondly, that a genuine problem develop within this situation as a stimulus to thought; third, that he possess the information and make the observations needed to deal with it; fourth, that suggested solutions occur to him which he shall be responsible for developing in an orderly way; fifth, that he have opportunity and occasion to test his ideas by application, to make their meaning clear and to discover for himself their validity.

QUESTIONS FOR CRITICAL READING

1. What is the relationship of experience to thought? Why does experience precede thought?
2. Why is "learning more about ourselves and the world" (para. 1) crucial to thought and education?
3. In what ways does Dewey concern himself with nature in the classroom?
4. Dewey states that for some people thinking is cut off from experience. How could this be true? What are its consequences?
5. What is the relationship between a student being given something to do and being given something to learn?
6. What is the difference between genuine and mock problems in a classroom?

7. What is the importance of data in the classroom?
8. How does Dewey define creative originality?

SUGGESTIONS FOR WRITING

1. In paragraphs 2 and 3, Dewey discusses the question of experience in mathematics, reminding us that "it has nothing to do with physical existences." If you were teaching in an elementary school classroom, how could you introduce experiences that would help children learn mathematics as part of a practical, real-life experience? How would your methods relate to children's personal experiences?

2. In paragraph 3 Dewey makes some important comments on the nature of the child's experience in the classroom. He says that in the classroom "[w]hat is here insisted upon is the necessity of an actual empirical situation as the initiating phase of thought." This is a fundamental idea in his essay. What does he mean by it? How can a teacher help produce such a situation? How well would it help develop real thought in the classroom?

3. In paragraph 8 Dewey addresses the circumstances of the classroom in which the student "has a problem, but it is the problem of meeting the peculiar requirements set by the teacher. His problem becomes that of finding out what the teacher wants, what will satisfy the teacher in recitation and examination and outward deportment." Judging from your own experience, is this situation still common in the early grades? Is it common in later grades? What has been your experience with this "problem"? Does it extend to the college level too?

4. The kind of education Dewey advocated was called progressive, and among its tenets were the questioning of authority and an emphasis on independence of thought on the part of the student. Throughout the twentieth century, schools of education at universities around the world were influenced by Dewey's ideas about education. Is it possible they are responsible for the current breakdown in respect for authority on the part of young people? Is it possible that Dewey can be held responsible for the permissiveness that is common in society today? Is this the ultimate empirical result of his educational ideas?

5. What examples do you have from your own learning experience that help validate Dewey's concepts of how learning should occur in a classroom? Since Dewey's theories are still extant (like Montessori's), it is reasonable that some of your teachers would have used his techniques. Describe any such techniques that you recall having been used in your classroom and from which you feel you profited.

6. In paragraph 11 Dewey states, "The accumulation and acquisition of information for purposes of reproduction in recitation and examination is made too much of." Under what conditions is this statement true of education? Under what conditions is it not true? Do you think that the process he describes is still common in education, or have Dewey's

theories tended to make it rare in the classroom? What are its effects, either for good or for bad?

7. **CONNECTIONS**   Dewey comments briefly on the Montessori method, which he feels moves too quickly from the child's sensory experiences to the transformation of those experiences into intellectual activity. Apart from that quibble, what ideas about education do Montessori and Dewey have that seem compatible? Assuming that Dewey may have read Montessori's book or visited her schools, in what particular ways does he seem to take account of her recommendations? Does he improve upon Montessori's ideas, or does he strike out in a different direction?

8. **CONNECTIONS**   Both Ralph Waldo Emerson and Maria Montessori write about respecting nature in the educational process. While Dewey does not invoke that term specifically, is it possible that he is also developing their thoughts on this point? What would be considered natural about the processes Dewey describes? What would be a natural situation in a Dewey-led classroom?

PAULO FREIRE
The Banking Concept of Education

PAULO FREIRE (1921–1997) was one of the most influential educators of the latter half of the twentieth century. In some ways he built on ideas originally propounded by both Maria Montessori and John Dewey. However, he focused his attention on illiterate peasants in underdeveloped countries and the problems they faced. His sympathies were always with the poor and the disenfranchised, for whom he hoped to be a voice. His method depended in large part on the fact that he understood the world of the poor and disenfranchised firsthand and could see ways to change their views of themselves. His landmark book on education, *Pedagogy of the Oppressed* (1970), immediately became a best-seller.

Freire, a Brazilian, began working in programs to help peasants learn to read and write. In the process, he also introduced political ideas and began to help the peasants liberate their minds and imagine a better life. Freire's methods, which included learning and using his students' language in his instruction, proved exceptionally effective. In just forty-five days Freire taught three hundred peasants in the city of Recife to read and write. In 1962 the Brazilian government gave Freire considerable financial support to set up similar programs in other parts of the country.

However, after a military coup in Brazil in 1964, Freire's work came to be seen as subversive because it threatened to upend the social order by educating and thus empowering the country's peasants. Because the new Brazilian military leaders feared his influence on the peasants, Freire was jailed in June 1964. When he was released some two months later, Freire was sent into exile. He went to nearby Chile and worked for agrarian reform, also focusing on education. It was there that he wrote his first book, *Education as the*

From *Pedagogy of the Oppressed*. Translated by Myra Bergman Ramos.

Practice of Freedom (1967). As a result of the acclaim this book received, as well as the remarkable success of his programs in Chile, Freire was made professor at Harvard in 1969. A year later *Pedagogy of the Oppressed* (which he wrote in 1968) secured his international reputation. The book was not published in Brazil until 1974.

In 1970 Freire began working for the World Congress of Churches, traveling widely while training teachers. He spent part of his time in the west African nation of Guinea-Bissau; his book *Pedagogy in Progress: The Letters to Guinea-Bissau* (1978) resulted from his work there. In Africa, as elsewhere, Freire's methods produced favorable results. Through learning to read, his students gained a much larger sense of themselves and of their opportunities for change and growth.

Freire was permitted to return to Brazil in 1979. He was appointed minister of education for the city of São Paulo, where, in 1991, the Paulo Freire Institute was founded. The institute continues to this day. Its mission remains international in scope, with many educational centers throughout the world.

Freire's Rhetoric

One of Freire's techniques is the use of specialized terminology. The term "oppressed" is used for those who are dominated by others. Likewise, the oppressor is someone who dominates. When the oppressed recognize their position, they may rise and overthrow their oppressors. But the result is often, as Freire notes, that they then become the oppressors. Freire's ideal is a world in which equals do not oppress one another. Another term is "praxis," which means action. A theory that is not turned into action is essentially a failure.

In the selection included here, the most important rhetorical device Freire uses is metaphor. His metaphor of the banking concept of education is famous and quite useful in explaining the kind of education that he does not favor: education that is rendered remote from life. The banking metaphor implies that the learner "deposits" knowledge transferred from a teacher, but the knowledge does not inform the learner about the realities of life. It remains in a depository for a while, but it does not rise to the level of critical thought. It is not a transforming or liberating force in the mind of the student. Rhetorically, this metaphor functions to convince us that traditional methods of teaching aid the oppressor, not the oppressed. The oppressor possesses the wealth of knowledge and deposits only some of it into the "account" of the oppressed, thus always keeping the edge of power over the oppressed.

The term "dialogue" implies a give and take between teacher and student. Freire borrows the term from the philosopher Hegel and uses it to emphasize an alternative to the banking concept. Dialogue implies an interaction in which the student may become the teacher and the teacher the student. It also implies that the learning experience is dynamic rather than static, that it can change both student and teacher. This line of thought leads to his "problem-posing," a term that is the alternative to "depositing" information. Posing a problem that students can address on their own terms will then produce new "cognition," which implies both an awareness of knowledge and a more useful possession of knowledge than in the banking concept because it encourages critical thinking. For Freire the act of thinking is much more important than the act of stashing away information provided by a teacher. Critical thinking is essential to real education because it is liberating.

Because Freire writes from the perspective of the poor, one realizes that his view of the oppressor implies a minority elite oppressing the majority of the poor. This view reflects reality in many underdeveloped nations, including some in South America, in which the wealth and power is in the hands of the few. In those societies it is to the advantage of the elite that the poor remain content in their social situation. As Simone de Beauvoir states, in the lines Freire quotes, the aim of education in such societies is to change the consciousness of the poor, but not to change the conditions that oppress them (para 11). The banking concept of education is not liberating because it does not produce critical thinking or involve problem-solving: it involves rote memorization and retention of facts.

In paragraph 17 Freire clarifies the banking concept by establishing that the teacher is the depositor and the student is the empty container into which the knowledge is placed for safekeeping. There is no dialogue because the transmission of knowledge is a one-way transaction. Likewise, the choice of what is transmitted is entirely up to the teacher or the institution that chooses the curriculum. There can be no enlightened critique of the information because it is not discussed; it is imparted. The passivity of this process is clarified in paragraph 18: "And since men 'receive' the world as passive entities, education should make them more passive still, and adapt them to the world. . . . Translated into practice, this concept is well suited to the purposes of the oppressors." At this point, one can see that Freire's approach is essentially revolutionary in that it implies a change in which the oppressed become more aware of the nature of their political realities. This was the reason Brazilian military leaders knew they had to put an end to Freire's work. Revolution implies change, and the military leaders demanded, now that they were the oppressors, that change be denied the poor and the oppressed.

PREREADING QUESTIONS: WHAT TO READ FOR

The following prereading questions may help you anticipate key issues in the discussion of Paulo Freire's "The Banking Concept of Education." Keeping them in mind during your first reading of the selection should help focus your attention.

- What is the banking concept of education?

- Why is the banking concept of education the preferred means of the oppressor?

- Who are the oppressed and what does Freire want for them?

The Banking Concept of Education

A careful analysis of the teacher-student relationship at any 1
level, inside or outside the school, reveals its fundamentally *narrative* character. This relationship involves a narrating Subject (the teacher) and patient, listening objects (the students). The contents, whether values or empirical dimensions of reality, tend in the process of being narrated to become lifeless and petrified. Education is suffering from narration sickness.

The teacher talks about reality as if it were motionless, static, 2
compartmentalized, and predictable. Or else he expounds on a topic completely alien to the existential experience of the students. His task is to "fill" the students with the contents of his narration— contents which are detached from reality, disconnected from the totality that engendered them and could give them significance. Words are emptied of their concreteness and become a hollow, alienated, and alienating verbosity.

The outstanding characteristic of this narrative education, then, 3
is the sonority of words, not their transforming power. "Four times

four is sixteen; the capital of Pará is Belem."[1] The student records, memorizes, and repeats these phrases without perceiving what four times four really means, or realizing the true significance of "capital" in the affirmation "the capital of Pará is Belém," that is, what Belém means for Pará and what Pará means for Brazil.

Narration (with the teacher as narrator) leads the students to   4 memorize mechanically the narrated content. Worse yet, it turns them into "containers," into "receptacles" to be "filled" by the teacher. The more completely he fills the receptacles, the better a teacher he is. The more meekly the receptacles permit themselves to be filled, the better students they are.

Education thus becomes an act of depositing, in which the stu-   5 dents are the depositories and the teacher is the depositor. Instead of communicating, the teacher issues communiqués and makes deposits which the students patiently receive, memorize, and repeat. This is the "banking" concept of education, in which the scope of action allowed to the students extends only as far as receiving, filing, and storing the deposits. They do, it is true, have the opportunity to become collectors or cataloguers of the things they store. But in the last analysis, it is men themselves who are filed away through the lack of creativity, transformation, and knowledge in this (at best) misguided system. For apart from inquiry, apart from the praxis, men cannot be truly human. Knowledge emerges only through invention and re-invention, through the restless, impatient, continuing, hopeful inquiry men pursue in the world, with the world, and with each other.

In the banking concept of education, knowledge is a gift be-   6 stowed by those who consider themselves knowledgeable upon those whom they consider to know nothing. Projecting an absolute ignorance onto others, a characteristic of the ideology of oppression, negates education and knowledge as processes of inquiry. The teacher presents himself to his students as their necessary opposite; by considering their ignorance absolute, he justifies his own existence. The students, alienated like the slave in the Hegelian dialectic,[2] accept their ignorance as justifying the teacher's existence—but, unlike the slave, they never discover that they educate the teacher.

The *raison d'être*[3] of libertarian education, on the other hand,   7 lies in its drive towards reconciliation. Education must begin with

---

[1] **Belém** Capital of Brazil's Pará State on the southern Amazon.

[2] **Hegelian dialectic** Hegel's view of history as the result of an opposition of two forces that results in a third force that then collides with a new force to repeat the process. The dialectic Freire refers to is the master/slave relationship, wherein each defines the other.

[3] ***raison d'être*** The reason for being.

the solution of the teacher-student contradiction, by reconciling the poles of the contradiction so that both are simultaneously teachers *and* students.

This solution is not (nor can it be) found in the banking con- 8 cept. On the contrary, banking education maintains and even stimulates the contradiction through the following attitudes and practices, which mirror oppressive society as a whole:

(a) the teacher teaches and the students are taught;

(b) the teacher knows everything and the students know nothing;

(c) the teacher thinks and the students are thought about;

(d) the teacher talks and the students listen—meekly;

(e) the teacher disciplines and the students are disciplined;

(f) the teacher chooses and enforces his choice, and the students comply;

(g) the teacher acts and the students have the illusion of acting through the action of the teacher;

(h) the teacher chooses the program content, and the students (who were not consulted) adapt to it;

(i) the teacher confuses the authority of knowledge with his own professional authority, which he sets in opposition to the freedom of the students;

(j) the teacher is the Subject of the learning process, while the pupils are mere objects.

It is not surprising that the banking concept of education re- 9 gards men as adaptable, manageable beings. The more students work at storing the deposits entrusted to them, the less they develop the critical consciousness which would result from their intervention in the world as transformers of that world. The more completely they accept the passive role imposed on them, the more they tend simply to adapt to the world as it is and to the fragmented view of reality deposited in them.

The capability of banking education to minimize or annul the 10 students' creative power and to stimulate their credulity serves the interests of the oppressors, who care neither to have the world revealed nor to see it transformed. The oppressors use their "humanitarianism" to preserve a profitable situation. Thus they react almost instinctively against any experiment in education which stimulates the critical faculties and is not content with a partial view of reality but always seeks out the ties which link one point to another and one problem to another.

Indeed, the interests of the oppressors lie in "changing the con-   11
sciousness of the oppressed, not the situation which oppresses
them";[4] for the more the oppressed can be led to adapt to that situation, the more easily they can be dominated. To achieve this end, the
oppressors use the banking concept of education in conjunction with
a paternalistic social action apparatus, within which the oppressed receive the euphemistic title of "welfare recipients." They are treated as
individual cases, as marginal men who deviate from the general configuration of a "good, organized, and just" society. The oppressed are
regarded as the pathology of the healthy society, which must therefore
adjust these "incompetent and lazy" folk to its own patterns by changing their mentality. These marginals need to be "integrated," "incorporated" into the healthy society that they have "forsaken."

The truth is, however, that the oppressed are not "marginals,"   12
are not men living "outside" society. They have always been
"inside"—inside the structure which made them "beings for others."
The solution is not to "integrate" them into the structure of oppression, but to transform that structure so that they can become "beings
for themselves." Such transformation, of course, would undermine
the oppressors' purposes; hence their utilization of the banking concept of education to avoid the threat of student *conscientização*.[5]

The banking approach to adult education, for example, will never   13
propose to students that they critically consider reality. It will deal instead with such vital questions as whether Roger gave green grass to
the goat, and insist upon the importance of learning that, on the contrary, Roger gave green grass to the rabbit. The "humanism" of the
banking approach masks the effort to turn men into automatons—
the very negation of their ontological vocation to be more fully
human.

Those who use the banking approach, knowingly or unknow-   14
ingly (for there are innumerable well-intentioned bank-clerk
teachers who do not realize that they are serving only to dehuman-
ize), fail to perceive that the deposits themselves contain contradictions about reality. But, sooner or later, these contradictions
may lead formerly passive students to turn against their domestication and the attempt to domesticate reality. They may discover
through existential experience that their present way of life is

---

[4] Simone de Beauvoir, *La Pensée de Droite, Aujourd'hui* (Paris); ST, *El Pensamiento
político de la Derecha* (Buenos Aires, 1963) *Political Thought of The Right* [1963],
p. 34. [Freire's note]

[5] **conscientização** Conscientization, a made-up word. It is the moment the
oppressed become aware of their oppression.

irreconcilable with their vocation to become fully human. They may perceive through their relations with reality that reality is really a *process*, undergoing constant transformation. If men are searchers and their ontological vocation[6] is humanization, sooner or later they may perceive the contradiction in which banking education seeks to maintain them, and then engage themselves in the struggle for their liberation.

But the humanist, revolutionary educator cannot wait for this 15 possibility to materialize. From the outset, his efforts must coincide with those of the students to engage in critical thinking and the quest for mutual humanization. His efforts must be imbued with a profound trust in men and their creative power. To achieve this, he must be a partner of the students in his relations with them.

The banking concept does not admit to such partnership—and 16 necessarily so. To resolve the teacher-student contradiction, to exchange the role of depositor, prescriber, domesticator, for the role of student among students would be to undermine the power of oppression and serve the cause of liberation.

Implicit in the banking concept is the assumption of a dichotomy 17 between man and the world: man is merely *in* the world, not *with* the world or with others; man is spectator, not re-creator. In this view, man is not a conscious being (*corpo consciente*); he is rather the possessor of *a* consciousness: an empty "mind" passively open to the reception of deposits of reality from the world outside. For example, my desk, my books, my coffee cup, all the objects before me—as bits of the world which surrounds me—would be "inside" me, exactly as I am inside my study right now. This view makes no distinction between being accessible to consciousness and entering consciousness. The distinction, however, is essential: the objects which surround me are simply accessible to my consciousness, not located within it. I am aware of them, but they are not inside me.

It follows logically from the banking notion of consciousness 18 that the educator's role is to regulate the way the world "enters into" the students. His task is to organize a process which already occurs spontaneously, to "fill" the students by making deposits of information which he considers to constitute true knowledge.[7] And since

---

[6] **ontological vocation** The calling in life that best fits their nature. Ontology refers to Existence.

[7] This concept corresponds to what Sartre calls the "digestive" or "nutritive" concept of education, in which knowledge is "fed" by the teacher to the students to "fill them out." See Jean-Paul Sartre, "Une idée fundamentale de la phénomenologie de Husserl: L'intentionalité" (Intentionality: A Fundamental Idea of Husserl's Phenomenology), *Situations I* (Paris, 1947). [Freire's note]

men "receive" the world as passive entities, education should make them more passive still, and adapt them to the world. The educated man is the adapted man, because he is better "fit" for the world. Translated into practice, this concept is well suited to the purposes of the oppressors, whose tranquility rests on how well men fit the world the oppressors have created, and how little they question it.

The more completely the majority adapt to the purposes which   19
the dominant minority prescribe for them (thereby depriving them of the right to their own purposes), the more easily the minority can continue to prescribe. The theory and practice of banking education serve this end quite efficiently. Verbalistic lessons, reading requirements,[8] the methods for evaluating "knowledge," the distance between the teacher and the taught, the criteria for promotion: everything in this ready-to-wear approach serves to obviate thinking.

The bank-clerk educator does not realize that there is no true   20
security in his hypertrophied role, that one must seek to live *with* others in solidarity. One cannot impose oneself, nor even merely coexist with one's students. Solidarity requires true communication, and the concept by which such an educator is guided fears and proscribes communication.

Yet only through communication can human life hold meaning.   21
The teacher's thinking is authenticated only by the authenticity of the students' thinking. The teacher cannot think for his students, nor can he impose his thought on them. Authentic thinking, thinking that is concerned about *reality*, does not take place in ivory tower isolation, but only in communication. If it is true that thought has meaning only when generated by action upon the world, the subordination of students to teachers becomes impossible.

Because banking education begins with a false understanding of   22
men as objects, it cannot promote the development of what Fromm[9] calls "biophily," but instead produces its opposite: "necrophily."

> While life is characterized by growth in a structured, functional manner, the necrophilous person loves all that does not grow, all that is mechanical. The necrophilous person is driven by the desire to transform the organic into the inorganic, to approach life mechanically, as if all living persons were things. . . . Memory, rather than experience; having, rather than being, is what counts. The necrophilous person can relate to an object—a flower or a person—only if he possesses it; hence a threat to his possession is

---

[8] For example, some professors specify in their reading lists that a book should be read from pages 10 to 15—and do this to "help" their students! [Freire's note]

[9] **Erich Fromm (1900–1980)** An influential psychologist. The book Freire refers to is *The Heart of Man* (1964).

a threat to himself; if he loses possession he loses contact with the world. . . . He loves control, and in the act of controlling he kills life.[10]

Oppression—overwhelming control—is necrophilic; it is nour- 23 ished by love of death, not life. The banking concept of education, which serves the interests of oppression, is also necrophilic. Based on a mechanistic, static, naturalistic, spatialized view of consciousness, it transforms students into receiving objects. It attempts to control thinking and action, leads men to adjust to the world, and inhibits their creative power.

When their efforts to act responsibly are frustrated, when they 24 find themselves unable to use their faculties, men suffer. "This suffering due to impotence is rooted in the very fact that the human equilibrium has been disturbed."[11] But the inability to act which causes men's anguish also causes them to reject their impotence, by attempting

> . . . to restore [their] capacity to act. But can [they], and how? One way is to submit to and identify with a person or group having power. By this symbolic participation in another person's life, [men have] the illusion of acting, when in reality [they] only submit to and become a part of those who act.[12]

Populist manifestations perhaps best exemplify this type of 25 behavior by the oppressed, who, by identifying with charismatic leaders, come to feel that they themselves are active and effective. The rebellion they express as they emerge in the historical process is motivated by that desire to act effectively. The dominant elites consider the remedy to be more domination and repression, carried out in the name of freedom, order, and social peace (that is, the peace of the elites). Thus they can condemn—logically, from their point of view—"the violence of a strike by workers and [can] call upon the state in the same breath to use violence in putting down the strike."[13]

Education as the exercise of domination stimulates the credulity 26 of students, with the ideological intent (often not perceived by educators) of indoctrinating them to adapt to the world of oppression. This accusation is not made in the naïve hope that the dominant elites will thereby simply abandon the practice. Its objective is to call the attention of true humanists to the fact that they cannot use

---

[10] Fromm, *op. cit.*, p. 41. [Freire's note]

[11] *Ibid.*, p. 31. [Freire's note]

[12] *Ibid.* [Freire's note]

[13] Reinhold Niebuhr, *Moral Man and Immoral Society* (New York, 1960), p. 130. [Freire's note]

banking educational methods in the pursuit of liberation, for they would only negate that very pursuit. Nor may a revolutionary society inherit these methods from an oppressor society. The revolutionary society which practices banking education is either misguided or mistrusting of men. In either event, it is threatened by the specter of reaction.

Unfortunately, those who espouse the cause of liberation are themselves surrounded and influenced by the climate which generates the banking concept, and often do not perceive its true significance or its dehumanizing power. Paradoxically, then, they utilize this same instrument of alienation in what they consider an effort to liberate. Indeed, some "revolutionaries" brand as "innocents," "dreamers," or even "reactionaries" those who would challenge this educational practice. But one does not liberate men by alienating them. Authentic liberation—the process of humanization—is not another deposit to be made in men. Liberation is a praxis: the action and reflection of men upon their world in order to transform it. Those truly committed to the cause of liberation can accept neither the mechanistic concept of consciousness as an empty vessel to be filled, nor the use of banking methods of domination (propaganda, slogans—deposits) in the name of liberation. 27

Those truly committed to liberation must reject the banking concept in its entirety, adopting instead a concept of men as conscious beings, and consciousness as consciousness intent upon the world. They must abandon the educational goal of deposit-making and replace it with the posing of the problems of men in their relations with the world. "Problem-posing" education, responding to the essence of consciousness—*intentionality*—rejects communiqués and embodies communication. It epitomizes the special characteristic of consciousness: being *conscious of*, not only as intent on objects but as turned in upon itself in a Jasperian[14] "split" — consciousness as consciousness *of* consciousness. 28

Liberating education consists in acts of cognition, not transferrals of information. It is a learning situation in which the cognizable object (far from being the end of the cognitive act) intermediates the cognitive actors—teacher on the one hand and students on the other. Accordingly, the practice of problem-posing education entails at the outset that the teacher-student contradiction be resolved. Dialogical relations—indispensable to the capacity of cognitive actors to cooperate in perceiving the same cognizable object—are otherwise impossible. 29

---

[14]**Jasperian: Karl Jaspers (1883–1969)**, German philosopher and psychiatrist.

Indeed, problem-posing education, which breaks with the verti-   30
cal patterns characteristic of banking education, can fulfill its function
as the practice of freedom only if it can overcome the above contradiction. Through dialogue, the teacher-of-the-students and the students-
of-the-teacher cease to exist and a new term emerges: teacher-student
with students-teachers. The teacher is no longer merely the-one-
who-teaches, but one who is himself taught in dialogue with the students, who in turn while being taught also teach. They become
jointly responsible for a process in which all grow. In this process,
arguments based on "authority" are no longer valid; in order to function, authority must be *on the side of* freedom, not *against* it. Here, no
one teaches another, nor is anyone self-taught. Men teach each other,
mediated by the world, by the cognizable objects which in banking
education are "owned" by the teacher.

The banking concept (with its tendency to dichotomize every-   31
thing) distinguishes two stages in the action of the educator. During
the first, he cognizes a cognizable object while he prepares his
lessons in his study or his laboratory; during the second, he expounds to his students about that object. The students are not called
upon to know, but to memorize the contents narrated by the teacher.
Nor do the students practice any act of cognition, since the object towards which that act should be directed is the property of the
teacher rather than a medium evoking the critical reflection of
both teacher and students. Hence in the name of the "preservation of
culture and knowledge" we have a system which achieves neither
true knowledge nor true culture.

The problem-posing method does not dichotomize the activity of   32
the teacher-student: he is not "cognitive" at one point and "narrative"
at another. He is always "cognitive," whether preparing a project or
engaging in dialogue with the students. He does not regard cognizable objects as his private property, but as the object of reflection by
himself and the students. In this way, the problem-posing educator
constantly re-forms his reflections in the reflection of the students.
The students—no longer docile listeners—are now critical co-
investigators in dialogue with the teacher. The teacher presents the
material to the students for their consideration, and re-considers his
earlier considerations as the students express their own. The role of
the problem-posing educator is to create, together with the students,
the conditions under which knowledge at the level of the *doxa* is superseded by true knowledge, at the level of the *logos*.[15]

---

[15] **doxa . . . logos** *Doxa* are teachings handed down by a higher authority. *Logos*
is the word at the level of experience.

Whereas banking education anesthetizes and inhibits creative   33
power, problem-posing education involves a constant unveiling of
reality. The former attempts to maintain the *submersion* of consciousness; the latter strives for the *emergence* of consciousness and *critical
intervention* in reality.

Students, as they are increasingly posed with problems relating   34
to themselves in the world and with the world, will feel increasingly
challenged and obliged to respond to that challenge. Because they
apprehend the challenge as interrelated to other problems within a
total context, not as a theoretical question, the resulting comprehension tends to be increasingly critical and thus constantly less
alienated. Their response to the challenge evokes new challenges,
followed by new understandings; and gradually the students come
to regard themselves as committed.

Education as the practice of freedom—as opposed to education   35
as the practice of domination—denies that man is abstract, isolated,
independent, and unattached to the world; it also denies that the
world exists as a reality apart from men. Authentic reflection considers neither abstract man nor the world without men, but men in their
relations with the world. In these relations consciousness and world
are simultaneous: consciousness neither precedes the world nor follows it.

> La conscience et le monde sont dormés d'un même coup: ex-
> térieur par essence à la conscience, le monde est, par essence re-
> latif à elle.[16]

In one of our culture circles in Chile, the group was discussing
(based on a codification) the anthropological concept of culture. In
the midst of the discussion, a peasant who by banking standards
was completely ignorant said: "Now I see that without man there is
no world." When the educator responded: "Let's say, for the sake
of argument, that all the men on earth were to die, but that the
earth itself remained, together with trees, birds, animals, rivers,
seas, the stars . . . wouldn't all this be a world?" "Oh no," the peasant replied emphatically. "There would be no one to say: 'This is a
world.'"

The peasant wished to express the idea that there would be   36
lacking the consciousness of the world which necessarily implies
the world of consciousness. *I* cannot exist without a *not-I*. In turn,
the *not-I* depends on that existence. The world which brings

---

[16] Sartre, *op. cit.* (*Situations I*), p. 32. [Freire's note] ("Consciousness and the
world are put to sleep by the same blow; beyond consciousness, the world is essentially relative to itself.")

consciousness into existence becomes the world *of* that consciousness. Hence, the previously cited affirmation of Sartre: "*La conscience et le monde sont dormés d'un même coup.*"

As men, simultaneously reflecting on themselves and on the world, increase the scope of their perception, they begin to direct their observations towards previously inconspicuous phenomena:

> In perception properly so-called, as an explicit awareness [*Gewahren*], I am turned towards the object, to the paper, for instance. I apprehend it as being this here and now. The apprehension is a singling out, every object having a background in experience. Around and about the paper lie books, pencils, ink-well, and so forth, and these in a certain sense are also "perceived," perceptually there, in the "field of intuition"; but whilst I was turned towards the paper there was no turning in their direction, nor any apprehending of them, not even in a secondary sense. They appeared and yet were not singled out, were not posited on their own account. Every perception of a thing has such a zone of background intuitions or background awareness, if "intuiting" already includes the state of being turned towards, and this also is a "conscious experience," or more briefly a "consciousness of" all indeed that in point of fact lies in the co-perceived objective background.[17]

That which had existed objectively but had not been perceived in its deeper implications (if indeed it was perceived at all) begins to "stand out," assuming the character of a problem and therefore of challenge. Thus, men begin to single out elements from their "background awarenesses" and to reflect upon them. These elements are now objects of men's consideration, and, as such, objects of their action and cognition.

In problem-posing education, men develop their power to perceive critically *the way they exist* in the world *with which* and *in which* they find themselves; they come to see the world not as a static reality, but as a reality in process, in transformation. Although the dialectical relations of men with the world exist independently of how these relations are perceived (or whether or not they are perceived at all), it is also true that the form of action men adopt is to a large extent a function of how they perceive themselves in the world. Hence, the teacher-student and the students-teachers reflect simultaneously on themselves and the world without dichotomizing this reflection from action, and thus establish an authentic form of thought and action.

---

[17] Edmund Husserl, *Ideas—General Introduction to Pure Phenomenology* (London, 1969), pp. 105–106. [Freire's note]

Once again, the two educational concepts and practices under   39
analysis come into conflict. Banking education (for obvious reasons)
attempts, by mythicizing reality, to conceal certain facts which explain the way men exist in the world; problem-posing education sets
itself the task of demythologizing. Banking education resists dialogue; problem-posing education regards dialogue as indispensable
to the act of cognition which unveils reality. Banking education treats
students as objects of assistance; problem-posing education makes
them critical thinkers. Banking education inhibits creativity and do-
mesticates (although it cannot completely destroy) the *intentionality*
of consciousness by isolating consciousness from the world, thereby
denying men their ontological and historical vocation of becoming
more fully human. Problem-posing education bases itself on creativity and stimulates true reflection and action upon reality, thereby responding to the vocation of men as beings who are authentic only
when engaged in inquiry and creative transformation. In sum: banking theory and practice, as immobilizing and fixating forces, fail to
acknowledge men as historical beings; problem-posing theory and
practice take man's historicity as their starting point.

Problem-posing education affirms men as beings in the process of   40
becoming—as unfinished, uncompleted beings in and with a likewise
unfinished reality. Indeed, in contrast to other animals who are unfinished, but not historical, men know themselves to be unfinished;
they are aware of their incompletion. In this incompletion and this
awareness lie the very roots of education as an exclusively human
manifestation. The unfinished character of men and the transforma-
tional character of reality necessitate that education be an ongoing
activity.

Education is thus constantly remade in the praxis. In order to   41
be, it must *become*. Its "duration" (in the Bergsonian[18] meaning of the
word) is found in the interplay of the opposites *permanence* and
change. The banking method emphasizes permanence and becomes
reactionary; problem-posing education—which accepts neither a
"well-behaved" present nor a predetermined future—roots itself in
the dynamic present and becomes revolutionary.

Problem-posing education is revolutionary futurity. Hence it is   42
prophetic (and, as such, hopeful). Hence, it corresponds to the historical nature of man. Hence, it affirms men as beings who transcend
themselves, who move forward and look ahead, for whom immobility

---

[18]**Bergsonian: Henri Bergson (1859–1941),** French philosopher who regarded duration as a "succession of conscious states, intermingling and unmea-
sured."

represents a fatal threat, for whom looking at the past must only be a means of understanding more clearly what and who they are so that they can more wisely build the future. Hence, it identifies with the movement which engages men as beings aware of their incompletion — an historical movement which has its point of departure, its Subjects and its objective.

The point of departure of the movement lies in men themselves. But since men do not exist apart from the world, apart from reality, the movement must begin with the men-world relationship. Accordingly, the point of departure must always be with men in the "here and now," which constitutes the situation within which they are submerged, from which they emerge, and in which they intervene. Only by starting from this situation — which determines their perception of it — can they begin to move. To do this authentically they must perceive their state not as fated and unalterable, but merely as limiting — and therefore challenging. 43

Whereas the banking method directly or indirectly reinforces men's fatalistic perception of their situation, the problem-posing method presents this very situation to them as a problem. As the situation becomes the object of their cognition, the naïve or magical perception which produced their fatalism gives way to perception which is able to perceive itself even as it perceives reality, and can thus be critically objective about that reality. 44

A deepened consciousness of their situation leads men to apprehend that situation as an historical reality susceptible of transformation. Resignation gives way to the drive for transformation and inquiry, over which men feel themselves to be in control. If men, as historical beings necessarily engaged with other men in a movement of inquiry, did not control that movement, it would be (and is) a violation of men's humanity. Any situation in which some men prevent others from engaging in the process of inquiry is one of violence. The means used are not important; to alienate men from their own decision-making is to change them into objects. 45

This movement of inquiry must be directed towards humanization — man's historical vocation. The pursuit of full humanity, however, cannot be carried out in isolation or individualism, but only in fellowship and solidarity; therefore it cannot unfold in the antagonistic relations between oppressors and oppressed. No one can be authentically human while he prevents others from being so. Attempting *to be more* human, individualistically, leads to *having more*, egotistically: a form of dehumanization. Not that it is not fundamental *to have* in order *to be* human. Precisely because it *is* necessary, some men's *having* must not be allowed to constitute an obstacle to others' *having*, must not consolidate the power of the former to crush the latter. 46

Problem-posing education, as a humanist and liberating praxis, 47 posits as fundamental that men subjected to domination must fight for their emancipation. To that end, it enables teachers and students to become Subjects of the educational process by overcoming authoritarianism and an alienating intellectualism; it also enables men to overcome their false perception of reality. The world—no longer something to be described with deceptive words—becomes the object of that transforming action by men which results in their humanization.

Problem-posing education does not and cannot serve the interests 48 of the oppressor. No oppressive order could permit the oppressed to begin to question: Why? While only a revolutionary society can carry out this education in systematic terms, the revolutionary leaders need not take full power before they can employ the method. In the revolutionary process, the leaders cannot utilize the banking method as an interim measure, justified on grounds of expediency, with the intention of *later* behaving in a genuinely revolutionary fashion. They must be revolutionary—that is to say, dialogical—from the outset.

QUESTIONS FOR CRITICAL READING

1. What is the narrative character of the teacher-student relationship?
2. What does Freire mean by depositing knowledge? Are you familiar with the practice?
3. Why is it a problem to think of knowledge as a gift?
4. What does Freire seem to mean by recommending a libertarian education?
5. Why would the banking concept in education tend to "annul the students' creative power" (para. 10)?
6. What do the oppressors seem to want from the process of education?
7. Does your own education seem to have been the product of a social group of oppressors?
8. Freire says the banking concept of education stimulates the credulity of the student. Is he correct?

SUGGESTIONS FOR WRITING

1. In paragraph 8, Freire lists ten "attitudes and practices" of education that he says "mirror oppressive society as a whole." Examine each of these practices and describe any experience you have had with them. What was their effect on your own education? Which of these practices have you never experienced? Which do you feel may have some value,

in general, to education? Are there other "attitudes and practices" you can add to this list that would help reinforce Freire's thinking?

2. Freire says a liberating education involves the give and take between teacher and student. He recommends a classroom environment in which the student can sometimes be the teacher and the teacher can sometimes be the student. Have you experienced such a classroom? What was the result of the experience? Do you feel your education was opened up, that you connected with real-world experience in the process? How liberating was it for you? Was it successful?

3. In paragraph 19 Freire states, "Verbalistic lessons, reading require-ments, the methods for evaluating 'knowledge,' the distance between the teacher and the taught, the criteria for promotion: everything in this ready-to-wear approach serves to obviate thinking." In your expe-rience, is this statement true about the kind(s) of education you have experienced? If so, is it more true of one level of education than of an-other? At what level—elementary, secondary, or college—were you most challenged creatively in your education? How was it different from what Freire describes?

4. In paragraph 28 Freire states, "Those truly committed to liberation must reject the banking concept in its entirety." Do you think that is possible? Is it possible that one can be committed to a liberal education while also relying to an extent on the banking concept? How could an educator justify the banking concept while also defending a libera-tionist attitude toward education?

5. Examine any current recommendations by local or federal government agencies for changes in U.S. schools. How sympathetic would Freire be to plans, such as standardized testing, that government has for "im-proving" education? How might he react to enforced summer school? Examine recent articles in newspapers, magazines, journals, and online sources for statements that tend to support the banking concept of ed-ucation. To what extent might current educational thinking lead to a pedagogy of the oppressed? To what extent are you concerned?

6. **CONNECTIONS**   To what extent does Frederick Douglass's exam-ple support Freire's views on the importance of problem-posing in education? And to what extent does it support his views that say edu-cation must be connected to life experiences? To what extent was Douglass's experience in education dialogic? With whom or what did he have a dialogue? How did education help him free his mind and his body?

7. **CONNECTIONS**   John Dewey in "Thinking in Education" seems to have some of the same views as Freire, especially in terms of Freire's ideas about problem-posing. Compare their views and see what is sim-ilar and what is dissimilar in their concepts of thinking in education. Would you think it likely that Freire had read Dewey's book? What are your reasons? In the process, discuss some of the apparent political ideas that are implied in each of their works. How much do they have in common politically?

8. **CONNECTIONS**   Consider Freire's ideas about the dehumanization of the oppressed student in relation to the kind of oppression Hannah Arendt discusses in her essay "Total Domination" in Part One. How much do they have in common in their conception of what it means to be human and what it means to lose one's sense of humanity? How much do Arendt and Freire seem to have in common in terms of their political outlook? Why would one think that the Germans of Arendt's experience depended on the banking concept of education?

PART FOUR

WEALTH AND POVERTY

Adam Smith

Karl Marx

John Maynard Keynes

John Kenneth Galbraith

Robert B. Reich

INTRODUCTION

Wealth and poverty: the one is the parent of luxury and indolence, and the other of meanness and viciousness, and both of discontent.

–PLATO (428–347 B.C.)

What difference does it make how much you have? What you do not have amounts to much more.

–SENECA (4 B.C.–A.D. 65)

Great eagerness in the pursuit of wealth, pleasure, or honor, cannot exist without sin.

–DESIDERIUS ERASMUS (1466–1536)

In any country where talent and virtue produce no advancement, money will be the national god. Its inhabitants will either have to possess money or make others believe that they do. Wealth will be the highest virtue, poverty the greatest vice.

–DENIS DIDEROT (1713–1784)

Poverty in itself does not make men into a rabble; a rabble is created only when there is joined to poverty a disposition of mind, an inner indignation against the rich, against society, against the government.

–GEORG WILHELM FRIEDRICH HEGEL (1770–1831)

Animals struggle with each other for food or for leadership, but they do not, like human beings, struggle with each other for that that stands for food or leadership: such things as our paper symbols of wealth (money, bonds, titles), badges of rank to wear on our clothes, or low-number license plates, supposed by some people to stand for social precedence.

–S. I. HAYAKAWA (1906–1992)

Ancient writers talk about wealth in terms of a surplus of necessary or desirable goods and products. After the invention of coins — which historians attribute to the Lydians, whose civilization flourished in the eastern Mediterranean region from 800 to 200 B.C.—wealth also became associated with money. However, the relationship of wealth to money has long been debated. According to Aristotle, people misunderstand wealth when they think of it as "only a quantity of coin." For him, money was useful primarily as a means of representing and purchasing goods but was not sustaining in and of itself.

Writers like Aristotle have argued that wealth benefits the state by ensuring stability, growth, security, and cultural innovations and that it benefits the individual by providing leisure time, mobility, and luxury. Most societies, however, have struggled with the problems

336

caused by unequal distribution of wealth, either among individuals or between citizens and the state. The Spartan leader Lycurgus is said to have tackled the problem in the ninth century B.C. by convincing the inhabitants of the Greek city-state of Sparta that they needed to redistribute their wealth. Land and household goods were redistributed among the citizens, and Lycurgus was hailed as a hero. However, Lycurgus's model has not been the norm in subsequent civilizations, and questions about the nature of wealth and its role and distribution in society have persisted.

The selections in this section present ideas on wealth and poverty from a variety of perspectives. Adam Smith begins by tracing the natural evolution of wealth from farming to trade. Karl Marx expounds on what he feels are the corrosive effects of excessive wealth on the individual and on the problems caused by unequal distribution of wealth between laborers and business owners. John Maynard Keynes explains how changes in the value of money affect social classes. John Kenneth Galbraith and Robert B. Reich further investigate the problems that an unequal distribution of wealth poses for society as a whole.

Adam Smith was known originally as a moral philosopher with a professorship at Glasgow, but he wrote at a time of extraordinary expansion in Great Britain. As industrial power grew in the late eighteenth century, England became more wealthy and began to dominate trade in important areas of commerce. In his own mind, Smith's interest in wealth may have been connected with his studies in morality, or it may have grown from his considerable curiosity about a broad range of subjects. Regardless, he produced one of the century's most important and extensive books on economics, *The Wealth of Nations*. It is still consulted by economists today.

Smith's "Of the Natural Progress of Opulence" is an attempt to understand the "natural" steps to wealth. Smith posits an interesting relationship between the country, where food and plants, such as cotton and flax, supply the necessities of life, and the city, which produces no food but takes the surplus from the country and turns it into manufactured goods. Smith's ideas concerning this process center on surplus. The farmers produce more than they can consume, and therefore they can market their goods to the city. The city takes some of the goods from the farmers and turns them into manufactured products, which can be sold back to the people in the country. When there is a surplus of manufactured goods, they can be sold abroad. That process can produce wealth—on a grand scale.

Karl Marx's *Communist Manifesto* clarifies the relationship between a people's condition and the economic system in which they live. Marx saw that capitalism provided opportunities for the

wealthy and powerful to take advantage of labor. He argued that because labor cannot efficiently sell its product, management can keep
labor in perpetual economic bondage.

Marx knew poverty firsthand, but one of his close associates,
Friedrich Engels, who collaborated on portions of the *Manifesto*, was
the son of a factory owner and so was able to observe closely how the
rich can oppress the poor. For both of them, the economic system of
capitalism produced a class struggle between the rich (bourgeoisie)
and the laboring classes (proletariat).

One of the chief architects of contemporary capitalism, John
Maynard Keynes, addresses one of capitalism's most important issues: the stability of the value of money. As he points out, during the
nineteenth century Europe was enjoying a period of essential stability, with the changes to the value of money oscillating very moderately. The result was that people were encouraged to invest and save
on a large scale, and wealth increased greatly until the calamity of
Word War I. After the war, inflation so severely ravaged many nations that a great deal of wealth was wiped out. Inflation and deflation, Keynes explains, are the chief culprits in lowering or raising the
value of money in any given period. When sudden or extreme
changes in these forces occur, then there is disruption in the economy. These changes can be extremely damaging to capitalist nations
and to the individuals living in them. Government intervention, he
feels, can help keep the value of money as stable as possible.

John Kenneth Galbraith's selection, "The Position of Poverty,"
dates from the middle of the twentieth century and addresses an issue
that earlier thinkers avoided: the question of poverty. It is not that earlier writers were unaware that poverty existed—most mention it in
passing—but their main concern was the accumulation and preservation of wealth. Galbraith, in his study of the economics of contemporary America, also focuses on wealth; the title of his most famous book
is *The Affluent Society* (1958; rev. 1998). He, however, points toward
something greater than the issue of attaining affluence. His concern is
with the allocation of the wealth that American society has produced.
His fears that selfishness and waste will dominate the affluent society
have led him to write about what he considers the most important social issue related to economics: poverty and its effects. If Smith was
correct in seeing wealth as appropriate subject matter for economic
study, then Galbraith has pointed to the opposite of wealth as being
equally worthy of close examination.

Robert B. Reich, a lecturer at Harvard University until he was
appointed secretary of labor in the first Clinton administration, has
taught courses in economics and published widely. His 1991 book
The Work of Nations echoes the title of Adam Smith's eighteenth-century

masterpiece of capitalist theory, *The Wealth of Nations*. Although Reich's views on labor are distinct from Smith's, his essay focuses on labor with the same intensity Smith brings to money. His views consider how worldwide economic developments will affect labor in the next decades. According to Reich, labor falls into three groups—routine workers, in-person servers, and symbolic analysts—each of which will fare differently in the coming years.

Most of these theorists agree that a healthy economy can relieve the misery and suffering of a population. Most agree that wealth and plenty are preferable to impoverishment and want. But some are also concerned with the effects of materialism and greed on the spiritual life of a nation. Galbraith sees a society with enormous power to bring about positive social change and the capacity to make positive moral decisions. But, for all his optimism, Galbraith reminds us that we have made very little progress in an area of social concern that has been a focus of thought and action for a generation.

ADAM SMITH
Of the Natural Progress
of Opulence

ADAM SMITH (1723–1790) was born in Kirkcaldy on the eastern coast of Scotland. He attended Glasgow University and received a degree from Oxford, after which he gave a successful series of lectures on rhetoric in his hometown. This resulted in his appointment as professor of logic at Glasgow in 1751. A year later he moved to a professorship in moral philosophy that had been vacated by Thomas Craggie, one of his former teachers. He held this position for twelve years. Smith's early reputation was built entirely on his work in moral philosophy, which included theology, ethics, justice, and political economy.

In many ways Adam Smith's views are striking in their modernity; in fact, his work continues to inform our understanding of current economic trends. His classic and best-known book, *An Inquiry into the Nature and Causes of the Wealth of Nations* (1776), examines the economic system of the modern nation that has reached, as England had, the commercial level of progress. According to Smith, a nation has to pass through a number of levels of culture—from hunter-gatherer to modern commercial—on its way to becoming modern. In this sense, he was something of an evolutionist in economics.

Wealth of Nations is quite different in both tone and concept from Smith's earlier success, *Theory of Moral Sentiments* (1759). The earlier work postulates a social order based, in part, on altruism—an order in which individuals aid one another—whereas *Wealth of Nations* asserts that the best economic results are obtained when individuals work for their own interests and their own

---

From *An Inquiry into the Nature and Causes of the Wealth of Nations*.

gain. This kind of effort, Smith assures us, results in the general improvement of a society because the industry of the individual benefits everyone in the nation by producing more wealth; the greater the wealth of the nation, the better the lot of every individual in the nation.

There is no question that Smith was an ardent capitalist who felt an almost messianic need to spread the doctrine of capitalism. He maintained throughout his life that *Wealth of Nations* was one with his writings on moral and social issues and that when his work was complete it would encompass the basic elements of any society.

In "Of the Natural Progress of Opulence," Smith outlines a microcosm of the progress of capitalism as he understood it. His purpose is to establish the steps by which a nation creates its wealth and the steps by which a region becomes wealthy. For the most part, he is interested in the development of capitalism in Great Britain, including his native Scotland. His perspective includes the natural developments that he observed in his own time in the late eighteenth century as well as developments that he could imagine from earlier times. Because he wrote and published his book just before the American Revolution and the subsequent industrial revolution, his primary concerns are farming and agriculture. In earlier sections of *Wealth of Nations*, Smith focused on metal—silver and gold—as a measure of wealth, then later on corn (by which he usually meant wheat or barley) as a measure of wealth. In this selection, he is more emphatic about land as a convenient instrument of wealth.

His primary point is related to what he sees as a natural progression. People in the country have land on which they plant crops, which they sell, in part, to people in the town. The people in the town, lacking land but possessing skills such as weaving, building, and the like, create a market for the goods from the country. They take the product of the land and, with the surplus beyond their daily needs for food and sustenance, manufacture useful goods. In turn, they sell the desirable goods to people in the country, and both manage to accumulate wealth in the process. In this view the manufactures of the town are important but by no means as essential as the food that sustains the nation. Indeed, Smith regards surplus production as the key to the move toward wealth, which accumulates into opulence.

It is interesting that Smith does not emphasize the trade of goods among nations. He does emphasize the fact that the interchange between the country and the town in England also has a counterpart in international trade. However, Smith seems a bit uneasy in contemplating the usefulness of international trade as a means to accumulate wealth. Land, he reminds the reader, is secure, controllable, and not likely to yield to the whimsy of foul winds, leaky ships, or dishonest foreign merchants. One realizes that regardless of what he might say in praise of other possibilities, Smith himself would likely prefer a life in the country on a spread of his own land, collecting rent from tenants who produce food and flax and other goods that help him accumulate wealth.

Smith's Rhetoric

Adam Smith is widely regarded as one of the most influential economic thinkers of the eighteenth century. His *Wealth of Nations* is a gigantic book with many complex arguments regarding the nature of money and the role of capital in trade. This selection is a relatively straightforward statement regarding what he feels is the usual progress that all nations experience in the creation and accumulation of wealth. However, the normal eighteenth-century paragraph is much longer than those of today. By the same token, the normal eighteenth-century sentence is more complex in structure than we are used to today. For that reason, many readers will pause for reflection as they read Smith's work.

Still, his sentences are ultimately clear and direct. His opening sentence, for example, is a mighty declaration: "The great commerce of every civilized society, is that carried on between the inhabitants of the town and those of the country." In this sentence Smith makes a clear pronouncement, a statement about *every* society. Such a sweeping generalization is likely to invite attack and skepticism, but he feels totally secure in his assertion and proceeds to argue his position point by point.

On a more modest note, when Smith says, "Upon equal, or nearly equal profits, most men will chuse to employ their capitals rather in the improvement and cultivation of land, than either in manufactures or in foreign trade" (para. 3), he expects the reader to see the simple wisdom of trusting the land and distrusting instruments of trade. However, many readers—even in his own time—would see this sentence as revealing a personal preference rather than a general rule. Even in the eighteenth century, many merchants were growing rich by ignoring land and trusting trade on the high seas.

Smith's view on this issue reflects an aspect of his conservatism, a stance that remains recognizably conservative even by today's standards. Nevertheless, his principles have guided traders as well as farmers for more than two hundred years. In his time, the workers in agriculture outnumbered workers in manufactures by a factor of eighty or ninety. But today, workers in agriculture have decreased progressively since the industrial revolution. Now, as a result of more efficient farming methods, only two or three people out of a hundred work on farms producing food and other goods. It would be interesting to know how Smith might react to this dramatic shift in occupations.

In helping the reader to work through his argument, Smith includes inset "summaries" of the content of each paragraph. For paragraph 2, he includes two insets. The first—"*The cultivation of the country must be prior to the increase of the town,*"—alerts the reader to look for his explanation of why this claim is true. The second inset—"*though the town may sometimes be distant from the country from which it derives its subsistence.*"—helps readers focus on the implications of distances from agriculture and manufacture for the local population. Those who grow corn nearest the city will make more money than those who live at a distance and must pay for its transportation to market. It is interesting to note that later ages developed relatively inexpensive means of transport—such as canals and railroads—to even out the cost of carriage in relation to fixed prices.

Smith depends on the clear, step-by-step argument to hold the attention of his reader. He establishes and examines each major point, clarifies his own position, then moves on to the next related point. For example, he talks about nations with uncultivated land, or large areas of land, and how the procedure he outlines works. Then he introduces the situation of a nation that has no uncultivated land available, or land available only at very high cost. Under such circumstances, people will turn to manufacture but not rely on selling their products locally. In those conditions, they will risk foreign sales.

It is also worth noting that when Smith talks about the American colonies, he reminds the reader that there is plenty of land for people to work. As a result, little or no manufacture is produced for sale abroad. He sees this as an indication that the Americans are fiercely independent, demanding land of their own so as to guarantee that they will have adequate sustenance in the future. Throughout the selection Smith establishes a clear sense of the progress of nations toward the accumulation of wealth, and he provides the reader with a blueprint for financial success.

PREREADING QUESTIONS:
WHAT TO READ FOR

The following prereading questions may help you anticipate key issues in the discussion of Adam Smith's "Of the Natural Progress of Opulence." Keeping them in mind during your first reading of the selection should help focus your attention.

- What is the nature of the commerce between the country and the town?
- What does Smith think is the natural order of things in the development of commerce?

Of the Natural Progress of Opulence

The great commerce is that between town and country, which is obviously advantageous to both.

The great commerce of every civilized society, is that carried on between the inhabitants of the town and those of the country. It consists in the exchange of rude for manufactured produce, either immediately, or by the intervention of money, or of some sort of paper which represents money. The country supplies the town with the means of subsistence, and the materials of manufacture. The town repays this supply by sending back a part of the manufactured produce to the inhabitants of the country. The town, in which there neither is nor can be any reproduction of substances, may very properly be said to gain its whole wealth and subsistence from the country. We must not, however, upon this account, imagine that the gain of the town is the loss of the country. The gains of both are mutual and reciprocal, and the division of labour is in this, as in all other cases, advantageous to all the different persons employed in the various occupations into which it is subdivided. The inhabitants of the country purchase of the town a greater quantity of manufactured goods, with the produce of a much smaller quantity of their own labour, than they must have employed had they attempted to prepare them themselves. The town affords a market for the surplus produce of the country, or what is over and above the maintenance of the cultivators, and it is there that the inhabitants of the country exchange it for something else which is in demand among them. The greater the number

1

and revenue of the inhabitants of the town, the more extensive is the market which it affords to those of the country; and the more extensive that market, it is always the more advantageous to a great number. The corn which grows within a mile of the town, sells there for the same price with that which comes from twenty miles distance. But the price of the latter must generally, not only pay the expence of raising and bringing it to market, but afford too the ordinary profits of agriculture to the farmer. The proprietors and cultivators of the country, therefore, which lies in the neighbourhood of the town, over and above the ordinary profits of agriculture, gain, in the price of what they sell, the whole value of the carriage of the like produce that is brought from more distant parts, and they save, besides, the whole value of this carriage in the price of what they buy. Compare the cultivation of the lands in the neighbourhood of any considerable town, with that of those which lie at some distance from it, and you will easily satisfy yourself how much the country is benefited by the commerce of the town. Among all the absurd speculations that have been propagated concerning the balance of trade, it has never been pretended that either the country loses by its commerce with the town, or the town by that with the country which maintains it.

The cultivation of the country must be prior to the increase of the town,

As subsistence is, in the nature of things, prior to conveniency and luxury, so the industry which procures the former, must necessarily be prior to that which ministers to the latter. The cultivation and improvement of the country, therefore, which affords subsistence, must, necessarily, be prior to the increase of the town, which furnishes only the means of conveniency and luxury. It is the surplus produce of the country only, or what is over and above the maintenance of the cultivators, that constitutes the subsistence of the town, which can therefore increase only with the increase of this surplus produce. The town, indeed, may not always derive its whole subsistence from the country in its neighbourhood, or even from the territory to which it belongs, but from very distant countries; and this, though it forms no exception from the

though the town may sometimes be distant from the country

from which it derives its subsistence.

This order of things is favoured by the natural preference of man for agriculture.

general rule, has occasioned considerable variations in the progress of opulence in different ages and nations.

That order of things which necessity imposes 3 in general, though not in every particular country, is, in every particular country, promoted by the natural inclinations of man. If human institutions had never thwarted those natural inclinations, the towns could no-where have increased beyond what the improvement and cultivation of the territory in which they were situated could support; till such time, at least, as the whole of that territory was completely cultivated and improved. Upon equal, or nearly equal profits, most men will chuse to employ their capitals rather in the improvement and cultivation of land, than either in manufactures or in foreign trade. The man who employs his capital in land, has it more under his view and command, and his fortune is much less liable to accidents, than that of the trader, who is obliged frequently to commit it, not only to the winds and the waves, but to the more uncertain elements of human folly and injustice, by giving great credits in distant countries to men, with whose character and situation he can seldom be thoroughly acquainted. The capital of the landlord, on the contrary, which is fixed in the improvement of his land, seems to be as well secured as the nature of human affairs can admit of. The beauty of the country besides, the pleasures of a country life, the tranquillity of mind which it promises, and wherever the injustice of human laws does not disturb it, the independency which it really affords, have charms that more or less attract every body; and as to cultivate the ground was the original destination of man, so in every stage of his existence he seems to retain a predilection for this primitive employment.

Cultivators require the assistance of artificers, who settle together and form a village,

Without the assistance of some artificers, 4 indeed, the cultivation of land cannot be carried on, but with great inconveniency and continual interruption. Smiths, carpenters, wheel-wrights, and plough-wrights, masons, and bricklayers, tanners, shoemakers, and taylors, are people, whose service the farmer has frequent occasion for. Such artificers

*and their
employment
augments
with the
improvement
of the country.*

too stand, occasionally, in need of the assistance of one another; and as their residence is not, like that of the farmer, necessarily tied down to a precise spot, they naturally settle in the neighbourhood of one another, and thus form a small town or village. The butcher, the brewer, and the baker, soon join them, together with many other artificers and retailers, necessary or useful for supplying their occasional wants, and who contribute still further to augment the town. The inhabitants of the town and those of the country are mutually the servants of one another. The town is a continual fair or market, to which the inhabitants of the country resort in order to exchange their rude for manufactured produce. It is this commerce which supplies the inhabitants of the town both with the materials of their work, and the means of their subsistence. The quantity of the finished work which they sell to the inhabitants of the country, necessarily regulates the quantity of the materials and provisions which they buy. Neither their employment nor subsistence, therefore, can augment, but in proportion to the augmentation of the demand from the country for finished work; and this demand can augment only in proportion to the extension of improvement and cultivation. Had human institutions, therefore, never disturbed the natural course of things, the progressive wealth and increase of the towns would, in every political society, be consequential, and in proportion to the improvement and cultivation of the territory or country.

*In the American
colonies an
artificer who
has acquired
sufficient stock
becomes a
planter instead
of manufac-
turing for
distant sale,*

In our North American colonies, where uncultivated land is still to be had upon easy terms, no manufactures for distant sale have ever yet been established in any of their towns. When an artificer has acquired a little more stock than is necessary for carrying on his own business in supplying the neighbouring country, he does not, in North America, attempt to establish with it a manufacture for more distant sale, but employs it in the purchase and improvement of uncultivated land. From artificer he becomes planter, and neither the large wages nor the easy subsistence which that country affords to artificers, can bribe him rather to work   5 for other people than for himself. He feels that an artificer is the servant of his customers, from whom he derives his subsistence; but that a planter who cultivates his own land, and derives his necessary subsistence from the labour of his own family, is really a master, and independent of all the world.

as in countries where no uncultivated land can be procured.

In countries, on the contrary, where there is either no uncultivated land, or none that can be had upon easy terms, every artificer who has acquired more stock than he can employ in the occasional jobs of the neighbourhood, endeavours to prepare work for more distant sale. The smith erects some sort of iron, the weaver some sort of linen or woollen manufactory. Those different manufactures come, in process of time, to be gradually subdivided, and thereby improved and refined in a great variety of ways, which may easily be conceived, and which it is therefore unnecessary to explain any further.   6

Manufactures are naturally preferred to foreign commerce.

In seeking for employment to a capital, manufactures are, upon equal or nearly equal profits, naturally preferred to foreign commerce, for the same reason that agriculture is naturally preferred to manufactures. As the capital of the landlord or farmer is more secure than that of the manufacturer, so the capital of the manufacturer, being at all times more within his view and command, is more secure than that of the foreign merchant. In every period, indeed, of every society, the surplus part both of the rude and manufactured produce, or that for which there is no demand at home, must be sent abroad in order to be exchanged for something for which there is some demand at home. But whether the capital, which carries this surplus produce abroad, be a foreign or a domestic one, is of very little importance. If the society has not acquired sufficient capital both to cultivate all its lands, and to manufacture in the completest manner the whole of its rude produce, there is even a considerable advantage that that rude produce should be exported by a foreign capital, in order that the whole stock of the society may be employed in more useful purposes. The wealth of ancient Egypt, that of China and Indostan, sufficiently   7 demonstrate that a nation may attain a very high degree of opulence, though the greater part of its exportation trade be carried on by foreigners. The progress of our North American and West Indian colonies would have been much less rapid, had no capital but what belonged to themselves been employed in exporting their surplus produce.

So the natural course of things is first agriculture, then manufactures, and finally foreign commerce.

According to the natural course of things, there- 8 fore, the greater part of the capital of every growing society is, first, directed to agriculture, afterwards to manufactures, and last of all to foreign commerce. This order of things is so very natural, that in every society that had any territory, it has always, I believe, been in some degree observed. Some of their lands must have been cultivated before any considerable towns could be established, and some sort of coarse industry of the manufacturing kind must have been carried on in those towns, before they could well think of employing themselves in foreign commerce.

But this order has been in many respects inverted.

But though this natural order of things must 9 have taken place in some degree in every such society, it has, in all the modern states of Europe, been, in many respects, entirely inverted. The foreign commerce of some of their cities has introduced all their finer manufactures, or such as were fit for distant sale; and manufactures and foreign commerce together, have given birth to the principal improvements of agriculture. The manners and customs which the nature of their original government introduced, and which remained after that government was greatly altered, necessarily forced them into this unnatural and retrograde order.

QUESTIONS FOR CRITICAL READING

1. How does manufacture eventually help agriculture?
2. Why is it more important to cultivate land than foreign trade?
3. What is special about the civilizations of Egypt, China, and Indostan?
4. Why did the American and West Indian colonies grow so rapidly?
5. In unpopulated countries, what is the natural way people treat the land?
6. How do the town manufactures profit from the country's surplus goods?
7. What is an artificer?

SUGGESTIONS FOR WRITING

1. Explain how you know that Adam Smith favors country living over town life. What seems to be his opinion of each way of living?

2. Explain what Smith means by "subsistence is, in the nature of things, prior to conveniency and luxury, so the industry which procures the former, must necessarily be prior to that which ministers to the latter" (para. 2). Smith makes this claim several times. Is he correct even today?

3. Examine Smith's discussion and write an essay that takes issue with his conclusions. Base your argument on the changes that have occurred in world economy since Smith's time. How have things changed economically to render his arguments less valid or less applicable?

4. In paragraph 3, Smith talks about the "natural inclinations of man." What are they? What relevance do they have to Smith's argument? Have man's "natural inclinations" changed substantially since Smith wrote *Wealth of Nations*?

5. Smith says, "The town affords a market for the surplus produce of the country" (para 1). What does he mean by this statement? Is it still true today? What are the implications of this statement for the theories that Smith attempts to establish? Why is a surplus essential for his theory on the natural progress of opulence to be persuasive?

6. **CONNECTIONS** Examine Thomas Jefferson's Declaration of Independence (p. 78) for issues that relate well to the questions that Adam Smith raises. What are the economic and capitalist underpinnings of Jefferson's statements? In what ways does Jefferson agree or disagree with Smith's concepts of the development of opulence?

7. **CONNECTIONS** Smith is the most important theorist of capitalism prior to the twentieth century. How do his ideas contrast with Karl Marx's views about capitalism and how capitalists work? What would Marx take issue with in Smith's argument? What can you tell about the nature of capitalism in the worlds of Adam Smith in 1776 and of Karl Marx in 1850?

8. **CONNECTIONS** How does Robert B. Reich's analysis of the "new economy" alter the basic wisdom of Adam Smith's views on the natural progress of an economy's development from agriculture to manufactures to foreign trade? What novelties in the "new economy" alter your view of Smith's theory?

KARL MARX
The Communist Manifesto

KARL MARX (1818–1883) was born in Germany to Jewish parents who converted to Lutheranism. A scholarly man, Marx studied literature and philosophy, ultimately earning a doctorate in philosophy at the University of Jena. After being denied a university position, however, he turned to journalism to earn a living.

Soon after beginning his journalistic career, Marx came into conflict with Prussian authorities because of his radical social views, and after a period of exile in Paris he moved to Brussels. After several more moves, Marx found his way to London, where he finally settled in absolute poverty; his friend Friedrich Engels (1820–1895) contributed money to prevent Marx and his family from starving. During this time in London, Marx wrote the books for which he is famous while also writing for and editing newspapers. His contributions to the *New York Daily Tribune* number over 300 items between the years 1851 and 1862.

Marx is best known for his theories of socialism, as expressed in *The Communist Manifesto* (1848)—which, like much of his important work, was written with Engels's help—and in the three-volume *Das Kapital* (*Capital*), the first volume of which was published in 1867. In his own lifetime he was not well known, nor were his ideas widely debated. Yet he was part of an ongoing movement composed mainly of intellectuals. Vladimir Lenin (1870–1924) was a disciple whose triumph in the Russian Revolution of 1917 catapulted Marx to the forefront of world thought. Since 1917 Marx's thinking has been scrupulously analyzed, debated, and argued. Capitalist thinkers have found him unconvincing, whereas Communist thinkers have found him a prophet and keen analyst of social structures.

Translated by Samuel Moore. Part III of *The Communist Manifesto*, "Socialist and Communist Literature," is omitted here.

In England, Marx's studies centered on the concept of an ongoing class struggle between those who owned property — the bourgeoisie — and those who owned nothing but whose work produced wealth — the proletariat. Marx was concerned with the forces of history, and his view of history was that it is progressive and, to an extent, inevitable. This view is prominent in *The Communist Manifesto*, particularly in Marx's review of the overthrow of feudal forms of government by the bourgeoisie. He thought it inevitable that the bourgeoisie and the proletariat would engage in a class struggle, from which the proletariat would emerge victorious. In essence, Marx took a materialist position. He denied the providence of God in the affairs of humans and defended the view that economic institutions evolve naturally and that, in their evolution, they control the social order. Thus, communism was an inevitable part of the process, and in the *Manifesto* he worked to clarify the reasons for its inevitability.

One of Marx's primary contentions was that capital is "not a personal, it is a social power" (para. 78). Thus, according to Marx, the "past dominates the present" (para. 83), because the accumulation of past capital determines how people will live in the present society. Capitalist economists, however, see capital as a personal power, but a power that, as John Kenneth Galbraith might say, should be used in a socially responsible way.

Marx's Rhetoric

The selection included here omits one section, the least important for the modern reader. The first section has a relatively simple rhetorical structure that depends on comparison. The title, "Bourgeois and Proletarians," tells us that the section will clarify the nature of each class and then go on to make some comparisons and contrasts. These concepts were by no means as widely discussed or thought about in 1848 as they are today, so Marx is careful to define his terms. At the same time, he establishes his theories regarding history by making further comparisons with class struggles in earlier ages.

Marx's style is simple and direct. He moves steadily from point to point, establishing his views on the nature of classes, on the nature of bourgeois society, and on the questions of industrialism and its effects on modern society. He considers wealth, worth, nationality, production, agriculture, and machinery. Each point is addressed in turn, usually in its own paragraph.

The organization of the next section, "Proletarians and Communists" (paras. 60–133), is not, despite its title, comparative in nature. Rather, with the proletariat defined as the class of the future, Marx tries to show that the Communist cause is the proletarian cause. In the process, Marx uses a clever rhetorical strategy. He assumes that he is addressed by an antagonist—presumably a bourgeois or a proletarian who is in sympathy with the bourgeoisie. He then proceeds to answer each popular complaint against communism. He shows that it is not a party separate from other workers' parties (para. 61). He clarifies the question of abolishing existing property relations (paras. 68–93). He emphasizes the antagonism between capital and wage labor (para. 76); he discusses the disappearance of culture (para. 94); he clarifies the questions of the family (paras. 98–100) and of the exploitation of children (para. 101). He brings up the new system of public education (paras. 102–4). He raises the touchy issue of the "community of women" (paras. 105–10), as well as the charge that Communists want to abolish nations (paras. 111–15). He brushes aside religion (para. 116). When he is done with the complaints, he gives us a rhetorical signal: "But let us have done with the bourgeois objections to Communism" (para. 126).

The rest of the second section contains a brief summary, and then Marx presents his ten-point program (para. 131). The structure is simple, direct, and effective. In the process of answering the charges against communism, Marx is able to clarify exactly what it is and what it promises. In contrast to his earlier arguments, the ten points of his Communist program seem clear, easy, and (again by contrast) almost acceptable. Although the style is not dashing (despite a few memorable lines), the rhetorical structure is extraordinarily effective for the purposes at hand.

In the last section (paras. 135–45), in which Marx compares the Communists with other reform groups such as those agitating for redistribution of land and other agrarian reforms, he indicates that the Communists are everywhere fighting alongside existing groups for the rights of people who are oppressed by their societies. As Marx says, "In short, the Communists everywhere support every revolutionary movement against the existing social and political order of things" (para. 141). Nothing could be a more plain and direct declaration of sympathies.

PREREADING QUESTIONS: WHAT TO READ FOR

The following prereading questions may help you anticipate key issues in the discussion of Karl Marx's *Communist Manifesto*. Keeping them in mind during your first reading of the selection should help focus your attention.

- What is the economic condition of the bourgeoisie? What is the economic condition of the proletariat?

- How does the expanding world market for goods affect national identity?

- What benefits does Marx expect communism to provide the proletariat?

The Communist Manifesto

A specter is haunting Europe — the specter of Communism. All   1
the Powers of old Europe have entered into a holy alliance to exorcise this specter; Pope and Czar, Metternich[1] and Guizot,[2] French Radicals[3] and German police-spies.

Where is the party in opposition that has not been decried as   2
communistic by its opponents in power? Where the Opposition that has not hurled back the branding reproach of Communism against the more advanced opposition parties, as well as against its reactionary adversaries?

Two things result from this fact.   3

I. Communism is already acknowledged by all European Pow-   4
ers to be itself a Power.

II. It is high time that Communists should openly, in the face of   5
the whole world, publish their views, their aims, their tendencies, and meet this nursery tale of the specter of Communism with a Manifesto of the party itself.

To this end, Communists of various nationalities have assem-   6
bled in London and sketched the following Manifesto, to be published in the English, French, German, Italian, Flemish and Danish languages.

---

[1] **Prince Klemens von Metternich (1773–1859)** Foreign minister of Austria (1809–1848), who had a hand in establishing the peace after the final defeat in 1815 of Napoleon (1769–1821); Metternich was highly influential in the crucial Congress of Vienna (1814–1815).

[2] **François Pierre Guizot (1787–1874)** Conservative French statesman, author, and philosopher. Like Metternich, he was opposed to communism.

[3] **French Radicals** Actually middle-class liberals who wanted a return to a republic in 1848 after the eighteen-year reign of Louis-Philippe (1773–1850), the "citizen king."

Bourgeois and Proletarians[4]

The history of all hitherto existing society is the history of class   7
struggles.

Freeman and slave, patrician and plebeian, lord and serf, guild-   8
master and journeyman, in a word, oppressor and oppressed, stood in
constant opposition to one another, carried on uninterrupted, now
hidden, now open fight, a fight that each time ended, either in a revolutionary re-constitution of society at large, or in the common ruin of
the contending classes.

In the earlier epochs of history we find almost everywhere a   9
complicated arrangement of society into various orders, a manifold
gradation of social rank. In ancient Rome we have patricians, knights,
plebeians, slaves; in the Middle Ages, feudal lords, vassals, guild-
masters, journeymen, apprentices, serfs; in almost all of these classes,
again, subordinate gradations.

The modern bourgeois society that has sprouted from the ruins of   10
feudal society, has not done away with class antagonisms. It has but
established new classes, new conditions of oppression, new forms of
struggle in place of the old ones.

Our epoch, the epoch of the bourgeoisie, possesses, however, this   11
distinctive feature; it has simplified the class antagonisms. Society as a
whole is more and more splitting up into two great hostile camps, into
two great classes directly facing each other: Bourgeoisie and Proletariat.

From the serfs of the Middle Ages sprang the chartered burghers   12
of the earliest towns. From these burgesses the first elements of the
bourgeoisie were developed.

The discovery of America, the rounding of the Cape,[5] opened   13
up fresh ground for the rising bourgeoisie. The East Indian and Chinese markets, the colonization of America, trade with the colonies,
the increase in the means of exchange and in commodities generally,
gave to commerce, to navigation, to industry, an impulse never before
known, and thereby, to the revolutionary element in the tottering
feudal society, a rapid development.

The feudal system of industry, under which industrial production   14
was monopolized by closed guilds, now no longer sufficed for the

---

[4] By bourgeois is meant the class of modern Capitalists, owners of the means of
social production and employers of wage labor. By proletarians, the class of modern
wage laborers who, having no means of production of their own, are reduced to selling their labor-power in order to live. [Engels's note]

[5] **the Cape** The Cape of Good Hope, at the southern tip of Africa. This was a
main sea route for trade with India and the Orient. Europe profited immensely from
the opening up of these new markets in the sixteenth century.

growing wants of the new market. The manufacturing system took
its place. The guild-masters were pushed on one side by the manufacturing middle-class: division of labor between the different corporate
guilds vanished in the face of division of labor in each single workshop.

Meantime the markets kept ever growing, the demand ever ris-   15
ing. Even manufacture no longer sufficed. Thereupon, steam and
machinery revolutionized industrial production. The place of manufacture was taken by the giant, Modern Industry, the place of the industrial middle-class, by industrial millionaires, the leaders of whole
industrial armies, the modern bourgeois.

Modern industry has established the world-market, for which the   16
discovery of America paved the way. This market has given an immense development to commerce, to navigation, to communication
by land. This development has, in its turn, reacted on the extension of
industry; and in proportion as industry, commerce, navigation, railways extended, in the same proportion the bourgeoisie developed, increased its capital, and pushed into the background every class
handed down from the Middle Ages.

We see, therefore, how the modern bourgeoisie is itself the   17
product of a long course of development, of a series of revolutions in
the modes of production and of exchange.

Each step in the development of the bourgeoisie was accompa-   18
nied by a corresponding political advance of that class. An oppressed
class under the sway of the feudal nobility, an armed and self-
governing association in the medieval commune,[6] here independent
urban republic (as in Italy and Germany), there taxable "third estate"[7]
of the monarchy (as in France), afterwards, in the period of manufacture proper, serving either the semi-feudal or the absolute monarchy
as a counterpoise against nobility, and, in fact, corner stone of the
great monarchies in general, the bourgeoisie has at last, since the establishment of Modern Industry and of the world-market, conquered
for itself, in the modern representative State, exclusive political sway.
The executive of the modern State is but a committee for managing
the common affairs of the whole bourgeoisie.

The bourgeoisie, historically, has played a most revolutionary part.   19

The bourgeoisie, wherever it has got the upper hand, has put   20
an end to all feudal, patriarchal, idyllic relations. It has pitilessly
torn asunder the motley feudal ties that bound man to his "natural
superiors," and has left no other nexus between man and man than

---

[6] **the medieval commune** Refers to the growth in the eleventh century of
towns whose economy was highly regulated by mutual interest and agreement.

[7] **"third estate"** The clergy was the first estate, the aristocracy the second estate, and the bourgeoisie the third estate.

naked self-interest, than callous "cash payment." It has drowned the most heavenly ecstasies of religious fervor,[8] of chivalrous enthusiasm, of Philistine sentimentalism, in the icy water of egotistical calculation. It has resolved personal worth into exchange value, and in place of the numberless indefeasible chartered freedoms, has set up that single, unconscionable freedom — Free Trade. In one word, for exploitation, veiled by religious and political illusions, it has substituted naked, shameless, direct, brutal exploitation.

The bourgeoisie has stripped of its halo every occupation hith-   21
erto honored and looked up to with reverent awe. It has converted the physician, the lawyer, the priest, the poet, the man of science, into its paid wage laborers.

The bourgeoisie has torn away from the family its sentimental   22
veil, and has reduced the family relation to a mere money relation.

The bourgeoisie has disclosed how it came to pass that the brutal   23
display of vigor in the Middle Ages, which reactionists so much admire, found its fitting complement in the most slothful indolence. It has been the first to show what man's activity can bring about. It has accomplished wonders far surpassing Egyptian pyramids, Roman aqueducts and Gothic cathedrals; it has conducted expeditions that put in the shade all former Exoduses of nations and crusades.

The bourgeoisie cannot exist without constantly revolutionizing   24
the instruments of production, and thereby the relations of production, and with them the whole relations of society. Conservation of the old modes of production in unaltered form was, on the contrary, the first condition of existence for all earlier industrial classes. Constant revolutionizing of production, uninterrupted disturbance of all social conditions, everlasting uncertainty and agitation distinguish the bourgeois epoch from all earlier ones. All fixed, fast frozen relations, with their train of ancient and venerable prejudices and opinions, are swept away, all new formed ones become antiquated before they can ossify. All that is solid melts into the air, all that is holy is profaned, and man is at last compelled to face with sober senses, his real conditions of life, and his relations with his kind.

The need of a constantly expanding market for its products   25
chases the bourgeoisie over the whole surface of the globe. It must

---

[8] **religious fervor** This and other terms in this sentence contain a compressed historical observation. "Religious fervor" refers to the Middle Ages; "chivalrous enthusiasm" refers to the rise of the secular state and to the military power of knights; "Philistine sentimentalism" refers to the development of popular arts and literature in the sixteenth, seventeenth, and eighteenth centuries. "Philistine" refers to those who were generally uncultured, that is, the general public. "Sentimentalism" is a code word for the encouragement of emotional response rather than rational thought.

nestle everywhere, settle everywhere, establish connections everywhere.

The bourgeoisie has through its exploitation of the world-market [26] given a cosmopolitan character to production and consumption in every country. To the great chagrin of reactionists, it has drawn from under the feet of industry the national ground on which it stood. All old-established national industries have been destroyed or are daily being destroyed. They are dislodged by new industries, whose introduction becomes a life and death question for all civilized nations, by industries that no longer work up indigenous raw material, but raw material drawn from the remotest zones; industries whose products are consumed, not only at home, but in every quarter of the globe. In place of the old wants, satisfied by the productions of the country, we find new wants, requiring for their satisfaction the products of distant lands and climes. In place of the old local and national seclusion and self-sufficiency, we have intercourse in every direction, universal interdependence of nations. And as in material, so also in intellectual production. The intellectual creations of individual nations become common property. National onesidedness and narrowmindedness become more and more impossible, and from the numerous national and local literatures there arises a world-literature.

The bourgeoisie, by the rapid improvement of all instruments of [27] production, by the immensely facilitated means of communication, draws all, even the most barbarian nations into civilization. The cheap prices of its commodities are the heavy artillery with which it batters down all Chinese walls, with which it forces the barbarians' intensely obstinate hatred of foreigners to capitulate. It compels all nations, on pain of extinction, to adopt the bourgeois mode of production; it compels them to introduce what it calls civilization into their midst, i.e., to become bourgeois themselves. In a word, it creates a world after its own image.

The bourgeoisie has subjected the country to the rule of the [28] towns. It has created enormous cities, has greatly increased the urban population as compared with the rural and has thus rescued a considerable part of the population from the idiocy of rural life. Just as it has made the country dependent on the towns, so it has made barbarian and semi-barbarian countries dependent on civilized ones, nations of peasants on nations of bourgeois, the East on the West.

The bourgeoisie keeps more and more doing away with the [29] scattered state of the population, of the means of production, and of property. It has agglomerated population, centralized means of production, and has concentrated property in a few hands. The necessary consequence of this was political centralization. Independent, or but loosely connected provinces, with separate interests, laws, governments and systems of taxation, became lumped together in one nation, with one government, one code of laws, one national class interest, one frontier and one customs tariff.

The bourgeoisie, during its rule of scarce one hundred years, 30 has created more massive and more colossal productive forces than have all preceding generations together. Subjection of Nature's forces to man, machinery, application of chemistry to industry and agriculture, steam-navigation, railways, electric telegraphs, clearing of whole continents for cultivation, canalization of rivers, whole populations conjured out of the ground—what earlier century had even a presentiment that such productive forces slumbered in the lap of social labor?

We see then: the means of production and of exchange on whose 31 foundation the bourgeoisie built itself up, were generated in feudal society. At a certain stage in the development of these means of production and of exchange, the conditions under which feudal society produced and exchanged, the feudal organization of agriculture and manufacturing industry, in one word, the feudal relations of property became no longer compatible with the already developed productive forces; they became so many fetters. They had to burst asunder; they were burst asunder.

Into their place stepped free competition, accompanied by a so- 32 cial and political constitution adapted to it, and by the economical and political sway of the bourgeois class.

A similar movement is going on before our own eyes. Modern 33 bourgeois society with its relations of production, of exchange and of property, a society that has conjured up such gigantic means of production and of exchange, is like the sorcerer, who is no longer able to control the powers of the nether world whom he has called up by his spells. For many a decade past, the history of industry and commerce is but the history of the revolt of modern productive forces against modern conditions of production, against the property relations that are the conditions for the existence of the bourgeoisie and of its rule. It is enough to mention the commercial crises that by their periodical return put on its trial, each time more threateningly, the existence of the entire bourgeois society. In these crises a great part not only of the existing products, but also of the previously created productive forces, are periodically destroyed. In these crises there breaks out an epidemic that, in all earlier epochs, would have seemed an absurdity—the epidemic of overproduction. Society suddenly finds itself put back into a state of momentary barbarism; it appears as if a famine, a universal war of devastation, had cut off the supply of every means of subsistence; industry and commerce seem to be destroyed; and why? Because there is too much civilization, too much means of subsistence, too much industry, too much commerce. The productive forces at the disposal of society no longer tend to further the development of the conditions of the bourgeois property; on the contrary, they have become too powerful for these conditions by which they are fettered, and as soon as they overcome these fetters they bring disorder into the whole of bourgeois society, endanger the existence of bourgeois property. The conditions of bourgeois society are too narrow to comprise the wealth created by them. And how does the bourgeoisie get over these crises? On the one hand by enforced destruction of a mass of productive forces; on the other, by the conquest of new markets, and by the more thorough exploitation of the old ones. That is to say, by paving the way for more extensive and more destructive crises, and by diminishing the means whereby crises are prevented.

The weapons with which the bourgeoisie felled feudalism to the 34
ground are now turned against the bourgeoisie itself.

But not only has the bourgeoisie forged the weapons that bring 35
death to itself; it has also called into existence the men who are to wield those weapons—the modern working class—the proletarians.

In proportion as the bourgeoisie, i.e., capital, is developed, in 36
the same proportion is the proletariat, the modern working class, developed, a class of laborers who live only so long as they find work, and who find work only so long as their labor increases capital. These laborers, who must sell themselves piecemeal, are a commodity, like every other article of commerce, and are consequently exposed to all the vicissitudes of competition, to all the fluctuations of the market.

Owing to the extensive use of machinery and to division of 37
labor, the work of the proletarians has lost all individual character, and, consequently, all charm for the workman. He becomes an appendage of the machine, and it is only the most simple, most monotonous and most easily acquired knack that is required of him. Hence, the cost of production of a workman is restricted almost entirely to the means of subsistence that he requires for his maintenance, and for the propagation of his race. But the price of a commodity, and also of labor, is equal to its cost of production. In proportion, therefore, as the repulsiveness of the work increases the wage decreases. Nay more, in proportion as the use of machinery and division of labor increases, in the same proportion the burden of toil increases, whether by prolongation of the working hours, by increase of the

work enacted in a given time, or by increased speed of the machinery, etc.

Modern industry has converted the little workshop of the patri- 38
archal master into the great factory of the industrial capitalist.
Masses of laborers, crowded into factories, are organized like soldiers. As privates of the industrial army they are placed under the
command of a perfect hierarchy of officers and sergeants. Not only
are they the slaves of the bourgeois class and of the bourgeois state,
they are daily and hourly enslaved by the machine, by the over-
looker, and, above all, by the individual bourgeois manufacturer
himself. The more openly this despotism proclaims gain to be its
end and aim, the more petty, the more hateful and the more embit-
tering it is.

The less the skill and exertion or strength implied in manual 39
labor, in other words, the more modern industry becomes developed, the more is the labor of men superseded by that of women.
Differences of age and sex have no longer any distinctive social validity for the working class. All are instruments of labor, more or less
expensive to use, according to their age and sex.

No sooner is the exploitation of the laborer by the manufacturer, 40
so far at an end, that he receives his wages in cash, than he is set
upon by the other portions of the bourgeoisie, the landlord, the
shopkeeper, the pawnbroker, etc.

The lower strata of the middle class—the small trades-people, 41
shopkeepers and retired tradesmen generally, the handicraftsmen
and peasants—all these sink gradually into the proletariat, partly
because their diminutive capital does not suffice for the scale on
which Modern Industry is carried on, and is swamped in the competition with the large capitalists, partly because their specialized
skill is rendered worthless by new methods of production. Thus the
proletariat is recruited from all classes of the population

The proletariat goes through various stages of development. 42
With its birth begins its struggle with the bourgeoisie. At first the
contest is carried on by individual laborers, then by the workpeople
of a factory, then by the operatives of one trade, in one locality,
against the individual bourgeois who directly exploits them. They
direct their attacks not against the bourgeois conditions of production, but against the instruments of production themselves; they destroy imported wares that compete with their labor, they smash to
pieces machinery, they set factories ablaze, they seek to restore by
force the vanished status of the workman of the Middle Ages.

At this stage the laborers still form an incoherent mass scattered 43
over the whole country, and broken up by their mutual competition. If anywhere they unite to form more compact bodies, this is

not yet the consequence of their own active union, but of the union of the bourgeoisie, which class, in order to attain its own political ends, is compelled to set the whole proletariat in motion, and is moreover yet, for a time, able to do so. At this stage, therefore, the proletarians do not fight their enemies, but the enemies of their enemies, the remnants of absolute monarchy, the landowners, the non-industrial bourgeois, the petty bourgeoisie. Thus the whole historical movement is concentrated in the hands of the bourgeoisie, every victory so obtained is a victory for the bourgeoisie.

But with the development of industry the proletariat not only 44 increases in number; it becomes concentrated in greater masses, its strength grows and it feels that strength more. The various interests and conditions of life within the ranks of the proletariat are more and more equalized, in proportion as machinery obliterates all distinctions of labor, and nearly everywhere reduces wages to the same low level. The growing competition among the bourgeois, and the resulting commercial crisis, make the wages of the workers even more fluctuating. The unceasing improvement of machinery, ever more rapidly developing, makes their livelihood more and more precarious; the collisions between individual workmen and individual bourgeois take more and more the character of collisions between two classes. Thereupon the workers begin to form combinations (Trades' Unions)[9] against the bourgeois; they club together in order to keep up the rate of wages; they found permanent associations in order to make provision beforehand for these occasional revolts. Here and there the contest breaks out into riots.

Now and then the workers are victorious, but only for a time. 45 The real fruit of their battle lies not in the immediate result but in the ever-expanding union of workers. This union is helped on by the improved means of communication that are created by modern industry, and that places the workers of different localities in contact with one another. It was just this contact that was needed to centralize the numerous local struggles, all of the same character, into one national struggle between classes. But every class struggle is a political struggle. And that union, to attain which the burghers of the Middle Ages with their miserable highways, required centuries, the modern proletarians, thanks to railways, achieve in a few years.

This organization of the proletarians into a class, and conse- 46 quently into a political party, is continually being upset again by the

---

[9]**combinations (Trades' Unions)** The labor movement was only beginning in 1848. It consisted of trades' unions that started as social clubs but soon began agitating for labor reform. They represented an important step in the growth of socialism in Europe.

competition between the workers themselves. But it ever rises up again, stronger, firmer, mightier. It compels legislative recognition of particular interests of the workers by taking advantage of the divisions among the bourgeoisie itself. Thus the ten hours' bill in England[10] was carried.

Altogether collisions between the classes of the old society fur-   47
ther, in many ways, the course of development of the proletariat. The bourgeoisie finds itself involved in a constant battle. At first with the aristocracy; later on, with those portions of the bourgeoisie itself whose interests have become antagonistic to the progress of industry; at all times, with the bourgeoisie of foreign countries. In all these battles it sees itself compelled to appeal to the proletariat, to ask for its help, and thus, to drag it into the political arena. The bourgeoisie itself, therefore, supplies the proletariat with its own elements of political and general education; in other words, it furnishes the proletariat with weapons for fighting the bourgeoisie.

Further, as we have already seen, entire sections of the ruling   48
classes are, by the advance of industry, precipitated into the proletariat, or are at least threatened in their conditions of existence. These also supply the proletariat with fresh elements of enlightenment and progress.

Finally, in times when the class struggle nears the decisive hour,   49
the process of dissolution going on within the ruling class—in fact, within the whole range of an old society—assumes such a violent, glaring character that a small section of the ruling class cuts itself adrift and joins the revolutionary class, the class that holds the future in its hands. Just as, therefore, at an earlier period, a section of the nobility went over to the bourgeoisie, so now a portion of the bourgeoisie goes over to the proletariat, and in particular, a portion of the bourgeois ideologists, who have raised themselves to the level of comprehending theoretically the historical movements as a whole.

Of all the classes that stand face to face with the bourgeoisie   50
today the proletariat alone is a really revolutionary class. The other classes decay and finally disappear in the face of Modern Industry; the proletariat is its special and essential product.

The lower middle class, the small manufacturer, the shopkeep-   51
er, the artisan, the peasant, all these fight against the bourgeoisie, to save from extinction their existence as fractions of the middle class.

---

[10] **the ten hours' bill in England** This bill (1847) was an important labor reform. It limited the working day for women and children in factories to only ten hours, at a time when it was common for some people to work sixteen hours a day. The bill's passage was a result of political division, not of benevolence on the managers' part.

They are therefore not revolutionary, but conservative. Nay, more; they are reactionary, for they try to roll back the wheel of history. If by chance they are revolutionary, they are so only in view of their impending transfer into the proletariat; they thus defend not their present, but their future interests; they desert their own standpoint to place themselves at that of the proletariat.

The "dangerous class," the social scum, that passively rotting 52 mass thrown off by the lowest layers of old society, may, here and there, be swept into the movement by a proletarian revolution; its conditions of life, however, prepare it far more for the part of a bribed tool of reactionary intrigue.

In the conditions of the proletariat, those of the old society at large 53 are already virtually swamped. The proletarian is without property; his relation to his wife and children has no longer anything in common with the bourgeois family relations; modern industrial labor, modern subjection to capital, the same in England as in France, in America as in Germany, has stripped him of every trace of national character. Law, morality, religion, are to him so many bourgeois prejudices, behind which lurk in ambush just as many bourgeois interests.

All the preceding classes that got the upper hand sought to for- 54 tify their already acquired status by subjecting society at large to their conditions of appropriation. The proletarians cannot become masters of the productive forces of society, except by abolishing their own previous mode of appropriation, and thereby also every other previous mode of appropriation. They have nothing of their own to secure and to fortify; their mission is to destroy all previous securities for and insurances of individual property.

All previous historical movements were movements of minori- 55 ties, or in the interest of minorities. The proletarian movement is the self-conscious, independent movement of the immense majority. The proletariat, the lowest stratum of our present society, cannot stir, cannot raise itself up without the whole superincumbent strata of official society being sprung into the air.

Though not in substance, yet in form, the struggle of the prole- 56 tariat with the bourgeoisie is at first a national struggle. The proletariat of each country must, of course, first of all settle matters with its own bourgeoisie.

In depicting the most general phases of the development of the 57 proletariat, we traced the more or less veiled civil war, raging within existing society, up to the point where that war breaks out into open revolution, and where the violent overthrow of the bourgeoisie, lays the foundations for the sway of the proletariat.

Hitherto every form of society has been based, as we have al- 58 ready seen, on the antagonism of oppressing and oppressed classes.

But in order to oppress a class, certain conditions must be assured to it under which it can, at least, continue its slavish existence. The serf, in the period of serfdom, raised himself to membership in the commune, just as the petty bourgeois, under the yoke of feudal absolutism, managed to develop into a bourgeois. The modern laborer, on the contrary, instead of rising with the progress of industry, sinks deeper and deeper below the conditions of existence of his own class. He becomes a pauper, and pauperism develops more rapidly than population and wealth. And here it becomes evident that the bourgeoisie is unfit any longer to be the ruling class in society, and to impose its conditions of existence upon society as an over-riding law. It is unfit to rule, because it is incompetent to assure an existence to its slave within his slavery, because it cannot help letting him sink into such a state that it has to feed him, instead of being fed by him. Society can no longer live under this bourgeoisie; in other words, its existence is no longer compatible with society.

The essential condition for the existence, and for the sway of the   59 bourgeois class, is the formation and augmentation of capital; the condition for capital is wage labor. Wage labor rests exclusively on competition between the laborers. The advance of industry, whose involuntary promoter is the bourgeoisie, replaces the isolation of the laborers, due to competition, by their involuntary combination, due to association. The development of Modern Industry, therefore, cuts from under its feet the very foundation on which the bourgeoisie produces and appropriates products. What the bourgeoisie therefore produces, above all, are its own grave diggers. Its fall and the victory of the proletariat are equally inevitable.

Proletarians and Communists

In what relation do the Communists stand to the proletarians as   60 a whole?

The Communists do not form a separate party opposed to other   61 working class parties.

They have no interests separate and apart from those of the pro-   62 letariat as a whole.

They do not set up any sectarian principles of their own, by   63 which to shape and mold the proletarian movement.

The Communists are distinguished from the other working class   64 parties by this only: 1. In the national struggles of the proletarians of the different countries, they point out and bring to the front the common interests of the entire proletariat, independently of all nationality. 2. In the various stages of development which the struggle of the working class against the bourgeoisie has to pass through, they always and everywhere represent the interests of the movement as a whole.

The Communists, therefore, are on the one hand practically the 65 most advanced and resolute section of the working class parties of every country, that section which pushes forward all others; on the other hand, theoretically, they have over the great mass of the proletariat the advantage of clearly understanding the line of march, the conditions, and the ultimate general results of the proletarian movement.

The immediate aim of the Communists is the same as that of all 66 the other proletarian parties: formation of the proletariat into a class, overthrow of the bourgeois of supremacy, conquest of political power by the proletariat.

The theoretical conclusions of the Communists are in no way 67 based on ideas or principles that have been invented or discovered by this or that would-be universal reformer.

They merely express, in general terms, actual relations springing 68 from an existing class struggle, from a historical movement going on under our very eyes. The abolition of existing property relations is not at all a distinctive feature of Communism.

All property relations in the past have continually been subject to 69 historical change consequent upon the change in historical conditions.

The French Revolution, for example, abolished feudal property 70 in favor of bourgeois property.

The distinguishing feature of Communism is not the abolition 71 of property generally, but the abolition of bourgeois property. But modern bourgeois private property is the final and most complete expression of the system of producing and appropriating products, that is based on class antagonism, on the exploitation of the many by the few.

In this sense, the theory of the Communists may be summed up 72 in the single sentence: Abolition of private property.

We Communists have been reproached with the desire of abol- 73 ishing the right of personally acquiring property as the fruit of a man's own labor, which property is alleged to be the groundwork of all personal freedom, activity and independence.

Hard won, self-acquired, self-earned property! Do you mean the 74 property of the petty artisan and of the small peasant, a form of property that preceded the bourgeois form? There is no need to abolish that; the development of industry has to a great extent already destroyed it, and is still destroying it daily.

Or do you mean modern bourgeois private property?   75

But does wage labor create any property for the laborer? Not a 76 bit. It creates capital, i.e., that kind of property which exploits wage labor, and which cannot increase except upon condition of getting a new supply of wage labor for fresh exploitation. Property, in its present form, is based on the antagonism of capital and wage labor. Let us examine both sides of this antagonism.

To be a capitalist is to have not only a purely personal, but a social status in production. Capital is a collective product, and only by the united action of many members, nay, in the last resort, only by the united action of all members of society, can it be set in motion. 77

Capital is therefore not a personal, it is a social power. 78

When, therefore, capital is converted into common property, into the property of all members of society, personal property is not thereby transformed into social property. It is only the social character of the property that is changed. It loses its class character. 79

Let us now take wage labor. 80

The average price of wage labor is the minimum wage, i.e., that quantum of the means of subsistence which is absolutely requisite to keep the laborer in bare existence as a laborer. What, therefore, the wage laborer appropriates by means of his labor, merely suffices to prolong and reproduce a bare existence. We by no means intend to abolish this personal appropriation of the products of labor, an appropriation that is made for the maintenance and reproduction of human life, and that leaves no surplus wherewith to command the labor of others. All that we want to do away with is the miserable character of this appropriation, under which the laborer lives merely to increase capital and is allowed to live only in so far as the interests of the ruling class require it. 81

In bourgeois society, living labor is but a means to increase accumulated labor. In Communist society accumulated labor is but a means to widen, to enrich, to promote the existence of the laborer. 82

In bourgeois society, therefore, the past dominates the present; in Communist society the present dominates the past. In bourgeois society, capital is independent and has individuality, while the living person is dependent and has no individuality. 83

And the abolition of this state of things is called by the bourgeois abolition of individuality and freedom! And rightly so. The abolition of bourgeois individuality, bourgeois independence and bourgeois freedom is undoubtedly aimed at. 84

By freedom is meant, under the present bourgeois conditions of production, free trade, free selling and buying. 85

But if selling and buying disappears, free selling and buying disappears also. This talk about free selling and buying, and all the other "brave words" of our bourgeoisie about freedom in general have a meaning, if any, only in contrast with restricted selling and buying, with the fettered traders of the Middle Ages, but have no meaning 86 when opposed to the Communistic abolition of buying and selling, of the bourgeois conditions of production, and of the bourgeoisie itself.

You are horrified at our intending to do away with private prop- 87
erty. But in your existing society private property is already done away with for nine-tenths of the population; its existence for the few is solely due to its non-existence in the hands of those nine-tenths. You reproach us, therefore, with intending to do away with a form of property, the necessary condition for whose existence is the non-existence of any property for the immense majority of society.

In one word, you reproach us with intending to do away with 88
your property. Precisely so: that is just what we intend.

From the moment when labor can no longer be converted into 89
capital, money, or rent, into a social power capable of being monopolized, i.e., from the moment when individual property can no longer be transformed into bourgeois property, into capital, from that moment, you say, individuality vanishes.

You must, therefore, confess that by "individual" you mean no 90
other person than the bourgeois, than the middle-class owner of property. This person must, indeed, be swept out of the way and made impossible.

Communism deprives no man of the power to appropriate the 91
products of society: all that it does is to deprive him of the power to subjugate the labor of others by means of such appropriation.

It has been objected that upon the abolition of private property 92
all work will cease and universal laziness will overtake us.

According to this, bourgeois society ought long ago to have 93
gone to the dogs through sheer idleness; for those of its members who work acquire nothing, and those who acquire anything do not work. The whole of this objection is but another expression of the tautology:[11] that there can no longer be any wage labor when there is no longer any capital.

All objections urged against the Communistic mode of produc- 94
ing and appropriating material products have, in the same way, been urged against the Communistic modes of producing and appropriating intellectual products. Just as, to the bourgeois, the disappearance of class property is the disappearance of production itself, so the disappearance of class culture is to him identical with the disappearance of all culture.

That culture, the loss of which he laments, is, for the enormous 95
majority, a mere training to act as a machine.

---

[11] **tautology** A statement whose two parts say essentially the same thing. The second half of the previous sentence is a tautology.

But don't wrangle with us so long as you apply, to our intended 96
abolition of bourgeois property, the standard of your bourgeois notions of freedom, culture, law, etc. Your very ideas are but the out-
growth of the conditions of your bourgeois production and bourgeois
property, just as your jurisprudence is but the will of your class made
into a law for all, a will whose essential character and direction are determined by the economical conditions of existence of your class.

The selfish misconception that induces you to transform into 97
eternal laws of nature and of reason the social forms springing from
your present mode of production and form of property — historical
relations that rise and disappear in the progress of production — this
misconception you share with every ruling class that has preceded
you. What you see clearly in the case of ancient property, what you
admit in the case of feudal property, you are of course forbidden to
admit in the case of your own bourgeois form of property.

Abolition of the family! Even the most radical flare up at this in- 98
famous proposal of the Communists.

On what foundation is the present family, the bourgeois family, 99
based? On capital, on private gain. In its completely developed form
this family exists only among the bourgeoisie. But this state of things
finds its complement in the practical absence of the family among
the proletarians, and in public prostitution.

The bourgeois family will vanish as a matter of course when its 100
complement vanishes, and both will vanish with the vanishing of
capital.

Do you charge us with wanting to stop the exploitation of chil- 101
dren by their parents? To this crime we plead guilty.

But, you will say, we destroy the most hallowed of relations 102
when we replace home education by social.

And your education! Is not that also social, and determined by 103
the social conditions under which you educate; by the intervention,
direct or indirect, of society by means of schools, etc.? The Communists have not invented the intervention of society in education; they
do but seek to alter the character of that intervention, and to rescue
education from the influence of the ruling class.

The bourgeois clap-trap about the family and education, about 104
the hallowed correlation of parent and child, become all the more
disgusting, the more, by the action of Modern Industry, all family ties
among the proletarians are torn asunder and their children transformed into simple articles of commerce and instruments of labor.

But you Communists would introduce community of women, 105
screams the whole bourgeoisie chorus.

The bourgeois sees in his wife a mere instrument of production. 106
He hears that the instruments of production are to be exploited in

common, and, naturally, can come to no other conclusion, than that the lot of being common to all will likewise fall to the women.

He has not even a suspicion that the real point aimed at is 107 to do away with the status of women as mere instruments of production.

For the rest, nothing is more ridiculous than the virtuous indig- 108 nation of our bourgeois at the community of women which, they pretend, is to be openly and officially established by the Communists. The Communists have no need to introduce community of women, it has existed almost from time immemorial.

Our bourgeois, not content with having the wives and daughters 109 of their proletarians at their disposal, not to speak of common prostitutes, take the greatest pleasure in seducing each others' wives.

Bourgeois marriage is in reality a system of wives in common, 110 and thus, at the most, what the Communists might possibly be reproached with, is that they desire to introduce, in substitution for a hypocritically concealed, an openly legalized community of women. For the rest, it is self-evident that the abolition of the present system of production must bring with it the abolition of the community of women springing from that system, i.e., of prostitution both public and private.

The Communists are further reproached with desiring to abolish 111 countries and nationalities.

The working men have no country. We cannot take from them 112 what they don't possess. Since the proletariat must first of all acquire political supremacy, must rise to be the leading class of the nation, must constitute itself the nation, it is, so far, itself national, though not in the bourgeois sense of the word.

National differences and antagonisms between peoples are daily 113 more and more vanishing, owing to the development of the bourgeoisie, to freedom of commerce, to the world-market, to uniformity in the mode of production and in the conditions of life corresponding thereto.

The supremacy of the proletariat will cause them to vanish still 114 faster. United action, of the leading civilized countries at least, is one of the first conditions for the emancipation of the proletariat.

In proportion as the exploitation of one individual by another is 115 put an end to, the exploitation of one nation by another will also be put an end to. In proportion as the antagonism between classes within the nation vanishes, the hostility of one nation to another will come to an end.

The charges against Communism made from a religious, a 116 philosophical, and generally, from an ideological standpoint, are not deserving of serious examination.

Does it require deep intuition to comprehend that man's ideas, 117
views and conceptions, in one word, man's consciousness, changes
with every change in the conditions of his material existence, in his social relations and in his social life?

What else does the history of ideas prove than that intellectual 118
production changes in character in proportion as material production
is changed? The ruling ideas of each age have ever been the ideas of
its ruling class.

When people speak of ideas that revolutionize society they do 119
but express the fact that within the old society the elements of a new
one have been created, and that the dissolution of the old ideas keeps
even pace with the dissolution of the old conditions of existence.

When the ancient world was in its last throes the ancient reli- 120
gions were overcome by Christianity. When Christian ideas suc-
cumbed in the 18th century to rationalist ideas, feudal society fought
its death battle with the then revolutionary bourgeoisie. The ideas of
religious liberty and freedom of conscience merely gave expression to
the sway of free competition within the domain of knowledge.

"Undoubtedly," it will be said, "religious, moral, philosophical 121
and judicial ideas have been modified in the course of historical development. But religion, morality, philosophy, political science, and
law, constantly survived this change.

"There are, besides, eternal truths such as Freedom, Justice, etc., 122
that are common to all states of society. But Communism abolishes
eternal truths, it abolishes all religion and all morality, instead of
constituting them on a new basis; it therefore acts in contradiction to
all past historical experience."

What does this accusation reduce itself to? The history of all 123
past society has consisted in the development of class antagonisms,
antagonisms that assumed different forms at different epochs.

But whatever form they may have taken, one fact is common to 124
all past ages, viz., the exploitation of one part of society by the other.
No wonder, then, that the social consciousness of past ages, despite
all the multiplicity and variety it displays, moves within certain common forms, or general ideas, which cannot completely vanish except
with the total disappearance of class antagonisms.

The Communist revolution is the most radical rupture with tra- 125
ditional property relations; no wonder that its development involves
the most radical rupture with traditional ideas.

But let us have done with the bourgeois objections to Com- 126
munism.

We have seen above that the first step in the revolution by the 127
working class is to raise the proletariat to the position of ruling class,
to win the battle of democracy.

The proletariat will use its political supremacy to wrest, by de- 128
grees, all capital from the bourgeoisie, to centralize all instruments of
production in the hands of the State, i.e., of the proletariat organized
as a ruling class; and to increase the total productive forces as
rapidly as possible.

Of course, in the beginning, this cannot be effected except by 129
means of despotic inroads on the rights of property, and on the conditions of bourgeois production; by means of measures, therefore,
which appear economically insufficient and untenable, but which in
the course of the movement outstrip themselves, necessitate further
inroads upon the old social order, and are unavoidable as a means of
entirely revolutionizing the mode of production.

These measures will of course be different in different countries. 130

Nevertheless in the most advanced countries the following will 131
be pretty generally applicable:

1. Abolition of property in land and application of all rents of land
   to public purposes.
2. A heavy progressive or graduated income tax.
3. Abolition of all right of inheritance.
4. Confiscation of the property of all emigrants and rebels.
5. Centralization of credit in the hands of the State, by means of a
   national bank with State capital and an exclusive monopoly.
6. Centralization of the means of communication and transport in
   the hands of the State.
7. Extension of factories and instruments of production owned
   by the State; the bringing into cultivation of waste lands, and the
   improvement of the soil generally in accordance with a common
   plan.
8. Equal liability of all to labor. Establishment of industrial armies,
   especially for agriculture.
9. Combination of agriculture with manufacturing industries; gradual abolition of the distinction between town and country by a
   more equable distribution of the population over the country.
10. Free education for all children in public schools. Abolition of
    children's factory labor in its present form. Combination of edu-
    cation with industrial production, etc., etc.

When, in the course of development, class distinctions have dis- 132
appeared, and all production has been concentrated in the hands of
a vast association of the whole nation, the public power will lose its
political character. Political power, properly so called, is merely the organized power of one class for oppressing another. If the proletariat
during its contest with the bourgeoisie is compelled, by the force of
circumstances, to organize itself as a class, if, by means of a revolution,
it makes itself the ruling class, and, as such, sweeps away by force

the old conditions of production, then it will, along with these conditions, have swept away the conditions for the existence of class antagonism, and of classes generally, and will thereby have abolished its own supremacy as a class.

In place of the old bourgeois society, with its classes and class   133
antagonisms, we shall have an association in which the free development of each is the condition for the free development of all. . . .

Position of the Communists in Relation to the Various Existing Opposition Parties

[The preceding section] has made clear the relations of the Com-   134
munists to the existing working class parties, such as the Chartists in England and the Agrarian Reforms[12] in America.

The Communists fight for the attainment of the immediate aims,   135
for the enforcement of the momentary interests of the working class; but in the movement of the present they also represent and take care of the future of that movement. In France the Communists ally themselves with the Social-Democrats[13] against the conservative and radical bourgeoisie, reserving, however, the right to take up a critical position in regard to phrases and illusions traditionally handed down from the great Revolution.

In Switzerland they support the Radicals,[14] without losing sight of   136
the fact that this party consists of antagonistic elements, partly of Democratic Socialists, in the French sense, partly of radical bourgeois.

In Poland they support the party that insists on an agrarian rev-   137
olution, as the prime condition for national emancipation, that party which fomented the insurrection of Cracow in 1846.[15]

In Germany they fight with the bourgeoisie whenever it acts in   138
a revolutionary way, against the absolute monarchy, the feudal squirearchy, and the petty bourgeoisie.

---

[12] **Agrarian Reforms** Agrarian reform was a very important issue in America after the Revolution. The Chartists were a radical English group established in 1838; they demanded political and social reforms. They were among the more violent revolutionaries of the day. Agrarian reform, or redistribution of the land, was slow to come, and the issue often sparked violence between social classes.

[13] **Social-Democrats** In France in the 1840s, a group that proposed the ideal of labor reform through the establishment of workshops supplied with government capital.

[14] **Radicals** By 1848, European Radicals, taking their name from the violent revolutionaries of the French Revolution (1789–1799), were a nonviolent group content to wait for change.

[15] **the insurrection of Cracow in 1846** Cracow was an independent city in 1846. The insurrection was designed to join Cracow with Poland and to further large-scale social reforms.

But they never cease for a single instant to instill into the work-   139
ing class the clearest possible recognition of the hostile antagonism
between bourgeoisie and proletariat, in order that the German workers may straightway use, as so many weapons against the bourgeoisie,
the social and political conditions that the bourgeoisie must necessarily introduce along with its supremacy, and in order that, after
the fall of the reactionary classes in Germany, the fight against the
bourgeoisie itself may immediately begin.

The Communists turn their attention chiefly to Germany, be-   140
cause that country is on the eve of a bourgeois revolution,[16] that is
bound to be carried out under more advanced conditions of European civilization, and with a more developed proletariat, than that
of England was in the seventeenth and of France in the eighteenth
century, and because the bourgeois revolution in Germany will
be but the prelude to an immediately following proletarian revolution.

In short, the Communists everywhere support every revolution-   141
ary movement against the existing social and political order of things.

In all these movements they bring to the front, as the leading   142
question in each, the property question, no matter what its degree of
development at the time.

Finally, they labor everywhere for the union and agreement of   143
the democratic parties of all countries.

The Communists disdain to conceal their views and aims. They   144
openly declare that their ends can be attained only by the forcible
overthrow of all existing social conditions. Let the ruling classes tremble at a Communistic revolution. The proletarians have nothing to
lose but their chains. They have a world to win.

Working men of all countries, unite!   145

---

[16] **on the eve of a bourgeois revolution** Ferdinand Lassalle (1825–1864) developed the German labor movement and was in basic agreement with Marx, who
was nevertheless convinced that Lassalle's approach was wrong. The environment in
Germany seemed appropriate for revolution, in part because of its fragmented political structure and in part because no major revolution had yet occurred there.

QUESTIONS FOR CRITICAL READING

1. Begin by establishing your understanding of the terms *bourgeois* and
   proletarian. Does Marx make a clear distinction between the terms? Are
   such terms applicable to American society today? Which of these
   groups, if any, do you feel that you belong to?

2. Marx makes the concept of social class fundamental to his theories. Can "social class" be easily defined? Are social classes evident in our society? Are they engaged in a struggle of the sort Marx assumes to be inevitable?
3. What are Marx's views about the value of work in the society he describes? What is his attitude toward wealth?
4. Marx says that every class struggle is a political struggle. Do you agree?
5. Examine the first part. Which class gets more paragraphs—the bourgeoisie or the proletariat? Why?
6. Is the modern proletariat a revolutionary class?
7. Is Marx's analysis of history clear? Try to summarize his views on the progress of history.
8. Is capital a social force, or is it a personal force? Do you think of your savings (either now or in the future) as belonging to you alone or as in some way belonging to your society?
9. What, in Marx's view, is the responsibility of wealthy citizens?

SUGGESTIONS FOR WRITING

1. Defend or attack Marx's statement: "The executive of the modern State is but a committee for managing the common affairs of the whole bourgeoisie" (para. 18). Is this generally true? Take three "affairs of the whole bourgeoisie" and test each one in turn.
2. Examine Marx's statements regarding women. Refer especially to paragraphs 39, 98, 105, and 110. Does he imply that his views are in conflict with those of his general society? After you have a list of his statements, see if you can establish exactly what he is recommending. Do you approve of his recommendations?
3. Marx's program of ten points is listed in paragraph 131. Using the technique that Marx himself uses—taking each point in its turn, clarifying the problems with the point, and finally deciding for or against the point—evaluate his program. Which points do you feel are most beneficial to society? Which are detrimental to society? What is your overall view of the general worth of the program? Do you think it would be possible to put such a program into effect?
4. All Marx's views are predicated on the present nature of property ownership and the changes that communism will institute. He claims, for example, that a rupture with property relations "involves the most radical rupture with traditional ideas" (para. 125). And he discusses in depth his proposal for the rupture of property relations (paras. 68–93). Clarify traditional property relations—what can be owned and by whom—and then contrast with these the proposals Marx makes. Establish your own views as you go along. Include your reasons for taking issue or expressing agreement with Marx. What kinds of property relations do you see around you? What kinds are most desirable for a healthy society?

5. What is the responsibility of the state toward the individual in the kind of economic circumstances that Marx describes? How can the independence of individuals who have amassed great wealth and wish to operate freely be balanced against the independence of those who are poor and have no wealth to manipulate? What kinds of abuse are possible in such circumstances, and what remedies can a state achieve through altering the economic system? What specific remedies does Marx suggest? Are they workable?

6. Do you feel that Marx's suggestions are desirable? Or that they are likely to produce the effects he desires? Critics sometimes complain about Marx's misunderstanding of human nature. Do you feel he has an adequate understanding of human nature? What do you see as impediments to the full success of his program?

7. How accurate is Marx's view of the bourgeoisie? He identifies the bourgeoisie with capital and capitalists. He also complains that the bourgeoisie has established a world market for goods and by doing so has destroyed national and regional identities. Examine his analysis in paragraphs 22–36 in terms of what you see happening in the economic world today and decide whether or not his ideas about how the bourgeoisie functions still apply and ring true. Did Marx foresee the problems of globalization that incited protests and riots such as those aimed at the World Bank, the World Trade Organization, and the International Monetary Fund during the last years of the twentieth century into the early part of the twenty-first century?

8. **CONNECTIONS** Marx's philosophy differs from that of Robert B. Reich. How would Marx respond to Reich's analysis of the future of labor in the next few decades? Would Marx see signs of a coming class struggle in the distinctions Reich draws between the routine workers, the in-person servers, and the symbolic analysts? Does Reich's essay take any of Marx's theories into account?

9. **SEEING CONNECTIONS** The following cartoon by Pulitzer Prize–winning cartoonist Edmund Valtman (b. 1914) depicts Karl Marx as God seated in a cloudy, heaven-like "communist paradise." Below Marx are the Soviet Union's first two leaders, (right) Vladimir Lenin (1870–1924) and (left) Joseph Stalin (1879–1953). The three men are watching a funeral procession for Soviet communism led by Mikhail Gorbachev (b. 1931), the Soviet Communist Party secretary general (1985–1991) and Soviet president (1990–1991) whose reforms helped end the Cold War and led to the downfall of Soviet communism and the breakup of the Soviet Union itself. This cartoon was published in September 1991, just months before the Soviet Union was formally dissolved. (To learn more about this period in Soviet history, go to http://memory.loc.gov/frd/cs/rutoc.html.)

In paragraph 144 Marx states, "Let the ruling classes tremble at a Communist revolution. The proletarians have nothing to lose but their chains. They have a world to win." Given Marx's confident tone in *The Communist Manifesto*, how do you think he would have reacted to the

fall of communism in the Soviet Union? To this cartoon's depiction of
him? Why? Begin your essay with the words, "I can't believe my eyes!"

JOHN MAYNARD KEYNES
Social Consequences of Changes in the Value of Money

JOHN MAYNARD KEYNES (1883–1946) became one of the most influential economists in modern times after his extraordinary analyses of economic decisions following World War I. He advised his own government, Great Britain, between the two world wars and during and after World War II. His advice to the United States government was responsible for policies that helped to restore economic prosperity in Europe.

His first famous book, *The Economic Consequences of the Peace* (1919), was written after he left his official position with the government in Britain during negotiations leading to the Treaty of Versailles. That document clarified the political and economic terms of the surrender of Germany and its allies at the end of World War I. He was outraged at the plans for demanding reparations from Germany for damages during the war, and he was especially appalled at the behavior of President Woodrow Wilson, whom he thought was both stupid and hypocritical. The publication of *The Economic Consequences of the Peace* immediately established him not only as the most original economic mind of his generation but also as a kind of prophet. He pointed out that the economic strictures imposed on Germany would produce economic collapse and social disorder. He, like many others, was fearful that Germany might become Communist — as Karl Marx predicted it would — as did Russia during a period of war and social upheaval.

His views were prophetic, but his analysis of the situation in Germany was not completely accurate. He felt that the Treaty of Versailles had been motivated by political and military considerations

From *The Collected Writings of John Maynard Keynes*, vol. IX.

and that it had ignored the impact of economic issues. This he feared would lead to collapse, and to an extent it did. But the fact is that Britain and France had modified their demands for reparations, and the economic conditions of most Germans before the Great Depression of 1929 were not as bad as he predicted they would be.

He pointed out that four factors were essential to guarantee continued economic prosperity: control of population; avoidance of wars and civil dissensions; permitting science to be unimpeded in matters proper to it; and ensuring that production continue to exceed consumption at the proper rate. One of his major contributions to United States economic policy was his view that during a depression the government must spend vast sums of money on social programs and on programs that would pump money into the economy. President Franklin D. Roosevelt partially followed his advice, which was best articulated in *General Theory of Employment, Interest and Money* (1936). This treatise still forms the basis of most of our theories of how capitalism works. In 1936, however, the prevailing philosophy for ending a depression was to stop government spending and wait for the system to correct itself; in this way inflation could be kept under control. Keynes reasoned that a major depression was a form of deflation; he believed, therefore, that the prevailing theory was wrong. Following his advice, the United States began to achieve economic recovery before Great Britain did. World War II ended the depression in part by requiring the spending of even greater amounts of government money.

Another of Keynes's views was that economic prosperity is linked to spending on the part of the average citizen. He championed easy credit—certainly one of the chief reasons for prosperity among average citizens today—and discouraged the practice of saving at the then current interest rates. Savings could only help the economy if they were lent out for investment in industry. He was especially negative in his attitude toward hoarding gold, which does not produce interest. It is barren, just as an economic system based on the gold standard would be. Since 1937, the United States has not had a gold standard. The government controls the nation's money supply, and our policies are guided by Keynesian monetarism and resultant views concerning the government's role in spending.

In the final analysis, Keynes remained a highly optimistic economist. He perceived that economists were capable of affecting social policy and that they could make a mark on the culture. His views about money and spending were designed to help spread the wealth of a nation among the greatest number of people. He advised Great Britain on how it could finance World War II in part by taking large tax contributions from the very wealthy and keeping them in a kind of "savings" account so that the general mass of people during wartime would not have much money to spend. Doing this would prevent massive inflation. Britain followed his plans in modified form and has generally done so since.

Keynes's Rhetoric

Keynes is capable of being an elegant stylist (see the last part of paragraph 10), but the material he discusses here is sometimes difficult to absorb. So his most effective rhetorical strategy is to enumerate the important points and to structure the essay so that it focuses on one issue at a time. Once the reader understands his organization, most of what he has to say will become clear.

He begins with an introduction (paragraphs 1–5) on the advantage of a stable value of money in terms of buying power; the problems of fluctuations in the value of money that do not benefit everyone; a review of problems of inflation and deflation from the Napoleonic Wars (early 1800s) to 1923; and a reminder that periods of inflation and deflation—which represent changes in the value of money—affect the distribution of wealth among classes.

Two very large sections follow, A and B. Section A, subsection I, talks about how the investing class fares when the value of money changes (paragraphs 6–23). Section A, subsection II, treats the same question from the point of view of how the business class is affected (paragraphs 24–31). Section A, subsection III, then considers the question from the point of view of the wage earner or working class (paragraphs 32–36). Section B considers the entire question of how changes in the value of money affect the production of goods (paragraphs 37–43). Paragraphs 44–46 act as a summation of the essay's major points.

Each of the sections can be broken down into parts because Keynes is systematic in considering as many important issues as possible for each economic class. For instance, in paragraph 7 he states that there are three kinds of investors: 1. those who maintain ownership and sell stocks in a company, 2. those who lease property or a company for a fixed sum and a fixed period; and 3. those who part with property entirely in return for an annuity in the form of a mortgage or other fixed income. Each of these kinds of investing was successful for a very long time in nineteenth-century England because the value of money was stable over that period. On the other hand, as he explains in paragraph 13, the real value of money over very long periods of time has gone down, whether its standard is gold or paper. Essentially, as he tells us in the following paragraphs, the government has had a hand in steady depreciation of the value of money because the debtor class has brought political pressure to bear (para. 16). People who have to pay back long-term debts are helped by the depreciation of money over a period of years because the dollar they pay back in 2010 would be worth only a fraction of the dollar they borrowed in 1950.

Keynes offers some historical comparisons in paragraphs 17–18 to help us understand the stability of the nineteenth century. Government securities, in England called "consols," were a great means of investing for the wealthy, so long as the value of money was relatively stable. While the money was stable, however, a great many people became wealthy "who owned neither buildings, nor land, nor businesses, nor precious metals, but titles to an annual income in legal-tender money" (para. 20). Legal tender money is essentially the dollar bill we have in our pocket, which, as Keynes states, "is only important for what it will procure" (para. 1). When the value of money decreased, consols became bad investments.

When Keynes points to the current age—1923 at the time he is writing—he explains that the expenses of World War I have essentially ravaged Europe and caused inflation, which made the consols much less valuable. People relying on fixed investments lost their wealth because the value of money had changed dramatically. In paragraph 23, Keynes argues in favor of some form of government intervention: "[W]e must make it a prime object of deliberate State policy that the standard of value, in terms of which they are expressed, should be kept stable." However, he does not explain how this can be accomplished.

The business class, those who operate and own businesses, will profit "while prices are rising" (para. 26)—a situation that implies a depreciation of money. The profit will be especially large if the business class borrows money, because inflation permits debtors to pay later with depreciated money. Keynes analyzes the reaction of the public to undue windfall profits in paragraphs 27–28. He then explains that investment in business is discouraged when the value of money falls, but things are even worse when prices fall sharply, as in a depression, and the business class sells at a loss.

Subsection III explains that wage earners lose out when prices go up and the value of money goes down because wages go up much more slowly than prices. The one protection wage earners have is union organization. After World War I workers' wages went up in part, Keynes states, because the large profits of the business class made it possible for business owners to respond to the demands of unions. Unemployment during the postwar depression had hurt earners more than a reduction in wages.

In Part B, Keynes discusses the risks entrepreneurs take in planning long-term development of products when the stability of the value of money is in question. Generally, "the business world as a whole must always be in a position where it stands to gain by a rise of price and to lose by a fall of price" (para. 39). But entrepreneurs need to be able to plan ahead, because some of their ideas may take years to plan and produce. If there is a period of deflation, as in periods of recession and depression, the entrepreneur loses. If entrepreneurs do not go ahead with their plans, unemployment results.

Keyne's summary reminds us "that rising prices and falling prices each have their characteristic disadvantage" (para. 44). Investors, business owners, and wage earners will all have unequal results when the value of money changes. Inflation hurts investors, especially those in fixed annuities, such as bonds. Deflation harms entrepreneurs and results in unemployment. As Keynes states, "Thus inflation is unjust and deflation is inexpedient" (para. 45).

PREREADING QUESTIONS: WHAT TO READ FOR

The following prereading questions may help you anticipate key issues in the discussion of John Maynard Keynes's "Social Consequences of Changes in the Value of Money." Keeping them in mind during your first reading of the selection should help focus your attention.

- How do inflation and deflation change the value of money?
- How do changes in the value of money affect the investor? The businessman? The wage earner?
- How is the production of goods affected by inflation and deflation?

Social Consequences of Changes in the Value of Money

Money is only important for what it will procure. Thus a change   1
in the monetary unit, which is uniform in its operation and affects all transactions equally, has no consequences. If, by a change in the established standard of value, a man received and owned twice as much money as he did before in payment for all rights and for all efforts, and if he also paid out twice as much money for all acquisitions and for all satisfactions, he would be wholly unaffected.

It follows, therefore, that a change in the value of money, that is   2
to say in the level of prices, is important to society only in so far as
its incidence is unequal. Such changes have produced in the past,
and are producing now, the vastest social consequences, because, as
we all know, when the value of money changes, it does *not* change
equally for all persons or for all purposes. A man's receipts and his
outgoings are not all modified in one uniform proportion. Thus a
change in prices and rewards, as measured in money, generally
affects different classes unequally, transfers wealth from one to another, bestows affluence here and embarrassment there, and redis-
tributes Fortune's favours so as to frustrate design and disappoint
expectation.

The fluctuations in the value of money since 1914 have been on   3
a scale so great as to constitute, with all that they involve, one of the
most significant events in the economic history of the modern
world. The fluctuation of the standard, whether gold, silver, or
paper, has not only been of unprecedented violence, but has been
visited on a society of which the economic organisation is more dependent than that of any earlier epoch on the assumption that the
standard of value would be moderately stable.

During the Napoleonic Wars and the period immediately suc-   4
ceeding them the extreme fluctuation of English prices within a
single year was 22 per cent; and the highest price level reached during the first quarter of the nineteenth century, which we used to
reckon the most disturbed period of our currency history, was less
than double the lowest and with an interval of thirteen years. Compare with this the extraordinary movements of the past nine years.
From 1914 to 1920 all countries experienced an expansion in the
supply of money to spend relatively to the supply of things to purchase, that is to say *inflation*. Since 1920 those countries which have
regained control of their financial situation, not content with bringing the inflation to an end, have contracted their supply of money
and have experienced the fruits of *deflation*. Others have followed
inflationary courses more riotously than before.

Each process, inflation and deflation alike, has inflicted great in-   5
juries. Each has an effect in altering the *distribution* of wealth between
different classes, inflation in this respect being the worse of the two.
Each has also an effect in overstimulating or retarding the *production*
of wealth, though here deflation is the more injurious. The division of
our subject thus indicated is the most convenient for us to follow—
examining first the effect of changes in the value of money on the distribution of wealth with most of our attention on inflation, and next
their effect on the production of wealth with most of our attention on
deflation.

A   Changes in the Value of Money, As Affecting Distribution

I   The Investing Class

Of the various purposes which money serves, some essentially 6
depend upon the assumption that its real value is nearly constant
over a period of time. The chief of these are those connected,
in a wide sense, with contracts for the *investment of money*. Such
contracts — namely, those which provide for the payment of fixed
sums of money over a long period of time — are the characteristic
of what it is convenient to call the *investment system*, as distinct
from the property system generally.

Under this phase of capitalism, as developed during the nine- 7
teenth century, many arrangements were devised for separating the
management of property from its ownership. These arrangements
were of three leading types: (1) Those in which the proprietor, while
parting with the management of his property, retained his ownership
of it — i.e. of the actual land, buildings, and machinery, or of whatever else it consisted in, this mode of tenure being typified by a holding of ordinary shares in a joint-stock company; (2) those in which
he parted with the property temporarily, receiving a fixed sum of
money annually in the meantime, but regained his property eventually, as typified by a lease; and (3) those in which he parted with his
real property permanently, in return either for a perpetual annuity
fixed in terms of money, or for a terminable annuity and the repay-
ment of the principal in money at the end of the term, as typified
by mortgages, bonds, debentures,[1] and preference shares. This third
type represents the full development of *investment.*

Contracts to receive fixed sums of money at future dates (made 8
without provision for possible changes in the real value of money at
those dates) must have existed as long as money has been lent and
borrowed. In the form of leases and mortgages, and also of permanent
loans to governments and to a few private bodies, such as the East
India Company, they were already frequent in the eighteenth century.
But during the nineteenth century they developed a new and increased importance, and had, by the beginning of the twentieth, divided the propertied classes into two groups — the "business men" and
the "investors" — with partly divergent interests. The division was not
sharp as between individuals; for business men might be investors also,
and investors might hold ordinary shares; but the division was nevertheless real, and not the less important because it was seldom noticed.

---

[1]**debentures** Similar to a bond, a debenture is a long-term investment in a
company.

By this system the active business class could call to the aid of 9
their enterprises not only their own wealth but the savings of the
whole community; and the professional and propertied classes, on
the other hand, could find an employment for their resources,
which involved them in little trouble, no responsibility, and (it was
believed) small risk.

For a hundred years the system worked, throughout Europe, 10
with an extraordinary success and facilitated the growth of wealth
on an unprecedented scale. To save and to invest became at once the
duty and the delight of a large class. The savings were seldom drawn
on and, accumulating at compound interest, made possible the material triumphs which we now all take for granted. The morals, the
politics, the literature, and the religion of the age joined in a grand
conspiracy for the promotion of saving. God and Mammon were
reconciled. Peace on earth to men of good means. A rich man could,
after all, enter into the Kingdom of Heaven—if only he saved. A
new harmony sounded from the celestial spheres. "It is curious to
observe how, through the wise and beneficent arrangement of Providence, men thus do the greatest service to the public, when they are
thinking of nothing but their own gain";[2] so sang the angels.

The atmosphere thus created well harmonised the demands of 11
expanding business and the needs of an expanding population with
the growth of a comfortable non-business class. But amidst the general enjoyment of ease and progress, the extent to which the system
depended on the stability of the money to which the investing classes
had committed their fortunes, was generally overlooked; and an un-
questioning confidence was apparently felt that this matter would
look after itself. Investments spread and multiplied, until, for the
middle classes of the world, the gilt-edged bonds came to typify all
that was most permanent and most secure. So rooted in our day has
been the conventional belief in the stability and safety of a money
contract that, according to English law, trustees have been encouraged to embark their trust funds exclusively in such transactions,
and are indeed forbidden, except in the case of real estate (an exception which is itself a survival of the conditions of an earlier age), to
employ them otherwise.[3]

As in other respects, so also in this, the nineteenth century re- 12
lied on the future permanence of its own happy experiences and

---

[2] *Easy Lessons on Money Matters for the Use of Young People*, published by the Society for Promoting Christian Knowledge. Twelfth Edition, 1850. [Keynes's note]

[3] German trustees were not released from a similar obligation until 1923, by
which date the value of trust funds invested in titles to money had entirely disappeared. [Keynes's note]

disregarded the warning of past misfortunes. It chose to forget that there is no historical warrant for expecting money to be represented even by a constant quantity of a particular metal, far less by a constant purchasing power. Yet money is simply that which the State declares from time to time to be a good legal discharge of money contracts. In 1914 gold had not been the English standard for a century or the sole standard of any other country for half a century. There is no record of a prolonged war or a great social upheaval which has not been accompanied by a change in the legal tender, but an almost unbroken chronicle in every country which has a history, back to the earliest dawn of economic record, of a progressive deterioration in the real value of the successive legal tenders which have represented money.

Moreover, this progressive deterioration in the value of money   13 through history is not an accident, and has had behind it two great driving forces—the impecuniosity[4] of governments and the superior political influence of the debtor class.

The power of taxation by currency depreciation is one which   14 has been inherent in the state since Rome discovered it. The creation of legal tender has been and is a government's ultimate reserve; and no state or government is likely to decree its own bankruptcy or its own downfall so long as this instrument still lies at hand unused.

Besides this, as we shall see below, the benefits of a depreciating   15 currency are not restricted to the government. Farmers and debtors and all persons liable to pay fixed money dues share in the advantage. As now in the persons of business men, so also in former ages these classes constituted the active and constructive elements in the economic scheme. Those secular changes, therefore, which in the past have depreciated money, assisted the new men and emancipated them from the dead hand; they benefited new wealth at the expense of old, and armed enterprise against accumulation. The tendency of money to depreciate has been in past times a weighty counterpoise against the cumulative results of compound interest and the inheritance of fortunes. It has been a loosening influence against the rigid distribution of old-won wealth and the separation of ownership from activity. By this means each generation can disinherit in part its predecessors' heirs; and the project of founding a perpetual fortune must be disappointed in this way, unless the community with conscious deliberation provides against it in some other way, more equitable and more expedient.

At any rate, under the influence of these two forces—the finan-   16 cial necessities of governments and the political influence of the

---

[4]**impecuniosity** Lack of money.

debtor class—sometimes the one and sometimes the other, the progress of inflation has been *continuous*, if we consider long periods, ever since money was first devised in the sixth century B.C. Sometimes the standard of value has depreciated of itself; failing this, debasements have done the work.

Nevertheless it is easy at all times, as a result of the way we use money in daily life, to forget all this and to look on money as itself the absolute standard of value; and, when besides, the actual events of a hundred years have not disturbed his illusions, the average man regards what has been normal for three generations as a part of the permanent social fabric.   17

The course of events during the nineteenth century favoured such ideas. During its first quarter, the very high prices of the Napoleonic Wars were followed by a somewhat rapid improvement in the value of money. For the next seventy years, with some temporary fluctuations, the tendency of prices continued to be downwards, the lowest point being reached in 1896. But while this was the tendency as regards direction, the remarkable feature of this long period was the relative *stability* of the price level. Approximately the *same* level of price ruled in or about the years 1826, 1841, 1855, 1862, 1867, 1871, and 1915. Prices were also level in the years 1844, 1881, and 1914.[5] If we call the index number of these latter years 100, we find that, for the period of close on a century from 1826 to the outbreak of war, the maximum fluctuation in either direction was 30 points, the index number never rising above 130 and never falling below 70. No wonder that we came to believe in the stability of money contracts over a long period. The metal *gold* might not possess all the theoretical advantages of an artificially regulated standard, but it could not be tampered with and had proved reliable in practice.   18

At the same time, the investor in consols[6] in the early part of the century had done very well in three different ways. The "security" of his investment had come to be considered as near absolute perfection as was possible. Its capital value had uniformly appreciated, partly for the reason just stated, but chiefly because the steady fall in the rate of interest increased the number of years' purchase of the annual income which represented the capital.[7] And the annual money income had a purchasing power which on the whole was increasing. If, for example, we consider the seventy years from 1826 to   19

---

[5] [And again, it is now possible to add, in 1931.] [Keynes's note]

[6] **consols** Consolidated annuities; British government securities.

[7] If, for example, the rate of interest falls from 4½ per cent to 3 per cent, 3 per cent Consols rise in value from 66 to 100. [Keynes's note]

1896 (and ignore the great improvement immediately after Water-
loo), we find that the capital value of consols rose steadily, with only
temporary setbacks, from 79 to 109 (in spite of Goschen's[8] conver-
sion from a 3 per cent rate to a $2\frac{3}{4}$ per cent rate in 1889 and a $2\frac{1}{2}$
per cent rate effective in 1903), while the purchasing power of the
annual dividends, even after allowing for the reduced rates of interest, had increased 50 per cent. But consols, too, had added the
virtue of stability to that of improvement. Except in years of crisis
consols never fell below 90 during the reign of Queen Victoria; and
even in 1848, when thrones were crumbling, the mean price of the
year fell but 5 points. Ninety when she ascended the throne, they
reached their maximum with her in the year of Diamond Jubilee.[9]
What wonder that our parents thought consols a good investment!

Thus there grew up during the nineteenth century a large,   20
powerful, and greatly respected class of persons, well-to-do individually and very wealthy in the aggregate, who owned neither buildings, nor land, nor businesses, nor precious metals, but titles to an
annual income in legal-tender money. In particular, that peculiar
creation and pride of the nineteenth century, the savings of the middle class, had been mainly thus embarked. Custom and favourable
experience had acquired for such investments an unimpeachable
reputation for security.

Before the war these medium fortunes had already begun to suf-   21
fer some loss (as compared with the summit of their prosperity in
the middle nineties) from the rise in prices and also in the rate of interest. But the monetary events which have accompanied and have
followed the war[10] have taken from them about one-half of their real
value in England, seven-eighths in France, eleven-twelfths in Italy,
and virtually the whole in Germany and in the succession states of
Austria-Hungary and Russia.

Thus the effect of the war, and of the monetary policy which has   22
accompanied and followed it, has been to take away a large part of
the real value of the possessions of the investing class. The loss has
been so rapid and so intermixed in the time of its occurrence with
other worse losses that its full measure is not yet separately apprehended. But it has effected, nevertheless, a far-reaching change in
the relative position of different classes. Throughout the Continent
the pre-war savings of the middle class, so far as they were invested

---

[8] **George Joachim Goschen, First Viscount (1831–1907)** When chancellor of the exchequer, he converted the British national debt by reducing interest
rates.
[9] **Diamond Jubilee** In 1897, sixty years after Victoria took the throne.
[10] World War I (1914–1918).

in bonds, mortgages, or bank deposits, have been largely or entirely wiped out. Nor can it be doubted that this experience must modify social psychology towards the practice of saving and investment. What was deemed most secure has proved least so. He who neither spent nor "speculated," who made "proper provision for his family," who sang hymns to security and observed most straitly the morals of the edified and the respectable injunctions of the worldly-wise—he, indeed, who gave fewest pledges to Fortune has yet suffered her heaviest visitations.

What moral for our present purpose should we draw from this?   23
Chiefly, I think, that it is not safe or fair to combine the social organisation developed during the nineteenth century (and still retained) with a *laissez-faire*[11] policy towards the value of money. It is not true that our former arrangements have worked well. If we are to continue to draw the voluntary savings of the community into "investments," we must make it a prime object of deliberate State policy that the standard of value, in terms of which they are expressed, should be kept stable; adjusting in other ways (calculated to touch all forms of wealth equally and not concentrated on the relatively helpless "investors") the redistribution of the national wealth, if, in course of time, the laws of inheritance and the rate of accumulation have drained too great a proportion of the income of the active classes into the spending control of the inactive.

II   The Business Class

It has long been recognised, by the business world and by   24
economists alike, that a period of rising prices acts as a stimulus to enterprise and is beneficial to business men.

In the first place there is the advantage which is the counter-   25
part of the loss to the investing class which we have just examined. When the value of money falls, it is evident that those persons who have engaged to pay fixed sums of money yearly out of the profits of active business must benefit, since their fixed money outgoings will bear a smaller proportion than formerly to their money turnover. This benefit persists not only during the transitional period of change, but also, so far as old loans are concerned, when prices have settled down at their new and higher level. For example, the farmers throughout Europe, who had raised by mortgage the funds to purchase the land they farmed, now find themselves almost freed from the burden at the expense of the mortgages.

---

[11] **laissez-faire** Noninterference of government with stabilizing the value of money.

But during the period of change, while prices are rising month   26
by month, the business man has a further and greater source of
windfall. Whether he is a merchant or a manufacturer, he will generally buy before he sells, and on at least a part of his stock he will
run the risk of price changes. If, therefore, month after month his
stock appreciates on his hands, he is always selling at a better price
than he expected and securing a windfall profit upon which he had
not calculated. In such a period the business of trade becomes unduly easy. Any one who can borrow money and is not exceptionally
unlucky must make a profit, which he may have done little to deserve. Thus, when prices are rising, the business man who borrows
money is able to repay the lender with what, in terms of real value,
not only represents no interest, but is even less than the capital originally advanced.

But if the depreciation of money is a source of gain to the busi-   27
ness man, it is also the occasion of opprobrium. To the consumer
the business man's exceptional profits appear as the cause (instead
of the consequence) of the hated rise of prices. Amidst the rapid
fluctuations of his fortunes he himself loses his conservative instincts, and begins to think more of the large gains of the moment
than of the lesser, but permanent, profits of normal business. The
welfare of his enterprise in the relatively distant future weighs less
with him than before, and thoughts are excited of a quick fortune
and clearing out. His excessive gains have come to him unsought
and without fault or design on his part, but once acquired he does not
lightly surrender them, and will struggle to retain his booty. With
such impulses and so placed, the business man is himself not free
from a suppressed uneasiness. In his heart he loses his former self-
confidence in his relation to society, in his utility and necessity in
the economic scheme. He fears the future of his business and his
class, and the less secure he feels his fortune to be the tighter he
clings to it. The business man, the prop of society and the builder of
the future, to whose activities and rewards there had been accorded,
not long ago, an almost religious sanction, he of all men and classes
most respectable, praiseworthy, and necessary, with whom interfer
ence was not only disastrous but almost impious, was now to suffer
sidelong glances, to feel himself suspected and attacked, the victim
of unjust and injurious laws—to become, and know himself half
guilty, a profiteer.

No man of spirit will consent to remain poor if he believes his   28
betters to have gained their goods by lucky gambling. To convert the
business man into the profiteer is to strike a blow at capitalism, because it destroys the psychological equilibrium which permits the
perpetuance of unequal rewards. The economic doctrine of normal

profits, vaguely apprehended by every one, is a necessary condition
for the justification of capitalism. The business man is only tolerable
so long as his gains can be held to bear some relation to what,
roughly and in some sense, his activities have contributed to society.

This, then, is the second disturbance to the existing economic   29
order for which the depreciation of money is responsible. If the fall
in the value of money discourages investment, it also discredits enterprise.

Not that the business man was allowed, even during the period of   30
boom, to retain the whole of his exceptional profits. A host of popular
remedies vainly attempted to cure the evils of the day; which remedies
themselves—subsidies, price and rent fixing, profiteer hunting, and
excess profits duties—eventually became not the least part of the
evils.

In due course came the depression, with falling prices, which   31
operate on those who hold stocks in a manner exactly opposite to
rising prices. Excessive losses, bearing no relation to the efficiency of
the business, took the place of windfall gains; and the effort of every
one to hold as small stocks as possible brought industry to a standstill, just as previously their efforts to accumulate stocks had over-
stimulated it. Unemployment succeeded profiteering as the problem
of the hour.

III   The Earner

It has been a commonplace of economic textbooks that wages   32
tend to lag behind prices, with the result that the real earnings of the
wage earner are diminished during a period of rising prices. This has
often been true in the past, and may be true even now of certain
classes of labour which are ill-placed or ill-organised for improving
their position. But in Great Britain, at any rate, and in the United
States also, some important sections of labour were able to take advantage of the situation not only to obtain money wages equivalent in
purchasing power to what they had before, but to secure a real improvement, to combine this with a diminution in their hours of work
(and, so far, of the work done), and to accomplish this (in the case of
Great Britain) at a time when the total wealth of the community as a
whole had suffered a decrease. This reversal of the usual course has
not been due to an accident and is traceable to definite causes.

The organisation of certain classes of labour—railwaymen,   33
miners, dockers, and others—for the purpose of securing wage increases is better than it was. Life in the army, perhaps for the first
time in the history of wars, raised in many respects the conventional
standard of requirements—the soldier was better clothed, better

shod, and often better fed than the labourer, and his wife, adding in wartime a separation allowance to new opportunities to earn, had also enlarged her ideas.

But these influences, while they would have supplied the mo- 34 tive, might have lacked the means to the result if it had not been for another factor—the windfalls of the profiteer. The fact that the business man had been gaining, and gaining notoriously, consider-able windfall profits in excess of the normal profits of trade, laid him open to pressure, not only from his employees but from public opinion generally; and enabled him to meet this pressure without fi-nancial difficulty. In fact, it was worth his while to pay ransom, and to share with his workmen the good fortune of the day.

Thus the working classes improved their *relative* position in the 35 years following the war, as against all other classes except that of the "profiteers." In some important cases they improved their absolute position—that is to say, account being taken of shorter hours, in-creased money wages, and higher prices, some sections of the work-ing classes secured for themselves a higher real remuneration for each unit of effort or work done. But we cannot estimate the *stability* of this state of affairs, as contrasted with its desirability, unless we know the source from which the increased reward of the working classes was drawn. Was it due to a permanent modification of the economic factors which determine the distribution of the national product between different classes? Or was it due to some temporary and exhaustible influence connected with inflation and with the re-sulting disturbance in the standard of value?

The period of depression has exacted its penalty from the work- 36 ing classes more in the form of unemployment than by a lowering of real wages, and state assistance to the unemployed has greatly mod-erated even this penalty. Money wages have followed prices down-wards. But the depression of 1921–2 did not reverse or even greatly diminish the relative advantage gained by the working classes over the middle class during the previous years. In 1923 British wage rates stood at an appreciably higher level above the pre-war rates than did the cost of living, if allowance is made for the shorter hours worked.

B   Changes in the Value of Money, as Affecting Production

If, for any reason right or wrong, the business world *expects* that 37 prices will fall, the processes of production tend to be inhibited; and if it expects that prices will rise, they tend to be over-stimulated.

A fluctuation in the measuring-rod of value does not alter in the least the wealth of the world, the needs of the world, or the productive capacity of the world. It ought not, therefore, to affect the character or the volume of what is produced. A movement of *relative* prices, that is to say of the comparative prices of different commodities, *ought* to influence the character of production, because it is an indication that various commodities are not being produced in the exactly right proportions. But this is not true of a change, as such, in the *general* price level.

The fact that the expectation of changes in the *general* price level   38 affects the processes of production, is deeply rooted in the peculiarities of the existing economic organisation of society. We have already seen that a change in the general level of prices, that is to say a change in the measuring-rod, which fixes the obligation of the borrowers of money (who make the decisions which set production in motion) to the lenders (who are inactive once they have lent their money), effects a redistribution of real wealth between the two groups. Furthermore, the active group can, if they foresee such a change, alter their action in advance in such a way as to minimize their losses to the other group or to increase their gains from it, if and when the expected change in the value of money occurs. If they expect a fall, it may pay them, as a group, to damp production down, although such enforced idleness impoverishes society as a whole. If they expect a rise, it may pay them to increase their borrowings and to swell production beyond the point where the real return is just sufficient to recompense society as a whole for the effort made. Sometimes, of course, a change in the measuring-rod, especially if it is unforeseen, may benefit one group at the expense of the other disproportionately to any influence it exerts on the volume of production; but the tendency, in so far as the active group anticipate a change, will be as I have described it. This is simply to say that the intensity of production is largely governed in existing conditions by the anticipated real profit of the entrepreneur. Yet this criterion is the right one for the community as a whole only when the delicate adjustment of interests is not upset by fluctuations in the standard of value.

There is also a considerable risk directly arising out of instability   39 in the value of money. During the lengthy process of production the business world is incurring outgoings in terms of *money* — paying out in money for wages and other expenses of production — in the expectation of recouping this outlay by disposing of the product for *money* at a later date. That is to say, the business world as a whole must always be in a position where it stands to gain by a rise of price and to lose by a fall of price. Whether it likes it or not, the technique of production under a régime of money-contract forces the business world always to carry a big speculative position; and if it is reluctant to carry this position, the productive process must be slackened. The argument is not affected by the fact that there is some degree of specialisation of function within the business world, in so far as the professional speculator comes to the assistance of the producer proper by taking over from him a part of his risk.

Now it follows from this, not merely that the *actual occurrence* of price changes profits some classes and injuries others (which has been the theme of the first section of this chapter), but that a *general fear* of falling prices may inhibit the productive process altogether. For if prices are expected to fall, not enough risk-takers can be found who are willing to carry a speculative "bull" position, and this means that entrepreneurs will be reluctant to embark on lengthy productive processes involving a money outlay long in advance of money recoupment—whence unemployment. The *fact* of falling prices injures entrepreneurs; consequently the *fear* of falling prices causes them to protect themselves by curtailing their operations; yet it is upon the aggregate of their individual estimations of the risk, and their willingness to run the risk, that the activity of production and of employment mainly depends. 40

There is a further aggravation of the case, in that an expectation about the course of prices tends, if it is widely held, to be cumulative in its results up to a certain point. If prices are expected to rise and the business world acts on this expectation, that very fact causes them to rise for a time and, by verifying the expectation, reinforces it; and similarly, if it expects them to fall. Thus a comparatively weak initial impetus may be adequate to produce a considerable fluctuation. 41

The best way to cure this mortal disease of individualism must be to provide that there shall never exist any confident expectation either that prices generally are going to fall or that they are going to rise; and also that there shall be no serious risk that a movement, if it does occur, will be a big one. If, unexpectedly and accidentally, a moderate movement were to occur, wealth, though it might be redistributed, would not be diminished thereby. 42

To procure this result by removing all possible influences towards an initial movement would seem to be a hopeless enterprise. The remedy would lie, rather, in so controlling the standard of value that whenever something occurred which, left to itself, would create an expectation of a change in the general level of prices, the controlling authority should take steps to counteract this expectation by setting in motion some factor of a contrary tendency. Even if such a policy were not wholly successful, either in counteracting expectations or in 43 avoiding actual movements, it would be an improvement on the policy of sitting quietly by whilst a standard of value, governed by chance causes and deliberately removed from central control, produces expectations which paralyse or intoxicate the government of production.

We see, therefore, that rising prices and falling prices each have   44
their characteristic disadvantage. The inflation which causes the former means injustice to individuals and to classes—particularly to rentiers;[12] and is therefore unfavourable to saving. The deflation which causes falling prices means impoverishment to labour and to enterprise by leading entrepreneurs to restrict production, in their endeavour to avoid loss to themselves; and is therefore disastrous to employment. The counterparts are, of course, also true—namely that deflation means injustice to borrowers, and that inflation leads to the over-stimulation of industrial activity. But these results are not so marked as those emphasised above, because borrowers are in a better position to protect themselves from the worst effects of deflation than lenders are to protect themselves from those of inflation, and because labour is in a better position to protect itself from over-exertion in good times than from under-employment in bad times.

Thus inflation is unjust and deflation is inexpedient. Of the two   45
perhaps deflation is, if we rule out exaggerated inflations such as that of Germany, the worse; because it is worse, in an impoverished world, to provoke unemployment than to disappoint the rentier. But it is not necessary that we should weigh one evil against the other. It is easier to agree that both are evils to be shunned. The individualistic capitalism of today, precisely because it entrusts saving to the individual investor and production to the individual employer, *presumes* a stable measuring-rod of value, and cannot be efficient—perhaps cannot survive—without one.

For these grave causes we must free ourselves from the deep   46
distrust which exists against allowing the regulation of the standard of value to be the subject of *deliberate decision*. We can no longer afford to leave it in the category of which the distinguishing characteristics are possessed in different degrees by the weather, the birth-rate, and the Constitution—matters which are settled by natural causes, or are the resultant of the separate action of many individuals acting independently, or require a revolution to change them.

---

[12] **rentier** One who depends on a fixed income from investments.

QUESTIONS FOR CRITICAL READING

1. What effects do inflation and deflation have on the value of money?
2. Why do changes in the value of money affect different groups of people differently?
3. Why was the rate of change in the value of money from 1914 to 1923 so dramatically different from the rate during the previous one hundred years?
4. How does inflation affect the investor who lives on a fixed income?
5. How does inflation affect the individual's attitude toward saving money?
6. What seems to be the main reason for the stability of the value of money in England throughout the nineteenth century?
7. What is Keynes's view of the value of business people to society?

SUGGESTIONS FOR WRITING

1. In a short essay, explain the basic principles that Keynes outlines here. Assume you are writing to someone who has heard of this essay but has not read it. First explain what the value of money is and why a stable value of money is helpful to an economy. Explain the effects inflation and deflation have on the value of money. Then describe the reactions investors, business people, and wage earners have to changes in the value of money. Given your plans for the future, which will be worse for you: inflation or deflation?
2. Interview several people who are at least thirty years older than you. Friends, relatives, or acquaintances would be good subjects. Ask them what they think has happened to the value of money since they were your age. Ask them how much specific items would have cost when they were your age: houses, cars, television sets, basic grocery orders, tuition, or medical expenses. Then ask them how their wages have changed. How much did they make a year in their first real job? What do their answers reveal about changes in the value of money in the last thirty years?
3. Research the history of Germany from 1918 to 1928. Germany experienced a form of inflation that stunned the world. Write an essay that explains what happened to the German economy in this period and how the general public in Germany reacted. What were the effects on the politics of Germany at this time? Were the predictions Keynes made accurate in terms of how various classes were affected by the severe changes in the stability of German money?
4. Assume that you are about to embark on a life of investing. You are to be a member of the investor class Keynes describes at the beginning of his essay. What strategies would you adopt now that you know what the risks are for the investor in any society in which there is a chance

that the stability of money can be affected negatively? Do you think your long-term prospects as an investor—starting today—are good or bad?

5. Go to the government Web site http://www.bls.gov/cpi/home.htm and examine the details about the consumer price index for the United States, calculated each year since 1913. Keynes says that over long periods of time money will depreciate in value. Does the consumer price index confirm his views? What patterns do you see in the changes in the consumer price index? Are there any periods of rapid change? Are they related to historic events, such as wars? What classes of people, using Keynes's terminology, would be most affected by these changes? What do you think the consumer price index will be in ten years? How would such a change affect the value of a dollar ten years from now?

6. In paragraph 27 Keynes describes the "business man" as "the prop of society and the builder of the future." To what extent do you agree or disagree with Keynes's views on members of the business class? What have you experienced in business that would help you make a judgment that would qualify Keynes's comments? What have you read or learned in the news about members of the business class that helps you decide on the validity of Keynes's view?

7. Keynes states, "The business man is only tolerable so long as his gains can be held to bear some relation to what, roughly and in some sense, his activities have contributed to society" (para. 28). Today it is possible for individual business people to earn more than a hundred million dollars a year. Would Keynes have thought that amount to be intolerable? Research the annual income of the highest-paid executives as reported in magazines such as *Fortune*, *Worth*, or *Money*. Do some of the executives get paid much more than their contribution to society warrants?

8. **CONNECTIONS**   How would Marx react to Keynes's views of capitalism? What would be his critique of Keynes's position on the value of money? In light of Keynes's essay, what would Marx have to say about fluctuations in the value of money? Write an essay that distinguishes between the capitalist view of Keynes and the communist view of Marx. Which of these writers is more idealistic? Which of them is more optimistic about the economy?

9. **CONNECTIONS**   Keynes has a great deal to say about the effect on production of changes in the value of money. What would Robert Reich have to say on this issue? Reich writes almost seventy years after Keynes. How much have things changed regarding production of goods in the United States, according to Reich? If Keynes were writing today, would he take a different position on the problems of production in a time of inflation or deflation? Is Reich concerned with the value of money in his essay?

JOHN KENNETH GALBRAITH
The Position of Poverty

JOHN KENNETH GALBRAITH (b. 1908) was born in Canada but has been an American citizen since 1937. He grew up on a farm in Ontario and received his first university degree in agricultural science. This background may have contributed to the success of his many books on subjects such as economics, the State Department, Indian art, and government, which have always explained complex concepts with a clarity easily grasped by laypeople. Sometimes he has been criticized for oversimplifying issues, but on the whole, he has made a brilliant success of writing with wit and humor about perplexing and sometimes troubling issues.

Galbraith was professor of economics at Harvard University for many years. During the presidential campaigns of Adlai Stevenson in 1952 and 1956, he assisted the Democrats as a speechwriter and economics adviser. He performed the same tasks for John F. Kennedy in 1960. Kennedy appointed Galbraith ambassador to India, a post that he maintained for a little over two years, including the period during which India and China fought a border war. His experiences in India resulted in *Ambassador's Journal: A Personal Account of the Kennedy Years* (1969). Kennedy called Galbraith his finest ambassadorial appointment.

Galbraith's involvement with politics was somewhat unusual for an academic economist at that time. It seems to have stemmed from strongly held personal views on the social issues of his time. One of the most important contributions of his best-known and probably most significant book, *The Affluent Society* (1958; rev. eds. 1969, 1976, 1998), was its analysis of America's economic ambitions. He pointed out that at that time the economy was entirely focused on the

---

From *The Affluent Society*.

403

measurement and growth of the gross national product. Economists
and government officials concentrated on boosting output, a goal that
he felt was misdirected because it would result in products that people really did not need and that would not benefit them. Creating artificial needs for things that had no ultimate value, and building in a
"planned obsolescence," seemed to him to be wasteful and ultimately
destructive.

Galbraith suggested that America concentrate on genuine
needs and satisfy them immediately. He was deeply concerned
about the environment and suggested that clean air was a priority
that should take precedence over industry. He supported development of the arts and stressed the importance of improving housing
across the nation. His effort was directed at trying to help Americans change certain basic values by giving up the pursuit of useless
consumer novelties and substituting a program of genuine social
development. The commitment to consumer products as the basis
of the economy naturally argued against a redirection of effort toward the solution of social problems.

Galbraith is so exceptionally clear in his essay that little commentary is needed to establish its importance. He is insightful in
clarifying two kinds of poverty: case poverty and insular poverty.
Case poverty is restricted to an individual and his or her family
and often seems to be caused by alcoholism, ignorance, mental deficiency, discrimination, or specific handicaps. It is an individual,
not a group, disorder. Insular poverty affects a group in a given
area—an "island" within the larger society. He points to poverty in
Appalachia and in the slums of major cities, where most of the people in those "islands" are at or below the poverty level. Insular
poverty is linked to the environment, and its causes are somehow
derived from that environment.

Galbraith's analysis is perceptive and influential, and although
little or no progress has been made in solving the problem of poverty since 1959, he assures us that there are steps that can be taken
to help eradicate it. Such steps demand the nation's will, however,
and he warns that the nation may lack the will. He also reasons
that because the poor are a minority, few politicians make their
plight a campaign issue. Actually, in this belief he is wrong.
Kennedy in 1960, Lyndon Johnson in 1964, and Jimmy Carter
in 1976 made programs for the poor central among their governmental concerns. Because of the war in Vietnam and other
governmental policies, however, the 1960s and early 1970s were a
time of staggering inflation, wiping out any of the advances the
poor had made.

Galbraith's Rhetoric

The most important rhetorical achievement of the piece is its style. This is an example of the elevated plain style: a clear, direct, and basically simple approach to language that only occasionally admits a somewhat learned vocabulary—as in the use of a very few words such as *opulent, unremunerative,* and *ineluctable.* Most of the words he uses are ordinary ones.

He breaks the essay into five carefully numbered sections. In this way he highlights its basic structure and informs us that he has clearly separated its elements into related groups so that he can speak directly to aspects of his subject rather than to the entire topic. This rhetorical technique of division contributes to clarity and confers a sense of authority on the writer.

Galbraith relies on statistical information that the reader can examine if necessary. This information is treated in the early stages of the piece as a prologue. Once such information has been given, Galbraith proceeds in the manner of a logician establishing premises and deriving the necessary conclusions. The subject is sober and sobering, involving issues that are complex, uncertain, and difficult, but the style is direct, confident, and essentially simple. This is the secret of the success of the book from which this selection comes. *The Affluent Society* has been translated into well over a dozen languages and has been a best-seller around the globe, and almost fifty years after its first publication it remains an influential book. Its fundamental insights are such that it is likely to be relevant to the economy of the United States for generations to come.

PREREADING QUESTIONS: WHAT TO READ FOR

The following prereading questions may help you anticipate key issues in the discussion of John Kenneth Galbraith's "The Position of Poverty." Keeping them in mind during your first reading of the selection should help focus your attention.

- Why is modern poverty different from that of a century ago?
- What is case poverty?
- What is insular poverty?

The Position of Poverty

"The study of the causes of poverty," Alfred Marshall observed at   1
the turn of the century, "is the study of the causes of the degradation
of a large part of mankind." He spoke of contemporary England as
well as of the world beyond. A vast number of people both in town
and country, he noted, had insufficient food, clothing and house-
room; they were: "Overworked and undertaught, weary and care-
worn, without quiet and without leisure." The chance of their
succor, he concluded, gave to economic studies "their chief and
their highest interest."[1]

No contemporary economist would be likely to make such an   2
observation about the United States. Conventional economic discourse makes obeisance to the continued existence of some poverty.
"We must remember that we still have a great many poor people." In
the nineteen-sixties, poverty promised, for a time, to become a subject of serious political concern. Then the Vietnam war came and the
concern evaporated or was displaced. For economists of conventional mood, the reminders that the poor still exist are a useful way
of allaying uneasiness about the relevance of conventional economic
goals. For some people, wants must be synthesized. Hence, the importance of the goods to them is not *per se* very high. So much may
be conceded. But others are far closer to physical need. And hence
we must not be cavalier about the urgency of providing them with
the most for the least. The sales tax may have merit for the opulent,
but it still bears heavily on the poor. The poor get jobs more easily
when the economy is expanding. Thus poverty survives in economic discourse partly as a buttress to the conventional economic
wisdom.

The privation of which Marshall spoke was, going on to a cen-   3
tury ago, the common lot at least of all who worked without special
skill. As a general affliction, it was ended by increased output which,
however imperfectly it may have been distributed, nevertheless ac-
crued in substantial amount to those who worked for a living. The
result was to reduce poverty from the problem of a majority to that
of a minority. It ceased to be a general case and became a special
case. It is this which has put the problem of poverty into its peculiar
modern form.

---

[1]*Principles of Economics*, 8th ed. (London: Macmillan, 1927), pp. 2–4. [Gal-
braith's note] Alfred Marshall (1842–1924) was an English economist whose *Principles
of Economics* (1890) was long a standard text and is still relied on by some economists
for its theories of costs, values, and distribution.

II

For poverty does survive. In part, it is a physical matter; those af-   4
flicted have such limited and insufficient food, such poor clothing,
such crowded, cold and dirty shelter that life is painful as well as comparatively brief. But just as it is far too tempting to say that, in matters
of living standards, everything is relative, so it is wrong to rest everything on absolutes. People are poverty-stricken when their income,
even if adequate for survival, falls radically behind that of the community. Then they cannot have what the larger community regards as
the minimum necessary for decency; and they cannot wholly escape, therefore, the judgment of the larger community that they are
indecent. They are degraded for, in the literal sense, they live outside
the grades or categories which the community regards as acceptable.

Since the first edition of this book appeared, and one hopes   5
however slightly as a consequence, the character and dimension of
this degradation have become better understood. There have also
been fulsome promises that poverty would be eliminated. The performance on these promises has been less eloquent.

The degree of privation depends on the size of the family, the   6
place of residence—it will be less with given income in rural areas
than in the cities—and will, of course, be affected by changes in living costs. One can usefully think of deprivation as falling into two
broad categories. First, there is what may be called *case* poverty.
This one encounters in every community, rural or urban, however
prosperous that community or the times. Case poverty is the poor
farm family with the junk-filled yard and the dirty children playing
in the bare dirt. Or it is the gray-black hovel beside the railroad tracks.
Or it is the basement dwelling in the alley.

Case poverty is commonly and properly related to some charac-   7
teristic of the individuals so afflicted. Nearly everyone else has mastered his or her environment, this proves that it is not intractable
But some quality peculiar to the individual or family involved—
mental deficiency, bad health, inability to adapt to the discipline of
industrial life, uncontrollable procreation, alcohol, discrimination involving a very limited minority, some educational handicap unrelated
to community shortcoming, or perhaps a combination of several of
theses handicaps—has kept these individuals from participating
in the general well-being.

Second, there is what may be called *insular* poverty—that which   8
manifests itself as an "island" of poverty. In the island, everyone or
nearly everyone is poor. Here, evidently, it is not easy to explain matters by individual inadequacy. We may mark individuals down as intrinsically deficient in social performance; it is not proper or even

wise so to characterize an entire community. The people of the island have been frustrated by some factor common to their environment.

Case poverty exists. It has also been useful to those who have   9 needed a formula for keeping the suffering of others from causing suffering to themselves. Since this poverty is the result of the deficiencies, including the moral shortcomings, of the persons concerned, it is possible to shift the responsibility to them. They are worthless and, as a simple manifestation of social justice, they suffer for it. Or, at a somewhat higher level of social perception and compassion, it means that the problem of poverty is sufficiently solved by private and public charity. This rescues those afflicted from the worst consequences of their inadequacy or misfortune; no larger social change or reorganization is suggested. Except as it may be insufficient in its generosity, the society is not at fault.

Insular poverty yields to no such formulas. In earlier times, when   10 agriculture and extractive industries were the dominant sources of livelihood, something could be accomplished by shifting the responsibility for low income to a poor natural endowment and thus, in effect, to God. The soil was thin and stony, other natural resources absent and hence the people were poor. And, since it is the undoubted preference of many to remain in the vicinity of the place of their birth, a homing instinct that operates for people as well as pigeons, the people remained in the poverty which heaven had decreed for them. It is an explanation that is nearly devoid of empirical application. Connecticut is very barren and stony and incomes are very high. Similarly Wyoming. West Virginia is well watered with rich mines and forests and the people are very poor. The South is much favored in soil and climate and similarly poor and the very richest parts of the South, such as the Mississippi-Yazoo Delta, have long had a well-earned reputation for the greatest deprivation. Yet so strong is the tendency to associate poverty with natural causes that even individuals of some modest intelligence will still be heard, in explanation of insular poverty, to say, "It's basically a poor country." "It's a pretty barren region."

Most modern poverty is insular in character and the islands are   11 the rural and urban slums. From the former, mainly in the South, the southern Appalachians and Puerto Rico, there has been until recent times a steady flow of migrants, some white but more black, to the latter. Grim as life is in the urban ghetto, it still offers more hope, income and interest than in the rural slum.

The most important characteristic of insular poverty is forces,   12 common to all members of the community, that restrain or prevent participation in economic life at going rates of return. These restraints are several. Race, which acts to locate people by their color rather than by the proximity to employment, is obviously one. So are poor educational facilities. (And this effect is further exaggerated when the poorly educated, endemically a drug on the labor market, are brought together in dense clusters by the common inadequacy of the schools available to blacks and the poor.) So is the disintegration of family life in the slum which leaves households in the hands of women. Family life itself is in some measure a manifestation of affluence. And so, without doubt, is the shared sense of helplessness and rejection and the resulting demoralization which is the product of the common misfortune.

The most certain thing about this poverty is that it is not reme-   13
died by a general advance in income. Case poverty is not remedied because the specific individual inadequacy precludes employment and participation in the general advance. Insular poverty is not directly alleviated because the advance does not remove the specific frustrations of environment to which the people of these areas are subject. This is not to say that it is without effect. If there are jobs outside the ghetto or away from the rural slum, those who are qualified, and not otherwise constrained, can take them and escape. If there are no such jobs, none can escape. But it remains that advance cannot improve the position of those who, by virtue of self or environment, cannot participate.

III

With the transition of the very poor from a majority to a com-   14
parative minority position, there has been a change in their political position. Any tendency of a politician to identify himself with those of the lowest estate usually brought the reproaches of the well-to-do. Political pandering and demagoguery were naturally suspected. But, for the man so reproached, there was the compensating advantage of alignment with a large majority. Now any politician who speaks for the very poor is speaking for a small and generally inarticulate minority. As a result, the modern liberal politician regularly aligns himself not with the poverty-ridden members of the community but with the far more numerous people who enjoy the far more affluent income of (say) the modern trade union member or the intellectual. Ambrose Bierce, in *The Devil's Dictionary*, called poverty "a file provided for the teeth of the rats of reform."[2] It is so no longer. Reform now concerns itself with the needs of people who are relatively well-to-do—whether the comparison be with their own past or with those who are really at the bottom of the income ladder.

---

[2] **Ambrose Bierce (1842–1914)** A southern American writer noted for satirical writings such as the one quoted.

In consequence, a notable feature of efforts to help the very   15
poor is their absence of any very great political appeal.[3] Politicians
have found it possible to be indifferent where they could not be de-
risory. And very few have been under a strong compulsion to support these efforts.

The concern for inequality and deprivation had vitality only   16
so long as the many suffered while a few had much. It did not survive as a decisive political issue in a time when the many had
much even though others had much more. It is our misfortune
that when inequality declined as an issue, the slate was not left
clean. A residual and in some ways rather more hopeless problem
remained.

IV

An affluent society that is also both compassionate and rational   17
would, no doubt, secure to all who needed it the minimum income
essential for decency and comfort. The corrupting effect on the
human spirit of unearned revenue has unquestionably been exaggerated as, indeed, have the character-building values of hunger
and privation. To secure to each family a minimum income, as a
normal function of the society, would help ensure that the misfortunes of parents, deserved or otherwise, were not visited on their
children. It would help ensure that poverty was not self-perpetuating.
Most of the reaction, which no doubt would be adverse, is based on
obsolete attitudes. When poverty was a majority phenomenon,
such action could not be afforded. A poor society, as this essay has
previously shown, had to enforce the rule that the person who did
not work could not eat. And possibly it was justified in the added
cruelty of applying the rule to those who could not work or whose
efficiency was far below par. An affluent society has no similar excuse for such rigor. It can use the forthright remedy of providing
income for those without. Nothing requires such a society to be
compassionate. But it no longer has a high philosophical justification for callousness.

The notion that income is a remedy for indigency has a certain   18
forthright appeal.[4] It would also ease the problems of economic
management by reducing the reliance on production as a source of

---

[3] This was true of the Office of Economic Opportunity—the so called poverty
program—and was ultimately the reason for its effective demise. [Galbraith's note]

[4] As earlier noted, in the first edition the provision of a guaranteed income was
discussed but dismissed as "beyond reasonable hope." [Galbraith's note]

income. The provision of such a basic source of income must henceforth be the first and the strategic step in the attack on poverty.

But it is only one step. In the past, we have suffered from the supposition that the only remedy for poverty lies in remedies that allow people to look after themselves—to participate in the economy. Nothing has better served the conscience of people who wished to avoid inconvenient or expensive action than an appeal, on this issue, to Calvinist precept—"The only sound way to solve the problem of poverty is to help people help themselves." But this does not mean that steps to allow participation and to keep poverty from being self-perpetuating are unimportant. On the contrary. It requires that the investment in children from families presently afflicted be as little below normal as possible. If the children of poor families have first-rate schools and school attendance is properly enforced; if the children, though badly fed at home, are well nourished at school; if the community has sound health services, and the physical well-being of the children is vigilantly watched; if there is opportunity for advanced education for those who qualify regardless of means; and if, especially in the case of urban communities, housing is ample and housing standards are enforced, the streets are clean, the laws are kept, and recreation is adequate—then there is a chance that the children of the very poor will come to maturity without inhibiting disadvantage. In the case of insular poverty, this remedy requires that the services of the community be assisted from outside. Poverty is self-perpetuating partly because the poorest communities are poorest in the services which would eliminate it. To eliminate poverty efficiently, we must, indeed, invest more than proportionately in the children of the poor community. It is there that high-quality schools, strong health services, special provision for nutrition and recreation are most needed to compensate for the very low investment which families are able to make in their own offspring.   19

The effect of education and related investment in individuals is to help them overcome the restraints that are imposed by their environment. These need also to be attacked even more directly—by giving the mobility that is associated with plentiful, good and readily available housing, by provision of comfortable, efficient and economical mass transport, by making the environment pleasant and safe, and by eliminating the special health handicaps that afflict the poor.   20

Nor is case poverty entirely resistant to such remedies. Much can be done to treat those characteristics which cause people to reject or be rejected by the modern industrial society. Educational deficiencies can be overcome. Mental deficiencies can be treated. Physical handicaps can be remedied. The limiting factor is not a lack of knowledge of what can be done. Overwhelmingly, it is a shortage of money.   21

V

It will be clear that, to a remarkable extent, the remedy for   22
poverty leads to the same requirements as those for social balance.
The restraints that confine people to the ghetto are those that result
from insufficient investment in the public sector. And the means to
escape from these constraints and to break their hold on subsequent
generations just mentioned—better nutrition and health, better education, more and better housing, better mass transport, an environment more conducive to effective social participation—all, with
rare exceptions, call for massively greater investment in the public
sector. In recent years, the problems of the urban ghetto have been
greatly discussed but with little resultant effect. To a certain extent,
the search for deeper social explanations of its troubles has been
motivated by the hope that these (together with more police) might
lead to solutions that would somehow elide the problem of cost. It is
an idle hope. The modern urban household is an extremely expensive thing. We have not yet taken the measure of the resources that
must be allocated to its public tasks if it is to be agreeable or even
tolerable. And first among the symptoms of an insufficient allocation is the teeming discontent of the modern ghetto.

A further feature of these remedies is to be observed. Their con-   23
sequence is to allow of participation in the economic life of the
larger community—to make people and the children of people who
are now idle productive. This means that they will add to the total
output of goods and services. We see once again that even by its
own terms the present preoccupation with the private sector of the
economy as compared with the whole spectrum of human needs is
inefficient. The parallel with investment in the supply of trained and
educated manpower discussed above will be apparent.

But increased output of goods is not the main point. Even to the   24
most intellectually reluctant reader, it will now be evident that enhanced productive efficiency is not the motif of this volume. The
very fact that increased output offers itself as a by-product of the
effort to eliminate poverty is one of the reasons. No one would
be called upon to write at such length on a problem so easily solved
as that of increasing production. The main point lies elsewhere.
Poverty—grim, degrading and ineluctable—is not remarkable in
India. For relatively few, the fate is otherwise. But in the United
States, the survival of poverty is remarkable. We ignore it because
we share with all societies at all times the capacity for not seeing
what we do not wish to see. Anciently this has enabled the noble-
man to enjoy his dinner while remaining oblivious to the beggars

around his door. In our own day, it enables us to travel in comfort through the South Bronx and into the lush precincts of midtown Manhattan. But while our failure to notice can be explained, it cannot be excused. "Poverty," Pitt[5] exclaimed, "is no disgrace but it is damned annoying." In the contemporary United States, it is not annoying but it is a disgrace.

---

[5]**William Pitt, the Younger (1759–1806)** British prime minister from 1783 to 1801 and, briefly, again in 1804 and 1805.

QUESTIONS FOR CRITICAL READING

1. What is the fundamental difference between the attitude Alfred Marshall held toward the poor (para. 1) and the attitude contemporary economists hold?
2. Galbraith avoids a specific definition of poverty because he says it changes from society to society. How would you define poverty as it exists in our society? What are its major indicators?
3. According to Galbraith, what is the relationship of politics to poverty?
4. What, according to this essay, seem to be the causes of poverty?
5. Clarify the distinctions Galbraith makes between case poverty and insular poverty. Are they reasonable distinctions?
6. Does Galbraith oversimplify the issues of poverty in America?
7. Galbraith first published this piece in 1958. How much have attitudes toward poverty changed since then? What kinds of progress seem to have been made toward eradicating poverty?

SUGGESTIONS FOR WRITING

1. In paragraph 4, Galbraith says, "People are poverty-stricken when their income, even if adequate for survival, falls radically behind that of the community. Then they cannot have what the larger community regards as the minimum necessary for decency; and they cannot wholly escape, therefore, the judgment of the larger community that they are indecent. They are degraded for, in the literal sense, they live outside the grades or categories which the community regards as acceptable." Examine what he says here, and explain what he means. Is this an accurate description of poverty? How would you amend it? If you accept his description of poverty, what public policy would you recommend to deal with it? What would be the consequences of accepting Galbraith's description?

2. Galbraith points out some anomalies of poverty and place. For example, he notes that West Virginia is rich in resources but that its people have been notable for their poverty. Connecticut, on the other hand, is poor in resources, with stony, untillable land, yet its people have been notable for their wealth. Some economists have also pointed out that when the Americas were settled, South America had gold, was home to lush tropics that yielded food and fruit for the asking, and held the promise of immense wealth. North America had a harsh climate, stubborn soil conditions, and dense forests that needed clearing. Yet North America has less poverty now than does South America. Write a brief essay in which you consider whether what is said above is too simplified to be useful. If it is not, what do you think is the reason for the economic distinctions that Galbraith and others point out?

3. What personal experiences have you had with poverty? Are you familiar with examples of case poverty? If so, describe them in such a way as to help others understand them. What causes produced the poverty? What is the social situation of the people in your examples? How might they increase their wealth?

4. Examine the newspapers for the last several days, and look through back issues of magazines such as *Time*, *Newsweek*, the *New Republic*, the *New Leader*, or *U.S. News & World Report*. How many stories does each devote to the question of poverty? Present a survey of the views you find, and compare them with Galbraith's. How much agreement or disagreement is there? Would the level of the nation's concern with poverty please Galbraith?

5. Write a brief essay about current political attitudes toward poverty. If possible, gather some recent statements made by politicians. Analyze them to see how closely they tally with Galbraith's concerns and views. Do any specific politicians act as spokespeople for the poor?

6. Galbraith says that poverty has undergone a dramatic change in our society: once most people were poor and only a few were affluent, and now most people are affluent and only a few are poor. Is Galbraith correct in this assessment? Interview your parents and grandparents and their friends to establish or disprove the validity of Galbraith's claim, and then explain what you feel are the problems the poor face as a result of their minority status. If possible, during your interviews ask what feelings your parents and their friends have about the poor. What feelings do you have? Are they shared by your friends?

7. **CONNECTIONS** What might Karl Marx say in reaction to Galbraith's definition of poverty and his terms for case poverty and insular poverty? Should Galbraith have examined the role of the bourgeoisie in creating, maintaining, or ignoring poverty? Galbraith wrote the original version of this piece during the 1950s, while world communism was at its height. How might he have accommodated the issues that Marx felt were most important for the working person?

8. **CONNECTIONS** Galbraith's focus on poverty is unusual for a capitalist economist. What might John Maynard Keynes's reaction be to Galbraith's views on poverty? How would he respond to Galbraith's chief points? How might Robert Reich respond to Galbraith's sense that certain kinds of poverty are likely to be long-term in the United States? Would Keynes and Reich agree that poverty is a natural condition in a modern capitalist society?

ROBERT B. REICH
Why the Rich Are Getting Richer and the Poor, Poorer

ROBERT B. REICH (b. 1946), University Professor in the Heller Graduate School at Brandeis University, who served as secretary of labor in the first Clinton administration, holds a graduate degree from Yale Law School, and, unlike his former colleagues in the John F. Kennedy School of Government at Harvard, he does not hold a Ph.D. in economics. Nonetheless, he has written numerous books on economics and has been a prominent lecturer for more than a dozen years. One of his most recent books, *Locked in the Cabinet* (1997), is a memoir of his four years as secretary of labor. *The Work of Nations* (1991), from which this essay comes, is the distillation of many years' analysis of modern economic trends.

As a college student, Reich was an activist but not a radical. In 1968 he was a Rhodes scholar, studying at Oxford University with Bill Clinton and a number of others who became influential American policymakers. Reich is a specialist in policy studies — that is, the relationship of governmental policy to the economic health of the nation. Unlike those who champion free trade and unlimited expansion, Reich questions the existence of free trade by pointing to the effect of government taxation on business enterprise. Taxation — like many governmental policies regarding immigration, tariffs, and money supply — directly shapes the behavior of most companies. Reich feels that government must establish and execute an industrial policy that will benefit the nation.

Even though organized labor groups, such as industrial unions, have rejected much of his theorizing about labor, Reich has developed a reputation as a conciliator who can see opposite sides of a

From *The Work of Nations*.

question and resolve them. He is known for his denunciation of
mergers, lawsuits, takeovers, and other deals that he believes simply churn money around rather than produce wealth. He feels that
such maneuvers enrich a few predatory people but do not benefit
labor in general—and, indeed, that the debt created by such deals
harms labor in the long run.

In *The Next American Frontier* (1983), Reich insists that government, unions, and businesses must cooperate to create a workable program designed to improve the economy. Trusting to chance
and free trade, he argues, will not work in the current economy.
He also has said that the old assembly-line methods must give way
to what he calls "flexible production," involving smaller, cus-
tomized runs of products for specific markets.

Reich's *The Work of Nations* (1991), whose title draws on
Adam Smith's classic *The Wealth of Nations* (1776), examines the
borderless nature of contemporary corporations. Multinational corporations are a reality, and as he points out in the following essay,
their flexibility makes it possible for them to thrive by moving
manufacturing plants from nation to nation. The reasons for moving are sometimes connected to lower wages but more often are
connected to the infrastructure of a given nation. Reliable roads,
plentiful electricity, well-educated workers, low crime rates, and
political stability are all elements that make a location attractive to
a multinational corporation.

Reich's Rhetoric

The structure of "Why the Rich Are Getting Richer and the
Poor, Poorer" is built on a metaphor: that of boats rising or falling
with the tide. As Reich notes, "All Americans used to be in roughly
the same economic boat" (para. 2), and when the economic tide
rose, most people rose along with it. However, today "national borders no longer define our economic fates"; Reich therefore views
Americans today as being in different boats, depending on their role
in the economy, and his essay follows the fates of three distinct
kinds of workers.

Examining the routine worker, he observes, "The boat containing routine producers is sinking rapidly" (para. 3). As he demonstrates, the need for routine production has declined in part because
of improvements in production facilities. Much labor-intensive work
has been replaced by machines. Modern factories often scramble to
locate in places where production costs are lowest. People in other
nations work at a fraction of the hourly rate of American workers,

and because factories are relatively cheap to establish, they can be easily moved.

Reich continues the boat metaphor with "in-person servers." The boat that carries these workers, he says, "is sinking as well, but somewhat more slowly and unevenly" (para. 20). Workers in restaurants, retail outlets, car washes, and other personal service industries often work part-time and have few health or other benefits. Their jobs are imperiled by machines as well, although not as much as manufacturing jobs are. Although the outlook for such workers is buoyed by a declining population, which will reduce competition for their jobs, increased immigration may cancel this benefit.

Finally, Reich argues that the "vessel containing America's symbolic analysts is rising" (para. 28). This third group contains the population that identifies and solves problems and brokers ideas. "Almost everyone around the world is buying the skills and insights of Americans who manipulate oral and visual symbols" (para. 33). Engineers, consultants, marketing experts, publicists, and those in entertainment fields all manage to cross national boundaries and prosper at a rate that is perhaps startling. As a result of an expanding world market, symbolic analysts do not depend only on the purchasing power of routine and in-service workers. Instead, they rely on the same global web that dominates the pattern of corporate structure.

Reich's essay follows the fate of these three groups in turn to establish the pattern of change and expectation that will shape America's economic future. His metaphor is deftly handled, and he includes details, examples, facts, and careful references to support his position.

PREREADING QUESTIONS:
WHAT TO READ FOR

The following prereading questions may help you anticipate key issues in the discussion of Robert B. Reich's "Why the Rich Are Getting Richer and the Poor, Poorer." Keeping them in mind during your first reading of the selection should help focus your attention.

- Why and how does an individual's position in the world economy depend on the function he/she performs in it?

- What are "routine producers"? What will be their fate in the future?

- Who are the "symbolic analysts" in our economy? How does one become a symbolic analyst?

Why the Rich Are Getting Richer
and the Poor, Poorer

The division of labour is limited by the extent of the market.
–ADAM SMITH
An Inquiry into the Nature
and Causes of the Wealth of Nations (1776)

Regardless of how your job is officially classified (manufactur-   1
ing, service, managerial, technical, secretarial, and so on), or the industry in which you work (automotive, steel, computer, advertising,
finance, food processing), your real competitive position in the
world economy is coming to depend on the function you perform in
it. Herein lies the basic reason why incomes are diverging. The fortunes of routine producers are declining. In-person servers are also
becoming poorer, although their fates are less clear-cut. But symbolic analysts—who solve, identify, and broker new problems—
are, by and large, succeeding in the world economy.

All Americans used to be in roughly the same economic boat.   2
Most rose or fell together as the corporations in which they were
employed, the industries comprising such corporations, and the national economy as a whole became more productive—or languished. But national borders no longer define our economic fates.
We are now in different boats, one sinking rapidly, one sinking
more slowly, and the third rising steadily.

The boat containing routine producers is sinking rapidly. Re-   3
call that by midcentury routine production workers in the United
States were paid relatively well. The giant pyramidlike organizations at the core of each major industry coordinated their prices
and investments—avoiding the harsh winds of competition and
thus maintaining healthy earnings. Some of these earnings, in turn,
were reinvested in new plant and equipment (yielding ever-larger-
scale economies); another portion went to top managers and investors. But a large and increasing portion went to middle managers
and production workers. Work stoppages posed such a threat to
high-volume production that organized labor was able to exact an
ever-larger premium for its cooperation. And the pattern of wages
established within the core corporations influenced the pattern
throughout the national economy. Thus the growth of a relatively
affluent middle class, able to purchase all the wondrous things
produced in high volume by the core corporations.

But, as has been observed, the core is rapidly breaking down   4
into global webs which earn their largest profits from clever
problem-solving, -identifying, and brokering. As the costs of transporting standard things and of communicating information about
them continue to drop, profit margins on high-volume, standardized production are thinning, because there are few barriers to
entry. Modern factories and state-of-the-art machinery can be installed almost anywhere on the globe. Routine producers in the
United States, then, are in direct competition with millions of routine producers in other nations. Twelve thousand people are added
to the world's population every hour, most of whom, eventually,
will happily work for a small fraction of the wages of routine producers in America.[1]

The consequence is clearest in older, heavy industries, where   5
high-volume, standardized production continues its ineluctable move
to where labor is cheapest and most accessible around the world.
Thus, for example, the Maquiladora factories cluttered along the
Mexican side of the U.S. border in the sprawling shanty towns of Ti-
juana, Mexicali, Nogales, Agua Prieta, and Ciudad Juárez—factories
owned mostly by Americans, but increasingly by Japanese—in
which more than a half million routine producers assemble parts
into finished goods to be shipped into the United States.

The same story is unfolding worldwide. Until the late 1970s,   6
AT&T had depended on routine producers in Shreveport, Louisiana,
to assemble standard telephones. It then discovered that routine producers in Singapore would perform the same tasks at a far lower
cost. Facing intense competition from other global webs, AT&T's
strategic brokers felt compelled to switch. So in the early 1980s they
stopped hiring routine producers in Shreveport and began hiring
cheaper routine producers in Singapore. But under this kind of pressure for ever-lower high-volume production costs, today's Singa-
porean can easily end up as yesterday's Louisianan. By the late
1980s, AT&T's strategic brokers found that routine producers in
Thailand were eager to assemble telephones for a small fraction of
the wages of routine producers in Singapore. Thus, in 1989, AT&T
stopped hiring Singaporeans to make telephones and began hiring
even cheaper routine producers in Thailand.

---

[1] The reader should note, of course, that lower wages in other areas of the
world are of no particular attraction to global capital unless workers there are sufficiently productive to make the labor cost of producing *each unit* lower there than in
higher-wage regions. Productivity in many low-wage areas of the world has improved due to the ease with which state-of-the-art factories and equipment can be
installed there. [Reich's note]

The search for ever-lower wages has not been confined to heavy   7
industry. Routine data processing is equally footloose. Keypunch
operators located anywhere around the world can enter data into
computers, linked by satellite or transoceanic fiber-optic cable, and
take it out again. As the rates charged by satellite networks continue
to drop, and as more satellites and fiber-optic cables become available (reducing communication costs still further), routine data processors in the United States find themselves in ever more direct
competition with their counterparts abroad, who are often eager to
work for far less.

By 1990, keypunch operators in the United States were earning,   8
at most, $6.50 per hour. But keypunch operators throughout the rest
of the world were willing to work for a fraction of this. Thus, many
potential American data-processing jobs were disappearing, and the
wages and benefits of the remaining ones were in decline. Typical
was Saztec International, a $20-million-a-year data-processing firm
headquartered in Kansas City, whose American strategic brokers contracted with routine data processors in Manila and with American-
owned firms that needed such data-processing services. Compared
with the average Philippine income of $1,700 per year, data-entry
operators working for Saztec earn the princely sum of $2,650. The
remainder of Saztec's employees were American problem-solvers and
-identifiers, searching for ways to improve the worldwide system and
find new uses to which it could be put.[2]

By 1990, American Airlines was employing over 1,000 data pro-   9
cessors in Barbados and the Dominican Republic to enter names and
flight numbers from used airline tickets (flown daily to Barbados
from airports around the United States) into a giant computer bank
located in Dallas. Chicago publisher R. R. Donnelley was sending
entire manuscripts to Barbados for entry into computers in preparation for printing. The New York Life Insurance Company was dis-
patching insurance claims to Castleisland, Ireland, where routine
producers, guided by simple directions, entered the claims and determined the amounts due, then instantly transmitted the computations back to the United States. (When the firm advertised in Ireland
for twenty-five data-processing jobs, it received six hundred applications.) And McGraw-Hill was processing subscription renewal
and marketing information for its magazines in nearby Galway. Indeed, literally millions of routine workers around the world were
receiving information, converting it into computer-readable form,

---

[2] John Maxwell Hamilton, "A Bit Player Buys into the Computer Age," *New York Times Business World*, December 3, 1989, p. 14. [Reich's note]

and then sending it back—at the speed of electronic impulses—whence it came.

The simple coding of computer software has also entered into world commerce. India, with a large English-speaking population of technicians happy to do routine programming cheaply, is proving to be particularly attractive to global webs in need of this service. By 1990, Texas Instruments maintained a software development facility in Bangalore, linking fifty Indian programmers by satellite to TI's Dallas headquarters. Spurred by this and similar ventures, the Indian government was building a teleport in Poona, intended to make it easier and less expensive for many other firms to send their routine software design specifications for coding.[3]

This shift of routine production jobs from advanced to developing nations is a great boon to many workers in such nations who otherwise would be jobless or working for much lower wages. These workers, in turn, now have more money with which to purchase symbolic-analytic services from advanced nations (often embedded within all sorts of complex products). The trend is also beneficial to everyone around the world who can now obtain high-volume, standardized products (including information and software) more cheaply than before.

But these benefits do not come without certain costs. In particular the burden is borne by those who no longer have good-paying routine production jobs within advanced economies like the United States. Many of these people used to belong to unions or at least benefited from prevailing wage rates established in collective bargaining agreements. But as the old corporate bureaucracies have flattened into global webs, bargaining leverage has been lost. Indeed, the tacit national bargain is no more.

Despite the growth in the number of new jobs in the United States, union membership has withered. In 1960, 35 percent of all nonagricultural workers in America belonged to a union. But by 1980 that portion had fallen to just under a quarter, and by 1989 to about 17 percent. Excluding government employees, union membership was down to 13.4 percent.[4] This was a smaller proportion even than in the early 1930s, before the National Labor Relations Act created a legally protected right to labor representation. The drop in membership has been accompanied by a growing number of

---

[3] Udayan Gupta, "U.S.-Indian Satellite Link Stands to Cut Software Costs," *Wall Street Journal*, March 6, 1989, p. B2. [Reich's note]

[4] *Statistical Abstract of the United States* (Washington, D.C.: U.S. Government Printing Office, 1989), p. 416, table 684. [Reich's note]

collective bargaining agreements to freeze wages at current levels, reduce wage levels of entering workers, or reduce wages overall. This is an important reason why the long economic recovery that began in 1982 produced a smaller rise in unit labor costs than any of the eight recoveries since World War II—the low rate of unemployment during its course notwithstanding.

Routine production jobs have vanished fastest in traditional 14 unionized industries (autos, steel, and rubber, for example), where average wages have kept up with inflation. This is because the jobs of older workers in such industries are protected by seniority; the youngest workers are the first to be laid off. Faced with a choice of cutting wages or cutting the number of jobs, a majority of union members (secure in the knowledge that there are many who are junior to them who will be laid off first) often have voted for the latter.

Thus the decline in union membership has been most striking 15 among young men entering the work force without a college education. In the early 1950s, more than 40 percent of this group joined unions; by the late 1980s, less than 20 percent (if public employees are excluded, less than 10 percent).[5] In steelmaking, for example, although many older workers remained employed, almost half of all routine steelmaking jobs in America vanished between 1974 and 1988 (from 480,000 to 260,000). Similarly with automobiles: During the 1980s, the United Auto Workers lost 500,000 members— one-third of their total at the start of the decade. General Motors alone cut 150,000 American production jobs during the 1980s (even as it added employment abroad). Another consequence of the same phenomenon: the gap between the average wages of unionized and nonunionized workers widened dramatically—from 14.6 percent in 1973 to 20.4 percent by end of the 1980s.[6] The lesson is clear. If you drop out of high school or have no more than a high school diploma, do not expect a good routine production job to be awaiting you.

Also vanishing are lower- and middle-level management jobs 16 involving routine production. Between 1981 and 1986, more than 780,000 foremen, supervisors, and section chiefs lost their jobs through plant closings and layoffs.[7] Large numbers of assistant

---

[5] Calculations from Current Population Surveys by L. Katz and A. Revenga, "Changes in the Structure of Wages: U.S. and Japan," National Bureau of Economic Research, September 1989. [Reich's note]

[6] U.S. Department of Commerce, Bureau of Labor Statistics, "Wages of Unionized and Non-Unionized Workers," various issues. [Reich's note]

[7] U.S. Department of Labor, Bureau of Labor Statistics, "Reemployment Increases Among Displaced Workers," BLS News, USDL 86–414, October 14, 1986, table 6. [Reich's note]

division heads, assistant directors, assistant managers, and vice presidents also found themselves jobless. GM shed more than 40,000 white-collar employees and planned to eliminate another 25,000 by the mid-1990s.[8] As America's core pyramids metamorphosed into global webs, many middle-level routine producers were as obsolete as routine workers on the line.

As has been noted, foreign-owned webs are hiring some   17
Americans to do routine production in the United States. Philips, Sony, and Toyota factories are popping up all over—to the self-congratulatory applause of the nation's governors and mayors, who have lured them with promises of tax abatements and new sewers, among other amenities. But as these ebullient politicians will soon discover, the foreign-owned factories are highly automated and will become far more so in years to come. Routine production jobs account for a small fraction of the cost of producing most items in the United States and other advanced nations, and this fraction will continue to decline sharply as computer-integrated robots take over. In 1977 it took routine producers thirty-five hours to assemble an automobile in the United States; it is estimated that by the mid-1990s, Japanese-owned factories in America will be producing finished automobiles using only eight hours of a routine producer's time.[9]

The productivity and resulting wages of American workers who   18
run such robotic machinery may be relatively high, but there may not be many such jobs to go around. A case in point: in the late 1980s, Nippon Steel joined with America's ailing Inland Steel to build a new $400 million cold-rolling mill fifty miles west of Gary, Indiana. The mill was celebrated for its state-of-the-art technology, which cut the time to produce a coil of steel from twelve days to about one hour. In fact, the entire plant could be run by a small team of technicians, which became clear when Inland subsequently closed two of its old cold rolling mills, laying off hundreds of routine workers. Governors and mayors take note: your much-ballyhooed foreign factories may end up employing distressingly few of your constituents.

Overall, the decline in routine jobs has hurt men more than   19
women. This is because the routine production jobs held by men in high-volume metal-bending manufacturing industries had paid higher wages than the routine production jobs held by women in

---

[8] *Wall Street Journal*, February 16, 1990, p. A5. [Reich's note]

[9] Figures from the International Motor Vehicles Program, Massachusetts Institute of Technology, 1989. [Reich's note]

textiles and data processing. As both sets of jobs have been lost,
American women in routine production have gained more equal
footing with American men — equally poor footing, that is. This is a
major reason why the gender gap between male and female wages
began to close during the 1980s.

The second of the three boats, carrying in-person servers, is   20
sinking as well, but somewhat more slowly and unevenly. Most in-
person servers are paid at or just slightly above the minimum
wage and many work only part-time, with the result that their take-
home pay is modest, to say the least. Nor do they typically receive
all the benefits (health care, life insurance, disability, and so forth)
garnered by routine producers in large manufacturing corporations
or by symbolic analysts affiliated with the more affluent threads of
global webs.[10] In-person servers are sheltered from the direct effects
of global competition and, like everyone else, benefit from access to
lower-cost products from around the world. But they are not im-
mune to its indirect effects.

For one thing, in-person servers increasingly compete with   21
former routine production workers, who, no longer able to find well-
paying routine production jobs, have few alternatives but to seek in-
person service jobs. The Bureau of Labor Statistics estimates that of
the 2.8 million manufacturing workers who lost their jobs during
the early 1980s, fully one-third were rehired in service jobs paying
at least 20 percent less.[11] In-person servers must also compete with
high school graduates and dropouts who years before had moved
easily into routine production jobs but no longer can. And if demographic predictions about the American work force in the first decades of the twenty-first century are correct (and they are likely to
be, since most of the people who will comprise the work force are
already identifiable), most new entrants into the job market will
be black or Hispanic men, or women — groups that in years past
have possessed relatively weak technical skills. This will result in an
even larger number of people crowding into in-person services. Finally, in-person servers will be competing with growing numbers of
immigrants, both legal and illegal, for whom in-person services will
comprise the most accessible jobs. (It is estimated that between the

---

[10] The growing portion of the American labor force engaged in in-person services, relative to routine production, thus helps explain why the number of Americans lacking health insurance increased by at least 6 million during the 1980s.
[Reich's note]

[11] U.S. Department of Labor, Bureau of Labor Statistics, "Reemployment Increases Among Disabled Workers," October 14, 1986. [Reich's note]

mid-1980s and the end of the century, about a quarter of all workers entering the American labor force will be immigrants.[12])

Perhaps the fiercest competition that in-person servers face   22
comes from labor-saving machinery (much of it invented, designed, fabricated, or assembled in other nations, of course). Automated tellers, computerized cashiers, automatic car washes, robotized vending machines, self-service gasoline pumps, and all similar gadgets substitute for the human beings that customers once encountered. Even telephone operators are fast disappearing, as electronic sensors and voice simulators become capable of carrying on conversations that are reasonably intelligent and always polite. Retail sales workers—among the largest groups of in-person servers—are similarly imperiled. Through personal computers linked to television screens, tomorrow's consumers will be able to buy furniture, appliances, and all sorts of electronic toys from their living rooms—examining the merchandise from all angles, selecting whatever color, size, special features, and price seem most appealing, and then transmitting the order instantly to warehouses from which the selections will be shipped directly to their homes. So, too, with financial transactions, airline and hotel reservations, rental car agreements, and similar contracts, which will be executed between consumers in their homes and computer banks somewhere else on the globe.[13]

Advanced economies like the United States will continue to   23
generate sizable numbers of new in-person service jobs, of course, the automation of older ones notwithstanding. For every bank teller who loses her job to an automated teller, three new jobs open for aerobics instructors. Human beings, it seems, have an almost insatiable desire for personal attention. But the intense competition nevertheless ensures that the wages of in-person servers will remain relatively low. In-person servers—working on their own, or else dispersed widely amid many small establishments, filling all sorts of personal-care niches—cannot readily organize themselves into labor unions or create powerful lobbies to limit the impact of such competition.

In two respects, demographics will work in favor of in-person   24
servers, buoying their collective boat slightly. First, as has been noted, the rate of growth of the American work force is slowing. In particular, the number of young workers is shrinking. Between 1985 and

---

[12] Federal Immigration and Naturalization Service, *Statistical Yearbook* (Washington, D.C.: U.S. Government Printing Office, 1986, 1987). [Reich's note]

[13] See Claudia H. Deutsch, "The Powerful Push for Self-Service," *New York Times*, April 9, 1989, section 3, p. 1. [Reich's note]

1995, the number of the eighteen- to twenty-four-year-olds will
have declined by 17.5 percent. Thus, employers will have more
incentive to hire and train in-person servers whom they might previously have avoided. But this demographic relief from the competitive pressures will be only temporary. The cumulative procreative
energies of the postwar baby-boomers (born between 1946 and
1964) will result in a new surge of workers by 2010 or there-
abouts.[14] And immigration—both legal and illegal—shows every
sign of increasing in years to come.

Next, by the second decade of the twenty-first century, the   25
number of Americans aged sixty-five and over will be rising precipi-
tously, as the baby-boomers reach retirement age and live longer.
Their life expectancies will lengthen not just because fewer of them
will have smoked their way to their graves and more will have eaten
better than their parents, but also because they will receive all sorts
of expensive drugs and therapies designed to keep them alive—
barely. By 2035, twice as many Americans will be elderly as in 1988,
and the number of octogenarians is expected to triple. As these decaying baby-boomers ingest all the chemicals and receive all the
treatments, they will need a great deal of personal attention. Millions
of deteriorating bodies will require nurses, nursing-home operators,
hospital administrators, orderlies, home-care providers, hospice
aides, and technicians to operate and maintain all the expensive
machinery that will monitor and temporarily stave off final disintegration. There might even be a booming market for euthanasia
specialists. In-person servers catering to the old and ailing will be in
strong demand.[15]

One small problem: the decaying baby-boomers will not have   26
enough money to pay for these services. They will have used up
their personal savings years before. Their Social Security payments
will, of course, have been used by the government to pay for the
previous generation's retirement and to finance much of the budget
deficits of the 1980s. Moreover, with relatively fewer young Americans in the population, the supply of housing will likely exceed the
demand, with the result that the boomers' major investments—
their homes—will be worth less (in inflation-adjusted dollars) when
they retire than they planned for. In consequence, the huge cost of

---

[14] U.S. Bureau of the Census, Current Population Reports, Series P-23, no. 138,
tables 2-1, 4-6. See W. Johnson, A. Packer, et al., *Workforce 2000: Work and Workers
for the 21st Century* (Indianapolis: Hudson Institute, 1987). [Reich's note]

[15] The Census Bureau estimates that by the year 2000, at least 12 million Americans will work in health services—well over 6 percent of the total work force.
[Reich's note]

caring for the graying boomers will fall on many of the same people who will be paid to care for them. It will be like a great sump pump: in-person servers of the twenty-first century will have an abundance of health-care jobs, but a large portion of their earnings will be devoted to Social Security payments and income taxes, which will in turn be used to pay their salaries. The net result: no real improvement in their standard of living.

The standard of living of in-person servers also depends, indi- 27 rectly, on the standard of living of the Americans they serve who are engaged in world commerce. To the extent that these Americans are richly rewarded by the rest of the world for what they contribute, they will have more money to lavish upon in-person services. Here we find the only form of "trickle-down" economics that has a basis in reality. A waitress in a town whose major factory has just been closed is unlikely to earn a high wage or enjoy much job security; in a swank resort populated by film producers and banking moguls, she is apt to do reasonably well. So, too, with nations. In-person servers in Bangladesh may spend their days performing roughly the same tasks as in-person servers in the United States, but have a far lower standard of living for their efforts. The difference comes in the value that their customers add to the world economy.

Unlike the boats of routine producers and in-person servers, 28 however, the vessel containing America's symbolic analysts is rising. Worldwide demand for their insights is growing as the ease and speed of communicating them steadily increases. Not every symbolic analyst is rising as quickly or as dramatically as every other, of course; symbolic analysts at the low end are barely holding their own in the world economy. But symbolic analysts at the top are in such great demand worldwide that they have difficulty keeping track of all their earnings. Never before in history has opulence on such a scale been gained by people who have earned it, and done so legally.

Among symbolic analysts in the middle range are American sci- 29 entists and researchers who are busily selling their discoveries to global enterprise webs. They are not limited to American customers. If the strategic brokers in General Motors' headquarters refuse to pay a high price for a new means of making high-strength ceramic engines dreamed up by a team of engineers affiliated with Carnegie Mellon University in Pittsburgh, the strategic brokers of Honda or Mercedes-Benz are likely to be more than willing.

So, too, with the insights of America's ubiquitous management 30 consultants, which are being sold for large sums to eager entrepreneurs in Europe and Latin America. Also, the insights of America's energy consultants, sold for even larger sums to Arab sheikhs. American design engineers are providing insights to Olivetti, Mazda, Siemens, and other global webs; American marketers, techniques for learning what worldwide consumers will buy; American advertisers, ploys for ensuring that they actually do. American architects are issuing designs and blueprints for opera houses, art galleries, museums, luxury hotels, and residential complexes in the world's major cities; American commercial property developers, marketing these properties to worldwide investors and purchasers.

Americans who specialize in the gentle art of public relations are 31 in demand by corporations, governments, and politicians in virtually every nation. So, too, are American political consultants, some of whom, at this writing, are advising the Hungarian Socialist Party, the remnant of Hungary's ruling Communists, on how to salvage a few parliamentary seats in the nation's first free election in more than forty years. Also at this writing, a team of American agricultural consultants is advising the managers of a Soviet farm collective employing 1,700 Russians eighty miles outside Moscow. As noted, American investment bankers and lawyers specializing in financial circumnavigations are selling their insights to Asians and Europeans who are eager to discover how to make large amounts of money by moving large amounts of money.

Developing nations, meanwhile, are hiring American civil engi- 32 neers to advise on building roads and dams. The present thaw in the Cold War will no doubt expand these opportunities. American engineers from Bechtel (a global firm notable for having employed both Caspar Weinberger and George Shultz for much larger sums than either earned in the Reagan administration) have begun helping the Soviets design and install a new generation of nuclear reactors. Nations also are hiring American bankers and lawyers to help them renegotiate the terms of their loans with global banks, and Washington lobbyists to help them with Congress, the Treasury, the World Bank, the IMF, and other politically sensitive institutions. In fits of obvious desperation, several nations emerging from communism have even hired American economists to teach them about capitalism.

Almost everyone around the world is buying the skills and 33 insights of Americans who manipulate oral and visual symbols— musicians, sound engineers, film producers, makeup artists, directors, cinematographers, actors and actresses, boxers, scriptwriters, songwriters, and set designers. Among the wealthiest of symbolic analysts are Steven Spielberg, Bill Cosby, Charles Schulz, Eddie Murphy, Sylvester Stallone, Madonna, and other star directors and performers—who are almost as well known on the streets of Dresden and Tokyo as in the Back Bay of Boston. Less well rewarded but no less renowned are the unctuous anchors on Turner Broadcasting's Cable News, who appear daily, via satellite, in places ranging from Vietnam to Nigeria. Vanna White is the world's most-watched game-show hostess. Behind each of these familiar faces is a collection of American problem-solvers, -identifiers, and brokers who train, coach, advise, promote, amplify, direct, groom, represent, and otherwise add value to their talents.[16]

There are also the insights of senior American executives who   34
occupy the world headquarters of global "American" corporations and the national or regional headquarters of global "foreign" corporations. Their insights are duly exported to the rest of the world through the webs of global enterprise. IBM does not export many machines from the United States, for example. Big Blue makes machines all over the globe and services them on the spot. Its prime American exports are symbolic and analytic. From IBM's world headquarters in Armonk, New York, emanate strategic brokerage and related management services bound for the rest of the world. In return, IBM's top executives are generously rewarded.

The most important reason for this expanding world market   35
and increasing global demand for the symbolic and analytic insights of Americans has been the dramatic improvement in worldwide communication and transportation technologies. Designs, instructions, advice, and visual and audio symbols can be communicated more and more rapidly around the globe, with ever-greater precision and at ever-lower cost. Madonna's voice can be transported to billions of listeners, with perfect clarity, on digital compact discs. A new invention emanating from engineers in Battelle's laboratory in Columbus, Ohio, can be sent almost anywhere via modem, in a form that will allow others to examine it in three dimensions through enhanced computer graphics. When face-to-face meetings are still required—and videoconferencing will not suffice—it is relatively easy for designers, consultants, advisers, artists, and executives to board supersonic jets and, in a matter of hours, meet directly with their worldwide clients, customers, audiences, and employees.

With rising demand comes rising compensation. Whether in   36
the form of licensing fees, fees for service, salaries, or shares in final profits, the economic result is much the same. There are also

---

[16] In 1989, the entertainment business summoned to the United States $5.5 billion in foreign earnings—making it among the nation's largest export industries, just behind aerospace. U.S. Department of Commerce, International Trade Commission, "Composition of U.S. Exports," various issues. [Reich's note]

nonpecuniary rewards. One of the best-kept secrets among symbolic analysts is that so many of them enjoy their work. In fact, much of it does not count as work at all, in the traditional sense. The work of routine producers and in-person servers is typically monotonous; it causes muscles to tire or weaken and involves little independence or discretion. The "work" of symbolic analysts, by contrast, often involves puzzles, experiments, games, a significant amount of chatter, and substantial discretion over what to do next. Few routine producers or in-person servers would "work" if they did not need to earn the money. Many symbolic analysts would "work" even if money were no object.

At midcentury, when America was a national market dominated 37 by core pyramid-shaped corporations, there were constraints on the earnings of people at the highest rungs. First and most obviously, the market for their services was largely limited to the borders of the nation. In addition, whatever conceptual value they might contribute was small relative to the value gleaned from large scale—and it was dependent on large scale for whatever income it was to summon. Most of the problems to be identified and solved had to do with enhancing the efficiency of production and improving the flow of materials, parts, assembly, and distribution. Inventors searched for the rare breakthrough revealing an entirely new product to be made in high volume; management consultants, executives, and engineers thereafter tried to speed and synchronize its manufacture, to better achieve scale efficiencies; advertisers and marketers sought then to whet the public's appetite for the standard item that emerged. Since white-collar earnings increased with larger scale, there was considerable incentive to expand the firm; indeed, many of America's core corporations grew far larger than scale economies would appear to have justified.

By the 1990s, in contrast, the earnings of symbolic analysts 38 were limited neither by the size of the national market nor by the volume of production of the firms with which they were affiliated. The marketplace was worldwide, and conceptual value was high relative to value added from scale efficiencies.

There had been another constraint on high earnings, which 39 also gave way by the 1990s. At midcentury, the compensation awarded to top executives and advisers of the largest of America's core corporations could not be grossly out of proportion to that of low-level production workers. It would be unseemly for executives who engaged in highly visible rounds of bargaining with labor unions, and who routinely responded to government requests to moderate prices, to take home wages and benefits wildly in excess of what other Americans earned. Unless white-collar executives restrained themselves, moreover, blue-collar production workers could not be expected to restrain their own demands for higher wages. Unless both groups exercised restraint, the government could not be expected to forbear from imposing direct controls and regulations.

At the same time, the wages of production workers could not be   40
allowed to sink too low, lest there be insufficient purchasing power in the economy. After all, who would buy all the goods flowing out of American factories if not American workers? This, too, was part of the tacit bargain struck between American managers and their workers.

Recall the oft-repeated corporate platitude of the era about the   41
chief executive's responsibility to carefully weigh and balance the interests of the corporation's disparate stakeholders. Under the stewardship of the corporate statesman, no set of stakeholders—least of all white-collar executives —was to gain a disproportionately large share of the benefits of corporate activity; nor was any stakeholder—especially the average worker—to be left with a share that was disproportionately small. Banal though it was, this idea helped to maintain the legitimacy of the core American corporation in the eyes of most Americans, and to ensure continued economic growth.

But by the 1990s, these informal norms were evaporating, just   42
as (and largely because) the core American corporation was vanishing. The links between top executives and the American production worker were fading: an ever-increasing number of subordinates and contractees were foreign, and a steadily growing number of American routine producers were working for foreign-owned firms. An entire cohort of middle-level managers, who had once been deemed "white collar," had disappeared; and, increasingly, American executives were exporting their insights to global enterprise webs.

As the American corporation itself became a global web almost   43
indistinguishable from any other, its stakeholders were turning into a large and diffuse group, spread over the world. Such global stakeholders were less visible, and far less noisy, than national stakeholders. And as the American corporation sold its goods and services all over the world, the purchasing power of American workers became far less relevant to its economic survival.

Thus have the inhibitions been removed. The salaries and   44
benefits of America's top executives, and many of their advisers and consultants, have soared to what years before would have been unimaginable heights, even as those of other Americans have declined.

QUESTIONS FOR CRITICAL READING

1. What are symbolic analysts? Give some examples from your own experience.
2. What is the apparent relationship between higher education and an educated worker's prospects for wealth?
3. To what extent do you agree or disagree with Reich's description and analysis of routine workers and in-service workers?
4. If Reich's analysis is correct, which gender or social groups are likely to be most harmed by modern economic circumstances in America? Which are most likely to become wealthy? Why?
5. Are symbolic analysts inherently more valuable to our society than routine or in-service workers? Why do symbolic analysts command so much more wealth?
6. Which of the three groups Reich mentions do you see as having the greatest potential for growth in the next thirty years?

SUGGESTIONS FOR WRITING

1. Judging from the views that Reich holds about decreasing job opportunities for all three groups of workers, how will increased immigration affect the American economy? Is immigration a hopeful sign? Is it a danger to the economy? How do most people seem to perceive the effect of increased immigration?
2. To what extent do you think Reich is correct about the growing wealth of symbolic analysts? He says, "Never before in history has opulence on such a scale been gained by people who have earned it, and done so legally" (para. 28). Do you see yourself as a symbolic analyst? How do you see your future in relation to the three economic groups Reich describes?
3. Reich says, "Few routine producers or in-person servers would 'work' if they did not need to earn the money. Many symbolic analysts would 'work' even if money were no object" (para. 36). Is this true? Examine your own experience—along with the experience of others you know—and defend or attack this view. How accurate do you consider Reich to be in his analysis of the way various workers view their work?
4. Describe the changes that have taken place in the American economy since 1960, according to this essay. How have they affected the way Americans work and the work that Americans can expect to find? How have your personal opportunities been broadened or narrowed by the changes? Do you feel the changes have been good for the country or not? Why?
5. Reich's view of the great success of Japanese corporations and of their presence as manufacturing giants in the United States and elsewhere is largely positive. He has pointed out elsewhere that Honda and other manufacturers in the United States provide jobs and municipal income

that would otherwise go to other nations. What is your view of the presence of large Japanese corporations in the United States? What is your view of other nations' manufacturing facilities in the United States?

6. Why are the rich getting richer and the poor, poorer? Examine the kinds of differences between the rich and the poor that Reich describes. Is the process of increasing riches for the rich and increasing poverty for the poor inevitable, or will it begin to change in the near future?

7. **CONNECTIONS**   Compare Robert Reich's views of the new economy with those of John Maynard Keynes. Keynes's economic analysis was based on the idea that nations largely produce consumer goods domestically. How do the changes in our current economy, as described by Reich, affect Keynes's concepts regarding the value of money? Consider Keynes's three basic groups: the investor class, the business class, the wage earner class. Are Keynes and Reich the same kind of capitalist?

PART FIVE

MIND

Plato
René Descartes
Sigmund Freud
Carl Jung
Melanie Klein
Howard Gardner

INTRODUCTION

We are shaped by our thoughts; we become what we think.
When the mind is pure, joy follows like a shadow that never
leaves.
— SIDDHARTHA GAUTAMA (563–483 B.C.)

That in the soul which is called the mind is, before it thinks, not
actually any real thing.
— ARISTOTLE (384–322 B.C.)

Distinctions drawn by the mind are not necessarily equivalent to
distinctions in reality.
— ST. THOMAS AQUINAS (1225–1274)

Consciousness is the perception of what passes in a man's own
mind. Can another man perceive that I am conscious of any
thing, when I perceive it not myself? No man's knowledge here
can go beyond his experience.
— JOHN LOCKE (1632–1704)

The difference in mind between man and the higher animals,
great as it is, is one of degree and not of kind.
— CHARLES DARWIN (1809–1882)

The computer takes up where psychoanalysis left off. It takes the
ideas of a decentered self and makes it more concrete by
modeling mind as a multiprocessing machine.
— SHERRY TURKLE (b. 1948)

Ideas about the nature of the human mind have abounded
throughout history. Philosophers and scientists have sought to discern the mind's components and functions and have distinguished
humans from other animals according to the qualities associated
with the mind, such as reason and self-awareness. The ancient
Greeks formulated the concept of the psyche (from which we derive
the term *psychology*) as the center of consciousness and reason as well
as emotions. During the Renaissance, René Descartes (1596–1650)
concluded *Cogito ergo sum* ("I think, therefore I am") and proposed
that the mind was the source of human identity and that reason was
the key to comprehending the material world. Influenced by
Descartes, John Locke (1632–1704) developed a theory of the mind
as a *tabula rasa*, or blank slate, that was shaped entirely by external
experiences. The selections in this section further explore these
questions about the nature of the mind and its relationship to consciousness, knowledge, intellect, and the other means by which we
work to understand ourselves and our world.

The first selection, by Plato, contains one of the seminal ideas about the nature of mind. Plato posited that the world of sensory experience is not the real world and that our senses are in fact incapable of experiencing reality. In Plato's view, reality is an ideal that exists only in an environment that is somewhat akin to the concept of heaven. He suggested that people are born with knowledge of that reality. The infant, in other words, possesses the ideas of reality to start with, having gained them from heaven and retaining them in memory. For Plato, education was the process by which students regained such "lost" memories and made them part of their conscious understanding. Although he never uses the terms *conscious* and *unconscious* in describing the mind, Plato's views foreshadow the later theories of psychologists such as William James (1842–1910), Sigmund Freud, and Carl Jung.

René Descartes wrote in an age that was influenced by a revival of attention to Greek philosophers. His views were consistent in some ways with those of Plato and Aristotle, especially in the quest for a form of certainty in knowledge on which all thought could be based. His primary motive was to prove the existence of God, which he felt he could do if he could establish one absolute truth on which to build a clear argument. His solution was *Cogito ergo sum*, which translates as "I think, therefore I am." Having established his own existence without a doubt, he was able to move toward a defensible proof of the existence of God. However, in the process of developing his argument, he introduced a long-lasting idea that influenced thought for many years: that the mind and the body are separate entities. The mind/body split had been apparent in the work of earlier writers, but it never had such a forceful champion as in Descartes. His influence has continued to modern times despite the current view that the mind and body are much more closely integrated than earlier investigators had assumed.

One of the best-known results of Freud's study of dreams is his conclusion that all people suffer from an Oedipus complex when they are extremely young. Freud explains that Oedipus, thinking he was escaping his fate, killed his father and married his mother, both of whom were strangers to him. Freud takes this familiar Greek myth and explores its significance in the lives of very young children, showing that it is common for them to wish to do away with their parent of the same sex and have their opposite-sex parent all to themselves. As people grow older, both the memory and the desire to follow through on this feeling are repressed and forgotten. They become part of our unconscious and, in some cases, may resurface in the form of guilt. As adults we know that such feelings are completely unacceptable, and the guilt that results can create psychological illness.

Carl Jung began his studies with Freud's views of the content of the unconscious, but one of his analyses led him in a novel direction. He concluded that some of the content of the unconscious mind could not have begun in the conscious mind because it was not the product of the individual's conscious experience. Jung reasoned that certain images present in the unconscious were common to all members of a culture. He called these images *archetypal* because they seemed fundamental and universal, such as the archetype of the father and the archetype of the mother. He then hypothesized that part of the mind's content is derived from cultural history. Unlike Freud, Jung saw the unconscious as containing images that represent deep instinctual longings belonging to an entire culture, not just to the individual.

One of the twentieth century's most important psychologists, Melanie Klein established herself as a pioneer in the psychoanalysis of children as young as two or three years old. She demonstrated that, contrary to the established position of her profession, such children were developed enough to be able to respond to the Freudian techniques she used. She did not rely on Freud's couch for her studies, but invented what is now known as play technique, an approach in which the analyst actually plays with the child and examines his or her speech and behavior for signs of problems or fears. Although she and Freud did not agree on everything, their views on the Oedipus complex were comparable. But whereas Freud concentrated almost entirely on male children, Klein demonstrated that the complex was equally significant in female children. Her work in the 1920s continues to be influential to this day.

Howard Gardner's interest is in intelligence, which he approaches from a pluralist point of view. His idea of seven distinct intelligences, as opposed to the conventional views represented by standardized IQ tests, is at once traditional and revolutionary. In drawing on the model of ancient Greek education, he urges us to examine the virtues of all seven forms of intelligence and not rely on the logical-mathematical model that dominates contemporary education. Gardner notes that certain forms of intelligence are culturally linked, but he leaves open the question of whether they are gender-linked.

These essays approach the problem of mind from different positions and are concerned with different questions of consciousness, thought, limitation, and intelligence. They raise some of the most basic questions concerning the mind, such as, What are its components? What can it know? What should we most value in its function? In answering these questions, each essay provides us with ideas that provoke more thought and still more questions.

PLATO

The Allegory of the Cave

PLATO (428–347 B.C.) was born into an aristocratic, probably Athenian, family and educated according to the best precepts available. He eventually became a student of Socrates and later involved himself closely with Socrates' work and teaching. Plato was not only Socrates' finest student but also the one who immortalized Socrates in his works. Most of Plato's works are philosophical essays in which Socrates speaks as a character in a dialogue with one or more students or listeners.

Both Socrates and Plato lived in turbulent times. In 404 B.C. Athens was defeated by Sparta, and its government was taken over by tyrants. Political life in Athens became dangerous. Plato felt, however, that he could effect positive change in Athenian politics — until Socrates was tried unjustly for corrupting the youth of Athens and sentenced to death in 399 B.C. After that, Plato withdrew from public life and devoted himself to writing and to the Academy he founded in an olive grove in Athens. The Academy endured for almost a thousand years, which tells us how greatly Plato's thought was valued.

Although it is not easy to condense Plato's views, he may be said to have held the world of sense perception to be inferior to the world of ideal entities that exist only in a pure spiritual realm. These ideals, or forms, Plato argued, are perceived directly by everyone before birth and then dimly remembered here on earth. But the memory, dim as it is, enables people to understand what the senses perceive, despite the fact that the senses are unreliable and their perceptions imperfect.

This view of reality has long been important to philosophers because it gives a philosophical basis to antimaterialistic thought.

From *The Republic*. Translated and glossed by Benjamin Jowett.

It values the spirit first and frees people from the tyranny of sensory perception and sensory reward. In the case of love, Plato held that Eros leads individuals to revere the body and its pleasures; but the thrust of his teaching is that the body is a metaphor for spiritual delights. Plato maintains that the body is only a starting point, which eventually can lead to both spiritual fulfillment and the appreciation of true beauty.

On the one hand, "The Allegory of the Cave" is a discussion of politics: *The Republic*, from which it is taken, is a treatise on justice and the ideal government. On the other hand, it has long stood as an example of the notion that if we rely on our perceptions to know the truth about the world, then we will know very little about it. In order to live ethically, it is essential to know what is true and, therefore, what is important beyond the world of sensory perception.

Plato's allegory has been persuasive for centuries and remains at the center of thought that attempts to counter the pleasures of the sensual life. Most religions aim for spiritual enlightenment and praise the qualities of the soul, which lies beyond perception. Thus, it comes as no surprise that Christianity and other religions have developed systems of thought that bear a close resemblance to Plato's. Later refinements of his thought, usually called Neo-Platonism, have been influential even into modern times.

Plato's Rhetoric

Two important rhetorical techniques are at work in the following selection. The first and more obvious—at least on one level— is the device of the allegory, a story in which the characters and situations actually represent people and situations in another context. It is a difficult technique to sustain, although Aesop's fables were certainly successful in using animals to represent people and their foibles. The advantage of the technique is that a complex and sometimes unpopular argument can be fought and won before the audience realizes that an argument is under way. The disadvantage of the technique is that the terms of the allegory may only approximate the situation it represents; thus, the argument may fail to be convincing.

The second rhetorical technique Plato uses is the dialogue. In fact, this device is a hallmark of Plato's work; indeed, most of his writings are called dialogues. The *Symposium*, *Apology*, *Phaedo*, *Crito*, *Meno*, and most of his famous works are written in dialogue form. Usually in these works Socrates is speaking to a student or a friend about highly abstract issues, asking questions that require simple answers. Slowly, the questioning proceeds to elucidate the answers to complex issues.

This question-and-answer technique basically constitutes the Socratic method. Socrates analyzes the answer to each question, examines its implications, and then asserts the truth. The method works partly because Plato believes that people do not learn things but remember them. That is, people originate from heaven, where they knew the truth; they already possess knowledge and must recover it by means of the dialogue. Socrates' method is ideally suited to that purpose.

Beyond these techniques, however, we must look at Plato's style. It is true that he is working with difficult ideas, but his style is so clear, simple, and direct that few people would have trouble understanding what he is saying. Considering the influence this work has had on world thought, and the reputation Plato had earned by the time he wrote *The Republic*, its style is remarkably plain and accessible. Plato's respect for rhetoric and its proper uses is part of the reason he can express himself with such impressive clarity.

PREREADING QUESTIONS:
WHAT TO READ FOR

The following prereading questions may help you anticipate key issues in the discussion of Plato's "The Allegory of the Cave." Keeping them in mind during your first reading of the selection should help focus your attention.

- In what ways are we like the people in the cave looking at shadows?
- Why is the world of sensory perception somewhat illusory?
- For Plato, what is the difference between the upper world and the lower world?

The Allegory of the Cave

SOCRATES,
GLAUCON. *The
den, the prison-
ers: the light at
a distance;*

And now, I said, let me show in a figure how 1 far our nature is enlightened or unenlightened:— Behold! human beings living in an underground den, which has a mouth open towards the light and reaching all along the den; here they have been from their childhood, and have their legs and necks chained so that they cannot move, and can only see before them, being prevented by the chains from turning round their heads. Above and behind them a fire is blazing at a distance, and between the fire and the prisoners there is a raised way; and you will see, if you look, a low wall built along the way, like the screen which marionette players have in front of them, over which they show the puppets.

I see.   2

And do you see, I said, men passing along the 3 wall carrying all sorts of vessels, and statues and figures of animals made of wood and stone and various materials, which appear over the wall? Some of them are talking, others silent.

the low wall, and the moving figures of which the shadows are seen on the opposite wall of the den.

You have shown me a strange image, and they 4 are strange prisoners.

Like ourselves, I replied; and they see only 5 their own shadows, or the shadows of one another, which the fire throws on the opposite wall of the cave?

True, he said; how could they see anything but 6 the shadows if they were never allowed to move their heads?

And of the objects which are being carried in 7 like manner they would only see the shadows?

Yes, he said.   8

And if they were able to converse with one an- 9 other, would they not suppose that they were naming what was actually before them?

Very true.   10

The prisoners would mistake the shadows for realities.

And suppose further that the prison had an 11 echo which came from the other side, would they not be sure to fancy when one of the passers-by spoke that the voice which they heard came from the passing shadow?

No question, he replied.   12

To them, I said, the truth would be literally 13 nothing but the shadows of the images.

That is certain.   14

And now look again, and see what will naturally 15 follow if the prisoners are released and disabused of their error. At first, when any of them is liberated and compelled suddenly to stand up and turn his neck round and walk and look towards the light, he will suffer sharp pains; the glare will distress him, and he will be unable to see the realities of which in his former state he had seen the shadows; and then conceive someone saying to him, that what he saw before was an illusion, but that now, when he is approaching nearer to being and his eye is turned towards more real existence, he has a clearer vision—what will be his reply? And you may further imagine that his instructor is pointing to the objects as they pass and requiring him to name them,—will he not be perplexed? Will he not fancy that the shadows which he formerly saw are truer than the objects which are now shown to him?

And when released, they would still persist in maintaining the superior truth of the shadows.

Far truer.   16

And if he is compelled to look straight at the   17
light, will he not have a pain in his eyes which will make him turn away to take refuge in the objects of vision which he can see, and which he will conceive to be in reality clearer than the things which are now being shown to him?

True, he said.   18

When dragged upwards, they would be dazzled by excess of light.

And suppose once more, that he is reluctantly   19
dragged up a steep and rugged ascent, and held fast until he is forced into the presence of the sun himself, is he not likely to be pained and irritated? When he approaches the light his eyes will be dazzled, and he will not be able to see anything at all of what are now called realities.

Not all in a moment, he said.   20

He will require to grow accustomed to the   21
sight of the upper world. And first he will see the shadows best, next the reflections of men and other objects in the water, and then the objects themselves; then he will gaze upon the light of the moon and the stars and the spangled heaven; and he will see the sky and the stars by night better than the sun or the light of the sun by day?

Certainly.   22

Last of all he will be able to see the sun, and   23
not mere reflections of him in the water, but he

will see him in his own proper place, and not in another; and he will contemplate him as he is.

Certainly.   24

He will then proceed to argue that this is he   25
who gives the season and the years, and is the guardian of all that is in the visible world, and in a certain way the cause of all things which he and his fellows have been accustomed to behold?

Clearly, he said, he would first see the sun and   26
then reason about him.

And when he remembered his old habitation,   27
and the wisdom of the den and his fellow prison-ers, do you not suppose that he would felicitate himself on the change, and pity them?

Certainly, he would.   28

And if they were in the habit of conferring   29
honors among themselves on those who were quickest to observe the passing shadows and to re-mark which of them went before, and which fol-lowed after, and which were together; and who were therefore best able to draw conclusions as to the future, do you think that he would care for such honors and glories, or envy the possessors of them? Would he not say with Homer,

> Better to be the poor servant of a poor master,

and to endure anything, rather than think as they do and live after their manner?

Yes, he said, I think that he would rather suffer   30
anything than entertain these false notions and live in this miserable manner.

Imagine once more, I said, such an one coming   31
suddenly out of the sun to be replaced in his old situation; would he not be certain to have his eyes full of darkness?

To be sure, he said.   32

And if there were a contest, and he had to   33
compete in measuring the shadows with the pris-oners who had never moved out of the den, while his sight was still weak, and before his eyes had be-come steady (and the time which would be needed to acquire this new habit of sight might be very considerable), would he not be ridiculous? Men would say of him that up he went and down he

came without his eyes; and that it was better not even to think of ascending; and if any one tried to loose another and lead him up to the light, let them only catch the offender, and they would put him to death.

No question, he said. 34

The prison is the world of sight, the light of the fire is the sun.

This entire allegory, I said, you may now ap- 35 pend, dear Glaucon, to the previous argument; the prison house is the world of sight, the light of the fire is the sun, and you will not misapprehend me if you interpret the journey upwards to be the ascent of the soul into the intellectual world according to my poor belief, which, at your desire, I have expressed—whether rightly or wrongly God knows. But, whether true or false, my opinion is that in the world of knowledge the idea of good appears last of all, and is seen only with an effort; and, when seen, is also inferred to be the universal author of all things beautiful and right, parent of light and of the lord of light in this visible world, and the immediate source of reason and truth in the intellectual; and that this is the power upon which he who would act rationally either in public or private life must have his eye fixed.

I agree, he said, as far as I am able to under- 36 stand you.

Moreover, I said, you must not wonder that 37 those who attain to this beatific vision are unwilling to descend to human affairs; for their souls are ever hastening into the upper world where they desire to dwell; which desire of theirs is very natural, if our allegory may be trusted.

Yes, very natural. 38

Nothing extraordinary in the philosopher being unable to see in the dark.

And is there anything surprising in one who 39 passes from divine contemplations to the evil state of man, misbehaving himself in a ridiculous manner; if, while his eyes are blinking and before he has become accustomed to the surrounding darkness, he is compelled to fight in courts of law, or in other places, about the images or the shadows of images of justice, and is endeavoring to meet the conceptions of those who have never yet seen absolute justice?

Anything but surprising, he replied. 40

*The eyes may
be blinded in
two ways, by
excess or by
defect of light.*

Anyone who has common sense will remember   41
that the bewilderments of the eyes are of two kinds,
and arise from two causes, either from coming out
of the light or from going into the light, which is
true of the mind's eye, quite as much as of the bodily eye; and he who remembers this when he sees
anyone whose vision is perplexed and weak, will
not be too ready to laugh; he will first ask whether
that soul of man has come out of the brighter life,
and is unable to see because unaccustomed to the
dark, or having turned from darkness to the day
is dazzled by excess of light. And he will count the
one happy in his condition and state of being, and
he will pity the other; or, if he have a mind to laugh
at the soul which comes from below into the light,
there will be more reason in this than in the
laugh which greets him who returns from above
out of the light into the den.

That, he said, is a very just distinction.   42

*The conversion
of the soul is
the turning
round the eye
from darkness
to light.*

But then, if I am right, certain professors of ed-   43
ucation must be wrong when they say that they can
put a knowledge into the soul which was not there
before, like sight into blind eyes.

They undoubtedly say this, he replied.   44

Whereas, our argument shows that the power   45
and capacity of learning exists in the soul already;
and that just as the eye was unable to turn from
darkness to light without the whole body, so too
the instrument of knowledge can only by the
movement of the whole soul be turned from the
world of becoming into that of being, and learn by
degrees to endure the sight of being, and of the
brightest and best of being, or in other words, of
the good.

Very true.   46

And must there not be some art which will ef-   47
fect conversion in the easiest and quickest manner;
not implanting the faculty of sight, for that exists
already, but has been turned in the wrong direction, and is looking away from the truth?

Yes, he said, such an art may be presumed.   48

And whereas the other so-called virtues of the   49
soul seem to be akin to bodily qualities, for even
when they are not originally innate they can be

The virtue of wisdom has a divine power which may be turned either towards good or towards evil.

implanted later by habit and exercise, the virtue of wisdom more than anything else contains a divine element which always remains, and by this conversion is rendered useful and profitable; or, on the other hand, hurtful and useless. Did you never observe the narrow intelligence flashing from the keen eye of a clever rogue—how eager he is, how clearly his paltry soul sees the way to his end; he is the reverse of blind, but his keen eyesight is forced into the service of evil, and he is mischievous in proportion to his cleverness?

Very true, he said.   50

But what if there had been a circumcision of   51 such natures in the days of their youth; and they had been severed from those sensual pleasures, such as eating and drinking, which, like leaden weights, were attached to them at their birth, and which drag them down and turn the vision of their souls upon the things that are below—if, I say, they had been released from these impediments and turned in the opposite direction, the very same faculty in them would have seen the truth as keenly as they see what their eyes are turned to now.

Very likely.   52

Neither the uneducated nor the over-educated will be good servants of the State.

Yes, I said; and there is another thing which is   53 likely, or rather a necessary inference from what has preceded, that neither the uneducated and uninformed of the truth, nor yet those who never make an end of their education, will be able ministers of State; not the former, because they have no single aim of duty which is the rule of all their actions, private as well as public; nor the latter, because they will not act at all except upon compulsion, fancying that they are already dwelling apart in the islands of the blessed.

Very true, he replied.   54

Then, I said, the business of us who are the   55 founders of the State will be to compel the best minds to attain that knowledge which we have already shown to be the greatest of all—they must continue to ascend until they arrive at the good; but when they have ascended and seen enough we must not allow them to do as they do now.

Men should
ascend to the
upper world,
but they should
also return to
the lower.

What do you mean?   56

I mean that they remain in the upper world: 57
but this must not be allowed; they must be made to
descend again among the prisoners in the den, and
partake of their labors and honors, whether they
are worth having or not.

But is not this unjust? he said; ought we to give   58
them a worse life, when they might have a better?

You have again forgotten, my friend, I said, the   59
intention of the legislator, who did not aim at making any one class in the State happy above the rest;
the happiness was to be in the whole State, and he
held the citizens together by persuasion and necessity, making them benefactors of the State, and
therefore benefactors of one another; to this end he
created them, not to please themselves, but to be
his instruments in binding up the State.

True, he said, I had forgotten.   60

The duties of
philosophers.

Observe, Glaucon, that there will be no injus-   61
tice in compelling our philosophers to have a care
and providence of others; we shall explain to them
that in other States, men of their class are not
obliged to share in the toils of politics: and this is
reasonable, for they grow up at their own sweet
will, and the government would rather not have
them. Being self-taught, they cannot be expected to
show any gratitude for a culture which they have
never received. But we have brought you into the
world to be rulers of the hive, kings of yourselves
and of the other citizens, and have educated you
far better and more perfectly than they have been
educated, and you are better able to share in the
double duty. Wherefore each of you, when his turn
comes, must go down to the general underground
abode, and get the habit of seeing in the dark.

Their
obligations to
their country
will induce
them to take
part in her
government.

When you have acquired the habit, you will see ten
thousand times better than the inhabitants of the
den, and you will know what the several images
are, and what they represent, because you have
seen the beautiful and just and good in their truth.
And thus our State, which is also yours, will be a
reality, and not a dream only, and will be administered in a spirit unlike that of other States, in
which men fight with one another about shadows

only and are distracted in the struggle for power, which in their eyes is a great good. Whereas the truth is that the State in which the rulers are most reluctant to govern is always the best and most quietly governed, and the State in which they are most eager, the worst.

Quite true, he replied. 62

And will our pupils, when they hear this, 63 refuse to take their turn at the toils of State, when they are allowed to spend the greater part of their time with one another in the heavenly light?

They will be willing but not anxious to rule.

Impossible, he answered; for they are just 64 men, and the commands which we impose upon them are just; there can be no doubt that every one of them will take office as a stern necessity, and not after the fashion of our present rulers of State.

The statesman must be provided with a better life than that of a ruler; and then he will not covet office.

Yes, my friend, I said; and there lies the 65 point. You must contrive for your future rulers another and a better life than that of a ruler, and then you may have a well-ordered State; for only in the State which offers this, will they rule who are truly rich, not in silver and gold, but in virtue and wisdom, which are the true blessings of life. Whereas if they go to the administration of public affairs, poor and hungering after their own private advantage, thinking that hence they are to snatch the chief good, order there can never be; for they will be fighting about office, and the civil and domestic broils which thus arise will be the ruin of the rulers themselves and of the whole State.

Most true, he replied. 66

And the only life which looks down upon the 67 life of political ambition is that of true philosophy. Do you know of any other?

Indeed, I do not, he said. 68

QUESTIONS FOR CRITICAL READING

1. What is the relationship between Socrates and Glaucon? Are they equal in intellectual authority? Are they concerned with the same issues?

2. How does the allegory of the prisoners in the cave watching shadows on a wall relate to us today? What shadows do we see, and how do they distort our sense of what is real?
3. Are we prisoners in the same sense that Plato's characters are?
4. If Plato is right that the material world is an illusion, how would too great a reliance on materialism affect ethical decisions?
5. What ethical issues, if any, are raised by Plato's allegory?
6. In paragraph 49, Plato states that the virtue of wisdom "contains a divine element." What is "a divine element"? What does this statement seem to mean? Do you agree with Plato?
7. What distinctions does Plato make between the public and the private? Would you make the same distinctions (see paras. 53–55)?

SUGGESTIONS FOR WRITING

1. Analyze the allegory of the cave for its strengths and weaknesses. Consider what the allegory implies for people living in a world of the senses and for what might lie behind that world. To what extent are people like (or unlike) the figures in the cave? To what extent is the world we know like the cave?
2. Socrates ends the dialogue by saying that rulers of the state must be able to look forward to a better life than that of being rulers. He and Glaucon agree that only one life "looks down upon the life of political ambition" — "that of true philosophy" (para. 67). What is the life of true philosophy? Is it superior to that of governing (or anything else)? How would you define its superiority? What would its qualities be? What would its concerns be? Would you be happy leading such a life?
3. In what ways would depending on the material world for one's highest moral values affect ethical behavior? What is the connection between ethics and materialism? Write a brief essay that defends or attacks materialism as a basis for ethical action. How can people aspire to the good if they root their greatest pleasures in the senses? What alternatives do modern people have if they choose to base their actions on nonmaterialistic, or spiritual, values? What are those values? How can they guide our ethical behavior? Do you think they should?
4. In paragraph 61, Socrates outlines a program that would assure Athens of having good rulers and good government. Clarify exactly what the program is, what its problems and benefits are, and how it could be put into action. Then decide whether the program would work. You may consider whether it would work for our time, for Socrates' time, or both. If possible, use examples (hypothetical or real) to bolster your argument.
5. Socrates states unequivocally that Athens should compel the best and the most intelligent young men to be rulers of the state. Review his reasons for saying so, consider what his concept of the state is, and then take a stand on the issue. Is it right to compel the best and most

intelligent young people to become rulers? If so, would it be equally proper to compel those well suited for the professions of law, medicine, teaching, or religion to follow those respective callings? Would an ideal society result if all people were forced to practice the calling for which they had the best aptitude?

6. **CONNECTIONS** Plato has a great deal to say about goodness as it relates to government. Compare his views with those of Lao-tzu and Niccolò Machiavelli. Which of those thinkers would Plato have agreed with most? In comparing these three writers and their political views, consider the nature of goodness they required in a ruler. Do you think that we hold similar attitudes today in our expectations for the goodness of our government?

7. **CONNECTIONS** Plato is concerned with the question of how we know what we know. Francis Bacon in "The Four Idols" (see Part 6) is concerned with the same question, although he poses it in different terms. Examine the fundamental issues each author raises. How well do these thinkers agree on basic issues? To what extent, for example, does Bacon warn us to beware the evidence of our senses? To what extent is Bacon concerned about getting to the truth as Plato is?

RENÉ DESCARTES
Discourse Four

RENÉ DESCARTES (1596–1650), credited with founding modern philosophy, was educated in Jesuit schools in France, beginning with Jesuit college at La Flèche, which was established by the king for the education of the brightest children of the upper classes. In time he came to reject certain principles of his education and developed his Method, the intellectual system expounded in his *Discourse on the Method of Rightly Conducting One's Reason and Seeking Truth in the Sciences* (1637). This work was followed by *Meditations on First Philosophy* (1641), which discuss the "first philosophy" — the nature of God.

For many thinkers *Discourse on Method* represents the beginning of the end of the domination of Aristotle and the scholastics. The scholastic philosophers (churchmen teaching throughout Europe) followed Aristotle and St. Thomas Aquinas in a rigid system governed by rules of logic. Although sensory evidence was sometimes relied upon, the final authority was the church. Descartes wished on the contrary to substitute the authority of his own reasoning in his investigations into the nature of truth.

His discovery of Method came to him suddenly in 1619 in a "blinding flash" of insight. Seeing the need for a unity of thought in science, he realized that the step-by-step proofs used by geometricians could be employed in all aspects of science. In "Discourse Two" he explains the four rules of his Method and ends with a summary of his insight into geometry:

> The first was never to accept anything as true that I did not know to be evidently so: that is to say, carefully to avoid precipitancy and prejudice, and to include in my judgements nothing more

From *Discourse on the Method of Rightly Conducting One's Reason and Seeking Truth in the Sciences.* Translated by F. E. Sutcliffe.

than what presented itself so clearly and so distinctly to my mind that I might have no occasion to place it in doubt.

The second, to divide each of the difficulties that I was examining into as many parts as might be possible and necessary in order best to solve it.

The third, to conduct my thoughts in an orderly way, beginning with the simplest objects and the easiest to know, in order to climb gradually, as by degrees, as far as the knowledge of the most complex, and even supposing some order among those objects which do not precede each other naturally.

And the last, everywhere to make such complete enumerations and such general reviews that I would be sure to have omitted nothing.

These long chains of reasonings, quite simple and easy, which geometers are accustomed to using to teach their most difficult demonstrations, had given me cause to imagine that everything which can be encompassed by man's knowledge is linked in the same way, and that, provided only that one abstains from accepting any for true which is not true, and that one always keeps the right order to one thing to be deduced from that which precedes it, there can be nothing so distant that one does not reach it eventually, or so hidden that one cannot discover it.

Descartes insisted that if each step of the inquiry were free from error, the darkest secrets of nature could be discovered. What he needed once he established this principle was an unassailable position from which to begin. That first point reached, his chain of reasoning could stretch to the stars; without it, true knowledge was impossible. Descartes describes that point in the following selection, "Discourse Four." It contains the most famous catch-phrase in philosophy: "*Cogito, ergo sum*" (I think, therefore I am). After rejecting many other possible points of departure, Descartes hit upon the statement that was for him unassailable: if he thought about something, then he knew that he must exist, that he was a "thing that thinks," and that he could not be deceived about the fact that he thought. After establishing this basic truth, he moved toward a proof of the existence of God that did not depend on sensory evidence. It is sometimes described as an intuitive proof, because it depends on a chain of reasoning that starts neither from observation nor from an outside authority.

Descartes was influenced by the skepticism of Michel Eyquem de Montaigne (1533–1592), who, in his essays, accepted the view that certainty was impossible because the senses were unreliable and the very existence of the individual unprovable. In the latter part of the sixteenth century, the discovery of important classical texts—especially Sextus Empiricus's translation of the work of the ancient Greek philosopher Pyrrho—was enormously influential in Europe because they cast doubt on all things. The fracturing of the Christian Church into several sects called into question the most authoritative truths of all, most notably when Martin Luther challenged the authority of the church on the question of the truth. Doubt and uncertainty were therefore part of a crisis in European thought. Descartes worked out his theories a hundred years after Luther, and with the publication of *Discourse on Method* he seemed to have begun to offer a way out of the crisis.

Ironically, Descartes's reliance on intuitive chains of reasoning did not work in his favor in scientific investigations of the kind we now rely upon. He was uncomfortable with evidence gathered by the senses—what is now called *empirical evidence*—and therefore made little contribution to the development of modern science. However, he did not hold science back. He especially admired Galileo (1564–1642), the most renowned scientist of his time.

Another legacy of Descartes is the body-mind split. He states in "Discourse Four" that he is aware of the distinctions between his body and his mind and sees them as different in certain essentials. Eventually, he postulates that the mind's existence may not depend on the body. Such a view was widely developed in poetry and literature and is for some critics a lamentable fact. However, Descartes remains a philosopher who confronted difficult problems in a very personal way. His "Discourse" records his personal development as a thinker, indulging at times in biographical detail that may seem superfluous. However, it is essential to his approach, since the individual, like him, must be in a position to acquire reliable knowledge in an effort to reach the truth.

PREREADING QUESTIONS: WHAT TO READ FOR

The following prereading questions may help you anticipate key issues in the discussion of René Descartes's "Discourse Four." Keeping them in mind during your first reading of the selection should help focus your attention.

- What is Descartes's first principle of philosophy?
- How does Descartes prove the existence of God?
- Why does Descartes discuss dreams?

Discourse Four

I do not know if I ought to tell you about the first meditations I   1
pursued there, for they are so abstract and unusual that they will
probably not be to the taste of everyone; and yet, so that one may
judge if the foundations I have laid are firm enough, I find myself to
some extent forced to speak of them. I had long ago noticed that, in
matters relating to conduct, one needs sometimes to follow, just as if
they were absolutely indubitable, opinions one knows to be very un-
sure, as has been said above; but as I wanted to concentrate solely
on the search for truth, I thought I ought to do just the opposite,
and reject as being absolutely false everything in which I could suppose the slightest reason for doubt, in order to see if there did not
remain after that anything in my belief which was entirely indubitable. So, because our senses sometimes play us false, I decided to
suppose that there was nothing at all which was such as they cause
us to imagine it; and because there are men who make mistakes in
reasoning, even with the simplest geometrical matters, and make
paralogisms,[1] judging that I was as liable to error as anyone else, I
rejected as being false all the reasonings I had hitherto accepted as
proofs. And finally, considering that all the same thoughts that we
have when we are awake can also come to us when we are asleep,
without any one of them then being true, I resolved to pretend that
nothing which had ever entered my mind was any more true than
the illusions of my dreams. But immediately afterwards I became
aware that, while I decided thus to think that everything was false,
it followed necessarily that I who thought thus must be something;
and observing that this truth: *I think, therefore I am*, was so certain
and so evident that all the most extravagant suppositions of the
sceptics were not capable of shaking it, I judged that I would accept
it without scruple as the first principle of the philosophy I was
seeking.

Then, examining attentively what I was, and seeing that I could   2
pretend that I had no body and that there was no world or place
that I was in, but that I could not, for all that, pretend that I did not
exist, and that, on the contrary, from the very fact that I thought of
doubting the truth of other things, it followed very evidently and
very certainly that I existed; while, on the other hand, if I had only
ceased to think, although all the rest of what I had ever imagined
had been true, I would have had no reason to believe that I existed;
I thereby concluded that I was a substance, of which the whole

---

[1] **paralogisms** Illogical reasonings.

essence or nature consists in thinking, and which, in order to exist, needs no place and depends on no material thing; so that this 'I,' that is to say, the mind, by which I am what I am, is entirely distinct from the body, and even that it is easier to know than the body, and moreover, that even if the body were not, it would not cease to be all that it is.

After this, I considered in general what is needed for a proposi- 3 tion to be true and certain; for, since I had just found one which I knew to be so, I thought that I ought also to know what this certainty consisted of. And having noticed that there is nothing at all in this, *I think, therefore I am*, which assures me that I am speaking the truth, except that I see very clearly that in order to think one must exist, I judged that I could take it to be a general rule that the things we conceive very clearly and very distinctly are all true, but that there is nevertheless some difficulty in being able to recognize for certain which are the things we see distinctly.

Following this, reflecting on the fact that I had doubts, and that 4 consequently my being was not completely perfect, for I saw clearly that it was a greater perfection to know than to doubt, I decided to inquire whence I had learned to think of something more perfect than myself; and I clearly recognized that this must have been from some nature which was in fact more perfect. As for the notions I had of several other things outside myself, such as the sky, the earth, light, heat, and a thousand others, I had not the same concern to know their source, because, seeing nothing in them which seemed to make them superior to myself, I could believe that, if they were true, they were dependencies of my nature, in as much as it had some perfection; and, if they were not, that I held them from nothing, that is to say that they were in me because of an imperfection in my nature. But I could not make the same judgment concerning the idea of a being more perfect than myself; for to hold it from nothing was something manifestly impossible; and because it is no less contradictory that the more perfect should proceed from and depend on the less perfect, than it is that something should emerge out of nothing, I could not hold it from myself; with the result that it remained that it must have been put into me by a being whose nature was truly more perfect than mine and which even had in itself all the perfections of which I could have any idea, that is to say, in a single word, which was God. To which I added that, since I knew some perfections that I did not have, I was not the only being which existed (I shall freely use here, with your permission, the terms of the School) but that there must of necessity be another more perfect, upon whom I depended, and from whom I had acquired all I had; for, if I had been alone and independent of all other, so as to have had from myself this small portion of perfection that I had by participation in the perfection of God, I could have given myself, by the same reason, all the remainder of perfection that I knew myself to lack, and thus to be myself infinite, eternal, immutable, omniscient, all-powerful, and finally to have all the perfections that I could observe to be in God. For, consequentially upon the reasonings by which I had proved the existence of God, in order to understand the nature of God as far as my own nature was capable of doing, I had only to consider, concerning all the things of which I found in myself some idea, whether it was a perfection or not to have them: and I was assured that none of those which indicated some imperfection was in him, but that all the others were. So I saw that doubt, inconstancy, sadness, and similar things could not be in him, seeing that I myself would have been very pleased to be free from them. Then, further, I had ideas of many sensible and bodily things; for even supposing that I was dreaming, and that everything I saw or imagined was false, I could not, nevertheless, deny that the ideas were really in my thoughts. But, because I had already recognized in myself very clearly that intelligent nature is distinct from the corporeal, considering that all composition is evidence of dependency, and that dependency is manifestly a defect, I thence judged that it could not be a perfection in God to be composed of these two natures, and that, consequently, he was not so composed; but that, if there were any bodies in the world or any intelligences or other natures which were not wholly perfect, their existence must depend on his power, in such a way that they could not subsist without him for a single instant.

I set out after that to seek other truths; and turning to the object   5
of the geometers, which I conceived as a continuous body, or a space extended indefinitely in length, width, and height or depth, divisible into various parts, which could have various figures and sizes and be moved or transposed in all sorts of ways—for the geometers take all that to be in the object of their study—I went through some of their simplest proofs. And having observed that the great certainty that everyone attributes to them is based only on the fact that they are clearly conceived according to the rule I spoke of earlier, I noticed also that they had nothing at all in them which might assure me of the existence of their object. Thus, for example, I very well perceived that, supposing a triangle to be given, its three angles must be equal to two right angles, but I saw nothing, for all that, which assured me that any such triangle existed in the world; whereas, reverting to the examination of the idea I had of a perfect Being, I found that existence was comprised in the idea in the same way that the equality of the three angles of a triangle to two right

angles is comprised in the idea of a triangle or, as in the idea of a sphere, the fact that all its parts are equidistant from its center, or even more obviously so; and that consequently it is at least as certain that God, who is this perfect Being, is, or exists, as any geometric demonstration can be.

But what persuades many people that it is difficult to know this, and even also to know what their soul is, is that they never lift their minds above tangible things, and that they are so accustomed not to think of anything except by imagining it, which is a mode of thinking peculiar to material objects, that everything which is not within the realm of imagination seems to them unintelligible. This is evident enough from the fact that even the philosophers hold as a maxim in the Schools, that there is nothing in the understanding which has not first been in the senses, in which, however, it is certain that ideas about God and the soul have never been; and it seems to me that those who wish to use their imagination to understand them are doing just the same as if, to hear sounds or smell odors, they attempted to use their eyes; except that there is still this difference, that the sense of light assures us no less of the truth of its objects than do the senses of smell and hearing, whereas neither our imagination nor our senses could ever assure us of anything, if our understanding did not intervene. Finally, if there are still men who are not sufficiently persuaded of the existence of God and of their soul by the reasons I have given, I would like them to know that all the other things of which they think themselves perhaps more assured, such as having a body, and that there are stars and an earth, and such like, are less certain; for, although we may have a moral assurance of these things, which is such that it seems that, short of being foolish, no one can doubt their existence, at the same time also, short of being unreasonable, when it is a question of a metaphysical certainty, one cannot deny that there are not sufficient grounds for being absolutely assured, when one observes that one can in the same way imagine, being asleep, that one has another body, and that one sees other stars and another earth, without there being anything of the sort. For how does one know that the thoughts which come while one dreams are false rather than the others, seeing that they are often no less strong and clear? And may the most intelligent men study this question as much as they please, I do not believe that they can give any reason which would be sufficient to remove this doubt, unless they presuppose the existence of God. For, firstly, even the rule which I stated above that I held, namely, that the things we grasp very clearly and very distinctly are all true, is assured only because God is or exists, and because he is a perfect Being, and because everything that is in us comes from him; whence it follows that our ideas and notions, being real things and coming from God, in so far as they are clear and distinct, cannot to this extent be other than true. Accordingly, if we often enough have ideas which contain errors, they can only be those which contain something confused and obscure, because in this they participate in nothingness, that is to say that they are in us in this confused way only because we are not completely perfect. And it is evident that it is no less contradictory that error or imperfection, as such, should proceed from God, than that truth or perfection should come from nothingness. But, if we did not know that all that is in us which is real and true comes from a perfect and infinite Being, we would have no reason which would assure us that, however clear and distinct our ideas might be, they had the perfection of being true.

But, after knowledge of God and of the soul has thus made us certain of this rule, it is a simple matter to understand that the dreams we imagine when we are asleep should not in any way make us doubt the truth of the thoughts we have when we are awake. For, even if it should happen that, while sleeping, one should have some quite distinct idea, as, for example, if a geometer were to discover some new demonstration, his being asleep would not prevent it from being true; and as for the most ordinary error of our dreams, which consists in representing to us various objects in the same way as our waking senses do, it does not matter that they give us occasion to doubt the truth of such ideas, because they can also lead us into error often enough without our being asleep, as when those who have jaundice see everything yellow, or when the stars or other very distant bodies seem to us much smaller than they are. For, finally, whether we are awake or asleep, we should never let ourselves be persuaded except on the evidence of our reason. And it is to be observed that I say: of our reason, and not: of our imagination or our senses. For, although we see the sun very clearly, we should not on that account judge that it is only as large as we see it; and we can well imagine distinctly a lion's head grafted on to the body of a goat, without concluding on that account that there is any such chimera in the world; for reason does not dictate that what we see or imagine thus is true, but it does tell us that all our ideas and notions must have some basis in truth, for it would not be possible that God, who is all perfect and true, should have put them in us unless it were so. And because our reasonings are never so clear or complete while we sleep as when we are awake, even though sometimes our imaginations are as vivid and distinct or even more so, reason tells us that, it not being possible that our thoughts should all be true, because we are

7

not absolutely perfect, what truth there is in them will undoubtedly be found in those we have when we are awake rather than in those we have in our dreams.

QUESTIONS FOR CRITICAL READING

1. Do you perceive a difference between your thoughts when you are awake and your thoughts when you are asleep? Why does Descartes worry about this distinction?
2. Why did Descartes resolve "to pretend that nothing which had ever entered my mind was any more true than the illusions of my dreams" (para. 1)?
3. Why is "I think, therefore I am" a powerful statement guaranteeing certainty on the part of the person who says it?
4. In paragraph 2, Descartes realizes he "was a substance, of which the whole essence or nature consists in thinking . . . so that this 'I,' . . . the mind . . . is entirely distinct from the body." Do you perceive this to be true?
5. Why, in paragraph 4, does he inquire "of something more perfect than myself"?
6. How does Descartes prove the existence of God (paras. 4 and 5)?
7. Do you feel Descartes is right to be suspicious of information gathered through the senses? Under what conditions can the senses be deceiving?

SUGGESTIONS FOR WRITING

1. In paragraph 6, Descartes complains that the "philosophers hold as a maxim in the Schools, that there is nothing in the understanding which has not first been in the senses." Examine that statement for accuracy and then explain in a brief essay why it is important to Descartes's search for the truth.
2. Explain the way in which Descartes, according to his explanations in this "Discourse," proceeded to move toward certainty. He states that his quest is for truth and that in order to begin thinking truthfully he needs to have a statement whose validity is unquestionably true. Once he has that statement, what does he do?
3. One of the problems Descartes faced was the absence of an ironclad way to argue that one is not dreaming all the time. Common sense tells most people whether they are awake or dreaming, but it is certainly possible to dream that one is awake. Examine this question with an eye toward clarifying the issues. Can anyone know positively that he or she is not dreaming?

4. About the most important questions of certainty Descartes says, "Whether we are awake or asleep, we should never let ourselves be persuaded except on the evidence of our reason. And it is to be observed that I say: of our reason, and not: of our imagination or our senses" (para. 7). Explain what Descartes means (you may wish to point to his example, geometry), and then give an example of the process of establishing an important truth by using your reason and not your imagination or senses.

5. Examine Descartes's proof of the existence of God. Does Descartes depend on imagination and the senses, or does he depend only on reason? Is it possible to prove the existence of God using only reason? Would you find it easier to prove the existence of God if you also used your imagination and your senses?

6. **CONNECTIONS**   What intellectual principles does Descartes share with Francis Bacon? You may want to consider the relationship of his four rules of Method—excerpted in the introduction to this piece—with Bacon's four idols. Would Bacon have felt at ease with Descartes's way of thinking, or has Descartes fallen into some of the traps that Bacon warns of?

7. **CONNECTIONS**   Descartes has an interest in dreams, but he dos not assign them much value in his search for knowledge. How would he have reacted to Sigmund Freud's contentions in his selection on the Oedipus complex? Would he have been sympathetic to Freud's view that we can know a great deal about our true nature by analyzing our dreams? Why or why not? Do you think Descartes and Freud are compatible thinkers, or are they simply worlds apart? Explain.

SIGMUND FREUD
The Oedipus Complex

SIGMUND FREUD (1856–1939) is, in the minds of many, the founder of modern psychiatry. He developed the psychoanalytic method: the examination of the mind using dream analysis, the analysis of the unconscious through free association, and the correlation of findings with attitudes toward sexuality and sexual development. His theories changed the way people treated neurosis and most other mental disorders. Today we use terms he either invented or championed, such as *psychoanalysis*, *penis envy*, *Oedipus complex*, and *wish-fulfillment*.

Freud was born in Freiberg, Moravia (now Pribor in the Czech Republic), and moved to Vienna, Austria, when he was four. He pursued a medical career and soon began exploring neurology, which stimulated him to begin his psychoanalytic methods. *The Interpretation of Dreams* (1899) is one of his first important books. It was followed in rapid succession by a number of ground-breaking studies: *The Psychopathology of Everyday Life* (1904), *Three Essays on the Theory of Sexuality* (1905), *Totem and Taboo* (1913), *Beyond the Pleasure Principle* (1920), and *Civilization and Its Discontents* (1930). Freud's personal life in Vienna was essentially uneventful until he was put under house arrest by the Nazis in 1938 because he was Jewish. He was released and then moved to London, where he died the following year.

As a movement, psychoanalysis shocked most of the world by postulating a superego, which establishes high standards of personal behavior; an ego, which corresponds to the apparent personality; an id, which includes the deepest primitive forces of life; and an unconscious, into which thoughts and memories we cannot face are repressed or sublimated. The origin of much mental illness, the

From *The Interpretation of Dreams*. Translated by James Strachey.

theory presumes, lies in the inability of the mind to find a way to sublimate — to express in harmless and creative ways — the painful thoughts that have been repressed. Dreams and unconscious actions sometimes act as releases or harmless expressions of these thoughts and memories.

As Freud states in *The Interpretation of Dreams*, the unconscious works in complex ways to help us cope with feelings and desires that our superego deems unacceptable. Dreams are mental events, not necessarily connected to physical events. The repression of important emotions, a constant process, often results in dreams that express repressed feelings in a harmless and sometimes symbolic way. In a sense, dreams help us maintain our mental health.

Further, dreams are a primary subject matter of psychoanalysis because they reveal a great deal about the unconscious mind, especially the material that we repress from our consciousness. His discussion of the Oedipus complex, which follows, is a classic case in point. Most people found Freud's theory of the Oedipus complex very compelling once they began to understand the details of its expression. Freud assumed that when we are infants we love our opposite-sex parent and hate our same-sex parent. These feelings of love and hate change as we grow, but they can still linger and cause neurotic behavior. Because these feelings are repressed into the unconscious, we are not aware of them as adults.

Freud's Rhetoric

This selection comes from a section of *The Interpretation of Dreams* in which Freud discusses what he calls "typical dreams." It is here that he speaks directly about his theory of the Oedipus complex and links it specifically with two major pieces of Western literature. *Oedipus Rex* by Sophocles (496–406 B.C.) and *Hamlet* by William Shakespeare (1564–1616) are tragedies in which some of the unconscious desires of the hero to marry his mother are either carried out, as in *Oedipus Rex*, or strongly hinted at, as in *Hamlet*.

Freud realizes that many readers will not be convinced that such a compulsion exists. He explains, however, that because most young people outgrow the compulsion and thereafter repress it, most adults are unaware of their own oedipal feelings.

The rhetorical strategy of introducing two classic dramatic works that are centuries apart and demonstrating what they have in common is effective in helping the reader understand that the psychological condition Freud refers to is not unknown to Western culture. His analysis of his patients' dreams has helped dredge up the original content and the connection with the oedipal urge, thus freeing them of a sense of guilt and a need for self-punishment. Paragraphs 2–6 detail the story of King Oedipus and the strange way in which he eventually married his mother and thus brought a plague upon his land. Freud's point is that this ancient text reveals an aspect of the inner nature of the human mind that has not changed for many thousands of years.

As he tells us, his patients have dreams of intercourse with parents and then feel such torrents of guilt and shame that they sometimes become neurotic. The fact that Oedipus severely punishes himself at the end of the play corresponds with the sense of guilt that Freud's patients experience. Hamlet is even more severely punished and suffers even more psychological anguish throughout the play, even though he never commits incest with his mother. The power of thought is enough. Hamlet is described as "a pathologically irresolute character which might be classed as neurasthenic" (para. 7). In other words, he could have benefited from Freud's psychoanalysis.

Freud uses these two great plays as examples of his theories because he sees them as imaginative constructs that work out the repressed feelings people have always had. They are similar to dreams in that they are written by poets; and poets who rely on inspiration have traditionally drawn on the unconscious. Because these two tragedies are so important to Western literature, they have a special value that no minor literature could have. Consequently, they have been enormously convincing to those interested in the way the mind works. What Freud has done with these works is to hold them up as a mirror. In that mirror one can see quite clearly the evidence for the Oedipus complex that would be totally invisible in any self-examination. It is one of Freud's great rhetorical achievements.

In paragraph 8 Freud makes some other observations about the dreams some of his patients have had in which they imagined themselves killing their parents. This is such a horrible idea for most people that Freud is surprised that our internal censor permits such dreams to occur. His theory is that the thought is so monstrous that the dream censor "is not armed to meet" it (para. 8). His analysis suggests that worry about a parent may disguise the unconscious wish that the parent should die. Freud mentions "our explanation of dreams in general" (para. 8), by which he means that dreams are wish-fulfillments. If that is true, those who dream about killing a parent are likely to be deeply upset and may make themselves neurotic by their own sense of guilt.

Though most people go through an infantile Oedipal stage, they usually grow out of it early in life. Freud suggests, however, that those who do not grow out of it may need psychoanalytic help.

PREREADING QUESTIONS: WHAT TO READ FOR

The following prereading questions may help you anticipate key issues in the discussion of Sigmund Freud's "The Oedipus Complex." Keeping them in mind during your first reading of the selection should help focus your attention.

- What, exactly, is the Oedipus complex ?
- How does the Oedipus complex express itself in dreams?
- How do *Oedipus Rex* and *Hamlet* illustrate the Oedipus complex?

The Oedipus Complex

In my experience, which is already extensive, the chief part in   1
the mental lives of all children who later become psychoneurotics is played by their parents. Being in love with the one parent and hating the other are among the essential constituents of the stock of psychical impulses which is formed at that time and which is of such importance in determining the symptoms of the later neurosis. It is not my belief, however, that psychoneurotics differ sharply in this respect from other human beings who remain normal—that they are able, that is, to create something absolutely new and peculiar to themselves. It is far more probable—and this is confirmed by occasional observations on normal children—that they are only distinguished by exhibiting on a magnified scale feelings of love and hatred to their parents which occur less obviously and less intensely in the minds of most children.

This discovery is confirmed by a legend that has come down to   2
us from classical antiquity: a legend whose profound and universal power to move can only be understood if the hypothesis I have put forward in regard to the psychology of children has an equally universal validity. What I have in mind is the legend of King Oedipus and Sophocles' drama which bears his name.

Oedipus, son of Laïus, King of Thebes, and of Jocasta, was ex- 3
posed as an infant because an oracle had warned Laïus that the still
unborn child would be his father's murderer. The child was rescued,
and grew up as a prince in an alien court, until, in doubts as to his origin, he too questioned the oracle and was warned to avoid his home
since he was destined to murder his father and take his mother in marriage. On the road leading away from what he believed was his home,
he met King Laïus and slew him in a sudden quarrel. He came next to
Thebes and solved the riddle set him by the Sphinx who barred his
way. Out of gratitude the Thebans made him their king and gave him
Jocasta's hand in marriage. He reigned long in peace and honour, and
she who, unknown to him, was his mother bore him two sons and
two daughters. Then at last a plague broke out and the Thebans made
enquiry once more of the oracle. It is at this point that Sophocles'
tragedy opens. The messengers bring back the reply that the plague
will cease when the murderer of Laïus has been driven from the land.

> But he, where is he? Where shall now be read
> The fading record of this ancient guilt?

The action of the play consists in nothing other than the process of
revealing, with cunning delays and ever-mounting excitement—a
process that can be likened to the work of a psycho-analysis—that
Oedipus himself is the murderer of Laïus, but further that he is the
son of the murdered man and of Jocasta. Appalled at the abomina-
tion which he has unwittingly perpetrated, Oedipus blinds himself
and forsakes his home. The oracle has been fulfilled.

Oedipus Rex is what is known as a tragedy of destiny. Its tragic 4
effect is said to lie in the contrast between the supreme will of the
gods and the vain attempts of mankind to escape the evil that threatens them. The lesson which, it is said, the deeply moved spectator
should learn from the tragedy is submission to the divine will and
realization of his own impotence. Modern dramatists have accordingly tried to achieve a similar tragic effect by weaving the same contrast into a plot invented by themselves. But the spectators have
looked on unmoved while a curse or an oracle was fulfilled in spite
of all the efforts of some innocent man: later tragedies of destiny
have failed in their effect.

If *Oedipus Rex* moves a modern audience no less than it did the 5
contemporary Greek one, the explanation can only be that its effect
does not lie in the contrast between destiny and human will, but is to
be looked for in the particular nature of the material on which that
contrast is exemplified. There must be something which makes a voice
within us ready to recognize the compelling force of destiny in the
Oedipus, while we can dismiss as merely arbitrary such dispositions as

are laid down in *Die Ahnfrau*[1] or other modern tragedies of destiny.
And a factor of this kind is in fact involved in the story of King Oedipus. His destiny moves us only because it might have been ours—
because the oracle laid the same curse upon us before our birth as
upon him. It is the fate of all of us, perhaps, to direct our first sexual
impulse towards our mother and our first hatred and our first murder-
ous wish against our father. Our dreams convince us that that is so.
King Oedipus, who slew his father Laïus and married his mother Jocasta, merely shows us the fulfilment of our own childhood wishes.
But, more fortunate than he, we have meanwhile succeeded, in so far
as we have not become psychoneurotics, in detaching our sexual impulses from our mothers and in forgetting our jealousy of our fathers.
Here is one in whom these primaeval wishes of our childhood have
been fulfilled, and we shrink back from him with the whole force of
the repression by which those wishes have since that time been held
down within us. While the poet, as he unravels the past, brings to light
the guilt of Oedipus, he is at the same time compelling us to recognize
our own inner minds, in which those same impulses, though suppressed, are still to be found. The contrast with which the closing Chorus leaves us confronted—

> . . Fix on Oedipus your eyes,
> Who resolved the dark enigma, noblest champion and most wise.
> Like a star his envied fortune mounted beaming far and wide:
> Now he sinks in seas of anguish, whelmed beneath a raging tide . . .

—strikes as a warning at ourselves and our pride, at us who since
our childhood have grown so wise and so mighty in our own eyes.
Like Oedipus, we live in ignorance of these wishes, repugnant to
morality, which have been forced upon us by Nature, and after their
revelation we may all of us well seek to close our eyes to the scenes
of our childhood.[2]

---

[1] **Die Ahnfrau** Franz Grillparzer (1791–1872) wrote *Die Ahnfrau* (The An-
cesstress).

[2] [*Footnote added* 1914:] None of the findings of psychoanalytic research has
provoked such embittered denials, such fierce opposition—or such amusing
contortions—on the part of critics as this indication of the childhood impulses towards incest which persist in the unconscious. An attempt has even been made recently to make out, in the face of all experience, that the incest should only be taken
as "symbolic."—Ferenczi (1912) has proposed an ingenious "over-interpretation" of
the Oedipus myth, based on a passage in one of Schopenhauer's letters.—[*Added*
1919:] Later studies have shown that the "Oedipus complex," which was touched
upon for the first time in the above paragraphs in the *Interpretation of Dreams*, throws
a light of undreamt-of importance on the history of the human race and the evolution
of religion and morality. (See my *Totem and Taboo*, 1912–13.) [Freud's notes]

There is an unmistakable indication in the text of Sophocles' 6 tragedy itself that the legend of Oedipus sprang from some primaeval dream-material which had as its content the distressing disturbance of a child's relation to his parents owing to the first stirrings of sexuality. At a point when Oedipus, though he is not yet enlightened, has begun to feel troubled by his recollection of the oracle, Jocasta consoles him by referring to a dream which many people dream, though, as she thinks, it has no meaning:

> Many a man ere now in dreams hath lain
> With her who bare him. He hath least annoy
> Who with such omens troubleth not his mind.

To-day, just as then, many men dream of having sexual relations with their mothers, and speak of the fact with indignation and astonishment. It is clearly the key to the tragedy and the complement to the dream of the dreamer's father being dead. The story of Oedipus is the reaction of the imagination to these two typical dreams. And just as these dreams, when dreamt by adults, are accompanied by feelings of repulsion, so too the legend must include horror and self-punishment. Its further modification originates once again in a misconceived secondary revision of the material, which has sought to exploit it for theological purposes. The attempt to harmonize divine omnipotence with human responsibility must naturally fail in connection with this subject-matter just as with any other.

Another of the great creations of tragic poetry, Shakespeare's *Hamlet*, has its roots in the same soil as *Oedipus Rex*. But the changed treatment of the same material reveals the whole difference in the mental life of these two widely separated epochs of civilization: the secular advance of repression in the emotional life of mankind. In the *Oedipus* the child's wishful phantasy that underlies it is brought into the open and realized as it would be in a dream. In *Hamlet* it remains repressed; and —just as in the case of a neurosis—we only learn of its existence from its inhibiting consequences. Strangely enough, the overwhelming effect produced by the more modern tragedy has turned out to be compatible with the fact that people have remained completely in the dark as to the hero's character. The play is built up on Hamlet's hesitations over fulfilling the task of revenge that is assigned to him; but its text offers no reasons or motives for these hesitations and an immense variety of attempts at interpreting them have failed to produce a result. According to the view which was originated by Goethe[3] and is still the

---

[3]**Johann Wolfgang Von Goethe (1749–1832)** One of Germany's greatest writers.

prevailing one to-day, Hamlet represents the type of man whose power of direct action is paralysed by an excessive development of his intellect. (He is "sicklied o'er with the pale cast of thought.") According to another view, the dramatist has tried to portray a pathologically irresolute character which might be classed as neurasthenic. The plot of the drama shows us, however, that Hamlet is far from being represented as a person incapable of taking any action. We see him doing so on two occasions: first in a sudden outburst of temper, when he runs his sword through the eavesdropper behind the arras, and secondly in a premeditated and even crafty fashion, when, with all the callousness of a Renaissance prince, he sends the two courtiers to the death that had been planned for himself. What is it, then, that inhibits him in fulfilling the task set him by his father's ghost? The answer, once again, is that it is the peculiar nature of the task. Hamlet is able to do anything—except take vengeance on the man who did away with his father and took that father's place with his mother, the man who shows him the repressed wishes of his own childhood realized. Thus the loathing which should drive him on to revenge is replaced in him by self-reproaches, by scruples of conscience, which remind him that he himself is literally no better than the sinner whom he is to punish. Here I have translated into conscious terms what was bound to remain unconscious in Hamlet's mind; and if anyone is inclined to call him a hysteric, I can only accept the fact as one that is implied by my interpretation. The distaste for sexuality expressed by Hamlet in his conversation with Ophelia fits in very well with this: the same distaste which was destined to take possession of the poet's mind more and more during the years that followed, and which reached its extreme expression in *Timon of Athens*. For it can of course only be the poet's own mind which confronts us in Hamlet. I observe in a book on Shakespeare by Georg Brandes (1896) a statement that *Hamlet* was written immediately after the death of Shakespeare's father (in 1601), that is, under the immediate impact of his bereavement and, as we may well assume, while his childhood feelings about his father had been freshly revived. It is known, too, that Shakespeare's own son who died at an early age bore the name of "Hamnet," which is identical with "Hamlet." Just as *Hamlet* deals with the relation of a son to his parents, so *Macbeth* (written at approximately the same period) is concerned with the subject of childlessness. But just as all neurotic symptoms, and, for that matter, dreams, are capable of being "over-interpreted" and indeed need to be, if they are to be fully understood, so all genuinely creative writings are the product of more than a single motive and more than a single impulse in the poet's mind, and are open to more than a single interpretation. In what I have written I have only attempted to interpret the deepest layer of impulses in the mind of the creative writer.[4]

I cannot leave the subject of typical dreams of the death of loved relatives, without adding a few more words to throw light on their significance for the theory of dreams in general. In these dreams we find the highly unusual condition realized of a dream-thought formed by a repressed wish entirely eluding censorship and passing into the dream without modification. There must be special factors at work to make this event possible, and I believe that the occurrence of these dreams is facilitated by two such factors. Firstly, there is no wish that seems more remote from us than this one: "we couldn't even *dream*"—so we believe—of wishing such a thing. For this reason the dream-censorship is not armed to meet such a monstrosity, just as Solon's[5] penal code contained no punishment for parricide. Secondly, in this case the repressed and unsuspected wish is particularly often met half-way by a residue from the previous day in the form of a *worry* about the safety of the person concerned. This worry can only make its way into the dream by availing itself of the corresponding wish; while the wish can disguise itself behind the worry that has become active during the day. We may feel inclined to think that things are simpler than this and that one merely carries on during the night and in dreams with what one has been turning over in one's mind during the day; but if so we shall be leaving dreams of the death of people of whom the dreamer is fond completely in the air and without any connection with our explanation of dreams in general, and we shall thus be clinging quite unnecessarily to a riddle which is perfectly capable of solution.

It is also instructive to consider the relation of these dreams to anxiety-dreams. In the dreams we have been discussing, a repressed wish has found a means of evading censorship—and the distortion which censorship involves. The invariable concomitant is that painful feelings are experienced in the dream. In just the same way

---

[4][*Footnote added* 1919:] The above indications of a psycho-analytic explanation of *Hamlet* have since been amplified by Ernest Jones and defended against the alternative views put forward in the literature of the subject. [*Added* 1930:] Incidentally, I have in the meantime ceased to believe that the author of Shakespeare's works was the man from Stratford. [*Added* 1919:] Further attempts at an analysis of *Macbeth* will be found in a paper of mine [Freud, 1916d] and in one by Jekels (1917). [Freud's notes]

[5]**Solon (638–558 B.C.)** Greek known as the law giver. His ideas on law continue to influence us today.

anxiety-dreams only occur if the censorship has been wholly or partly overpowered; and, on the other hand, the overpowering of the censorship is facilitated if anxiety has already been produced as an immediate sensation arising from somatic[6] sources. We can thus plainly see the purpose for which the censorship exercises its office and brings about the distortion of dreams: it does so *in order to prevent the generation of anxiety or other forms of distressing affect.*

---

[6] **Somatic** Having to do with the physical body.

QUESTIONS FOR CRITICAL READING

1. What role do parents play in the lives of those who become neurotics?
2. Do psychoneurotics differ substantially from normal people?
3. What does Freud expect his example of *Oedipus Rex* to call up in the mind of the reader?
4. What is a tragedy of destiny?
5. In what ways are all of us like Oedipus?
6. How is literature related to dreams, according to Freud?
7. Why do dreams sometimes need to be overinterpreted?
8. How does censorship operate in dreams?

SUGGESTIONS FOR WRITING

1. Most adults have absolutely no awareness of having had an oedipal period in their infancy. However, you may have observed oedipal behavior in young children. If so, describe how the children behaved and if possible describe how they have grown up and whether they have left the oedipal stage behind. Do your observations help to bolster Freud's views, or do they help to weaken them?
2. Describe in as much detail as possible any anxiety dreams you may have had. Often anxiety dreams are repetitive and recurrent. What are the circumstances in which you find yourself in your dream? What worries you most in the dream? What threatens you most? How does the dream resolve itself? Does the dream provoke guilt or shame? How would you interpret the dream in the light of what you have read here?
3. If you find yourself unable to remember your dreams, interview some friends and "collect" dreams from them. Ask them for dreams that make them feel uneasy—anxiety dreams. Have them write down their dreams and then ask them to talk about events in their waking life that preceded the dreams. See if there are contributing events or anticipations in the mind of the dreamers that would lead them to have anxiety

dreams. See, too, if there are any patterns to dreams of different people. Are there any "typical dreams" shared by your friends?

4. What are your typical dreams? Try to write them out as if they were plays. Identify characters, setting, and time, and then write the dialogue and stage directions that would give a good approximation of the content of the dreams. Do not censor your dreams or try to "overanalyze" them (despite Freud's recommendation). Do your best to make the dreams clear in their expression. Does this approach make your dreams any more meaningful to you? Explain.

5. Does your reading of *Hamlet* help to bear out Freud's theory that suggests Hamlet is suffering from an Oedipus complex? What is his relationship to his mother? How does she regard him? Is his killing of King Claudius an act of parricide? Is Hamlet's punishment warranted? Argue for or against Freud's view of the play.

6. **SEEING CONNECTIONS** The following photograph shows Sigmund Freud and his dog in his study in Vienna, the room in which he psychoanalyzed his patients. In the background can be seen a framed picture of a dog, book-lined shelves, glass-fronted cabinets filled with curios, and several masks and small statues. Freud occupied this study for forty-seven years, until the Nazi German annexation of Austria in March 1938 forced him and his family to flee to London.

   Examine the photograph closely. How does this it compare with the portrait of Freud on p. 468? Based on the objects that surround him, what can you tell about Freud and his interests? If you were a patient visiting Freud's office, how at ease do you think you would be about disclosing your innermost thoughts in this environment? Why?

7. In paragraph 6 Freud states, "There is an unmistakable indication in the text of Sophocles' tragedy itself that the legend of Oedipus sprang from some primaeval dream-material." Examine his evidence for this claim and decide yourself whether this seems a reasonable conclusion.

8. Most horror films involve monstrous actions and severe punishment. Is it possible that one of the functions of horror films is to reveal some of the inner nature of our minds somewhat the way *Oedipus Rex* and *Hamlet* do? Choose a favorite film and analyze it in terms of its revealing hidden desires that might trouble us if we felt them consciously and acted on them in life.

9. **CONNECTIONS**   Freud's early discussion of the Oedipus complex concentrated on the masculine dimensions of the mental state he describes. Oedipus and Hamlet are obviously male. But Melanie Klein focuses on her female child patients with no specific reference to literature of any kind. To what extent do Freud and Klein agree about the force of the Oedipus complex in individuals' lives? What are the similarities and differences in their observations of their patients?

CARL JUNG
The Personal and
the Collective Unconscious

CARL GUSTAV JUNG (1875–1961), Freud's most famous disciple, was a Swiss physician who collaborated with Freud from 1907 to 1912, when the two argued about the nature of the unconscious. Jung's *Psychology of the Unconscious* (1912) posits an unconscious that is composed of more than the ego, superego, and id. According to Jung, an additional aspect of the unconscious is a collection of archetypal images that can be inherited by members of the same group. Experience clarifies these images, but the images in turn direct experience.

In one of his essays on the collective unconscious, Jung asserts that the great myths express the archetypes of actions and heroes stored in the unconscious by elucidating them for the individual and society. These archetypes represent themselves in mythic literature in images, such as the great father or the great mother, or in patterns of action, such as disobedience and self-sacrifice. They transcend social barriers and exemplify themselves similarly in most people in any given cultural group. For Jung, the individual must adapt to the archetypes that reveal themselves in the myths in order to be psychically healthy.

Like Freud, Jung postulates a specific model of the way the mind works: he claims the existence not only of a conscious mind—which all of us can attest to from experience and common sense—but also of an unconscious component to the mind. He argues that we are unaware of the content of our unconscious mind except, perhaps, in dreams (which occur when we are unconscious), which Freud and others insist speak to us in symbols rather than in direct language.

From *The Basic Writings of C. G. Jung.* Translated by Cary F. Baynes.

Jung also acknowledges the symbolic nature of the unconscious but disagrees with the source of the content of the unconscious mind.

In "The Personal and the Collective Unconscious" (1916), Jung describes the pattern of psychological transference that most psychoanalysts experience with their patients. In the case presented here, the patient's problems were associated with her father, and the transference was the normal one of conceiving of the doctor—in this case, Jung—in terms of the father. When this transference occurs, the patient often is cured of the problems that brought her to the psychoanalyst, but in this case the transference was incomplete. Jung offers a detailed analysis of the dreams that revealed the problems with the transference and describes the intellectual state of the woman whose dreams form the basis of the discussion. She is intelligent, conscious of the mechanism of transference, and careful about her own inner life. Yet the dream that Jung analyzes had a content that he could not relate to her personal life.

In an attempt to explain his inability to analyze the woman's dream strictly in terms of her personal life, Jung reexamines Freud's definition of the unconscious. As Jung explains Freud's view, the unconscious is a repository for material that is produced by the conscious mind and later repressed so as not to interfere with the function of the conscious mind. Thus, painful memories and unpleasant fears are often repressed and rarely become problems because they are sublimated—transformed into harmless activity, often dreams— and released. According to Freud, the material in the unconscious mind develops solely from personal experience.

Jung, however, argues that personal experiences form only part of the individual's unconscious, what he calls the "personal unconscious" (para. 17). For the patient in this essay, the images in the dream that he and the patient at first classified as a transference dream (in which the doctor became the father/lover figure) had qualities that could not be explained fully by transference. Instead, the dream seemed to represent a primordial figure, a god. From this, Jung develops the view that such a figure is cultural in nature and not personal. Nothing in the patient's life pointed to her concern for a god of the kind that developed in her dream. Jung proposes that the images that constituted the content of her dream were not a result of personal experience or education but, instead, were inherited. Jung defines this portion of the unconscious as the "collective unconscious" (para. 19).

Jung's theories proved unacceptable to Freud. After their collaboration ended, Jung studied the world's myths and mythic systems, including alchemy and occult literature. In them he saw many of the archetypal symbols that he felt were revealed in dreams— including symbolic quests, sudden transformations, dramatic or threatening landscapes, and images of God. His conclusions were that this literature, most or all of which was suppressed or rejected by modern religions such as Christianity, was a repository for the symbols of the collective unconscious—at least of Western civilization and perhaps of other civilizations.

Jung's Rhetoric

Like Freud, Jung tells a story. His selection is a narrative beginning with a recapitulation of Freud's view of the unconscious. Jung tells us that according to the conventional view, the contents of the unconscious have passed "the threshold of consciousness" (para. 2): in other words they were once in the conscious mind of the individual. However, Jung also asserts that "the unconscious also contains components that have *not yet* reached the threshold of consciousness" (para. 3). At least two questions arise from this assertion: What is that content, and where did it come from?

Jung then provides the "example" (para. 5) of the woman whose therapy he was conducting. He tells us, as one would tell a story, about the woman's treatment and how such treatment works in a general sense. He explains the phenomenon of transference, claiming that "a successful transference can . . . cause the whole neurosis to disappear" (para. 5). Near the end of this patient's treatment he analyzed her dreams and found something he did not expect. He relates the narrative of the dream (para. 10), which includes the image of a superhuman father figure in a field of wheat swaying in the wind. From this he concludes that the image of the dream is not the doctor/father/lover figure that is common to transference—and that the patient was thoroughly aware of—but something of an entirely different order. He connects it to an archetype of God and proceeds to an analysis that explains the dream in terms of a collective unconscious whose content is shared by groups of people rather than created by the individual alone.

Jung's rhetorical strategy here is an argument proceeding from both example and analysis. The example is given in detail, along with enough background to make it useful to the reader. Then the example is narrated carefully, and its content is examined through a process of analysis familiar to those in psychiatry.

Some of the material in this selection is relatively challenging because Jung uses technical language and occasionally obscure references. However, the simplicity of the technique of narrative, telling a story of what happened, makes the selection intelligible, even though it deals with highly complex and controversial ideas.

The Personal and
the Collective Unconscious

In Freud's view, as most people know, the contents of the un- 1
conscious are limited to infantile tendencies which are repressed because of their incompatible character. Repression is a process that begins in early childhood under the moral influence of the environment and lasts throughout life. Through analysis the repressions are removed and the repressed wishes made conscious.

According to this theory, the unconscious contains only those 2
parts of the personality which could just as well be conscious and are in fact suppressed only through upbringing. Although from one point of view the infantile tendencies of the unconscious are the most conspicuous, it would nonetheless be incorrect to define or evaluate the unconscious entirely in these terms. The unconscious has still another side to it: it includes not only repressed contents, but also all psychic material that lies below the threshold of consciousness. It is impossible to explain the subliminal nature of all this material on the principle of repression; otherwise, through the removal of repressions, a man would acquire a phenomenal memory which would thenceforth forget nothing.

We therefore emphatically say that in addition to the repressed 3
material the unconscious contains all those psychic components that have fallen below the threshold, including subliminal sense perceptions. Moreover we know, from abundant experience as well as for theoretical reasons, that the unconscious also contains components that have *not yet* reached the threshold of consciousness.

These are the seeds of future conscious contents. Equally we have reason to suppose that the unconscious is never at rest in the sense of being inactive, but is continually engaged in grouping and regrouping its contents. Only in pathological cases can this activity be regarded as completely autonomous; normally it is co-ordinated with the conscious mind in a compensatory relationship.

It is to be assumed that all these contents are personal in so far   4
as they are acquired during the individual's life. Since this life is limited, the number of acquired contents in the unconscious must also be limited. This being so, it might be thought possible to empty the unconscious either by analysis or by making a complete inventory of unconscious contents, on the ground that the unconscious cannot produce anything more than is already known and accepted in the conscious mind. We should also have to infer, as already indicated, that if one could stop the descent of conscious contents into the unconscious by doing away with repression, unconscious productivity would be paralyzed. This is possible only to a very limited extent, as we know from experience. We urge our patients to hold fast to repressed contents that have been re-associated with consciousness, and to assimilate them into their plan of life. But this procedure, as we may daily convince ourselves, makes no impression on the unconscious, since it calmly continues to produce dreams and fantasies which, according to Freud's original theory, must arise from personal repressions. If in such cases we pursue our observations systematically and without prejudice, we shall find material which, although similar in form to the previous personal contents, yet seems to contain allusions that go far beyond the personal sphere.

Casting about in my mind for an example to illustrate what I   5
have just said, I have a particularly vivid memory of a woman patient with a mild hysterical neurosis which, as we expressed it in those days, had its principal cause in a "father complex." By this we wanted to denote the fact that the patient's peculiar relationship to her father stood in her way. She had been on very good terms with her father, who had since died. It was a relationship chiefly of feeling. In such cases it is usually the intellectual function that is developed, and this later becomes the bridge to the world. Accordingly our patient became a student of philosophy. Her energetic pursuit of knowledge was motivated by her need to extricate herself from the emotional entanglement with her father. This operation may succeed if her feelings can find an outlet on the new intellectual level, perhaps in the formation of an emotional tie with a suitable man, equivalent to the former tie. In this particular case, however, the transition refused to take place, because the patient's feelings remained

suspended, oscillating between her father and a man who was not altogether suitable. The progress of her life was thus held up, and that inner disunity so characteristic of a neurosis promptly made its appearance. The so-called normal person would probably be able to break the emotional bond in one or the other direction by a powerful act of will, or else—and this is perhaps the more usual thing—he would come through the difficulty unconsciously, on the smooth path of instinct, without ever being aware of the sort of conflict that lay behind his headaches or other physical discomforts. But any weakness of instinct (which may have many causes) is enough to hinder a smooth unconscious transition. Then all progress is delayed by conflict, and the resulting stasis of life is equivalent to a neurosis. In consequence of the standstill, psychic energy flows off in every conceivable direction, apparently quite uselessly. For instance, there are excessive innervations of the sympathetic system, which lead to nervous disorders of the stomach and intestines; or the vagus (and consequently the heart) is stimulated; or fantasies and memories, uninteresting enough in themselves, become overvalued and prey on the conscious mind (mountains out of molehills). In this state a new motive is needed to put an end to the morbid suspension. Nature herself paves the way for this, unconsciously and indirectly, through the phenomenon of the transference (Freud). In the course of treatment the patient transfers the father imago[1] to the doctor, thus making him, in a sense, the father, and in the sense that he is *not* the father, also making him a substitute for the man she cannot reach. The doctor therefore becomes both a father and a kind of lover—in other words, the object of conflict. In him the opposites are united, and for this reason he stands for a quasi-ideal solution of the conflict. Without in the least wishing it, he draws upon himself an overvaluation that is almost incredible to the outsider, for to the patient he seems like a savior or a god. This way of speaking is not altogether so laughable as it sounds. It is indeed a bit much to be a father and lover at once. Nobody could possibly stand up to it in the long run, precisely because it is too much of a good thing. One would have to be a demigod at least to sustain such a role without a break, for all the time one would have to be the giver. To the patient in the state of transference, this provisional solution naturally seems ideal, but only at first; in the end she comes to a standstill that is just as bad as the neurotic conflict was. Fundamentally, nothing has yet happened that might lead to a real solution. The conflict has merely been

---

[1] **imago** Idealized image of a person.

transferred. Nevertheless a successful transference can—at least temporarily—cause the whole neurosis to disappear, and for this reason
it has been very rightly recognized by Freud as a healing factor of first-
rate importance, but, at the same time, as a provisional state only, for
although it holds out the possibility of a cure, it is far from being the
cure itself.

  This somewhat lengthy discussion seemed to me essential if my   6
example was to be understood, for my patient had arrived at the
state of transference and had already reached the upper limit where
the standstill begins to make itself disagreeable. The question now
arose: what next? I had of course become the complete savior, and
the thought of having to give me up was not only exceedingly dis-
tasteful to the patient, but positively terrifying. In such a situation
"sound common sense" generally comes out with a whole repertory
of admonitions: "you simply must," "you really ought," "you just
cannot," etc. So far as sound common sense is, happily, not too rare
and not entirely without effect (pessimists, I know, exist), a rational
motive can, in the exuberant feeling of health you get from transference, release so much enthusiasm that a painful sacrifice can be
risked with a mighty effort of will. If successful—and these things
sometimes are—the sacrifice bears blessed fruit, and the erstwhile
patient leaps at one bound into the state of being practically cured.
The doctor is generally so delighted that he fails to tackle the theoretical difficulties connected with this little miracle.

  If the leap does not succeed—and it did not succeed with   7
my patient—one is then faced with the problem of severing the
transference. Here "psychoanalytic" theory shrouds itself in a thick
darkness. Apparently we are to fall back on some nebulous trust in
fate: somehow or other the matter will settle itself. "The transference
stops automatically when the patient runs out of money," as a
slightly cynical colleague once remarked to me. Or the ineluctable
demands of life make it impossible for the patient to linger on in the
transference—demands which compel the involuntary sacrifice,
sometimes with a more or less complete relapse as a result. (One
may look in vain for accounts of such cases in the books that sing
the praises of psychoanalysis!)

  To be sure, there are hopeless cases where nothing helps; but   8
there are also cases that do not get stuck and do not inevitably leave
the transference situation with bitter hearts and sore heads. I told
myself, at this juncture with my patient, that there must be a clear
and respectable way out of the impasse. My patient had long since
run out of money—if indeed she ever possessed any—but I was
curious to know what means nature would devise for a satisfactory

way out of the transference deadlock. Since I never imagined that I was blessed with that "sound common sense" which always knows exactly what to do in every tangled situation, and since my patient knew as little as I, I suggested to her that we could at least keep an eye open for any movements coming from a sphere of the psyche uncontaminated by our superior wisdom and our conscious plannings. That meant first and foremost her dreams.

Dreams contain images and thought associations which we do   9 not create with conscious intent. They arise spontaneously without our assistance and are representatives of a psychic activity withdrawn from our arbitrary will. Therefore the dream is, properly speaking, a highly objective, natural product of the psyche, from which we might expect indications, or at least hints, about certain basic trends in the psychic process. Now, since the psychic process, like any other life process, is not just a causal sequence, but is also a process with a teleological orientation,[2] we might expect dreams to give us certain indicia about the objective causality as well as about the objective tendencies, because they are nothing less than self-portraits of the psychic life process.

On the basis of these reflections, then, we subjected the dreams   10 to a careful examination. It would lead too far to quote word for word all the dreams that now followed. Let it suffice to sketch their main character: the majority referred to the person of the doctor, that is to say, the actors were unmistakably the dreamer herself and her doctor. The latter, however, seldom appeared in this natural shape, but was generally distorted in a remarkable way. Sometimes his figure was of supernatural size, sometimes he seemed to be extremely aged, then again he resembled her father, but was at the same time curiously woven into nature, as in the following dream: *Her father (who in reality was of small stature) was standing with her on a hill that was covered with wheat fields. She was quite tiny beside him, and he seemed to her like a giant. He lifted her up from the ground and held her in his arms like a little child. The wind swept over the wheat fields, and as the wheat swayed in the wind, he rocked her in his arms.*

From this dream and from others like it I could discern various   11 things. Above all I got the impression that her unconscious was holding unshakably to the idea of my being the father-lover, so that the fatal tie we were trying to undo appeared to be doubly strengthened. Moreover one could hardly avoid seeing that the unconscious placed a special emphasis on the supernatural, almost "divine" nature

---

[2] **teleological orientation** Possessing a sense of design; directed toward an end or purpose.

of the father-lover, thus accentuating still further the overvaluation occasioned by the transference. I therefore asked myself whether the patient had still not understood the wholly fantastic character of her transference, or whether perhaps the unconscious could never be reached by understanding at all, but must blindly and idiotically pursue some nonsensical chimera. Freud's idea that the unconscious can "do nothing but wish," Schopenhauer's[3] blind and aimless Will, the gnostic demi-urge who in his vanity deems himself perfect and then in the blindness of his limitation creates something lamentably imperfect—all these pessimistic suspicions of an essentially negative background to the world and the soul came threateningly near. And indeed there would be nothing to set against this except a well-meaning "you ought," reinforced by a stroke of the ax that would cut down the whole phantasmagoria for good and all.

But as I turned the dreams over and over in my mind, there 12 dawned on me another possibility. I said to myself: it cannot be denied that the dreams continue to speak in the same old metaphors with which our conversations have made both doctor and patient sickeningly familiar. But the patient has an undoubted understanding of her transference fantasy. She knows that I appear to her as a semidivine father-lover, and she can, at least intellectually, distinguish this from my factual reality. Therefore the dreams are obviously reiterating the conscious standpoint minus the conscious criticism, which they completely ignore. They reiterate the conscious contents, not *in toto*, but insist on the fantastic standpoint as opposed to "sound common sense."

I naturally asked myself what was the source of this obstinacy 13 and what was its purpose? That it must have some purposive meaning I was convinced, for there is no truly living thing that does not have a final meaning, that can in other words be explained as a mere leftover from antecedent facts. But the energy of the transference is so strong that it gives one the impression of a vital instinct. That being so, what is the purpose of such fantasies? A careful examination and analysis of the dreams, especially of the one just quoted, revealed a very marked tendency—in contrast to conscious criticism, which always seeks to reduce things to human proportions—to endow the person of the doctor with superhuman attributes. He had to be gigantic, primordial, huger than the father, like the wind that sweeps over the earth—was he then to be made into a god? Or, I said to myself, was it rather the case that the unconscious was trying to *create* a god out of the person of the doctor, as it were to free a vision of God from the veils of the personal, so that the transference to

---

[3] **Arthur Schopenhauer (1788–1860)** German pessimistic philosopher.

the person of the doctor was no more than a misunderstanding on the part of the conscious mind, a stupid trick played by "sound common sense"? Was the urge of the unconscious perhaps only apparently reaching out towards the person, but in a deeper sense towards a god? Could the longing for a god be a *passion* welling up from our darkest, instinctual nature, a passion unswayed by any outside influences, deeper and stronger perhaps than the love for a human person? Or was it perhaps the highest and truest meaning of that inappropriate love we call transference, a little bit of real *Gottesminne*,[4] that has been lost to consciousness ever since the fifteenth century?

No one will doubt the reality of a passionate longing for a human person; but that a fragment of religious psychology, an historical anachronism, indeed something of a medieval curiosity—we are reminded of Mechtild of Magdeburg[5]—should come to light as an immediate living reality in the middle of the consulting room, and be expressed in the prosaic figure of the doctor, seems almost too fantastic to be taken seriously.   14

A genuinely scientific attitude must be unprejudiced. The sole criterion for the validity of an hypothesis is whether or not it possesses an heuristic—i.e., explanatory—value. The question now is, can we regard the possibilities set forth above as a valid hypothesis? There is no a priori[6] reason why it should not be just as possible that the unconscious tendencies have a goal beyond the human person, as that the unconscious can "do nothing but wish." Experience alone can decide which is the more suitable hypothesis.   15

This new hypothesis was not entirely plausible to my very critical patient. The earlier view that I was the father-lover, and as such presented an ideal solution of the conflict, was incomparably more attractive to her way of feeling. Nevertheless her intellect was sufficiently clear to appreciate the theoretical possibility of the new hypothesis. Meanwhile the dreams continued to disintegrate the person of the doctor and swell them to ever vaster proportions. Concurrently with this there now occurred something which at first I alone perceived, and with the utmost astonishment, namely a kind of subterranean undermining of the transference. Her relations with a certain friend deepened perceptibly, notwithstanding the fact that consciously she still clung to the transference. So that when the time came for leaving   16

---

[4] **Gottesminne** Love of God.
[5] **Mechtild of Magdeburg (1207–1282)** Thirteenth-century German mystic, writer, and saint.
[6] **a priori** Based on theory rather than on experiment or evidence.

me, it was no catastrophe, but a perfectly reasonable parting. I had the privilege of being the only witness during the process of severance. I saw how the transpersonal control point developed—I cannot call it anything else—a *guiding function* and step by step gathered to itself all the former personal overvaluations; how, with this afflux of energy, it gained influence over the resisting conscious mind without the patient's consciously noticing what was happening. From this I realized that the dreams were not just fantasies, but self-representations of unconscious developments which allowed the psyche of the patient gradually to grow out of the pointless personal tie.

This change took place, as I showed, through the unconscious   17
development of a transpersonal control point; a virtual goal, as it were, that expressed itself symbolically in a form which can only be described as a vision of God. The dreams swelled the human person of the doctor to superhuman proportions, making him a gigantic primordial father who is at the same time the wind, and in whose protecting arms the dreamer rests like an infant. If we try to make the patient's conscious, and traditionally Christian, idea of God responsible for the divine image in the dreams, we would still have to lay stress on the distortion. In religious matters the patient had a critical and agnostic attitude, and her idea of a possible deity had long since passed into the realm of the inconceivable, i.e., had dwindled into a complete abstraction. In contrast to this, the god-image of the dreams corresponded to the archaic conception of a nature demon, something like Wotan.[7] *Theos to pneûma*, "God is spirit," is here translated back into its original form where *pneûma* means "wind": God is the wind, stronger and mightier than man, an invisible breath-spirit. As in the Hebrew *ruach*, so in Arabic *ruh* means breath and spirit. Out of the purely personal form the dreams developed an archaic god-image that is infinitely far from the conscious idea of God. It might be objected that this is simply an infantile image, a childhood memory. I would have no quarrel with this assumption if we were dealing with an old man sitting on a golden throne in heaven. But there is no trace of any sentimentality of that kind; instead, we have a primitive conception that can correspond only to an archaic mentality. These primitive conceptions, of which I have given a large number of examples in my *Symbols of Transformation*, tempt one to make, in regard to unconscious material, a distinction very different from that between "preconscious" and "unconscious" or "subconscious" and "unconscious." The justification for these distinctions need not be discussed here. They have a definite

---

[7] **Wotan** Supreme God; character in Richard Wagner's *Ring* cycle of operas.

value and are worth refining further as points of view. The fundamental distinction which experience has forced upon me merely
claims the value of a further point of view. From what has been said
it is clear that we have to distinguish in the unconscious a layer
which we may call the *personal unconscious*. The materials contained
in this layer are of a personal nature in so far as they have the character partly of acquisitions derived from the individual's life and
partly of psychological factors which could just as well be conscious.
It is readily understandable that incompatible psychological elements are liable to repression and therefore become unconscious;
but on the other hand we also have the possibility of making and
keeping the repressed contents conscious, once they have been recognized. We recognize them as personal contents because we can
discover their effects, or their partial manifestation, or their specific
origin in our personal past. They are the integral components of the
personality, they belong to its inventory, and their loss to consciousness produces an inferiority in one or the other respect — an inferiority, moreover, that has the psychological character not so much of
an organic mutilation or an inborn defect as of a want which gives
rise to a feeling of moral resentment. The sense of moral inferiority
always indicates that the missing element is something which, one
feels, should not be missing, or which could be made conscious if
only one took enough trouble. The feeling of moral inferiority does
not come from a collision with the generally accepted and, in a
sense, arbitrary moral law, but from the conflict with one's own self
which, for reasons of psychic equilibrium, demands that the deficit
be redressed. Whenever a sense of moral inferiority appears, it
shows that there is not only the demand to assimilate an unconscious component, but also the possibility of assimilating it. In the
last resort it is a man's moral qualities which force him, either
through direct recognition of the necessity to do so, or indirectly
through a painful neurosis, to assimilate his unconscious self and to
keep himself fully conscious. Whoever progresses along this road of
realizing the unconscious self must inevitably bring into consciousness the contents of the personal unconscious, thus widening the
scope of his personality. I should add at once that this "widening"
primarily concerns the moral consciousness, one's self-knowledge,
for the unconscious contents that are released and brought into consciousness by analysis are usually unpleasant — which is precisely
why these wishes, memories, tendencies, plans, etc. were repressed.
These are the contents that are brought to light in much the same
way by a thorough confession, though to a much more limited extent. The rest comes out as a rule in dream analysis. It is often very
interesting to watch how the dreams fetch up the essential points, bit

by bit and with the nicest choice. The total material that is added to consciousness causes a considerable widening of the horizon, a deepened self-knowledge which, more than anything else, is calculated to humanize a man and make him modest. But even self-knowledge, assumed by all wise men to be the best and most efficacious, has different effects on different characters. We make very remarkable discoveries in this respect in practical analysis, but I shall deal with this question in the next chapter.

As my example of the archaic idea of God shows, the uncon-   18 scious seems to contain other things besides personal acquisitions and belongings. My patient was quite unconscious of the derivation of "spirit" from "wind," or of the parallelism between the two. This content was not the product of her thinking, nor had she ever been taught it. The critical passage in the New Testament was inaccessible to her—*to pneûma pneî hopou thelei*[8]—since she knew no Greek. If we must take it as a wholly personal acquisition, it might be a case of so-called cryptomnesia,[9] the unconscious recollection of a thought which the dreamer had once read somewhere. I have nothing against such a possibility in this particular case; but I have seen a sufficient number of other cases—many of them are to be found in the book mentioned above—where cryptomnesia can be excluded with certainty. Even if it were a case of cryptomnesia, which seems to me very improbable, we should still have to explain what the predisposition was that caused just this image to be retained and later, as Semon puts it, "ecphorated" (*ekphorein*, Latin *efferre*, "to produce"). In any case, cryptomnesia or no cryptomnesia, we are dealing with a genuine and thoroughly primitive god image that grew up in the unconscious of a civilized person and produced a living effect— an effect which might well give the psychologist of religion food for reflection. There is nothing about this image that could be called personal: it is a wholly collective image, the ethnic origin of which has long been known to us. Here is an historical image of worldwide distribution that has come into existence again through a natural psychic function. This is not so very surprising, since my patient was born into the world with a human brain which presumably still functions today much as it did of old. We are dealing with a reactivated archetype, as I have elsewhere called these primordial images. These ancient images are restored to life by the primitive, analogical

---

[8] *to pneûma pneî hopou thelei* the wind blows where it wishes (John 3:8).
[9] Cf. Théodore Flournoy, *Des Indes à la planète Mars: Étude sur un cas de somnambulisme avec glossolalie* (Paris and Geneva, 1900; trans. by D. B. Vermilye as *From India to the Planet Mars*, New York, 1900), and Jung, "Psychology and Pathology of So-called Occult Phenomena," *Coll. Works*, Vol. 1, pp. 81ff. [Jung's note]

mode of thinking peculiar to dreams. It is not a question of inherited ideas, but of inherited thought patterns.

In view of these facts we must assume that the unconscious con-   19
tains not only personal, but also impersonal, collective components in the form of inherited categories or archetypes. I have therefore advanced the hypothesis that at its deeper levels the unconscious possesses collective contents in a relatively active state. That is why I speak of the collective unconscious.

QUESTIONS FOR CRITICAL READING

1. What is Jung's view of the relationship of the unconscious mind to the conscious mind? How does it compare to Freud's?
2. What is repression? Why does repression work as it does?
3. How does transference work in psychoanalytic treatment? Is it a good thing or not?
4. What is unusual about Jung's patient's dream? What about it can he not fit into a normal pattern of transference?
5. What is the distinction between the personal unconscious and the collective unconscious?
6. Do you agree that "Dreams contain images and thought associations which we do not create with conscious intent" (para. 9)? Why or why not?

SUGGESTIONS FOR WRITING

1. Jung talks about common sense and its limitations. For some people, common sense denies the existence of an unconscious mind. Relying on Jung, your own personal experiences, and any other sources you choose, defend the existence of an unconscious mind. At the same time, do your best to explain the content of the unconscious and why it is important to the individual.
2. With reference to your own dreams, argue for or against the belief that dreams are products of the conscious mind. Have you had dreams whose content did not pass the "threshold" of your conscious mind?
3. Although the adult Jung was not religious, as the son of a Swiss pastor he was well acquainted with religion. In paragraph 13, Jung asserts that his patient's dream reveals a fundamental human longing for God. As he puts it, "Could the longing for a god be a *passion* welling up from our darkest, instinctual nature?" Examine the possibility that such a psychological phenomenon has affected your attitude toward religion and religious belief.

4. Jung suggests that mythic literature maintains some of the images that make up the collective unconscious of a group of people. Select a myth (consult Ovid's *Metamorphosis*, Grimm's fairy tales, or the Greek myths, or choose a pattern of mythic behavior repeated in popular films) and analyze the instinctual longing it represents for us. What does the myth reveal about our culture?

5. **CONNECTIONS** Jung was a follower of Freud until he eventually broke from him. The break was not altogether friendly, and the feelings between the two—on professional matters—were often strained. Compare Jung's approach to the subject of the unconscious with Freud's. In what respects do they differ? In what ways are their methods either compatible or incompatible with each other? Do you find Jung's methods more or less useful than Freud's? Explain why.

6. **CONNECTIONS** In "Natural Selection" (see Part 6), Charles Darwin suggests that as humans developed over a long period of time they may have continued many traditions that began early in history. How would Darwin's ideas help reinforce the concept of an unconscious that might transcend the ages and thus become part of our collective "memory" gathered through eons of evolution? Would Jung have found Darwin's ideas congenial, or would he have discounted them? Does he show any evidence of having been influenced by Darwin? Explain.

MELANIE KLEIN
The Psychological Principles of Infant Analysis

MELANIE KLEIN (1882–1960) has been described as one of the most important child psychologists of the twentieth century. She was born in Austria and lived there while Freud practiced, although she did not learn of his work until she went to Budapest in 1910 with her husband, Arthur Klein, an engineer. She had studied for two years at the University of Vienna, planning to be a doctor like her father, but her plans were upset when she married. She read Freud's landmark book *On Dreams* (1900) and soon began analysis with Sandor Ferenczi (1873–1933), an associate of Freud. She began then to devote her life to the practice of psychoanalysis.

Klein's work over a period of years in the 1920s began to convince the Freudian community that while the child's mind might be somewhat different from the adult's, there were definitely ways in which young children could be successfully analyzed. She specialized in analyzing children at a time when the general view was that it was impossible to analyze children younger than seven. Like Freud, Klein analyzed her own child, Eric, whose characteristics of play and construction of fantasies convinced her that children had to be approached in special ways.

She developed the "play technique" that is still used by child psychologists today. Instead of expecting the child to approach analysis verbally, in the manner of an adult, Klein saw that children's play revealed much about their unconscious. The trick was for the analyst to engage in play with the child and to go along with the child's fantasies while watching carefully for their significance.

From *The Selected Melanie Klein*. Edited by Juliet Mitchell.

As she demonstrates in her essay, the process of play reveals children's fantasies, desires, and inner lives.

The symbols that arise in play sometimes suggest the kind of symbols common in dream studies. Freudian technique depends on a process of free association in which the patient talks and the analyst listens without interference. Free association brings up symbols, dreams, or anxieties that have no apparent connection, but which, if the process is conducted properly, may reveal the causes of neurosis. The child cannot lie on a couch and free associate, but Klein discovered that children as young as two and three-quarters can, in the course of play with the analyst, essentially mimic the process of free association. The content of children's play reveals their deepest concerns and pathologies.

The theory of "object relations," which asserts that children begin to develop their senses of identity by establishing relations first with their mothers or caretakers and then with other people, is one of Klein's most important contributions to the field of psychology.

Controversy was almost commonplace in Klein's life. She had a bad relationship with Anna Freud (1895–1982), Sigmund Freud's daughter and a renowned psychoanalyst in her own right, who did not believe young children could be analyzed successfully. This public disagreement was compounded by Anna Freud's influence in the Viennese psychoanalysis community. In addition, many psychoanalysts had a low opinion of Klein's work because she was not a medical doctor. In fact, Klein was widely known to have had an extremely contentious relationship with her daughter Melitta, a doctor practicing psychoanalysis.

Once she became established as a child analyst, Klein left her husband, and in 1927 she moved from Vienna to London. Despite the controversy surrounding her, a few important psychoanalysts took up Klein's cause, helping her to amass an impressive and lasting body of work.

Klein's Rhetoric

In her essay, Klein summarizes some of her most important findings concerning the analysis of children. She had already presented papers on the subject to psychoanalytic congresses, but this piece, in 1926, was one of the most forceful statements of her findings. She avoids, as much as possible, the professional jargon of the psychologist. When she must resort to such terminology, such as the terms *libido* and *narcissistic*, she tries to establish them in a clear context. She speaks directly to her audience, clarifying her purpose from the start. She tells us that there is a difference between the mind of the child and that of the adult, but that she has developed a technique that permits her to use Freudian analytic methods with children.

Klein introduces the concept of "play technique" in the first paragraph. She introduces the concept of "object relations" in the second paragraph when she states, "As we know, children form relations with the outside world by directing to objects, from which pleasure is obtained, the libido that was originally attached exclusively to the child's own ego." In other words, from the first the child is aware only of him- or herself; as he or she becomes aware of others, the child forms pleasurable and meaningful relationships. Klein begins to explore the nature of the relationships the child forms with the parent. She describes the early stage of oedipal attraction in which a child expresses affection for his or her opposite-sex parent. At each stage of the child's development, beginning with two-year-olds, Klein describes the nature of the child's observations and anxieties.

Klein uses case study followed by discussion and analysis to establish the success of her approach. Each child she discusses is an example of a problem she felt she was able to solve by analyzing that child's play and object relations. Her first example is "Trude, a child of three and a quarter" (para. 3), through whom Klein introduces the problems associated with "deprivation," or not getting what one wants. She discusses deprivation in paragraphs 4–7, linking it to Freud's ideas about the Oedipus complex. Klein saw evidence of this development at very early ages. Her discussion in these paragraphs clarifies her views on the "Oedipus situation" (para. 4).

Her discussion of Trude in paragraphs 8–10 focuses on the child's overdeveloped sense of guilt, which Klein felt had sexual overtones that expressed themselves in fear of darkness (*pavor nocturnus*). Klein's description of Trude's play reveals the child's considerable anxiety and a highly developed superego, which, according to Freud, is the mind's censor at work. In paragraph 11, Rita reveals some of the same issues.

In paragraphs 12–19, Klein offers a discussion of the psychological issues that are revealed by the analysis of these children, focusing on the sexual implications of the oedipal forces, which she sees at work at a very early age. A discussion of Ruth follows in paragraph 20, and then Klein discusses the famous case of an obsessive six-year-old named Erna whose analysis had been widely discussed and that impressed a number of skeptical psychologists. Erna exploded in rage and exhibited a quality that Klein felt was very important: the urge to repeat actions over and over.

Klein ends her essay by emphasizing the need for action or play when analyzing children because, as she states in paragraph 22, "We cannot appeal to the sense of reality in little patients as we can in older ones."

PREREADING QUESTIONS: WHAT TO READ FOR

The following prereading questions may help you anticipate key issues in the discussion of Melanie Klein's "The Psychological Principles of Infant Analysis." Keeping them in mind during your first reading of the selection should help focus your attention.

- How does the play technique help Klein observe the mental state of the child?
- What objects do children form relations with besides people?
- Why do young children have problems dealing with reality?

The Psychological Principles of Infant Analysis

In the following paper I propose to discuss in detail certain dif-   1
ferences between the mental life of young children and that of adults. These differences require us to use a technique adapted to the mind of the young child, and I shall try to show that there is a certain analytical *play technique* which fulfils this requirement. This technique is planned in accordance with certain points of view which I shall discuss in some detail in this paper.

As we know, children form relations with the outside world by   2
directing to objects, from which pleasure is obtained, the libido[1] that was originally attached exclusively to the child's own ego. A child's relation to these objects, whether they be living or inanimate, is in the first instance purely narcissistic.[2] It is in this way, however,

---

[1] **libido** Psychic energy of biological drives, such as the sexual drive.
[2] **narcissistic** Self-admiring or self-centered.

that children arrive at their relations with reality also. I should like to illustrate the relation of young children to reality by means of an example.

Trude, a child of three and a quarter, went on a journey with 3 her mother, having previously had a single hour's analysis. Six months later the analysis was continued. It was only after some considerable time that she spoke of anything that had happened to her in the interval, the occasion of her touching on it being a dream which she related to me. She dreamt that she was with her mother again in Italy, in a familiar restaurant. The waitress did not give her any raspberry-syrup, for there was none left. The interpretation of this dream showed, amongst other things, that the child was still suffering from the deprivation of the mother's breast when she was weaned; further, it revealed her envy of her little sister. As a rule Trude told me all sorts of apparently irrelevant things, and also repeatedly mentioned details of her first hour's analysis six months previously, but it was only the connection with the deprivation she had experienced which caused her to think of her travels, otherwise they were of no interest to her.

At a very early age children become acquainted with reality 4 through the deprivations which it imposes on them. They try to defend themselves against it by repudiating it. The fundamental thing, however, and the criterion of all later capacity for adaptation to reality, is the degree in which they are able to tolerate the deprivations that result from the Oedipus situation. Hence, even in little children, an exaggerated repudiation of reality (often disguised under an apparent "adaptability" and "docility") is an indication of neurosis and differs from the flight from reality of adult neurotics only in the forms in which it manifests itself. Even in the analysis of young children, therefore, one of the final results to be attained is successful adaptation to reality. One way in which this shows itself in children is in the disappearance of the difficulties encountered in their education. In other words, such children have become capable of tolerating real deprivations.

Observation of children often shows, as early as in the begin- 5 ning of their second year, a marked preference for the parent of the opposite sex and other indications of incipient Oedipus tendencies. When the ensuing conflicts begin, that is, at what point the child actually becomes dominated by the Oedipus complex, is less clear; for we infer its existence only from certain changes which we notice in the child.

The analysis of one child of two years and nine months, another 6 of three years and a quarter, and several children of about four years old, has led me to conclude that, in them, the Oedipus complex

exercised a powerful influence as early as their second year. I will illustrate this from the development of a little patient. Rita showed a
preference for her mother up to the beginning of her second year;
after that she showed a striking preference for her father. For instance, at the age of fifteen months she would constantly demand to
stay alone in the room with him and, sitting on his knee, look at
books with him. At the age of eighteen months, however, her attitude changed again, and once more she preferred her mother. Simultaneously she began to suffer from *pavor nocturnus*[3] and a dread
of animals. She developed an excessive fixation to her mother and a
very pronounced father identification. At the beginning of her third
year she displayed increasing ambivalence, and was more and more
difficult to train, so that when she was two years and nine months
she was brought for analytic treatment. At this time she had for
some months shown very considerable inhibition in play, as well as
an inability to tolerate deprivations, an excessive sensitivity to pain,
and marked moodiness. The following experiences had contributed
to this development. Up till the age of nearly two years Rita had
slept in her parents' room, and the effects of the primal scene[4]
showed plainly in her analysis. The occasion of the outbreak of her
neurosis, however, was the birth of her little brother. Soon after this,
still greater difficulties manifested themselves and constantly increased. There can be no doubt that there is a close connection between neurosis and such profound effects of the Oedipus complex
experienced at so early an age. I cannot determine whether it is neurotic children whom the early working of the Oedipus complex affects so intensely, or whether children become neurotic because this
happens to them. It is, however, certain that experiences such as I
have mentioned here make the conflict more severe and therefore either increase the neurosis or cause it to break out.

I will now select from this case the features which the analysis of
children of different ages has taught me are typical. They are seen
most directly in the analysis of *little* children. In several cases in
which I analysed anxiety attacks in quite little children, these attacks
proved to be the repetition of a *pavor nocturnus* which had occurred
in the second half of the child's second year and at the beginning of
its third year. This fear was at once an effect and a neurotic elaboration of the Oedipus complex. There are innumerable elaborations of
this sort and they lead us to certain positive conclusions as to the effects of the Oedipus complex.

---

[3] ***pavor nocturnus*** Fear of darkness.
[4] **primal scene** Witnessing parents having sex.

Amongst such elaborations, in which the connection with the   8
Oedipus situation was quite clear, are to be reckoned the way in
which children constantly fall and hurt themselves, their exaggerated
sensitivity, their incapacity to tolerate deprivations, their inhibitions
in play, their highly ambivalent attitude towards festive occasions
and presents, and finally, various difficulties in education which
often make their appearance at a surprisingly early age. But I found
that the cause of these very common phenomena was a particularly
strong sense of guilt, the development of which I will now examine
in detail.

How strongly the sense of guilt operates even in *pavor nocturnus* I   9
will show from an example. Trude, at the age of four and a quarter,
constantly played in the analytic hour that it was night. We both had
to go to sleep. Then she came out of the particular corner which
she called her room, stole up to me and made all sorts of threats. She
would stab me in the throat, throw me into the courtyard, burn me
up, or give me to the policeman. She tried to tie my hands and feet,
she lifted the sofa-cover and said she was making "*po-kacki-kucki*."

It turned out that she was looking into the mother's "popo" for   10
the kackis, which to her represented children. Another time she
wanted to hit me on the stomach and declared that she was taking
out the "a-a's" (faeces) and making me poor. She then pulled down
the cushions, which she constantly called "children," and hid herself with them in the corner of the sofa, where she crouched down
with vehement signs of fear, covered herself up, sucked her thumb
and wetted herself. This always directly followed her attacks on me.
Her attitude was, however, similar to that which, at the age of not
quite two, she had adopted in bed when she began to suffer from
intense *pavor nocturnus*. At that time, too, she used constantly to
run into her parents' bedroom in the night without being able to tell
them what she wanted. When her sister was born she was two years
old, and the analysis succeeded in revealing what was in her mind
at the time and also what were the causes of her anxiety and of her
wetting and dirtying her bed. Analysis also succeeded in getting rid
of these symptoms. At that time she had already wished to rob her
mother, who was pregnant, of her children, to kill her and to take
her place in coitus with the father. These tendencies to hate and aggression were the cause of her fixation to her mother (which, at the
age of two years, was becoming peculiarly strong), the cause also of
her sense of anxiety and guilt. At the time when these phenomena
were so prominent in Trude's analysis, she managed to hurt herself
almost always just before the analytic hour. I found out that the
objects against which she hurt herself (tables, cupboards, stoves,
etc.), signified to her (in accordance with the primitive childish

identification) her mother, or at times her father who was punishing her. In general I have found, especially in very little children,
that constantly "being in the wars" and falling and hurting themselves is closely connected with the castration complex and the sense
of guilt.

Children's games enable us to form certain special conclusions   11
about the infantile sense of guilt. As early as her second year, those
with whom Rita came into contact were struck by her remorse for
every naughtiness, however small, and her hypersensitiveness to any
sort of blame. For instance, she burst into tears when her father
playfully threatened a bear in a picture-book. Here, what determined her identification with the bear was her fear of blame from
her *real* father. Again, her inhibition in play proceeded from her
sense of guilt. When she was only two and a half she repeatedly declared when playing with her doll (a game which she did not much
enjoy), that she was not the baby doll's mother. Analysis showed
that she did not *dare* to play at being the mother because the baby
doll stood to her amongst other things for the little brother whom
she had wanted to take away from her mother, even during the
pregnancy. But here the prohibition of the childish wish no longer
emanated from the *real* mother, but from an introjected[5] mother,
whose role she enacted for me in many ways and who exercised a
harsher and more cruel influence upon her than her real mother had
ever done. One obsessional symptom which Rita developed at the
age of two was a sleep ceremonial which wasted a great deal of time.
The main point of this was that she insisted on being tightly rolled
up in the bedclothes for fear that "a mouse or a butty might come
through the window and bite off her butty (genital)." Her games
revealed other determinants: the doll had always to be rolled up in the
same way as Rita herself, and on one occasion an elephant was put
beside its bed. This elephant was supposed to prevent the baby doll
from getting up; otherwise it would steal into the parents' bedroom
and do some harm or take something away from them. The
elephant (a father-imago) was intended to take over the part of hin-
derer. This part the introjected father had played within her since
the time when, between the ages of eighteen months and two years,
she had wanted to usurp her mother's place with her father, to steal
from her mother the child with which she was pregnant, and to
injure and castrate the parents. The reactions of rage and anxiety
which followed on the punishment of the "child" during such
games showed, too, that Rita was inwardly playing both parts: that

---

[5] **introjected** Projected imaginatively.

of the authorities who sit in judgement and that of the child who is punished.

A fundamental and universal mechanism in the game of acting a   12
part serves to separate those different identifications at work in the child which are tending to form a single whole. By the division of roles the child succeeds in expelling the father and mother whom, in the elaboration of the Oedipus complex, it has absorbed into itself and who are now tormenting it inwardly by their severity. The result of this expulsion is a sensation of relief, which contributes in great measure to the pleasure derived from the game. Though this game of acting often appears quite simple and seems to represent only primary identifications, this is only the surface appearance. To penetrate behind this appearance is of great importance in the analysis of children. It can, however, have its full therapeutic effect only if the investigation reveals all the underlying identifications and determinations and, above all, if we have found our way to the sense of guilt which is here at work.

In the cases which I have analysed the inhibitory effect of feel-   13
ings of guilt was clear at a very early age. What we here encounter corresponds to that which we know as the super-ego[6] in adults. The fact that we assume the Oedipus complex to reach its zenith somewhere about the fourth year of life and that we recognize the development of the super-ego as the end-result of the complex seems to me in no way to contradict these observations. Those definite, typical phenomena, the existence of which in the most clearly developed form we can establish when the Oedipus complex has reached its zenith and which precede its waning, are simply the termination of a development which occupies *years*. The analysis of little children shows that, immediately the Oedipus complex arises, they begin to work it through and thereby to develop the super-ego.

The effects of this childish super-ego upon the child are analo-   14
gous to those of the super-ego upon the adult, but they weigh far more heavily upon the weaker, childish ego. As the analysis of children teaches us, we strengthen that ego when the analytic procedure curbs the excessive demands of the super-ego. There can be no doubt that the ego of little children differs from that of older children or of adults. But, when we have freed the little child's ego from neurosis, it proves perfectly equal to such demands of reality as it encounters—demands as yet less serious than those made upon adults.

---

[6]**super-ego** The faculty of mind that polices undesirable feelings; a form of conscience.

Just as the minds of little children differ from those of older   15
children, so their reaction to psycho-analysis is different in early
childhood from what it is later. We are often surprised at the facility
with which *for the time being* our interpretations are accepted: sometimes children even express considerable pleasure in them. The reason why this process is different from that met with in the analysis
of adults is that in certain strata of the child-mind there is a much
easier communication between *Cs* and *Ucs* (the system conscious
and unconscious), and therefore it is much simpler to retrace the
steps from the one to the other. This accounts for the rapid effect of
our interpretation, which of course is never given except on the
basis of adequate material. Children, however, often produce such
material surprisingly quickly and in amazing variety. The effect, too,
is often astonishing, even when the children have not seemed at all
receptive of the interpretation. The play which was interrupted
owing to the setting-up of resistances is resumed; it deepens, expands and expresses deeper strata of the mind; the relation between
the child and the analyst is strengthened. The pleasure in play, which
visibly ensues after an interpretation has been given, is also due to
the fact that the expenditure necessitated by a repression is no longer
required after the interpretation. But soon we once more encounter
resistances for a time, and here matters are no longer made easy by
what has gone before. On the contrary, we have to wrestle with the
greatest possible difficulties. This is especially the case when we encounter the sense of guilt.

In their play children represent symbolically phantasies, wishes   16
and experiences. Here they are employing the same language, the
same archaic, phylogenetically acquired[7] mode of expression as we are
familiar with from dreams. We can only fully understand it if we approach it by the method Freud has evolved for unravelling dreams.
Symbolism is only a part of it; if we want rightly to comprehend
children's play in connection with their whole behaviour during the
analytic hour, we must take into account not only the symbolism
which often appears so clearly in their games, but also all the means
of representation and the mechanisms employed in dream work,
and we must bear in mind the necessity of examining the whole
nexus of phenomena.

If we employ this technique we soon find that children produce   17
no fewer associations to the separate features of their games than do
adults to the fragments of their dreams. The details of the play point

---

[7] **phylogenetically acquired** Developed over a long period of time in the development of the human race.

the way for an attentive observer; and, in between, the child tells all sorts of things which must be given their full weight as associations.

Besides this archaic mode of representation children employ another primitive mechanism, that is to say, they substitute actions (which were the original precursors of thoughts) for words: with children, *acting* plays a prominent part. 18

In *The History of an Infantile Neurosis*, Freud says: "An analysis which is conducted upon a neurotic child itself must, as a matter of course, appear to be more trustworthy, but it cannot be very rich in material; too many words and thoughts have to be lent to the child, and even so the deepest strata may turn out to be impenetrable to consciousness." 19

If we approach children with the technique appropriate to the analysis of adults we shall assuredly not succeed in penetrating to the deepest layers of the child's mental life. But it is precisely these layers which are of moment for the value and success of an analysis. If, however, we take into account the psychological differences between children and adults and bear in mind the fact that in children we find *Ucs* still in operation side by side with *Cs*, the most primitive tendencies side by side with those most complicated developments known to us, such as the super-ego—if, that is to say, we rightly understand the child's mode of expression, all these doubtful points and unfavourable factors vanish. For we find that, as regards the depth and scope of the analysis, we may expect as much from children as from adults. And more still, in the analysis of children we can go back to experiences and fixations which in analysing adults we can only *reconstruct*, while in children they are *directly* represented. Take for instance, the case of Ruth who, as an infant, had gone hungry for some time because her mother had little milk to give her. At the age of four years and three months, when playing with the wash-basin, she called the water-tap a milk-tap. She declared that the milk was running into mouths (the holes of the waste-pipe), but that only a very little was flowing. This unsatisfied oral demand made its appearance in countless games and dramatizations and showed itself in her whole attitude. For instance, she asserted that she was poor, that she only had one coat, and that she had very little to eat—none of these statements being in the least in accordance with reality. 20

Another little patient who suffered from obsessional neurosis was the six-year-old Erna, whose neurosis was based on impressions received during the period of training in cleanliness. These impressions she dramatized for me in the minutest detail. Once she placed a little doll on a stone, pretended that it was defecating and stood other dolls round it which were supposed to be admiring it. After this 21 dramatization Erna brought the same material into a game of acting. She wanted me to be a baby in long clothes which made itself dirty, while she was the mother. The baby was a spoilt child and an object of admiration. This was followed by a reaction of rage in Erna, and she played the part of a cruel teacher who knocked the child about. In this way Erna enacted before me one of the first traumata in her experience: the heavy blow her narcissism received when she imagined that the measures taken to train her meant the loss of the excessive affection bestowed on her in her infancy.

In general, in the analysis of children we cannot over-estimate   22 the importance of translation into action and of phantasy at the bidding of the compulsion to repetition. Naturally, *little* children use the vehicle of action to a far greater extent, but even older ones constantly have recourse to this primitive mechanism, especially when analysis has removed some of their repressions. It is indispensable for carrying on the analysis that children should have the pleasure that is bound up with this mechanism, but the pleasure must always remain only a means to the end. It is just here that we see the predominance of the pleasure principle over the reality principle. We cannot appeal to the sense of reality in little patients as we can in older ones.

Just as children's means of expression differ from those of   23 adults, so the analytic situation in the analysis of children is of a wholly different character. It is, however, in both cases *essentially* the same. Constant interpretation, the gradual solving of resistances and the constant tracing of the transference to earlier situations—these constitute in children as in adults the correct analytic situation.

I have said that in the analysis of young children I have again   24 and again proved how rapidly the interpretations take effect. It is a striking fact that, though there are numerous unmistakable indications of this effect: the development of play, the consolidating of the transference, the lessening of anxiety, etc., nevertheless for quite a long time the child does not consciously elaborate the interpretations. I have been able, however, to prove that this elaboration does set in later. For instance, children begin to distinguish between the "pretence" mother and the real mother and between the wooden baby doll and the live baby brother. They then firmly insist that they wanted to do this or that injury to the toy baby only—the real baby, they say, of course they love. Only when very powerful and long-standing resistances have been overcome, do children admit that their aggressive acts were directed against the *real* objects. When this admission is made, however, the result, even in quite little children, is generally a notable step forward in adaptation to reality. My impression is that the interpretation is at first only unconsciously assimilated. It is not till later that its relation to reality gradually penetrates the child's understanding. The process of enlightenment is analogous. For a long time analysis brings to light only the material for sexual theories and birth phantasies and interprets this material without any "explanation." Thus, enlightenment takes place bit by bit with the removal of the unconscious resistances which operate against it.

Hence, the first thing that happens as a result of psycho-analysis   25
is that the emotional relation to the parents improves; it is only when this has taken place that understanding comes. This understanding is admitted at the bidding of the super-ego, whose demands have been modified by analysis so that it can tolerate and comply with an ego which is less oppressed and therefore stronger. Thus the child is not *suddenly* confronted with the situation of admitting a new knowledge of its relation to the parents or, in general, of being obliged to absorb knowledge which burdens it. It has always been my experience that the effect of such knowledge, gradually elaborated, is simply to *relieve* the child, to establish a fundamentally more favourable relation to the parents and thus to increase its power of social adaptation.

When this has taken place children also are quite able to replace   26
repression to some extent by reasoned rejection. We see this from the fact that at a later stage of the analysis children have advanced so far from various anal-sadistic or cannibalistic cravings (which at an earlier stage were still so powerful) that they can now at times adopt an attitude of humorous criticism towards them. When this happens I hear even very little children making jokes to the effect, for instance, that some time ago they really wanted to eat up their mummy or cut her into bits. When this change takes place, not only is the sense of guilt inevitably lessened, but at the same time the children are enabled to *sublimate* the wishes which previously were wholly repressed. This manifests itself in practice in the disappearance of inhibitions in play and in a beginning of numerous interests and activities.

To sum up what I have said: the special primitive peculiarities   27
of the mental life of children necessitate a separate technique adapted to them, consisting of the analysis of their play. By means of this technique we can reach the deepest repressed experiences and fixations and this enables us fundamentally to influence the children's development.

It is a question simply of a difference of *technique*, not of the   28
principles of treatment. The criteria of the psycho-analytic method proposed by Freud, namely, that we should use as our starting-point the facts of transference and resistance, that we should take into account infantile impulses, repression and its effects, amnesia and

the compulsion to repetition and, further, that we should discover the primal scene, as he requires in the "History of an Infantile Neurosis"—all these criteria are maintained in their entirety in the play technique. The method of play preserves all the principles of psycho-analysis and leads to the same results as the classic technique. Only it is adapted to the minds of children in the technical means employed.

QUESTIONS FOR CRITICAL READING

1. What is the connection between play technique and the Freudian technique of free association?
2. Why would play be an effective means of psychoanalyzing a child?
3. What connection is there between the child's unconscious and conscious mind?
4. How do the children in the essay exhibit behavior that suggests the "Oedipus situation" (para. 4) is at work?
5. How convinced are you that the children Klein discusses had disturbances that had psychosexual origins?
6. Why does the experience of deprivation affect a child's sense of reality? How do fantasies protect a child from deprivation?
7. What seems to be the source of *pavor nocturnus*—fear of the dark?
8. What function does the superego serve? Can it be problematic in one's life?

SUGGESTIONS FOR WRITING

1. Before Freud, people believed that no child under seven had sexual awareness or erotic experiences. However, both Freud and Klein observed such qualities in children as young as two. If you have had the chance to observe young children—as a parent, sibling, teacher, or babysitter—describe the evidence you have that would support Klein's views or the views of those who believe such feelings do not develop in children until some time after the age of seven. Argue for one side or the other and use, where possible, concrete examples from your own observations.
2. Do you think the violent fantasies these children developed in regard to their mothers were signs of neurosis? Is it possible that these fantasies are natural to developing children? Calling on your own experience, or on the experiences of others (which you can gather by interview), decide how much children's fantasies reveal clues about their true feelings toward parents or other people in their circle. Is it possible that fantasies, even violent ones, are necessary for growing into a healthy adult?

3. Klein discusses the Oedipus complex in relation to most of the children she analyzes. The Oedipus complex is a fixation on the parent of the opposite sex accompanied by the desire to kill (metaphorically) the parent of the same sex. Examine Klein's evidence of the existence of this "Oedipus situation" (para. 4), as she calls it. Judging from your own observation of children, do you believe the complex exists? Where do you stand on this issue?

4. One thing Klein emphasizes is the narcissism of the child. Narcissism is the state of being so self-involved that one has few concerns about others. It is an early development of the ego, but it persists in some cases into later childhood. Look up the term in a dictionary of psychology and, once you feel you understand it, write an essay that explains it to others. Use where possible any personal observations you have had of narcissism in children or even adults. Why would narcissism be a problem for children as they grow up?

5. Klein discusses guilt and focuses to some extent on the kind of guilt that goes to extremes, thus causing illness. Write an essay that tries to examine how guilt is instilled in people, how they react to it, and what effect it has on society. Klein talks about the superego, which monitors guilt to some extent. Learn what you can about the concept of the superego and, drawing on your own experience where possible, take a stand on whether or not guilt is productive or damaging for society.

6. Deprivation of all sorts—not getting one's way, being forced to follow a prescribed ritual (such as potty training), and any restraint from any activity—tends to frustrate children. Klein states that without the proper kinds of deprivation the child may be able to avoid the demands of reality well into adulthood. Given your own experience and your observations of children and people, argue either for or against her position. Use her own rhetorical method of the case study, or use an example of behavior as you have observed it.

7. **CONNECTIONS** Klein's discussion of the Oedipus complex comes more than twenty years after Sigmund Freud's discussion of it in *The Interpretation of Dreams*. Compare the ways in which Freud and Klein treat the basic concepts of the "Oedipus situation" (para. 4). What advances, if any, does Klein make on Freud's theory? To what extent does her analysis of her child patients reinforce Freud's basic views? Is there any aspect of Freud's position that Klein seems uncomfortable with? Explain.

8. **CONNECTIONS** Read Simone de Beauvoir's "Woman: Myth and Reality" and Carol Gilligan's "Woman's Place in Man's Life Cycle" in Part 8. How might they respond to Klein's discussion of the analysis of young girls? How do you think they would have reacted to Klein's conclusions? Would they consider Klein a feminist or an antifeminist? Why? What do you think they would consider to be Klein's contribution, if any, to feminism? Explain.

HOWARD GARDNER
A Rounded Version: The Theory
of Multiple Intelligences

HOWARD GARDNER (b. 1943), Hobbs Professor of Cognition and Education at the Harvard Graduate School of Education, is codirector of Harvard's Project Zero, a program dedicated to improving education in schools by emphasizing creativity in thinking and problem solving. By emphasizing the arts and the newer electronic technologies associated with learning, the program cultivates a "culture of thinking" in the classroom as opposed to a culture of rote learning. Gardner has received a MacArthur Foundation award (1981), which supported his research for five years, and has won a number of important awards in the field of education, including the Grawemeyer Award in Education (1990), given for the first time to an American. Among his many books are *Leading Minds: An Anatomy of Leadership* (1995) and *Extraordinary Minds: Portraits of Exceptional Individuals and an Examination of Our Extraordinariness* (1997).

Perhaps the most important and best-known product of Project Zero is the theory of multiple intelligences, which Gardner first published in *Frames of Mind* (1983). (His more recent book, *Intelligence Reframed: Multiple Intelligence for the 21st Century* [1999], offers a revisitation and more detailed elaboration on multiple intelligence theory and its application.) In *Frames of Mind*, he noted that the general attitude toward intelligence centers on the IQ (intelligence quotient) test that Alfred Binet (1857–1911) devised. Binet believed that intelligence is measurable and that IQ tests result in numerical scores that are reliable indicators of a more or less permanent basic intelligence. Gardner offered several objections to that

From *Multiple Intelligences: The Theory in Practice*.

515

view. One was that IQ predictors might point to achievement in schools and colleges but not necessarily to achievement in life. For example, students with middling scores performed at extraordinary levels in business, politics, and other walks of life, whereas high-achieving students often settled for middling careers. The reports on high-performing executives indicated a considerable intelligence at work, but it was not necessarily the kind of intelligence that could be measured by the Binet tests.

Gardner also was intrigued by findings that local regions of the brain controlled specific functions of the mind. For example, studies had established that certain regions of the brain were specialized for language functions, whereas others were specialized for physical movement, music, mathematics, and other skills. When those portions of the brain suffered damage, as with stroke or accident, the functions for which they were specialized were adversely affected. These observations, which were plentiful in the work of neurologists during and after World War II, led Gardner to propose the existence of a variety of intelligences rather than only one.

As he explains in the following essay from his book *Multiple Intelligences: The Theory in Practice* (1993), his studies led him to propose seven distinct intelligences. The first is linguistic, which naturally includes language. This intelligence applies not only to learning languages but also to using language well—as, for example, in the case of poets and writers. The second is logical-mathematical, which refers to the applications of mathematics and of logical reasoning. Our society uses these verbal-mathematical forms of intelligence as the practical measure of intelligence: the SATs, for instance, depend almost entirely on measuring these forms.

Gardner adds five more forms of intelligence. Spatial intelligence concerns the ways in which we perceive and imagine spatial relations. Some people, such as architects and sculptors, are clearly more gifted than others at imagining space. Musical intelligence is seen as distinct from other forms of intelligence if only because some people, such as child prodigies, are apparently born with superior musical abilities. Bodily-kinesthetic intelligence shows up in dancers and athletes, like Mikhail Barishnikov and the late Jackie Joyner-Kersee, who perform extraordinarily with their bodies. But bodily-kinesthetic intelligence also applies to detailed physical work, such as the manipulations necessary for the work of surgeons, dentists, and craftspeople, such as weavers, potters, metal-workers, and jewelers.

Finally, Gardner also defines two kinds of personal intelligence that are difficult to isolate and study but that he feels must be regarded as forms of intelligence. Interpersonal intelligence concerns the way we get along with other people. People with high interpersonal intelligence might be salespeople, teachers, politicians, or evangelists. They respond to others and are sensitive to their needs and their concerns. They understand cooperation, compromise, and respect for other people's views. The second kind of personal intelligence—intrapersonal—refers to how one understands oneself. The self-knowledge to recognize one's strengths and weaknesses and to avoid an inflated sense of self-importance constitutes a high degree of intrapersonal intelligence.

Gardner sees all these intelligences working together in the individual. As he says, when one of them dominates, the individual can appear freakish, as in the person with autism who easily multiplies huge numbers in his head but cannot relate to other human beings. Because the individual must nurture all these intelligences to develop into a complete person, Gardner is working to revise educational practices to reflect all varieties of intelligence.

Greeks in the time of Plato and Aristotle seem to have understood much of what Gardner says. They included music and dance, for example, in the curriculum of their schools. They developed linguistic and interpersonal skills in the teaching of rhetoric and made logic and mathematics central to their teaching. One of Socrates' most famous statements, in fact—"Know thyself"—admonishes us to develop intrapersonal intelligence.

Gardner's Rhetoric

Rather than open the essay by describing the multiple intelligences, Gardner starts with a dramatic scene and a hypothetical story. He describes two eleven-year-old children who take an IQ test and then are regarded in special ways by their teachers: one is expected to do well in school, the other is expected to do less well. The expectations are met. But years later the student with the lower IQ is vastly more successful in business than the student who scored higher. Why is this so? The rest of the essay answers that implied rhetorical question.

One of the most important devices Gardner relies on is enumeration. He has seven different kinds of intelligence to discuss and takes each one in turn. The reader is not aware of a special range of importance to the seven forms of intelligence: the first, musical intelligence, is not necessarily the most important or the first to be recognized in an individual. Bodily-kinesthetic is not necessarily less important because it comes after musical intelligence. By placing logical-mathematical intelligence in the middle of the sequence, Gardner suggests that this form of intelligence, which our society traditionally treats as first in importance, should take its place beside a range of intelligences that are all more or less equal in value.

Just as important as the use of enumeration is Gardner's use of parallelism in the structure of each of the intelligences he enumerates. For each he offers a subhead that identifies the specific intelligence and then a "sketch with a thumbnail biography" that helps establish the nature of the intelligence. Then Gardner discusses the details of each intelligence and suggests ways in which it may relate to other forms of intelligence. This method has the advantage of extreme clarity. Likewise, paralleling examples and quotations in describing each intelligence makes the point over and over and ultimately produces a convincing argument without the appearance of argument.

Gardner makes another important rhetorical decision regarding the size and nature of the paragraphs. Modern readers, conditioned by newspapers and magazines, expect paragraphs to be short and direct. Gardner's paragraphs reflect a decision to communicate with a general reading audience rather than an audience of specialists or specially educated readers. For that reason, a single subject may sometimes be discussed in two or more adjacent paragraphs, with the paragraph break acting as a "breather" (see paras. 19–20 and 22–23).

All these rhetorical devices aid the reader in absorbing complex material. Gardner's primary efforts in this essay are to facilitate communication. He keeps his language simple, his sentences direct, and his paragraphs brief. For the modern reader, this is a recipe for understanding.

PREREADING QUESTIONS: WHAT TO READ FOR

The following prereading questions may help you anticipate key issues in the discussion of Howard Gardner's "A Rounded Version: The Theory of Multiple Intelligences." Keeping them in mind during your first reading of the selection should help focus your attention.

- What constitutes an intelligence, according to Gardner?
- What is the most compelling evidence for the theory of multiple intelligences?

A Rounded Version: The Theory of Multiple Intelligences

Coauthored by Joseph Walters

Two eleven-year-old children are taking a test of "intelligence."   1
They sit at their desks laboring over the meanings of different words,
the interpretation of graphs, and the solutions to arithmetic problems. They record their answers by filling in small circles on a single
piece of paper. Later these completed answer sheets are scored objectively: the number of right answers is converted into a standardized
score that compares the individual child with a population of children of similar age.

The teachers of these children review the different scores. They   2
notice that one of the children has performed at a superior level; on
all sections of the test, she answered more questions correctly than
did her peers. In fact, her score is similar to that of children three to
four years older. The other child's performance is average—his
scores reflect those of other children his age.

A subtle change in expectations surrounds the review of these   3
test scores. Teachers begin to expect the first child to do quite well
during her formal schooling, whereas the second should have only
moderate success. Indeed these predictions come true. In other
words, the test taken by the eleven-year-olds serves as a reliable predictor of their later performance in school.

How does this happen? One explanation involves our free use of   4
the word "intelligence": the child with the greater "intelligence" has
the ability to solve problems, to find the answers to specific questions,
and to learn new material quickly and efficiently. These skills in turn
play a central role in school success. In this view, "intelligence" is a
singular faculty that is brought to bear in any problem solving situation. Since schooling deals largely with solving problems of various
sorts, predicting this capacity in young children predicts their future
success in school.

"Intelligence," from this point of view, is a general ability that is   5
found in varying degrees in all individuals. It is the key to success in
solving problems. This ability can be measured reliably with standardized pencil-and-paper tests that, in turn, predict future success
in school.

What happens after school is completed? Consider the two indi-   6
viduals in the example. Looking further down the road, we find that
the "average" student has become a highly successful mechanical

engineer who has risen to a position of prominence in both the professional community of engineers as well as in civic groups in his
community. His success is no fluke—he is considered by all to be a
talented individual. The "superior" student, on the other hand, has
had little success in her chosen career as a writer; after repeated rejec-
tions by publishers, she has taken up a middle management position
in a bank. While certainly not a "failure," she is considered by her
peers to be quite "ordinary" in her adult accomplishments. So what
happened?

This fabricated example is based on the facts of intelligence   7
testing. IQ tests predict school performance with considerable accuracy, but they are only an indifferent predictor of performance in
a profession after formal schooling.[1] Furthermore, even as IQ tests
measure only logical or logical-linguistic capacities, in this society
we are nearly "brain-washed" to restrict the notion of intelligence to
the capacities used in solving logical and linguistic problems.

To introduce an alternative point of view, undertake the fol-   8
lowing "thought experiment." Suspend the usual judgment of what
constitutes intelligence and let your thoughts run freely over the capabilities of humans—perhaps those that would be picked out by
the proverbial Martian visitor. In this exercise, you are drawn to
the brilliant chess player, the world-class violinist, and the champion athlete; such outstanding performers deserve special consideration. Under this experiment, a quite different view of *intelligence*
emerges. Are the chess player, violinist, and athlete "intelligent" in
these pursuits? If they are, then why do our tests of "intelligence"
fail to identify them? If they are not "intelligent," what allows them
to achieve such astounding feats? In general, why does the contemporary construct "intelligence" fail to explain large areas of human
endeavor?

In this chapter we approach these problems through the theory   9
of multiple intelligences (MI). As the name indicates, we believe that
human cognitive competence is better described in terms of a set of
abilities, talents, or mental skills, which we call "intelligences." All
normal individuals possess each of these skills to some extent; individuals differ in the degree of skill and in the nature of their combination. We believe this theory of intelligence may be more humane
and more veridical[2] than alternative views of intelligence and that it
more adequately reflects the data of human "intelligent" behavior.

---

[1] Jencks, C. (1972). *Inequality*. New York: Basic Books. [Gardner's note]
[2] **veridical** Telling the truth.

Such a theory has important educational implications, including ones for curriculum development.

What Constitutes an Intelligence?

The question of the optimal definition of intelligence looms large in our inquiry. Indeed, it is at the level of this definition that the theory of multiple intelligences diverges from traditional points of view. In a traditional view, intelligence is defined operationally as the ability to answer items on tests of intelligence. The inference from the test scores to some underlying ability is supported by statistical techniques that compare responses of subjects at different ages; the apparent correlation of these test scores across ages and across different tests corroborates the notion that the general faculty of intelligence, g, does not change much with age or with training or experience. It is an inborn attribute or faculty of the individual.   10

Multiple intelligences theory, on the other hand, pluralizes the traditional concept. An intelligence entails the ability to solve problems or fashion products that are of consequence in a particular cultural setting or community. The problem-solving skill allows one to approach a situation in which a goal is to be obtained and to locate the appropriate route to that goal. The creation of a *cultural* product is crucial to such functions as capturing and transmitting knowledge or expressing one's views or feelings. The problems to be solved range from creating an end for a story to anticipating a mating move in chess to repairing a quilt. Products range from scientific theories to musical compositions to successful political campaigns.   11

MI theory is framed in light of the biological origins of each problem-solving skill. Only those skills that are universal to the human species are treated. Even so, the biological proclivity to participate in a particular form of problem solving must also be coupled with the cultural nurturing of that domain. For example, language, a universal skill, may manifest itself particularly as writing in one culture, as oratory in another culture, and as the secret language of anagrams in a third.   12

Given the desire of selecting intelligences that are rooted in biology, and that are valued in one or more cultural settings, how does one actually identify an "intelligence"? In coming up with our list, we consulted evidence from several different sources: knowledge about normal development and development in gifted individuals; information about the breakdown of cognitive skills under conditions of brain damage; studies of exceptional populations, including   13 prodigies, idiots savants, and autistic children; data about the evolution of cognition over the millennia; cross-cultural accounts of cognition; psychometric studies, including examinations of correlations among tests; and psychological training studies, particularly measures of transfer and generalization across tasks. Only those candidate intelligences that satisfied all or a majority of the criteria were selected as bona fide intelligences. A more complete discussion of each of these criteria for an "intelligence" and the seven intelligences that have been proposed so far, is found in *Frames of Mind*.[3] This book also considers how the theory might be disproven and compares it to competing theories of intelligence.

In addition to satisfying the aforementioned criteria, each intel-   14
ligence must have an identifiable core operation or set of operations. As a neutrally based computational system, each intelligence is activated or "triggered" by certain kinds of internally or externally presented information. For example, one core of musical intelligence is the sensitivity to pitch relations, whereas one core of linguistic intelligence is the sensitivity to phonological features.

An intelligence must also be susceptible to encoding in a symbol   15
system—a culturally contrived system of meaning, which captures and conveys important forms of information. Language, picturing, and mathematics are but three nearly worldwide symbol systems that are necessary for human survival and productivity. The relationship of a candidate intelligence to a human symbol system is no accident. In fact, the existence of a core computational capacity anticipates the existence of a symbol system that exploits that capacity. While it may be possible for an intelligence to proceed without an accompanying symbol system, a primary characteristic of human intelligence may well be its gravitation toward such an embodiment.

The Seven Intelligences

Having sketched the characteristics and criteria of an intelli-   16
gence, we turn now to a brief consideration of each of the seven intelligences. We begin each sketch with a thumbnail biography of a person who demonstrates an unusual facility with that intelligence. These biographies illustrate some of the abilities that are central to the fluent operation of a given intelligence. Although each biography illustrates a particular intelligence, we do not wish to imply that in

---

[3] Gardner, H. (1983). *Frames of Mind: The Theory of Multiple Intelligences.* New York: Basic Books. [Gardner's note]

adulthood intelligences operate in isolation. Indeed, except for ab-
normal individuals, intelligences always work in concert, and any
sophisticated adult role will involve a melding of several of them.
Following each biography we survey the various sources of data that
support each candidate as an "intelligence."

Musical Intelligence

When he was three years old, Yehudi Menuhin was smuggled into
the San Francisco Orchestra concerts by his parents. The sound of
Louis Persinger's violin so entranced the youngster that he insisted on a violin for his birthday and Louis Persinger as his
teacher. He got both. By the time he was ten years old, Menuhin
was an international performer.[4]

Violinist Yehudi Menuhin's musical intelligence manifested itself   17
even before he had touched a violin or received any musical training.
His powerful reaction to that particular sound and his rapid progress
on the instrument suggest that he was biologically prepared in some
way for that endeavor. In this way evidence from child prodigies
supports our claim that there is a biological link to a particular intelligence. Other special populations, such as autistic children who can
play a musical instrument beautifully but who cannot speak, under-
score the independence of musical intelligence.

A brief consideration of the evidence suggests that musical skill   18
passes the other tests for an intelligence. For example, certain parts
of the brain play important roles in perception and production of
music. These areas are characteristically located in the right hemisphere, although musical skill is not as clearly "localized," or located
in a specifiable area, as language. Although the particular susceptibility of musical ability to brain damage depends on the degree of
training and other individual differences, there is clear evidence for
"amusia" or loss of musical ability.

Music apparently played an important unifying role in Stone   19
Age (Paleolithic) societies. Birdsong provides a link to other species.
Evidence from various cultures supports the notion that music is a
universal faculty. Studies of infant development suggest that there is
a "raw" computational ability in early childhood. Finally, musical
notation provides an accessible and lucid symbol system.

In short, evidence to support the interpretation of musical ability   20
as an "intelligence" comes from many different sources. Even though
musical skill is not typically considered an intellectual skill like
mathematics, it qualifies under our criteria. By definition it deserves

---

[4] Menuhin, Y. (1977). *Unfinished Journey*. New York: Knopf. [Gardner's note]

consideration; and in view of the data, its inclusion is empirically justified.

Bodily-Kinesthetic Intelligence

Fifteen-year-old Babe Ruth played third base. During one game his team's pitcher was doing very poorly and Babe loudly criticized him from third base. Brother Mathias, the coach, called out, "Ruth, if you know so much about it, YOU pitch!" Babe was surprised and embarrassed because he had never pitched before, but Brother Mathias insisted. Ruth said later that at the very moment he took the pitcher's mound, he KNEW he was supposed to be a pitcher and that it was "natural" for him to strike people out. Indeed, he went on to become a great major league pitcher (and, of course, attained legendary status as a hitter).[5]

Like Menuhin, Babe Ruth was a child prodigy who recognized   21 his "instrument" immediately upon his first exposure to it. This recognition occurred in advance of formal training.

Control of bodily movement is, of course, localized in the motor   22 cortex, with each hemisphere dominant or controlling bodily movements on the contra-lateral side. In right-handers, the dominance for such movement is ordinarily found in the left hemisphere. The ability to perform movements when directed to do so can be impaired even in individuals who can perform the same movements reflexively or on a nonvoluntary basis. The existence of specific *apraxia* constitutes one line of evidence for a bodily-kinesthetic intelligence.

The evolution of specialized body movements is of obvious   23 advantage to the species, and in humans this adaptation is extended through the use of tools. Body movement undergoes a clearly defined developmental schedule in children. And there is little question of its universality across cultures. Thus it appears that bodily-kinesthetic "knowledge" satisfies many of the criteria for an intelligence.

The consideration of bodily-kinesthetic knowledge as "problem   24 solving" may be less intuitive. Certainly carrying out a mime sequence or hitting a tennis ball is not solving a mathematical equation. And yet, the ability to use one's body to express an emotion (as in a dance), to play a game (as in a sport), or to create a new product (as in devising an invention) is evidence of the cognitive features of body usage. The specific computations required to solve a particular

---

[5] Connor, A. (1982). *Voices from Cooperstown*. New York: Collier. (Based on a quotation taken from *The Babe Ruth Story*, Babe Ruth & Bob Considine. New York: Dutton, 1948.) [Gardner's note]

bodily-kinesthetic *problem*, hitting a tennis ball, are summarized by Tim Gallwey:

> At the moment the ball leaves the server's racket, the brain calculates approximately where it will land and where the racket will intercept it. This calculation includes the initial velocity of the ball, combined with an input for the progressive decrease in velocity and the effect of wind and after the bounce of the ball. Simultaneously, muscle orders are given: not just once, but constantly with refined and updated information. The muscles must cooperate. A movement of the feet occurs, the racket is taken back, the face of the racket kept at a constant angle. Contact is made at a precise point that depends on whether the order was given to hit down the line or cross-court, an order not given until after a split-second analysis of the movement and balance of the opponent.
>
> To return an average serve, you have about one second to do this. To hit the ball at all is remarkable and yet not uncommon. The truth is that everyone who inhabits a human body possesses a remarkable creation.[6]

Logical-Mathematical Intelligence. In 1983 Barbara McClin- 25 tock won the Nobel Prize in medicine or physiology for her work in microbiology. Her intellectual powers of deduction and observation illustrate one form of logical-mathematical intelligence that is often labeled "scientific thinking." One incident is particularly illuminating. While a researcher at Cornell in the 1920s McClintock was faced one day with a problem: while *theory* predicted 50-percent pollen sterility in corn, her research assistant (in the "field") was finding plants that were only 25- to 30-percent sterile. Disturbed by this discrepancy, McClintock left the cornfield and returned to her office, where she sat for half an hour, thinking:

> Suddenly I jumped up and ran back to the (corn) field. At the top of the field (the others were still at the bottom) I shouted "Eureka, I have it! I know what the 30% sterility is!" . . . They asked me to prove it. I sat down with a paper bag and a pencil and I started from scratch, which I had not done at all in my laboratory. It had all been done so fast; the answer came and I ran. Now I worked it out step by step—it was an intricate series of steps—and I came out with [the same result]. [They] looked at the material and it was exactly as I'd said it was; it worked out exactly as I had diagrammed it. Now, why did I know, without having done it on paper? Why was I so sure?[7]

---

[6] Gallwey, T. (1976). *Inner Tennis.* New York: Random House. [Gardner's note]
[7] Keller, E. (1983). *A Feeling for the Organism* (p. 104). Salt Lake City: W. H. Freeman. [Gardner's note]

This anecdote illustrates two essential facts of the logical- 26
mathematical intelligence. First, in the gifted individual, the process of
problem solving is often remarkably rapid—the successful scientist
copes with many variables at once and creates numerous hypotheses
that are each evaluated and then accepted or rejected in turn.

The anecdote also underscores the *nonverbal* nature of the intelli- 27
gence. A solution to a problem can be constructed *before* it is articulated. In fact, the solution process may be totally invisible, even to the
problem solver. This need not imply, however, that discoveries of this
sort—the familiar "Aha!" phenomenon—are mysterious, intuitive, or
unpredictable. The fact that it happens more frequently to some people (perhaps Nobel Prize winners) suggests the opposite. We interpret
this as the work of the logical-mathematical intelligence.

Along with the companion skill of language, logical-mathematical 28
reasoning provides the principal basis for IQ tests. This form of intelligence has been heavily investigated by traditional psychologists, and it
is the archetype of "raw intelligence" or the problem-solving faculty
that purportedly cuts across domains. It is perhaps ironic, then, that
the actual mechanism by which one arrives at a solution to a logical-
mathematical problem is not as yet properly understood.

This intelligence is supported by our empirical criteria as well. 29
Certain areas of the brain are more prominent in mathematical calculation than others. There are idiots savants who perform great
feats of calculation even though they remain tragically deficient in
most other areas. Child prodigies in mathematics abound. The development of this intelligence in children has been carefully docu-
mented by Jean Piaget and other psychologists.

Linguistic Intelligence

At the age of ten, T. S. Eliot created a magazine called "Fireside" to
which he was the sole contributor. In a three-day period during
his winter vacation, he created eight complete issues. Each one included poems, adventure stories, a gossip column, and humor.
Some of this material survives and it displays the talent of the
poet.[8]

As with the logical intelligence, calling linguistic skill an "intelli- 30
gence" is consistent with the stance of traditional psychology. Linguistic intelligence also passes our empirical tests. For instance, a
specific area of the brain, called "Broca's Area," is responsible for the
production of grammatical sentences. A person with damage to this

---

[8] Soldo, J. (1982). Jovial juvenilia: T. S. Eliot's first magazine. *Biography*, 5,
25–37. [Gardner's note]

area can understand words and sentences quite well but has difficulty putting words together in anything other than the simplest of sentences. At the same time, other thought processes may be entirely unaffected.

The gift of language is universal, and its development in chil- 31 dren is strikingly constant across cultures. Even in deaf populations where a manual sign language is not explicitly taught, children will often "invent" their own manual language and use it surreptitiously! We thus see how an intelligence may operate independently of a specific input modality or output channel.

Spatial Intelligence

Navigation around the Caroline Islands in the South Seas is accomplished without instruments. The position of the stars, as viewed from various islands, the weather patterns, and water color are the only sign posts. Each journey is broken into a series of segments; and the navigator learns the position of the stars within each of these segments. During the actual trip the navigator must envision mentally a reference island as it passes under a particular star and from that he computes the number of segments completed, the proportion of the trip remaining, and any corrections in heading that are required. The navigator cannot *see* the islands as he sails along; instead he maps their locations in his mental "picture" of the journey.[9]

Spatial problem solving is required for navigation and in the use 32 of the notational system of maps. Other kinds of spatial problem solving are brought to bear in visualizing an object seen from a different angle and in playing chess. The visual arts also employ this intelligence in the use of space.

Evidence from brain research is clear and persuasive. Just as the 33 left hemisphere has, over the course of evolution, been selected as the site of linguistic processing in right-handed persons, the right hemisphere proves to be the site most crucial for spatial processing. Damage to the right posterior regions causes impairment of the ability to find one's way around a site, to recognize faces or scenes, or to notice fine details.

Patients with damage specific to regions of the right hemisphere 34 will attempt to compensate for their spacial deficits with linguistic strategies. They will try to reason aloud, to challenge the task, or even make up answers. But such nonspatial strategies are rarely successful.

---

[9] Gardner, H. (1983). *Frames of Mind: The Theory of Multiple Intelligences*. New York: Basic Books. [Gardner's note]

Blind populations provide an illustration of the distinction be- 35
tween the spatial intelligence and visual perception. A blind person
can recognize shapes by an indirect method: running a hand along
the object translates into length of time of movement, which in turn
is translated into the size of the object. For the blind person, the
perceptual system of the tactile modality parallels the visual modality in the seeing person. The analogy between the spatial reasoning
of the blind and the linguistic reasoning of the deaf is notable.

There are few child prodigies among visual artists, but there are 36
idiots savants such as Nadia.[10] Despite a condition of severe autism,
this preschool child made drawings of the most remarkable repre-
sentational accuracy and finesse.

Interpersonal Intelligence. With little formal training in special 37
education and nearly blind herself, Anne Sullivan began the intimi-
dating task of instructing a blind and deaf seven-year-old Helen
Keller. Sullivan's efforts at communication were complicated by the
child's emotional struggle with the world around her. At their first
meal together, this scene occurred:

> Annie did not allow Helen to put her hand into Annie's plate and
> take what she wanted, as she had been accustomed to do with her
> family. It became a test of wills—hand thrust into plate, hand
> firmly put aside. The family, much upset, left the dining room.
> Annie locked the door and proceeded to eat her breakfast while
> Helen lay on the floor kicking and screaming, pushing and
> pulling at Annie's chair. [After half an hour] Helen went around
> the table looking for her family. She discovered no one else was
> there and that bewildered her. Finally, she sat down and began to
> eat her breakfast, but with her hands. Annie gave her a spoon.
> Down on the floor it clattered, and the contest of wills began
> anew.[11]

Anne Sullivan sensitively responded to the child's behavior. She 38
wrote home: "The greatest problem I shall have to solve is how to discipline and control her without breaking her spirit. I shall go rather
slowly at first and try to win her love."

In fact, the first "miracle" occurred two weeks later, well before 39
the famous incident at the pumphouse. Annie had taken Helen to a
small cottage near the family's house, where they could live alone.

---

[10] Selfe, L. (1977). *Nadia: A Case of Extraordinary Drawing in an Autistic Child.*
New York: Academic Press. [Gardner's note]

[11] Lash, J. (1980). *Helen and Teacher: The Story of Helen Keller and Anne Sullivan
Macy* (p. 52). New York: Delacorte. [Gardner's note]

After seven days together, Helen's personality suddenly underwent a profound change—the therapy had worked:

> My heart is singing with joy this morning. A miracle has happened! The wild little creature of two weeks ago has been transformed into a gentle child.[12]

It was just two weeks after this that the first breakthrough in 40
Helen's grasp of language occurred; and from that point on, she progressed with incredible speed. The key to the miracle of language was Anne Sullivan's insight into the *person* of Helen Keller.

Interpersonal intelligence builds on a core capacity to notice 41
distinctions among others; in particular, contrasts in their moods, temperaments, motivations, and intentions. In more advanced forms, this intelligence permits a skilled adult to read the intentions and desires of others, even when these have been hidden. This skill appears in a highly sophisticated form in religious or political leaders, teachers, therapists, and parents. The Helen Keller–Anne Sullivan story suggests that this interpersonal intelligence does not depend on language.

All indices in brain research suggest that the frontal lobes play a 42
prominent role in interpersonal knowledge. Damage in this area can cause profound personality changes while leaving other forms of problem solving unharmed—a person is often "not the same person" after such an injury.

Alzheimer's disease, a form of presenile dementia, appears to 43
attack posterior brain zones with a special ferocity, leaving spatial, logical, and linguistic computations severely impaired. Yet, Alzheimer's patients will often remain well groomed, socially proper, and continually apologetic for their errors. In contrast, Pick's disease, another variety of presenile dementia that is more frontally oriented, entails a rapid loss of social graces.

Biological evidence for interpersonal intelligence encompasses 44
two additional factors often cited as unique to humans. One factor is the prolonged childhood of primates, including the close attachment to the mother. In those cases where the mother is removed from early development, normal interpersonal development is in serious jeopardy. The second factor is the relative importance in humans of social interaction. Skills such as hunting, tracking, and killing in prehistoric societies required participation and cooperation of large numbers of people. The need for group cohesion, leadership, organization, and solidarity follows naturally from this.

---

[12] Lash (p. 54). [Gardner's note]

Intrapersonal Intelligence. In an essay called "A Sketch of   45
the Past," written almost as a diary entry, Virginia Woolf discusses the
"cotton wool of existence"—the various mundane events of life. She
contrasts this "cotton wool" with three specific and poignant memories from her childhood: a fight with her brother, seeing a particular
flower in the garden, and hearing of the suicide of a past visitor:

> These are three instances of exceptional moments. I often tell
> them over, or rather they come to the surface unexpectedly. But
> now for the first time I have written them down, and I realize
> something that I have never realized before. Two of these moments
> ended in a state of despair. The other ended, on the contrary, in a
> state of satisfaction.
>
> The sense of horror (in hearing of the suicide) held me pow-
> erless. But in the case of the flower, I found a reason; and was thus
> able to deal with the sensation. I was not powerless.
>
> Though I still have the peculiarity that I receive these sudden
> shocks, they are now always welcome; after the first surprise, I al-
> ways feel instantly that they are particularly valuable. And so I go
> on to suppose that the shock-receiving capacity is what makes me
> a writer. I hazard the explanation that a shock is at once in my
> case followed by the desire to explain it. I feel that I have had a
> blow; but it is not, as I thought as a child, simply a blow from an
> enemy hidden behind the cotton wool of daily life; it is or will be-
> come a revelation of some order; it is a token of some real thing
> behind appearances; and I make it real by putting it into words.[13]

This quotation vividly illustrates the intrapersonal intelligence—   46
knowledge of the internal aspects of a person: access to one's own
feeling life, one's range of emotions, the capacity to effect discrimi-
nations among these emotions and eventually to label them and to
draw upon them as a means of understanding and guiding one's
own behavior. A person with good intrapersonal intelligence has a
viable and effective model of himself or herself. Since this intelligence is the most private, it requires evidence from language, music,
or some other more expressive form of intelligence if the observer is
to detect it at work. In the above quotation, for example, linguistic
intelligence is drawn upon to convey intrapersonal knowledge; it
embodies the interaction of intelligences, a common phenomenon
to which we will return later.

We see the familiar criteria at work in the intrapersonal intelli-   47
gence. As with the interpersonal intelligence, the frontal lobes play a
central role in personality change. Injury to the lower area of the

---

[13] Woolf, V. (1976). *Moments of Being* (pp. 69–70). Sussex: The University Press.
[Gardner's note]

frontal lobes is likely to produce irritability or euphoria; while injury to the higher regions is more likely to produce indifference, listlessness, slowness, and apathy—a kind of depressive personality. In such "frontal-lobe" individuals, the other cognitive functions often remain preserved. In contrast, among aphasics who have recovered sufficiently to describe their experiences, we find consistent testimony: while there may have been a diminution of general alertness and considerable depression about the condition, the individual in no way felt himself to be a different person. He recognized his own needs, wants, and desires and tried as best he could to achieve them.

The autistic child is a prototypical example of an individual   48
with impaired intrapersonal intelligence; indeed, the child may not even be able to refer to himself. At the same time, such children often exhibit remarkable abilities in the musical, computational, spatial, or mechanical realms.

Evolutionary evidence for an intrapersonal faculty is more diffi-   49
cult to come by, but we might speculate that the capacity to transcend the satisfaction of instinctual drives is relevant. This becomes increasingly important in a species not perennially involved in the struggle for survival.

In sum, then, both interpersonal and intrapersonal faculties pass   50
the tests of an intelligence. They both feature problem-solving endeavors with significance for the individual and the species. Interpersonal intelligence allows one to understand and work with others; intrapersonal intelligence allows one to understand and work with oneself. In the individual's sense of self, one encounters a melding of inter- and intrapersonal components. Indeed, the sense of self emerges as one of the most marvelous of human inventions—a symbol that represents all kinds of information about a person and that is at the same time an invention that all individuals construct for themselves.

Summary: The Unique Contributions
of the Theory

As human beings, we all have a repertoire of skills for solving   51
different kinds of problems. Our investigation has begun, therefore, with a consideration of these problems, the contexts they are found in, and the culturally significant products that are the outcome. We have not approached "intelligence" as a reified[14] human faculty that is brought to bear in literally any problem setting; rather, we have

----

[14] **reified** Regarding an abstraction (e.g., intelligence) as if it were a concrete thing.

begun with the problems that humans *solve* and worked back to the "intelligences" that must be responsible.

Evidence from brain research, human development, evolution, 52 and cross-cultural comparisons was brought to bear in our search for the relevant human intelligences: a candidate was included only if reasonable evidence to support its membership was found across these diverse fields. Again, this tack differs from the traditional one: since no candidate faculty is *necessarily* an intelligence, we could choose on a motivated basis. In the traditional approach to "intelligence," there is no opportunity for this type of empirical decision.

We have also determined that these multiple human faculties, 53 the intelligences, are to a significant extent *independent*. For example, research with brain-damaged adults repeatedly demonstrates that particular faculties can be lost while others are spared. This independence of intelligences implies that a particularly high level of ability in one intelligence, say mathematics, does not require a similarly high level in another intelligence, like language or music. This independence of intelligences contrasts sharply with traditional measures of IQ that find high correlations among test scores. We speculate that the usual correlations among subtests of IQ tests come about because all of these tasks in fact measure the ability to respond rapidly to items of a logical-mathematical or linguistic sort; we believe that these correlations would be substantially reduced if one were to survey in a contextually appropriate way the full range of human problem-solving skills.

Until now, we have supported the fiction that adult roles depend 54 largely on the flowering of a single intelligence. In fact, however, nearly every cultural role of any degree of sophistication requires a combination of intelligences. Thus, even an apparently straightforward role, like playing the violin, transcends a reliance on simple musical intelligence. To become a successful violinist requires bodily-kinesthetic dexterity and the interpersonal skills of relating to an audience and, in a different way, choosing a manager; quite possibly it involves an intrapersonal intelligence as well. Dance requires skills in bodily-kinesthetic, musical, interpersonal, and spatial intelligences in varying degrees. Politics requires an interpersonal skill, a linguistic facility, and perhaps some logical aptitude. Inasmuch as nearly every cultural role requires several intelligences, it becomes important to consider individuals as a collection of aptitudes rather than as having a singular problem-solving faculty that can be measured directly through pencil-and-paper tests. Even given a relatively small number of such intelligences, the diversity of human ability is created through the differences in these profiles. In fact, it may well be that the "total is greater than the sum of the parts." An individual may not be particularly gifted in any intelligence; and yet, because of a particular combination or blend of skills, he or she may be able to fill some niche uniquely well. Thus it is of paramount importance to assess the particular combination of skills that may earmark an individual for a certain vocational or avocational niche.

QUESTIONS FOR CRITICAL READING

1. In the heading preceding paragraph 10, Gardner asks, "What Constitutes an Intelligence?" After reading this essay, how would you answer that question? How effectively does Gardner answer it?
2. What is the relation of culture to intelligence? See paragraph 11.
3. Why does society value logical-mathematical intelligence so highly? Do you feel it is reasonable to do so? Why?
4. What relationship do you see between intelligence and problem solving? What relationship do you see between education and problem solving?
5. Do you think that education can enhance these seven forms of intelligence? What evidence can you cite that intelligence is not fixed but can be altered by experience?
6. Why is it important "to assess the particular combination of skills that may earmark an individual" (para. 54)?

SUGGESTIONS FOR WRITING

1. Gardner says that his theory of MI (multiple intelligences) was shaped by his observations of "the biological origins of each problem-solving skill" (para. 12). Why is this important to his theory? How has he connected each of the intelligences to a biological origin? What biological issues are not fully accounted for in the theory of multiple intelligences?
2. In which of these seven forms of intelligence do you excel? Describe your achievements in these forms by giving specific examples that help your reader relate your abilities to the intelligences you have cited. Now that you have identified your primary intelligences, what implications do they suggest for your later life?
3. Gardner is keenly interested in reforming education in light of his theory of multiple intelligences. How could education be altered to best accommodate the seven forms of intelligence? What would be done differently in schools? Who would benefit from the differences you propose? How would society in general benefit from those differences?
4. Describe a problem-solving situation that requires two or more of the intelligences that Gardner describes. If possible, draw your example from your own experience or the experience of someone you know.

Describe how the several intelligences work together to help solve the problem.

5. In some discussions of the forms of intelligence, commentators add an eighth—the naturalist's ability to recognize fine distinctions and patterns in the natural world. What might be the biological origin for that intelligence? In what cultural context might that intelligence be crucial? Do you feel that there is such an intelligence as represented by the naturalist or that it is included in other forms of intelligence?

6. **CONNECTIONS**   What relationship do you see between Plato's discussion of the soul and Gardner's discussion of intelligence? See paragraphs 41–55 in Plato's essay. Which of Gardner's intelligences does Socrates seem to favor in Plato's dialogue?

7. **CONNECTIONS**   Read Maria Montessori's "The Montessori Method" in Part 3. How might she have responded to Gardner's theory of multiple intelligences? Would she have welcomed it, or would she have felt it to be irrelevant to her mission? What evidence, if any, is there in Montessori's essay to suggest that she might have anticipated Gardner's observations? In the light of Gardner's theory, what changes, if any, do you suspect Montessori might have made to her views on education? Explain.

PART SIX

NATURE

Francis Bacon
Charles Darwin
Rachel Carson
Stephen Jay Gould
Michio Kaku

INTRODUCTION

If there be light, then there is darkness; if cold, heat; if height,
depth; if solid, fluid; if hard, soft; if rough, smooth; if calm,
tempest; if prosperity, adversity; if life, death.
                              —PYTHAGORAS (C. 580–C. 500 B.C.)

The life of a man in a state of nature is solitary, poor, nasty,
brutish, and short.
                              —THOMAS HOBBES (1588–1679)

Nature and nature's laws lay hid in the night.
God said, Let Newton be! and all was light!
                              —ALEXANDER POPE (1688–1744)

Some see nature all ridicule and deformity . . . and some scarce
see nature at all. But to the eyes of the man of imagination, nature
is imagination itself.
                              —WILLIAM BLAKE (1757–1827)

The old question of whether there is design is idle. The real
question is what is the world, whether or not it have a
designer—and that can be revealed only by the study of all
nature's particulars.
                              —WILLIAM JAMES (1842–1910)

There are no accidents, only nature throwing her weight around.
Even the bomb merely releases energy that nature has put there.
Nuclear war would be just a spark in the grandeur of space. Nor
can radiation "alter" nature: she will absorb it all. After the bomb,
nature will pick up the cards we have spilled, shuffle them, and
begin her game again.
                              —CAMILLE PAGLIA (b. 1947)

Ideas of nature—of the world that exists outside human
invention—have formed the core of human inquiry since the beginning of society. Early civilizations viewed nature as a willfully creative and destructive force and structured their religions around
gods and goddesses who personified components of the natural
world. For example, many early Egyptian and Greek religions wor-
shiped a sun god, such as Ra or Apollo, and performed rituals meant
to gain the favor of these gods.

This affiliation of nature with divine forces was gradually joined
by a new approach: scientific inquiry. The basic premise of scientific
inquiry was that the physical world could be understood through
careful observation and described through consistent and logical
rules. Lucretius, a prominent Roman thinker who lived during the

536

first century B.C., wrote one of the first treatises on natural science. In his work *On the Nature of Things*, he argued that nature should be viewed in purely materialistic terms and that the universe was composed of minute pieces of matter, or "atoms." During the Renaissance the pursuit of a scientific understanding of the world culminated with Nicolaus Copernicus's (1473–1543) heliocentric (sun-centered) model of the universe. In the seventeenth century Sir Isaac Newton (1642–1727) further developed these methods of objective observation while formulating his laws of physics. Although nature was still believed to be the creation of a divine force, its workings were gradually becoming more and more accessible to human understanding. In the process, humans began to reevaluate their own place in nature.

The five writers in this section offer various ideas on nature, from the origin of life to the structure of the universe. Many of their theories were contended in their time and continue to be debated and rethought, but they share the underlying mission of deciphering the forces that shape our world and our lives.

At the time Francis Bacon wrote, before the advent of sophisticated scientific instruments, most scientists relied on their five senses and their theoretical preconceptions to investigate the workings of the world around them. In "The Four Idols," Bacon raises questions about these modes of scientific inquiry by asking, What casts of mind are essential to gaining knowledge? What prevents us from understanding nature clearly? By thus critiquing traditional presumptions and methods of investigation, Bacon challenges his readers to examine nature with new mental tools.

In "Natural Selection," Charles Darwin proposes a theory that is still controversial today. While on a voyage around South America on HMS *Beagle*, Darwin observed remarkable similarities in the structures of various animals. He approached these discoveries with the advantages of a good education, a deep knowledge of the Bible and theology (he was trained as a minister), and a systematic and inquiring mind. Ultimately, he developed his theories of evolution to explain the significance of resemblances he detected among his scientific samples of insects and flowers and other forms of life. Explaining the nature of nature forms the underpinnings of Darwin's work.

Rachel Carson's "The Sunless Sea" is a masterpiece of description and exploration. Carson gives us a view of the darkest depths of the ocean, a span of almost half the world where there has never been any sunlight at all. Scientists originally thought that without sunlight there could be no life, but Carson points out that not only were they wrong, but that life in the deep is incredibly abundant, beyond what anyone could have imagined. As a result of her early writing on the ocean, more and more attention has been paid to the very issues she raised. Now, much more is known about the deepest parts of the ocean because new submersible robots have made it possible to explore miles below the surface. Her own research demonstrated that there were numerous mysteries in the ocean depths, particularly involving the different forms of life at different depths of the ocean. Carson whets our appetite to know more about the least-explored area of the planet.

Stephen Jay Gould, in "Nonmoral Nature," examines the results of the kind of thinking that Bacon deplored in the seventeenth century but that nevertheless flourished in the nineteenth century. Interpreting the world of nature as if it were fashioned by someone with the same prejudices as the Victorian scientist—usually also a minister—led people to see good and evil in animal and insect behavior. Even today most of us see the world in such terms. To Gould, however, moral issues relate to people—not to, say, dolphins or sharks. For him, thinking like a naturalist means achieving detachment: how we approach the evidence before us, in other words, is as important as what we actually observe. Gould wants us to give up anthropomorphic ways of interpreting evidence in favor of a more rational approach. As he demonstrates, this is not easy to achieve.

Puzzling out the most current thinking in theoretical physics requires speculation that borders on what Michio Kaku calls craziness. One of the craziest theories concerns dark matter, a form of matter in the universe that cannot be seen or touched. Yet according to the calculations of physicists and astronomers, more than 90 percent of the universe may be made up of dark matter. In "The Mystery of Dark Matter," Kaku explains that were it not for the existence of dark matter, our galaxy would spin apart and the universe itself would not hold together. In passing, Kaku alludes to another theory that contradicts common sense: the superstring theory. Instead of postulating hard particles at the heart of the atom, Kaku suggests that the smallest entities in the atom are vibrating strings of energy. This theory not only explains why there are so many particles but also resolves the inherent contradictions between the two great theories in modern physics, quantum theory and the theory of relativity.

Although Francis Bacon probably would not understand the astonishing theories that the other writers in this section discuss, he would appreciate the methods they used to reason about their hypotheses and to establish their conclusions. All these writers are joined in their desire to understand the workings of nature and in their profound respect for the questions that remain.

FRANCIS BACON
The Four Idols

FRANCIS BACON, Lord Verulam (1561–1626), lived during one of the most exciting times in history. Among his contemporaries were the essayist Michel Eyquem de Montaigne; the playwrights Christopher Marlowe and William Shakespeare; the adventurer Sir Francis Drake; and Queen Elizabeth I, in whose reign Bacon held several high offices. He became lord high chancellor of England in 1618 but fell from power in 1621 through a complicated series of events, among which was his complicity in a bribery scheme. His so-called crimes were minor, but he paid dearly for them. His book *Essayes* (1597) was exceptionally popular during his lifetime, and when he found himself without a proper job, he devoted himself to what he declared to be his own true work: writing about philosophy and science.

His purpose in *Novum Organum* (The new organon), published in 1620, was to replace the old organon, or instrument of thought, Aristotle's treatises on logic and thought. Despite Aristotle's pervasive influence on sixteenth- and seventeenth-century thought—his texts were used in virtually all schools and colleges—Bacon thought that Aristotelian deductive logic produced error. In *Novum Organum* he tried to set the stage for a new attitude toward logic and scientific inquiry. He proposed a system of reasoning usually referred to as induction. This quasi-scientific method involves collecting and listing observations from nature. Once a mass of observations is gathered and organized, Bacon believed, the truth about what is observed will become apparent.

Bacon is often mistakenly credited with having invented the scientific method of inquiring into nature; but although he was right about the need for collecting and observing, he was wrong

---

From *Novum Organum*. Translated by Francis Headlam and R. L. Ellis.

about the outcome of such endeavors. After all, one could watch an infinite number of apples (and oranges, too) fall to the ground without ever having the slightest sense of why they do so. What Bacon failed to realize — and he died before he could become scientific enough to realize it — is the creative function of the scientist as expressed in the hypothesis. The hypothesis — an educated guess about why something happens — must be tested by the kinds of observations Bacon recommended.

Nonetheless, "The Four Idols" is a brilliant work. It does establish the requirements for the kind of observation that produces true scientific knowledge. Bacon despaired of any thoroughly objective inquiry in his own day, in part because no one paid attention to the ways in which the idols, limiting preconceptions, strangled thought, observation, and imagination. He realized that the would-be natural philosopher was foiled even before he began. Bacon was a farsighted man. He was correct about the failures of science in his time; and he was correct, moreover, in his assessment that advancement would depend on sensory perception and on aids to perception, such as microscopes and telescopes. The real brilliance of "The Four Idols" lies in Bacon's focus not on what is observed but on the instrument of observation — the human mind. Only when the instrument is freed of error can we rely on its observations to reveal the truth.

Bacon's Rhetoric

Bacon was trained during the great age of rhetoric, and his prose (even though in this case it is translated from Latin) shows the clarity, balance, and organization that characterize the prose writing of seventeenth-century England. The most basic device Bacon uses is enumeration: stating clearly that there are four idols and implying that he will treat each one in turn.

Enumeration is one of the most common and most reliable rhetorical devices. The listener hears a speaker say "I have only three things I want to say today" and is alerted to listen for all three, while feeling secretly grateful that there are only three. When encountering complex material, the reader is always happy to have such "road signs" as "The second aspect of this question is . . ."

"The Four Idols," after a three-paragraph introduction, proceeds with a single paragraph devoted to each idol, so that we have an early definition of each and a sense of what to look for. Paragraphs 8 to 16 cover only the issues related to the Idols of the Tribe: the problems all people have simply because they are people. Paragraphs 17 to 22 consider the Idols of the Cave: those particular fixations individuals have because of their special backgrounds or limitations. Paragraphs 23 to 26 address the questions related to Idols of the Marketplace, particularly those that deal with the way people misuse words and abuse definitions. The remainder of the selection treats the Idols of the Theater, which relate entirely to philosophic systems and preconceptions — all of which tend to narrow the scope of research and understanding.

Enumeration is used within each of these groups of paragraphs as well. Bacon often begins a paragraph with such statements as "There is one principal . . . distinction between different minds" (para. 19). Or he says, "The idols imposed by words on the understanding are of two kinds" (para. 24). The effect is to ensure clarity where confusion could easily reign.

As an added means of achieving clarity, Bacon sets aside a single paragraph — the last — to summarize the main points that he has made, in the order in which they were made.

Within any section of this selection, Bacon depends on observation, example, and reason to make his points. When he speaks of a given idol, he defines it, gives several examples to make it clearer, discusses its effects on thought, and then dismisses it as dangerous. He then goes on to the next idol. Where appropriate, in some cases he names those who are victims of a specific idol. In each case he tries to be thorough, explanatory, and convincing.

Not only is this work a landmark in thought; it is also, because of its absolute clarity, a beacon. We can still benefit from its light.

PREREADING QUESTIONS: WHAT TO READ FOR

The following prereading questions may help you anticipate key issues in the discussion of Francis Bacon's "The Four Idols." Keeping them in mind during your first reading of the selection should help focus your attention.

- What are the four idols?
- Why do the four idols make it difficult for us to see the truth?
- What are some chief characteristics of human understanding?

The Four Idols

The idols[1] and false notions which are now in possession of the   1
human understanding, and have taken deep root therein, not only
so beset men's minds that truth can hardly find entrance, but even
after entrance obtained, they will again in the very instauration[2] of
the sciences meet and trouble us, unless men being forewarned of
the danger fortify themselves as far as may be against their assaults.

There are four classes of idols which beset men's minds. To these   2
for distinction's sake I have assigned names—calling the first class
Idols of the Tribe; the second, *Idols of the Cave*; the third, *Idols of the Marketplace*; the fourth, *Idols of the Theater*.

The formation of ideas and axioms by true induction[3] is no   3
doubt the proper remedy to be applied for the keeping off and clearing away of idols. To point them out, however, is of great use; for
the doctrine of idols is to the interpretation of nature what the doctrine of the refutation of sophisms[4] is to common logic.

The *Idols of the Tribe* have their foundation in human nature it-   4
self, and in the tribe or race of men. For it is a false assertion that the
sense of man is the measure of things. On the contrary, all perceptions as well of the sense as of the mind are according to the measure
of the individual and not according to the measure of the universe.
And the human understanding is like a false mirror, which, receiving
rays irregularly, distorts and discolors the nature of things by min-
gling its own nature with it.

The *Idols of the Cave* are the idols of the individual man. For   5
everyone (besides the errors common to human nature in general)
has a cave or den of his own, which refracts[5] and discolors the light
of nature; owing either to his own proper and peculiar nature; or to
his education and conversation with others; or to the reading of books,
and the authority of those whom he esteems and admires; or to the

---

[1] **idols** By this term Bacon means phantoms or illusions. The Greek philosopher Democritus spoke of *eidola*, tiny representations of things that impressed
themselves on the mind (see note 21).

[2] **instauration** Institution.

[3] **induction** Bacon championed induction as the method by which new
knowledge is developed. As he saw it, induction involved a patient gathering and
categorizing of facts in the hope that a large number of them would point to the
truth. As a process of gathering evidence from which inferences are drawn, induction is contrasted with Aristotle's method, *deduction*, according to which a theory is
established and the truth deduced. Deduction places the stress on the authority of
the expert; induction places the stress on the facts themselves.

[4] **sophisms** Apparently intelligent statements that are wrong; false wisdom.

[5] **refracts** Deflects, bends back, alters.

differences of impressions, accordingly as they take place in a mind preoccupied and predisposed or in a mind indifferent and settled; or the like. So that the spirit of man (according as it is meted out to different individuals) is in fact a thing variable and full of perturbation,[6] and governed as it were by chance. Whence it was well observed by Heraclitus[7] that men look for sciences in their own lesser worlds, and not in the greater or common world.

There are also idols formed by the intercourse and association of   6
men with each other, which I call *Idols of the Marketplace*, on account of the commerce and consort of men there. For it is by discourse that men associate; and words are imposed according to the apprehension of the vulgar.[8] And therefore the ill and unfit choice of words wonderfully obstructs the understanding. Nor do the definitions or explanations wherewith in some things learned men are wont[9] to guard and defend themselves, by any means set the matter right. But words plainly force and overrule the understanding, and throw all into confusion and lead men away into numberless empty controversies and idle fancies.

Lastly, there are idols which have immigrated into men's minds   7
from the various dogmas of philosophies, and also from wrong laws of demonstration.[10] These I call *Idols of the Theater*; because in my judgment all the received systems[11] are but so many stage-plays, representing worlds of their own creation after an unreal and scenic fashion. Nor is it only of the systems now in vogue, or only of the ancient sects and philosophies, that I speak; for many more plays of the same kind may yet be composed and in like artificial manner set forth; seeing that errors the most widely different have nevertheless causes for the most part alike. Neither again do I mean this only of entire systems, but also of many principles and axioms in science, which by tradition, credulity, and negligence, have come to be received.

But of these several kinds of idols I must speak more largely and   8
exactly, that the understanding may be duly cautioned.

The human understanding is of its own nature prone to sup   9
pose the existence of more order and regularity in the world than

---

[6] **perturbation** Uncertainty, disturbance. In astronomy, the motion caused by the gravity of nearby planets.

[7] **Heraclitus (535?–475? B.C.)** Greek philosopher who believed that there was no reality except in change; all else was illusion. He also believed that fire was the basis of all the world and that everything we see is a transformation of it.

[8] **vulgar** Common people.

[9] **wont** Accustomed.

[10] **laws of demonstration** Bacon may be referring to Aristotle's logical system of syllogism and deduction.

[11] **received systems** Official or authorized views of scientific truth.

it finds. And though there be many things in nature which are singular and unmatched, yet it devises for them parallels and conjugates and relatives[12] which do not exist. Hence the fiction that all
celestial bodies move in perfect circles; spirals and dragons being
(except in name) utterly rejected. Hence too the element of fire
with its orb is brought in, to make up the square with the other
three which the sense perceives. Hence also the ratio of density[13] of
the so-called elements is arbitrarily fixed at ten to one. And so on of
other dreams. And these fancies affect not dogmas only, but simple
notions also.

The human understanding when it has once adopted an opin-   10
ion (either as being the received opinion or as being agreeable to itself) draws all things else to support and agree with it. And though
there be a greater number and weight of instances to be found on
the other side, yet these it either neglects and despises, or else by
some distinction sets aside and rejects; in order that by this great
and pernicious predetermination the authority of its former conclusions may remain inviolate. And therefore it was a good answer that
was made by one who when they showed him hanging in a temple a
picture of those who had paid their vows as having escaped ship-
wreck, and would have him say whether he did not now acknowledge the power of the gods—"Ay," asked he again, "but where are
they painted that were drowned after their vows?" And such is the
way of all superstition, whether in astrology, dreams, omens, divine
judgments, or the like; wherein men having a delight in such vani-
ties, mark the events where they are fulfilled, but where they fail,
though this happen much oftener, neglect and pass them by. But
with far more subtlety does this mischief insinuate itself into philosophy and the sciences; in which the first conclusion colors and
brings into conformity with itself all that come after, though far
sounder and better. Besides, independently of that delight and vanity which I have described, it is the peculiar and perpetual error of
the human intellect to be more moved and excited by affirmatives
than by negatives; whereas it ought properly to hold itself indiffer-
ently disposed towards both alike. Indeed, in the establishment of
any true axiom, the negative instance is the more forcible of the two.

---

[12] **parallels and conjugates and relatives** A reference to the habit of assuming that phenomena are regular and ordered, consisting of squares, triangles, circles,
and other regular shapes.
[13] **ratio of density** The false assumption that the relationship of mass or weight
to volume was ten to one. This is another example of Bacon's complaint, establishing
a convenient regular "relative," or relationship.

The human understanding is moved by those things most which 11
strike and enter the mind simultaneously and suddenly, and so fill
the imagination; and then it feigns and supposes all other things to
be somehow, though it cannot see how, similar to those few things
by which it is surrounded. But for that going to and fro to remote
and heterogeneous instances, by which axioms are tried as in the
fire,[14] the intellect is altogether slow and unfit, unless it be forced
thereto by severe laws and overruling authority.

The human understanding is unquiet; it cannot stop or rest,   12
and still presses onward, but in vain. Therefore it is that we cannot
conceive of any end or limit to the world, but always as of necessity it occurs to us that there is something beyond. Neither again
can it be conceived how eternity has flowed down to the present
day; for that distinction which is commonly received of infinity in
time past and in time to come can by no means hold; for it would
thence follow that one infinity is greater than another, and that infinity is wasting away and tending to become finite. The like subtlety arises touching the infinite divisibility of lines,[15] from the
same inability of thought to stop. But this inability interferes more
mischievously in the discovery of causes:[16] for although the most
general principles in nature ought to be held merely positive, as
they are discovered, and cannot with truth be referred to a cause;
nevertheless, the human understanding being unable to rest still
seeks something prior in the order of nature. And then it is that in
struggling towards that which is further off, it falls back upon that
which is more nigh at hand; namely, on final causes: which have
relation clearly to the nature of man rather than to the nature of

---

[14] **tried as in the fire** Trial by fire is a figure of speech representing thorough, rigorous testing even to the point of risking what is tested. An axiom is a
statement of apparent truth that has not yet been put to the test of examination
and investigation.

[15] **infinite divisibility of lines** This gave rise to the paradox of Zeno, the
Greek philosopher of the fifth century B.C. who showed that it was impossible to get
from one point to another because one had to pass the midpoint of the line determined by the two original points, and then the midpoint of the remaining distance,
and then of that remaining distance, down to an infinite number of points. By using
accepted truths to "prove" an absurdity about motion, Zeno actually hoped to prove
that motion itself did not exist. This is the "subtlety," or confusion, Bacon says is
produced by the "inability of thought to stop."

[16] **discovery of causes** Knowledge of the world was based on four causes: efficient (who made it?), material (what is it made of?), formal (what is its shape?), and
final (what is its purpose?). The scholastics concentrated their thinking on the first
and last, whereas the "middle causes," related to matter and shape, were the proper
subject matter of science because they alone yielded to observation. (See para. 34.)

the universe, and from this source have strangely defiled philosophy. But he is no less an unskilled and shallow philosopher who seeks causes of that which is most general, than he who in things subordinate and subaltern[17] omits to do so.

The human understanding is no dry light, but receives an infusion   13
from the will and affections;[18] whence proceed sciences which may be called "sciences as one would." For what a man had rather were true he more readily believes. Therefore he rejects difficult things from impatience of research; sober things, because they narrow hope; the deeper things of nature, from superstition; the light of experience, from arrogance and pride, lest his mind should seem to be occupied with things mean and transitory; things not commonly believed, out of deference to the opinion of the vulgar. Numberless in short are the ways, and sometimes imperceptible, in which the affections color and infect the understanding.

But by far the greatest hindrance and aberration of the human   14
understanding proceeds from the dullness, incompetency, and deceptions of the senses; in that things which strike the sense outweigh things which do not immediately strike it, though they be more important. Hence it is that speculation commonly ceases where sight ceases; insomuch that of things invisible there is little or no observation. Hence all the working of the spirits[19] enclosed in tangible bodies lies hid and unobserved of men. So also all the more subtle changes of form in the parts of coarser substances (which they commonly call alteration, though it is in truth local motion through exceedingly small spaces) is in like manner unobserved. And yet unless these two things just mentioned be searched out and brought to light, nothing great can be achieved in nature, as far as the production of works is concerned. So again the essential nature of our common air, and of all bodies less dense than air (which are very many) is almost unknown. For the sense by itself is a thing infirm and erring; neither can instruments for enlarging or sharpening the senses do much; but all the truer kind of interpretation of nature is effected by instances and experiments fit and apposite;[20] wherein the sense decides touching the experiment only, and the experiment touching the point in nature and the thing itself.

The human understanding is of its own nature prone to abstrac-   15
tions and gives a substance and reality to things which are fleeting. But to resolve nature into abstractions is less to our purpose than to

_____

[17] **subaltern** Lower in status.
[18] **will and affections** Human free will and emotional needs and responses.
[19] **spirits** The soul or animating force.
[20] **apposite** Appropriate; well related.

dissect her into parts; as did the school of Democritus,[21] which went further into nature than the rest. Matter rather than forms should be the object of our attention, its configurations and changes of configuration, and simple action, and law of action or motion; for forms are figments of the human mind, unless you will call those laws of action forms.

Such then are the idols which I call *Idols of the Tribe*; and which take their rise either from the homogeneity of the substance of the human spirit,[22] or from its preoccupation, or from its narrowness, or from its restless motion, or from an infusion of the affections, or from the incompetency of the senses, or from the mode of impression.   16

The *Idols of the Cave* take their rise in the peculiar constitution, mental or bodily, of each individual; and also in education, habit, and accident. Of this kind there is a great number and variety; but I will instance those the pointing out of which contains the most important caution, and which have most effect in disturbing the clearness of the understanding.   17

Men become attached to certain particular sciences and speculations, either because they fancy themselves the authors and inventors thereof, or because they have bestowed the greatest pains upon them and become most habituated to them. But men of this kind, if they betake themselves to philosophy and contemplations of a general character, distort and color them in obedience to their former fancies; a thing especially to be noticed in Aristotle,[23] who made his natural philosophy[24] a mere bondservant to his logic, thereby rendering it contentious and well nigh useless. The race of chemists[25] again out of a few experiments of the furnace have built up a fantastic philosophy, framed with reference to a few things; and Gilbert[26] also,   18

---

[21]**Democritus (460?–370? B.C.)** Greek philosopher who thought the world was composed of atoms. Bacon felt such "dissection" to be useless because it was impractical. Yet Democritus's concept of the *eidola*, the mind's impressions of things, may have contributed to Bacon's idea of "the idol."

[22]**human spirit** Human nature.

[23]**Aristotle (384–322 B.C.)** Greek philosopher whose *Organon* (system of logic) dominated the thought of Bacon's time. Bacon sought to overthrow Aristotle's hold on science and thought.

[24]**natural philosophy** The scientific study of nature in general — biology, zoology, geology, etc.

[25]**chemists** Alchemists had developed a "fantastic philosophy" from their experimental attempts to transmute lead into gold.

[26]**William Gilbert (1544–1603)** An English scientist who studied magnetism and codified many laws related to magnetic fields. He was particularly ridiculed by Bacon for being too narrow in his researches.

after he had employed himself most laboriously in the study and observation of the loadstone, proceeded at once to construct an entire system in accordance with his favorite subject.

There is one principal and, as it were, radical distinction be- 19
tween different minds, in respect of philosophy and the sciences, which is this: that some minds are stronger and apter to mark the differences of things, others to mark their resemblances. The steady and acute mind can fix its contemplations and dwell and fasten on the subtlest distinctions: the lofty and discursive mind recognizes and puts together the finest and most general resemblances. Both kinds however easily err in excess, by catching the one at gradations, the other at shadows.

There are found some minds given to an extreme admiration of 20
antiquity, others to an extreme love and appetite for novelty; but few so duly tempered that they can hold the mean, neither carping at what has been well laid down by the ancients, nor despising what is well introduced by the moderns. This however turns to the great injury of the sciences and philosophy; since these affectations of antiquity and novelty are the humors[27] of partisans rather than judgments; and truth is to be sought for not in the felicity of any age, which is an unstable thing, but in the light of nature and experience, which is eternal. These factions therefore must be abjured,[28] and care must be taken that the intellect be not hurried by them into assent.

Contemplations of nature and of bodies in their simple form 21
break up and distract the understanding, while contemplations of nature and bodies in their composition and configuration overpower and dissolve the understanding: a distinction well seen in the school of Leucippus[29] and Democritus as compared with the other philosophies. For that school is so busied with the particles that it hardly attends to the structure; while the others are so lost in admiration of the structure that they do not penetrate to the simplicity of nature. These kinds of contemplation should therefore be alternated and taken by turns; that so the understanding may be rendered at once penetrating and comprehensive, and the inconveniences above mentioned, with the idols which proceed from them, may be avoided.

Let such then be our provision and contemplative prudence for 22
keeping off and dislodging the *Idols of the Cave*, which grow for the most part either out of the predominance of a favorite subject, or out

---

[27] **humors** Used in a medical sense to mean a distortion caused by imbalance.

[28] **abjured** Renounced, sworn off, repudiated.

[29] **Leucippus (fifth century B.C.)** Greek philosopher; teacher of Democritus and inventor of the atomistic theory. His works survive only in fragments.

of an excessive tendency to compare or to distinguish, or out of partiality for particular ages, or out of the largeness or minuteness of the objects contemplated. And generally let every student of nature take this as a rule—that whatever his mind seizes and dwells upon with peculiar satisfaction is to be held in suspicion, and that so much the more care is to be taken in dealing with such questions to keep the understanding even and clear.

But the *Idols of the Marketplace* are the most troublesome of all: 23 idols which have crept into the understanding through the alliances of words and names. For men believe that their reason governs words; but it is also true that words react on the understanding; and this it is that has rendered philosophy and the sciences sophistical and inactive. Now words, being commonly framed and applied according to the capacity of the vulgar, follow those lines of division which are most obvious to the vulgar understanding. And whenever an understanding of greater acuteness or a more diligent observation would alter those lines to suit the true divisions of nature, words stand in the way and resist the change. Whence it comes to pass that the high and formal discussions of learned men end oftentimes in disputes about words and names; with which (according to the use and wisdom of the mathematicians) it would be more prudent to begin, and so by means of definitions reduce them to order. Yet even definitions cannot cure this evil in dealing with natural and material things; since the definitions themselves consist of words, and those words beget others: so that it is necessary to recur to individual instances, and those in due series and order; as I shall say presently when I come to the method and scheme for the formation of notions and axioms.[30]

The idols imposed by words on the understanding are of two   24 kinds. They are either names of things which do not exist (for as there are things left unnamed through lack of observation, so likewise are there names which result from fantastic suppositions and to which nothing in reality responds), or they are names of things which exist, but yet confused and ill-defined, and hastily and irregularly derived from realities. Of the former kind are Fortune, the Prime Mover, Planetary Orbits, Element of Fire, and like fictions which owe their origin to false and idle theories.[31] And this class of idols is more easily expelled, because to get rid of them it is only

---

[30] **notions and axioms** Conceptions and definitive statements of truth.

[31] **idle theories** These are things that cannot be observed and thus do not exist. Fortune is fate; the Prime Mover is God or some "first" force; the notion that planets orbited the sun was considered as "fantastic" as these others or as the idea that everything was made up of fire and its many permutations.

necessary that all theories should be steadily rejected and dismissed as obsolete.

But the other class, which springs out of a faulty and unskillful 25 abstraction, is intricate and deeply rooted. Let us take for example such a word as *humid*; and see how far the several things which the word is used to signify agree with each other; and we shall find the word *humid* to be nothing else than a mark loosely and confusedly applied to denote a variety of actions which will not bear to be reduced to any constant meaning. For it both signifies that which easily spreads itself round any other body; and that which in itself is indeterminate and cannot solidize; and that which readily yields in every direction; and that which easily divides and scatters itself; and that which easily unites and collects itself; and that which readily flows and is put in motion; and that which readily clings to another body and wets it; and that which is easily reduced to a liquid, or being solid easily melts. Accordingly when you come to apply the word—if you take it in one sense, flame is humid; if in another, air is not humid; if in another, fine dust is humid; if in another, glass is humid. So that it is easy to see that the notion is taken by abstraction only from water and common and ordinary liquids, without any due verification.

There are however in words certain degrees of distortion and 26 error. One of the least faulty kinds is that of names of substances, especially of lowest species and well-deduced (for the notion of *chalk* and of *mud* is good, of *earth* bad);[32] a more faulty kind is that of actions, as *to generate, to corrupt, to alter*; the most faulty is of qualities (except such as are the immediate objects of the sense), as *heavy, light, rare, dense*, and the like. Yet in all these cases some notions are of necessity a little better than others, in proportion to the greater variety of subjects that fall within the range of the human sense.

But the *Idols of the Theater* are not innate, nor do they steal into 27 the understanding secretly, but are plainly impressed and received into the mind from the play-books of philosophical systems and the perverted rules of demonstration.[33] To attempt refutations in this case would be merely inconsistent with what I have already said: for since we agree neither upon principles nor upon demonstrations, there is no place for argument. And this is so far well, inasmuch as it leaves the honor of the ancients untouched. For they are no wise

---

[32] *earth* **bad** Chalk and mud were useful in manufacture; hence they were terms of approval. *Earth* is used here in the sense we use *dirt*, as in "digging in the dirt."

[33] **perverted rules of demonstration** Another complaint against Aristotle's logic as misapplied in Bacon's day.

disparaged—the question between them and me being only as to the way. For as the saying is, the lame man who keeps the right road outstrips the runner who takes a wrong one. Nay, it is obvious that when a man runs the wrong way, the more active and swift he is the further he will go astray.

But the course I propose for the discovery of sciences is such as leaves but little to the acuteness and strength of wits, but places all wits[34] and understandings nearly on a level. For as in the drawing of a straight line or perfect circle, much depends on the steadiness and practice of the hand, if it be done by aim of hand only, but if with the aid of rule or compass, little or nothing; so is it exactly with my plan. But though particular confutations[35] would be of no avail, yet touching the sects and general divisions of such systems I must say something; something also touching the external signs which show that they are unsound; and finally something touching the causes of such great infelicity and of such lasting and general agreement in error; that so the access to truth may be made less difficult, and the human understanding may the more willingly submit to its purgation and dismiss its idols. 28

Idols of the Theater, or of systems, are many, and there can be and perhaps will be yet many more. For were it not that now for many ages men's minds have been busied with religion and theology; and were it not that civil governments, especially monarchies, have been averse to such novelties, even in matters speculative; so that men labor therein to the peril and harming of their fortunes— not only unrewarded, but exposed also to contempt and envy; doubtless there would have arisen many other philosophical sects like to those which in great variety flourished once among the Greeks. For as on the phenomena of the heavens many hypotheses may be constructed, so likewise (and more also) many various dogmas may be set up and established on the phenomena of philosophy. And in the plays of this philosophical theater you may observe the same thing which is found in the theater of the poets, that stories invented for the stage are more compact and elegant, and more as one would wish them to be, than true stories out of history. 29

In general, however, there is taken for the material of philosophy either a great deal out of a few things, or a very little out of many things; so that on both sides philosophy is based on too narrow a foundation of experiment and natural history, and decides on 30

---

[34] **wits** Intelligence, powers of reasoning.
[35] **confutations** Specific counterarguments. Bacon means that he cannot offer particular arguments against each scientific sect; thus he offers a general warning.

the authority of too few cases. For the rational school of philosophers[36] snatches from experience a variety of common instances, neither duly ascertained nor diligently examined and weighed, and leaves all the rest to meditation and agitation of wit.

There is also another class of philosophers,[37] who having be- 31 stowed much diligent and careful labor on a few experiments, have thence made bold to educe and construct systems; wresting all other facts in a strange fashion to conformity therewith.

And there is yet a third class,[38] consisting of those who out of 32 faith and veneration mix their philosophy with theology and traditions; among whom the vanity of some has gone so far aside as to seek the origin of sciences among spirits and genii.[39] So that this parent stock of errors—this false philosophy—is of three kinds; the sophistical, the empirical, and the superstitious. . . .

But the corruption of philosophy by superstition and an admix- 33 ture of theology is far more widely spread, and does the greatest harm, whether to entire systems or to their parts. For the human understanding is obnoxious to the influence of the imagination no less than to the influence of common notions. For the contentious and sophistical kind of philosophy ensnares the understanding; but this kind, being fanciful and tumid[40] and half poetical, misleads it more by flattery. For there is in man an ambition of the understanding, no less than of the will, especially in high and lofty spirits.

Of this kind we have among the Greeks a striking example in 34 Pythagoras, though he united with it a coarser and more cumbrous superstition; another in Plato and his school,[41] more dangerous and subtle. It shows itself likewise in parts of other philosophies, in the introduction of abstract forms and final causes and first causes, with

---

[36] **rational school of philosophers** Platonists who felt that human reason alone could discover the truth and that experiment was unnecessary. Their observation of experience produced only a "variety of common instances" from which they reasoned.

[37] **another class of philosophers** William Gilbert (1544–1603) experimented tirelessly with magnetism, from which he derived numerous odd theories. Though Gilbert was a true scientist, Bacon thought of him as limited and on the wrong track.

[38] **a third class** Pythagoras (c. 580–500 B.C.) was a Greek philosopher who experimented rigorously with mathematics and a tuned string. He is said to have developed the musical scale. His theory of reincarnation, or the transmigration of souls, was somehow based on his travels in India and his work with scales. The superstitious belief in the movement of souls is what Bacon complains of.

[39] **genii** Oriental demons or spirits; a slap at Pythagoras, who traveled in the Orient.

[40] **tumid** Overblown, swollen.

[41] **Plato and his school** Plato's religious bent was further developed by Plotinus (A.D. 205–270) in his *Enneads*. Although Plotinus was not a Christian, his Neo-Platonism was welcomed as a philosophy compatible with Christianity.

the omission in most cases of causes intermediate, and the like. Upon this point the greatest caution should be used. For nothing is so mischievous as the apotheosis of error; and it is a very plague of the understanding for vanity to become the object of veneration. Yet in this vanity some of the moderns have with extreme levity indulged so far as to attempt to found a system of natural philosophy on the first chapter of Genesis, on the book of Job, and other parts of the sacred writings; seeking for the dead among the living: which also makes the inhibition and repression of it the more important, because from this unwholesome mixture of things human and divine there arises not only a fantastic philosophy but also an heretical religion. Very meet it is therefore that we be sober-minded, and give to faith that only which is faith's. . . .

So much concerning the several classes of Idols, and their 35 equipage: all of which must be renounced and put away with a fixed and solemn determination, and the understanding thoroughly freed and cleansed; the entrance into the kingdom of man, founded on the sciences, being not much other than the entrance into the kingdom of heaven, whereunto none may enter except as a little child.

QUESTIONS FOR CRITICAL READING

1. Which of Bacon's idols is the most difficult to understand? Do your best to define it.
2. Which of these idols do we still need to worry about? Why? What dangers does it present?
3. What does Bacon mean by implying that our senses are weak (para. 14)? In what ways do you agree or disagree with that opinion?
4. Occasionally Bacon says something that seems a bit like an aphorism (see the introduction to Machiavelli, p. 37). Find at least one such expression in this selection. On examination, does the expression have as much meaning as it seems to have?
5. What kind of readers did Bacon expect for this piece? What clues does his way of communicating provide regarding the nature of his anticipated readers?

SUGGESTIONS FOR WRITING

1. Which of Bacon's idols most seriously affects the way you as a person observe nature? Using enumeration, arrange the idols in order of their effect on your own judgment. If you prefer, you may write about the idol you believe is most effective in slowing investigation into nature.

2. Is it true, as Bacon says in paragraph 10, that people are in general "more moved and excited by affirmatives than by negatives"? Do we really stress the positive and deemphasize the negative in the conduct of our general affairs? Find at least three instances in which people seem to gravitate toward the positive or the negative in everyday situations. Try to establish whether Bacon has, in fact, described what is a habit of mind.

3. In paragraph 13, Bacon states that the "will and affections" enter into matters of thought. By this he means that our understanding of what we observe is conditioned by what we want and what we feel. Thus, when he says, "For what a man had rather were true he more readily believes," he tells us that people tend to believe what they want to believe. Test this statement by means of observation. Find out, for example, how many older people are convinced that the world is deteriorating, how many younger people feel that there is a plot on the part of older people to hold them back, how many women feel that men consciously oppress women, and how many men feel that feminists are not as feminine as they should be. What other beliefs can you discover that seem to have their origin in what people want to believe rather than in what is true?

4. Bacon's views on religion have always been difficult to define. He grew up in a very religious time, but his writings rarely discuss religion positively. In this work he talks about giving "to faith that only which is faith's" (para. 34). He seems to feel that scientific investigation is something quite separate from religion. Examine the selection carefully to determine what you think Bacon's view on this question is. Then take a stand on the issue of the relationship between religion and science. Should science be totally independent of religious concerns? Should religious issues control scientific experimentation? What does Bacon mean when he complains about the vanity of founding "a system of natural philosophy on the first chapter of Genesis, on the book of Job, and other parts of the sacred writings" (para. 34)? "Natural philosophy" means biology, chemistry, physics, and science in general. Are Bacon's complaints justified? Would his complaints be relevant today?

5. **CONNECTIONS** How has the reception of Charles Darwin's work been affected by a general inability of the public to see beyond Bacon's four idols? Read both Darwin's essay and that of Stephen Jay Gould. Which of those two writers is more concerned with the lingering effects of the four idols? Do you feel that the effects have seriously affected people's beliefs regarding Darwinian theory?

6. **CONNECTIONS** Read any essay in Part 8, the Feminism section, and decide how much public resistance to feminist views depends on the types of thinking Bacon condemns in his essay. Which of the four idols do you think is the most damaging to the feminist cause? Why? How, if at all, does an examination of Bacon's four idols help you clarify your own thoughts on feminist issues? Explain.

CHARLES DARWIN
Natural Selection

CHARLES DARWIN (1809–1882) was trained as a minister in the Church of England, but he was also the grandson of one of England's greatest horticulturists, Erasmus Darwin. Partly as a way of putting off ordination in the church and partly because of his natural curiosity, Darwin found himself performing the functions of a naturalist on HMS *Beagle*, which was engaged in scientific explorations around South America during the years 1831 to 1836. Darwin's book *Journal of Researches into the Geology and Natural History of the Various Countries Visited by H. M. S. Beagle, 1832–36* (1839) details the experiences he had and offers some views of his self-education as a naturalist.

His journeys on the *Beagle* led him to note variations in species of animals he found in various separate locales, particularly between remote islands and the mainland. Varieties—his term for any visible (or invisible) differences in markings, coloration, size or shape of appendages, organs, or bodies—were of some peculiar use, he believed, for animals in the environment in which he found them. He was not certain about the use of these varieties, and he did not know whether the changes that created the varieties resulted from the environment or from some chance operation of nature. Ultimately, he concluded that varieties in nature were caused by three forces: (1) natural selection, in which varieties occur spontaneously by chance but are then "selected for" because they are aids

---

From *On the Origin of Species by Means of Natural Selection*. This text is from the first edition, published in 1859. In the five subsequent editions, Darwin hedged more and more on his theory, often introducing material in defense against objections. The first edition is vigorous and direct; this edition jolted the worlds of science and religion out of their complaisance. In later editions, this chapter was titled "Natural Selection; or, Survival of the Fittest."

to survival; (2) direct action of the environment, in which nonadaptive varieties do not survive because of climate, food conditions, or the like; and (3) the effects of use or disuse of a variation (for example, the short beak of a bird mentioned in para. 9). Darwin later regarded sexual selection, which figures prominently in this work, as less significant.

The idea of evolution—the gradual change of species through some kind of modification of varieties—had been in the air for many years when Darwin began his work. The English scientists W. C. Wells in 1813 and Patrick Matthew in 1831 had both proposed theories of natural selection, although Darwin was unaware of their work. Alfred Russel Wallace (1823–1913), a younger English scientist, revealed in 1858 that he was about to propose the same theory of evolution as was Darwin. They jointly published brief versions of their theories in 1858, and the next year Darwin rushed the final version of his book *On the Origin of Species by Means of Natural Selection* to press.

Darwin did not mention human beings as part of the evolutionary process in *On the Origin of Species*; because he was particularly concerned about the probable adverse reactions of theologians, he merely promised later discussion of that subject. It came in *The Descent of Man and Selection in Relation to Sex* (1871), the companion to *On the Origin of Species*.

When Darwin returned to England after completing his research on the *Beagle*, he supplemented his knowledge with information gathered from breeders of pigeons, livestock, dogs, and horses. This research, it must be noted, involved relatively few samples and was conducted according to comparatively unscientific practices. Yet although limited, it corresponded with his observations of nature. Humans could and did cause changes in species; Darwin's task was to show that nature—through the process of natural selection— could do the same thing.

The Descent of Man stirred up a great deal of controversy between the church and Darwin's supporters. Not since the Roman Catholic Church denied the fact that the earth went around the sun, which Galileo proved scientifically by 1632 (and was placed under house arrest for his pains), had there been a more serious confrontation between science and religion. Darwin was ridiculed by ministers and doubted by older scientists; but his views were stoutly defended by younger scientists, many of whom had arrived at similar conclusions. In the end, Darwin's views were accepted by the Church of England, and when he died in 1882 he was lionized and buried at Westminster Abbey in London. Only recently has controversy concerning his work arisen again.

Darwin's Rhetoric

Despite the complexity of the material it deals with, Darwin's writing is fluent, smooth, and stylistically sophisticated and keeps the reader engaged. Darwin's rhetorical method depends entirely on the yoking of thesis and demonstration. He uses definition frequently, but most often he uses testimony, gathering information and instances, both real and imaginary, from many different sources.

Interestingly enough, Darwin claimed that he used Francis Bacon's method of induction in his research, gathering evidence of many instances of a given phenomenon, from which the truth—or a natural law—emerges. In fact, Darwin did not quite follow this path. Like most modern scientists, he established a hypothesis after a period of observation, and then he looked for evidence that confirmed or refuted the hypothesis. He was careful to include examples that argued against his view, but like most scientists, he emphasized the importance of the supportive samples.

Induction plays a part in the rhetoric of this selection in that it is dominated by examples from bird breeding, birds in nature, domestic farm animals and their breeding, and botany, including the breeding of plants and the interdependence of certain insects and certain plants. Erasmus Darwin was famous for his work with plants, and it is natural that such observations would play an important part in his grandson's thinking.

The process of natural selection is carefully discussed, particularly in paragraph 8 and thereafter. Darwin emphasizes its positive nature and its differences from selection by human breeders. The use of comparison, which appears frequently in the selection, is most conspicuous in these paragraphs. He postulates a nature in which the fittest survive because they are best adapted for survival, but he does not dwell on the fate of those who are unfit individuals. It was left to later writers, often misapplying his theories, to do that.

PREREADING QUESTIONS: WHAT TO READ FOR

The following prereading questions may help you anticipate key issues in the discussion of Charles Darwin's "Natural Selection." Keeping them in mind during your first reading of the selection should help focus your attention.

- What is the basic principle of natural selection?
- How does "human" selection differ from nature's selection?

Natural Selection

How will the struggle for existence . . . act in regard to variation? Can the principle of selection, which we have seen is so potent in the hands of man, apply in nature? I think we shall see that it can act most effectually. Let it be borne in mind in what an endless number of strange peculiarities our domestic productions, and, in a lesser degree, those under nature, vary; and how strong the hereditary tendency is. Under domestication, it may be truly said that the whole organization becomes in some degree plastic.[1] Let it be borne in mind how infinitely complex and close-fitting are the mutual relations of all organic beings to each other and to their physical conditions of life. Can it, then, be thought improbable, seeing that variations useful to man have undoubtedly occurred, that other variations useful in some way to each being in the great and complex battle of life, should sometimes occur in the course of thousands of generations? If such do occur, can we doubt (remembering that many more individuals are born than can possibly survive) that individuals having any advantage, however slight, over others, would have the best chance of surviving and or procreating their kind? On the other hand, we may feel sure that any variation in the least degree injurious would be rigidly destroyed. This preservation of favorable variations and the rejection of injurious variations, I call Natural Selection. Variations neither useful nor injurious would not be affected by natural selection, and would be left a fluctuating element, as perhaps we see in the species called polymorphic.[2]

We shall best understand the probable course of natural selection by taking the case of a country undergoing some physical change, for instance, of climate. The proportional numbers of its inhabitants would almost immediately undergo a change, and some species might become extinct. We may conclude, from what we have seen of the intimate and complex manner in which the inhabitants of each country are bound together, that any change in the numerical proportions of some of the inhabitants, independently of the change of climate itself, would most seriously affect many of the others. If the country were open on its borders, new forms would certainly immigrate, and this also would seriously disturb the relations of some of the former inhabitants. Let it be remembered how powerful the influence of a single introduced tree or mammal has been shown

---

[1] **plastic** Capable of being shaped and changed.
[2] **species called polymorphic** Species that have more than one form over the course of their lives, such as butterflies.

to be. But in the case of an island, or of a country partly surrounded by barriers, into which new and better adapted forms could not freely enter, we should then have places in the economy of nature which would assuredly be better filled up, if some of the original inhabitants were in some manner modified; for, had the area been open to immigration, these same places would have been seized on by intruders. In such case, every slight modification, which in the course of ages chanced to arise, and which in any way favored the individuals of any of the species, by better adapting them to their altered conditions, would tend to be preserved; and natural selection would thus have free scope for the work of improvement.

We have reason to believe . . . that a change in the conditions of   3 life, by specially acting on the reproductive system, causes or increases variability; and in the foregoing case the conditions of life are supposed to have undergone a change, and this would manifestly be favorable to natural selection, by giving a better chance of profitable variations occurring; and unless profitable variations do occur, natural selection can do nothing. Not that, as I believe, any extreme amount of variability is necessary; as man can certainly produce great results by adding up in any given direction mere individual differences, so could Nature, but far more easily, from having incomparably longer time at her disposal. Nor do I believe that any great physical change, as of climate, or any unusual degree of isolation to check immigration, is actually necessary to produce new and unoccupied places for natural selection to fill up by modifying and improving some of the varying inhabitants. For as all the inhabitants of each country are struggling together with nicely balanced forces, extremely slight modifications in the structure or habits of one inhabitant would often give it an advantage over others; and still further modifications of the same kind would often still further increase the advantage. No country can be named in which all the native inhabitants are now so perfectly adapted to each other and to the physical conditions under which they live, that none of them could anyhow be improved; for in all countries, the natives have been so far conquered by naturalized productions, that they have allowed foreigners to take firm possession of the land. And as foreigners have thus everywhere beaten some of the natives, we may safely conclude that the natives might have been modified with advantage, so as to have better resisted such intruders.

As man can produce and certainly has produced a great result   4 by his methodical and unconscious means of selection, what may not nature effect? Man can act only on external and visible characters; nature cares nothing for appearances, except in so far as they may be useful to any being. She can act on every internal organ, on every shade of constitutional difference, on the whole machinery of life. Man selects only for his own good; Nature only for that of the being which she tends. Every selected character is fully exercised by her; and the being is placed under well-suited conditions of life. Man keeps the natives of many climates in the same country; he seldom exercises each selected character in some peculiar and fitting manner; he feeds a long and a short beaked pigeon on the same food; he does not exercise a long-backed or long-legged quadruped in any peculiar manner; he exposes sheep with long and short wool to the same climate. He does not allow the most vigorous males to struggle for the females. He does not rigidly destroy all inferior animals, but protects during each varying season, as far as lies in his power, all his productions. He often begins his selection by some half-monstrous form; or at least by some modification prominent enough to catch the eye, or to be plainly useful to him. Under nature, the slightest difference of structure or constitution may well turn the nicely balanced scale in the struggle for life, and so be preserved. How fleeting are the wishes and efforts of man! how short his time! and consequently how poor will his products be, compared with those accumulated by nature during whole geological periods. Can we wonder, then, that nature's productions should be far "truer" in character than man's productions; that they should be infinitely better adapted to the most complex conditions of life, and should plainly bear the stamp of far higher workmanship?

It may be said that natural selection is daily and hourly scrutinizing, throughout the world, every variation, even the slightest; rejecting that which is bad, preserving and adding up all that is good; silently and insensibly working, whenever and wherever opportunity offers, at the improvement of each organic being in relation to its organic and inorganic conditions of life. We see nothing of these slow changes in progress, until the hand of time has marked the long lapse of ages, and then so imperfect is our view into long past geological ages, that we only see that the forms of life are now different from what they formerly were. 5

Although natural selection can act only through and for the good of each being, yet characters and structures, which we are apt to consider as of very trifling importance, may thus be acted on. When we see leaf-eating insects green, and bark-feeders mottled-grey; the alpine ptarmigan white in winter, the red-grouse the color of heather, and the black-grouse that of peaty earth, we must believe that these tints are of service to these birds and insects in preserving them from danger. Grouse, if not destroyed at some period of their lives, would increase in countless numbers; they are known to suffer 6 largely from birds of prey; and hawks are guided by eyesight to their prey—so much so that on parts of the Continent[3] persons are warned not to keep white pigeons, as being the most liable to destruction. Hence I can see no reason to doubt that natural selection might be most effective in giving the proper color to each kind of grouse, and in keeping that color, when once acquired, true and constant. Nor ought we to think that the occasional destruction of an animal of any particular color would produce little effect; we should remember how essential it is in a flock of white sheep to destroy every lamb with the faintest trace of black. In plants, the down on the fruit and the color of the flesh are considered by botanists as characters of the most trifling importance; yet we hear from an excellent horticulturist, Downing,[4] that in the United States, smooth-skinned fruits suffer far more from a beetle, a curculio,[5] than those with down; that purple plums suffer far more from a certain disease than yellow plums; whereas another disease attacks yellow-fleshed peaches far more than those with other colored flesh. If, with all the aids of art, these slight differences make a great difference in cultivating the several varieties, assuredly, in a state of nature, where the trees would have to struggle with other trees and with a host of enemies, such differences would effectually settle which variety, whether a smooth or downy, a yellow or purple fleshed fruit, should succeed.

In looking at many small points of difference between species, which, as far as our ignorance permits us to judge, seem to be quite unimportant, we must not forget that climate, food, etc., probably produce some slight and direct effect. It is, however, far more necessary to bear in mind that there are many unknown laws of correlation[6] of growth, which, when one part of the organization is modified through variation and the modifications are accumulated by natural selection for the good of the being, will cause other modifications, often of the most unexpected nature. 7

As we see that those variations which under domestication appear at any particular period of life, tend to reappear in the offspring at the same period—for instance, in the seeds of the many varieties 8

---

[3] **Continent** European continent; the contiguous land mass of Europe, which excludes the British Isles.

[4] **Andrew Jackson Downing (1815–1852)** American horticulturist and specialist in fruit and fruit trees.

[5] **curculio** A weevil.

[6] **laws of correlation** In certain plants and animals, one condition relates to another, as in the case of blue-eyed white cats, which are often deaf; the reasons are not clear but have to do with genes and their locations.

of our culinary and agricultural plants; in the caterpillar and cocoon stages of the varieties of the silkworm; in the eggs of poultry, and in the color of the down of their chickens; in the horns of our sheep and cattle when nearly adult — so in a state of nature, natural selection will be enabled to act on and modify organic beings at any age, by the accumulation of profitable variations at that age, and by their inheritance at a corresponding age. If it profit a plant to have its seeds more and more widely disseminated by the wind, I can see no greater difficulty in this being effected through natural selection than in the cotton-planter increasing and improving by selection the down in the pods on his cotton-trees. Natural selection may modify and adapt the larva of an insect to a score of contingencies, wholly different from those which concern the mature insect. These modifications will no doubt effect, through the laws of correlation, the structure of the adult; and probably in the case of those insects which live only for a few hours, and which never feed, a large part of their structure is merely the correlated result of successive changes in the structure of their larvae. So, conversely, modifications in the adult will probably often affect the structure of the larva; but in all cases natural selection will ensure that modifications consequent on other modifications at a different period of life, shall not be in the least degree injurious: for if they became so, they would cause the extinction of the species.

Natural selection will modify the structure of the young in relation to the parent, and of the parent in relation to the young. In social animals it will adapt the structure of each individual for the benefit of the community, if each in consequence profits by the selected change. What natural selection cannot do is to modify the structure of one species, without giving it any advantage, for the good of another species; and though statements to this effect may be found in works of natural history, I cannot find one case which will bear investigation. A structure used only once in an animal's whole life, if of high importance to it, might be modified to any extent by natural selection; for instance, the great jaws possessed by certain insects, and used exclusively for opening the cocoon — or the hard tip to the beak of nestling birds, used for breaking the egg. It has been asserted that of the best short-beaked tumbler-pigeons, more perish in the egg than are able to get out of it; so that fanciers[7] assist in the act of hatching. Now, if nature had to make the beak of a full-grown pigeon very short for the bird's own advantage, the process of modification would be very slow, and there would be simultaneously the most

9

---

[7] **fanciers** Amateurs who raise and race pigeons.

rigorous selection of the young birds within the egg, which had the most powerful and hardest beaks, for all with weak beaks would inevitably perish; or, more delicate and more easily broken shells might be selected, the thickness of the shell being known to vary like every other structure.

Sexual Selection

Inasmuch as peculiarities often appear under domestication in one sex and become hereditarily attached to that sex, the same fact probably occurs under nature, and if so, natural selection will be able to modify one sex in its functional relations to the other sex, or in relation to wholly different habits of life in the two sexes, as is sometimes the case with insects. And this leads me to say a few words on what I call Sexual Selection. This depends, not on a struggle for existence, but on a struggle between the males for possession of the females; the result is not death to the unsuccessful competitor, but few or no offspring. Sexual selection is, therefore, less rigorous than natural selection. Generally, the most vigorous males, those which are best fitted for their places in nature, will leave most progeny. But in many cases, victory will depend not on general vigor, but on having special weapons, confined to the male sex. A hornless stag or spurless cock would have a poor chance of leaving offspring. Sexual selection by always allowing the victor to breed might surely give indomitable courage, length to the spur, and strength to the wing to strike in the spurred leg, as well as the brutal cock fighter,[8] who knows well that he can improve his breed by careful selection of the best cocks. How low in the scale of nature this law of battle descends, I know not; male alligators have been described as fighting, bellowing, and whirling round, like Indians in a wardance, for the possession of the females; male salmons have been seen fighting all day long; male stag-beetles often bear wounds from the huge mandibles[9] of other males. The war is, perhaps, severest between the males of polygamous animals,[10] and these seem oftenest provided with special weapons. The males of carnivorous animals are already well armed; though to them and to others, special means of defense may be given through means of sexual selection, as the mane to the lion, the shoulder-pad to the boar, and the hooked jaw to the male

10

---

[8] **brutal cock fighter** Cockfights were a popular spectator sport in England, especially for gamblers, but many people considered them a horrible brutality.

[9] **mandibles** Jaws.

[10] **polygamous animals** Animals that typically have more than one mate.

salmon; for the shield may be as important for victory as the sword
or spear.

Among birds, the contest is often of a more peaceful character. 11
All those who have attended to the subject believe that there is the
severest rivalry between the males of many species to attract, by
singing, the females. The rock-thrush of Guiana,[11] birds of paradise,
and some others, congregate; and successive males display their gor-
geous plumage and perform strange antics before the females, which
standing by as spectators, at last choose the most attractive partner.
Those who have closely attended to birds in confinement well know
that they often take individual preferences and dislikes: thus Sir
R. Heron[12] has described how one pied peacock was eminently
attractive to all his hen birds. It may appear childish to attribute any
effect to such apparently weak means: I cannot here enter on the
details necessary to support this view; but if man can in a short time
give elegant carriage and beauty to his bantams,[13] according to his
standard of beauty, I can see no good reason to doubt that female
birds, by selecting, during thousands of generations, the most melo-
dious or beautiful males, according to their standard of beauty, might
produce a marked effect. I strongly suspect that some well-known
laws with respect to the plumage of male and female birds, in comparison with the plumage of the young, can be explained on the view
of plumage having been chiefly modified by sexual selection, acting
when the birds have come to the breeding age or during the breeding
season; the modifications thus produced being inherited at corresponding ages or seasons, either by the males alone, or by the males
and females; but I have not space here to enter on this subject.

Thus it is, as I believe, that when the males and females of any 12
animal have the same general habits of life, but differ in structure,
color, or ornament, such differences have been mainly caused by
sexual selection; that is, individual males have had, in successive generations, some slight advantage over other males, in their weapons,
means of defense, or charms; and have transmitted these advantages
to their male offspring. Yet, I would not wish to attribute all such
sexual differences to this agency: for we see peculiarities arising and
becoming attached to the male sex in our domestic animals (as the
wattle in male carriers, horn-like protuberances in the cocks of certain fowls, etc.), which we cannot believe to be either useful to the

---

[11] **Guiana** Formerly British Guiana, now Guyana, on the northeast coast of
South America.
[12] **Sir Robert Heron (1765–1854)** English politician who maintained a
menagerie of animals.
[13] **bantams** Cocks bred for fighting.

males in battle, or attractive to the females. We see analogous cases under nature, for instance, the tuft of hair on the breast of the turkey-cock, which can hardly be either useful or ornamental to this bird; indeed, had the tuft appeared under domestication, it would have been called a monstrosity.

Illustrations of the Action of Natural Selection

In order to make it clear how, as I believe, natural selection acts, I must beg permission to give one or two imaginary illustrations. Let us take the case of a wolf, which preys on various animals, securing some by craft, some by strength, and some by fleetness; and let us suppose that the fleetest prey, a deer for instance, had from any change in the country increased in numbers, or that other prey had decreased in numbers, during that season of the year when the wolf is hardest pressed for food. I can under such circumstances see no reason to doubt that the swiftest and slimmest wolves would have the best chance of surviving, and so be preserved or selected, provided always that they retained strength to master their prey at this or at some other period of the year, when they might be compelled to prey on other animals. I can see no more reason to doubt this, than that man can improve the fleetness of his greyhounds by careful and methodical selection, or by that unconscious selection which results from each man trying to keep the best dogs without any thought of modifying the breed. 13

Even without any change in the proportional numbers of the animals on which our wolf preyed, a cub might be born with an innate tendency to pursue certain kinds of prey. Nor can this be thought very improbable; for we often observe great differences in the natural tendencies of our domestic animals; one cat, for instance, taking to catch rats, another mice; one cat, according to Mr. St. John,[14] bringing home winged game, another hares or rabbits, and another hunting on marshy ground and almost nightly catching woodcocks or snipes. The tendency to catch rats rather than mice is known to be inherited. Now, if any slight innate change of habit or of structure benefited an individual wolf, it would have the best chance of surviving and of leaving offspring. Some of its young would probably inherit the same habits or structure, and by the repetition of this process, a new variety might be formed which would either supplant or 14

---

[14] **Charles George William St. John (1809–1856)** An English naturalist whose book *Wild Sports and Natural History of the Highlands* was published in 1846.

coexist with the parent-form of wolf. Or, again, the wolves inhabiting a mountainous district, and those frequenting the lowlands, would naturally be forced to hunt different prey; and from the continued preservation of the individuals best fitted for the two sites, two varieties might slowly be formed. These varieties would cross and blend where they met; but to this subject of intercrossing we shall soon have to return. I may add, that, according to Mr. Pierce,[15] there are two varieties of the wolf inhabiting the Catskill Mountains in the United States, one with a light greyhound-like form, which pursues deer, and the other more bulky, with shorter legs, which more frequently attacks the shepherd's flocks.

Let us now take a more complex case. Certain plants excrete a sweet juice, apparently for the sake of eliminating something injurious from their sap; this is effected by glands at the base of the stipules[16] in some Leguminosæ, and at the back of the leaf of the common laurel. This juice, though small in quantity, is greedily sought by insects. Let us now suppose a little sweet juice or nectar to be excreted by the inner bases of the petals of a flower. In this case insects in seeking the nectar would get dusted with pollen, and would certainly often transport the pollen from one flower to the stigma of another flower. The flowers of two distinct individuals of the same species would thus get crossed; and the act of crossing, we have good reason to believe (as will hereafter be more fully alluded to), would produce very vigorous seedlings, which consequently would have the best chance of flourishing and surviving. Some of these seedlings would probably inherit the nectar-excreting power. Those individual flowers which had the largest glands or nectaries, and which excreted most nectar, would be oftenest visited by insects, and would be oftenest crossed; and so in the long-run would gain the upper hand. Those flowers, also, which had their stamens and pistils[17] placed, in relation to the size and habits of the particular insects which visited them, so as to favor in any degree the transportal of their pollen from flower to flower, would likewise be favored or selected. We might have taken the case of insects visiting flowers for the sake of collecting pollen instead of nectar; and as pollen is formed for the sole object of fertilization, its destruction appears a simple loss to the plant; yet if a little pollen were carried, at first occasionally and then habitually, by the pollen-devouring insects from flower to flower, and a cross thus effected, although nine-tenths of

15

---

[15] **Mr. Pierce** Unidentified.

[16] **stipules** Spines at the base of a leaf.

[17] **stamens and pistils** Sexual organs of plants. The male and female organs appear together in the same flower.

the pollen were destroyed, it might still be a great gain to the plant; and those individuals which produced more and more pollen, and had larger and larger anthers,[18] would be selected.

When our plant, by this process of the continued preservation or natural selection of more and more attractive flowers, had been rendered highly attractive to insects, they would, unintentionally on their part, regularly carry pollen from flower to flower; and that they can most effectually do this, I could easily show by many striking instances. I will give only one — not as a very striking case, but as likewise illustrating one step in the separation of the sexes of plants, presently to be alluded to. Some holly-trees bear only male flowers, which have four stamens producing rather a small quantity of pollen, and a rudimentary pistil; other holly-trees bear only female flowers; these have a full-sized pistil, and four stamens with shrivelled anthers, in which not a grain of pollen can be detected. Having found a female tree exactly sixty yards from a male tree, I put the stigmas[19] of twenty flowers, taken from different branches, under the microscope, and on all, without exception, there were pollengrains, and on some a profusion of pollen. As the wind had set for several days from the female to the male tree, the pollen could not thus have been carried. The weather had been cold and boisterous, and therefore not favorable to bees; nevertheless every female flower which I examined had been effectually fertilized by the bees, accidentally dusted with pollen, having flown from tree to tree in search of nectar. But to return to our imaginary case: as soon as the plant had been rendered so highly attractive to insects that pollen was regularly carried from flower to flower, another process might commence. No naturalist doubts the advantage of what has been called the "physiological division of labor"; hence we may believe that it would be advantageous to a plant to produce stamens alone in one flower or on one whole plant, and pistils alone in another flower or on another plant. In plants under culture and placed under new conditions of life, sometimes the male organs and sometimes the female organs become more or less impotent; now if we suppose this to occur in ever so slight a degree under nature, then as pollen is already carried regularly from flower to flower, and as a more complete separation of the sexes of our plant would be advantageous on the principle of the division of labor, individuals with this tendency more and more increased, would be continually favored or selected, until at last a complete separation of the sexes would be effected.

16

---

[18] **anthers** That part of the stamen that contains pollen.
[19] **stigmas** Where the plant's pollen develops.

Let us now turn to the nectar-feeding insects in our imaginary   17
case: we may suppose the plant of which we have been slowly increasing the nectar by continued selection, to be a common plant;
and that certain insects depended in main part on its nectar for food.
I could give many facts, showing how anxious bees are to save time;
for instance, their habit of cutting holes and sucking the nectar at
the bases of certain flowers, which they can, with a very little more
trouble, enter by the mouth. Bearing such facts in mind, I can see no
reason to doubt that an accidental deviation in the size and form of
the body, or in the curvature and length of the proboscis,[20] etc., far
too slight to be appreciated by us, might profit a bee or other insect,
so that an individual so characterized would be able to obtain its
food more quickly, and so have a better chance of living and leaving
descendants. Its descendants would probably inherit a tendency to a
similar slight deviation of structure. The tubes of the corollas[21] of
the common red and incarnate clovers (Trifolium pratense and in-
carnatum) do not on a hasty glance appear to differ in length; yet the
hive-bee can easily suck the nectar out of the incarnate clover, but
not out of the common red clover, which is visited by humble-
bees[22] alone; so that whole fields of the red clover offer in vain an
abundant supply of precious nectar to the hive-bee. Thus it might
be a great advantage to the hive-bee to have a slightly longer or differently constructed proboscis. On the other hand, I have found by
experiment that the fertility of clover greatly depends on bees visiting and moving parts of the corolla, so as to push the pollen on to
the stigmatic surface. Hence, again, if humble-bees were to become
rare in any country, it might be a great advantage to the red clover to
have a shorter or more deeply divided tube to its corolla, so that the
hive-bee could visit its flowers. Thus I can understand how a flower
and a bee might slowly become, either simultaneously or one after
the other, modified and adapted in the most perfect manner to each
other, by the continued preservation of individuals presenting mutual and slightly favorable deviations of structure.

I am well aware that this doctrine of natural selection, exempli-   18
fied in the above imaginary instances, is open to the same objections
which were at first urged against Sir Charles Lyell's noble views[23] on

---

[20] **proboscis** Snout.
[21] **corollas** Inner set of floral petals.
[22] **humble-bees** Bumblebees.
[23] **Sir Charles Lyell's noble views** Lyell (1797–1875) was an English geologist whose landmark work, *Principles of Geology* (1830–1833), Darwin read while on
the *Beagle*. The book inspired Darwin, and the two scientists became friends. Lyell
was shown portions of *On the Origin of Species* while Darwin was writing it.

"the modern changes of the earth, as illustrative of geology"; but we now very seldom hear the action, for instance, of the coast-waves, called a trifling and insignificant cause, when applied to the excavation of gigantic valleys or to the formation of the longest lines of inland cliffs. Natural selection can act only by the preservation and accumulation of infinitesimally small inherited modifications, each profitable to the preserved being; and as modern geology has almost banished such views as the excavation of a great valley by a single diluvial[24] wave, so will natural selection, if it be a true principle, banish the belief of the continued creation of new organic beings, or of any great and sudden modification in their structure.

---

[24] **diluvial** Pertaining to a flood. Darwin means that geological changes, such as those that caused the Grand Canyon, were no longer thought of as occurring instantly by flood (or other catastrophes) but were considered to have developed over a long period of time, as he imagines happened in the evolution of the species.

QUESTIONS FOR CRITICAL READING

1. Darwin's metaphor "battle of life" (para. 1) introduces issues that might be thought extraneous to a scientific inquiry. What is the danger of using such a metaphor? What is the advantage of doing so?
2. Many religious groups reject Darwin's concept of natural selection, but they heartily accept human selection in the form of controlled breeding. Why would there be such a difference between the two?
3. Do you feel that the theory of natural selection is a positive force? Could it be directed by divine power?
4. In this work, there is no reference to human beings in terms of the process of selection. How might the principles at work on animals also work on people? Do you think that Darwin assumes this?
5. When this chapter was published in a later edition, Darwin added to its title "Survival of the Fittest." What issues or emotions does that new title raise that "Natural Selection" does not?

SUGGESTIONS FOR WRITING

1. In paragraph 13, Darwin uses imaginary examples. Compare the value of his genuine examples and these imaginary ones. How effective is the use of imaginary examples in an argument? What requirements should an imaginary example meet to be forceful in an argument? Do you find Darwin's imaginary examples to be strong or weak?
2. From paragraph 14 on, Darwin discusses the process of modification of a species through its beginning in the modification of an individual.

Explain, insofar as you understand the concept, how a species could be modified by a variation occurring in just one individual. In your explanation, use Darwin's rhetorical technique of the imaginary example.

3. Write an essay that takes as its thesis statement the following sentence from paragraph 18: "Natural selection can act only by the preservation and accumulation of infinitesimally small inherited modifications, each profitable to the preserved being." Be sure to examine the work carefully for other statements by Darwin that add strength, clarity, and meaning to this one. You may also employ the Darwinian device of presenting imaginary instances in your essay.

4. A controversy exists concerning the Darwinian theory of evolution. Explore the *Readers' Guide to Periodical Literature* (a reference book you can find at your local or college library), and the Internet for up-to-date information on the creationist-evolutionist conflict in schools. Look up either or both terms to see what articles you can find. Define the controversy and take a stand on it. Use your knowledge of natural selection gained from this piece. Remember, too, that Darwin was trained as a minister of the church and was concerned about religious opinion.

5. When Darwin wrote this piece, he believed that sexual selection was of great importance in evolutionary changes in species. Assuming that this belief is true, establish the similarities between sexual selection in plants and animals and sexual selection, as you have observed it, in people. Paragraphs 10 to 12 discuss this issue. Darwin does not discuss selection in human beings, but it is clear that physical and stylistic distinctions between the sexes have some bearing on selection. Assuming that to be true, what qualities in people (physical and mental) are likely to survive? Why?

6. **CONNECTIONS**   Which of Francis Bacon's four idols would have made it most difficult for Darwin's contemporaries to accept the theory of evolution, despite the mass of evidence he presented? Do the idols interfere with people's ability to evaluate evidence?

7. **CONNECTIONS**   To what extent are Darwin's theories a threat to public morality? Consider Iris Murdoch's "Morality and Religion" and the Dalai Lama's "The Ethics of Compassion" in Part 7. How do their ideas on morality relate to Darwin's ideas on the survival of the fittest? Some people in the mid nineteenth century feared that Darwin's theories could undermine religion and therefore religious codes of ethics and morality. Why do you think some people felt that way? Explain. Do you think such fears were legitimate? Why or why not?

8. **SEEING CONNECTIONS**   Charles Darwin's *On the Origin of Species* (1859) and *The Descent of Man* (1871) were met with a storm of protest and controversy in the United States and Europe. In response to Darwin's theory of evolution, which posits that humans and apes descended from a common ancestor, Princeton University theologian Charles Hodge published *What Is Darwinism?* (1874). Hodge claimed that the "denial of [God's] design in nature is virtually the denial of God." This was a core argument among many of Darwin's critics.

Examine the following image, an 1871 cover of the French satirical journal *La petite lune* (The Little Moon), carefully. How does this depiction of Darwin compare with his portrait on p. 558? Why do you think the artist chose to caricaturize Darwin this way? Read Genesis 2–3 in the Bible and explain the significance of the apples and tree in the image below. Does this caricature support or refute Hodge's claim that Darwin's theories deny the existence of God? Why?

DARWIN

(Voir à la page 2.)

RACHEL CARSON
The Sunless Sea

RACHEL CARSON (1907–1964) was educated at the Pennsylvania College for Women (now Chatham College) and Johns Hopkins University, where she received a master's degree in zoology in 1932. She continued her studies at the Marine Biological Laboratory of the Woods Hole Oceanographic Institute in Massachusetts. After teaching biology at the University of Maryland, Carson joined the Bureau of Fisheries (now the United States Fish and Wildlife Service) in 1936. She became editor-in-chief of its publications in 1949. Her first bestselling book on science, *The Sea Around Us* (1951), earned her a National Book Award, among many other prizes. In 1952 she left government service to devote herself to research and writing.

Although Rachel Carson was not a scientist, she was frequently praised for her science writing, which distinguished her from others in her field. She was a painstaking writer who, by her own admission, wrote late into the night and subjected her work to many revisions. In addition to magazine articles, she wrote a number of books, including *Under the Sea-Wind: A Naturalist's Picture of Ocean Life* (1941), *The Edge of the Sea* (1955), and *Silent Spring* (1962). She was eventually elected to the British Royal Society of Literature and the American Institute of Arts and Letters.

Her most successful book, *Silent Spring*, brought to the attention of the nation and the world the harmful effects of widespread use of pesticides. It sold more than 500,000 copies, which astonished Carson. The book had an enormous influence on the curtailment of the use of pesticides such as DDT, which had wreaked havoc on numerous species, especially birds. Only in recent years have some species begun to recover to normal populations.

From *The Sea Around Us*.

When she wrote *Silent Spring*, Carson realized that many scientists knew that the long-term effects of the pesticides they were developing would be devastating. The reason for their silence, according to Carson, was clear: the insecticide manufacturers supported entomologists with generous research grants, essentially "buying off" the very scientists who might have made a difference by informing the public about the dangers of spraying.

In *The Sea Around Us* (1951), Carson was not so much sounding an alarm as she was presenting a picture of a world that at the time was not known to the general public. Naturally, much has been discovered about the sea since the book's publication, but most of what Carson wrote is still quite relevant today. Indeed, when she wrote these pages she was a pioneer in oceanic ecology.

Carson's Rhetoric

Carson was praised for her ability to communicate matters of science to a wide audience. In college, she was an English major before she switched to biology; her rhetorical style, although not specifically literary in this essay, is characterized by careful writing, vivid description, and metaphors designed to move, as well as inform, her audience.

Her technique is straightforward. After establishing the expanse and depth of the world's oceans, Carson begins a survey of those who have tried to discover its secrets. She mentions William Beebe and Otis Barton, followed by French divers in the 1950s (she updated her details in a later edition of the book). She then goes through history to point to Sir John Ross in 1818, Edward Forbes in the 1850s, the surveying ship *Bulldog* in 1860, the *Challenger* in 1872 — all to show that people had been gradually learning that life existed at depths that had seemed unlikely if not impossible.

Beginning in paragraph 10, Carson describes the contemporary situation in which a "'layer' of some sort" (para. 12) indicated that there were reflective bodies in the water that postwar sonic equipment was able to detect. But no one could identify what the layer consisted of. The likelihood, she suggests, is that the layer may be comprised of plankton or perhaps tiny squid that undulate upward toward the night sky, then downward away from daylight. In paragraphs 12–16, she describes attempts to observe the ocean depths and to discover what the "phantom bottom" (para. 13) actually was.

By paragraph 25 Carson has established that there are abundant sources of food at very deep levels of the ocean. Whales, seals, and other animals had been feeding at great depths for millions of years, so it should have been no surprise. Yet until recently there had been no way to study the truly great depths of the oceans. Paragraphs 26–30 examine the development and habits of whales and seals, reporting on their strange and unusual habits. Paragraphs 31–34 examine the phenomenon of very high pressures experienced in the ocean's depths.

Then, surprisingly, she turns to the ocean lights that appear in depths that seemed to be entirely without light. In paragraphs 36–41 we find that fish of various sorts sometimes have vivid colors, although rays of light hardly reach their depths. Some aquatic species are luminescent, and others have only a sense of touch to inform them of their whereabouts. In paragraph 43 she states, "Pressure, darkness, and— we should have added only a few years ago—silence, are the conditions of life in the deep sea." She notes that military hydrophones— sound sensors planted throughout the oceans to detect submarines during World War II—picked up a wide variety of sounds emanating from many different species all through the oceans.

She ends her essay with some speculation on the age and range of the life in the depths of the seas, focusing on sharks, fossils, and fossil fish, such as the coelacanths, which were first discovered in 1938 after being assumed to have been extinct for 60 million years. Since the publication of her book, numerous other coelacanths have been fished from the sea, but they still remain mysterious animals.

Carson's rhetorical methods are marked by extensive description of historical explorations of the ocean, followed by a review of modern and contemporary reports of discovery and oceanic activity. Her capacity to describe the discoveries is part of her style and part of the appeal of this essay. She makes the information much more accessible by gathering it carefully and organizing it effectively, beginning with the earliest exploration, ending with the current understanding of explorers and scientists. To that she adds details concerning the life found at various levels of the deep. Here, too, she pauses to describe phenomena in detail so that we have a more tangible understanding of what is known about the darkest environments of the ocean.

PREREADING QUESTIONS: WHAT TO READ FOR

The following prereading questions may help you anticipate key issues in the discussion of Rachel Carson's "The Sunless Sea." Keeping them in mind during your first reading of the selection should help focus your attention.

- What had been known about the depths of the ocean in the nineteenth century?

- Which mysteries seem yet to be resolved?
- What had been learned about the ocean in Carson's time that had not been known before?

The Sunless Sea

> Where great whales come sailing by,
> Sail and sail, with unshut eye.
> — MATTHEW ARNOLD

Between the sunlit surface waters of the open sea and the hidden hills and valleys of the ocean floor lies the least known region of the sea. These deep, dark waters, with all their mysteries and their unsolved problems, cover a very considerable part of the earth. The whole world ocean extends over about three-fourths of the surface of the globe. If we subtract the shallow areas of the continental shelves and the scattered banks and shoals, where at least the pale ghost of sunlight moves over the underlying bottom, there still remains about half the earth that is covered by miles-deep, lightless water, that has been dark since the world began.

This region has withheld its secrets more obstinately than any other. Man, with all his ingenuity, has been able to venture only to its threshold. Carrying tanks of compressed air, he can swim down to depths of about 300 feet. He can descend about 500 feet wearing a diving helmet and a rubberized suit. Only a few men in all the history of the world have had the experience of descending, alive, beyond the range of visible light. The first to do so were William Beebe[1] and Otis Barton; in the bathysphere, they reached a depth of 3028 feet in the open ocean off Bermuda, in the year 1934. Barton alone, in the summer of 1949, descended to a depth of 4500 feet off California, in a steel sphere of somewhat different design; and in 1953 French divers penetrated depths greater than a mile, existing for several hours in a zone of cold and darkness where the presence of living man had never before been known.

Although only a fortunate few can ever visit the deep sea, the precise instruments of the oceanographer, recording light penetration, pressure, salinity, and temperature, have given us the materials with

---

[1] **William Beebe (1877–1962)** With Otis Barton (1899–?), was the first explorer to reach depths of half a mile in the 1930s.

which to reconstruct in imagination these eerie, forbidding regions. Unlike the surface waters, which are sensitive to every gust of wind, which know day and night, respond to the pull of sun and moon, and change as the seasons change, the deep waters are a place where change comes slowly, if at all. Down beyond the reach of the sun's rays, there is no alternation of light and darkness. There is rather an endless night, as old as the sea itself. For most of its creatures, groping their way endlessly through its black waters, it must be a place of hunger, where food is scarce and hard to find, a shelterless place where there is no sanctuary from ever-present enemies, where one can only move on and on, from birth to death, through the darkness, confined as in a prison to his own particular layer of the sea.

They used to say that nothing could live in the deep sea. It was a belief that must have been easy to accept, for without proof to the contrary, how could anyone conceive of life in such a place? 4

A century ago the British biologist Edward Forbes wrote: "As we descend deeper and deeper into this region, the inhabitants become more and more modified, and fewer and fewer, indicating our approach to an abyss where life is either extinguished, or exhibits but a few sparks to mark its lingering presence." Yet Forbes urged further exploration of "this vast deep-sea region" to settle forever the question of the existence of life at great depths. 5

Even then the evidence was accumulating. Sir John Ross, during his exploration of the arctic seas in 1818, had brought up from a depth of 1000 fathoms mud in which there were worms, "thus proving there was animal life in the bed of the ocean notwithstanding the darkness, stillness, silence, and immense pressure produced by more than a mile of superincumbent water." 6

Then from the surveying ship *Bulldog*, examining a proposed northern route for a cable from Faroe to Labrador in 1860, came another report. The *Bulldog's* sounding line, which at one place had been allowed to lie for some time on the bottom at a depth of 1260 fathoms, came up with 13 starfish clinging to it. Through these starfish, the ship's naturalist wrote, "the deep has sent forth the long coveted message." But not all the zoologists of the day were prepared to accept the message. Some doubters asserted that the starfish had "convulsively embraced" the line somewhere on the way back to the surface. 7

In the same year, 1860, a cable in the Mediterranean was raised for repairs from a depth of 1200 fathoms. It was found to be heavily encrusted with corals and other sessile[2] animals that had attached themselves at an early stage of development and grown to maturity 8

---

[2] **sessile** Attached directly at the base.

over a period of months or years. There was not the slightest chance that they had become entangled in the cable as it was being raised to the surface.

Then the *Challenger*, the first ship ever equipped for oceano- 9 graphic exploration, set out from England in the year 1872 and traced a course around the globe. From bottoms lying under miles of water, from silent deeps carpeted with red clay ooze, and from all the lightless intermediate depths, net-haul after net-haul of strange and fantastic creatures came up and were spilled out on the decks. Poring over the weird beings thus brought up for the first time into the light of day, beings no man had ever seen before, the *Challenger* scientists realized that life existed even on the deepest floor of the abyss.

The recent discovery that a living cloud of some unknown crea- 10 tures is spread over much of the ocean at a depth of several hundred fathoms below the surface is the most exciting thing that has been learned about the ocean for many years.

When, during the first quarter of the twentieth century, echo 11 sounding was developed to allow ships while under way to record the depth of the bottom, probably no one suspected that it would also provide a means of learning something about deep-sea life. But operators of the new instruments soon discovered that the sound waves, directed downward from the ship like a beam of light, were reflected back from any solid object they met. Answering echoes were returned from intermediate depths, presumably from schools of fish, whales, or submarines; then a second echo was received from the bottom.

These facts were so well established by the late 1930's that fish- 12 ermen had begun to talk about using their fathometers to search for schools of herring. Then the war brought the whole subject under strict security regulations, and little more was heard about it. In 1946, however, the United States Navy issued a significant bulletin. It was reported that several scientists, working with sonic equipment in deep water off the California coast, had discovered a widespread "layer" of some sort, which gave back an answering echo to the sound waves. This reflecting layer, seemingly suspended between the surface and the floor of the Pacific, was found over an area 300 miles wide. It lay from 1000 to 1500 feet below the surface. The discovery was made by three scientists, C. F. Eyring, R. J. Christensen, and R. W. Raitt, aboard the U.S.S. *Jasper* in 1942, and for a time this mysterious phenomenon, of wholly unknown nature, was called the ECR layer. Then in 1945 Martin W. Johnson, marine biologist of the Scripps Institution of Oceanography, made a further discovery which gave the first clue to the nature of the layer. Working aboard the vessel, *E. W. Scripps*, Johnson found that whatever sent back the echoes moved upward and downward in rhythmic fashion, being found near the surface at night, in deep water during the day. This discovery disposed of speculations that the reflections came from something inanimate, perhaps a mere physical discontinuity in the water, and showed that the layer is composed of living creatures capable of controlled movement.

From this time on, discoveries about the sea's "phantom bottom" came rapidly. With widespread use of echo-sounding instruments, it has become clear that the phenomenon is not something peculiar to the coast of California alone. It occurs almost universally in deep ocean basins—drifting by day at a depth of several hundred fathoms, at night rising to the surface, and again, before sunrise, sinking into the depths.

On the passage of the U.S.S. *Henderson* from San Diego to the Antarctic in 1947, the reflecting layer was detected during the greater part of each day, at depths varying from 150 to 450 fathoms, and on a later run from San Diego to Yokosuka, Japan, the *Henderson's* fathometer again recorded the layer every day, suggesting that it exists almost continuously across the Pacific.

During July and August 1947, the U.S.S. *Nereus* made a continuous fathogram from Pearl Harbor to the Arctic and found the scattering layer over all deep waters along this course. It did not develop, however, in the shallow Bering and Chuckchee seas. Sometimes in the morning, the *Nereus'* fathogram showed two layers, responding in different ways to the growing illumination of the water; both descended into deep water, but there was an interval of twenty miles between the two descents.

Despite attempts to sample it or photograph it, no one is sure what the layer is, although the discovery may be made any day. There are three principal theories, each of which has its group of supporters. According to these theories, the sea's phantom bottom may consist of small planktonic shrimps, of fishes, or of squids.

As for the plankton theory, one of the most convincing arguments is the well-known fact that many plankton creatures make regular vertical migrations of hundreds of feet, rising toward the surface at night, sinking down below the zone of light penetration very early in the morning. This is, of course, exactly the behavior of the scattering layer. Whatever composes it is apparently strongly repelled by sunlight. The creatures of the layer seem almost to be held prisoner at the end—or beyond the end—of the sun's rays throughout the hours of daylight, waiting only for the welcome return of darkness to hurry upward into the surface waters. But what is the power that repels; and what the attraction that draws them surfaceward once the inhibiting force is removed? Is it comparative safety from enemies that makes them seek darkness? Is it more abundant food near the surface that lures them back under cover of night?

Those who say that fish are the reflectors of the sound waves   18
usually account for the vertical migrations of the layer as suggesting that the fish are feeding on planktonic shrimp and are following their food. They believe that the air bladder of a fish is, of all structures concerned, most likely from its construction to return a strong echo. There is one outstanding difficulty in the way of accepting this theory: we have no other evidence that concentrations of fish are universally present in the oceans. In fact, almost everything else we know suggests that the really dense populations of fish live over the continental shelves or in certain very definite determined zones of the open ocean where food is particularly abundant. If the reflecting layer is eventually proved to be composed of fish, the prevailing views of fish distribution will have to be radically revised.

The most startling theory (and the one that seems to have the   19
fewest supporters) is that the layer consists of concentrations of squid, "hovering below the illuminated zone of the sea and awaiting the arrival of darkness in which to resume their raids into the plankton-rich surface waters." Proponents of this theory argue that squid are abundant enough, and of wide enough distribution, to give the echoes that have been picked up almost everywhere from the equator to the two poles. Squid are known to be the sole food of the sperm whale, found in the open oceans in all temperate and tropical waters. They also form the exclusive diet of the bottlenosed whale and are eaten extensively by most other toothed whales, by seals, and by many sea birds. All these facts argue that they must be prodigiously abundant.

It is true that men who have worked close to the sea surface at   20
night have received vivid impressions of the abundance and activity of squids in the surface waters in darkness. Long ago Johan Hjort[3] wrote:

"One night we were hauling long lines on the Faroe slope,   21
working with an electric lamp hanging over the side in order to see the line, when like lightning flashes one squid after another shot towards the light . . . In October 1902 we were one night steaming outside the slopes of the coast banks of Norway, and for many miles we could see the squids moving in the surface waters like luminous

---

[3] **Johan Hjort (1869–1948)** A Norwegian marine biologist.

bubbles, resembling large milky white electric lamps being constantly lit and extinguished."[4]

Thor Heyerdahl[5] reports that at night his raft was literally bombarded by squids; and Richard Fleming says that in his oceanographic work off the coast of Panama it was common to see immense schools of squid gathering at the surface at night and leaping upward toward the lights that were used by the men to operate their instruments. But equally spectacular surface displays of shrimp have been seen, and most people find it difficult to believe in the ocean-wide abundance of squid.   22

Deep-water photography holds much promise for the solution of the mystery of the phantom bottom. There are technical difficulties, such as the problem of holding a camera still as it swings at the end of a long cable, twisting and turning, suspended from a ship which itself moves with the sea. Some of the pictures so taken look as though the photographer has pointed his camera at a starry sky and swung it in an arc as he exposed the film. Yet the Norwegian biologist Gunnar Rollefson had an encouraging experience in correlating photography with echograms. On the research ship *Johan Hjort* off the Lofoten Islands, he persistently got reflection of sound from schools of fish in 20 to 30 fathoms. A specially constructed camera was lowered to the depth indicated by the echogram. When developed, the film showed moving shapes of fish at a distance, and a large and clearly recognizable cod appeared in the beam of light and hovered in front of the lens.   23

Direct sampling of the layer is the logical means of discovering its identity, but the problem is to develop large nets that can be operated rapidly enough to capture swift-moving animals. Scientists at Woods Hole, Massachusetts, have towed ordinary plankton nets in the layer and have found that euphausiid[6] shrimps, glassworms, and other deep-water plankton are concentrated there; but there is still a possibility that the layer itself may actually be made up of larger forms feeding on the shrimps—too large or swift to be taken in the presently used nets. New nets may give the answer. Television is another possibility.   24

Shadowy and indefinite though they be, these recent indications of an abundant life at mid-depths agree with the reports of the only   25

---

[4] From *The Depths of the Ocean*, by Sir John Murray and Johan Hjort, 1912 edition, Macmillan & Co., p. 649. [Carson's note]

[5] **Thor Heyerdahl (1914–2002)** A famous Norwegian explorer.

[6] **euphausiid** A small luminescent shrimp that migrates up and down in the ocean.

observers who have actually visited comparable depths and brought back eyewitness accounts of what they saw. William Beebe's impressions from the bathysphere were of a life far more abundant and varied than he had been prepared to find, although, over a period of six years, he had made many hundreds of net hauls in the same area. More than a quarter of a mile down, he reported aggregations of living things "as thick as I have ever seen them." At half a mile — the deepest descent of the bathysphere — Dr. Beebe recalled that "there was no instant when a mist of plankton . . . was not swirling in the path of the beam."

The existence of an abundant deep-sea fauna was discovered, probably millions of years ago, by certain whales and also, it now appears, by seals. The ancestors of all whales, we know by fossil remains, were land mammals. They must have been predatory beasts, if we are to judge by their powerful jaws and teeth. Perhaps in their foragings about the deltas of great rivers or around the edges of shallow seas, they discovered the abundance of fish and other marine life and over the centuries formed the habit of following them farther and farther into the sea. Little by little their bodies took on a form more suitable for aquatic life; their hind limbs were reduced to rudiments, which may be discovered in a modern whale by dissection, and the forelimbs were modified into organs for steering and balancing.   26

Eventually the whales, as though to divide the sea's food resources among them, became separated into three groups: the plankton-eaters, the fish-eaters, and the squid-eaters. The plankton-eating whales can exist only where there are dense masses of small shrimp or copepods to supply their enormous food requirements. This limits them, except for scattered areas, to arctic and antarctic waters and the high temperate latitudes. Fish-eating whales may find food over a somewhat wider range of ocean, but they are restricted to places where there are enormous populations of schooling fish. The blue water of the tropics and of the open ocean basins offers little to either of these groups. But that immense, square-headed, formidably toothed whale known as the cachalot or sperm whale discovered long ago what men have known for only a short time — that hundreds of fathoms below the almost untenanted surface waters of these regions there is an abundant animal life. The sperm whale has taken these deep waters for his hunting grounds; his quarry is the deep-water population of squids including the giant squid Architeuthis, which lives pelagically[7] at depths of 1500 feet or   27

---

[7] **pelagically** Living in the open ocean.

more. The head of the sperm whale is often marked with long stripes, which consist of a great number of circular scars made by the suckers of the squid. From this evidence we can imagine the battles that go on, in the darkness of the deep water, between these two huge creatures—the sperm whale with its 70-ton bulk, the squid with a body as long as 30 feet, and writhing, grasping arms extending the total length of the animal to perhaps 50 feet.

The greatest depth at which the giant squid lives is not definitely known, but there is one instructive piece of evidence about the depth to which sperm whales descend, presumably in search of the squids. In April 1932, the cable repair ship *All America* was investigating an apparent break in the submarine cable between Balboa in the Canal Zone and Esmeraldas, Ecuador. The cable was brought to the surface off the coast of Colombia. Entangled in it was a dead 45-foot male sperm whale. The submarine cable was twisted around the lower jaw and was wrapped around one flipper, the body, and the caudal flukes. The cable was raised from a depth of 540 fathoms, or 3240 feet. 28

Some of the seals also appear to have discovered the hidden food reserves of the deep ocean. It has long been something of a mystery where, and on what, the northern fur seals of the eastern Pacific feed during the winter, which they spend off the coast of North America from California to Alaska. There is no evidence that they are feeding to any great extent on sardines, mackerel, or other commercially important fishes. Presumably four million seals could not compete with commercial fishermen for the same species without the fact being known. But there is some evidence on the diet of the fur seals, and it is highly significant. Their stomachs have yielded the bones of a species of fish that has never been seen alive. Indeed, not even its remains have been found anywhere except in the stomachs of seals. Ichthyologists say that this "seal fish" belongs to a group that typically inhabits very deep water, off the edge of the continental shelf. 29

How either whales or seals endure the tremendous pressure changes involved in dives of several hundred fathoms is not definitely known. They are warm-blooded mammals like ourselves. Caisson disease, which is caused by the rapid accumulation of nitrogen bubbles in the blood with sudden release of pressure, kills human divers if they are brought up rapidly from depths of 200 feet or so. Yet, according to the testimony of whalers, a baleen whale, when harpooned, can dive straight down to a depth of half a mile, as measured by the amount of line carried out. From these depths, where it has sustained a pressure of half a ton on every inch of body, it returns almost immediately to the surface. The most plausible 30 explanation is that, unlike the diver, who has air pumped to him while he is under water, the whale has in its body only the limited supply it carries down, and does not have enough nitrogen in its blood to do serious harm. The plain truth is, however, that we really do not know, since it is obviously impossible to confine a living whale and experiment on it, and almost as difficult to dissect a dead one satisfactorily.

At first thought it seems a paradox that creatures of such great 31 fragility as the glass sponge and the jellyfish can live under the conditions of immense pressure that prevail in deep water. For creatures at home in the deep sea, however, the saving fact is that the pressure inside their tissues is the same as that without, and as long as this balance is preserved, they are no more inconvenienced by a pressure of a ton or so than we are by ordinary atmospheric pressure. And most abyssal creatures, it must be remembered, live out their whole lives in a comparatively restricted zone, and are never required to adjust themselves to extreme changes of pressure.

But of course there are exceptions, and the real miracle of sea 32 life in relation to great pressure is not the animal that lives its whole life on the bottom, bearing a pressure of perhaps five or six tons, but those that regularly move up and down through hundreds or thousands of feet of vertical change. The small shrimps and other planktonic creatures that descend into deep water during the day are examples. Fish that possess air bladders, on the other hand, are vitally affected by abrupt changes of pressure, as anyone knows who has seen a trawler's net raised from a hundred fathoms. Apart from the accident of being captured in a net and hauled up through waters of rapidly diminishing pressures, fish may sometimes wander out of the zone to which they are adjusted and find themselves unable to return. Perhaps in their pursuit of food they roam upward to the ceiling of the zone that is theirs, and beyond whose invisible boundary they may not stray without meeting alien and inhospitable conditions. Moving from layer to layer of drifting plankton as they feed, they may pass beyond the boundary. In the lessened pressure of these upper waters the gas enclosed within the air bladder expands. The fish becomes lighter and more buoyant. Perhaps he tries to fight his way down again, opposing the upward lift with all the power of his muscles. If he does not succeed, he "falls" to the surface, injured and dying, for the abrupt release of pressure from without causes distension and rupture of the tissues.

The compression of the sea under its own weight is relatively 33 slight, and there is no basis for the old and picturesque belief that, at the deeper levels, the water resists the downward passage of objects from the surface. According to this belief, sinking ships, the bodies of drowned men, and presumably the bodies of the larger sea animals not consumed by hungry scavengers, never reach the bottom, but come to rest at some level determined by the relation of their own weight to the compression of the water, there to drift forever. The fact is that anything will continue to sink as long as its specific gravity is greater than that of the surrounding water, and all large bodies descend, in a matter of a few days, to the ocean floor. As mute testimony to this fact, we bring up from the deepest ocean basins the teeth of sharks and the hard ear bones of whales.

Nevertheless the weight of sea water—the pressing down of miles of water upon all the underlying layers—does have a certain effect upon the water itself. If this downward compression could suddenly be relaxed by some miraculous suspension of natural laws, the sea level would rise about 93 feet all over the world. This would shift the Atlantic coastline of the United States westward a hundred miles or more and alter other familiar geographic outlines all over the world. 34

Immense pressure, then, is one of the governing conditions of life in the deep sea; darkness is another. The unrelieved darkness of the deep waters has produced weird and incredible modifications of the abyssal fauna. It is a blackness so divorced from the world of the sunlight that probably only the few men who have seen it with their own eyes can visualize it. We know that light fades out rapidly with descent below the surface. The red rays are gone at the end of the first 200 or 300 feet, and with them all the orange and yellow warmth of the sun. Then the greens fade out, and at 1000 feet only a deep, dark, brilliant blue is left. In very clear waters the violet rays of the spectrum may penetrate another thousand feet. Beyond this is only the blackness of the deep sea. 35

In a curious way, the colors of marine animals tend to be related to the zone in which they live. Fishes of the surface waters, like the mackerel and herring, often are blue or green; so are the floats of the Portuguese men-of-war and the azure-tinted wings of the swimming snails. Down below the diatom[8] meadows and the drifting sargassum weed, where the water becomes ever more deeply, brilliantly blue, many creatures are crystal clear. Their glassy, ghostly forms blend with their surroundings and make it easier for them to elude the ever-present, ever-hungry enemy. Such are the transparent hordes 36

---

[8] **diatom** One-celled algae that congregate in layers in the ocean.

of the arrowworms or glassworms, the comb jellies, and the larvae of many fishes.

At a thousand feet, and on down to the very end of the sun's rays, 37 silvery fishes are common, and many others are red, drab brown, or black. Pteropods are a dark violet. Arrowworms, whose relatives in the upper layers are colorless, are here a deep red. Jellyfish medusae, which above would be transparent, at a depth of 1000 feet are a deep brown.

At depths greater than 1500 feet, all the fishes are black, deep 38 violet, or brown, but the prawns wear amazing hues of red, scarlet, and purple. Why, no one can say. Since all the red rays are strained out of the water far above this depth, the scarlet raiment of these creatures can only look black to their neighbors.

The deep sea has its stars, and perhaps here and there an eerie 39 and transient equivalent of moonlight, for the mysterious phenomenon of luminescence is displayed by perhaps half of all the fishes that live in dimly lit or darkened waters, and by many of the lower forms as well. Many fishes carry luminous torches that can be turned on or off at will, presumably helping them find or pursue their prey. Others have rows of lights over their bodies, in patterns that vary from species to species and may be a sort of recognition mark or badge by which the bearer can be known as friend or enemy. The deep-sea squid ejects a spurt of fluid that becomes a luminous cloud, the counterpart of the "ink" of his shallow-water relative.

Down beyond the reach of even the longest and strongest of the 40 sun's rays, the eyes of fishes become enlarged, as though to make the most of any chance illumination of whatever sort, or they may become telescopic, large of lens, and protruding. In deep-sea fishes, hunting always in dark waters, the eyes tend to lose the "cones" or color-perceiving cells of the retina, and to increase the "rods," which perceive dim light. Exactly the same modification is seen on land among the strictly nocturnal prowlers which, like abyssal fish, never see the sunlight.

In their world of darkness, it would seem likely that some of the 41 animals might have become blind, as has happened to some cave fauna. So, indeed, many of them have, compensating for the lack of eyes with marvelously developed feelers and long, slender fins and processes with which they grope their way, like so many blind men with canes, their whole knowledge of friends, enemies, or food coming to them through the sense of touch.

The last traces of plant life are left behind in the thin upper layer 42 of water, for no plant can live below about 600 feet even in very clear water, and few find enough sunlight for their food-manufacturing activities below 200 feet. Since no animal can make its own food, the creatures of the deeper waters live a strange, almost parasitic existence of utter dependence on the upper layers. These hungry carnivores prey fiercely and relentlessly upon each other, yet the whole community is ultimately dependent upon the slow rain of descending food particles from above. The components of this never-ending rain are the dead and dying plants and animals from the surface, or from one of the intermediate layers. For each of the horizontal zones or communities of the sea that lie, in tier after tier, between the surface and the sea bottom, the food supply is different and in general poorer than for the layer above. There is a hint of the fierce and uncompromising competition for food in the saber-toothed jaws of some of the small, dragonlike fishes of the deeper waters, in the immense mouths and in the elastic and distensible bodies that make it possible for a fish to swallow another several times its size, enjoying swift repletion after a long fast.

Pressure, darkness, and—we should have added only a few   43
years ago—silence, are the conditions of life in the deep sea. But we know now that the conception of the sea as a silent place is wholly false. Wide experience with hydrophones and other listening devices for the detection of submarines has proved that, around the shore lines of much of the world, there is the extraordinary uproar produced by fishes, shrimps, porpoises and probably other forms not yet identified. There has been little investigation as yet of sound in the deep, offshore areas, but when the crew of the *Atlantis* lowered a hydrophone into deep water off Bermuda, they recorded strange mewing sounds, shrieks, and ghostly moans, the sources of which have not been traced. But fish of shallower zones have been captured and confined in aquaria, where their voices have been recorded for comparison with sounds heard at sea, and in many cases satisfactory identification can be made.

During the Second World War the hydrophone network set up   44
by the United States Navy to protect the entrance to Chesapeake Bay was temporarily made useless when, in the spring of 1942, the speakers at the surface began to give forth, every evening, a sound described as being like "a pneumatic drill tearing up pavement." The extraneous noises that came over the hydrophones completely masked the sounds of the passage of ships. Eventually it was discovered that the sounds were the voices of fish known as croakers, which in the spring move into Chesapeake Bay from their offshore wintering grounds. As soon as the noise had been identified and analyzed, it was possible to screen it out with an electric filter, so that once more only the sounds of ships came through the speakers.

Later in the same year, a chorus of croakers was discovered off   45
the pier of the Scripps Institution at La Jolla. Every year from May

until late September the evening chorus begins about sunset, and "increases gradually to a steady uproar of harsh froggy croaks, with a background of soft drumming. This continues unabated for two to three hours and finally tapers off to individual outbursts at rare intervals." Several species of croakers isolated in aquaria gave sounds similar to the "froggy croaks," but the authors of the soft background drumming—presumably another species of croaker—have not yet been discovered.

One of the most extraordinarily widespread sounds of the undersea is the crackling, sizzling sound, like dry twigs burning or fat frying, heard near beds of the snapping shrimp. This is a small, round shrimp, about half an inch in diameter, with one very large claw which it uses to stun its prey. The shrimp are forever clicking the two joints of this claw together, and it is the thousands of clicks that collectively produce the noise known as shrimp crackle. No one had any idea the little snapping shrimps were so abundant or so widely distributed until their signals began to be picked up on hydrophones. They have been heard over a broad band that extends around the world, between latitudes 35° N and 35° S (for example, from Cape Hatteras to Buenos Aires) in ocean waters less than 30 fathoms deep.   46

Mammals as well as fishes and crustaceans contribute to the undersea chorus. Biologists listening through a hydrophone in an estuary of the St. Lawrence River heard "high-pitched resonant whistles and squeals, varied with the ticking and clucking sounds slightly reminiscent of a string orchestra tuning up, as well as mewing and occasional chirps." This remarkable medley of sounds was heard only while schools of the white porpoise were seen passing up or down the river, and so was assumed to be produced by them.   47

The mysteriousness, the eeriness, the ancient unchangingness of the great depths have led many people to suppose that some very old forms of life—some "living fossils"—may be lurking undiscovered in the deep ocean. Some such hope may have been in the minds of the *Challenger* scientists. The forms they brought up in their nets were weird enough, and most of them had never before been seen by man. But basically they were modern types. There was nothing like the trilobites of Cambrian[9] time or the sea scorpions of the Silurian,[10] nothing reminiscent of the great marine reptiles that invaded the sea in the Mesozoic.[11] Instead, there were modern   48

---

[9] **Cambrian** Geologic period of 544–2500 million years ago.
[10] **Silurian** Geologic period of 438–505 million years ago.
[11] **Mesozoic** Geologic era of 98–286 million years ago.

fishes, squids, and shrimps, strangely and grotesquely modified, to be sure, for life in the difficult deep-sea world, but clearly types that have developed in rather recent geologic time.

Far from being the original home of life, the deep sea has proba-   49
bly been inhabited for a relatively short time. While life was developing and flourishing in the surface waters, along the shores, and perhaps in the rivers and swamps, two immense regions of the earth still forbade invasion by living things. These were the continents and the abyss. As we have seen, the immense difficulties of surviving on land were first overcome by colonists from the sea about 300 million years ago. The abyss, with its unending darkness, its crushing pressures, its glacial cold, presented even more formidable difficulties. Probably the successful invasion of this region — at least by higher forms of life — occurred somewhat later.

Yet in recent years there have been one or two significant hap-   50
penings that have kept alive the hope that the deep sea may, after all, conceal strange links with the past. In December 1938, off the southeast tip of Africa, an amazing fish was caught alive in a trawl — a fish that was supposed to have been dead for at least 60 million years! This is to say, the last known fossil remains of its kind date from the Cretaceous,[12] and no living example had been recognized in historic time until this lucky net-haul.

The fishermen who brought it up in their trawl from a depth of   51
only 40 fathoms realized that this five-foot, bright blue fish, with its large head and strangely shaped scales, fins, and tail, was different from anything that they ever caught before, and on their return to port they took it to the nearest museum, where it was christened Latimeria. It was identified as a coelacanth, or one of an incredibly ancient group of fishes that first appeared in the seas some 300 million years ago. Rocks representing the next 200 million and more years of earth history yielded fossil coelacanths; then, in the Cretaceous, the record of these fishes came to an end. After 60 million years of mysterious oblivion, one of the group, Latimeria, then appeared before the eyes of the South African fishermen, apparently little changed in structure from its ancient ancestors. But where had these fishes been in the meantime?

The story of the coelacanths did not end in 1938. Believing there   52
must be other such fish in the sea, an ichthyologist in South Africa, Professor J. L. B. Smith, began a patient search that lasted 14 years before it was successful. Then, in December 1952, a second coelacanth was captured near the island of Anjouan, off the northwestern tip of Madagascar. It differed enough from Latimeria to be placed in

---

[12] **Cretaceous** Geologic period of 65–208 million years ago.

a separate genus, but like the first coelacanth known in modern
times, it can tell us much of a shadowy chapter in the evolution of
living things.

Occasionally a very primitive type of shark, known from its   53
puckered gills as a "frillshark," is taken in waters between a quarter
of a mile and half a mile down. Most of these have been caught in
Norwegian and Japanese waters—there are only about 50 preserved
in the museums of Europe and America—but recently one was captured off Santa Barbara, California. The frillshark has many anatomi-
cal features similar to those of the ancient sharks that lived 25 to 30
million years ago. It has too many gills and too few dorsal fins for a
modern shark, and its teeth, like those of fossil sharks, are three-
pronged and briarlike. Some ichthyologists regard it as a relic derived
from very ancient shark ancestors that have died out in the upper
waters but, through this single species, are still carrying on their
struggle for earthly survival, in the quiet of the deep sea.

Possibly there are other such anachronisms lurking down in these   54
regions of which we know so little, but they are likely to be few and
scattered. The terms of existence in these deep waters are far too uncompromising to support life unless that life is plastic, molding itself
constantly to the harsh conditions, seizing every advantage that makes
possible the survival of living protoplasm in a world only a little less
hostile than the black reaches of interplanetary space.

QUESTIONS FOR CRITICAL READING

1. How much of the earth has been "dark since the world began" (para. 1)?
2. What is a bathysphere?
3. Why did people think there was no life in the deep sea?
4. What were the earliest signs that there might be life in the great depths
   of the sea?
5. What is the ECR layer?
6. How did the "phantom bottom" behave?
7. Why was the squid theory so startling?
8. What does Carson tell us about whale behavior in the deep?

SUGGESTIONS FOR WRITING

1. Use the term "ocean depths" to perform an online search. Based on
   your findings, write an essay in which you update at least one aspect of
   Carson's essay. For example, what new discoveries have been made

about the nature of the deep sea? What new technologies have been developed to aid in the explanation of the ocean floor?

2. What is known today about whales? How many species of whales are known to exist and how many are in peril of extinction or have become extinct? Use Carson's technique of reviewing what has been known historically about whales, and then bring us up to date with what is known today.

3. In three pages summarize the most important points in Carson's essay. Assume that you are writing to someone who does not know much about the ocean and who knows nothing about Rachel Carson. What, for you, are the most impressive points that she makes and the points that should most concern the person for whom you are writing?

4. Jacques Cousteau is probably the most famous ocean explorer. What did he discover that would add to the information Carson details in "The Sunless Sea"? Was he able to solve any of the problems that Carson suggests remain to be solved? How important was his work to our understanding of the ocean? Explain.

5. **CONNECTIONS** What are the similarities in the rhetorical techniques of Rachel Carson and Stephen Jay Gould? Consider their subject matter, their interest in mysteries, their concern for history, and their capacity for description. On what points about nature do they seem to differ? Would Gould be sympathetic to Carson's purposes in this essay? What might he have done differently?

6. **CONNECTIONS** In paragraphs 26 and 27 Carson talks about some ways in which sea life changed over time. How would Darwin have reacted to what Carson describes? Does Carson seem to accept Darwin's views on the evolution of species, or is her research independent of Darwin? What contribution, if any, do you think she makes toward validating Darwin's theory that life evolves over time? Explain.

STEPHEN JAY GOULD
Nonmoral Nature

Stephen Jay Gould (1941–2002) was Alexander Agassiz professor of zoology, professor of geology, and curator of invertebrate paleontology in the Museum of Comparative Zoology at Harvard University, where his field of interest centered on the special evolutionary problems related to species of Bahamian snails. He decided to become a paleontologist when he was five years old, after he visited the American Museum of Natural History in New York City and first saw reconstructed dinosaurs.

Gould became well known for essays on science written with the clarity needed to explain complex concepts to a general audience and also informed by a superb scientific understanding. His articles for *Natural History* magazine have been widely quoted and collected in book form. His books have won both praise and prizes; they include *Ever Since Darwin* (1977), *The Panda's Thumb* (1980), *The Mismeasure of Man* (1981), *The Flamingo's Smile* (1985), *Bully for Brontosaurus* (1991), *Eight Little Piggies* (1993), *Dinosaur in a Haystack* (1995), *Full House: The Spread of Excellence from Plato to Darwin* (1996), and *Questioning the Millennium* (1997). In much of his writing, Gould pointed to the significance of the work of the scientist he most frequently cited, Charles Darwin. His books have been celebrated around the world, and in 1981 Gould won a MacArthur Fellowship—a stipend of more than $38,000 a year for five years that permitted him to do any work he wished.

"Nonmoral Nature" examines a highly controversial issue—the religious "reading" of natural events. Gould opposes the position of creationists who insist that the Bible's version of creation be taught in science courses as scientific fact. Moreover, he views the account of the creation in Genesis as religious, not scientific, and

From *Natural History*, vol. 91, no. 2, 1982.

points out that Darwin (who was trained as a minister) did not see a conflict between his theories and religious beliefs.

Gould's primary point in this selection is that the behavior of animals in nature—with ruthless and efficient predators inflicting pain on essentially helpless prey—has presented theologians with an exacting dilemma: If God is good and if creation reveals his goodness, why do nature's victims suffer?

Gould examines in great detail specific issues that plagued nineteenth-century theologians. One of these, the behavior of the ichneumon wasp, an efficient wasp that plants its egg in a host caterpillar or aphid, is his special concern. Gould describes the behavior of the ichneumon in detail to make it plain that the total mechanism of the predatory, parasitic animal is complex, subtle, and brilliant. The ichneumon paralyzes its host and then eats it from the inside out, taking care not to permit a victim to die until the last morsel is consumed. He also notes that because there are so many species of ichneumons, their behavior cannot be regarded as an isolated phenomenon.

It is almost impossible to read this selection without developing respect for the predator, something that was extremely difficult, if not impossible, for nineteenth-century theologians to do. Their problem, Gould asserts, was that they anthropomorphized the behavior of these insects. That is, they thought of them in human terms. The act of predation was seen as comparable to the acts of human thugs who toy with their victims, or as Gould puts it, the acts of executioners in Renaissance England who inflicted as much pain as possible on traitors before killing them. This model is the kind of lens through which the behavior of predators was interpreted and understood.

Instead of an anthropocentric—human-centered—view, Gould suggests a scientific view that sees the behavior of predators as sympathetically as that of victims. In this way, he asserts, the ichneumon—and nature—will be seen as nonmoral, and the act of predation seen as neither good nor evil. The concept of evil, he says, is limited to human beings. The world of nature is unconcerned with it, and if we apply morality to nature, we see nature as merely a reflection of our own beliefs and values. Instead, he wishes us to conceive of nature as he thinks it is, something apart from strictly human values.

Gould's Rhetoric

Gould's writing is distinguished for its clarity and directness. In this essay, he relies on the testimony of renowned authorities, establishing at once a remarkable breadth of interest and revealing considerably detailed learning about his subject. He explores a number of theories with sympathy and care, demonstrating their limits before offering his own views.

Because his field of interest is advanced biology, he runs the risk of losing the attention of the general reader. To avoid doing this, he could have oversimplified his subject, but he does not: he does not shrink from using Latin classifications to identify his subject matter, but he defines each specialized term when he first uses it. He clarifies each opposing argument and demonstrates, in his analysis, its limitations and potential.

Instead of using a metaphor to convince us of a significant fact or critical opinion, Gould "deconstructs" a metaphor that was once in wide use — that the animal world, like the human world, is ethical. He reveals the metaphor to us, shows how it has affected belief, and then asks us to reject it in favor of seeing the world as it actually is. Although acknowledging that the metaphor is inviting and can be irresistible, Gould says we must resist it.

Gould also makes widespread use of the rhetorical device of metonymy, in which a part of something stands for the whole. Thus, the details of nature, which is God's creation, are made to reflect the entirety, which is God. Therefore, the behavior of the ichneumon comes to stand for the nature of God; and because the ichneumon's behavior is adjudged evil by those who think that animal behavior is metaphorically like that of people, there is a terrible contradiction that cannot be rationalized by theological arguments.

Gould shows us just how difficult the problem of the theologian is. Then he shows us a way out. But his way out depends on the capacity to think in a new way, a change that some readers may not be able to achieve.

PREREADING QUESTIONS: WHAT TO READ FOR

The following prereading questions may help you anticipate key issues in the discussion of Stephen Jay Gould's "Nonmoral Nature." Keeping them in mind during your first reading of the selection should help focus your attention.

- What are the consequences of anthropomorphizing nature?
- What does it mean for nature to be nonmoral?

Nonmoral Nature

When the Right Honorable and Reverend Francis Henry, earl of   1
Bridgewater,[1] died in February, 1829, he left £8,000 to support a series of books "on the power, wisdom and goodness of God, as manifested in the creation." William Buckland,[2] England's first official
academic geologist and later dean of Westminster, was invited to
compose one of the nine Bridgewater Treatises. In it he discussed
the most pressing problem of natural theology: If God is benevolent
and the Creation displays his "power, wisdom and goodness," then
why are we surrounded with pain, suffering, and apparently senseless cruelty in the animal world?

Buckland considered the depredation of "carnivorous races" as   2
the primary challenge to an idealized world in which the lion might
dwell with the lamb. He resolved the issue to his satisfaction by arguing that carnivores actually increase "the aggregate of animal enjoyment" and "diminish that of pain." The death of victims, after all, is
swift and relatively painless, victims are spared the ravages of de-
crepitude and senility, and populations do not outrun their food supply to the greater sorrow of all. God knew what he was doing when
he made lions. Buckland concluded in hardly concealed rapture:

> The appointment of death by the agency of carnivora, as the ordi-
> nary termination of animal existence, appears therefore in its main
> results to be a dispensation of benevolence; it deducts much from
> the aggregate amount of the pain of universal death; it abridges,
> and almost annihilates, throughout the brute creation, the misery
> of disease, and accidental injuries, and lingering decay; and im-
> poses such salutary restraint upon excessive increase of numbers,
> that the supply of food maintains perpetually a due ratio to the
> demand. The result is, that the surface of the land and depths of
> the waters are ever crowded with myriads of animated beings, the
> pleasures of whose life are co-extensive with its duration; and
> which throughout the little day of existence that is allotted to
> them, fulfill with joy the functions for which they were created.

We may find a certain amusing charm in Buckland's vision   3
today, but such arguments did begin to address "the problem of

---

[1]**Reverend Francis Henry, earl of Bridgewater (1756–1829)** He was the
eighth and last earl of Bridgewater. He was also a naturalist and a Fellow at All Souls
College, Oxford, before he became earl of Bridgewater in 1823. On his death, he left
a fund to be used for the publication of the Bridgewater Treatises, essay discussions
of the moral implications of scientific research and discoveries.

[2]**William Buckland (1784–1856)** An English clergyman and also a geologist. His essay "Geology and Mineralogy" was a Bridgewater Treatise in 1836.

evil" for many of Buckland's contemporaries—how could a benevolent God create such a world of carnage and bloodshed? Yet these claims could not abolish the problem of evil entirely, for nature includes many phenomena far more horrible in our eyes than simple predation. I suspect that nothing evokes greater disgust in most of us than slow destruction of a host by an internal parasite—slow ingestion, bit by bit, from the inside. In no other way can I explain why *Alien*, an uninspired, grade-C, formula horror film, should have won such a following. That single scene of Mr. Alien, popping forth as a baby parasite from the body of a human host, was both sickening and stunning. Our nineteenth-century forebears maintained similar feelings. Their greatest challenge to the concept of a benevolent deity was not simple predation—for one can admire quick and efficient butcheries, especially since we strive to construct them ourselves— but slow death by parasitic ingestion. The classic case, treated at length by all the great naturalists, involved the so-called ichneumon fly. Buckland had sidestepped the major issue.

The ichneumon fly, which provoked such concern among natural theologians, was a composite creature representing the habits of an enormous tribe. The Ichneumonoidea are a group of wasps, not flies, that include more species than all the vertebrates combined (wasps, with ants and bees, constitute the order Hymenoptera; flies, with their two wings—wasps have four—form the order Diptera). In addition, many related wasps of similar habits were often cited for the same grisly details. Thus, the famous story did not merely implicate a single aberrant species (perhaps a perverse leakage from Satan's realm), but perhaps hundreds of thousands of them—a large chunk of what could only be God's creation.

The ichneumons, like most wasps, generally live freely as adults but pass their larval life as parasites feeding on the bodies of other animals, almost invariably members of their own phylum, Arthropoda. The most common victims are caterpillars (butterfly and moth larvae), but some ichneumons prefer aphids and others attack spiders. Most hosts are parasitized as larvae, but some adults are attacked, and many tiny ichneumons inject their brood directly into the egg of their host.

The free-flying females locate an appropriate host and then convert it to a food factory for their own young. Parasitologists speak of ectoparasitism when the uninvited guest lives on the surface of its host, and endoparasitism when the parasite dwells within. Among endoparasitic ichneumons, adult females pierce the host with their ovipositor and deposit eggs within it. (The ovipositor, a thin tube extending backward from the wasp's rear end, may be many times as long as the body itself.) Usually, the host is not otherwise inconvenienced for the moment, at least until the eggs hatch and the ichneumon larvae begin their grim work of interior excavation. Among ectoparasites, however, many females lay their eggs directly upon the host's body. Since an active host would easily dislodge the egg, the ichneumon mother often simultaneously injects a toxin that paralyzes the caterpillar or other victim. The paralysis may be permanent, and the caterpillar lies, alive but immobile, with the agent of its future destruction secure on its belly. The egg hatches, the helpless caterpillar twitches, the wasp larva pierces and begins its grisly feast.

Since a dead and decaying caterpillar will do the wasp larva no 7 good, it eats in a pattern that cannot help but recall, in our inappropriate, anthropocentric interpretation, the ancient English penalty for treason—drawing and quartering, with its explicit object of extracting as much torment as possible by keeping the victim alive and sentient. As the king's executioner drew out and burned his client's entrails, so does the ichneumon larva eat fat bodies and digestive organs first, keeping the caterpillar alive by preserving intact the essential heart and central nervous system. Finally, the larva completes its work and kills its victim, leaving behind the caterpillar's empty shell. Is it any wonder that ichneumons, not snakes or lions, stood as the paramount challenge to God's benevolence during the heyday of natural theology?

As I read through the nineteenth- and twentieth-century litera- 8 ture on ichneumons, nothing amused me more than the tension between an intellectual knowledge that wasps should not be described in human terms and a literary or emotional inability to avoid the familiar categories of epic and narrative, pain and destruction, victim and vanquisher. We seem to be caught in the mythic structures of our own cultural sagas, quite unable, even in our basic descriptions, to use any other language than the metaphors of battle and conquest. We cannot render this corner of natural history as anything but story, combining the themes of grim horror and fascination and usually ending not so much with pity for the caterpillar as with admiration for the efficiency of the ichneumon.

I detect two basic themes in most epic descriptions: the strug- 9 gles of prey and the ruthless efficiency of parasites. Although we acknowledge that we witness little more than automatic instinct or physiological reaction, still we describe the defenses of hosts as though they represented conscious struggles. Thus, aphids kick and caterpillars may wriggle violently as wasps attempt to insert their ovipositors. The pupa of the tortoise-shell butterfly (usually considered an inert creature silently awaiting its conversion from duckling to swan) may contort its abdominal region so sharply that attacking wasps are thrown into the air. The caterpillars of *Hapalia*, when attacked by the wasp *Apanteles machaeralis*, drop suddenly from their leaves and suspend themselves in air by a silken thread. But the wasp may run down the thread and insert its eggs nonetheless. Some hosts can encapsulate the injected egg with blood cells that aggregate and harden, thus suffocating the parasite.

J.-H. Fabre,[3] the great nineteenth-century French entomologist, 10 who remains to this day the preeminently literate natural historian of insects, made a special study of parasitic wasps and wrote with an unabashed anthropocentrism about the struggles of paralyzed victims (see his books *Insect Life* and *The Wonders of Instinct*). He describes some imperfectly paralyzed caterpillars that struggle so violently every time a parasite approaches that the wasp larvae must feed with unusual caution. They attach themselves to a silken strand from the roof of their burrow and descend upon a safe and exposed part of the caterpillar:

> The grub is at dinner: head downwards, it is digging into the limp belly of one of the caterpillars. . . . At the least sign of danger in the heap of caterpillars, the larva retreats . . . and climbs back to the ceiling, where the swarming rabble cannot reach it. When peace is restored, it slides down [its silken cord] and returns to table, with its head over the viands and its rear upturned and ready to withdraw in case of need.

In another chapter, he describes the fate of a paralyzed cricket: 11

> One may see the cricket, bitten to the quick, vainly move its antennae and abdominal styles, open and close its empty jaws, and even move a foot, but the larva is safe and searches its vitals with impunity. What an awful nightmare for the paralyzed cricket!

Fabre even learned to feed some paralyzed victims by placing a 12 syrup of sugar and water on their mouthparts—thus showing that they remained alive, sentient, and (by implication) grateful for any palliation of their inevitable fate. If Jesus, immobile and thirsting on the cross, received only vinegar from his tormentors, Fabre at least could make an ending bittersweet.

The second theme, ruthless efficiency of the parasites, leads to 13 the opposite conclusion—grudging admiration for the victors. We learn of their skill in capturing dangerous hosts often many times larger than themselves. Caterpillars may be easy game, but the

---

[3] **Jean-Henri Fabre (1823–1915)** A French entomologist whose patient study of insects earned him the nickname "the Virgil of Insects." His writings are voluminous and, at times, elegant.

psammocharid wasps prefer spiders. They must insert their ovipositors in a safe and precise spot. Some leave a paralyzed spider in its own burrow. *Planiceps hirsutus*, for example, parasitizes a California trapdoor spider. It searches for spider tubes on sand dunes, then digs into nearby sand to disturb the spider's home and drive it out. When the spider emerges, the wasp attacks, paralyzes its victim, drags it back into its own tube, shuts and fastens the trapdoor, and deposits a single egg upon the spider's abdomen. Other psammocharids will drag a heavy spider back to a previously prepared cluster of clay or mud cells. Some amputate a spider's legs to make the passage easier. Others fly back over water, skimming a buoyant spider along the surface.

Some wasps must battle with other parasites over a host's body. 14 *Rhyssella curvipes* can detect the larvae of wood wasps deep within alder wood and drill down to its potential victims with its sharply ridged ovipositor. *Pseudorhyssa alpestris*, a related parasite, cannot drill directly into wood since its slender ovipositor bears only rudimentary cutting ridges. It locates the holes made by *Rhyssella*, inserts its ovipositor, and lays an egg on the host (already conveniently paralyzed by *Rhyssella*), right next to the egg deposited by its relative. The two eggs hatch at about the same time, but the larva of *Pseudorhyssa* has a bigger head bearing much larger mandibles. *Pseudorhyssa* seizes the smaller *Rhyssella* larva, destroys it, and proceeds to feast upon a banquet already well prepared.

Other praises for the efficiency of mothers invoke the themes of 15 early, quick, and often. Many ichneumons don't even wait for their hosts to develop into larvae, but parasitize the egg directly (larval wasps may then either drain the egg itself or enter the developing host larva). Others simply move fast. *Apanteles militaris* can deposit up to seventy-two eggs in a single second. Still others are doggedly persistent. *Aphidius gomezi* females produce up to 1,500 eggs and can parasitize as many as 600 aphids in a single working day. In a bizarre twist upon "often," some wasps indulge in polyembryony, a kind of iterated supertwinning. A single egg divides into cells that aggregate into as many as 500 individuals. Since some polyembryonic wasps parasitize caterpillars much larger than themselves and may lay up to six eggs in each, as many as 3,000 larvae may develop within, and feed upon, a single host. These wasps are endoparasites and do not paralyze their victims. The caterpillars writhe back and forth, not (one suspects) from pain, but merely in response to the commotion induced by thousands of wasp larvae feeding within.

The efficiency of mothers is matched by their larval offspring. I 16 have already mentioned the pattern of eating less essential parts first, thus keeping the host alive and fresh to its final and merciful dispatch.

After the larva digests every edible morsel of its victim (if only to prevent later fouling of its abode by decaying tissue), it may still use the outer shell of its host. One aphid parasite cuts a hole in the belly of its victim's shell, glues the skeleton to a leaf by sticky secretions from its salivary gland, and then spins a cocoon to pupate within the aphid's shell.

In using inappropriate anthropocentric language in this romp 17
through the natural history of ichneumons, I have tried to emphasize just why these wasps became a preeminent challenge to natural theology—the antiquated doctrine that attempted to infer God's essence from the products of his creation. I have used twentieth-century examples for the most part, but all themes were known and stressed by the great nineteenth-century natural theologians. How then did they square the habits of these wasps with the goodness of God? How did they extract themselves from this dilemma of their own making?

The strategies were as varied as the practitioners; they shared 18
only the theme of special pleading for an a priori doctrine[4]—they knew that God's benevolence was lurking somewhere behind all these tales of apparent horror. Charles Lyell[5] for example, in the first edition of his epochal *Principles of Geology* (1830–1833), decided that caterpillars posed such a threat to vegetation that any natural checks upon them could only reflect well upon a creating deity, for caterpillars would destroy human agriculture "did not Providence put causes in operation to keep them in due bounds."

The Reverend William Kirby,[6] rector of Barham and Britain's 19
foremost entomologist, chose to ignore the plight of caterpillars and focused instead upon the virtue of mother love displayed by wasps in provisioning their young with such care.

> The great object of the female is to discover a proper nidus for her eggs. In search of this she is in constant motion. Is the caterpillar of a butterfly or moth the appropriate food for her young? You see

---

[4] **an a priori doctrine** *A priori* means "beforehand," and Gould refers to those who approach a scientific situation with a preestablished view in mind. He is suggesting that such an approach prevents the kind of objectivity and fairness that scientific examination is supposed to produce.

[5] **Charles Lyell (1797–1875)** An English geologist who established the glacial layers of the Eocene (dawn of recent), Miocene (less recent), and Pliocene (more recent) epochs during his excavations of Tertiary period strata in Italy. He was influential in urging Darwin to publish his theories. His work is still respected.

[6] **The Reverend William Kirby (1759–1850)** An English specialist in insects. He was the author of a Bridgewater Treatise, *On the power, wisdom, and goodness of God, as manifested in the creation of animals, and in their history, habits, and instincts* (2 vols., 1835).

her alight upon the plants where they are most usually to be met with, run quickly over them, carefully examining every leaf, and, having found the unfortunate object of her search, insert her sting into its flesh, and there deposit an egg. . . . The active Ichneumon braves every danger, and does not desist until her courage and address have insured subsistence for one of her future progeny.

Kirby found this solicitude all the more remarkable because the   20
female wasp will never see her child and enjoy the pleasures of parenthood. Yet her love compels her to danger nonetheless:

A very large proportion of them are doomed to die before their young come into existence. But in these the passion is not extinguished. . . . When you witness the solicitude with which they provide for the security and sustenance of their future young, you can scarcely deny to them love for a progeny they are never destined to behold.

Kirby also put in a good word for the marauding larvae, praising   21
them for their forbearance in eating selectively to keep their caterpillar prey alive. Would we all husband our resources with such care!

In this strange and apparently cruel operation one circumstance is truly remarkable. The larva of the Ichneumon, though every day, perhaps for months, it gnaws the inside of the caterpillar, and though at last it has devoured almost every part of it except the skin and intestines, carefully all this time it avoids injuring the vital organs, as if aware that its own existence depends on that of the insect upon which it preys! . . . What would be the impression which a similar instance amongst the race of quadrupeds would make upon us? If, for example, an animal . . . should be found to feed upon the inside of a dog, devouring only those parts not essential to life, while it cautiously left uninjured the heart, arteries, lungs, and intestines—should we not regard such an instance as a perfect prodigy, as an example of instinctive forebearance almost miraculous? [The last three quotes come from the 1856, and last pre-Darwinian, edition of Kirby and Spence's *Introduction to Entomology*.]

This tradition of attempting to read moral meaning from nature   22
did not cease with the triumph of evolutionary theory after Darwin published *On the Origin of Species* in 1859—for evolution could be read as God's chosen method of peopling our planet, and ethical messages might still populate nature. Thus, St. George Mivart,[7] one

---

[7] **St. George Mivart (1827–1900)** English anatomist and biologist who examined the comparative anatomies of insect-eating and meat-eating animals. A convert to Roman Catholicism in 1844, he was unable to reconcile religious and evolutionary theories and was excommunicated from the Catholic Church in 1900.

of Darwin's most effective evolutionary critics and a devout Catholic, argued that "many amiable and excellent people" had been misled by the apparent suffering of animals for two reasons. First, however much it might hurt, "physical suffering and moral evil are simply incommensurable." Since beasts are not moral agents, their feelings cannot bear any ethical message. But secondly, lest our visceral sensitivities still be aroused, Mivart assures us that animals must feel little, if any, pain. Using a favorite racist argument of the time—that "primitive" people suffer far less than advanced and cultured people— Mivart extrapolated further down the ladder of life into a realm of very limited pain indeed: Physical suffering, he argued,

> depends greatly upon the mental condition of the sufferer. Only during consciousness does it exist, and only in the most highly organized men does it reach its acme. The author has been assured that lower races of men appear less keenly sensitive to physical suffering than do more cultivated and refined human beings. Thus only in man can there really be any intense degree of suffering, because only in him is there that intellectual recollection of past moments and that anticipation of future ones, which constitute in great part the bitterness of suffering. The momentary pang, the present pain, which beasts endure, though real enough, is yet, doubtless, not to be compared as to its intensity with the suffering which is produced in man through his high prerogative of self-consciousness [from *Genesis of Species*, 1871].

It took Darwin himself to derail this ancient tradition—in that gentle way so characteristic of his radical intellectual approach to nearly everything. The ichneumons also troubled Darwin greatly and he wrote of them to Asa Gray[8] in 1860:

> I own that I cannot see as plainly as others do, and as I should wish to do, evidence of design and beneficence on all sides of us. There seems to me too much misery in the world. I cannot persuade myself that a beneficent and omnipotent God would have designedly created the Ichneumonidae with the express intention of their feeding within the living bodies of Caterpillars, or that a cat should play with mice.

23

---

[8] **Asa Gray (1810–1888)** America's greatest botanist. His works, which are still considered important, are *Structural Botany* (1879; originally published in 1842 as *Botanical Text-Book*), *The Elements of Botany* (1836), *How Plants Grow* (1858), and *How Plants Behave* (1872). Gray was a serious critic of Darwin and wrote a great number of letters to him, but he was also a firm believer in Darwinian evolution. Because he was also a well-known member of an evangelical Protestant faith, he was effective in countering religious attacks on Darwin by showing that there is no conflict between Darwinism and religion.

Indeed, he had written with more passion to Joseph Hooker[9] in   24
1856: "What a book a devil's chaplain might write on the clumsy,
wasteful, blundering, low, and horribly cruel works of nature!"

This honest admission—that nature is often (by our standards)   25
cruel and that all previous attempts to find a lurking goodness behind everything represent just so much absurd special pleading—
can lead in two directions. One might retain the principle that nature
holds moral messages for humans, but reverse the usual perspective and claim that morality consists in understanding the ways of
nature and doing the opposite. Thomas Henry Huxley[10] advanced
this argument in his famous essay on *Evolution and Ethics* (1893):

> The practice of that which is ethically best—what we call good-
> ness or virtue—involves a course of conduct which, in all respects,
> is opposed to that which leads to success in the cosmic struggle for
> existence. In place of ruthless self-assertion it demands self-
> restraint; in place of thrusting aside, or treading down, all competi-
> tors, it requires that the individual shall not merely respect, but
> shall help his fellows. . . . It repudiates the gladiatorial theory of
> existence. . . . Laws and moral precepts are directed to the end of
> curbing the cosmic process.

The other argument, more radical in Darwin's day but common   26
now, holds that nature simply is as we find it. Our failure to discern
the universal good we once expected does not record our lack of insight or ingenuity but merely demonstrates that nature contains no
moral messages framed in human terms. Morality is a subject for
philosophers, theologians, students of the humanities, indeed for all
thinking people. The answers will not be read passively from nature;
they do not, and cannot, arise from the data of science. The factual
state of the world does not teach us how we, with our powers for
good and evil, should alter or preserve it in the most ethical manner.

Darwin himself tended toward this view, although he could not,   27
as a man of his time, thoroughly abandon the idea that laws of nature
might reflect some higher purpose. He clearly recognized that the

---

[9]**Joseph Hooker (1817–1911)** English botanist who studied flowers in exotic locations such as Tasmania, the Antarctic, New Zealand, and India. He was,
along with Charles Lyell, a friend of Darwin and one of those who urged him to
publish *On the Origin of Species*. He was the director of London's Kew Gardens from
1865 to 1885.
[10]**Thomas Henry Huxley (1825–1895)** An English naturalist who, quite independent of organizations and formal support, became one of the most important
scientists of his time. He searched for a theory of evolution that was based on a rigorous examination of the facts and found, in Darwin's work, the theory that he could
finally respect. He was a strong champion of Darwin.

specific manifestations of those laws—cats playing with mice, and ichneumon larvae eating caterpillars—could not embody ethical messages, but he somehow hoped that unknown higher laws might exist "with the details, whether good or bad, left to the working out of what we may call chance."

Since ichneumons are a detail, and since natural selection is a law regulating details, the answer to the ancient dilemma of why such cruelty (in our terms) exists in nature can only be that there isn't any answer—and that the framing of the question "in our terms" is thoroughly inappropriate in a natural world neither made for us nor ruled by us. It just plain happens. It is a strategy that works for ichneumons and that natural selection has programmed into their behavioral repertoire. Caterpillars are not suffering to teach us something; they have simply been outmaneuvered, for now, in the evolutionary game. Perhaps they will evolve a set of adequate defenses sometime in the future, thus sealing the fate of ichneumons. And perhaps, indeed probably, they will not. 28

Another Huxley, Thomas's grandson Julian,[11] spoke for this position, using as an example—yes, you guessed it—the ubiquitous ichneumons: 29

> Natural selection, in fact, though like the mills of God in grinding slowly and grinding small, has few other attributes that a civilized religion would call divine. . . . Its products are just as likely to be aesthetically, morally, or intellectually repulsive to us as they are to be attractive. We need only think of the ugliness of *Sacculina* or a bladderworm, the stupidity of a rhinoceros or a stegosaur, the horror of a female mantis devouring its mate or a brood of ichneumon flies slowly eating out a caterpillar.

It is amusing in this context, or rather ironic since it is too serious to be amusing, that modern creationists accuse evolutionists of preaching a specific ethical doctrine called secular humanism and thereby demand equal time for their unscientific and discredited views. If nature is nonmoral, then evolution cannot teach any ethical theory at all. The assumption that it can has abetted a panoply of social evils that ideologues falsely read into nature from their beliefs— eugenics and (misnamed) social Darwinism prominently among them. Not only did Darwin eschew any attempt to discover an antireligious ethic in nature, he also expressly stated his personal bewilderment about such deep issues as the problem of evil. Just a few sentences after invoking the ichneumons, and in words that express

---

[11]**Thomas's grandson Julian** Julian Huxley (1887–1975), an English biologist and a brother of the novelist Aldous Huxley.

both the modesty of this splendid man and the compatibility, through lack of contact, between science and true religion, Darwin wrote to Asa Gray,

> I feel most deeply that the whole subject is too profound for the human intellect. A dog might as well speculate on the mind of Newton. Let each man hope and believe what he can.

QUESTIONS FOR CRITICAL READING

1. What does Gould reveal to us about the nature of insect life?
2. What scientific information does Gould provide that is most valuable in explaining how nature works?
3. What does it mean to anthropomorphize nature? What are some concrete results of doing so?
4. Describe the reaction you have to the process by which the ichneumon wasp parasitizes its host.
5. How might the behavior of the ichneumon wasp put at stake any genuine religious questions of today?
6. What counterassertions can you make to Gould's view that nature is nonmoral?

SUGGESTIONS FOR WRITING

1. In a brief essay, try to answer the question Gould examines in paragraph 1: "Why are we surrounded with pain, suffering, and apparently senseless cruelty in the animal world?"
2. Is the fact of such pain, suffering, and apparently senseless cruelty a religious issue? If so, in what way? If not, demonstrate why.
3. In paragraph 17, Gould describes natural theology as "the antiquated doctrine that attempted to infer God's essence from the products of his creation." Is this a reasonable description of natural theology as you understand it? What can a theology that bases its claims in an observation of nature assert about the essence of God? What kind of religion would support a theology that was based on the behavior of natural life, including ichneumons?
4. Gould points out that even after having established his theory of evolution, Darwin could not "thoroughly abandon the idea that laws of nature might reflect some higher purpose" (para. 27). Assuming that you agree with Darwin but also acknowledge the problems that Gould presents, clarify what the higher purpose of a nature such as Gould describes might be. Does Gould's description of the behavior of the ichneumon (or any other) predator in any way compromise the idea that nature has a higher purpose? Does Gould hold that it has a higher purpose?

5. **CONNECTIONS**   Compare this essay with Francis Bacon's "The Four Idols." What intellectual issues do the two essays share? What common ground do they share regarding attitudes toward science and religion? What might Bacon have decided about the ultimate ethical issues raised by a consideration of the ichneumon? Do you think that Bacon would have held the same views about the ichneumon's predatory powers as did the nineteenth-century theologians? That is, would he have conceived of nature in ethical/moral terms?

6. **CONNECTIONS**   Why would Gould's scientific subject matter involve issues of morality to a greater extent than, say, the subject matter of Francis Bacon, Charles Darwin, or Rachel Carson? Is it possible that the study of physics or chemistry is less fundamentally concerned with moral issues than the study of biology is? One result of Darwin's concerns is the possibility that apes and humans are related. Is this point less worthy of consideration from a moral viewpoint than the behavior of the ichneumon wasp? What are the major moral issues in science that you have observed from examining these writers?

MICHIO KAKU
The Mystery of Dark Matter

MICHIO KAKU (b. 1947) was born and raised in San Jose, California, received his undergraduate degree from Harvard, and returned to California for his Ph.D. in physics from Berkeley in 1972. Since 1973 he has been professor of theoretical physics at the City College and the Graduate Center of the City University of New York, publishing widely on superstring theory, supergravity, and string field theory. He hosts a weekly national radio show on science called *Explorations*, and his other science commentaries on Pacifica National Radio are carried by sixty radio stations in the United States. Kaku is deeply concerned about the practical ramifications of theoretical physics and has written several books on the dangers of nuclear war. He is active in groups that advocate disarmament.

"The Mystery of Dark Matter" is a chapter in his book entitled *Beyond Einstein* (1987, rev. 1995), written with Jennifer Trainer Thompson. In this work Kaku attempts to explain the circumstances of modern physics, with a special look at efforts to resolve the conflicts between two important theories: quantum theory and the theory of relativity. Quantum theory explains the physics of atoms and small particles. The theory of relativity explains cosmic phenomena such as gravity and the universe. However, neither theory works in the other's sphere of influence. Hence a new theory is needed to resolve the problems: superstring theory, which postulates that instead of hard particles existing at the center of atoms, "tiny strings of energy" vibrate at an infinite number of frequencies. These strings of energy are at the heart

---

From *Beyond Einstein*.

of atoms and consist of everything we know of as matter in the universe.

If superstring theory is correct, one of the tests will be a confirmation of the existence of—and perhaps an explanation of—dark matter. In this essay Kaku describes dark matter as matter that we know exists but that cannot be seen or perceived except in terms of its effect on other bodies, such as stars.

Because physics involves specialized, advanced mathematics, much of what Kaku says is simplified for a general audience. As a result we can understand the theories, but only in general terms. Therefore, without the mathematics, we must accept certain ideas at face value, making an effort to imagine, along with Kaku, how modern theories of physics work. Fortunately his co-author, Jennifer Trainer Thompson, is able to spell out the very complex theories in a fashion that makes them as intelligible as possible for readers who are not experts in mathematics.

Some of the ideas in this essay are also developed in Kaku's best-selling *Hyperspace* (1994), which discusses the so-called crazy theories of contemporary physicists. Kaku tells us that modern research by contemporary physicists has produced a view of the natural world that virtually defies common sense, just as facts such as the earth's roundness (rather than flatness) and its movement around the sun (rather than the reverse) initially contradicted common sense. Unfortunately, common sense does not help us understand modern physics or the world of the atom. Because we cannot directly perceive the atom or the molecule, we require sophisticated equipment to make their nature evident. Interestingly, Francis Bacon insisted in *Novum Organum* that until better tools were developed, people would not be able to perceive the truth about the complexities of nature.

In an early chapter of *Hyperspace*, Kaku tells a story about being a young boy and watching fish in a small pond. He realized that for the carp, it was inconceivable that anything existed outside the water in which they swam. Their perceptions were limited entirely to the watery environment of their home. The same is true for people. Our environment may seem larger and more capacious than a pond, but we, like the carp, are limited in our perceptions. Plato realized this when he postulated his allegory of the cave and theorized that human beings' profoundly limited sensory apparatus prevents us from imagining experiences beyond what we know from our senses.

In "The Mystery of Dark Matter," Kaku discusses a phenomenon that similarly defies common sense. He explains that experiments

and observations of a number of important astrophysicists throughout a period of more than twenty years have led physicists to conclude that the universe is made up of more than the matter that we
can perceive. Indeed, the best observations have suggested that as
much as 90 percent of the universe may be made up of dark matter,
even though this matter cannot be observed directly. If it were not
so, theorists say, the galaxies would spin apart and the stars would
drift into distant space, thereby cooling the universe to a temperature that would lead to its death.

Kaku's Rhetoric

Jennifer Trainer Thompson, a nonphysicist, has worked on a
number of Kaku's books meant for a general reading public, and she
employs techniques common to contemporary journalism. She uses
short paragraphs and intriguing subheads, such as "What Is the
World Made Of?"; "How Much Does a Galaxy Weigh?"; and "Hot and
Cold Dark Matter." These techniques help readers grasp the ideas
that the research of Michio Kaku and other modern physicists has
developed.

Because the essay offers a general overview of an interesting
and elusive subject, Kaku provides a considerable amount of background information. He tells us about the impact of the work of
early mathematicians and physicists, some of whom developed theories that were far ahead of their times and who did not benefit
from seeing their work validated. This technique is effective rhetorically, because it helps us understand the struggles of scientists on a
human level. We feel sympathy for Vera Rubin, for example, who
grew up wanting to be an astrophysicist and whose dreams were almost shattered by male scientists who tried to discourage her. Kaku
gives insight into her struggles and demonstrates that much of what
she thought was true has been borne out in contemporary observations. Kaku describes a number of other scientists who came up
with "crazy" early theories, again helping us see the human side of
the story.

The most important aspect of this essay's rhetoric involves the
explanation of complex theories in terms that readers can grasp
easily. Although we will not leave this essay with a full understanding of the complexities of dark matter, we will at least understand
the problems that physicists face in trying to both describe how the
universe works and postulate the existence of a kind of matter that
seems to defy all common sense.

PREREADING QUESTIONS:
WHAT TO READ FOR

The following prereading questions may help you anticipate key issues in the discussion of Michio Kaku's "The Mystery of Dark Matter." Keeping them in mind during your first reading of the selection should help focus your attention.

- Why do physicists call it "dark matter"?
- What evidence tells us dark matter exists?
- What are the primary forces in the universe?

The Mystery of Dark Matter

With the cancellation of the SSC,[1] some commentators have publicly speculated that physics will "come to an end." Promising ideas such as the superstring theory, no matter how compelling and elegant, will never be tested and, hence, can never be verified. Physicists, however, are optimists. If evidence for the superstring theory cannot be found on the earth, then one solution is to leave the earth and go into outer space. Over the coming years, physicists will rely increasingly on cosmology to probe the inner secrets of matter and energy. Their laboratory will be the cosmos and the Big Bang itself.

Already, cosmology has given us several mysteries that may very well provide clues to the ultimate nature of matter. The first is dark matter, which makes up 90 percent of the universe. And the second is cosmic strings.

What Is the World Made Of?

One of the greatest achievements of twentieth-century science was the determination of the chemical elements of the universe. With only a little over one hundred elements, scientists could explain the trillions upon trillions of possible forms of matter, from DNA to animals to exploding stars. The familiar elements that made up the earth — such as carbon, oxygen, and iron — were the same as

---

[1] **SSC** An acronym for Superconducting Super Collider, a huge cyclotron designed to test the string theory of matter. It was canceled by the U.S. government in 1993.

the elements making up the distant galaxies. Analyzing the light taken from blazing stars billions of light-years from our galaxy, scientists found precisely the same familiar elements found in our own backyards, no more, no less.

Indeed, no new mysterious elements were found anywhere in 4 the universe. The universe was made of atoms and their subatomic constituents. That was the final word in physics.

But by the late twentieth century, an avalanche of new data has 5 confirmed that over 90 percent of the universe is made of an invisible form of unknown matter, or dark matter. The stars we see in the heavens, in fact, are now known to make up only a tiny fraction of the real mass of the universe.

Dark matter is a strange substance, unlike anything ever en- 6 countered before. It has weight but cannot be seen. In theory, if someone held a clump of dark matter in their hand, it would appear totally invisible. The existence of dark matter is not an academic question, because the ultimate fate of the universe, whether it will die in a fiery Big Crunch or fade away in a Cosmic Whimper or Big Chill, depends on its precise nature.

High-mass subatomic vibrations predicted by the superstring 7 theory are a leading candidate for dark matter. Thus, dark matter may give us an experimental clue to probe the nature of the superstring. Even without the SSC, science may be able to explore the new physics beyond the Standard Model.

How Much Does a Galaxy Weigh?

The scientist who first suspected that there was something 8 wrong about our conception of the universe was Fritz Zwicky,[2] a Swiss-American astronomer at the California Institute of Technology. In the 1930s, he was studying the Coma cluster of galaxies, about 300 million light years away, and was puzzled by the fact that they were revolving about each other so fast that they should be unstable. To confirm his suspicions, he had to calculate the mass of a galaxy. Since galaxies can contain hundreds of billion stars, calculating their weight is a tricky question.

There are two simple ways of making this determination. The 9 fact that these two methods gave startlingly different results has created the present crisis in cosmology.

---

[2] **Fritz Zwicky (1898–1974)** A Swiss-American astronomer who studied supernovas (huge exploding stars) in distant galaxies.

First, we can count the stars. This may seem like an impossible   10
task, but it's really quite simple. We know the rough average density
of the galaxy, and then we multiply by the total volume of the
galaxy. (That's how, for example, we calculate the number of hairs
on the human head, and how we determine that blondes have fewer
hairs than brunettes.)

Furthermore, we know the average weight of the stars. Of   11
course, no one actually puts a star on a scale. Astronomers instead
look for binary star systems, where two stars rotate around each
other. Once we know the time it takes for a complete rotation, Newton's laws are then sufficient to determine the mass of each star. By
multiplying the number of stars in a galaxy by the average weight of
each star, we get a rough number for the weight of the galaxy.

The second method is to apply Newton's laws directly on the   12
galaxy. Distant stars on a spiral arm of the galaxy, for example, orbit
around the galactic center at different rates. Furthermore, galaxies
and clusters of stars rotate around each other. Once we know the
time it takes for these various revolutions, we can then determine
the total mass of the galaxy using Newton's laws of motion.

Zwicky calculated the mass necessary to bind this cluster of galax-   13
ies by analyzing the rate at which they orbited around each other. He
found that this mass was twenty times greater than the actual mass of
the luminous stars. In a Swiss journal, Zwicky reported that there was
a fundamental discrepancy between these two results. He postulated
that there had to be some form of mysterious "dunkle Materie," or
dark matter, whose gravitational pull held this galactic cluster together. Without this dark matter, the Coma galaxies should fly apart.

Zwicky was led to postulate the existence of dark matter be-   14
cause of his unshakable belief that Newton's laws were correct out to
galactic distances. (This is not the first time that scientists predicted
the presence of unseen objects based on faith in Newton's laws. The
planets Neptune and Pluto, in fact, were discovered because the
orbit of closer planets, such as Saturn, wobbled and deviated from
Newton's predictions. Rather than give up Newton's laws, scientists
simply predicted the existence of new outer planets.)

However, Zwicky's results were met with indifference, even hos-   15
tility, by the astronomical community. After all, the very existence of
galaxies beyond our own Milky Way galaxy had been determined
only nine years before by Edwin Hubble, so most astronomers were
convinced that his results were premature, that eventually they would
fade away as better, more precise observations were made.

So Zwicky's results were largely ignored. Over the years, as-   16
tronomers accidentally rediscovered them but dismissed them as an

aberration. In the 1970s, for example, astronomers using radio tele-scopes analyzed the hydrogen gas surrounding a galaxy and found that it rotated much faster than it should have, but discounted the result.

In 1973, Jeremiah Ostriker and James Peebles at Princeton Uni- 17 versity resurrected this theory by making rigorous theoretical calcula-tions about the stability of a galaxy. Up to that time, most astronomers thought that a galaxy was very much like our solar system, with the inner planets traveling much faster than the outer planets. Mercury, for example, was named after the Greek god for speed since it raced across the heavens (traveling at 107,000 miles per hour). Pluto, on the other hand, lumbers across the solar system at 10,500 miles per hour. If Pluto traveled around the sun as fast as Mercury, then it would quickly fly into outer space, never to return. The gravitational pull of the sun would not be enough to hold on to Pluto.

However, Ostriker and Peebles showed that the standard pic- 18 ture of a galaxy, based on our solar system, was unstable; by rights, the galaxy should fly apart. The gravitational pull of the stars was not enough to hold the galaxy together. They then showed that a galaxy can become stable if it is surrounded by a massive invisible halo that holds the galaxy together and if 90 percent of its mass was actually in the halo in the form of dark matter. Their paper was also met with indifference.

But after decades of skepticism and derision, what finally turned 19 the tide on dark matter was the careful, persistent results of as-tronomer Vera Rubin and her colleagues at the Carnegie Institution in Washington, D.C. The results of these scientists, who analyzed hun-dreds of galaxies, verified conclusively that the velocity of the outer stars in a galaxy did not vary much from that of the inner ones, con-trary to the planets in our solar system. This meant that the outer stars should fly into space, causing the galaxy to disintegrate into billions of individual stars, unless held together by the gravitational pull of invisible dark matter.

Like the history of dark matter itself, it took several decades for 20 Vera Rubin's lifetime of results to be recognized by the skeptical (and overwhelmingly male) astronomical community.

One Woman's Challenge

It has never been easy for a female scientist to be accepted by 21 her male peers. In fact, at every step of the way, Dr. Rubin's career came perilously close to being derailed by male hostility. She first became interested in the stars in the 1930s as a ten-year-old child, gazing at the night sky over Washington, D.C., for hours at a time, even making detailed maps of meteor trails across the heavens.

Her father, an electrical engineer, encouraged her to pursue her   22
interest in the stars, even helping her build her first telescope at the age of fourteen and taking her to amateur astronomy meetings in Washington. However, the warm encouragement she felt inside her family contrasted sharply with the icy reception she received from the outside world.

When she applied to Swarthmore College, the admissions offi-   23
cer tried to steer her away from astronomy, to a more "ladylike" career of painting astronomical subjects. That became a standard joke around her family. She recalled, "Whenever anything went wrong for me at work, someone would say, 'Have you ever thought of a career in which you paint? . . . '"[3]

When accepted at Vassar, she proudly told her high school   24
physics teacher in the hallway, who replied bluntly, "You'll do all right as long as you stay away from science." (Years later, she recalled, "It takes an enormous amount of self-esteem to listen to things like that and not be demolished.")[4]

After graduating from Vassar, she applied to graduate school at   25
Princeton, which had a world-renowned reputation in astronomy. However, she never even received the school's catalog, since Princeton did not accept female graduate students in astronomy until 1971.

She was accepted at Harvard, but declined the offer because she   26
had just gotten married to Robert Rubin, a physical chemist, and followed him to Cornell University, where the astronomy department consisted of just two faculty members. (After she declined, she got a formal letter back from Harvard, with the handwritten words scrawled on the bottom, "Damn you women. Every time I get a good one ready, she goes off and gets married.")[5]

Going to Cornell, however, was a blessing in disguise, since   27
Rubin took graduate courses in physics from two Nobel laureates in physics, Hans Bethe, who decoded the complex fusion reactions which energize the stars, and Richard Feynman, who renormalized quantum electrodynamics. Her master's thesis met head-on the hostility of a male-dominated world. Her paper, which showed that the faraway galaxies deviated from the uniform expansion of a simplified version of the Big Bang model, was rejected for publication

---

[3] Marcia Bartusiak, *Discover* (October 1990): 89. [Kaku's note]

[4] Alan Lightman and Roberta Brawer, *Origins: The Lives and Worlds of Modern Cosmologists* (Cambridge: Harvard University Press, 1990), 305. [Kaku's note]

[5] *Ibid.*, 288. [Kaku's note]

because it was too far-fetched for its time. (Decades later, her paper would be considered prophetic.)

But after receiving her master's degree from Cornell, Rubin found 28 herself an unhappy housewife. "I actually cried every time the *Astrophysical Journal* came into the house . . . nothing in my education had taught me that one year after Cornell my husband would be out doing his science and I would be home changing diapers."[6]

Nonetheless, Rubin struggled to pursue her childhood dream, 29 especially after her husband took a job in Washington. Taking nighttime classes, she received her Ph.D. from Georgetown University. In 1954, she published her Ph.D. thesis, a landmark study that showed that the distribution of the galaxies in the heavens was not smooth and uniform, as previously thought, but actually clumpy.

Unfortunately, she was years ahead of her time. Over the years, 30 she gained a reputation of being something of an eccentric, going against the prevailing prejudice of astronomical thought. It would take years for her ideas to gain the recognition they deserved.

Distressed by the controversy her work was generating, Rubin 31 decided to take a respite and study one of the most mundane and unglamorous areas of astronomy, the rotation of galaxies. Innocently enough, Rubin began studying the Andromeda galaxy, our nearest neighbor in space. She and her colleagues expected to find that the gas swirling in the outer fringes of the Andromeda galaxy was traveling much slower than the gas near the center. Like our own solar system, the speed of the gas should slow down as one went farther from the galactic nuclei.

Much to their surprise, they found that the velocity of the gas 32 was a constant, whether it was near the center or near the rim of the galaxy. At first, they thought this peculiar result was unique to the Andromeda galaxy. Then they systematically began to analyze hundreds of galaxies (two hundred galaxies since 1978) and found the same curious result. Zwicky had been right all along.

The sheer weight of their observational results could not be de- 33 nied. Galaxy after galaxy showed the same, flat curve. Because astronomy had become technically much more sophisticated since the time of Zwicky, it was possible for other laboratories to verify Rubin's numbers rapidly. The constancy of velocity of a rotating galaxy was now a universal fact of galactic physics. Dark matter was here to stay.

For her pioneering efforts, Vera Rubin was elected to the presti- 34 gious National Academy of Science in 1981. (Since it was founded

---

[6] Bartusiak, *Discover*, 90. [Kaku's note]

in 1863, only 75 women among the 3,508 scientists have been elected to the academy.)

Today, Rubin is still pained by how little progress female scientists 35 have made. Her own daughter has a Ph.D. in cosmic ray physics. When she went to Japan for an international conference, she was the only woman there. "I really couldn't tell that story for a long time without weeping," Rubin recalled, "because certainly in one generation, between her generation and mine, not an awful lot has changed."[7]

Not surprisingly, Rubin is interested in stimulating the interest 36 of young girls to pursue scientific studies. She has even written a children's book, entitled *My Grandmother Is an Astronomer.*

Bending Starlight

Since Rubin's original paper, even more sophisticated analyses of 37 the universe have shown the existence of the dark matter halo, which may be as much as six times the size of the galaxy itself. In 1986, Bodhan Paczynski of Princeton University realized that if the starlight from a distant star traveled by a nearby clump of dark matter, the dark matter might bend the starlight and act as a magnifying lens, making the star appear much brighter. In this way, by looking for dim stars that suddenly got brighter, the presence of dark matter could be detected. In 1994, two groups independently reported photographing such a stellar brightening. Since then, other teams of astronomers have joined in, hoping to find more examples of stellar brightening.

In addition, the bending of starlight by a distant galaxy can be 38 used as another way in which to calculate the galaxy's weight. Anthony Tyson and his colleagues at the AT&T Bell Laboratories have analyzed light rays from dim blue galaxies at the rim of the visible universe. This cluster of galaxies acts like a gravitational lens, bending the light from other galaxies. Photos of distant galaxies have confirmed that the bending is much more than expected, meaning that their weight comes from much more than the sum of their individual stars. Ninety percent of the mass of these galaxies turns out to be dark, as predicted.

Hot and Cold Dark Matter

While the existence of dark matter is no longer in dispute, its 39 composition is a matter of lively controversy. Several schools of thought have emerged, none of them very satisfactory.

---

[7] Lightman, *Origins*, 305. [Kaku's note]

First, there is the "hot dark matter" school, which holds that 40
dark matter is made of familiar lightweight subparticles such as neutrinos, which are notoriously difficult to detect. Since the total flux
of neutrinos filling up the universe is not well known, the universe
may be bathed in a flood of neutrinos, making up the dark matter of
the universe.

If the electron-neutrino, for example, is found to have a tiny 41
mass, then there is a chance that it may have enough mass to make
up the missing mass problem. (In February 1995, physicists at the
Los Alamos National Laboratory in New Mexico announced that
they had found evidence that the electron-neutrino has a tiny mass:
one-millionth the weight of an electron. However, this result must
still be verified by other laboratories before it is finally accepted by
other physicists.)

Then there is the "cold dark matter" school, which suspects that 42
dark matter is made of heavier, slow-moving, and much more exotic
subparticles. For the past decade, physicists have been looking for
exotic candidates that might make up cold dark matter. These particles have been given strange, whimsical names, such as "axions,"
named after a household detergent. Collectively, they are called
WIMPs, for "weakly interacting massive particles." (The skeptics
have retaliated by pointing out that a significant part of dark matter
may consist of familiar but dim forms of ordinary matter, such as
red dwarf stars, neutron stars, black holes, and Jupiter-sized planets.
Not to be outdone, they have called these objects MACHOs, for
"massive astrophysical compact halo objects." However, even the
proponents of MACHOs admit that, at best, they can explain only
20 percent of the dark matter problem. In late 1994, however, a version of the MACHO theory was dealt a blow when the Hubble Space
Telescope, scanning the Milky Way galaxy for red dwarf stars, found
far fewer of these dim stars than expected.)

But perhaps the most promising candidate for WIMPs are the su- 43
perparticles, or "sparticles" for short. Supersymmetry,[8] we remember,
was first seen as a symmetry of particle physics in the superstring
theory. Indeed, the superstring is probably the only fully consistent
theory of superparticles.

---

[8] **supersymmetry** A mathematical theory that postulates the existence of a
"superpartner" for each physical particle discovered. Every particle has a spin and its
superparticle has a spin, sometimes the same, sometimes different. All particles are
either fermions (electrons, etc.) with a spin of $\frac{1}{2}$ or bosons (photons, etc.) with spins
from 0 to 2. Mathematical models match them with superpartners that can sometimes convert bosons into fermions. Fermions are the particles that make up all the
material world. Bosons make up gravity and light.

According to supersymmetry, every particle must have a super-   44
partner, with differing spin. The leptons (electrons and neutrinos)
for example, have spin $\frac{1}{2}$. Their superpartners are called "sleptons"
and have spin 0. Likewise, the superpartners of the quarks are called
"squarks" and also have spin 0.

Furthermore, the superpartner of the spin I photon (which de-   45
scribes light) is called the "photino." And the superpartner of the
gluons (which holds the quarks together) is called "gluino."

The main criticism of sparticles is that we have never seen them   46
in the laboratory. At present, there is no evidence that these superparticles exist. However, it is widely believed that this lack of evidence
is only because our atom smashers are too feeble to create superparticles. In other words, their mass is simply too large for our atom
smashers to produce them.

Lack of concrete evidence has not, however, prevented physicists   47
from trying to use particle physics to explain the mysteries of dark
matter and cosmology. For example, one of the leading candidates
for the WIMP is the photino.

The cancellation of the SSC, therefore, does not necessarily   48
doom our attempts to verify the correctness of the superstring. Within
the next decade, it is hoped that the increased accuracy of our astronomical observations, with the deployment of a new generation of
telescopes and satellites, may narrow down the candidates for dark
matter. If dark matter turns out to be composed, at least in part, of
sparticles, belief in the superstring theory would receive an enormous boost.

How Will the Universe Die?

Last, dark matter may prove decisive in understanding the ulti-   49
mate fate of the universe. One persistent controversy has been the fate
of an expanding universe. Some believe that there is enough matter
and gravity to reverse its expansion. Others believe that the universe is
too low in density, so that the galaxies will continue their expansion,
until temperatures around the universe approach absolute zero.

At present, attempts to calculate the average density of the uni-   50
verse show the latter to be true: The universe will die in a Cosmic
Whimper or a Big Chill, expanding forever. However, this theory is
open to experimental challenges. Specifically, there might be enough
missing matter to boost the average density of the universe.

To determine the fate of the universe, cosmologists use the pa-   51
rameter called "omega," which measures the matter density of the
universe. If omega is greater than one, then there is enough matter

in the universe to reverse the cosmic expansion, and the universe will begin to collapse until it reaches the Big Crunch.

However, if omega is less than one, then the gravity of the uni- 52 verse is too weak to change the cosmic expansion, and the universe will expand forever, until it reaches the near-absolute-zero temperatures of the Cosmic Whimper. If omega is equal to one, then the universe is balanced between these two scenarios, and the universe will appear to be perfectly flat, without any curvature. (For omega to equal one, the density of the universe must be approximately three hydrogen atoms per cubic meter.) Current astronomical data favors a value of .1 for omega, which is too small to reverse the cosmic expansion.

The leading modification of the Big Bang theory is the inflation- 53 ary universe, which predicts a value of omega of precisely 1. However, the visible stars in the heavens only give us 1 percent of the critical density. This is sometimes called the "missing mass" problem. (It is different from the dark matter problem, which was based on purely galactic considerations.) Dust, brown dwarfs, and nonluminous stars may boost this number a bit, but not by much. For example, the results from nucleosynthesis show that the maximum value of the density of this form of nonluminous matter cannot exceed 15 percent of the critical density.

Even if we add in the dark matter halos that surround the galaxies, 54 this only brings us up to 10 percent of the critical value. So the dark matter in halos cannot solve the missing mass problem by itself. . . .

QUESTIONS FOR CRITICAL READING

1. What is the Cosmic Whimper?
2. What are the qualities of dark matter? Why is it a "problem"?
3. How will cosmology help physicists understand more about "the inner secrets of matter and energy" (para. 1)?
4. When did scientists begin to notice "that there was something wrong about our conception of the universe" (para. 8)?
5. How do scientists count the stars?
6. What would make a galaxy like ours unstable enough to fly apart?
7. Which aspects of Kaku's presentation most defy common sense?

SUGGESTIONS FOR WRITING

1. In two pages, try to explain the nature of dark matter and the problems associated with it to a friend who has not read Kaku's essay and who does not have a technical background.

2. Why is it important to know how the universe will end? Which theory is more compelling, the Big Crunch or the Big Chill? Do your best to represent your view as the most likely view.

3. Michio Kaku has written in both *Beyond Einstein* and *Hyperspace* about the superstring theory, which insists that at the heart of the atom is not a hard particle but a vibrating string of energy. Consult either of those books (or other discussions of the theory) and explain it in clear terms so that your classmates will understand it. What is your view of the likelihood of such a theory being accurate?

4. After conducting a search on the Internet for information on black holes, construct an essay that clarifies the nature of the black hole. Try to integrate this information with Kaku's theories about the ways in which a study of the cosmos will contribute to an understanding of the atom's inner workings. How does the behavior of black holes defy common sense? How does it help us understand the nature of the universe?

5. Kaku mentions the decision to abandon the superconducting super collider (SSC) in 1993. Do a search in both popular and scientific journals for a discussion of the promise and purpose of the SSC. Write an essay describing the reasons the SSC was originally planned and its construction begun, as well as the reasons why it was abandoned. Do you think it was a wise decision to give up on the SSC? Are you as optimistic as Kaku regarding the possibility of high-level research continuing despite the SCC's cancellation?

6. **CONNECTIONS** How does Plato's "Allegory of the Cave" (in Part 5) prepare us for reading the work of Kaku? What does Plato say about the human mind that has special relevance to Kaku's theories? In what ways would the four idols of Francis Bacon come into play in our efforts to make sense of the theories of physics that Kaku discusses?

7. **CONNECTIONS** To what extent could the concept of dark matter be compared with Carl Jung's views in "The Personal and the Collective Unconscious" (in Part 5)? Is dark matter a metaphorical celestial unconscious? Since neither dark matter nor the unconscious can be perceived directly, and since both seem to be profoundly influential on our daily life, what ought we to think about the information that our senses gather? How far can we rely on our sensory apprehension? What are the limits of sense perception? What intellectual processes permit us to go beyond sensory perception?

PART SEVEN

ETHICS AND MORALITY

The Torah
Aristotle
St. Matthew
The Koran
Friedrich Nietzsche
Iris Murdoch
His Holiness the Dalai Lama

INTRODUCTION

A system of morality which is based on relative emotional values is a mere illusion, a thoroughly vulgar conception which has nothing sound in it and nothing true.

—SOCRATES (469–399 B.C.)

God considered not action, but the spirit of the action. It is the intention, not the deed, wherein the merit or praise of the doer consists.

—PETER ABELARD (1079–1142)

If men were born free, they would, so long as they remained free, form no conception of good and evil.

—BARUCH SPINOZA (1632–1677)

All morality depends upon our sentiments; and when any action or quality of the mind pleases us after a certain manner we say it is virtuous; and when the neglect or nonperformance of it displeases us after a like manner, we say that we lie under an obligation to perform it.

—DAVID HUME (1711–1776)

There are no whole truths; all truths are half-truths. It is trying to treat them as whole truths that plays the devil

—ALFRED NORTH WHITEHEAD (1861–1947)

To set up as a standard of public morality a notion which can neither be defined nor conceived is to open the door to every kind of tyranny.

—SIMONE WEIL (1909–1943)

The establishment of ethical principles that translate into moral behavior constitutes a major step forward for civilization. To be sure, ancient civilizations maintained rules and laws governing behavior, and in some cases those rules were written down and adhered to by the majority of citizens. But the move that major religions made was to go beyond simple rules or laws—to penetrate deeper layers of emotion to make people want to behave well toward each other. The writers and writings in this section have all examined the nature of morality and have come to some interesting conclusions, focusing on various aspects of the ethical nature of humankind.

The Torah is comprised of the first five books of the Bible—Genesis, Exodus, Leviticus, Numbers, and Deuteronomy. In the selection included here—"Moses and the Ten Commandments"—from Chapters 19–23 of the Book of Exodus, Moses ascends Mount Sinai to receive the Ten Commandments from God. Exodus reveals a powerful deity who singles out the Hebrews for survival and prosperity if they are willing to cleave to the Commandments. The further instruction from God helps to clarify the day-to-day management of life, with suggestions for proper behavior that add up to a pattern of ethical action. These additional instructions seem particularly suited to the culture of Moses and his people in the fourteenth century B.C., but most of them can be modified in such a way as to remain pertinent today. The Ten Commandments are the basis of Western morality, and while they are amplified in Exodus with further commands, they represent the basic points on which, for God, there is no negotiation.

Taking a much different approach, Aristotle, in the fourth century B.C., wrote a treatise on ethics aimed at instructing his son Nichomachus. The *Nichomachean Ethics* is the single most famous ancient document that attempts to clarify the nature of ethical behavior and its effect on the individual. In the selection from the *Ethics* included here, Aristotle focuses on defining the good in life, not in the abstract, but in terms of the individual's obligation to participate in statecraft—what we might call politics. Aristotle also felt that in a democracy it is everyone's duty to understand the principles by which people can live happily and well. Once he has defined the good he proceeds to examine the nature of human happiness, and eventually he connects it to "virtuous conduct" (para. 23). In the process, he examines virtuous conduct in an effort to enlighten his son on the kind of behavior that is likely to reward him with the most happiness and the best life.

Aristotle emphasizes the soul over the body, in the sense that he emphasizes the spiritual over the material world. Reason, his guide, must be followed if we are to live well, but he realizes it is often disregarded. Therefore he discusses at some length the irrational aspects of our minds that affect behavior. In the final analysis, Aristotle argues for a reasonable approach to guiding the individual's behavior with respect for others.

In the Sermon on the Mount, St. Matthew's gospel from the New Testament of the Bible, as in "Moses and the Ten Commandments," the specific behavior of the individual is measured and an examination of the laws of moral behavior is conducted for all humankind. St. Matthew was present when Jesus gave his sermon to the people, and he records it carefully for all to follow. The sermon begins somewhat differently from the passages of the Ten Commandments in that Jesus focuses first on what he calls beatitudes, the blessings that people enjoy from God. He then moves on to injunctions that resemble the Ten Commandments but that have a somewhat different edge to them. For example, Jesus warns people to "judge not, that ye be not judged" (7:1), and advises those who feel they have been harmed by a neighbor to turn the other cheek. In essence, the Sermon on the Mount represents a response and reinterpretation of the passages in Exodus concerning the Ten Commandments and offers a guide for holy living for the new age.

The Koran includes many passages from the Bible, and it recognizes Jesus as a prophet in the same way it recognizes Muhammad as a prophet. Written six hundred years after the Sermon on the Mount, "The Night Journey" takes on the task of updating the ethical commandments that are essential for the faithful to understand and follow. Many of the edicts are similar to those set forth by both Moses and Jesus, and some of the further instructions focus on the special concerns of the culture that Muhammad was part of. For example, the doctrine of fairness in dealings with others is much more clearly articulated than in earlier texts, which may be a result of changes in the culture's economy, since in Muhammad's time people were more likely to be traders or business people than farmers or herders. The Koran remains the principal source of proper ethical behavior for all Islam.

Friedrich Nietzsche, a nineteenth-century philosopher and critic of all social institutions, approaches the question of ethics from a completely unexpected angle. In "Morality as Anti-Nature" he argues that the moral and ethical views of traditional religions are "anti-life." He believes religious injunctions stifle individuals' natural behaviors and promote values of death rather than of life. He speculates that religion condemns certain behaviors in order to protect those who are too weak to protect themselves, and that the strong, whom Nietzsche calls "Supermen," are condemned to obey commandments that rob them of the vitality of existence. His complaint is that religions punish everyone for the sins of the few because the few are weak and unable to control themselves. Nietzsche's views have been very influential in modern thought, especially during the last decades of the nineteenth and the whole of the twentieth century.

Iris Murdoch, one of the twentieth century's most distinguished writers, spent part of her life as an Oxford don teaching philosophy. Her major interests were ethics and morals; in "Morality and Religion" she addresses the question: Can there be morality without religion? Murdoch explores the issues of virtue and duty, both of which she sees as aspects of what we think of as moral behavior, and connects them with the ideals of institutional religion. She then goes on to examine guilt, usually thought of as a religious concept, and the question of sin. That leads her to consider how religion conceives of the struggle of good and evil, aiming as it does to conquer evil through moral behavior. But a paradox arises: If evil can be totally conquered, can there still be a system of morals or a behavior that needs to be called ethical? Murdoch's method is to keep us questioning basic issues until we begin to grasp their significance.

His Holiness the Dalai Lama, the spiritual and political leader of the Tibetan people, has approached ethical issues from a special position. All of the Dalai Lamas (there have been fourteen) are considered reincarnations of Avalokiteshvara, the Bodhisattva of Compassion. A bodhisattva is a Buddha, an enlightened one. Therefore the Buddhist Dalai Lama naturally focuses on issues of compassion and how they affect ethical behavior. His message is not couched in terms of commandments that urge people not to do specific things, but rather it is dedicated to explaining why the compassion natural to everyone can be a guide to living a life of happiness and fulfillment. The Dalai Lama knows that not everyone can reach the levels of compassion that a truly enlightened person can. But he feels that a willingness to experiment by focusing on compassion in everyday life will improve the individual emotionally and spiritually. As the Dalai Lama argues, those who feel proper empathy and deep compassion certainly cannot behave unethically toward others.

Each of these selections offers insights into the ethical underpinnings of modern culture. They clarify the nature of the good, the holy, and the moral. If humankind's ultimate goal is happiness, then the path to that goal must go through the precincts of ethical and moral behavior.

THE TORAH
Moses and the Ten Commandments

THE PASSAGES IN THE BIBLE that record the Ten Commandments are considered by many to be the ethical basis for most of Western thought. Other figures, such as Solon (638–558 B.C.), a Greek statesman and poet, also laid down laws for ethical behavior, but the Ten Commandments have guided major religions in their establishment of moral principles since the time of Moses. In Exodus, the second book of the Bible, the Ten Commandments are delivered on Mount Sinai to Moses, and thereafter Moses outlines further laws guiding proper moral behavior.

Traditionally, the first five books of the Bible, known as the Torah and also as the Pentateuch, were written by Moses. There is some dispute about both authorship and dating, but the current thinking is that Moses was born sometime in the fourteenth century B.C. The exodus—the removal of the Hebrews from Egypt to Israel—probably took place early in the thirteenth century B.C. This dating is based on certain references in the Bible correlated with the known dates of Egyptian pharaohs who ruled before and after the Hebrews left Egypt.

Originally, Hebrews were laborers working in Egypt, but at some time in the fourteenth century B.C. their numbers grew so large that the pharaoh, Seti I (ruled 1318–1304 B.C.), demanded that male Hebrew children be killed at birth. Moses' parents placed him in a reed basket and floated him in the Nile. There he was found by pharaoh's daughter, who saved him and raised him as a member of the royal household. Moses' name is etymologically Egyptian, close in meaning to "is born." Moses' story of life in Egypt, and of leaving for Midian after he killed an Egyptian overlord who was bullying a Hebrew worker, is told in the early chapters of Exodus

From *The Oxford Study Edition of the New Age Bible* (1976).

and is familiar to many. He married and became a farmer in Midian, where he expected to remain until he heard the word of God and set out to free the Hebrews.

The portions of Exodus reprinted here—Chapters 19–23—concern the fate of the Hebrews, who, with Moses' leadership, escaped slavery in Egypt and determined to resettle in the "promised land" of Israel. After their escape from Egypt, the Hebrews—traditionally said to number about one and a half million—camped at Mount Sinai for some fourteen months. During this encampment, God appeared to Moses in the form of a burning bush. He commanded Moses to go into his presence on top of Mount Sinai (called Horeb). God then made the mountain itself appear to be burning so that the Hebrews would be in awe. It was there that Moses received the Ten Commandments. In some versions they are delivered to him engraved on stone tablets, in others they are delivered orally. Another version of the Ten Commandments appears in Chapter 5 of Deuteronomy, the fifth and last book of the Torah.

Moses led his people out of Egypt, helped them avoid a catastrophic rebellion while they were on the move, and successfully got them to Israel. But he himself did not go with them. He is said to have climbed Mount Pisgah, from whose summit he could see the promised land. Ironically, he went no further, and the Hebrews never saw him again. His death and burial are a mystery.

The Rhetoric of "Moses and the Ten Commandments"

Because the book of Exodus is a dramatic narrative, essentially a story of what happened to the Hebrews on their way to Israel, we have a setting in Chapter 19:1—"Israel at Mount Sinai"—and we have dialogue as well. In the opening verses of Chapter 19 the primary dialogue is between God and Moses. God explains his covenant, or agreement with the people: "[Y]ou shall become my special possession" (19:5), and says to Moses, "These are the words you shall speak to the Israelites" (19:6).

Chapter 19 is filled with warnings from God not to look directly at him. When he appears and the thunder and lightning frighten the Hebrews, Moses ascends Mount Sinai alone to speak to God. God asks that the Hebrews accompany Moses, but he warns Moses to erect a barrier to prevent them from ascending the mountain. In order for the people to hear what God has to say, Moses must return to the foot of the mountain to relay his message.

In Chapter 20 God speaks directly to Moses and delivers to him the Ten Commandments by which the Hebrews must live. These commandments, in comparison with those outlined in Deuteronomy, are full and detailed. The fifth commandment, to "keep the Sabbath day holy" (20:8), is elaborated with details and reasons so that Moses may interpret the commandment for the Hebrews. But the sixth commandment, "You shall not commit murder" (20:13), is a flat statement that offers no room for commentary or elaboration. This is true also of the seventh, eighth, and ninth commandments.

When Moses receives the Ten Commandments, trumpets sound, lightning flashes, thunder claps, and Mount Sinai emits smoke, reaffirming the Hebrews' confidence in Moses' ability to lead them to Israel.

Chapter 21 offers an elaboration and clarification of God's edicts. It is here that God sets down rules that govern behavior in unjust situations. As a measure of justice, God says, "Wherever hurt is done, you shall give life for life, eye for eye, tooth for tooth, hand for hand, foot for foot, burn for burn, bruise for bruise, wound for wound" (20:23–25). Chapter 22 concerns farming squabbles and crimes, as well as rules governing sexual behavior. Chapter 23 concerns spreading false rumor, giving false evidence, and how to behave toward your enemies, especially when they have lost livestock that must be returned to them.

Thus the original narrative in Chapter 19, which was essentially a dialogue between Moses and God, then between Moses and the Hebrews, evolves into a monologue in which God delivers a message filled with dire warnings that is softened by the promise of protection and blessing in exchange for fealty.

PREREADING QUESTIONS: WHAT TO READ FOR

The following prereading questions may help you anticipate key issues in the discussion of "Moses and the Ten Commandments" from the Torah. Keeping them in mind during your first reading of the selection should help focus your attention.

- What are the Ten Commandments?

- How does Moses receive the Ten Commandments?

- How do God's ancillary edicts help clarify the Ten Commandments?

Moses and the Ten Commandments

Israel at Mount Sinai

19

In the third month after Israel had left Egypt, they came to the wilderness of Sinai.

2   They set out from Rephidim and entered the wilderness of Sinai, where they encamped, pitching their tents opposite the mountain.

3   Moses went up to the mountain of God, and the Lord called to him from the mountain and said, "Speak thus to the house of Jacob, and tell this to the sons of Israel:

4   You have seen with your eyes what I did to Egypt, and how I have carried you on eagles' wings and brought you here to me.

5   If only you will now listen to me and keep my covenant, then out of all peoples you shall become my special possession; for the whole earth is mine.

6   You shall be my kingdom of priests, my holy nation. These are the words you shall speak to the Israelites."

7   Moses came and summoned the elders of the people and set before all these commands which the Lord had laid upon him.

8   The people all answered together, "Whatever the Lord has said we will do." Moses brought this answer back to the Lord.

9   The Lord said to Moses, "I am now coming to you in a thick cloud, so that I may speak to you in the hearing of the people, and their faith in you may never fail."

10   Moses told the Lord what the people had said, and the Lord said to him, "Go to the people and hallow them today and to-morrow and make them wash their clothes.

11   They must be ready by the third day, because on the third day the Lord will descend upon Mount Sinai in the sight of all the people.

12   You must put barriers round the mountain and say, 'Take care not to go up the mountain or even touch the edge of it.' Any man who touches the mountain must be put to death.

13   No hand shall touch him; he shall be stoned or shot dead: neither man nor beast may live. But when the ram's horn sounds, they may go up the mountain."

14   Moses came down from the mountain to the people. He hallowed them and they washed their clothes.

15   He said to the people, "Be ready by the third day; do not go near a woman."

16   On the third day, when morning came, there were peals of thunder and flashes of lightning, dense cloud on the mountain and a loud trumpet blast; the people in the camp were all terrified.

17   Moses brought the people out from the camp to meet God, and they took their stand at the foot of the mountain.

18   Mount Sinai was all smoking because the Lord had come down upon it in fire; the smoke went up like the smoke of a kiln; all the people were terrified, and the sound of the trumpet grew ever louder.

19   Whenever Moses spoke, God answered him in a peal of thunder.

20   The Lord came down upon the top of Mount Sinai and summoned Moses to the mountain-top, and Moses went up.

21   The Lord said to Moses, "Go down; warn the people solemnly that they must not force their way through to the Lord to see him, or many of them will perish.

22   Even the priests, who have access to the Lord, must hallow themselves, for fear that the Lord may break out against them."

23   Moses answered the Lord, "The people cannot come up Mount Sinai, because thou thyself didst solemnly warn us to set up a barrier to the mountain and so to keep it holy."

24   The Lord therefore said to him, "Go down; then come up and bring Aaron with you, but let neither priests nor people force their way up to the Lord, for fear that he may break out against them."

25   So Moses went down to the people and spoke to them.

20

God spoke, and these were his words:

2   I am the Lord your God who brought you out of Egypt, out of the land of slavery.

3   You shall have no other god to set against me.

4   You shall not make a carved image for yourself nor the likeness of anything in the heavens above, or on the earth below, or in the waters under the earth.

5   You shall not bow down to them or worship them; for I, the Lord your God, am a jealous god. I punish the children for the sins of the fathers to the third and fourth generations of those who hate me.

6   But I keep faith with thousands, with those who love me and keep my commandments.

7   You shall not make wrong use of the name of the Lord your God: the Lord will not leave unpunished the man who misuses my name.

8   Remember to keep the sabbath day holy.

9　You have six days to labour and do all your work.

10　But the seventh day is a sabbath of the Lord your God; that day you shall not do any work, you, your son or your daughter, your cattle or the alien within your gates;

11　for in six days the Lord made heaven and earth, the sea, and all that is in them, and on the seventh day he rested. Therefore the Lord blessed the sabbath day and declared it holy.

12　Honour your father and your mother, that you may live long in the land which the Lord your God is giving you.

13　You shall not commit murder.

14　You shall not commit adultery.

15　You shall not steal.

16　You shall not give false evidence against your neighbour.

17　You shall not covet your neighbour's house; you shall not covet your neighbour's wife, his slave, his slave-girl, his ox, his ass, or anything that belongs to him.

18　When all the people saw how it thundered and the lightning flashes, when they heard the trumpet sound and saw the mountain smoking, they trembled and stood at a distance.

19　"Speak to us yourself," they said to Moses, "and we will listen; but if God speaks to us we shall die."

20　Moses answered, "Do not be afraid. God has come only to test you, so that the fear of him may remain with you and keep you from sin."

21　So the people stood at a distance, while Moses approached the dark cloud where God was.

22　The Lord said to Moses, say this to the Israelites: "You know now that I have spoken to you from heaven.

23　I have spoken to you from heaven. You shall not make gods of silver to be worshipped as well as me, nor shall you make yourselves gods of gold.

24　You shall make an altar of earth for me, and you shall sacrifice on it both your whole-offerings and your shared-offerings, your sheep and your cattle. Wherever I cause my name to be invoked, I will come to you and bless you.

25　If you make an altar of stones for me, you must not build it of hewn stones, for if you use a chisel on it, you will profane it.

26　You must not mount up to my altar by steps, in case your private parts be exposed on it."

21

These are the laws you shall set before them:

2　When you buy a Hebrew slave, he shall be your slave for six years, but in the seventh year he shall go free and pay nothing.

3   If he comes to you alone, he shall go away alone; but if he is married, his wife shall go away with him.

4   If his master gives him a wife, and she bears him sons or daughters, the woman and her children shall belong to her master, and the man shall go away alone.

5   But if the slave should say, "I love my master, my wife, and my children; I will not go free,"

6   then his master shall bring him to God: he shall bring him to the door or the door-post, and his master shall pierce his ear with an awl, and the man shall be his slave for life.

7   When a man sells his daughter into slavery, she shall not go free as a male slave may.

8   If her master has not had intercourse with her and she does not please him, he shall let her be ransomed. He has treated her unfairly and therefore has no right to sell her to strangers.

9   If he assigns her to his son, he shall allow her the rights of a daughter.

10   If he takes another woman, he shall not deprive the first of meat, clothes, and conjugal rights.

11   If he does not provide her with these three things, she shall go free without any payment.

12   Whoever strikes another man and kills him shall be put to death.

13   But if he did not act with intent, but they met by act of God, the slayer may flee to a place which I will appoint for you.

14   But if a man has the presumption to kill another by treachery, you shall take him even from my altar to be put to death.

15   Whoever strikes his father or mother shall be put to death.

16   Whoever kidnaps a man shall be put to death, whether he has sold him, or the man is found in his possession.

17   Whoever reviles his father or mother shall be put to death.

18   When men quarrel and one hits another with a stone or with a spade, and the man is not killed but takes to his bed;

19   if he recovers so as to walk about outside with a stick, then the one who struck him has no liability, except that he shall pay for loss of time and shall see that he is cured.

20   When a man strikes his slave or his slave-girl with a stick and the slave dies on the spot, he must be punished.

21   But he shall not be punished if the slave survives for one day or two, because he is worth money to his master.

22   When, in the course of a brawl, a man knocks against a pregnant woman so that she has a miscarriage but suffers no further hurt, then the offender must pay whatever fine the woman's husband demands after assessment.

23   Wherever hurt is done, you shall give life for life,

24   eye for eye, tooth for tooth, hand for hand, foot for foot,

25   burn for burn, bruise for bruise, wound for wound.

26   When a man strikes his slave or slave-girl in the eye and destroys it, he shall let the slave go free in compensation for the eye.

27   When he knocks out the tooth of a slave or a slave-girl, he shall let the slave go free in compensation for the tooth.

28   When an ox gores a man or a woman to death, the ox shall be stoned, and its flesh may not be eaten; the owner of the ox shall be free from liability.

29   If, however, the ox has for some time past been a vicious animal, and the owner has been duly warned but has not kept it under control, and the ox kills a man or a woman, the ox shall be stoned, and the owner shall be put to death as well.

30   If, however, the penalty is commuted for a money payment, he shall pay in redemption of his life whatever is imposed upon him.

31   If the ox gores a son or a daughter, the same rule shall apply.

32   If the ox gores a slave or a slave-girl, its owner shall pay thirty shekels of silver to their master, and the ox shall be stoned.

33   When a man removes the cover of a well or digs a well and leaves it uncovered, then if an ox or an ass falls into it, the owner of the well shall make good the loss.

34   He shall repay the owner of the beast in silver, and the dead beast shall be his.

35   When one man's ox butts another's and kills it, they shall sell the live ox, share the price and also share the dead beast.

36   But if it is known that the ox has for some time past been vicious and the owner has not kept it under control, he shall make good the loss, ox for ox, but the dead beast is his.

22

When a man steals an ox or a sheep and slaughters or sells it, he shall repay five beasts for the ox and four sheep for the sheep.

2   He shall pay in full; if he has no means, he shall be sold to pay for the theft.

3   But if the animal is found alive in his possession, be it ox, ass, or sheep, he shall repay two.

4   If a burglar is caught in the act and is fatally injured, it is not murder; but if he breaks in after sunrise and is fatally injured, then it is murder.

5   When a man burns off a field or a vineyard and lets the fire spread so that it burns another man's field, he shall make restitution

from his own field according to the yield expected; and if the whole field is laid waste, he shall make restitution from the best part of his own field.

6   When a fire starts and spreads to a heap of brushwood, so that sheaves, or standing corn, or a whole field is destroyed, he who started the fire shall make full restitution.

7   When one man gives another silver or chattels for safe keeping, and they are stolen from that man's house, the thief, if he is found, shall restore twofold.

8   But if the thief is not found, the owner of the house shall appear before God, to make a declaration that he has not touched his neighbour's property.

9   In every case of law-breaking an ox, an ass, or a sheep, a cloak, or any lost property which may be claimed, each party shall bring his case before God; he whom God declares to be in the wrong shall restore twofold to his neighbour.

10   When a man gives an ass, an ox, a sheep or any beast into his neighbour's keeping, and it dies or is injured or is carried off, there being no witness,

11   the neighbour shall swear by the Lord that he has not touched the man's property. The owner shall accept this, and no restitution shall be made.

12   If it has been stolen from him, he shall make restitution to the owner.

13   If it has been mauled by a wild beast, he shall bring it in as evidence; he shall not make restitution for what has been mauled.

14   When a man borrows a beast from his neighbour and it is injured or dies while its owner is not with it, the borrower shall make full restitution;

15   but if the owner is with it, the borrower shall not make restitution. If it was hired, only the hire shall be due.

16   When a man seduces a virgin who is not yet betrothed, he shall pay the bride price for her to be his wife.

17   If her father refuses to give her to him, the seducer shall pay in silver a sum equal to the bride-price for virgins.

18   You shall not allow a witch to live.

19   Whoever has unnatural connection with a beast shall be put to death.

20   Whoever sacrifices to any god but the Lord shall be put to death under solemn ban.

21   You shall not wrong an alien, or be hard upon him; you were yourselves aliens in Egypt.

22   You shall not ill-treat any widow or fatherless child.

23   If you do, be sure that I will listen if they appeal to me;

24   my anger will be roused and I will kill you with the sword; your own wives shall become widows and your children fatherless.

25   If you advance money to any poor man amongst my people, you shall not act like a money-lender: you must not exact interest in advance from him.

26   If you take your neighbour's cloak in pawn, you shall return it to him by sunset, because it is his only covering.

27   It is the cloak in which he wraps his body; in what else can he sleep? If he appeals to me, I will listen, for I am full of compassion.

28   You shall not revile God, nor curse a chief of your own people.

29   You shall not hold back the first of your harvest, whether corn or wine. You shall give me your first-born sons.

30   You shall do the same with your oxen and your sheep. They shall stay with the mother for seven days; on the eighth day you shall give them to me.

31   You shall be holy to me: you shall not eat the flesh of anything in the open country killed by beasts, but you shall throw it to the dogs.

23

You shall not spread a baseless rumour. You shall not make common cause with a wicked man by giving malicious evidence.

2   You shall not be led into wrongdoing by the majority, nor, when you give evidence in a lawsuit, shall you side with the majority to pervert justice;

3   nor shall you favour the poor man in his suit.

4   When you come upon your enemy's ox or ass straying, you shall take it back to him.

5   When you see the ass of someone who hates you lying helpless under its load, however unwilling you may be to help it, you must give him a hand with it.

6   You shall not deprive the poor man of justice in his suit.

7   Avoid all lies, and do not cause the death of the innocent and the guiltless; for I the Lord will never acquit the guilty.

8   You shall not accept a bribe, for bribery makes the discerning man blind and the just man give a crooked answer.

9   You shall not oppress the alien, for you know how it feels to be an alien; you were aliens yourselves in Egypt.

10   For six years you may sow your land and gather its produce;

11   but in the seventh year you shall let it lie fallow and leave it alone. It shall provide food for the poor or your people, and what

they leave the wild animals may eat. You shall do likewise with your vineyard and your olive-grove.

12 For six days you may do your work, but on the seventh day you shall abstain from work, so that your ox and your ass may rest, and your home-born slave and the alien may refresh themselves.

13 Be attentive to every word of mine. You shall not invoke other gods: your lips shall not speak their names.

14 Three times a year you shall keep a pilgrim-feast to me.

15 You shall celebrate the pilgrim-feast of Unleavened Bread for seven days; you shall eat unleavened cakes as I have commanded you, at the appointed time in the month of Abib, for in that month you came out of Egypt. No one shall come into my presence empty-handed.

16 You shall celebrate the pilgrim-feast of Harvest, with the first-fruits of your work in sowing the land, and the pilgrim-feast of Ingathering at the end of the year, when you bring in the fruits of all your work on the land.

17 These three times a year shall all your males come into the presence of the Lord God.

18 You shall not offer the blood of my sacrifice at the same time as anything leavened. The fat of my festal offering shall not remain overnight till morning.

19 You shall bring the choicest first-fruits of your soil to the house of the Lord your God. You shall not boil a kid in its mother's milk.

20 And now I send an angel before you to guard you on your way and to bring you to the place I have prepared.

21 Take heed of him and listen to his voice. Do not defy him; he will not pardon your rebelliousness, for my authority rests in him.

22 If you will only listen to his voice and do all I tell you, then I will be an enemy to your enemies, and I will harass those who harass you.

23 My angel will go before you and bring you to the Amorites, the Hittites, the Perizzites, the Canaanites, the Hivites, and the Jebusites, and I will make an end of them.

24 You are not to bow down to their gods, nor worship them, nor observe their rites, but you shall tear down all their images and smash their sacred pillars.

25 Worship the Lord your God, and he will bless your bread and your water. I will take away all sickness out of your midst.

26 None shall miscarry or be barren in your land. I will grant you a full span of life.

27   I will send my terror before you and throw into confusion all the peoples whom you find in your path. I will make all your enemies turn their backs.

28   I will spread panic before you to drive out in front of you the Hivites, the Canaanites and the Hittites.

29   I will not drive them out in all one year, or the land would become waste and the wild beasts too many for you.

30   I will drive them out little by little until your numbers have grown enough to take possession of the whole country.

31   I will establish your frontiers from the Red Sea to the sea of the Philistines, and from the wilderness to the River. I will give the inhabitants of the country into your power, and you shall drive them out before you.

32   You shall make no covenant with them and their gods.

33   They shall not stay in your land for fear they make you sin against me; for then you would worship their gods, and in this way you would be ensnared.

QUESTIONS FOR CRITICAL READING

1. How do the elders react to Moses' report that God has selected them to be "my kingdom of priests" (19:6)?
2. Why do you think God came to Hebrews in a "thick cloud" (19:9)?
3. Where do the people go when they accompany Moses to meet God?
4. Which of the Ten Commandments seems to you most unexpected?
5. What are the reasons for keeping the Sabbath day?
6. Which commandment is most difficult to understand?
7. God commands the Hebrews not to make a chiseled stone altar. Is there a difference between a command and a commandment?
8. What assumptions about slavery seem to be made in the commandments?

SUGGESTIONS FOR WRITING

1. At the end of Chapter 20, God says, "You shall not make gods of silver to be worshipped as well as me, nor shall you make yourselves gods of gold" (20:23). What do you think is the purpose of this commandment? Is it possible that its intent is to prevent people from worshiping material goods as if they were God? Write an essay that explores the temptation that people even today have of substituting their love of things for their love of God. How much of a threat to religion is the adoration of wealth and possessions today?

2. Review the commands in Chapter 21 regarding slavery. What ethical problems, if any, do you find in these verses? What is your own position regarding the details provided in Chapter 21? Write a short essay in which you clarify, within the scope of your own beliefs, exactly what seems to be at stake in these verses.

3. If our modern justice system were to follow the instructions and commands in Exodus concerning rendering "hand for hand, foot for foot, burn for burn" (21:23–25), how would our courts and our penitentiaries function? What would our justice system look like? Is it possible that by not following these commands our justice system is antireligious or goes against the recorded word of God?

4. The Ten Commandments, as outlined in Chapter 20, may be grouped into those that guide people's attitudes toward God, their concern for themselves, and their concern for their neighbors. Take each commandment separately and explain how it relates to any or all of the other commandments. Do you view the Ten Commandments as a unified, inseparable whole or as individual, equally important units? Explain.

5. Read the first chapters of Exodus. Do you think God felt that Moses was the right man to choose to be his intermediary to the Hebrews? What were the qualities that Moses displayed earlier? What do you feel are his virtues and his limitations? Do you feel he was the right person? At one point, God commands Moses' brother Aaron to ascend the mountain as well, but we hear nothing of him later. What do we know about Aaron's capabilities to intervene with God?

6. The sixth commandment is "You shall not commit murder" (20:13). This is different from other translations that read: "Thou shalt not kill." Explain the difference and, in the light of all the other commandments and edicts laid down in this selection, decide which version is the preferred version. Which one is more in keeping with the God's advice and expectations? Why?

7. Which commandments specifically refer to women? Are any of the commandments explicitly aimed at women rather than men? What seems to be the culture's attitude toward women in light of the way the commandments consider them? Does Moses seem to be a feminist? How concerned is he for women's well-being? Explain.

8. **CONNECTIONS** Compare the Ten Commandments with the interpretation of moral behavior that Jesus, as recorded by St. Matthew, sets down in the Sermon on the Mount. Why do you think Jesus decides to give his sermon on a mountain? Does Jesus imply that Moses also heard a sermon on a mountain? Explain.

9. **SEEING CONNECTIONS** In Exodus 32, the Hebrews, fearing Moses will not return from Mount Sinai, ask Moses' brother Aaron to fashion an idol—a golden calf—to lead them into Israel. The following engraving, *Moses Breaking the Tablets of Law* by Gustave Doré (1832–1883), depicts Moses' return with the Ten Commandments and his and God's reaction to the Hebrews' violation of the commandment not to worship graven images.

What does Doré's engraving show you about the physical and emotional circumstances of Moses? Of his people? In Exodus 20:5 God declares, "I, the Lord your God, am a jealous god. I punish the children for the sins of the fathers to the third and fourth generations of those who hate me." What details does Doré use in this image to depict the nature of God as revealed in Exodus?

ARISTOTLE
The Aim of Man

ARISTOTLE (384–322 B.C.) is the great inheritor of Plato's influence in philosophical thought. He was a student at the Academy of Plato in Athens from age seventeen to thirty-seven, and by all accounts he was Plato's most brilliant pupil. He did not agree with Plato on all issues, however, and seems to have broken with his master around the time of Plato's death (347 B.C.). In certain of his writings he is careful to disagree with the Platonists while insisting on his friendship with them. In the *Nichomachean Ethics*, for example, the most difficult section (omitted here) demonstrates that Plato is not correct in assuming that the good exists in some ideal form in a higher spiritual realm.

One interesting point concerning Aristotle's career is that when he became a teacher, his most distinguished student was Alexander the Great, the youthful ruler who spread Greek values and laws throughout the rest of the known world. Much speculation has centered on just what Aristotle might have taught Alexander about politics. The emphasis on statecraft and political goals in the *Nichomachean Ethics* suggests that it may have been a great deal. A surviving fragment of a letter from Aristotle to Alexander suggests that he advised Alexander to become the leader of the Greeks and the master of the barbarians.

The *Nichomachean Ethics* is a difficult document. Aristotle may have written it with an eye to tutoring his son, Nichomachus, but it is also meant to be read by those who have thought deeply about human ethical behavior. "The Aim of Man" treats most of the basic issues raised in the entire document. It is difficult primarily because it is so thoroughly abstract. Abstract reason was thought to be the highest form of reason, because it is independent

From the *Nichomachean Ethics*. Translated by Martin Ostwald.

of sensory experience and because only human beings can indulge in it. Aristotle, whose studies included works on plants, physics, animals, law, rhetoric, and logic, to name only some subjects, reminds us often of what we have in common with the animal and vegetable worlds. But because he values abstract thought so much, his reasoning demands unusual attention from contemporary readers.

Moreover, because he wrote so much on scientific subjects— and, unlike Plato, emphasized the role of sensory perception in scientific matters—he is careful to warn that reasoning about humankind cannot entail the precision taken for granted in science. That warning is repeated several times in this selection. The study of humankind requires awareness of people's differences of background, education, habit, temperament, and other, similar factors. Such differences will impede the kinds of precision of definition and analysis taken for granted in other sciences.

Aristotle reveals an interesting Greek prejudice when he admits that the highest good for humankind is likely to be found in statecraft. He tells us that the well-ordered state—the pride of the Greek way of life—is of such noble value that other values must take second place to it. Because current thought somewhat agrees with this view, Aristotle sounds peculiarly modern in this passage. Unlike the Christian theorists of the Middle Ages, the theorists of the Islamic insurgence, or the theorists of the Judaic Scriptures, Aristotle does not put divinity or godliness first. He is a practical man whose concerns are with the life that human beings know here on earth. When he considers the question, for instance, of whether a man can be thought of as happy before he has died (tragedy can always befall the happy man), he is thoroughly practical and does not point to happiness in heaven as any substitute for happiness on earth.

Aristotle's Rhetoric

Even though Aristotle is the author of the single most influential treatise on rhetoric, this document does not have as eloquent a style as might be expected, which has suggested to some that the manuscript was taken from the lecture notes of a student. But, of course, he does use certain minor techniques that demonstrate his awareness of rhetorical effect. He makes careful use of aphorisms— for example, "One swallow does not make a spring" and "Perfect justice is noblest, health is best, / But to gain one's heart's desire is pleasantest" (para. 21).

In terms of style, Aristotle is at a disadvantage — or perhaps the modern world is — because he addresses an audience of those who have thought very deeply on the issues of human behavior, so that his style is elevated and complex. Fortunately, nothing he says here is beyond the grasp of the careful reader, although modern readers expect to be provided with a good many concrete examples to help them understand abstract principles. Aristotle purposely avoids using examples so as not to limit too sharply the truths he has to impart.

Aristotle's most prominent rhetorical technique is definition. His overall goal in this work is to define the aim of man. Thus, the first section of this work is entitled "Definition of the Good." In "Primacy of Statecraft" he begins to qualify various types of good. Later, he considers the relationship between good and happiness (paras. 8–9) and the various views concerning happiness and its definition (paras. 10–11). By then the reader is prepared for a "Functional Definition of Man's Highest Good" (paras. 12–18). He confirms his conclusions in the section entitled "Confirmation by Popular Beliefs" (paras. 19–22). After isolating happiness as the ultimate good, he devotes paragraphs 23–32 to its causes, its effects, and the events that will affect it, such as luck and human decision. The final section (paras. 33–39) constitutes an examination of the soul (the most human element) and its relationship to virtue; he begins that section by repeating, for the third time, his definition of happiness: "[H]appiness is a certain activity of the soul in accordance with perfect virtue."

It could be said that, rhetorically speaking, the body of the work is an exploration and definition of the highest good.

PREREADING QUESTIONS: WHAT TO READ FOR

The following prereading questions may help you anticipate key issues in the discussion of Aristotle's "The Aim of Man." Keeping them in mind during your first reading of the selection should help focus your attention.

- How does Aristotle define the good?
- What is the relationship of the good to human happiness?
- What are the two kinds of human happiness Aristotle discusses?

The Aim of Man

Definition of the Good

Every art and every "scientific investigation," as well as every ac-   1
tion and "purposive choice," appears to aim at some good; hence the
good has rightly been declared to be that at which all things aim. A
difference is observable, to be sure, among the several ends: some of
them are activities, while others are products over and above the activities that produce them. Wherever there are certain ends over and
above the actions themselves, it is the nature of such products to be
better than the activities.

As actions and arts and sciences are of many kinds, there must   2
be a corresponding diversity of ends: health, for example, is the aim
of medicine, ships of shipbuilding, victory of military strategy, and
wealth of domestic economics. Where several such arts fall under some
one faculty—as bridle-making and the other arts concerned with
horses' equipment fall under horsemanship, while this in turn along
with all other military matters falls under the head of strategy, and
similarly in the case of other arts—the aim of the master art is always
more choiceworthy than the aims of its subordinate arts, inasmuch
as these are pursued for its sake. And this holds equally good whether
the end in view is just the activity itself or something distinct from
the activity, as in the case of the sciences above mentioned.

Primacy of Statecraft

If in all our conduct, then, there is some end that we wish on its   3
own account, choosing everything else as a means to it; if, that is to
say, we do not choose everything as a means to something else (for
at that rate we should go on *ad infinitum*[1] and our desire would be
left empty and vain); then clearly this one end must be the good—
even, indeed, the highest good. Will not a knowledge of it, then,
have an important influence on our lives? Will it not better enable us
to hit the right mark, like archers who have a definite target to aim
at? If so, we must try to comprehend, in outline at least, what that
highest end is, and to which of the sciences or arts it belongs.

Evidently the art or science in question must be the most ab-   4
solute and most authoritative of all. Statecraft answers best to this
description; for it prescribes which of the sciences are to have a

---

[1] *ad infinitum* Endlessly; to infinity.

place in the state, and which of them are to be studied by the different classes of citizens, and up to what point; and we find that even
the most highly esteemed of the arts are subordinated to it, e.g.,
military strategy, domestic economics, and oratory. So then, since statecraft employs all the other sciences, prescribing also what the citizens are to do and what they are to refrain from doing, its aim must
embrace the aims of all the others; whence it follows that the aim of
statecraft is man's proper good. Even supposing the chief good to be
eventually the same for the individual as for the state, that of the
state is evidently of greater and more fundamental importance both
to attain and to preserve. The securing of even one individual's good
is cause for rejoicing, but to secure the good of a nation or of a city-
state[2] is nobler and more divine. This, then, is the aim of our present
inquiry, which is in a sense the study of statecraft.

Two Observations on the Study of Ethics

Our discussion will be adequate if we are content with as much   5
precision as is appropriate to the subject matter; for the same degree
of exactitude ought no more to be expected in all kinds of reasoning
than in all kinds of handicraft. Excellence and justice, the things with
which statecraft deals, involve so much disagreement and uncertainty
that they come to be looked on as mere conventions, having no natural foundation. The good involves a similar uncertainty, inasmuch
as good things often prove detrimental: there are examples of people
destroyed by wealth, of others destroyed by courage. In such matters,
then, and starting from such premises as we do, we must be content
with a rough approximation to the truth; for when we are dealing
with and starting out from what holds good only "as a general rule,"
the conclusions that we reach will have the same character. Let each
of the views put forward be accepted in this spirit, for it is the mark
of an educated mind to seek only so much exactness in each type of
inquiry as may be allowed by the nature of the subject matter. It is
equally wrong to accept probable reasoning from a mathematician
and to demand strict demonstrations from an orator.

A man judges well and is called a good judge of the things about   6
which he knows. If he has been educated in a particular subject he is a
good judge of that subject; if his education has been well-rounded he

---

[2] **city-state** Athens was an independent nation, a city-state (*polis*). Greece consisted of a great many independent states, which often leagued together in confed-
erations.

is a good judge in general. Hence no very young man is qualified to attend lectures on statecraft; for he is inexperienced in the affairs of life, and these form the data and subject matter of statecraft. Moreover, so long as he tends to be swayed by his feelings he will listen vainly and without profit, for the purport of these [lectures] is not purely theoretical but practical. Nor does it make any difference whether his immaturity is a matter of years or of character: the defect is not a matter of time, but consists in the fact that his life and all his pursuits are under the control of his passions. Men of this sort, as is evident from the case of those we call incontinent,[3] do not turn their knowledge to any account in practice; but those whose desires and actions are controlled by reason will derive much profit from a knowledge of these matters.

So much, then, for our prefatory remarks about the student, the 7
manner of inquiry, and the aim.

The Good as Happiness

To resume, then: since all knowledge and all purpose aims at 8
some good, what is it that we declare to be the aim of statecraft; or, in other words, what is the highest of all realizable goods? As to its name there is pretty general agreement: the majority of men, as well as the cultured few, speak of it as happiness; and they would maintain that to live well and to do well are the same thing as to be happy. They differ, however, as to what happiness is, and the mass of mankind give a different account of it from philosophers. The former take it to be something palpable and obvious, like pleasure or wealth or fame; they differ, too, among themselves, nor is the same man always of one mind about it: when ill he identifies it with health, when poor with wealth; then growing aware of his ignorance about the whole matter he feels admiration for anyone who proclaims some grand ideal above his comprehension. And to add to the confusion, there have been some philosophers who held that besides the various particular good things there is an absolute good which is the cause of all particular goods. As it would hardly be worthwhile to examine all the opinions that have been entertained, we shall confine our attention to those that are most popular or that appear to have some rational foundation.

One point not to be overlooked is the difference between argu- 9
ments that start from first principles[4] and arguments that lead up to

---

[3]**incontinent** Uncontrolled, in this case by reason.
[4]**first principles** Concepts such as goodness, truth, and justice. Arguments that lead to first principles usually begin with familiar, less abstract evidence.

first principles. Plato very wisely used to raise this question, and to ask whether the right way is from or toward first principles—as in the racecourse there is a difference between running from the judges to the boundary line and running back again. Granted that we must start with what is known, this may be interpreted in a double sense: as what is familiar to us or as what is intelligible in itself. Our own method, at any rate, must be to start with what is familiar to us. That is why a sound moral training is required before a man can listen intelligently to discussions about excellence and justice, and generally speaking, about statecraft. For in this field we must take as our "first principles" plain facts; if these are sufficiently evident we shall not insist upon the whys and wherefores. Such principles are in the possession of, or at any rate readily accessible to, the man with a sound moral training. As for the man who neither possesses nor can acquire them, let him hear the words of Hesiod:[5]

> Best is he who makes his own discoveries;
> Good is he who listens to the wise;
> But he who, knowing not, rejects another's wisdom
>   Is a plain fool.

Conflicting Views of Happiness

Let us now resume our discussion from the point at which we digressed. What is happiness, or the chief good? If it is permissible to judge from men's actual lives, we may say that the mass of them, being vulgarians, identify it with pleasure, which is the reason why they aim at nothing higher than a life of enjoyment. For there are three outstanding types of life: the one just mentioned, the political, and, thirdly, the contemplative. "The mass of men" reveal their utter slavishness by preferring a life fit only for cattle; yet their views have a certain plausibility from the fact that many of those in high places share the tastes of Sardanapalus.[6] Men of superior refinement and active disposition, on the other hand, identify happiness

10

---

[5]*Works and Days*, II. 293–297. [Translator's note] **Hesiod (eighth century B.C.)** was a well-known Greek author. His *Works and Days* is notable for its portraits of everyday shepherd life and for its moralizing fables. His *Theogony* is a description of the creation, widely taken as accurate in his day.

[6]An ancient Assyrian king to whom is attributed the saying, "Eat, drink, and be merry: nothing else is worth a snap of the fingers." [Translator's note] **Sardanapalus (d. 880 B.C.)** was noted for his slothful and decadent life. When it was certain that he was to die—the walls of his city had been breached by an opposing army—he had his wives, animals, and possessions burned with him in his palace.

with honor, this being more or less the aim of a statesman's life. It is evidently too superficial, however, to be the good that we are seeking; for it appears to depend rather on him who bestows than on him who receives it, while we may suspect the chief good to be something peculiarly a man's own, which he is not easily deprived of. Besides, men seem to pursue honor primarily in order to assure themselves of their own merit; at any rate, apart from personal acquaintances, it is by those of sound judgment that they seek to be appreciated, and on the score of virtue. Clearly, then, they imply that virtue is superior to honor: and so, perhaps, we should regard this rather than honor as the end and aim of the statesman's life. Yet even about virtue there is a certain incompleteness; for it is supposed that a man may possess it while asleep or during lifelong inactivity, or even while suffering the greatest disasters and misfortunes; and surely no one would call such a man happy, unless for the sake of a paradox. But we need not further pursue this subject, which has been sufficiently treated of in current discussions. Thirdly, there is the contemplative life, which we shall examine at a later point.

As for the life of money-making, it is something unnatural. 11 Wealth is clearly not the good that we are seeking, for it is merely useful as a means to something else. Even the objects above mentioned come closer to possessing intrinsic goodness than wealth does, for they at least are cherished on their own account. But not even they, it seems, can be the chief good, although much labor has been lost in attempting to prove them so. With this observation we may close the present subject.

Functional Definition of Man's Highest Good

Returning now to the good that we are seeking, let us inquire 12 into its nature. Evidently it is different in different actions and arts: it is not the same thing in medicine as in strategy, and so on. What definition of good will apply to all the arts? Let us say it is that for the sake of which all else is done. In medicine this is health, in the art of war victory, in building it is a house, and in each of the arts something different, although in every case, wherever there is action and choice involved, it is a certain end; because it is always for the sake of a certain end that all else is done. If, then, there is one end and aim of all our actions, this will be the realizable good; if there are several such ends, these jointly will be our realizable goods. Thus in a roundabout way the discussion has been brought back to the same point as before; which we must now try to explain more clearly.

As there is evidently a plurality of ends, and as some of these are   13
chosen only as means to ulterior ends (e.g., wealth, flutes, and instruments in general), it is clear that not all ends are final.[7] But the
supreme good must of course be something final. Accordingly, if
there is only one final end, this will be the good that we are seeking;
and if there is more than one such end, the most complete and final
of them will be this good. Now we call what is pursued as an end in
itself more final than what is pursued as a means to something else;
and what is never chosen as a means we call more final than what is
chosen both as an end in itself and as a means; in fact, when a thing
is chosen always as an end in itself and never as a means we call it
absolutely final. Happiness seems, more than anything else, to answer to this description: for it is something we choose always for its
own sake and never for the sake of something else; while honor,
pleasure, reason, and all the virtues, though chosen partly for themselves (for we might choose any one of them without heeding the
result), are chosen also for the sake of the happiness which we suppose they will bring us. Happiness, on the other hand, is never chosen for the sake of any of these, nor indeed as a means to anything
else at all.

We seem to arrive at the same conclusion if we start from the   14
notion of self-sufficiency; for the final good is admittedly self-sufficient.
To be self-sufficient we do not mean that an individual must live in
isolation. Parents, children, wife, as well as friends and fellow citizens
generally, are all permissible; for man is by nature political. To be
sure, some limit has to be set to such relationships, for if they are extended to embrace ancestors, descendants, and friends of friends, we
should go on *ad infinitum*. But this point will be considered later on;
provisionally we may attribute self-sufficiency to that which taken
by itself makes life choiceworthy and lacking in nothing. Such a thing
we conceive happiness to be. Moreover, we regard happiness as the
most choiceworthy of all things; nor does this mean that it is merely
one good thing among others, for if that were the case it is plain that
the addition of even the least of those other goods would increase its
desirability; since the addition would create a larger amount of good,
and of two goods the greater is always to be preferred. Evidently,
then, happiness is something final and self-sufficient, and is the end
and aim of all that we do.

---

[7]**not all ends are final** By *ends* Aristotle means purposes. Some purposes are
final—the most important; some are immediate—the less important. When a corporation contributes funds to Public Broadcasting, for example, its immediate purpose may be to fund a worthwhile program. Its final purpose may be to benefit from
the publicity gained from advertising.

But perhaps it will be objected that to call happiness the supreme   15
good is a mere truism, and that a clearer account of it is still needed.
We can give this best, probably, if we ascertain the proper function
of man. Just as the excellence and good performance of a flute player,
a sculptor, or any kind of artist, and generally speaking of anyone
who has a function or business to perform, lies always in that function, so man's good would seem to lie in the function of man, if he has
one. But can we suppose that while a carpenter and a cobbler each has
a function and mode of activity of his own, man qua man[8] has none,
but has been left by nature functionless? Surely it is more likely that
as his several members, eye and hand and foot, can be shown to have
each its own function, so man too must have a function over and
above the special functions of his various members. What will such
a function be? Not merely to live, of course: he shares that even with
plants, whereas we are seeking something peculiar to himself. We
must exclude, therefore, the life of nutrition and growth. Next comes
sentient[9] life, but this again is had in common with the horse, the
ox, and in fact all animals whatever. There remains only the "practical"[10] life of his rational nature; and this has two aspects, one of
which is rational in the sense that it obeys a "rational principle," the
other in the sense that it possesses and exercises reason. To avoid
ambiguity let us specify that by "rational" we mean the "exercise or
activity," not the mere possession, of reason; for it is the former that
would seem more properly entitled to the name. Thus we conclude
that man's function is an activity of the soul in conformity with, or
at any rate involving the use of, "rational principle."

An individual and a superior individual who belong to the same   16
class we regard as sharing the same function: a harpist and a good
harpist, for instance, are essentially the same. This holds true of any
class of individuals whatever; for superior excellence with respect to
a function is nothing but an amplification of that selfsame function:
e.g., the function of a harpist is to play the harp, while that of a good
harpist is to play it well. This being so, if we take man's proper function to be a certain kind of life, viz. an activity and conduct of the soul
that involves reason, and if it is the part of a good man to perform such
activities well and nobly, and if a function is well performed when it
is performed in accordance with its own proper excellence; we may
conclude that the good of man is an activity of the soul in accordance
with virtue, or, if there be more than one virtue, in accordance with

---

[8]**man qua man** Man as such, without reference to what he may be or do.
[9]**sentient** Knowing, aware, conscious.
[10]**"practical"** Aristotle refers to the actual practices that will define the ethical
nature of the individual.

the best and most perfect of them. And we must add, in a complete life. For one swallow does not make a spring, nor does one fine day; and similarly one day or brief period of happiness does not make a man happy and blessed.

So much, then, for a rough outline of the good: the proper 17 procedure being, we may suppose, to sketch an outline first and afterwards to fill in the details. When a good outline has been made, almost anyone presumably can expand it and fill it out; and time is a good inventor and collaborator in this work. It is in just such a way that progress has been made in the various "human techniques,"[11] for filling in the gaps is something anybody can do.

But in all this we must bear constantly in mind our previous 18 warning: not to expect the same degree of precision in all fields, but only so much as belongs to a given subject matter and is appropriate to a particular "type of inquiry." Both the carpenter and the geometer investigate the right angle, but in different ways: the one wants only such an approximation to it as will serve his work; the other, being concerned with truth, seeks to determine its essence or essential attributes. And so in other subjects we must follow a like procedure, lest we be so much taken up with side issues that we pass over the matter in hand. Similarly we ought not in all cases to demand the "reason why"; sometimes it is enough to point out the bare fact. This is true, for instance, in the case of "first principles"; for a bare fact must always be the ultimate starting point of any inquiry. First principles may be arrived at in a variety of ways: some by induction,[12] some by direct perception, some by a kind of habituation, and others in other ways. In each case we should try to apprehend them in whatever way is proper to them, and we should take care to define them clearly, because they will have a considerable influence upon the subsequent course of our inquiry. A good beginning is more than half of the whole inquiry, and once established clears up many of its difficulties.

Confirmation by Popular Beliefs

It is important to consider our ethical "first principle" not 19 merely as a conclusion drawn from certain premises, but also in its relation to popular opinion; for all data harmonize with a true principle, but with a false one they are soon found to be discordant.

---

[11]**"human techniques"** Arts or skills; in a sense, technology.

[12]**induction** A process of reasoning based on careful observation and collection of details upon which theories are based. "A kind of habituation" may refer to a combination of intellectual approaches characteristic of an individual.

Now it has been customary to divide good things into three classes: external goods on the one hand, and on the other goods of the soul and goods of the body; and those of the soul we call good in the highest sense, and in the fullest degree. "Conscious actions," i.e., "active expressions of our nature," we take, of course, as belonging to the soul; and thus our account is confirmed by the doctrine referred to, which is of long standing and has been generally accepted by students of philosophy. . . .

We are in agreement also with those who identify happiness   20
with virtue or with some particular virtue; for our phrase "activity in accordance with virtue" is the same as what they call virtue. It makes quite a difference, however, whether we conceive the supreme good as the mere possession of virtue or as its employment—i.e., as a state of character or as its active expression in conduct. For a state of character may be present without yielding any good result, as in a man who is asleep or in some other way inactive; but this is not true of its active expression, which must show itself in action, indeed in good action. As at the Olympic games it is not merely the fairest and strongest that receive the victory wreath, but those who compete (since the victors will of course be found among the competitors), so in life too those who carry off the finest prizes are those who manifest their excellence in their deeds.

Moreover, the life of those active in virtue is intrinsically pleas-   21
ant. For besides the fact that pleasure is something belonging to the soul, each man takes pleasure in what he is said to love—the horse lover in horses, the lover of sights in public spectacles, and similarly the lover of justice in just acts, and more generally, the lover of virtue in virtuous acts. And while most men take pleasure in things which, as they are not truly pleasant by nature, create warring factions in the soul, the lovers of what is noble take pleasure in things that are truly pleasant in themselves. Virtuous actions are things of this kind; hence they are pleasant for such men, as well as pleasant intrinsically. The life of such men, therefore, requires no adventitious[13] pleasures, but finds its own pleasure within itself. This is further shown by the fact that a man who does not enjoy doing noble actions is not a good man at all: surely no one would call a man just who did not enjoy performing just actions, nor generous who did not enjoy performing generous actions, and so on. On this ground too, then, actions in conformity with virtue must be intrinsically pleasant. And certainly they are good as well as noble, and both in the highest degree, if the judgment of the good man is any criterion; for he will judge them as

---

[13]**adventitious** Unnecessary; superfluous.

we have said. It follows, therefore, that happiness is at once the best and noblest and pleasantest of things, and that these attributes are not separable as the inscription at Delos[14] pretends:

> Perfect justice is noblest, health is best,
> But to gain one's heart's desire is pleasantest.

For our best activities possess all of these attributes; and it is in our best activities, or in the best one of them, that we say happiness consists.

22 Nevertheless, happiness plainly requires external goods as well; for it is impossible, or at least not easy, to act nobly without the proper equipment. There are many actions that can only be performed through such instruments as friends, wealth, or political influence; and there are some things, again, the lack of which must mar felicity, such as good birth, fine children, and personal comeliness: for the man who is repulsive in appearance, or ill-born, or solitary and childless does not meet the requirements of a happy man, and still less does one who has worthless children and friends, or who has lost good ones by death. As we have said, then, happiness seems to require the addition of external prosperity, and this has led some to identify it with "good fortune," just as others have made the opposite mistake of identifying it with virtue.

Sources of Happiness

23 For the same reason there are many who wonder whether happiness is attained by learning, or by habituation or some other kind of training, or whether it comes by some divine dispensation,[15] or even by chance. Well, certainly if the gods do give any gifts to men we may reasonably suppose that happiness is god-given, indeed, of all human blessings it is the most likely to be so, inasmuch as it is the best of them all. While this question no doubt belongs more properly to another branch of inquiry, we remark here that even if happiness is not god-sent but comes as a result of virtue or some kind of learning or training, still it is evidently one of the most divine things in the world, because that which is the reward as well as the end and aim of virtuous conduct must evidently be of supreme excellence, something divine and most blessed. If this is the case, happiness must further be something that can be generally shared; for with the exception of

---

[14]**inscription at Delos** Delos is the island that once held the Athenian treasury. It was the birthplace of Apollo, with whom the inscription would be associated.
[15]**divine dispensation** A gift of the gods.

those whose capacity for virtue has been stunted or maimed, everyone will have the ability, by study and diligence, to acquire it. And if it is better that happiness should be acquired in this way than by chance, we may reasonably suppose that it happens so; because everything in nature is arranged in the best way possible—just as in the case of man-made products, and of every kind of causation, especially the highest. It would be altogether wrong that what is greatest and noblest in the world should be left to the dispensation of chance.

Our present difficulty is cleared up by our previous definition of   24
happiness, as a certain activity of the soul in accordance with virtue; whereas all other sorts of good are either necessary conditions of, or cooperative with and naturally useful instruments of this. Such a conclusion, moreover, agrees with the proposition we laid down at the outset: that the end of statecraft is the best of all ends, and that the principal concern of statecraft is to make the citizens of a certain character—namely, good and disposed to perform noble actions.

Naturally, therefore, we do not call an ox or a horse or any other   25
brute happy, since none of them is able to participate in conduct of this kind. For the same reason a child is not happy, since at his age he too is incapable of such conduct. Or if we do call a child happy, it is in the sense of predicting for him a happy future. Happiness, as we have said, involves not only a completeness of virtue but also a complete lifetime for its fulfillment. Life brings many vicissitudes and chance happenings, and it may be that one who is now prosperous will suffer great misfortunes in his old age, as is told of Priam[16] in the Trojan legends; and a man who is thus buffeted by fortune and comes to a miserable end can scarcely be called happy.

Happiness and the Vicissitudes of Fortune

Are we, then, to call no one happy while he lives? Must we, as   26
Solon[17] advises, wait to see his end? And if we accept this verdict, are we to interpret it as meaning that a man actually becomes happy only after he is dead? Would not this be downright absurd, especially for us who define happiness as a kind of vital activity? Or if we reject this interpretation, and suppose Solon to mean rather that it is only after death, when beyond the reach of further evil and calamity that a man can safely be said to have been happy during his life, there is still a

---

[16]**Priam** King of Troy in Homer's *Iliad*. He suffered a terrible reversal of fortune when Troy was defeated by the Greeks.

[17]**Solon (638–558 B.C.)** Greek lawgiver and one of Greece's earliest poets. He was one of the Seven Sages of Athens.

possible objection that may be offered. For many hold that both good and evil may in a certain sense befall a dead man (just as they may befall a living man even when he is unconscious of them)—e.g., honors and disgraces, and the prosperity or misfortune of his children and the rest of his descendants. And this presents a further problem: suppose a man to have lived to a happy old age, and to have ended as he lived, there are still plenty of reverses that may befall his descendants—some of them will perhaps lead a good life and be dealt with by fortune as they deserve, others not. (It is clear, too, that a man's relationship to his descendants admits of various degrees.) It would be odd, then, if the dead man were to change along with the fortunes of his descendants, becoming happy and miserable by turns; although, to be sure, it would be equally odd if the fortunes of his descendants did not affect him at all, even for a brief time.

But let us go back to our earlier question,[18] which may perhaps 27 clear up the one we are raising at present. Suppose we agree that we must look to the end of a man's life, and only then call him happy, not because he then *is* happy but because we can only then know him to have been so: is it not paradoxical to have refused to call him happy during just the period when happiness was present to him? On the other hand, we are naturally loath to apply the term to living men, considering the vicissitudes to which they are liable. Happiness, we argue, must be something that endures without any essential change, whereas a living individual may experience many turns of fortune's wheel. Obviously if we judge by his changing fortunes we shall have to call the same man now happy now wretched, thereby regarding the happy man as a kind of chameleon and his happiness as built on no secure foundation; yet it surely cannot be right to regard a man's happiness as wholly dependent on his fortunes. True good and evil are not of this character; rather, as we have said, although good fortune is a necessary adjunct to a complete human life, it is virtuous activities that constitute happiness, and the opposite sort of activities that constitute its opposite.

The foregoing difficulty [that happiness can be judged of only 28 in retrospect] confirms, as a matter of fact, our theory. For none of man's functions is so permanent as his virtuous activities—indeed, many believe them to be more abiding even than a knowledge of the sciences; and of his virtuous activities those are the most abiding which are of highest worth, for it is with them that anyone blessed with supreme happiness is most fully and most continuously occupied, and hence never oblivious of. The happy man, then, will possess

---

[18] I.e., whether we are to call no one happy while he still lives. [Translator's note]

this attribute of permanence or stability about which we have been inquiring, and will keep it all his life; because at all times and in preference to everything else he will be engaged in virtuous action and contemplation, and he will bear the changes of fortune as nobly and in every respect as decorously as possible, inasmuch as he is truly good and "four-square beyond reproach."[19]

But the dispensations of fortune are many, some great, others small. Small ones do not appreciably turn the scales of life, but a multitude of great ones, if they are of the nature of blessings, will make life happier; for they add to life a grace of their own, provided that a man makes noble and good use of them. If, however, they are of an evil kind, they will crush and maim happiness, in that they bring pain and thereby hinder many of our natural activities. Yet true nobility shines out even here, if a multitude of great misfortunes be borne with calmness—not, to be sure, with the calmness of insensibility, but of nobility and greatness of soul.   29

If, as we have declared, it is our activities that give life its character, then no happy man can become miserable, inasmuch as he will never do what is hateful or base. For we hold that the truly good and wise man will bear with dignity whatever fortune sends, and will always make the best of his circumstances, as a good general makes the most effective use of the forces at his command, and a good shoemaker makes the best shoes out of the leather that is available, and so in the case of the other crafts. On this interpretation, the happy man can never become miserable—although of course he will not be blessed with happiness in the full sense of the word if he meets with such a fate as Priam's. At all events, he is not variable and always changing; for no ordinary misfortunes but only a multitude of great ones will dislodge him from his happy state, and should this occur he will not readily recover his happiness in a short time, but only, if at all, after a long period has run its course, during which he has achieved distinctions of a high order.   30

Is there any objection, then, to our defining a happy man as one whose activities are an expression of complete virtue, and who at the same time enjoys a sufficiency of worldly goods, not just for some limited period, but for his entire lifetime? Or perhaps we had better add the proviso that he shall be destined to go on living in this manner, and die as he has lived; for, whereas the future is obscure to us, we conceive happiness to be an end, something altogether   31

---

[19] A quotation from Simonides. [Translator's note] **Simonides (556?–469 B.C.)** was a Greek lyric poet who lived and wrote for a while in Athens. His works survive in a handful of fragments; this quotation is from fragment 5.

and in every respect final and complete. Granting all this, we may declare those living men to be "blessed with supreme happiness" in whom these conditions have been and are continuing to be fulfilled. Their blessedness, however, is of human order.

So much for our discussion of this question. 32

Derivation of the Two Kinds of Human Excellence

Since happiness is a certain activity of the soul in accordance with 33 perfect virtue, we must next examine the nature of virtue. Not only will such an inquiry perhaps clarify the problem of happiness; it will also be of vital concern to the true student of statecraft, whose aim is to make his fellow citizens good and law-abiding. The Cretan and Spartan lawgivers,[20] as well as such others as may have resembled them, exemplify this aim. And clearly, if such an inquiry has to do with statecraft, it will be in keeping with our original purpose to pursue it.

It goes without saying that the virtue we are to study is human 34 virtue, just as the good that we have been inquiring about is a human good, and the happiness a human happiness. By human virtue we mean virtue not of the body but of the soul, and by happiness too we mean an activity of the soul. This being the case, it is no less evident that the student of statecraft must have some knowledge of the soul, than that a physician who is to heal the eye or the whole body must have some knowledge of these organs; more so, indeed, in proportion as statecraft is superior to and more honorable than medicine. Now all physicians who are educated take much pains to know about the body. Hence as students of statecraft, too, we must inquire into the nature of the soul; but we must do so with reference to our own distinctive aim and only to the extent that it requires, for to go into minuter detail would be more laborious than is warranted by our subject matter.

We may adopt here certain doctrines about the soul that have 35 been adequately stated in our public discourses:[21] as that the soul may be distinguished into two parts, one of which is irrational while the other possesses reason. Whether these two parts are actually distinct like the parts of the body or any other divisible thing, or are distinct only in a logical sense, like convex and concave in the circumference of a circle, is immaterial to our present inquiry.

---

[20] **Cretan and Spartan lawgivers** Both Crete and Sparta were noted for their constitutions, based on the laws of Gortyn in Crete. These laws were aristocratic, not democratic as in Athens; they promoted a class system and a rigid code of personal behavior.

[21] **our public discourses** Aristotle may be referring to speeches at which the public is welcome, as opposed to his lectures to students.

Of the irrational part, again, one division is apparently of a veg-   36
etative nature and common to all living things: I mean that which is
the cause of nutrition and growth. It is more reasonable to postulate
a vital faculty of this sort, present in all things that take nourishment, even when in an embryo stage, and retained by the full-grown
organism, than to assume a special nutritive faculty in the latter.
Hence we may say that the excellence belonging to this part of the
soul is common to all species, and not specifically human: a point
that is further confirmed by the popular view that this part of the
soul is most active during sleep. For it is during sleep that the distinction between good men and bad is least apparent; whence the
saying that for half their lives the happy are no better off than the
wretched. This, indeed, is natural enough, for sleep is an inactivity
of the soul in those respects in which the soul is called good or bad.
(It is true, however, that to a slight degree certain bodily movements
penetrate to the soul; which is the reason why good men's dreams
are superior to those of the average person.) But enough of this subject: let us dismiss the nutritive principle, since it has by nature no
share in human excellence.

There seems to be a second part of the soul, which though ir-   37
rational yet in some way partakes of reason. For while we praise
the rational principle and the part of the soul that manifests it
in the case of the continent and incontinent man alike, on the
ground that it exhorts them rightly and urges them to do what is
best; yet we find within these men another element different in
nature from the rational element, and struggling against and resisting it. Just as ataxic limbs,[22] when we choose to move them to
the right, turn on the contrary to the left, so it is with the soul: the
impulses of the incontinent man run counter to his ruling part.
The only difference is that in the case of the body we see what it is
that goes astray, while in the soul we do not. Nevertheless the
comparison will doubtless suffice to show that there is in the soul
something besides the rational element, opposing and running
counter to it. (In what sense the two elements are distinct is immaterial.) But this other element, as we have said, seems also to
have some share in a rational principle: at any rate, in the continent man it submits to reason, while in the man who is at once
temperate and courageous it is presumably all the more obedient;
for in him it speaks on all matters harmoniously with the voice of
reason.

------

[22]**ataxic limbs** Aristotle refers to a nervous disorder of the limbs.

Evidently, then, the irrational part of the soul is twofold. 38
There is the vegetative element, which has no share in reason, and
there is the concupiscent,[23] or rather the appetitive element, which
does in a sense partake of reason, in that it is amenable and obedient to it: i.e., it is rational in the sense that we speak of "having
logos of" [paying heed to] father and friends, not in the sense of
"having *logos* of" [having a rational understanding of] mathematical truths. That this irrational element is in some way
amenable to reason is shown by our practice of giving admonish-
ment, and by rebuke and exhortation generally. If on this account
it is deemed more correct to regard this element as also possessing
reason, then the rational part of the soul, in turn, will have two
subdivisions: the one being rational in the strict sense as actually
possessing reason, the other merely in the sense that a child obeys
its father.

Virtue, too, is differentiated in accordance with this division of 39
the soul: for we call some of the virtues intellectual and others moral:
wisdom, understanding, and sagacity being among the former, liberality and temperance among the latter. In speaking of a man's character
we do not say that he is wise or intelligent, but that he is gentle
or temperate; yet we praise the wise man too for the disposition he has
developed within himself, and praiseworthy dispositions we call
virtues.

---

[23]**concupiscent** Sexual; Aristotle corrects himself to refer to the general nature
of desire.

QUESTIONS FOR CRITICAL READING

1. Define the following terms: "good," "virtue," "honor," "happiness,"
   "truth," "soul," "body."
2. In the first paragraphs of the selection, Aristotle talks about aims and
   ends. What does he mean by these terms?
3. Do you feel that Aristotle's view of the relationship of virtue to happiness is as relevant today as he argued it was in his day?
4. What is Aristotle's attitude toward most people?
5. What characteristics can we assume about the audience for whom
   Aristotle writes?
6. In what senses is the selection modern? In what senses is it antique or
   dated?

SUGGESTIONS FOR WRITING

1. Aristotle discusses the virtuous life in this selection. How would you apply his views to your own life? What ethical issues is Aristotle pointing us toward in this essay? To what extent does his guidance translate to modern life? Explain.

2. In his section on the primacy of statecraft, Aristotle makes a number of assertions regarding the relationship of the happiness of the individual to the welfare (or happiness) of the state. Clarify as much as possible the relationship of the individual's happiness to that of the state. How can a state be happy? Is the term relevant to anything other than an individual? Does Aristotle think that the individual's interests should be subservient to the state's?

3. In paragraph 15, Aristotle talks about the function of man. Relying on that discussion and other aspects of the work, write your own version of "The Function of Man." Be sure to use "man" as a collective term for both men and women. Once you have clarified the function of man, establish the connection between function and happiness. Is it true that the best-functioning person will be the happiest person? Aristotle implies that it is not enough to be, say, honorable or noble, but that one must act honorably or nobly. Is the implication true?

4. Take Aristotle's definition, "Happiness is a certain activity of the soul in accordance with perfect virtue." Define it in terms that are clear not only to you but also to your peers. Take care to include each part of the definition: "certain activity" (or lack of it), "soul" (which in modern terms may be "personality" or "psyche"), "in accordance with," "perfect virtue." You may rely on any parts of the selection that can be of help, but be sure to use the topic of definition to guide you through the selection. You certainly may disagree with Aristotle or amplify aspects of his definitions. In one sense, you will be defining "happiness" for yourself and your times.

5. In his "confirmation by popular beliefs" (para. 19 and following), Aristotle talks about the good. He mentions three classes of good, ranking them in order from lowest to highest: external goods, goods of the body, and goods of the soul. Using concrete examples, define each of these classes of good. Do you agree with Aristotle's order? Do you think that your peers agree with it? Where possible, give examples to help establish the validity of your opinion. Finally, do you think that our society in general puts the same value on these three classes of good that Aristotle does? Again, use examples where possible.

6. Analyze the following quotations from the selection, taking a stand on the question of whether or not Aristotle is generally correct in his assertion about the aim of man:

> It is in our best activities, or in the best one of them, that we say happiness consists. (para. 21)

> A man who does not enjoy doing noble actions is not a good man at all. (para. 21)

Even supposing the chief good to be eventually the same for the individual as for the state, that of the state is evidently of greater and more fundamental importance both to attain and to preserve. (para. 4)

In life . . . those who carry off the finest prizes are those who manifest their excellence in their deeds. (para. 20)

If, as we have declared, it is our activities that give life its character, then no happy man can become miserable, inasmuch as he will never do what is hateful or base. (para. 30)

7. **CONNECTIONS**   Among the selections in the Ethics and Morality section, what other writer takes as much interest in the nature of human happiness as Aristotle? Consider the view of happiness that Moses' chapters of Exodus provide for us. What are the major differences between these documents? Consider, too, the nature of happiness as expressed in the Sermon on the Mount. How do these ethical views differ? How do they help clarify the concept of human happiness?

8. **CONNECTIONS**   Write an essay in which you define happiness by comparing Aristotle's views with those in Jean-Jacques Rousseau's "The Origin of Civil Society" or in Thomas Jefferson's "The Declaration of Independence." Compare their attitudes toward material and spiritual happiness as well as their attitudes toward political freedom and the need for possessions. What does Aristotle leave out that others feel is important?

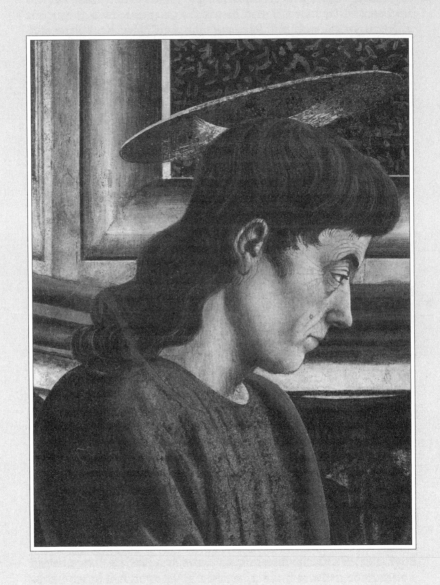

ST. MATTHEW
The Sermon on the Mount

Matthew, believed to be the author of the Gospel of St. Matthew, was also known as Levi, one of the twelve disciples of Jesus. He was a Jewish tax collector working for the Roman governors in Galilee, a region of what was then known as Palestine. His dates are uncertain, but he lived in the period of A.D. 10 to 80, and the best modern sources suggest that his gospel was composed sometime after A.D. 70 and probably written in Greek. Although some early church historians say this gospel was written originally in Hebrew, there is no evidence that a Hebrew text existed. This detail is important only because of the reputation of the Gospel of St. Matthew: it is said to be the most Jewish of the gospels. Even though it originally was addressed not to Jewish Christians but to Gentile Christians, it frequently quotes from and refers to Jewish law and the teachings and text of the Old Testament. Because the Romans repressed the Jews after their uprising in A.D. 66 to 70, few if any Jews were thought to remain in Palestine.

The Gospels of St. Matthew, St. Mark, and St. Luke are called synoptic, because they offer a common view of the same material: the story of the ministry of Jesus. The Gospel of St. Matthew may not have been written first, as it seems to rely in part on the Gospel of St. Mark. However, it has special authority because Matthew (and not Mark or Luke) was one of Jesus' twelve disciples. Despite his importance to the early church, very little is known about Matthew, and it is uncertain whether he wrote the Gospel that bears his name or whether he was the sole author. The strongest evidence in favor of his authorship is tradition, particularly the attribution of Papias, a second-century bishop of the church.

From the *King James Bible* (1611).

Matthew's plan in the gospel seems to have been to structure his observations in five parts, possibly emulating the Pentateuch (five books) of Moses, who is known as the lawgiver. Matthew is very knowledgeable about Jewish law and interprets that law through the teachings of Jesus. His focus, on at least one level, is on the details, or letter, of the law. Jesus felt the scribes and Pharisees — two groups of "righteous" citizens — concerned themselves with the details of following legal prescripts and not with the spirit of the law. For example, because it was against the law to work on the Sabbath, an act like pulling a donkey out of a hole on the Sabbath, thereby relieving its misery, was a crime according to the Pharisees — but not to Jesus.

The Gospel of St. Matthew tells of the early life of Jesus; his activity in Galilee, including the Sermon on the Mount, which appears here; his activity in Jerusalem; and his eventual crucifixion. Matthew emphasizes Jesus' powers as a healer and the spiritual value of his message. Part of the Sermon on the Mount includes the beatitudes (5:1–13), nine blessings that Jesus offers the multitude. The Gospel of St. Luke (6:20–23) includes four more beatitudes:

> Blessed are you poor, for yours is the kingdom of God.
> Blessed are you that hunger now, for you shall be satisfied.
> Blessed are you that weep now, for you shall laugh.
> Blessed are you when men hate you, and when they exclude you and revile you, and cast out your name as evil, on account of the Son of man! Rejoice in that day, and leap for joy, for behold, your reward is great in heaven; for so their fathers did to the prophets.

These blessings indicate the spiritual comfort that Matthew and the disciples received from the teachings of Jesus.

The Sermon on the Mount goes beyond spiritual comfort, however, by offering a guide for living as a Christian. In it, Jesus discourses on the law itself, the power of anger, adultery, lawsuits, loving one's enemies, charity, prayer, fasting, heaven, and God, as well as many other subjects. Some of this guidance is similar to the guidance that the Buddha gives in his efforts to point the way to enlightenment. Thus, the Sermon on the Mount offers the followers of Jesus a pattern for faith and a prescription for moral behavior.

St. Matthew's Rhetoric

The Gospel of St. Matthew is by far the most quoted of the four gospels. Matthew's style is crisp, sharpened, and pared to a remarkable economy of expression. By fashioning statements to make them memorable, he hopes to make the sayings of Jesus available to a multitude. Expressions such as "an eye for an eye" (5:38), "whosoever shall smite thee on thy right cheek, turn to him the other also" (5:39), "judge not, that ye be not judged" (7:1), "wide *is* the gate, and broad *is* the way, that leadeth to destruction" (7:13), "false prophets . . . in sheep's clothing" (7:15), and many more are found in the selection that is presented here. Even though he borrows or modifies expressions from the Old Testament, Matthew's Gospel shows him to be a gifted literary man as well as a spiritual guide.

The structure of the selection presented here is a narration of the story of Jesus' ministry, beginning with Jesus preaching to the multitude in Galilee (4:23–25). Chapter 5 contains the Sermon on the Mount ("he went up into a mountain," 5:1) and first examines the blessings — the beatitudes — that Jesus taught to the disciples. The Sermon on the Mount is an oral presentation of important teachings delivered directly to the disciples who have been chosen to carry out Jesus' work. The teachings continue in Chapters 6 and 7, which cover many of the important issues that concerned people who desired to learn how to live by proper precepts. Interestingly, when Jesus came down from the mount, one of his first acts was to cleanse a leper.

Most of the following selection records what Jesus said more than what he did, and part of Matthew's skill centers on getting Jesus' words, including his tone, "right." One reason for comparing the Gospel of St. Matthew with the Gospels of St. Mark and St. Luke is to see the nuances they each perceived in Jesus' tone and manner.

Partly because Matthew is economical in his recording of Jesus' sayings, later generations have pored over them carefully in an effort to decide exactly what they mean. Matthew is able to freight expressions with a considerable range of significance. An expression such as "an eye for an eye, and a tooth for a tooth" (5:38) needs careful examination, both in the context in which Jesus uses it and in the context of the entire Bible, because it also appears in the Torah in Exodus (21:23–24). The amplification that Jesus offers the expression effectively alters its meaning to help accomplish the reinterpretation of the law that is central to Matthew's understanding of Jesus' mission. Therefore, one of the rewards of reading St. Matthew lies in the invitation to read carefully and in depth.

PREREADING QUESTIONS:
WHAT TO READ FOR

The following prereading questions may help you anticipate key issues in the discussion of St. Matthew's the Sermon on the Mount. Keeping them in mind during your first reading of the selection should help focus your attention.

- How do the beatitudes help one learn to live a good life?
- What is Jesus' attitude toward the law?
- Which infractions of the law seem most serious?

The Sermon on the Mount

4

23   And Jesus went about all Galilee, teaching in their synagogues, and preaching the gospel of the kingdom, and healing all manner of sickness and all manner of disease among the people.

24   And his fame went throughout all Syria: and they brought unto him all sick people that were taken with divers diseases and torments, and those which were possessed with devils, and those which were lunatic, and those that had the palsy; and he healed them.

25   And there followed him great multitudes of people from Galilee, and *from* Decapolis, and *from* Jerusalem, and *from* Judea, and *from* beyond Jordan.

5

And seeing the multitudes, he went up into a mountain: and when he was set, his disciples came unto him:

2   And he opened his mouth, and taught them, saying,

3   Blessed *are* the poor in spirit: for theirs is the kingdom of heaven.

4   Blessed *are* they that mourn: for they shall be comforted.

5   Blessed *are* the meek: for they shall inherit the earth.

6   Blessed *are* they which do hunger and thirst after righteousness: for they shall be filled.

7   Blessed *are* the merciful: for they shall obtain mercy.

8   Blessed *are* the pure in heart: for they shall see God.

9   Blessed *are* the peacemakers: for they shall be called the children of God.

10   Blessed *are* they which are persecuted for righteousness' sake: for theirs is the kingdom of heaven.

11   Blessed are ye, when *men* shall revile you, and persecute *you*, and shall say all manner of evil against you falsely, for my sake.

12   Rejoice, and be exceeding glad: for great is your reward in heaven: for so persecuted they the prophets which were before you.

13   Ye are the salt of the earth: but if the salt have lost his savor, wherewith shall it be salted? It is thenceforth good for nothing, but to be cast out, and to be trodden under foot of men.

14   Ye are the light of the world. A city that is set on a hill cannot be hid.

15   Neither do men light a candle, and put it under a bushel, but on a candlestick; and it giveth light unto all that are in the house.

16   Let your light so shine before men, that they may see your good works, and glorify your Father which is in heaven.

17   Think not that I am come to destroy the law, or the prophets: I am not come to destroy, but to fulfil.

18   For verily I say unto you, Till heaven and earth pass, one jot or one tittle shall in no wise pass from the law, till all be fulfilled.

19   Whosoever therefore shall break one of these least commandments, and shall teach men so, he shall be called the least in the kingdom of heaven: but whosoever shall do and teach *them*, the same shall be called great in the kingdom of heaven.

20   For I say unto you, That except your righteousness shall exceed *the righteousness* of the scribes and Pharisees, ye shall in no case enter into the kingdom of heaven.

21   Ye have heard that it was said by them of old time, Thou shalt not kill; and whosoever shall kill shall be in danger of the judgment:

22   But I say unto you, That whosoever is angry with his brother without a cause shall be in danger of the judgment: and whosoever shall say to his brother, Raca, shall be in danger of the council: but whosoever shall say, Thou fool, shall be in danger of hell fire.

23   Therefore if thou bring thy gift to the altar, and there rememberest that thy brother hath aught against thee;

24   Leave there thy gift before the altar, and go thy way; first be reconciled to thy brother, and then come and offer thy gift.

25   Agree with thine adversary quickly, while thou art in the way with him; lest at any time the adversary deliver thee to the judge, and the judge deliver thee to the officer, and thou be cast into prison.

26   Verily I say unto thee, Thou shalt by no means come out thence, till thou hast paid the uttermost farthing.

27   Ye have heard that it was said by them of old time, Thou shalt not commit adultery:

28   But I say unto you, That whosoever looketh on a woman to lust after her hath committed adultery with her already in his heart.

29   And if thy right eye offend thee, pluck it out, and cast *it* from thee: for it is profitable for thee that one of thy members should perish, and not *that* thy whole body should be cast into hell.

30   And if thy right hand offend thee, cut it off, and cast *it* from thee: for it is profitable for thee that one of thy members should perish, and not *that* thy whole body should be cast into hell.

31   It hath been said, Whosoever shall put away his wife, let him give her a writing of divorcement:

32   But I say unto you, That whosoever shall put away his wife, saving for the cause of fornication, causeth her to commit adultery: and whosoever shall marry her that is divorced committeth adultery.

33   Again, ye have heard that it hath been said by them of old time, Thou shalt not forswear thyself, but shalt perform unto the Lord thine oaths:

34   But I say unto you, Swear not at all; neither by heaven; for it is God's throne:

35   Nor by the earth; for it is his footstool: neither by Jerusalem; for it is the city of the great King.

36   Neither shalt thou swear by thy head, because thou canst not make one hair white or black.

37   But let your communication be, Yea, yea; Nay, nay: for whatsoever is more than these cometh of evil.

38   Ye have heard that it hath been said, An eye for an eye, and a tooth for a tooth:

39   But I say unto you, That ye resist not evil: but whosoever shall smite thee on thy right cheek, turn to him the other also.

40   And if any man will sue thee at the law, and take away thy coat, let him have *thy* cloak also.

41   And whosoever shall compel thee to go a mile, go with him twain.

42   Give to him that asketh thee, and from him that would borrow of thee turn not thou away.

43   Ye have heard that it hath been said, Thou shalt love thy neighbor, and hate thine enemy.

44   But I say unto you, Love your enemies, bless them that curse you, do good to them that hate you, and pray for them which despitefully use you, and persecute you;

45   That ye may be the children of your Father which is in heaven: for he maketh his sun to rise on the evil and on the good, and sendeth rain on the just and on the unjust.

46   For if ye love them which love you, what reward have ye? do not even the publicans[1] the same?

47   And if ye salute your brethren only, what do ye more *than others?* do not even the publicans so?

48   Be ye therefore perfect, even as your Father which is in heaven is perfect.

6

Take heed that ye do not your alms before men, to be seen of them: otherwise ye have no reward of your Father which is in heaven.

2   Therefore when thou doest *thine* alms, do not sound a trumpet before thee, as the hypocrites do in the synagogues and in the streets, that they may have glory of men. Verily I say unto you, They have their reward.

3   But when thou doest alms, let not thy left hand know what thy right hand doeth:

4   That thine alms may be in secret: and thy Father which seeth in secret himself shall reward thee openly.

5   And when thou prayest, thou shalt not be as the hypocrites *are:* for they love to pray standing in the synagogues and in the corners of the streets, that they may be seen of men. Verily I say unto you, They have their reward.

6   But thou, when thou prayest, enter into thy closet, and when thou hast shut thy door, pray to thy Father which is in secret; and thy Father which seeth in secret shall reward thee openly.

7   But when ye pray, use not vain repetitions, as the heathen *do:* for they think that they shall be heard for their much speaking.

8   Be not ye therefore like unto them: for your Father knoweth what things ye have need of, before ye ask him.

9   After this manner therefore pray ye: Our father which art in heaven, Hallowed be thy name.

10   Thy kingdom come. Thy will be done in earth, as *it is* in heaven.

11   Give us this day our daily bread.

12   And forgive us our debts, as we forgive our debtors.

13   And lead us not into temptation, but deliver us from evil: For thine is the kingdom, and the power, and the glory, for ever. Amen.

14   For if ye forgive men their trespasses, your heavenly Father will also forgive you:

---

[1]**publicans** Tax collectors for the Roman Empire.

15   But if ye forgive not men their trespasses, neither will your Father forgive your trespasses.

16   Moreover when ye fast, be not, as the hypocrites, of a sad countenance: for they disfigure their faces, that they may appear unto men to fast. Verily I say unto you, They have their reward.

17   But thou, when thou fastest, anoint thine head, and wash thy face;

18   That thou appear not unto men to fast, but unto thy Father which is in secret: and thy Father which seeth in secret shall reward thee openly.

19   Lay not up for yourselves treasures upon earth, where moth and rust doth corrupt, and where thieves break through and steal:

20   But lay up for yourselves treasures in heaven, where neither moth nor rust doth corrupt, and where thieves do not break through nor steal:

21   For where your treasure is, there will your heart be also.

22   The light of the body is the eye: if therefore thine eye be single,[2] thy whole body shall be full of light.

23   But if thine eye be evil, thy whole body shall be full of darkness. If therefore the light that is in thee be darkness, how great is that darkness!

24   No man can serve two masters: for either he will hate the one, and love the other; or else he will hold to the one, and despise the other. Ye cannot serve God and mammon.[3]

25   Therefore I say unto you, Take no thought for your life, what ye shall eat, or what ye shall drink; nor yet for your body, what ye shall put on. Is not the life more than meat, and the body than raiment?[4]

26   Behold the fowls of the air: for they sow not, neither do they reap, nor gather into barns; yet your heavenly Father feedeth them. Are ye not much better than they?

27   Which of you by taking thought can add one cubit unto his stature?

28   And why take ye thought for raiment? Consider the lilies of the field, how they grow; they toil not, neither do they spin:

29   And yet I say unto you, That even Solomon in all his glory was not arrayed like one of these.

30   Wherefore, if God so clothe the grass of the field, which today is, and tomorrow is cast into the oven, *shall he* not much more *clothe* you, O ye of little faith?

---

[2]**single** Focused on proper things.
[3]**mammon** Pagan god, associated with materialism.
[4]**raiment** Clothing.

31   Therefore take no thought, saying, What shall we eat? or, What shall we drink? or, Wherewithal shall we be clothed?

32   (For after all these things do the Gentiles seek:) for your heavenly Father knoweth that ye have need of all these things.

33   But seek ye first the kingdom of God, and his righteousness; and all these things shall be added unto you.

34   Take therefore no thought for the morrow: for the morrow shall take thought for the things of itself. Sufficient unto the day *is* the evil thereof.

7

Judge not, that ye be not judged.

2   For with what judgment ye judge, ye shall be judged: and with what measure ye mete, it shall be measured to you again.

3   And why beholdest thou the mote that is in thy brother's eye, but considerest not the beam that is in thine own eye?

4   Or how wilt thou say to thy brother, Let me pull out the mote out of thine eye; and, behold, a beam *is* in thine own eye?

5   Thou hypocrite, first cast out the beam out of thine own eye; and then shalt thou see clearly to cast out the mote out of thy brother's eye.

6   Give not that which is holy unto the dogs, neither cast ye your pearls before swine, lest they trample them under their feet, and turn again and rend you.

7   Ask, and it shall be given you; seek, and ye shall find; knock, and it shall be opened unto you:

8   For every one that asketh receiveth; and he that seeketh findeth; and to him that knocketh it shall be opened

9   Or what man is there of you, whom if his son ask bread, will he give him a stone?

10   Or if he ask a fish, will he give him a serpent?

11   If ye then, being evil, know how to give good gifts unto your children, how much more shall your Father which is in heaven give good things to them that ask him?

12   Therefore all things whatsoever ye would that men should do to you, do ye even so to them: for this is the law and the prophets.

13   Enter ye in at the strait gate: for wide *is* the gate, and broad *is* the way, that leadeth to destruction, and many there be which go in thereat:

14   Because strait *is* the gate, and narrow *is* the way, which leadeth unto life, and few there be that find it.

15   Beware of false prophets, which come to you in sheep's clothing, but inwardly they are ravening wolves.

16   Ye shall know them by their fruits. Do men gather grapes of thorns, or figs of thistles?

17   Even so every good tree bringeth forth good fruit; but a corrupt tree bringeth forth evil fruit.

18   A good tree cannot bring forth evil fruit, neither *can* a corrupt tree bring forth good fruit.

19   Every tree that bringeth not forth good fruit is hewn down, and cast into the fire.

20   Wherefore by their fruits ye shall know them.

21   Not every one that saith unto me, Lord, Lord, shall enter into the kingdom of heaven; but he that doeth the will of my Father which is in heaven.

22   Many will say to me in that day, Lord, Lord, have we not prophesied in thy name? and in thy name have cast out devils? and in thy name done many wonderful works?

23   And then will I profess unto them, I never knew you: depart from me, ye that work iniquity.

24   Therefore whosoever heareth these sayings of mine, and doeth them, I will liken him unto a wise man, which built his house upon a rock:

25   And the rain descended, and the floods came, and the winds blew, and beat upon that house; and it fell not: for it was founded upon a rock.

26   And every one that heareth these sayings of mine, and doeth them not, shall be likened unto a foolish man, which built his house upon the sand:

27   And the rain descended, and the floods came, and the winds blew, and beat upon that house; and it fell: and great was the fall of it.

28   And it came to pass, when Jesus had ended these sayings, the people were astonished at his doctrine:

29   For he taught them as *one* having authority, and not as the scribes.

QUESTIONS FOR CRITICAL READING

1. What is a beatitude?
2. What is Jesus' attitude toward adultery?
3. What is the connection between "an eye for an eye" (5:38) and turning the other cheek?
4. What is Jesus' teaching on charity?
5. What is of importance in Jesus' references to the "lilies of the field" (6:28)?

SUGGESTIONS FOR WRITING

1. Describe what you feel is the central spiritual message of the selection. What prescription for living does the Sermon on the Mount offer the individual? What basis of faith does Jesus seem to require of his followers? Is faith a moral issue in this selection?

2. Why should a person's faith demand a specific manner of behavior? What is the connection between actions and beliefs as St. Matthew sees it?

3. Which of the teachings of Jesus is most difficult to follow? Why? Does the emphasis that Matthew gives that teaching imply its difficulty? Which of Jesus' teachings seem problematic for Matthew?

4. Apart from the fact that the Lord's Prayer begins with "Our father" (6:9), which of Jesus' teachings are patriarchal in implication? Would following his teachings produce a patriarchal society in which women are devalued? What implications for the modern world do you derive from your analysis of this issue?

5. The expression "eye for an eye" (5:38) appears in Exodus (21:23–24) as well as in the Sermon on the Mount. How does Jesus modify this expression? Read both versions to make your comparison. Analyze the text carefully in this selection (5:38–39) for the significance of the saying.

6. What are Jesus' teachings about lawbreakers? He speaks both of a higher law to which we are to adhere and also of the ordinary laws of the land. What distinctions does he make between those laws? And what are his directives regarding our responsibility to these laws? What contemporary legal cases can you think of that reveal important distinctions that would be of interest to St. Matthew or Jesus?

7. **CONNECTIONS** How compatible are the teachings of Jesus with the teachings of Moses? Are both equally moral in nature? Is the question of faith more important in one than in the other? How do the ultimate goals of each text differ? How are they similar? In what ways would the path of the disciples also be the path that follows Moses' law?

8. **CONNECTIONS** Consider the views of those who comment on government. How would this selection be interpreted by Thomas Jefferson? By Jean-Jacques Rousseau? By Niccolò Machiavelli? Which commentators on government could be considered in general alignment with the teachings of Jesus as imparted by St. Matthew?

THE KORAN
The Night Journey

THE PROPHET MUHAMMAD (A.D. c. 570–c. 632) was born in
Mecca in what is now Saudi Arabia. Mecca is the holiest city in
Islam in part for that reason. He was born a few months after his father died and became an orphan six years later when his mother
died. For health reasons he spent part of his early life with nomadic
tribes outside Mecca. Families in Mecca belonged to tight-knit clans,
some of which held great power. His family, led by an uncle, Abu
Talib, was part of the Hashim, a strong clan involved in trading with
Syria. In around 595, while in his middle twenties and on a trading
journey with his uncle, Muhammad managed the merchandise of a
wealthy older woman, Khadijah, who was so impressed with him
that she agreed to marriage. The marriage was successful and produced a number of children, two boys who died at a young age and
four daughters who survived. When Khadijah died in 619, Muhammad inherited her fortune and achieved independence.

Muhammad was a deeply religious man in early life. In Mecca
during his youth, religion was marked by idol worship and pagan-
ism centering on a sacred site called the Ka'bah. Sometime around
610 Muhammad began having visions and revelations, which he
believed were given to him by the Archangel Gabriel. He was
much shaken by these revelations, but his wife, Khadijah, reas-
sured him and encouraged him to welcome them. Gabriel told
him, "You are the messenger of God." The word *messenger* may
also be translated as "apostle." In Arabic, it is *rasūl*, and Muhammad was described as *rasūl Allah* (messenger of God). As far as is
known, because Muhammad was illiterate, he memorized these
revelations, which the Archangel Gabriel told him came directly
from God. They were written down by others early in the period

---

From the Koran. Translated by N. J. Dawood.

during which the revelations occurred. They were gathered together in written form around 650.

In 613, Muhammad began preaching in response to his revelations and became known as the Prophet. He faced derision at first. Meccans claimed he was possessed by spirits and that he was a shaman, not a true prophet, or a mere poet — because the Koran is in rhymed Arabic prose. In response he claimed this as proof that the Koran was a miracle, which his followers accepted. Nonetheless, he was generally ridiculed and rejected by people in his own clan and by others who denied him their business.

He eventually drew followers — about thirty-nine at first but growing soon to seventy. At the time of Muhammad, Mecca had no powerful central religion. The idols in the Ka'bah and the place itself were important, but most citizens were involved in mercantile activities and devoted little energy to religion. Muhammad, on the other hand, was fervent in his beliefs and seems to have represented a threat to the order of Mecca as early as 620, when he took the famous "night journey" to Jerusalem and envisioned heaven. In 622 he began the *Hejira*, the emigration from Mecca to Medina with his followers, sending them off in small groups and taking a circuitous route to avoid assassination. Muhammad's religion was known as Islam, meaning something close to "surrender to God's will," and his followers were known as Muslims — those who have surrendered. It is from this year, 622, that the Muslims begin their modern era.

The following years were filled with struggle as the number of Muslims increased. Raids on trading parties of both Meccans and Muslims led to battles between relatively large armies. Most of the struggles were won by Muhammad and his followers, but in 625 at the battle of Uhud the Muslims were defeated. Because Muhammad firmly believed that the will of God determines victory, the experience of defeat shook the faith of his followers. His opponents were unable to take advantage of their victory, however, and Muhammad soon restored faith in his followers and pressed forward.

In the year 627 Muhammad defeated a large Meccan army that attacked his party at Medina. In the same year he expelled a Jewish clan, al-Nadīr, from Medina on the grounds that it was conspiring against him, and he attacked and dispersed the Jewish clan of the Qurayzah on the same grounds. Although by 628 Muhammad and his followers were strong enough to enforce a truce with Mecca, his men soon were attacked by groups associated with Mecca, and as a result Muhammad gathered ten thousand men to attack Mecca. When he arrived in 630, however, the city essentially gave up without a fight, and Muhammad triumphed. Most Meccans converted to Islam even though Muhammad did not make that a condition of surrender. Thereafter he sent messengers to other parts of the Middle East to encourage other nations to convert to Islam and to recognize the Muslims as a formidable power in the Arab world.

By the time he died, his movement had grown enormously. Islam was destined to spread throughout the entire Arab world and beyond, rapidly becoming one of the world's largest religions.

The Rhetoric of the Koran

The Koran was composed in prose but with rhymes that were sometimes very close and sometimes rather distant. According to Arab scholars, there is no adequate way to translate the Koran, and therefore the English version that follows, like all non-Arabic versions, must be regarded as a paraphrase rather than a strict translation. The beauty of the original Arabic often depends on the sounds of words and their association with the words' meaning. But it also depends on the subtlety of possible interpretations resulting from purposeful ambiguities designed to produce a richly significant text. Many of these qualities are lost in English.

On the other hand, the sense that this is a text from a holy book is plain in terms of its resemblance to the Bible. Muhammad was aware of the Jewish Torah and the Christian New Testament. He also was aware that in the Koran the Muslims now had their own holy book. The Koran consists of 114 surahs, or chapters. The names of the surahs usually relate to a detail in the surah or to the subject of the surah. Examples are "The Ant," surah 27; "Smoke," surah 44; "The Hypocrites," surah 63; "The Soul-Snatchers," surah 79. The order of the surahs is not chronological but traditional. The order of composition is uncertain, although surah 93, "Daylight," is sometimes cited as the first.

"The Night Journey" is the seventeenth surah and records Muhammad's journey, in the year 620, aided by the Archangel Gabriel, from the "Sacred Temple" at Mecca to the "Farther Temple," the Dome of the Rock, in Jerusalem and then on to the seventh heaven. Believers are divided as to whether this records a vision or a historical event. God speaks directly to Muhammad, usually saying "we" but sometimes shifting to "I." The shifting point of view may imply the all-inclusive nature of God. Dialogue is an important rhetorical device, but, like the dialogue in Exodus, it is quite one-sided here. God tells Muhammad how one ought to live and gives him a careful list of moral principles to guide a believer toward a moral life.

Each of the numbered paragraphs in this text resembles the verses we encounter in biblical texts such as Exodus. Because we read the Koran in translation—just as we read Exodus in translation—it is all but impossible to make a comparison of the texts in terms of style. Obviously, though, each verse or paragraph is short and carefully worded so as to sustain very close reading.

The first part of "The Night Journey" (paras. 1–7) connects with Moses and the first five books of the Bible, whereas the next section (paras. 8–17) clarifies God's relationship with humankind in general. Starting with paragraph 20, the text reveals the commands that God imposes on his people—true believers. The first, "Serve no other God besides God" (para. 18), is conjoined with the command to "show kindness to your parents." Subsequent commands honor the relationships among kin, or family. Each of the commands aims to control a specific kind of behavior. A great deal has to do with contractual promises and fairness in business.

A considerable portion of text concerns unbelievers, reminding the faithful that the unbelievers will ridicule them (paras. 32–42), for Muhammad himself was reviled for his beliefs and understood the nature of rejection. A warning about Satan and his activities is apparent in paragraphs 45–55, and a vision of hell as a place of penitence and damnation contrasts with the promise of an afterlife of bliss in heaven.

Metaphors of sea journeys and merchant fleets help interpret the life of the average person as a sometimes tempest-tossed experience. The last part of the passage, from paragraph 69 to the end of the selection, concerns the nature of believers and unbelievers. The ways in which individuals react to God's gifts are the topic, and the general message is not good for those who do not remain steadfast. Because the matters at hand are of such great significance for every individual, the discourse is serious and the tone elevated. What is said here is intended to be a matter of life and death.

PREREADING QUESTIONS: WHAT TO READ FOR

The following prereading questions may help you anticipate key issues in the discussion of "The Night Journey" from the Koran. Keeping them in mind during your first reading of the selection will help focus your attention.

- What are the characteristics of God?
- Which statements are most like the Ten Commandments?
- What does God promise to true believers?

The Night Journey

In the Name of God, the Compassionate, the Merciful

Glory be to Him who made His servant go by night from the 1
Sacred Temple to the farther Temple whose surroundings We have
blessed, that We might show him some of Our signs. He alone hears
all and observes all.

We gave Moses the Book and made it a guide for the Israelites, 2
saying: "Take no other guardian than Myself. You are the descendants of those whom We carried in the Ark with Noah. He was a
truly thankful servant."

In the Book We solemnly declared to the Israelites: "Twice you 3
shall commit evil in the land. You shall become great transgressors."

And when the prophecy of your first transgression came to be ful- 4
filled, We sent against you a formidable army which ravaged your land
and carried out the punishment with which you had been threatened.

Then We granted you victory over them and multiplied your 5
riches and your descendants, so that once again you became a numerous people. We said: "If you do good, it shall be to your own advantage; but if you do evil, you shall sin against your own souls."

And when the prophecy of your second transgression came to be 6
fulfilled, We sent another army to afflict you and to enter the Temple
as the former entered it before, utterly destroying all that they laid
their hands on.

We said: "Your Lord may yet be merciful to you. If you again 7
transgress, you shall again be scourged. We have made Hell a prison-
house for the unbelievers."

This Koran will guide men to that which is most upright. It 8
promises the believers who do good works a rich reward, and
threatens those who deny the life to come with a grievous scourge.
Yet man prays for evil as fervently as he prays for good. Truly, man
is ever impatient.

We made the night and the day twin marvels. We enshrouded 9
the night with darkness and gave light to the day, so that you might
seek the bounty of your Lord and learn to compute the seasons and
the years. We have made all things manifestly plain to you.

The fate of each man We have bound about his neck. On the 10
Day of Resurrection We shall confront him with a book spread wide
open, saying: "Here is your book: read it. Enough for you this day
that your own soul should call you to account."

He that seeks guidance shall be guided to his own advantage, 11
but he that errs shall err at his own peril. No soul shall bear another's

burden. Nor do We punish a nation until We have sent forth an apostle to forewarn them.

When We resolve to destroy a city, We first give warning to 12 those of its people who live in comfort. If they persist in sin, judgement is irrevocably passed, and We destroy it utterly.

How many generations have We cut down since Noah's time! 13 Suffice it that your Lord is well aware of His servants' sins and observes them all.

He that desires this fleeting life shall soon receive in it whatever 14 We will for whomever We please. But then We have prepared Hell for him, where he will burn despised and helpless.

As for him that desires the life to come and strives for it as he 15 ought to, being a true believer, his endeavours shall be rewarded by God.

On all—on these and those—We bestow the bounty of your 16 Lord: none shall be denied the bounty of your Lord.

See how We have exalted some above others. Yet the life to 17 come has greater honours and is more exalted.

Serve no other god besides God, lest you incur disgrace and 18 ruin. Your Lord has enjoined you to worship none but Him, and to show kindness to your parents. If either or both of them attain old age in your dwelling, show them no sign of impatience, nor rebuke them; but speak to them kind words. Treat them with humility and tenderness and say: "Lord, be merciful to them. They nursed me when I was an infant."

Your Lord best knows what is in your hearts; He knows if you 19 are good. He will surely forgive those that turn to Him.

Give to the near of kin their due, and also to the destitute and 20 to the traveller in need. Do not squander your substance wastefully, for the wasteful are Satan's brothers; and Satan is ever ungrateful to his Lord. But if, while waiting for your Lord's bounty, you lack the means to assist them, then at least speak to them kindly.

Be neither miserly nor prodigal, for then you should either be 21 reproached or be reduced to penury.

Your Lord gives abundantly to whom He will and sparingly to 22 whom He pleases. He knows and observes His servants.

You shall not kill your children for fear of want. We will pro- 23 vide for them and for you. To kill them is a great sin.

You shall not commit adultery, for it is foul and indecent. 24

You shall not kill any man whom God has forbidden you to kill, 25 except for a just cause. If a man is slain unjustly, his heir shall be entitled to satisfaction. But let him not carry his vengeance too far, for his victim will in turn be assisted and avenged.

Do not interfere with the property of orphans except with the 26
best of motives, until they reach maturity. Keep your promises; you
are accountable for all that you promise.

Give full measure, when you measure, and weigh with even 27
scales. That is fair, and better in the end.

Do not follow what you do not know. Man's eyes, ears, and 28
heart—each of his senses shall be closely questioned.

Do not walk proudly on the earth. You cannot cleave the earth, 29
nor can you rival the mountains in stature.

Evil is all this in the sight of your Lord, and odious. 30

These injunctions are but a part of the wisdom your Lord has 31
inspired you with. Serve no other deity besides God, lest you should
be cast into Hell, condemned and rejected.

What! Has your Lord blessed *you* with sons and Himself adopted 32
daughters from among the angels? A monstrous blasphemy is that
which you utter.

We have made plain Our revelations in this Koran so that the 33
unbelievers may take warning. Yet it has only added to their aversion. Say: "If, as they affirm, there were other gods besides God, they
would surely seek to dethrone Him."

Glory to Him! Exalted be He, high above their false-hoods! 34

The seven heavens, the earth, and all who dwell in them give 35
glory to Him. All creatures celebrate His praises. Yet you cannot understand their praises. Benignant is He and forgiving.

When you recite the Koran, We place between you and those 36
who deny the life to come a hidden barrier. We have cast veils over
their hearts lest they understand it, and made them hard of hearing.
When you make mention of your Lord alone in the Koran, they turn
their backs with indignation.

We well know what they wish to hear when they listen to you, 37
and what they say when they converse in private; when the wrongdoers declare: "The man you follow is surely bewitched."

Behold what epithets they bestow upon you. They have surely 38
gone astray and cannot find the right path.

"What!" they say. "When we are turned to bones and dust, shall 39
we be restored in a new creation?"

Say: "Whether you turn to stone or iron, or any other substance 40
you may think unlikely to be given life."

They will ask: "Who will restore us?" 41

Say: "He that created you at first." 42

They will shake their heads at you and ask: "When will this be?" 43

Say: "It may be near at hand. On that day He will summon you 44
all, and you shall answer Him with praises. You shall think that you
have stayed away but for a little while."

Tell My servants to be courteous in their speech. Satan would   45
sow discord among them; Satan is surely the sworn enemy of
man.

Your Lord knows you best. He will show you mercy if He will,   46
and punish you if He pleases.

We have not charged you to be their guardian. Your Lord is best   47
aware of all who dwell in the heaves and the earth.

We have exalted some prophets above others. To David We   48
gave the Psalms.

Say: "Pray if you will to those whom you deify besides Him.   49
They cannot relieve your distress, nor can they change it."

Those to whom they pray, themselves seek to approach their   50
Lord, vying with each other to be near Him. They crave for His
mercy and fear His punishment; for your Lord's punishment is to be
feared indeed.

There is no nation but We shall destroy or sternly punish before   51
the Day of Resurrection. That is decreed in the Eternal Book.

Nothing hinders us from giving signs except that the ancients   52
disbelieved them. To Thamūd We gave the she-camel as a visible
sign, yet they laid violent hands on her. We give signs only by way
of warning.

We have told you that your Lord encompasses mankind. We   53
have made the vision which We showed you, as well as the tree
cursed in the Koran, but a test for men's faith. We seek to put fear in
their hearts, but their wickedness increases.

When We said to the angels: "Prostrate yourselves before   54
Adam," they all prostrated themselves, except Satan, who replied:
"Shall I bow to him whom You have made of clay? Do You see this
being whom You have exalted above me? If You give me respite till
the Day of Resurrection, I will exterminate all but a few of his descendants."

"Begone!" said He. "Hell is your reward, and the reward of those   55
that follow you. An ample reward it shall be. Rouse with your voice
whomever you are able. Muster against them all your forces. Be their
partner in their riches and in their offspring. Promise them what you
will. (Satan promises them only to deceive them.) But over My true
servants you shall have no power. Your Lord will be their all-
sufficient Guardian."

It is your Lord who drives for you the ships across the ocean,   56
so that you may seek His bounty. Surely He is ever merciful towards
you.

When at sea a misfortune befalls you, all but He of those to   57
whom you pray forsake you; yet when He brings you safe to dry
land you turn your backs upon Him. Truly, man is ever thankless.

Are you confident He will not cause the earth to cave in beneath 58
you, or let loose a deadly sand-storm upon you? Then you shall find
none to protect you.

Are you confident that when again you put to sea He will not 59
smite you with a violent tempest and drown you for your thankless-
ness? Then you shall find none to help you.

We have bestowed blessings on Adam's children and guided 60
them by land and sea. We have provided them with good things and
exalted them above many of Our creatures.

The day will surely come when We shall summon every nation 61
with its apostle. Those who are given their books in their right
hands will read their recorded doings, and shall not in the least be
wronged. But those who have been blind in this life, shall be blind
in the life to come and go farther astray.

They sought to entice you from Our revelations—they nearly 62
did—hoping that you might invent some other scripture in Our
name, and thus become their trusted friend. Indeed, had We not
strengthened your faith, you might have made some compromise
with them and thus incurred a double punishment in this life
and in the next. Then you should have found none to help you
against Us.

They sought to provoke you—they nearly did—and thus drive 63
you out of the land. Had they succeeded, they would have scarcely
survived your departure.

Such was Our way with the apostles whom We sent before you. 64
You shall find no change in Our way.

Recite your prayers at sunset, at nightfall, and at dawn; the dawn 65
prayer has its witnesses. Pray during the night as well; an additional
duty, for the fulfilment of which your Lord may exalt you to an honourable station.

Say: "Lord, grant me a goodly entrance and a goodly exit, and 66
sustain me with Your power."

Say: "Truth has come and Falsehood has been over-thrown. 67
Falsehood was bound to be discomfited."

That which We have revealed in the Koran is a balm and a 68
blessing to true believers, though it adds nothing but ruin to the
evil-doers.

When We bestow favours on man, he turns his back and holds 69
aloof. But when evil befalls him, he grows despondent.

Say: "Each man behaves after his own fashion. But your Lord 70
best knows who is best guided."

They put questions to you about the Spirit. Say: "The Spirit is 71
at my Lord's command. Little indeed is the knowledge vouchsafed
to you."

If We pleased We could take away that which We have revealed   72
to you: then you should find none to plead with Us on your behalf.
But your Lord has shown you mercy. His goodness to you has been
great indeed.

Say: "If men and jinn combined to write the like of this Koran,   73
they would surely fail to compose the like, though they helped one
another as best they could."

We have set forth for men in this Koran all manner of argu-   74
ments, yet most of them persist in unbelief. They say: "We will not
believe in you until you make a spring gush from the earth before
our very eyes, or cause rivers to flow in a grove of palms and vines;
until you cause the sky to fall upon us in pieces, as you have threatened to do, or bring down God and the angels in our midst; until
you build a house of gold, or ascend to heaven: nor will we believe
in your ascent until you have sent down for us a book which we can
read."

Say: "Glory to my Lord! Surely I am no more than an apostle   75
made of flesh and blood."

Nothing prevents men from having faith when guidance is re-   76
vealed to them but the excuse: "Can it be that God has sent a human
being as an apostle?"

Say: "Had the earth been safe enough for angels to walk on, We   77
would have sent down to them an angel from heaven as an apostle."

Say: "Sufficient is God as a judge between us. He knows and ob-   78
serves His servants."

Those whom God guides are rightly guided; but those whom   79
He confounds shall find no friend besides Him. We shall gather
them all on the Day of Resurrection, prostrate upon their faces,
blind, dumb, and deaf. Hell shall be their home: whenever its flames
die down We will rekindle them into a greater fire.

Thus shall they be rewarded: because they disbelieved Our rev-   80
elations and said: "When we are turned to bones and dust, shall we
be restored in a new creation?"

Do they not see that God, who has created the heavens and the   81
earth, has power to create their like? Their term He pre-ordained beyond all doubt. Yet the wrongdoers persist in unbelief.

Say: "Had you possessed the treasures of my Lord's mercy, you   82
would have covetously hoarded them. How niggardly is man!"

To Moses We gave nine clear signs. Ask the Israelites how he   83
first appeared among them.

Pharaoh said to him: "Moses, I can see that you are bewitched."   84

"You know full well," he replied, "that none but the Lord of   85
the heavens and the earth has revealed these visible signs. Indeed,
Pharaoh, I can see that you are doomed."

He sought to scare them out of the land: but We drowned him,   86
together with all who were with him. Then We said to the Israelites:
"Dwell in the land. When the promise of the hereafter comes to be
fulfilled, We shall assemble you all together."

We have revealed the Koran with the Truth, and with the Truth   87
it has come down. We have sent you forth only to proclaim good
news and to give warning.

We have divided the Koran into sections so that you may recite   88
it to the people with deliberation. We have imparted it by gradual
revelation.

Say: "It is for you to believe in it or to deny it. Those who were   89
endowed with knowledge before its revelation prostrate themselves
when it is recited and say: 'Glorious is our Lord. Our Lord's promise
has surely been fulfilled.' They fall down upon their faces, weeping;
and as they listen, their humility increases."

Say: "You may call on God or you may call on the Merciful: by   90
whatever name you call on Him, His are the most gracious names."

Pray neither with too loud a voice nor in silence, but, between   91
these extremes, seek a middle course. Say: "Praise be to God who has
never begotten a son; who has no partner in His Kingdom; who needs
none to defend Him from humiliation." Proclaim His greatness.

QUESTIONS FOR CRITICAL READING

1. What does this selection have to say about the soul?
2. What is the function of hell?
3. How important is the role of belief for the individual? What must be
   believed?
4. What is the result of human desire?
5. What promises does God make for the afterlife?
6. What is the function of the "hidden barrier" in paragraph 36?
7. What seems to be the role of Satan?
8. What is the significance of the references to Adam?

SUGGESTIONS FOR WRITING

1. Why in paragraph 18 is the command to serve no other god but God
   conjoined with the command to treat one's parents with extreme respect and care? What do God and one's parents have in common that
   makes it so essential that they be placed together in the most primary
   of commands? Do you feel that respecting one's parents serves a high
   moral purpose? Explain.

2. In paragraph 22 the Koran states, "Your Lord gives abundantly to whom He will and sparingly to whom He pleases. He knows and observes His servants." Offer an interpretation of this statement, explaining what important issues are dealt with in it. If you believed absolutely in this statement, how would your life be altered? If all our politicians believed it, how might our government be altered?

3. A great many of the "injunctions" (see the use of the word in paragraph 31) have to do with property and property rights. They are also closely related to concerns about doing business in honest way. Examine the injunctions that seem to relate to the life of the business person and analyze them for their significance. What can you tell about the business environment of the period when the Koran was written?

4. In paragraph 20 God says, "Do not squander your substance wastefully." What is implied by this injunction? Is it possible that modern people concerned about ecology could take this as a warning from God? What other injunctions that God confers on Muhammad contain ecological implications? Write an essay in which you cite examples from "The Night Journey" to support an ethical use of natural resources.

5. What ethical concerns seem to be foremost in "The Night Journey"? Write an essay in which you establish the proper behavior of people today, using the injunctions in this selection as your basis. According to your interpretation, how would you expect people to behave in their day-to-day lives? To what extent do the injunctions offered here apply to modern life?

6. To what extent does God seem concerned about the happiness of Muhammad and the true believers? What is the nature of the good in this selection? Write an essay in which you clarify the nature of the good as explained in "The Night Journey." What constitutes happiness for those who follow the injunctions outlined in this selection? Is it a happiness you can experience yourself? Explain.

7. **CONNECTIONS** Compare and contrast the injunctions in "The Night Journey" with those in the Sermon on the Mount. How are they similar? How are they different? What concerns raised in "The Night Journey" are not raised in the Sermon on the Mount? Explain.

8. **CONNECTIONS** How does the view of God in "The Night Journey" compare with the view of God in "Moses and the Ten Commandments"? Write an essay in which you describe the qualities of God as set forth in these two selections. What is his relationship with humankind? What are his concerns for humankind? How would you qualify his sense of his own power? What are his attitudes toward Satan?

FRIEDRICH NIETZSCHE
Morality as Anti-Nature

Friedrich Nietzsche (1844–1900), one of the most influential German philosophers, is the man who declared that God is dead (in *The Gay Science*, 1882). The statement came from his conviction that science had altered the balance between humans and nature, that psychology had begun to explain the unconscious mind, and that the commitment to religious belief of earlier times would give way. The result would be to leave people without a sense of hope or purpose unless they could create it for themselves. Like many historians and philosophers of the day, he feared that modern civilization itself was somehow hanging in the balance, and that unless people refashioned the spiritual energy that brought progress and prosperity, the foundations of society would collapse.

In some of his writing he characterized power as the driving force for most people. Two late works that have been influential in modern thought, *Daybreak: Reflections on Moral Prejudices* (1881) and *Thus Spoke Zarathustra* (1883–1885), begin to develop some of his most important thinking regarding what he called "the will to power." His solution to the problem of modernity was self-mastery, which he felt was the key to transcending the confusion of modern thought. Realizing that self-mastery was not an easy state to achieve, he called the man who could create his own moral and ethical values instead of blindly following conventional or societal standards "superman."

Nietzsche's personal life was difficult. Both his grandfathers were Lutheran ministers, and his paternal grandfather was a theological scholar whose book *Gamaliel* (1796) declared the permanency of Christianity. His father was also a Lutheran minister, but

From *The Twilight of the Idols* (1888) in *The Portable Nietzsche*. Translated by Walter Kaufmann.

he died when Friedrich was four years old. He and his younger sister had to leave their family home in the Prussian province of Saxony and live with relatives in Naumberg. When he was fourteen, he went to boarding school and prepared for the University of Bonn (1864), then the University of Leipzig (1865). His studies were in theology and philology—the study of the interpretation of primarily biblical and classical texts. He was also deeply fascinated by music—which he both played and composed—and eventually grew to love the music of Richard Wagner (1813–1883), which he felt expressed the spiritual realities of modern life.

Nietzsche's father died of an unspecified brain ailment. Nietzsche himself was ill much of his life. When he joined the army after university, he experienced a bad accident on a horse that left him weak and impaired. In 1870 during the Franco-Prussian War (1870–1871), Nietzsche served in a hospital unit and witnessed the carnage of war. He contracted illnesses in the wards that stayed with him for the rest of his life. He may have contracted syphilis either during this period or earlier, and in 1889 he began to show signs of brain sickness that made it necessary for him to be in a sanatorium. His mother and later his sister Elizabeth cared for him until his death.

Despite his short life, Nietzsche achieved much. In 1868, at the age of twenty-four, he became a professor of classical philology at the University of Basel in Switzerland. He published a considerable number of important and widely regarded books. *The Birth of Tragedy from the Spirit of Music* (1872), his first book, caught the eye of Wagner and helped establish Nietzsche's reputation. That book was an attempt to clarify the two basic religious forces in humankind: Apollonian intellectuality and Dionysian passion. Apollo was a god of conscience devoted to the arts and music. Dionysius, patron of Greek tragedy, was associated with vegetation, plentifulness, passion, and especially wine—and therefore inspiration. In 1873 Nietzsche published *Unfashionable Observations*, a critique of cultural critics. Before illness forced him to resign his professorship at the University of Basel in 1879, he published *Human, All-Too-Human* (1878), a collection of aphorisms—brief statements ranging from a single line to a page of text. This style, repeated in *Thus Spoke Zarathustra* and other works, became one of the hallmarks of his rhetorical approach. It gave him the appearance of a sage uttering wise sayings.

His production after leaving the university was not diminished. In 1882 he published one of his most impressive books, *The Gay Science*, which postulated an alternative to the Christian view that another world exists after death. His suggestion was known as "eternal recurrence," a view that says we are destined to live this life over and over again down to the slightest detail. The point of this observation was to make people take this life seriously enough to live it so well that they would not mind living it again. The concept of eternal recurrence influenced twentieth-century existentialists, who agreed that the way one lived life was the way one defined oneself.

The Genealogy of Morals (1887) was a critique of contemporary religion, especially Christianity. It emphasized his views about moral and ethical values and rejected the conventional views as being essentially based on an attack on our natural feelings and motives. A section of that book, "Beyond Good and Evil," attempts to neutralize those terms, which he sees as props of conventional religious thought.

The Twilight of the Idols: Or How One Philosophizes with a Hammer (1888), from which this selection is taken and one of his last books, is a careful attack on contemporary religious beliefs and an analysis of important philosophers such as Socrates and Plato as well as of more modern thinkers. Its title is a play on an opera by Wagner called *The Twilight of the Gods* and reveals his essential attitudes toward ethical values as maintained by most religions. Some of his basic views on ethics and morality are in evidence in the selection that follows.

Nietzsche's Rhetoric

"Morality as Anti-Nature" is a careful argument that attempts to prove that moral pronouncements by major religions are designed to stifle people's natural behaviors. According to Nietzsche, people give in to their natural, often destructive impulses because they are weak. Consequently, religions seek to enforce a moral code of conduct by threatening all people—even those who could easily control themselves—with damnation in the next world for any infraction of that code. Nietzsche regards passion as a good thing, but as he states in paragraph 1, "all the old moral monsters" agree that we must kill the passions. He opens by critiquing the Sermon on the Mount, reminding us that "it is said, for example, with particular reference to sexuality: 'If thy eye offend thee, pluck it out.' Fortunately, no Christian acts in accordance with this precept" (para. 1). This is a rhetorical salvo against many of his readers' standard views of religion.

He continues by demonstrating that religions prohibit various forms of sensuality in an effort to promote spirituality, stating,

"The spiritualization of sensuality is called *love*: it represents a great triumph over Christianity" (para. 5). This is an explosive statement, much like others he makes as he develops his argument. He then addresses another passion: hostility. This becomes an interesting political concept when he asserts that the success of the then German government, the Second Reich, depends on having enemies. As he states somewhat ironically in paragraph 5, "Another triumph is our spiritualization of *hostility*. It consists in a profound appreciation of the value of having enemies: in short, it means acting and thinking in the opposite way from that which has been the rule. The church always wanted the destruction of its enemies; we, we immoralists and Antichristians, find our advantage in this, that the church exists." His own writing in this selection demonstrates his position: he is opposed to conventional views of morals, and in order to clarify his own thoughts he needs to have the opposition of the church's views.

One of his rhetorical devices—in addition to the bald oppositional stance he takes in the opening of the selection—is the aphorism. He looks for opportunities to make a clear statement that capsulizes his views. The last sentence in paragraph 8 is an example: "Life has come to an end where the 'kingdom of God' begins." He describes himself as an immoralist—by which he means one who does not subscribe to conventional morals (but not one who acts immorally)—and states, "But we ourselves, we immoralists, are the answer" (para. 12). His most inflammatory aphorism is his last sentence: "Christianity is the metaphysics of the hangman" (para. 28). All this is rather shocking today; imagine what its effect was in 1888.

Among his less sensational rhetorical strategies is his careful enumeration of the elements of his argument. The first six sections examine specific details concerning the moral prohibitions of modern religions. His purpose here is to clarify his title, which he does in paragraph 8 when he states, "*Anti-natural* morality—that is, almost every morality which has so far been taught, revered, and preached—turns, conversely, *against* the instincts of life: it is *condemnation* of these instincts, now secret, now outspoken and impudent."

He then goes on to enumerate what he calls "The Four Great Errors": 1. the error of confusing cause and effect (paras. 13–15); 2. the error of false causality (paras. 16–18); 3. the error of imaginary causes (paras. 19–25); and 4. the error of free will (paras. 26–28). Each of these is treated carefully, sometimes with an example, but always with a clearly developed analysis.

Nietzsche offers modern readers a way of thinking that helps us avoid taking the views of Moses, Aristotle, Jesus, or Muhammad for granted. He provides modern thinkers with a challenge that many have gladly accepted.

PREREADING QUESTIONS: WHAT TO READ FOR

The following prereading questions may help you anticipate key issues in the discussion of Friedrich Nietzsche's "Morality as Anti-Nature." Keeping them in mind during your first reading of the selection should help focus your attention.

- What traditional moral views does Nietzsche attack?
- Why does Nietzsche think religious morals are anti-nature?
- What does Nietzsche say about the confusion of cause and effect?

Morality as Anti-Nature

1

All passions have a phase when they are merely disastrous, when they drag down their victim with the weight of stupidity—and a later, very much later phase when they wed the spirit, when they "spiritualize" themselves. Formerly, in view of the element of stupidity in passion, war was declared on passion itself, its destruction was plotted; all the old moral monsters are agreed on this: *il faut tuer les passions.*[1] The most famous formula for this is to be found in the New Testament, in that Sermon on the Mount, where, incidentally, things are by no means looked at from a height. There it is said, for example, with particular reference to sexuality: "If thy eye offend thee, pluck it out." Fortunately, no Christian acts in accordance with this precept. *Destroying* the passions and cravings, merely as a preventive measure against their stupidity and the unpleasant consequences of this stupidity—today this itself strikes us as merely another acute form of stupidity. We no longer admire dentists who "pluck out" teeth so that they will not hurt any more.

----

[1] *il faut tuer les passions* One must kill the passions.

To be fair, it should be admitted, however, that on the ground   2
out of which Christianity grew, the concept of the "*spiritualization* of
passion" could never have been formed. After all the first church, as is
well known, fought *against* the "intelligent" in favor of the "poor in
spirit." How could one expect from it an intelligent war against passion? The church fights passion with excision in every sense: its practice, its "cure," is *castratism*.[2] It never asks: "How can one spiritualize,
beautify, deify a craving?" It has at all times laid the stress of discipline
on extirpation[3] (of sensuality, of pride, of the lust to rule, of avarice, of
vengefulness). But an attack on the roots of passion means an attack
on the roots of life: the practice of the church is *hostile to life*.

2

The same means in the fight against a craving—castration,   3
extirpation—is instinctively chosen by those who are too weak-willed,
too degenerate, to be able to impose moderation on themselves; by
those who are so constituted that they require *La Trappe*,[4] to use a
figure of speech, or (without any figure of speech) some kind of definitive declaration of hostility, a *cleft* between themselves and the
passion. Radical means are indispensable only for the degenerate;
the weakness of the will—or, to speak more definitely, the inability
not to respond to a stimulus—is itself merely another form of de-
generation. The radical hostility, the deadly hostility against sensuality, is always a symptom to reflect on: it entitles us to suppositions
concerning the total state of one who is excessive in this manner.

This hostility, this hatred, by the way, reaches its climax only   4
when such types lack even the firmness for this radical cure, for this
renunciation of their "devil." One should survey the whole history of
the priests and philosophers, including the artists: the most poisonous things against the senses have been said not by the impotent,
nor by ascetics,[5] but by the impossible ascetics, by those who really
were in dire need of being ascetics.

3

The spiritualization of sensuality is called *love*: it represents a   5
great triumph over Christianity. Another triumph is our spiritualization of *hostility*. It consists in a profound appreciation of the value of
having enemies: in short, it means acting and thinking in the opposite way from that which has been the rule. The church always

---

[2] **castratism** Cutting off.
[3] **extirpation** Rooting out.
[4] ***La Trappe*** The Trappist order of monks. They do not speak.
[5] **ascetics** Those practicing extreme self-discipline, often hermits.

wanted the destruction of its enemies; we, we immoralists and Anti-christians, find our advantage in this, that the church exists. In the po-litical realm too, hostility has now become more spiritual—much more sensible, much more thoughtful, much more *considerate*. Almost every party understands how it is in the interest of its own self-preservation that the opposition should not lose all strength; the same is true of power politics. A new creation in particular—the new *Reich*,[6] for ex-ample—needs enemies more than friends: in opposition alone does it *feel* itself necessary, in opposition alone does it *become* necessary.

Our attitude to the "internal enemy" is no different: here too we   6
have spiritualized hostility; here too we have come to appreciate its value. The price of fruitfulness is to be rich in internal opposition; one remains young only as long as the soul does not stretch itself and desire peace. Nothing has become more alien to us than that desideratum[7] of former times, "peace of soul," the *Christian* desider-atum; there is nothing we envy less than the moralistic cow and the fat happiness of the good conscience. One has renounced the *great* life when one renounces war.

In many cases, to be sure, "peace of soul" is merely a   7
misunderstanding—something else, which lacks only a more hon-est name. Without further ado or prejudice, a few examples. "Peace of soul" can be, for one, the gentle radiation of a rich animality into the moral (or religious) sphere. Or the beginning of weariness, the first shadow of evening, of any kind of evening. Or a sign that the air is humid, that south winds are approaching. Or unrecognized gratitude for a good digestion (sometimes called "love of man"). Or the attain-ment of calm by a convalescent who feels a new relish in all things and waits. Or the state which follows a thorough satisfaction of our domi-nant passion, the well-being of a rare repletion. Or the senile weakness of our will, our cravings, our vices. Or laziness, persuaded by vanity to give itself moral airs. Or the emergence of certainty, even a dreadful certainty, after long tension and torture by uncertainty. Or the expres-sion of maturity and mastery in the midst of doing, creating, working, and willing—calm breathing, *attained* "freedom of the will." *Twilight of the Idols*—who knows? perhaps also only a kind of "peace of soul."

4

I reduce a principle to a formula. Every naturalism in morality—   8
that is, every healthy morality—is dominated by an instinct of life; some commandment of life is fulfilled by a determinate canon of

---

[6] **Reich** The Second Reich, 1871, founded by Wilhelm I as the German Empire.
[7] **desideratum** The thing that is desired.

"shalt" and "shalt not"; some inhibition and hostile element on the path of life is thus removed. *Anti-natural* morality—that is, almost every morality which has so far been taught, revered, and preached—turns, conversely, *against* the instincts of life: it is *condemnation* of these instincts, now secret, now outspoken and impudent. When it says, "God looks at the heart," it says No to both the lowest and the highest desires of life, and posits God as the *enemy of life*. The saint in whom God delights is the ideal eunuch. Life has come to an end where the "kingdom of God" begins.

5

Once one has comprehended the outrage of such a revolt against   9
life as has become almost sacrosanct in Christian morality, one has, fortunately, also comprehended something else: the futility, apparentness, absurdity, and *mendaciousness* of such a revolt. A condemnation of life by the living remains in the end a mere symptom of a certain kind of life: the question whether it is justified or unjustified is not even raised thereby. One would require a position *outside* of life, and yet have to know it as well as one, as many, as all who have lived it, in order to be permitted even to touch the problem of the *value* of life: reasons enough to comprehend that this problem is for us an unapproachable problem. When we speak of values, we speak with the inspiration, with the way of looking at things, which is part of life: life itself forces us to posit values; life itself values through us when we posit values. From this it follows that even that anti-natural morality which conceives of God as the counter-concept and condemnation of life is only a value judgment of life—but of what life? of what kind of life? I have already given the answer: of declining, weakened, weary, condemned life. Morality, as it has so far been understood—as it has in the end been formulated once more by Schopenhauer,[8] as "negation of the will to life"—is the very *instinct of decadence*, which makes an imperative of itself. It says: *"Perish!"* It is a condemnation pronounced by the condemned.

6

Let us finally consider how naïve it is altogether to say: "Man   10
ought to be such and such!" Reality shows us an enchanting wealth of types, the abundance of a lavish play and change of forms—and some wretched loafer of a moralist comments: "No! Man ought to be different." He even knows what man should be like, this

---

[8]**Arthur Schopenhauer (1788–1860)** German philosopher who believed reality was nothing but senseless will, having no divine origin.

wretched bigot and prig: he paints himself on the wall and comments, "*Ecce homo!*"[9] But even when the moralist addresses himself only to the single human being and says to him, "You ought to be such and such!" he does not cease to make himself ridiculous. The single human being is a piece of *fatum*[10] from the front and from the rear, one law more, one necessity more for all that is yet to come and to be. To say to him, "Change yourself!" is to demand that everything be changed, even retroactively. And indeed there have been consistent moralists who wanted man to be different, that is, virtuous—they wanted him remade in their own image, as a prig: to that end, they *negated* the world! No small madness! No modest kind of immodesty!

Morality, insofar as it *condemns* for its own sake, and *not* out of   11
regard for the concerns, considerations, and contrivances of life, is a specific error with which one ought to have no pity—an *idiosyncrasy of degenerates* which has caused immeasurable harm.

We others, we immoralists, have, conversely, made room in our   12
hearts for every kind of understanding, comprehending, and *approving*. We do not easily negate; we make it a point of honor to be *affirmers*. More and more, our eyes have opened to that economy which needs and knows how to utilize all that the holy witlessness of the priest, of the *diseased* reason in the priest, rejects—that economy in the law of life which finds an advantage even in the disgusting species of the prigs, the priests, the virtuous. *What* advantage? But we ourselves, we immoralists, are the answer.

The Four Great Errors

1

The error of confusing cause and effect. There is no more dangerous   13
error than that of mistaking the effect for the cause: I call it the real corruption of reason. Yet this error belongs among the most ancient and recent habits of mankind: it is even hallowed among us and goes by the name of "religion" or "morality." Every single sentence which religion and morality formulate contains it; priests and legislators of moral codes are the originators of this corruption of reason.

I give an example. Everybody knows the book of the famous   14
Cornaro[11] in which he recommends his slender diet as a recipe for a

---

[9] ***Ecce homo!*** Behold this man!

[10] ***fatum*** Prophecy, declaration.

[11] **Luigi Cornaro (1467–1566)** A Venetian who lived on a restricted diet. *The Sure and Certain Method of Attaining a Long and Healthful Life* (1550) was published when he was 83.

long and happy life—a virtuous one too. Few books have been read so much; even now thousands of copies are sold in England every year. I do not doubt that scarcely any book (except the Bible, as is meet) has done as much harm, has *shortened* as many lives, as this well-intentioned *curiosum*. The reason: the mistaking of the effect for the cause. The worthy Italian thought his diet was the *cause* of his long life, whereas the precondition for a long life, the extraordinary slowness of his metabolism, the consumption of so little, was the cause of his slender diet. He was not free to eat little *or* much; his frugality was not a matter of "free will": he became sick when he ate more. But whoever is no carp not only does well to eat properly, but needs to. A scholar in our time, with his rapid consumption of nervous energy, would simply destroy himself with Cornaro's diet. *Crede experto.*[12]

2

The most general formula on which every religion and morality   15 is founded is: "Do this and that, refrain from this and that—then you will be happy! Otherwise . . ." Every morality, every religion, *is* this imperative; I call it the great original sin of reason, the *immortal unreason*. In my mouth, this formula is changed into its opposite—first example of my "revaluation of all values": a well-turned-out human being, a "happy one," *must* perform certain actions and shrinks instinctively from other actions; he carries the order, which he represents physiologically, into his relations with other human beings and things. In a formula: his virtue is the *effect* of his happiness. A long life, many descendants—this is not the wages of virtue; rather virtue itself is that slowing down of the metabolism which leads, among other things, also to a long life, many descendants—in short, to *Cornarism.* . . .

3

The error of a false causality. People have believed at all times that   16 they knew what a cause is; but whence did we take our knowledge—or more precisely, our faith that we had such knowledge? From the realm of the famous "inner facts," of which not a single one has so far proved to be factual. We believed ourselves to be causal in the act of willing: we thought that here at least we caught causality in the act. Nor did one doubt that all the antecedents of an act, its causes, were to be sought in consciousness and would be found there once sought—as "motives": else one would not have

---

[12] **Crede experto** Believe him who has tried!

been free and responsible for it. Finally, who would have denied that a thought is caused? that the ego causes the thought?

Of these three "inward facts" which seem to guarantee causality, the first and most persuasive is that of the will as cause. The conception of a consciousness ("spirit") as a cause, and later also that of the ego as cause (the "subject"), are only afterbirths: first the causality of the will was firmly accepted as given, as *empirical*.   17

Meanwhile we have thought better of it. Today we no longer believe a word of all this. The "inner world" is full of phantoms and will-o'-the-wisps: the will is one of them. The will no longer moves anything, hence does not explain anything either—it merely accompanies events; it can also be absent. The so-called *motive*: another error. Merely a surface phenomenon of consciousness, something alongside the deed that is more likely to cover up the antecedents of the deeds than to represent them. And as for the *ego!* That has become a fable, a fiction, a play on words: it has altogether ceased to think, feel, or will! . . .   18

4

The error of imaginary causes. To begin with dreams: *ex post facto*,[13] a cause is slipped under a particular sensation (for example, one following a far-off cannon shot)—often a whole little novel in which the dreamer turns up as the protagonist. The sensation endures meanwhile in a kind of resonance: it waits, as it were, until the causal instinct permits it to step into the foreground—now no longer as a chance occurrence, but as "meaning." The cannon shot appears in a *causal* mode, in an apparent reversal of time. What is really later, the motivation, is experienced first—often with a hundred details which pass like lightning—and the shot *follows*. What has happened? The representations which were *produced* by a certain state have been misunderstood as its causes.   19

In fact, we do the same thing when awake. Most of our general feelings—every kind of inhibition, pressure, tension, and explosion in the play and counterplay of our organs, and particularly the state of the *nervus sympathicus*[14]—excite our causal instinct: we want to have a reason for feeling this way or that—for feeling bad or for feeling good. We are never satisfied merely to state the fact that we feel this way or that: we admit this fact only—become conscious of it only—when we have furnished some kind of motivation. Memory, which swings into action in such cases, unknown to us, brings   20

---

[13] *ex post facto* After the fact.
[14] *nervus sympathicus* System of sympathetic nerves that gives us a "gut feeling."

up earlier states of the same kind, together with the causal interpretations associated with them—not their real causes. The faith, to be
sure, that such representations, such accompanying conscious processes, are the causes, is also brought forth by memory. Thus originates a habitual acceptance of a particular causal interpretation,
which, as a matter of fact, inhibits any investigation into the real
cause—even precludes it.

5

The psychological explanation of this. To derive something un-   21
known from something familiar relieves, comforts, and satisfies, besides giving a feeling of power. With the unknown, one is confronted
with danger, discomfort, and care; the first instinct is to abolish these
painful states. First principle: any explanation is better than none.
Since at bottom it is merely a matter of wishing to be rid of oppressive representations, one is not too particular about the means of
getting rid of them: the first representation that explains the unknown
as familiar feels so good that one "considers it true." The proof of
pleasure ("of strength") as a criterion of truth.

The causal instinct is thus conditional upon, and excited by,   22
the feeling of fear. The "why?" shall, if at all possible, not give the
cause for its own sake so much as for *a particular kind of cause*—
a cause that is comforting, liberating, and relieving. That it is something already familiar, experienced, and inscribed in the memory,
which is posited as a cause, that is the first consequence of this need.
That which is new and strange and has not been experienced before,
is excluded as a cause. Thus one searches not only for some kind of
explanation to serve as a cause, but for a particularly selected and
preferred kind of explanation—that which has most quickly and
most frequently abolished the feeling of the strange, new, and hitherto unexperienced: the *most habitual* explanations. Consequence:
one kind of positing of causes predominates more and more, is concentrated into a system, and finally emerges as *dominant*, that is, as
simply precluding other causes and explanations. The banker immediately thinks of "business," the Christian of "sin," and the girl of
her love.

6

The whole realm of morality and religion belongs under this concept of   23
imaginary causes. The "explanation" of *disagreeable* general feelings.
They are produced by beings that are hostile to us (evil spirits: the
most famous case—the misunderstanding of the hysterical as witches).
They are produced by acts which cannot be approved (the feeling of
"sin," of "sinfulness," is slipped under a physiological discomfort; one

always finds reasons for being dissatisfied with oneself). They are produced as punishments, as payment for something we should not have done, for what we should not have *been* (impudently generalized by Schopenhauer into a principle in which morality appears as what it really is—as the very poisoner and slanderer of life: "Every great pain, whether physical or spiritual, declares what we deserve; for it could not come to us if we did not deserve it." *World as Will and Representation* II, 666). They are produced as effects of ill-considered actions that turn out badly. (Here the affects, the senses, are posited as causes, as "guilty"; and physiological calamities are interpreted with the help of other calamities as "deserved.")

The "explanation" of *agreeable* general feelings. They are produced by trust in God. They are produced by the consciousness of good deeds (the so-called "good conscience"—a physiological state which at times looks so much like good digestion that it is hard to tell them apart). They are produced by the successful termination of some enterprise (a naïve fallacy: the successful termination of some enterprise does not by any means give a hypochondriac or a Pascal[15] agreeable general feelings). They are produced by faith, charity, and hope—the Christian virtues. 24

In truth, all these supposed explanations are resultant states and, as it were, translations of pleasurable or unpleasurable feelings into a false dialect: one is in a state of hope *because* the basic physiological feeling is once again strong and rich; one trusts in God *because* the feeling of fullness and strength gives a sense of rest. Morality and religion belong altogether to the *psychology of error*: in every single case, cause and effect are confused; or truth is confused with the effects of *believing* something to be true; or a state of consciousness is confused with its causes. 25

7

The error of free will. Today we no longer have any pity for the concept of "free will": we know only too well what it really is—the foulest of all theologians' artifices, aimed at making mankind "responsible" in their sense, that is, *dependent upon them.* Here I simply supply the psychology of all "making responsible." 26

Wherever responsibilities are sought, it is usually the instinct of wanting to judge and punish which is at work. Becoming has been deprived of its innocence when any being-such-and-such is traced back to will, to purposes, to acts of responsibility: the doctrine of the will has been invented essentially for the purpose of punishment, 27

---

[15]**Blaise Pascal (1623–1662)** French mathematician and scientist.

that is, because one wanted to impute guilt. The entire old psychology, the psychology of will, was conditioned by the fact that its originators, the priests at the head of ancient communities, wanted to create for themselves the right to punish—or wanted to create this right for God. Men were considered "free" so that they might be judged and punished—so that they might become *guilty:* consequently, every act had to be considered as willed, and the origin of every act had to be considered as lying within the consciousness (and thus the most fundamental counterfeit *in psychologicis* was made the principle of psychology itself).

Today, as we have entered into the reverse movement and we   28
immoralists are trying with all our strength to take the concept of guilt and the concept of punishment out of the world again, and to cleanse psychology, history, nature, and social institutions and sanctions of them, there is in our eyes no more radical opposition than that of the theologians, who continue with the concept of a "moral world-order" to infect the innocence of becoming by means of "punishment" and "guilt." Christianity is a metaphysics of the hangman.

QUESTIONS FOR CRITICAL READING

1. What does Nietzsche mean when he says that passions "drag down their victim" (para. 1)?
2. Why does he claim there is a war on the passions?
3. Why does Nietzsche make several references to stupidity in the opening paragraph?
4. Is there such a thing as a spiritualization of passion?
5. Why does Nietzsche consider moderation an important quality?
6. In what sense is love a spiritualization of sensuality?
7. What is "the internal enemy" (para. 6)?
8. Is there such a thing as "healthy morality" (para. 8)?
9. What is Nietzsche's view of the Ten Commandments?

SUGGESTIONS FOR WRITING

1. Assume you are writing for an audience that knows a bit about Nietzsche but has not read this selection. Write an essay in which you clarify Nietzsche's attitudes toward conventional morality and explain why he feels it is anti-nature. Also explain his attitude toward people who, because they have no self-control, cannot keep themselves from acting in degenerate ways.

2. Do you think Nietzsche is correct in assuming that morality is anti-nature? Use other texts from this section of the book in your argument to help you convince your readers. Be sure to define the term "anti-nature" as carefully as possible.

3. What might Nietzsche's moral views be? It is clear that he does not intend to behave unethically as a result of his analysis of the moral views he condemns. But he does not go into detail about the moral position he might take. He talks about affirming life. How would this translate into an ethical position and thus into a clear moral purpose in life? Do you think he plans to live a moral life, or will he just do as he pleases? Explain.

4. Assuming that Nietzsche is correct that conventional morality is against our natural expression of passions, argue a case that suggests that while he is correct, the truth is that people must be restricted in their natural expression. Which moral statements clearly recognize dangerous natural inclinations and restrict them? What benefits do these restrictions provide to the individual as well as to society as a whole? How might Nietzsche react to your argument?

5. Do you believe Nietzsche is accurate when he declares in paragraph 15 that "every religion and morality" is founded on a general principle of "Do this and that, refrain from this and that—then you will be happy!"? Is he simply misreading the teachings of religion? Write an essay in which you take issue with or agree with Nietzsche's premise and conclusions.

6. In paragraphs 19 and 20 Nietzsche discusses the "error of imaginary causes." Are there instances in your own life when you made the mistake of assigning imaginary causes to effects you observed? If your examples have a moral implication, be sure to clarify the nature of the error and decide whether or not your experience helps to reinforce Nietzsche's argument or weaken it.

7. **CONNECTIONS** Examine "Moses and the Ten Commandments," the Sermon on the Mount, and "The Night Journey" to see if the views on morality they present are anti-nature, as Nietzsche claims. Do you agree with Nietzsche's position that these texts advocate behaviors that go against the natural forces of life? Are these the views of moral "hangmen"? Explain.

8. **CONNECTIONS** How would Niccolò Machiavelli respond to Nietzsche's argument? Would he agree or disagree with Nietzsche about morals promoted by the church? What might Machiavelli, in the light of reading Nietzsche, recommend as a moral path for the Prince? What would Nietzsche have to say about Machiavelli's Prince? Would he approve or disapprove of him? Why?

IRIS MURDOCH
Morality and Religion

IRIS MURDOCH (1919–1999) was born in Dublin, Ireland, but her family soon moved to London, where she grew up. Most people know Murdoch as one of the most important novelists in English in the twentieth century. She wrote twenty-six novels that explore interesting aspects of philosophy and psychology. She once said that while she distrusted psychoanalysis, she felt that she was analyzing herself in her novels. Critics have considered her one of the most important literary figures of her time.

Her early schooling prepared her for a degree in Oxford in classics and philosophy. In the 1930s she became a member of the Communist Party, but she soon rejected its principles and resigned from the party before World War II. During the war, she worked in the British Treasury offices, and afterwards she spent time in Belgium and Austria working with the United Nations Relief organization. Murdoch then spent a year trying to sort her life out. She had been given a scholarship to study at Vassar College, but could not get a visa because of her communist past. Eventually, in 1947, she accepted a studentship at Newnham College, Cambridge, to study philosophy under Ludwig Wittgenstein (1889–1951), one of the age's most influential philosophers. The next year she was elected Fellow of St. Anne's College, Oxford, and remained as a tutor (essentially a professor) until she retired in 1963 to write full time.

She won a number of important prizes for her literary work. Her novel *The Sea, The Sea* won Britain's most prestigious literary award, the Booker Prize, in 1978. The Divinity School at the University of Chicago honored her for "the religious depth of her novels" in 1992. Among the most important and interesting of her novels are *The Flight from the Enchanter* (1956), *The Red and the Green*

From *Metaphysics as a Guide to Morals*.

(1956), *The Black Prince* (1973), *The Sacred and Profane Love Machine* (1974), *The Book and the Brotherhood* (1987), and *The Green Knight* (1993).

In addition to novels, Iris Murdoch also wrote a number of influential philosophical studies. Her first book, *Sartre, Romantic Rationalist* (1953), resulted from her meeting Jean-Paul Sartre (1905–1980) in the 1940s and her interest in existentialism. *The Sovereignty of Good and Other Concepts* (1967) is considered a work of first importance in moral studies. *Metaphysics as a Guide to Morals* (1992) developed from the Gifford Lectures she gave at the University of Edinburgh in 1981–82. Her last book, *Existentialists and Mystics: Writings on Philosophy and Literature* (1997), was published near the end of her life when she was suffering from the final stages of Alzheimer's disease.

Murdoch's impressive work *Metaphysics as a Guide to Morals*, from which the following selection is taken, deals with how we interpret and understand the nature of morals. One of the questions she addresses is whether there can be a true moral position outside the confines of religion. Murdoch weighs the arguments on both sides of the issue and lets her readers decide how to resolve them. She herself thrived on contradictions and saw them as energy for understanding.

Murdoch's Rhetoric

The first thing one notices about Murdoch's writing is that she relies on very long paragraphs. Each paragraph addresses a position on how religion and morality are related. She does not pose an overarching argument, but how religion affects what we think of as moral behavior is one of the issues she pursues.

Another aspect of her writing is her many references to philosophers such as Kant, Plato, Bentham, and Wittgenstein, and to historical events such as the Cultural Revolution in Mao's China and the murder of kulaks—wealthy farmers—in Stalin's Soviet Union. But these are not essential to our understanding of the issues she discusses.

She begins in paragraph 2 with a consideration of the nature of virtue, which she sees as "[t]he most evident bridge between morality and religion." Yet there are problems with the very idea of virtue, as she points out. For some people in the modern world, the word *virtue* has lost its positive meaning and is related to rigidity and priggishness. Moreover, it is not capable of being applied universally to people because "fear, misery, deprivation" (para. 2) will alter the nature of virtue in people who experience those conditions. Those who suffer from hunger or political oppression may not have much interest in conventional bourgeois theories of virtue. Therefore, Murdoch suggests, virtue may be a relative concept rather than a fixed idea.

In paragraph 3 she continues her discussion of virtue but adds the concept of duty, a sense of obligation that is understood in a social context. According to Murdoch, "Dutifulness could be an account of a morality with no hint of religion" (para. 3). In this extensive paragraph Murdoch explores the idea of duty, connecting it to eighteenth-century principles of reason, showing that duty and reason fit together rather well. One understands one's duty to others, institutions, and nations, and one performs one's duty without religious intervention. Is that then a virtuous action? Is the performance of duty then irrelevant to the moral views of religion? As she says at the end of the paragraph, after exploring the issue it may be time to refer back to the "clear, rigid rules" of religions to find answers to these questions.

In paragraph 4 Murdoch contrasts secular idealism with religious belief. The question is whether one of these is more likely to produce moral good than the other. Is morality, she continually asks, dependent on religion, or can it be achieved outside religion? She points out a conundrum that continues in modern life: the criminal who constantly breaks the law and yet has a deep religious conviction. She criticizes religion indirectly by examining its nonrational elements, those of pure faith. But near the end of the paragraph she says, "Religion symbolizes high moral ideas which then travel with us and are more intimately and accessibly effective than the unadorned promptings of reason" (para. 4).

In paragraph 5 she begins to discuss the diary of Francis Kilvert (1840–1879), a simple clergyman who found in his rural community moments of intense beauty and moral uprightness. Kilvert is likened to another cleric, Julian of Norwich, who arrives at a deeply philosophical understanding when she holds a "little thing, the size of a hazel nut, which seemed to lie in the palm of my hand; and it was as round as any ball" (para. 5), and in it she saw a metaphor for the wholeness of creation, a sense that was at root a deep religious experience. Murdoch interprets this as a way of exhibiting "God's love for the world" (para. 5).

In paragraph 6 Murdoch proceeds to include religious philosophers such as Søren Kierkegaard (1813–1855), whose views on religion and morality are complex and not easily untangled. Her discussion reaches into the question of whether God exists and the Ontological Proof, a proof of God's existence that dates to the Middle

Ages. The proof asserts that we can imagine a perfect being, God, and that because we can imagine it, it must exist because perfection is consistent only with actual existence. Murdoch puts it this way: "Guilt, especially deep apparently incurable guilt, can be one of the worst of human pains. To cure such an ill, because of human sin, God *must* exist" (para. 6).

In her final paragraph Murdoch explores mysticism, which implies having a direct spiritual experience of God, achieved through prayer, religious discipline, fasting, or a variety of ascetic practices similar to meditation. As she says in her opening sentence, "Religion (even if 'primitive') is generally assumed to be in some sense moral. Mysticism is also assumed to be, by definition, moral" (para. 7). However, despite this assurance, she also points out that in some ages, such as the eighteenth-century Enlightenment period, "institutionalized religion [was] an enemy of morality, an enemy of freedom and free thought, guilty of cruelty and repression" (para. 7). In the remainder of this paragraph she attempts to work out some of the obvious conflicts inherent in these statements.

She ends with an interesting discussion of the relationship of two contradictory forces in the universe: good and evil. As she states in a rather paradoxical fashion: "Discord is essential to goodness" (para. 7). In other words, there can only be a concept of morality in an environment in which there is evil *and* goodness. Murdoch points out that "both morality and religion face the same insuperable difficulty": that if the goal of eradicating evil is achieved "the struggle, the need for devotion, would cease to be real. . . . If there is to be morality, there cannot altogether be an end to evil" (para. 7).

PREREADING QUESTIONS: WHAT TO READ FOR

The following prereading questions may help you anticipate key issues in the discussion of Iris Murdoch's "Morality and Religion." Keeping them in mind during your first reading of the selection should help focus your attention.

- How is the idea of virtue a bridge between religion and morality?
- In what senses do religion and morality seem to be different?
- Is morality impossible without religion?

Morality and Religion

In the background of many of these arguments lies a question   1
about the relation of morality to religion, the difference between
them, and the definition of religion. I have already suggested that
my whole argument can be read as moral philosophy. In any case
moral philosophy must include this dimension whether we call it religion or not. Someone may say that there is only one way to "acquire" religion and that is through being taught it as a small child.
You have to breathe it in. It is an ineffable attitude to the world which
cannot really be discussed. People who take up religion as adults are
merely playing at it, it remains at a level of illusion. So someone
could speak, being either a believer or an unbeliever. The unbeliever
might add that religion is imbibed in childhood, when it forms part
of the infantile child–parent relationship now well-known to psychology; only religion, being a soothing drug, is less easy to give up
in later life.

The most evident bridge between morality and religion is the   2
idea of virtue. Virtue is still treated in some quarters as something
precious to be positively pursued; yet the concept has also faded,
even tending to fall apart between "idealism" and "priggishness." It
may be seen as a self-indulgent luxury. It has, perhaps has always
had, many enemies. Fear of a perverted ideology or of a too fervent
"enthusiasm" may prevent a positive conception of virtue. Cynicism
and materialism and *dolce vita*[1] can occlude it, also fear, misery, deprivation and loss of concepts. Even in a religious context "personal
spirituality" may be something that has to be argued for. A utilitarian morality[2] may treat a concern with becoming virtuous as a waste
of energy which should be transmitted directly to the alleviation of
suffering. Of course numerous people are virtuous without thinking
about it, and sages may say that, if thought about, it may *ipso facto*[3]
diminish. A saint may perhaps be good by instinct and nature,
though saintly figures are also revered as reformed sinners. Perhaps
the word itself begins to seem pretentious and old-fashioned.

An idea (concept) of virtue which need not be formally reflective   3
or clarified bears some resemblance to religion, so that one might say
either that it is a shadow of religion, or religion is a shadow of it. The

---

[1] *dolce vita* The sweet life; the irresponsible life.
[2] **utilitarian morality** Utilitarianism professed a creed of the greatest good for
the greatest number and would insist that any moral principle produce the greatest
happiness and the least pain for all involved.
[3] *ipso facto* By the very fact itself.

demand that we should be virtuous or try to become good is something that goes beyond explicit calls of duty. One can of course extend the idea of duty into the area of generalised goodness (virtuous living) by making it a duty always to have pure thoughts and good motives. For reasons I have suggested I would rather keep the concept of duty nearer to its ordinary sense as something fairly strict, recognisable, intermittent, so that we can say that there may be time off from the call of duty, but no time off from the demand of good. These are conceptual problems which are important in the building up of a picture; that is, an overall extension of the idea of duty would blur a valuable distinction, and undermine the particular function of the concept. Duty then I take to be formal obligation, relating to occasions where it can be to some extent clarified. ("Why go?" "I promised." "Why go?" "He's an old friend." "Why go?" "Well, it's somehow that sort of situation.") Duty may be easily performed without strain or reflection, but may also prompt the well-known experience of the frustration of desire together with a sense of necessity to act, wherein there is a proper place for the concept of *will*. Dutifulness could be an account of a morality with no hint of religion. The rational formality of moral maxims made to govern particular situations might make them seem like separated interrupted points of insight rather than like a light which always shines. This could be a picture of human life. Yet Kant[4] also portrays us as *belonging* at every second to the noumenal world of rationality and freedom, the separated pure source. We are orderly because duty is duty, yet also behind the exercise of it we might (surely, after all) glimpse the inspiring light of pure goodness which Kant calls Reason, and sometimes even God. Beyond all this we may picture a struggle in Kant's religious soul over the concept of Reason, so essential, yet so awkward. The rationality (Pure Reason) which enables us to deal with objects and causes *must* be related to that (Practical Reason) which enables us to deal with right and wrong. Well, the concept of truth can relate them. . . . Perhaps Kant felt no awkwardness—it is we who feel awkward, when we connect morality with love and desire. Certainly it does seem possible to set up a contrast between the dutiful man and the virtuous man which is different from the contrast between the dutiful man and the religious man. Here we may think of Christ saying render unto Caesar what is Caesar's. Duty as order, relating morals to politics. Good decent men lead orderly

---

[4]**Immanuel Kant (1724–1804)** German philosopher who linked pure reason and experiential knowledge. *Noumenal* is a Kantian term that refers to the unknowable world as it is in itself. According to Kant, we can only know the world as it appears to us, as a phenomenon. We can never know it as it is in itself, as a noumenon.

lives. It might also be said in this context that given the abysmal sin-fulness of humans, only a strict list of rules can keep them from mu-tual destruction! The moral (or spiritual) life is both one and not one. There is the idea of a sovereign good, but there are also com-partments, obligations, rules, aims, whose identity may have to be respected. These separate aspects or modes of behaviour occasion some of the most difficult kinds of moral problems, as if we have to move between *styles*, or to change gear. We have to live a sin-gle moral existence, and also to retain the separate force of various kinds of moral vision. Jeanie Deans in Scott's novel[5] loves her sister, but cannot lie to save her life. Isabella in *Measure for Measure* will not save her brother by yielding her chastity to Angelo. Duty is one thing, love is another. These are dramatic examples; one can invent many more homely ones of the conflict of moral requirements of en-tirely different kinds, wherein one seems to have to choose between being two different kinds of person. This may be a choice between two paths in life, or it may be some everyday matter demanding an in-stant response. We tend to feel that these dissimilar demands and states of mind must somehow connect, there must be a deep con-nection, it must all somehow make a unified sense; this is a religious craving, God sees it all. What I earlier called axioms[6] are moral enti-ties whose force must not be overcome by, or dissolved into, other moral streams: a requirement in liberal politics. Axioms may not "win" but must remain in consideration, a Benthamite[7] utilitarian conception of happiness must not, as a frequently relevant feature, be eroded by high-minded considerations about quality of happi-ness or by theories which make happiness invisible, or of course by political objectives. (The Cultural Revolution, the liquidation of the kulaks.[8]) Equally of course, degraded or evil pleasure cannot count as simple or silly happiness. Such complexities, involving conflicts of moral discernment and moral style, are with us always. So, "keeping everything in mind" is not an easy matter in morals. This may be an argument for clear rigid rules. Modern clerics who

---

[5]**Scott's novel** *The Heart of Mid-Lothian* (1818) by Sir Walter Scott (1771–1832).

[6]**axioms** Statements of truth, as in geometry.

[7]**Benthamite: Jeremy Bentham (1748–1832)** proposed a scheme of "private ethics" in which the aim of one's actions should be to cause the greatest pleasure and least pain. He was influential in developing English Utilitarianism.

[8]**The Cultural Revolution . . . kulaks** The Cultural Revolution (1966–1976), begun by Mao Zedong (1893–1976), chairman of the Chinese communist party, was a period of political zealotry characterized by purges of intellectuals and anticommunists. The kulaks were relatively wealthy farmers who opposed Soviet collectivization of their land. Joseph Stalin (1879–1953), Soviet premier, sought to execute or deport the kulaks, whom he maligned as "exploiters."

do not feel able to tell newly married couples to be virtuous, tell them to have a sense of humour. This shift is a telling case of a change of style.

Religious belief may be a stronger motive to good conduct   4 than non-religious idealism. Corrupt immoral persons (for instance hardened criminals) who cheerfully break all the "moral rules," may retain the religious images of their childhood which can, at some juncture, affect their conduct. This idea has been (not unsentimentally) dealt with in various novels and films. Indeed, this retention of images, and sensibility to images, might suggest the importance of a religious childhood. (Is it easier to get out of religion, or to get in?) Parents who have had such a childhood themselves, but have "given up religion," may often think along these lines. A kind of sensible well-meaning tolerance is involved here. But, a sterner breed may say, what about *truth*? Religion just *isn't* true. A religious man, even a goodish one, is spoilt and flawed by irrational superstitious convictions; and it is held to be ridiculous for lapsed parents to let their innocent children be tainted with beliefs which the parents know to be false. It is no use talking of a "good atmosphere," what is fundamentally at stake is *truth*. Such arguments come near to familiar problems of today. Is the non-religious good man so like the religious good man that it is merely some point of terminology or superficial style which is at issue? Orthodoxly religious people often tolerantly compliment the unbeliever by saying, "He is *really* a true Christian"; which may well annoy the unbeliever. More positively attempting a distinction to form part of a definition, it might be suggested that religion is a form of heightened consciousness (Matthew Arnold[9] said it was "morality touched by emotion"), it is intense and highly toned, it is about what is deep, what is holy, what is absolute, the emotional imaginative image-making faculties are engaged, the whole man is engaged. Every moment matters, there is no time off. High morality without religion is too abstract, high morality craves for religion. Religion symbolises high moral ideas which then travel with us and are more intimately and accessibly effective than the unadorned promptings of reason. Religion suits the image-making human animal. Think what the image of Christ has done for us through centuries. Can such images *lie*? Do we not indeed adjust our attitudes to them, as time passes, so as to "make them true"? This continuous adjustment is an aspect of the history of religion.

---

[9]**Matthew Arnold (1822–1888)** Prominent English poet and social commentator.

I intended here, thinking about holiness and reverence, not the 5 exclusive property of believers, to quote from Francis Kilvert's[10] Diary (begun in 1870). Kilvert was a parson in country parishes on the Welsh border, a religious good man of simple faith. However, it is difficult to quote from the Diary because of the transparent artless lucidity of Kilvert's account of his days. Any particular quotation can sound naive, or sentimental. "I went to see my dear little lover Mary Tavener, the deaf and half dumb child. When I opened the door of the poor crazy old cottage in the yard the girl uttered a passionate inarticulate cry of joy and running to me flung her arms about my neck and covered me with kisses." (12 June 1875.) "Old William Price sat in his filthy den, unkempt, unshaven, shaggy and grey like a wild beast, and if possible filthier than the den. I read to him Faber's hymn of the Good Shepherd. He was much struck with it. 'That's what He has been telling me,' said the old man." (26 January 1872.) "The road was very still. No one seemed to be passing and the birds sang late and joyfully in the calm mild evening as if they thought it must be spring. A white mist gathered in the valley and hung low along the winding course of the river mingled with the rushing of the brooks, the distant voices of children at play came floating at intervals across the river and near at hand a pheasant screeched now and then and clapped its wings or changed his roost from tree to tree like a man turning in bed before he falls asleep." (27 January 1872.) Kilvert spent his days walking all over his terri- tory, visiting everyone, noticing everything (people, animals, birds, flowers) and describing it all in simple humble extremely readable detail. "How delightful on these sweet summer evenings to wander from cottage to cottage and farm to farm." It may be said that Kilvert was lucky, but also that he deserved his luck. There is a serene light and a natural kindly selfless love of people and of nature in what he writes. He felt secure. He had faith. Wittgenstein[11] was struck by a character in a play who seemed to him to feel safe, nothing that hap- pened could harm him. Wittgenstein's "Ontological Proof" or "state- ment" (*Tractatus* 6.41) places the sense of the world outside the

---

[10] **Francis Kilvert (1840–1879)** An English clergyman and diarist. Although after his death his widow destroyed many of his notebooks, the remainder were dis- covered by William Plomer (1903–1973), a South African writer, and published in 1938 and 1940.

[11] **Ludwig Wittgenstein (1889–1951)** Murdoch's philosophy professor. His *Tractatus* approaches problems of language in describing philosophical ideas. His concept of the "world outside of the world" implies that we imaginatively observe the world outside itself, much as we observe ourselves. Thus the "little thing" be- comes an observable metaphor for a little world.

world, outside *all* of the contingent facts. Thinking of Wittgenstein's picture of the world (all the facts) as a self-contained sphere, a sort of steel ball, outside which ineffable value roams, we might look at something similar but different. "He showed me a little thing, the size of a hazel nut, which seemed to lie in the palm of my hand; and it was as round as any ball. I looked upon it with my eye of understanding, and thought 'What may this be?' I was answered in a general way thus: 'It is all that is made.' I wondered how long it could last, for it seemed as though it might suddenly fade away to nothing, it was so small. And I was answered in my understanding: 'It lasts and ever shall last, for God loveth it. And even so hath everything being, by the love of God.'" (Julian of Norwich,[12] *Revelations of Divine Love*, chapter 5.) Julian's showing, besides exhibiting God's love for the world, also indicates our absolute dependence as created things. We are nothing, we owe our being to something not ourselves. We are enlivened from a higher source.

Kierkegaard[13] would object to a moral–religious continuum. 6 We, existing individuals, therefore sinners, feel guilt, feel in need of salvation, to be reborn into a new being. "If any man be in Christ he is a new creature: old things are passed away, behold all things are become new." (2 Corinthians 5:17.) In Kierkegaard's version of Hegelian dialectic[14] it is not endlessly evolving toward totality, but is a picture of levels in the soul, or of different kinds of people, or of the pilgrimage of a particular person. The aesthetic individual is private, the ethical man, including the tragic hero, is public, the religious individual, the man of faith, is once more private. This dramatic triad also suggests the dangerous link between the two private stages, the aesthetic and the religious, so deeply unlike, so easily confused. The idea of repentance and leading a better cleansed and renewed life is a generally understood moral idea; and the, however presented, granting of absolution, God's forgiveness, keeps many people inside religion, or invites them to enter. Guilt, especially deep apparently incurable guilt, can be one of the worst of

---

[12]**Julian of Norwich (1332–1416?)** English mystic and writer. Her book *Revelations of Divine Love* recounts her mystical religious experiences.

[13]**Søren Kierkegaard (1813–1855)** Danish philosopher whose concept of "Either/Or" explored the choice between an ethical life or one that ignored ethics.

[14]**Hegelian dialectic** Postulates that the conflict of two opposites ultimately resolves itself through synthesis (a third option). Georg Wilhelm Friedrich Hegel (1770–1831), a German philosopher, has been enormously influential on all modern philosophers. He felt that humans experienced a constant and irreconcilable conflict of reason and emotion.

human pains. To cure such an ill, because of human sin, God *must* exist. (As Norman Malcolm[15] suggested when discussing the Onto-logical Proof.) The condition of being changed and made anew is a general religious idea, sometimes appearing as magical instant sal-vation (as in suddenly "taking Christ as Saviour") or as the result of some lengthy ascesis.[16] Here salvation as spiritual change often goes with the conception of a *place* of purification and healing. (We light candles, we bring flowers, we go somewhere and kneel down.) This sense of a safe place is characteristic of religious imagery. Here the outer images the inner, and the inner images the outer. There is a literal place, the place of pilgrimage, the place of worship, the shrine, the sacred grove, there is also a psychological or spiritual place, a part of the soul. "Do not seek for God outside your soul." Religion provides a well-known well-tried procedure of rescue. Par-ticularly in relation to guilt and remorse or the obsessions which can be bred from these, the *mystery* of religion (respected, intuited) is a source of spiritual energy. An orientation toward the good in-volves a reorientation of desire. Here a meeting with a good person may bring about a change of direction. If Plato had never met Socrates and experienced his death perhaps western thinking might have been different. The mystical Christ too can be "met" with. (The idea of redemptive suffering is repugnant to some; but such suffer-ing is everywhere around us, where the innocent suffers through love of the guilty.) Of course it may well be argued that there are sound unmysterious secular equivalents to these devices, there are many resources for the afflicted who may use their enlightened common sense, or go to their friends, doctors, therapists, psycho-analysts, social workers, take refuge in art or nature, or say (as the religious too may say) to hell with it all. Many people hate religion, with its terrible history and its irrationality, and would regard re-sort to religious rituals as a false substitute for real morals and gen-uine amendment of life. Judaism and Islam, who have avoided the path of image-making, and have revered the name of [God], avoid many of the problems which now beset Christianity. Buddhists live with the mystical Buddha in the soul. (Like Eckhart's[17] God and Christ in the soul.) The Hindu religion also has its philosophical mysticism above its numerous gods. Religion has been fundamentally mystical, and this becomes, in this age, more evident. So will the

---

[15]**Norman Malcolm (1911–1990)** American philosopher whose book *Ludwig Wittgenstein: A Memoir* is referenced in Murdoch's text.

[16]**ascesis** Ascetic behavior, such as fasting, celibacy, or becoming a hermit.

[17]**Johannes Eckhart (1260?–1327?)** A German theologian who saw a unity in the soul and God: "the core of the soul and the core of God are one."

theologians invent new modes of speech, and will the churches fill with people who realise they do not need to believe in the supernatural?

Religion (even if "primitive") is generally assumed to be in some 7 sense moral. Mysticism is also assumed to be, by definition, moral. Thinkers of the Enlightenment however, and many since, have held, often rightly, that organised, institutionalised religion is an enemy of morality, an enemy of freedom and free thought, guilty of cruelty and repression. This has been so and in many quarters is so. Therefore the whole institution may be rationally considered to be discredited or outmoded. Many other influences from the past support such a line of thought. Kierkegaard saw Hegel as the enemy of religion and of, *ipso facto*, the existing individual. The vast force of Hegel's thinking, followed up by Marx, is inimical to both. The Romantic Movement and the liberal political thinking which went with it have tended to look after the individual, and we associate high morality (idealism, selflessness, goodness) with many people in this century and the last who assumed that religion was *finished*. It must be agreed that, in very many ways, western society has improved, become more tolerant, more free, more decently happy, in this period. It may also be agreed that with the decline of religious observance and religious "consciousness" (the practice of prayer and the fear of God for instance), some aspects of moral conduct may decline also. (Of course this decline can have other causes.) However that may be, Hegel and Marx, Nietzsche and Freud, have had influence. Virtues and values may give way to a more relaxed sense of determinism. There is a more "reasonable," ordinary, *available* relativism and "naturalism" about. Hegel's *Geist*[18] is the energy which perpetually urges the ever-unsatisfied intellect (and so the whole of being) onward toward Absolute reality. Everything is relative, incomplete, not yet fully real, not yet fully true, dialectic is a continual reformulation. Such is the history of thought, of civilisation, or of the "person" who, immersed in the process, is carried on toward some postulated self-consistent totality. Vaguely, such an image as something plausible may linger in the mind. I shall not discuss Hegel here, but look for a moment at a milder form of quasi-Hegelianism in F. H. Bradley's[19] *Appearance and Reality*. According to Bradley both morality and religion demand an unattainable unity. "Every separate aspect of the universe goes on to demand something

---

[18] *Geist* The reference is to Hegel's concept of the spirit/mind (geist). Hegel had three categories of spirit/mind: subjective, objective, and absolute. The absolute was reserved for contemplation of religion, fine arts, and philosophy.

[19] **F. H. Bradley (1846–1924)** English philosopher influenced by Hegel who emphasized the force of the mind over the physical world.

higher than itself." This is the dialectic, the overcoming of the incomplete, of appearance and illusion, the progress toward what is more true, more real, more harmoniously integrated. "And, like every other appearance, goodness implies that which, when carried out, must absorb it." Religion is higher than morality, being more unified, more expressive of a perfect wholeness. But both morality and religion face the same insuperable difficulty. Morality–religion believes in the reality of perfect good, and in the demand that good be victorious and evil destroyed. The postulated whole (good) is at once actually to be good, and at the same time to make itself good. Neither its perfect goodness nor its struggle may be degraded to an appearance (something incomplete and imperfect). But to unite these two aspects consistently is impossible. If the desired end were reached, the struggle, the need for devotion, would have ceased to be real. If there is to be morality, there cannot altogether be an end to evil. Discord is essential to goodness. Moral evil exists only in moral experience and that experience is essentially inconsistent. Morality desires unconsciously, with the suppression of evil, to become non-moral. It shrinks from this, yet it unknowingly desires the existence and perpetuity of evil. Morality, which makes evil, desires in evil to remove a condition of its own being; it labours to pass into a super-moral and therefore non-moral sphere. Moral–religious faith is make-believe: be sure that opposition to the good is overcome, but act as if it (the opposition) persists. "The religious consciousness rests on the felt unity of unreduced opposites."

QUESTIONS FOR CRITICAL READING

1. Can there be only one concept of virtue?
2. Why is virtue different from duty?
3. How is dutiful behavior different from religious behavior?
4. Does religion foster good behavior more than nonreligious idealism does?
5. How does guilt relate to morality?
6. Is religion essentially moral in nature?
7. Is high morality (idealism, selflessness, goodness) essentially religious?

SUGGESTIONS FOR WRITING

1. One question that underlies Murdoch's views is whether or not a high morality could ever be produced in a completely nonreligious environment. What is your view on this issue? What are the arguments in

defense of religion as the essential producer of the high morality Murdoch points to in paragraph 7? Why might it be difficult for such a high morality to be produced by secular means? In a nonreligious context, what would ultimately support high morality?

2. One of Murdoch's assertions is that moral–religious views depend on the existence of evil, otherwise there can be no good behavior. This assertion is commonly made by those who insist on a Hegelian dialectic — a condition in which two opposites collide and a third force emerges. What would the world be like if there were no evil? Would moral behavior then be possible? Would immoral behavior be possible? Would all behavior be morally neutral? Explain.

3. What effects do poverty and the absence of opportunity have on individuals' senses of virtue? Do you agree with Murdoch that virtue "may be seen as a self-indulgent luxury" (para. 2)? Why or why not? Should bourgeois concepts of morality be applied to those without hope of change in their lives? Is morality dependent on social condition? Explain.

4. In paragraph 3 Murdoch states: "Dutifulness could be an account of a morality with no hint of religion." Do you agree? She is obviously tentative in her statement. Examine your own sense of duty and that of someone you know and decide how much duty — as well as the expression of dutiful acts — satisfies our concept of a true morality.

5. Murdoch implies at the end of paragraph 3 that certain political complexities suggest there might be a need to have "clear rigid rules" of behavior in order to establish a morality. She implies that even clerics are viewing contemporary moral standards as flexible, perhaps alterable in some circumstances. How do you feel? Should morality follow the "rules" approach of the Ten Commandments? Or is there a more flexible, "realistic" alternative? Explain.

6. What do you consider virtuous behavior? Try to be as specific as possible. Do you find it difficult to apply your virtues in your everyday life? Why or why not? To what extent do you feel an individual's religious beliefs dictate his or her virtuousness? Is religious faith an accurate indicator of virtue? Why or why not? What is Murdoch's view of this issue?

7. **CONNECTIONS** How would Friedrich Nietzsche approach a critique of the views that Murdoch explores in this essay? Where would his sympathies lie in relation to her discussion of the relationship of virtue to duty? Where would he stand on the controversies that suggest that organized religion inhibits rather than fosters morality? What points in Murdoch's argument would he most take issue with?

8. **CONNECTIONS** Which of the selections in this section would most satisfy Murdoch's sense of the nature of morality and the relation of morality to religion? Who among these writers is most sympathetic to her views? Is she sympathetic to Aristotle's ideas is "The Aim of Man"? Does she share anything in common with Nietzsche in his "Morality as Anti-Nature"? Choose one and compare their views.

HIS HOLINESS THE DALAI LAMA
The Ethic of Compassion

HIS HOLINESS, TENZIN GYATSO (b. 1935), is the fourteenth Dalai Lama. He was selected Dalai Lama, which means
Ocean of Wisdom, when he was a young child because he was
assumed to be the reincarnation of the thirteenth Dalai Lama. Traditionally, the process of testing a child to see if he is the reincarnation of the Dalai Lama is careful and detailed, involving among
other things determining the child's familiarity with the belongings of the previous Dalai Lama. In the Tibetan Buddhist tradition,
the Dalai Lama is considered a reincarnation of the Bodhisattva of
Compassion, sometimes known as Avalokiteshvara. A Bodhisattva
is a Buddha, an enlightened one. The Dalai Lama has been the political as well as religious leader of the Tibetan people since the
fourteenth century.

In the early 1950s, the Chinese military threatened Tibet, which
is located between India and China. Despite many efforts by the
Dalai Lama to negotiate a settlement, China eventually invaded in
1959. As a result, the Dalai Lama now lives in exile in India.

The Dalai Lama was educated rigorously by scholars of Bud-
dhism and Tibetan thought. When he was sixteen he had to take on
the responsibilities of governing the state even though he was still
deeply involved with his religious studies. At the age of twenty-four,
just before he was forced into exile, he passed a series of complex
examinations conducted by dozens of scholars before he successfully qualified to earn his doctorate in Buddhist philosophy. When
he was twenty-five he established a Tibetan government in exile in
Dharamsala, India, where more than eighty thousand Tibetans had
followed him. Many more have left Tibet in reaction to the Chinese
invasion, which has markedly altered the character of the country.

From *Ethics for the New Millennium.*

Much of the Dalai Lama's political activity is aimed at restoring Tibet to its previous character and guaranteeing the safe return of Tibetan refugees. The Dalai Lama has been an advocate of human rights around the globe. His views are universal in nature and not limited to his own self-interest. He has figured in decisions made in the United Nations, and he has reached out to the religious leaders of other faiths, with personal communication with two Roman Catholic popes and the Archbishop of Canterbury, citing their common interest in the importance of religion in the modern world. His political views have been widely disseminated and base themselves in granting rights to all people in a democratic political system. He has said that if he is returned to Tibet, he will establish a democratic government and step down from its leadership.

Throughout the world, the Dalai Lama is respected as a scholarly, serious, and gifted man whose concerns focus on helping the poor and the disenfranchised. He won the Nobel Peace Prize in 1989 in recognition of the work he had done in encouraging peace among nations. Among his books are *My Land and My People* (1962), *Ocean of Wisdom: Guidelines for Living* (1989), *Freedom in Exile: The Autobiography of the Dalai Lama* (1990), *A Policy of Kindness: An Anthology of Writings by and about the Dalai Lama* (1990), and *Ethics for the New Millennium* (1999).

Today the Dalai Lama works to preserve Tibetan culture and to promote a policy that would establish Tibet as a "zone of peace" for the world.

The Dalai Lama's Rhetoric

The selection that follows is taken from *Ethics for the New Millennium* and focuses specifically on the meaning of compassion and its uses as a guide for ethical behavior. The Dalai Lama does not lay down any rules or proclaim any laws or commandments. One of the interesting qualities of this selection is that it does not prohibit undesirable behavior, but instead focuses entirely on the desirable behavior that one ought to consider in the interest of personal happiness and the overall well-being of the community.

The Dalai Lama begins by discussing compassion in terms of Buddhist practice and links it to the concept of empathy, the natural feeling one has for one's fellow beings. These first paragraphs both define and clarify compassion and empathy and relate them to the life of the individual. The Dalai Lama recognizes that not all people will be able to practice compassion unconditionally, but individuals can try to do so by emphasizing empathy in the course of their everyday lives.

The simplicity of the Dalai Lama's prose belies the complexity of his thought and message. He uses relatively few rhetorical flourishes and very little imagery. However, he does occasionally pose rhetorical questions, such as "Why is this?" (para. 4), as a way to elaborate on his major points.

His many references to "our" and "us" are inclusive of the reader, implying that he is not so different from us. He has said publicly that he is only a simple Buddhist monk, nothing more, and his humble attitude pervades this selection. When he states "Let us now consider the role of compassionate love and kind-heartedness in our daily lives" (para. 8), we realize that he has been including us all along in his discussion. His purpose is to show that we should choose to live compassionately, especially if we wish to live in peace with our neighbors.

In paragraph 9 he recognizes that some of his readers will find what he has to say relatively difficult to accept, even harder to practice. He considers some of the problems inherent in acting compassionately and practicing empathy. In addition, he connects his suggestions to the idea of virtue, which he sees as inalterably connected to the ideal of compassion. In paragraph 10 he reviews some of the problems he thinks we are likely to encounter if we follow his advice, even suggesting that in some situations people who would otherwise act compassionately find they cannot do so.

After reviewing the further objections to his program in paragraph 11, the Dalai Lama concludes by admitting that what he recommends is difficult, but absolutely worthwhile. As he states in paragraph 13, "Compassion and love are not mere luxuries. As the source both of inner and external peace, they are fundamental to the continued survival of our species."

PREREADING QUESTIONS: WHAT TO READ FOR

The following prereading questions may help you anticipate key issues in the discussion of the Dalai Lama's "The Ethic of Compassion." Keeping them in mind during your first reading of the selection should help focus your attention.

- What is compassion?
- Why is compassion important for us to have?
- What is the relationship of compassion to ethics?

The Ethic of Compassion

We noted earlier that all the world's major religions stress the 1
importance of cultivating love and compassion. In the Buddhist
philosophical tradition, different levels of attainment are described.
At a basic level, compassion (*nying je*) is understood mainly in terms
of empathy—our ability to enter into and, to some extent, share
others' suffering. But Buddhist—and perhaps others—believe that
this can be developed to such a degree that not only does our compassion arise without any effort, but it is unconditional, undifferen-
tiated, and universal in scope. A feeling of intimacy toward all other
sentient beings, including of course those who would harm us, is
generated, which is likened in the literature to the love a mother has
for her only child.

But this sense of equanimity toward all others is not seen as an 2
end in itself. Rather, it is seen as the springboard to a love still
greater. Because our capacity for empathy is innate, and because the
ability to reason is also an innate faculty, compassion shares the
characteristics of consciousness itself. The potential we have to develop it is therefore stable and continuous. It is not a resource which
can be used up—as water is used up when we boil it. And though it
can be described in terms of activity, it is not like a physical activity
which we train for, like jumping, where once we reach a certain
height we can go no further. On the contrary, when we enhance our
sensitivity toward others' suffering through deliberately opening
ourselves up to it, it is believed that we can gradually extend out
compassion to the point where the individual feels so moved by
even the subtlest suffering of others that they come to have an overwhelming sense of responsibility toward those others. This causes
the one who is compassionate to dedicate themselves entirely to
helping others overcome both their suffering and the causes of their
suffering. In Tibetan, this ultimate level of attainment is called *nying
je chenmo*, literally "great compassion."

Now I am not suggesting that each individual must attain 3
these advanced states of spiritual development in order to lead an
ethically wholesome life. I have described *nying je chenmo* not because it is a precondition of ethical conduct but rather because I
believe that pushing the logic of compassion to the highest level
can act as a powerful inspiration. If we can just keep the aspiration
to develop *nying je chenmo*, or great compassion, as an ideal, it will
naturally have a significant impact on our outlook. Based on the
simple recognition that, just as I do, so do all others desire to be
happy and not to suffer, it will serve as a constant reminder against

selfishness and partiality. It will remind us that there is little to be gained from being kind and generous because we hope to win something in return. It will remind us that actions motivated by the desire to create a good name for ourselves are still selfish, however much they may appear to be acts of kindness. It will also remind us that there is nothing exceptional about acts of charity toward those we already feel close to. And it will help us to recognize that the bias we naturally feel toward our families and friends is actually a highly unreliable thing on which to base ethical conduct. If we reserve ethical conduct for those whom we feel close to, the danger is that we will neglect our responsibilities toward those outside this circle.

Why is this? So long as the individuals in question continue to 4 meet our expectations, all is well. But should they fail to do so, someone we consider a dear friend one day can become our sworn enemy the next. As we saw earlier, we have a tendency to react badly to all who threaten fulfillment of our cherished desires, though they may be our closest relations. For this reason, compassion and mutual respect offer a much more solid basis for our relations with others. This is also true of partnerships. If our love for someone is based largely on attraction, whether it be their looks or some other superficial characteristic, our feelings for that person are liable, over time, to evaporate. When they lose the quality we found alluring, or when we find ourselves no longer satisfied by it, the situation can change completely, this despite their being the same person. This is why relationships based purely on attraction are almost always unstable. On the other hand, when we begin to perfect our compassion, neither the other's appearance nor their behavior affects our underlying attitude.

Consider, too, that habitually our feelings toward others depend 5 very much on their circumstances. Most people, when they see someone who is handicapped, feel sympathetic toward that person. But then when they see others who are wealthier, or better educated, or better placed socially, they immediately feel envious and competitive toward them. Our negative feelings prevent us from seeing the sameness of ourselves and all others. We forget that just like us, whether fortunate or unfortunate, distant or near, they desire to be happy and not to suffer.

The struggle is thus to overcome these feelings of partiality. Cer- 6 tainly, developing genuine compassion for our loved ones is the obvious and appropriate place to start. The impact our actions have on our close ones will generally be much greater than on others, and therefore our responsibilities toward them are greater. Yet we need to recognize that, ultimately, there are no grounds for discriminating in their favor. In this sense, we are all in the same position as a doctor confronted by ten patients suffering the same serious illness. They are each equally deserving of treatment. The reader should not suppose that what is being advocated here is a state of detached indifference, however. The further essential challenge, as we begin to extend our compassion toward all others, is to maintain the same level of intimacy as we feel toward those closest to us. In other words, what is being suggested is that we need to strive for even-handedness in our approach toward all others, a level ground into which we can plant the seed of *nying je chenmo*, of great love and compassion.

If we can begin to relate to others on the basis of such equa-   7
nimity, our compassion will not depend on the fact that so and so is my husband, my wife, my relative, my friend. Rather, a feeling of closeness toward all others can be developed based on the simple recognition that, just like myself, all wish to be happy and to avoid suffering. In other words, we will start to relate to others on the basis of their sentient nature. Again, we can think of this in terms of an ideal, one which it is immensely difficult to attain. But, for myself, I find it one which is profoundly inspiring and helpful.

Let us now consider the role of compassionate love and kind-   8
heartedness in our daily lives. Does the ideal of developing it to the point where it is unconditional mean that we must abandon our own interests entirely? Not at all. In fact, it is the best way of serving them—indeed, it could even be said to constitute the wisest course for fulfilling self-interest. For if it is correct that those qualities such as love, patience, tolerance, and forgiveness are what happiness consists in, and if it is also correct that *nying je*, or compassion, as I have defined it, is both the source and the fruit of these qualities, then the more we are compassionate, the more we provide for our own happiness. Thus, any idea that concern for others, though a noble quality, is a matter for our private lives only, is simply short-sighted. Compassion belongs to every sphere of activity, including, of course, the workplace.

Here, though, I must acknowledge the existence of a perception—   9
shared by many, it seems—that compassion is, if not actually an impediment, at least irrelevant to professional life. Personally, I would argue that not only is it relevant, but that when compassion is lacking, our activities are in danger of becoming destructive. This is because when we ignore the question of the impact our actions have on others' well-being, inevitably we end up hurting them. The ethic of compassion helps provide the necessary foundation and

motivation for both restraint and the cultivation of virtue. When we begin to develop a genuine appreciation of the value of compassion, our outlook on others begins automatically to change. This alone can serve as a powerful influence on the conduct of our lives. When, for example, the temptation to deceive others arises, our compassion for them will prevent us from entertaining the idea. And when we realize that our work itself is in danger of being exploited to the detriment of others, compassion will cause us to disengage from it. So to take an imaginary case of a scientist whose research seems likely to be a source of suffering, they will recognize this and act accordingly, even if this means abandoning the project.

I do not deny that genuine problems can arise when we dedi- 10 cate ourselves to the ideal of compassion. In the case of a scientist who felt unable to continue in the direction their work was taking them, this could have profound consequences both for themselves and for their families. Likewise, those engaged in the caring professions—in medicine, counseling, social work, and so on—or even those looking after someone at home may sometimes become so exhausted by their duties that they feel overwhelmed. Constant exposure to suffering, coupled occasionally with a feeling of being taken for granted, can induce feelings of helplessness and even despair. Or it can happen that individuals may find themselves performing outwardly generous actions merely for the sake of it— simply going through the motions, as it were. Of course this is better than nothing. But when left unchecked, this can lead to insensitivity toward others' suffering. If this starts to happen, it is best to disengage for a short while and make a deliberate effort to reawaken that sensitivity. In this it can be helpful to remember that despair is never a solution. It is, rather, the ultimate failure. Therefore, as the Tibetan expression has it, even if the rope breaks nine times, we must splice it back together a tenth time. In this way, even if ultimately we do fail, at least there will be no feelings of regret. And when we combine this insight with a clear appreciation of our potential to benefit others, we find that we can begin to restore our hope and confidence.

Some people may object to this ideal on the grounds that by en- 11 tering into others' suffering, we bring suffering on ourselves. To an extent, this is true. But I suggest that there is an important qualitative distinction to be made between experiencing one's own suffering and experiencing suffering in the course of sharing in others'. In the case of one's own suffering, given that it is involuntary, there is a sense of oppression: it seems to come from outside us. By contrast, sharing in someone else's suffering must at some level involve a degree of voluntariness, which itself is indicative of a certain inner strength. For this reason, the disturbance it may cause is considerably less likely to paralyze us than our own suffering.

Of course, even as an ideal, the notion of developing unconditional compassion is daunting. Most people, including myself, must struggle even to reach the point where putting others' interests on a par with our own becomes easy. We should not allow this to put us off, however. And while undoubtedly there will be obstacles on the way to developing a genuinely warm heart, there is the deep consolation of knowing that in doing so we are creating the conditions for our own happiness. As I mentioned earlier, the more we truly desire to benefit others, the greater the strength and confidence we develop and the greater the peace and happiness we experience. If this still seems unlikely, it is worth asking ourselves how else we are to do so. With violence and aggression? Of course not. With money? Perhaps up to a point, but no further. But with love, by sharing in others' suffering, by recognizing ourselves clearly in all others—especially those who are disadvantaged and those whose rights are not respected—by helping them to be happy: yes. Through love, through kindness, through compassion we establish understanding between ourselves and others. This is how we forge unity and harmony. 12

Compassion and love are not mere luxuries. As the source both of inner and external peace, they are fundamental to the continued survival of our species. On the one hand, they constitute non-violence in action. On the other, they are the source of all spiritual qualities: of forgiveness, tolerance, and all the virtues. Moreover, they are the very thing that gives meaning to our activities and makes them constructive. There is nothing amazing about being highly educated; there is nothing amazing about being rich. Only when the individual has a warm heart do these attributes become worthwhile. 13

So to those who say that the Dalai Lama is being unrealistic in advocating this ideal of unconditional love, I urge them to experiment with it nonetheless. They will discover that when we reach beyond the confines of narrow self-interest, our hearts become filled with strength. Peace and joy become our constant companion. It breaks down barriers of every kind and in the end destroys the notion of my interest as independent from others' interest. But most important, so far as ethics is concerned, where love of one's neighbor, affection, kindness, and compassion live, we find that ethical conduct is automatic. Ethically wholesome actions arise naturally in the context of compassion. 14

QUESTIONS FOR CRITICAL READING

1. How does compassion affect our ethical behavior?
2. Must one be specifically religious to feel compassion?
3. In what sense is empathy an inborn feeling?
4. Can one behave ethically if one does not feel compassion?
5. Do most religions promote love and compassion?
6. Are there degrees of compassion that one can feel?
7. What is the Tibetan *nying je chenmo*, the "great compassion" (para. 2)?
8. What is the effect of compassion on selfishness?

SUGGESTIONS FOR WRITING

1. Write a brief essay in which you establish what the ethic of compassion is for the average person, as outlined in this selection. Why is the concern for compassion an ethical issue? In what sense does the concern for compassion, in the terms that the Dalai Lama sets out, help in defining the nature of ethics in general?
2. What, according to the Dalai Lama, are the issues that limit a person's capacity to empathize and have compassion for others? Have you found yourself in situations in which you knew you should have compassion for someone but could not? If so, how did that disconnect make you feel? What do you think prevents us from feeling compassion or acting compassionately even when we know we should?
3. What elicits compassion in you? For whom do you feel empathy? Why? What factors do you think were influential in constructing your sense of compassion? To what extent might a lack of compassion affect an individual's emotional development? Explain.
4. The Dalai Lama states, "If our love for someone is based largely on attraction, whether it be their looks or some other superficial characteristic, our feelings for that person are liable, over time, to evaporate" (para. 4). Do you agree? Why or why not? Is it possible to control who you are attracted to? What suggestions does the Dalai Lama have for avoiding this problem in relationships?
5. The Dalai Lama urges us to feel the same kind of compassion for strangers as we do for our family and friends. What changes might a person have to make in order to practice the Dalai Lama's brand of compassion? Would you be willing to make those changes? Why or why not? To what extent is the choice to be compassionate a matter of morality? Explain.
6. **CONNECTIONS** How would Friedrich Nietzsche react to the Dalai Lama's views on compassion? Would Nietzsche agree with anything the Dalai Lama says? Do you think Nietzsche would find the ethics of compassion to be anti-nature? Why or why not?

7. **CONNECTIONS**   Which of the preceding writers in this section on
   ethics seems most in agreement with the Dalai Lama on the value of
   compassion? How do these views help you understand your moral
   obligations to your fellow human beings? What are the subtle differences between this selection's view of compassion and the selection
   you chose as closest in spirit to it?

PART EIGHT

FEMINISM

Mary Wollstonecraft
Virginia Woolf
Simone de Beauvoir
Carol Gilligan
bell hooks

INTRODUCTION

So it is naturally with the male and the female; the one is superior,
the other inferior; the one governs, the other is governed; and the
same rule must necessarily hold good with respect to all mankind.
                              —ARISTOTLE (384–322 B.C.)

If all men are born free, how is it that all women are born slaves?
                              —MARY ASTELL (1666–1731)

Male and female citizens, being equal in the eyes of the law,
must be equally admitted to all honors, positions, and public
employment according to their capacity and without other
distinctions besides those of their virtues and talents.
                              —OLYMPE DE GOUGES (1748–1793)

I have done a great deal of work, as much as a man, but did not
get so much pay. I used to work in the field and bind grain,
keeping up with the cradler; but men doing no more, got twice as
much pay. . . . We do as much, we eat as much, we want as much.
                              —SOJOURNER TRUTH (1787–1833)

Women need not always keep their mouths shut and their wombs
open.
                              —EMMA GOLDMAN (1869–1940)

Feminism is hated because women are hated. Anti-feminism is a
direct expression of misogyny; it is the political defense of women
hating.
                              —ANDREA DWORKIN (1946–2005)

Feminism is an issue that has long been important to the modern intellectual. Although it was only in the twentieth century that
many basic feminist ideas became accepted within the mainstream
of most societies, the history of feminist thought spans more than
three hundred years. Feminists were at work long before anarchist
and political idealist William Godwin (1756–1836) wrote about the
rights of women during the Romantic period in English literature.
Feminist writing has also traditionally extended into scholarly disciplines, from politics to philosophy to psychology to literature. For
example, in the nineteenth century, intense activity in Scandinavian
feminism produced a number of important literary artifacts, not the
least of which was Henrik Ibsen's play *A Doll's House*, which figures
in one of these essays. In our time, we associate feminism with important mid-twentieth-century writings by a diverse array of writers,
as well as with feminist groups organized in the 1960s and 1970s
such as the National Organization for Women. The essays included

here depict some of the most important eras in feminist thought. Readers should keep in mind, however, that these five essays represent only a fraction of the feminist works that have been written and published over the centuries. Like most feminist writers, the authors excerpted here echo some of the issues raised by Aristotle and Alexis de Tocqueville concerning equality. However, because the feminist writers take issues of gender, race, and class into account, they address the question of equality in more complex and concrete ways.

Mary Wollstonecraft wrote in a time of extreme political change: when revolution was erupting in the American colonies in 1776 and in France in 1789. Kings and aristocrats were losing their heads, literally. Monarchies were giving way to republics. During this period democracy in its modern forms began to grace the lives of some, whereas tyranny oppressed others. Even though radical changes took place in some areas, a conservative backlash in England and elsewhere threatened to heighten oppression rather than expand freedom. Although Wollstonecraft is known today chiefly for her feminist works, she was also engaged in the radical political thought of the time. For example, her defense of the ideals of the French Revolution in *A Vindication of the Rights of Men* (1790) brought her work to the attention of other radical thinkers such as William Godwin (whom she later married), Thomas Paine, William Blake, and William Wordsworth.

Still, Wollstonecraft's name remains a keystone in the history of feminism. She went on to write one of the most important books of the late eighteenth century, *Vindication of the Rights of Woman* (1792), and is remembered most for her careful analysis of a society that did not value the gifts and talents of women. Her complaint is based on a theory of efficiency and economics: it is a waste to limit the opportunities of women. By making her appeal in this fashion she may have expected to gain the attention of the men who held power in late eighteenth-century England. Some of them did listen. By the 1830s, at the height of the industrial revolution, women were often employed outside the home. However, they were frequently given the most wretched jobs (such as in mining) and were not accorded the kind of respect and opportunity that Wollstonecraft envisioned. They often became drudges in a process of industrial development that demeaned their humanity.

In 1929, the novelist and essayist Virginia Woolf considered the question of how gifted women could hope to achieve important works if the current and historical patterns of oppression were to continue. Her book *A Room of One's Own* was addressed originally to a group of women studying at Cambridge in the two colleges reserved for them at the time. Woolf regarded these women appropriately as gifted, but she worried for their future because their opportunities in postwar

England were quite limited. In a stroke of brilliance, Woolf demonstrates the pattern that oppresses gifted women by imagining for William Shakespeare an equally gifted sister named Judith and then tracing her probable development in sixteenth-century England. What chance would Judith have had to be a world-famous figure like her brother? Woolf's discussion is so lifelike and so well realized that it stands as a classic in modern feminist literature.

After the publication of her remarkable book *The Second Sex* (1949; 1953 in English), the French writer and philosopher Simone de Beauvoir was credited with inaugurating the modern feminist movement. Of course, the movement had been developing already in the work of countless women who fought for the right to vote (Russia, 1917; United States, 1920; Great Britain, 1928; France, 1945). Many years before Beauvoir began writing, numerous women had also sought better employment opportunities, improved wages and benefits, and better working conditions. Yet Beauvoir's book hit a nerve because it was one of the most scholarly and comprehensive works on the subject. *The Second Sex* was clearly the work of a gifted mind, brilliant in areas of philosophy, psychology, economics, and history. As a result, the book drew admiration from men as well as women. The essay included here considers one aspect of psychology: the negative effect of society's reliance on seemingly innocent cultural myths about women.

In her landmark work, *In a Different Voice* (1982), distinguished psychologist Carol Gilligan analyzes the basic male texts in psychology that explain the development of children into adults. She concludes that because the data came from studies of boys, "half the world was excluded." Experts in psychology insisted that these studies produced conclusions that were as true of women as they were of men. However, Gilligan felt they were wrong and went on to secure fresh data drawn from women and girls. When analyzed, her data gave new answers to old questions. The original studies of boys emphasized competitiveness and "liberal independence," whereas Gilligan's data showed that women often rejected these values in favor of communalism and a need for intimacy and cooperation. Gilligan shows how these qualities were interpreted to imply that women are somehow inferior to men—but only when one depends on data collected from men.

Gilligan has become a champion of feminists even though a number of respected critics disagree with her. Ultimately, much of what she has discovered about women's development has been shown to be true of men as well. Her work shows that a new model of human growth and development no longer supports a view that women are morally deficient in relation to men.

In "The Significance of Feminist Movement," bell hooks points to some of the limitations of the feminists of the 1960s and 1970s. She suggests that most of the women who spoke out on behalf of feminism at that time were white and middle class, and that these women assumed that all women—including women of color—were of the same mind and were in agreement on all the issues. She asserts that their attacks on men turned people away from the movement and oriented feminism as outside the mainstream. Hooks examines the root causes of sexism, which she feels is connected to classism, racism, and imperialism. Her analysis offers some interesting insights on the structure of the nuclear family and on the ways in which certain assumptions about family life can produce and reinforce the oppression of women. The fundamental problems, she states, are deep in the basic values of Western culture: "The primary contradiction in Western cultural thought is the belief that the superior should control the inferior" (para. 5).

These essays represent a wide variety of stances and cover a broad range of disciplines. Although they hardly cover the entire territory of feminism, they offer insights from diverse historical periods and from several important intellectual angles. Further, they reveal the resilience and strength of the feminist movement—a movement that continues today.

MARY WOLLSTONECRAFT
Pernicious Effects Which Arise from the Unnatural Distinctions Established in Society

MARY WOLLSTONECRAFT (1759–1797) was born into relatively modest circumstances, with a father whose heavy drinking and spending eventually ruined the family and left her and her sisters to support themselves. She became a governess, a teacher, and eventually a writer. Her views were among the most enlightened of her day, particularly regarding women and women's rights, giving her the reputation of being a very forward-looking feminist for her time, and even for ours. Her thinking, however, is comprehensive and not limited to a single issue.

She was known to the American patriot Thomas Paine (1737–1809), to Dr. Samuel Johnson (1709–1783), and to the English philosopher William Godwin (1756–1836), whom she eventually married. Her views on marriage were remarkable for her time; among other beliefs, she felt it unnecessary to marry a man in order to live happily with him. Her first liaison, with an American, Gilbert Imlay, gave her the opportunity to travel and learn something about commerce and capitalism at first hand. Her second liaison, with Godwin, brought her into the intellectual circles of her day. She married Godwin when she was pregnant, and died in childbirth. Her daughter, Mary, married the poet Percy Bysshe Shelley and wrote the novel *Frankenstein* (1818).

From *Vindication of the Rights of Woman.*

The excitement generated by the French Revolution (1789–1799) caused Wollstonecraft to react against the very conservative view put forward by the philosopher Edmund Burke. Her pamphlet A *Vindication of the Rights of Men* (1790) was well received. She followed it with *Vindication of the Rights of Woman* (1792), which was translated into French.

She saw feminism in political terms. The chapter reprinted here concentrates on questions of property, class, and law. As a person committed to the revolutionary principles of liberty, equality, and fraternity, Wollstonecraft linked the condition of women to the political and social structure of her society. Her aim was to point out the inequities in the treatment of women—which her society simply did not perceive—and to attempt to rectify them.

Wollstonecraft's Rhetoric

Mary Wollstonecraft wrote for an audience that did not necessarily appreciate brief, exact expression. Rather, they appreciated a more luxuriant and leisurely style than we use today. As a result, her prose can sometimes seem wordy to a modern audience. However, she handles imagery carefully (especially in the first paragraph) without overburdening her prose. She uses an approach that she calls "episodical observations" (para. 12). These are anecdotes—personal stories—and apparently casual cataloguings of thoughts on a number of related issues. She was aware that her structure was not tight, that it did not develop a specific argument, and that it did not force the reader to accept or reject her position. She also considered this a wise approach, because it was obvious to her that her audience was completely prejudiced against her view. To attempt to convince them of her views was to invite total defeat.

Instead, she simply puts forward several observations that stand by themselves as examples of the evils she condemns. Even those who stand against her will see that there is validity to her claims; and they will not be so threatened by her argument as to become defensive before they have learned something new. She appeals always to the higher intellectual capacities of both men and women, directing her complaints, too, against both men and women. This balance of opinion, coupled with a range of thought-provoking examples, makes her views clear and convincing.

Also distinctive in this passage is the use of metaphor. The second sentence of paragraph 1 is particularly heavy with metaphor: "For it is in the most polished society that noisome reptiles and venomous serpents lurk under the rank herbage; and there is voluptuousness pampered by the still sultry air, which relaxes every good disposition before it ripens into virtue." The metaphor presents society as a garden in which the grass is decaying and dangerous serpents are lurking. Good disposition—character—is a plant that might ripen, but—continuing the metaphor—it ripens into virtue, not just a fruit. A favorite source of metaphors for Wollstonecraft is drapery (dressmaking). When she uses one of these metaphors she is usually reminding the reader that drapery gives a new shape to things, that it sometimes hides the truth, and that it ought not to put a false appearance on what it covers.

One of her rhetorical techniques is that of literary allusion. By alluding to important literary sources—such as Greek mythology, William Shakespeare, Jean-Jacques Rousseau, and Samuel Johnson—she not only demonstrates her knowledge but also shows that she respects her audience, which she presumes shares the same knowledge. She does not show off by overquoting or by referring to very obscure writers. She balances her allusions perfectly, even transforming folk aphorisms into "homely proverbs" such as "whoever the devil finds idle he will employ."

Wollstonecraft's experiences with her difficult father gave her knowledge of gambling tables and card games, another source of allusions. She draws further on personal experience—shared by some of her audience—when she talks about the degradation felt by a woman of intelligence forced to act as a governess—a glorified servant—in a well-to-do family. Wollstonecraft makes excellent uses of these allusions, never overdoing them, always giving them just the right touch.

PREREADING QUESTIONS:
WHAT TO READ FOR

The following prereading questions may help you anticipate key issues in the discussion of Mary Wollstonecraft's "Pernicious Effects Which Arise from the Unnatural Distinctions Established in Society." Keeping them in mind during your first reading of the selection should help focus your attention.

- What are some of the pernicious effects that Wollstonecraft decries?

- What kinds of work are women fit for, in Wollstonecraft's view?

- What happens to people who are born to wealth and have nothing to do?

Pernicious Effects Which Arise from the Unnatural Distinctions Established in Society

From the respect paid to property flow, as from a poisoned foun- 1
tain, most of the evils and vices which render this world such a dreary
scene to the contemplative mind. For it is in the most polished society
that noisome reptiles and venomous serpents lurk under the rank
herbage; and there is voluptuousness pampered by the still sultry
air, which relaxes every good disposition before it ripens into virtue.

One class presses on another; for all are aiming to procure respect 2
on account of their property: and property, once gained, will procure
the respect due only to talents and virtue. Men neglect the duties in-
cumbent on man, yet are treated like demi-gods; religion is also separated from morality by a ceremonial veil, yet men wonder that the
world is almost, literally speaking, a den of sharpers or oppressors.

There is a homely proverb, which speaks a shrewd truth, that 3
whoever the devil finds idle he will employ. And what but habitual
idleness can hereditary wealth and titles produce? For man is so constituted that he can only attain a proper use of his faculties by exercising them, and will not exercise them unless necessity of some kind
first set the wheels in motion. Virtue likewise can only be acquired by
the discharge of relative duties; but the importance of these sacred
duties will scarcely be felt by the being who is cajoled out of his humanity by the flattery of sycophants.[1] There must be more equality
established in society, or morality will never gain ground, and this virtuous equality will not rest firmly even when founded on a rock, if
one half of mankind be chained to its bottom by fate, for they will be
continually undermining it through ignorance or pride.

It is vain to expect virtue from women till they are in some de- 4
gree independent of men; nay, it is vain to expect that strength of
natural affection which would make them good wives and mothers.
Whilst they are absolutely dependent on their husbands they will be
cunning, mean, and selfish, and the men who can be gratified by the
fawning fondness of spaniel-like affection have not much delicacy, for
love is not to be bought, in any sense of the words; its silken wings are
instantly shrivelled up when anything beside a return in kind is
sought. Yet whilst wealth enervates men, and women live, as it were,

---

[1] **sycophants** Toadies or false flatterers.

by their personal charms, how can we expect them to discharge those ennobling duties which equally require exertion and self-denial? Hereditary property sophisticates[2] the mind, and the unfortunate victims to it, if I may so express myself, swathed from their birth, seldom exert the locomotive faculty of body or mind; and, thus viewing everything through one medium, and that a false one, they are unable to discern in what true merit and happiness consist. False, indeed, must be the light when the drapery of situation hides the man, and makes him stalk in masquerade, dragging from one scene of dissipation to another the nerveless limbs that hang with stupid listlessness, and rolling round the vacant eye which plainly tells us that there is no mind at home.

I mean, therefore, to infer[3] that the society is not properly orga-   5
nized which does not compel men and women to discharge their respective duties, by making it the only way to acquire that countenance from their fellow-creatures which every human being wishes some way to attain. The respect, consequently, which is paid to wealth and mere personal charms, is a true north-east blast that blights the tender blossoms of affection and virtue. Nature has wisely attached affections to duties to sweeten toil, and to give that vigour to the exertions of reason which only the heart can give. But the affection which is put on merely because it is the appropriated insignia of a certain character, when its duties are not fulfilled, is one of the empty compliments which vice and folly are obliged to pay to virtue and the real nature of things.

To illustrate my opinion, I need only observe that when a woman   6
is admired for her beauty, and suffers herself to be so far intoxicated by the admiration she receives as to neglect to discharge the indispensable duty of a mother, she sins against herself by neglecting to cultivate an affection that would equally tend to make her useful and happy. True happiness, I mean all the contentment and virtuous satisfaction that can be snatched in this imperfect state, must arise from well regulated affections; and an affection includes a duty. Men are not aware of the misery they cause and the vicious weakness they cherish by only inciting women to render themselves pleasing; they do not consider that they thus make natural and artificial duties clash by sacrificing the comfort and respectability of a woman's life to voluptuous notions of beauty when in nature they all harmonize.

Cold would be the heart of a husband, were he not rendered un-   7
natural by early debauchery, who did not feel more delight at seeing his child suckled by its mother, than the most artful wanton tricks could ever raise; yet this natural way of cementing the matrimonial tie

---

[2] **sophisticates** Ruins or corrupts.
[3] **infer** Imply.

and twisting esteem with fonder recollections, wealth leads women to spurn. To preserve their beauty and wear the flowery crown of the day, which gives them a kind of right to reign for a short time over the sex, they neglect to stamp impressions on their husbands' hearts that would be remembered with more tenderness when the snow on the head began to chill the bosom than even their virgin charms. The maternal solicitude of a reasonable affectionate woman is very interesting, and the chastened dignity with which a mother returns the caresses that she and her child receive from a father who has been fulfilling the serious duties of his station, is not only a respectable but a beautiful sight. So singular indeed are my feelings, and I have endeavored not to catch factitious[4] ones, that after having been fatigued with the sight of insipid grandeur and the slavish ceremonies that with cumbrous pomp supplied the place of domestic affections, I have turned to some other scene to relieve my eye by resting it on the refreshing green everywhere scattered by nature. I have then viewed with pleasure a woman nursing her children, and discharging the duties of her station with, perhaps, merely a servant maid to take off her hands the servile part of the household business. I have seen her prepare herself and children, with only the luxury of cleanliness, to receive her husband, who returning weary home in the evening found smiling babes and a clean hearth. My heart has loitered in the midst of the group, and has even throbbed with sympathetic emotion, when the scraping of the well known foot has raised a pleasing tumult.

Whilst my benevolence has been gratified by contemplating this   8 artless picture, I have thought that a couple of this description, equally necessary and independent of each other, because each fulfilled the respective duties of their station, possessed all that life could give. Raised sufficiently above abject poverty not to be obliged to weigh the consequence of every farthing they spend, and having sufficient to prevent their attending to a frigid system of economy, which narrows both heart and mind, I declare, so vulgar[5] are my conceptions, that I know not what is wanted to render this the happiest as well as the most respectable situation in the world, but a taste for literature, to throw a little variety and interest into social converse, and some superfluous money to give to the needy and to buy books. For it is not pleasant when the heart is opened by compassion and the head active in arranging plans of usefulness, to have a prim urchin continually twitching back the elbow to prevent the hand from drawing out an almost empty purse, whispering at the same time some prudential maxim about the priority of justice.

---

[4]**factitious** False.
[5]**vulgar** Common.

Destructive, however, as riches and inherited honours are to the   9
human character, women are more debased and cramped, if possible, by them than men, because men may still, in some degree, unfold their faculties by becoming soldiers and statesmen.

As soldiers, I grant, they can now only gather, for the most part,   10
vainglorious laurels, whilst they adjust to a hair the European balance,
taking especial care that no bleak northern nook or sound incline the
beam.[6] But the days of true heroism are over, when a citizen fought
for his country like a Fabricius[7] or a Washington, and then returned
to his farm to let his virtuous fervour run in a more placid, but not a
less salutary, stream. No, our British heroes are oftener sent from the
gaming table than from the plough[8] and their passions have been
rather inflamed by hanging with dumb suspense on the turn of a
die, than sublimated by panting after the adventurous march of
virtue in the historic page.

The statesman, it is true, might with more propriety quit the faro   11
bank, or card table, to guide the helm, for he has still but to shuffle and
trick.[9] The whole system of British politics, if system it may courteously
be called, consisting in multiplying dependents and contriving taxes
which grind the poor to pamper the rich; thus a war, or any wild goose
chase, is, as the vulgar use the phrase, a lucky turn-up of patronage for
the minister, whose chief merit is the art of keeping himself in place. It
is not necessary then that he should have bowels for[10] the poor, so he
can secure for his family the odd trick. Or should some show of respect, for what is termed with ignorant ostentation an Englishman's
birthright, be expedient to bubble the gruff mastiff[11] that he has to lead
by the nose, he can make an empty show very safely by giving his single voice and suffering his light squadron to file off to the other side.
And when a question of humanity is agitated he may dip a sop in the
milk of human kindness to silence Cerberus,[12] and talk of the interest

---

[6] **incline the beam** The metaphor is of the balance—the scale that representations of blind justice hold up. Wollstonecraft's point is that in her time soldiers
fought to prevent the slightest changes in a balance of power that grew ever more
delicate, not in heroic wars with heroic consequences.

[7] **Fabricius (fl. 282 B.C.)** Gaius Fabricius, a worthy Roman general and statesman known for resistance to corruption.

[8] **from the plough** Worthy Roman heroes were humble farmers, not gamblers.

[9] **shuffle and trick** The upper class spent much of its time gambling: faro is a
high-stakes card game. Wollstonecraft is ironic when she says the statesman has "still
but to shuffle and trick," but she connects the "training" of faro with the practice of
politics in a deft, sardonic fashion. She is punning on the multiple meanings of *shuffle*—
to mix up a deck of cards and to move oneself or one's papers about slowly and
aimlessly—and *trick*—to win one turn of a card game and to do a devious deed.

[10] **bowels for** Feelings for; sense of pity.

[11] **to bubble the gruff mastiff** To fool even a guard dog.

[12] **Cerberus** The guard dog of Hades, the Greek hell or underworld.

which his heart takes in an attempt to make the earth no longer cry for
vengeance as it sucks in its children's blood, though his cold hand may
at the very moment rivet their chains by sanctioning the abominable
traffic. A minister is no longer a minister than while he can carry a
point which he is determined to carry. Yet it is not necessary that a
minister should feel like a man, when a bold push might shake his seat.

But, to have done with these episodical observations, let me re-   12
turn to the more specious slavery which chains the very soul of
woman, keeping her for ever under the bondage of ignorance.

The preposterous distinctions of rank, which render civilization a   13
curse by dividing the world between voluptuous tyrants and cunning
envious dependents, corrupt, almost equally, every class of people,
because respectability is not attached to the discharge of the relative
duties of life, but to the station, and when the duties are not fulfilled
the affections cannot gain sufficient strength to fortify the virtue of
which they are the natural reward. Still there are some loopholes out
of which a man may creep, and dare to think and act for himself; but
for a woman it is a herculean task, because she has difficulties peculiar
to her sex to overcome which require almost superhuman powers.

A truly benevolent legislator always endeavors to make it the   14
interest of each individual to be virtuous; and thus private virtue
becoming the cement of public happiness, an orderly whole is consolidated by the tendency of all the parts towards a common centre.
But, the private or public virtue of woman is very problematical; for
Rousseau, and a numerous list of male writers, insist that she should
all her life be subjected to a severe restraint, that of propriety. Why
subject her to propriety—blind propriety, if she be capable of acting
from a nobler spring, if she be an heir of immortality? Is sugar always
to be produced by vital blood? Is one half of the human species,
like the poor African slaves, to be subject to prejudices that brutalize
them, when principles would be a surer guard, only to sweeten the
cup of man? Is not this indirectly to deny woman reason? for a gift is
a mockery, if it be unfit for use.

Women are, in common with men, rendered weak and luxuri-   15
ous by the relaxing pleasures which wealth procures; but added to
this they are made slaves to their persons, and must render them alluring that man may lend them his reason to guide their tottering
steps aright. Or should they be ambitious, they must govern their
tyrants by sinister tricks, for without rights there cannot be any in-
cumbent duties. The laws respecting woman, which I mean to discuss in a future part, make an absurd unit of a man and his wife,[13]

---

[13] **absurd unit of a man and his wife** In English law man and wife were
legally one; the man spoke for both.

and then, by the easy transition of only considering him as responsible, she is reduced to a mere cypher.[14]

The being who discharges the duties of its station is independent; and, speaking of women at large, their first duty is to themselves as rational creatures, and the next in point of importance, as citizens, is that which includes so many, of a mother. The rank in life which dispenses with their fulfilling this duty necessarily degrades them by making them mere dolls. Or, should they turn to something more important than merely fitting drapery upon a smooth block, their minds are only occupied by some soft platonic attachment; or, the actual management of an intrigue may keep their thoughts in motion; for when they neglect domestic duties, they have it not in their own power to take the field and march and counter-march like soldiers, or wrangle in the senate to keep their faculties from rusting. 16

I know that, as a proof of the inferiority of the sex, Rousseau has exultingly exclaimed, How can they leave the nursery for the camp![15] And the camp has by some moralists been termed the school of the most heroic virtues; though, I think, it would puzzle a keen casuist[16] to prove the reasonableness of the greater number of wars that have dubbed heroes. I do not mean to consider this question critically; because, having frequently viewed these freaks of ambition as the first natural mode of civilization, when the ground must be torn up, and the woods cleared by fire and sword, I do not choose to call them pests; but surely the present system of war has little connection with virtue of any denomination, being rather the school of *finesse* and effeminacy than of fortitude. 17

Yet if defensive war, the only justifiable war, in the present advanced state of society, where virtue can show its face and ripen amidst the rigours which purify the air on the mountain's top, were alone to be adopted as just and glorious, the true heroism of antiquity might again animate female bosoms. But fair and softly, gentle reader, male or female, do not alarm thyself, for though I have compared the character of a modern soldier with that of a civilized woman, I am not going to advise them to turn their distaff[17] into a musket, though I sincerely wish to see the bayonet converted into a pruning-hook. I only recreated an imagination, fatigued by contemplating the vices and follies which all proceed from a feculent[18] stream of wealth that has muddied the pure rills of natural affection, by supposing that 18

---

[14] **cypher** Zero.

[15] **leave the nursery for the camp!** Rousseau's Émile complains that women cannot leave a nursery to go to war.

[16] **casuist** One who argues closely, persistently, and sometimes unfairly.

[17] **distaff** Instrument to wind wool in the act of spinning, notoriously a job only "fit for women."

[18] **feculent** Filthy, polluted; related to *feces*.

society will some time or other be so constituted, that man must necessarily fulfill the duties of a citizen or be despised, and that while he was employed in any of the departments of civil life, his wife, also an active citizen, should be equally intent to manage her family, educate her children, and assist her neighbours.

But, to render her really virtuous and useful, she must not, if she discharge her civil duties, want, individually, the protection of civil laws; she must not be dependent on her husband's bounty for her subsistence during his life or support after his death — for how can a being be generous who has nothing of its own? or virtuous, who is not free? 19

The wife, in the present state of things, who is faithful to her husband, and neither suckles nor educates her children, scarcely deserves the name of a wife, and has no right to that of a citizen. But take away natural rights, and duties become null. 20

Women then must be considered as only the wanton solace of men when they become so weak in mind and body that they cannot exert themselves, unless to pursue some frothy pleasure or to invent some frivolous fashion. What can be a more melancholy sight to a thinking mind than to look into the numerous carriages that drive helter-skelter about this metropolis in a morning full of pale-faced creatures who are flying from themselves. I have often wished, with Dr. Johnson,[19] to place some of them in a little shop with half a dozen children looking up to their languid countenances for support. I am much mistaken if some latent vigour would not soon give health and spirit to their eyes, and some lines drawn by the exercise of reason on the blank cheeks, which before were only undulated by dimples, might restore lost dignity to the character, or rather enable it to attain the true dignity of its nature. Virtue is not to be acquired even by speculation, much less by the negative supineness that wealth naturally generates. 21

Besides, when poverty is more disgraceful than even vice, is not morality cut to the quick? Still to avoid misconstruction, though I consider that women in the common walks of life are called to fulfill the duties of wives and mothers, by religion and reason, I cannot help lamenting that women of a superior cast have not a road open by which they can pursue more extensive plans of usefulness and independence. I may excite laughter by dropping a hint which I mean to pursue some future time, for I really think that women ought to have representatives, instead of being arbitrarily governed without having any direct share allowed them in the deliberations of government. 22

---

[19] **Dr. Samuel Johnson (1709–1784)** The greatest lexicographer and one of the most respected authors of England's eighteenth century. He was known to Mary Wollstonecraft and to her sister, Eliza, a teacher. The reference is to an item published in his *Rambler*, essay 85.

But, as the whole system of representation is now in this coun-   23
try only a convenient handle for despotism, they need not complain,
for they are as well represented as a numerous class of hard-working
mechanics, who pay for the support of royalty when they can scarcely
stop their children's mouths with bread. How are they represented
whose very sweat supports the splendid stud of an heir apparent, or
varnishes the chariot of some female favourite who looks down on
shame? Taxes on the very necessaries of life enable an endless tribe
of idle princes and princesses to pass with stupid pomp before
a gaping crowd, who almost worship the very parade which costs
them so dear. This is mere gothic grandeur, something like the barbarous useless parade of having sentinels on horseback at Whitehall,[20] which I could never view without a mixture of contempt and
indignation.

How strangely must the mind be sophisticated when this sort of   24
state impresses it! But, till these monuments of folly are levelled by
virtue, similar follies will leaven the whole mass. For the same character, in some degree, will prevail in the aggregate of society; and
the refinements of luxury, or the vicious repinings,[21] of envious
poverty, will equally banish virtue from society, considered as the
characteristic of that society, or only allow it to appear as one of the
stripes of the harlequin coat worn by the civilized man.

In the superior ranks of life every duty is done by deputies, as   25
if duties could ever be waived, and the vain pleasures which consequent idleness forces the rich to pursue appear so enticing to the next
rank that the numerous scramblers for wealth sacrifice everything to
tread on their heels. The most sacred trusts are then considered as
sinecures,[22] because they were procured by interest, and only sought
to enable a man to keep *good company*. Women in particular, all want
to be ladies. Which is simply to have nothing to do, but listlessly to
go they scarcely care where, for they cannot tell what.

But what have women to do in society? I may be asked, but   26
to loiter with easy grace; surely you would not condemn them all to
suckle fools and chronicle small beer![23] No. Women might certainly
study the art of healing, and be physicians as well as nurses. And
midwifery, decency seems to allot to them, though I am afraid the

---

[20] **sentinels on horseback at Whitehall** This is a reference to the expensive
demonstration of showmanship that continues to our day: the changing of the guard
at Whitehall.

[21] **repinings** Discontent, fretting.

[22] **sinecures** Jobs with few duties but good pay.

[23] **chronicle small beer!** *Othello* (II.i. 158). This means to keep the household
accounts.

word midwife in our dictionaries will soon give place to *accoucheur*,[24]
and one proof of the former delicacy of the sex be effaced from the
language.

They might also study politics, and settle their benevolence on   27
the broadest basis; for the reading of history will scarcely be more
useful than the perusal of romances, if read as mere biography; if the
character of the times, the political improvements, arts, &c., be not
observed. In short, if it be not considered as the history of man; and
not of particular men, who filled a niche in the temple of fame, and
dropped into the black rolling stream of time, that silently sweeps
all before it, into the shapeless void called—eternity. For shape, can
it be called, "that shape hath none"?[25]

Business of various kinds they might likewise pursue, if they   28
were educated in a more orderly manner, which might save many from
common and legal prostitution. Women would not then marry
for a support, as men accept of places under government, and neglect the implied duties; nor would an attempt to earn their own
subsistence—a most laudable one!—sink them almost to the level
of those poor abandoned creatures who live by prostitution. For are
not milliners and mantua-makers[26] reckoned the next class? The few
employments open to women, so far from being liberal, are menial;
and when a superior education enables them to take charge of the
education of children as governesses, they are not treated like the tutors of sons, though even clerical tutors are not always treated in a
manner calculated to render them respectable in the eyes of their
pupils, to say nothing of the private comfort of the individual. But as
women educated like gentlewomen are never designed for the humiliating situation which necessity sometimes forces them to fill,
these situations are considered in the light of a degradation; and
they know little of the human heart, who need to be told that nothing so painfully sharpens sensibility as such a fall in life.

Some of these women might be restrained from marrying by a   29
proper spirit or delicacy, and others may not have had it in their power
to escape in this pitiful way from servitude; is not that government
then very defective, and very unmindful of the happiness of one half of
its members, that does not provide for honest, independent women,
by encouraging them to fill respectable stations? But in order to render
their private virtue a public benefit, they must have a civil existence in

---

[24] *accoucheur* Male version of the female midwife.
[25] **"that shape hath none"** The reference is to *Paradise Lost* (II.667) by John
Milton (1608–1674); it is an allusion to death.
[26] **milliners and mantua-makers** Dressmakers, usually women (whereas
tailors were usually men).

the state, married or single; else we shall continually see some worthy woman, whose sensibility has been rendered painfully acute by undeserved contempt, droop like "the lily broken down by a plowshare."

It is a melancholy truth—yet such is the blessed effect of civilization!—the most respectable women are the most oppressed; and, unless they have understandings far superior to the common run of understandings, taking in both sexes, they must, from being treated like contemptible beings, become contemptible. How many women thus waste life away the prey of discontent, who might have practiced as physicians, regulated a farm, managed a shop, and stood erect, supported by their own industry, instead of hanging their heads surcharged with the dew of sensibility, that consumes the beauty to which it at first gave lustre; nay, I doubt whether pity and love are so near akin as poets feign, for I have seldom seen much compassion excited by the helplessness of females, unless they were fair; then, perhaps pity was the soft handmaid of love, or the harbinger of lust. 30

How much more respectable is the woman who earns her own bread by fulfilling any duty, than the most accomplished beauty!—beauty did I say?—so sensible am I of the beauty of moral loveliness, or the harmonious propriety that attunes the passions of a well regulated mind, that I blush at making the comparison; yet I sigh to think how few women aim at attaining this respectability by withdrawing from the giddy whirl of pleasure, or the indolent calm that stupefies the good sort of women it sucks in. 31

Proud of their weakness, however, they must always be protected, guarded from care, and all the rough toils that dignify the mind. If this be the fiat of fate, if they will make themselves insignificant and contemptible, sweetly to waste "life away," let them not expect to be valued when their beauty fades, for it is the fate of the fairest flowers to be admired and pulled to pieces by the careless hand that plucked them. In how many ways do I wish, from the purest benevolence, to impress this truth on my sex; yet I fear that they will not listen to a truth that dear-bought experience has brought home to many an agitated bosom, nor willingly resign the privileges of rank and sex for the privileges of humanity, to which those have no claim who do not discharge its duties. 32

Those writers are particularly useful, in my opinion, who make man feel for man, independent of the station he fills, or the drapery of factitious sentiments. I then would fain[27] convince reasonable men of the importance of some of my remarks; and prevail on them to weigh dispassionately the whole tenor of my observations. I appeal 33

---

[27] **fain** Happily, gladly.

to their understandings; and, as a fellow-creature, claim, in the name of my sex, some interest in their hearts. I entreat them to assist to emancipate their companion, to make her a *help meet*[28] for them!

Would men but generously snap our chains, and be content   34 with rational fellowship instead of slavish obedience, they would find us more observant daughters, more affectionate sisters, more faithful wives, more reasonable mothers—in a word, better citizens. We should then love them with true affection, because we should learn to respect ourselves; and, the peace of mind of a worthy man would not be interrupted by the idle vanity of his wife, nor the babes sent to nestle in a strange bosom, having never found a home in their mother's.

---

[28] ***help meet*** Helper, helpmate.

QUESTIONS FOR CRITICAL READING

1. Who is the audience for Wollstonecraft's writing? Is she writing more for men than for women? Is it clear from what she says that she addresses an explicit audience with specific qualities?
2. Analyze paragraph 1 carefully for the use of imagery, especially metaphor. What are the effects of these images? Are they overdone?
3. Wollstonecraft begins by attacking property, or the respect paid to it. What does she mean? Does she sustain that line of thought throughout the piece?
4. In paragraph 12, Wollstonecraft speaks of the "bondage of ignorance" in which women are held. Clarify precisely what she means by that expression.
5. In paragraph 30, Wollstonecraft says that people who are treated as if they were contemptible will become contemptible. Is this a political or a psychological judgment?
6. What is the substance of Wollstonecraft's complaint concerning the admiration of women for their beauty?

SUGGESTIONS FOR WRITING

1. Throughout the piece Wollstonecraft attacks the unnatural distinctions made between men and women. Establish carefully what those unnatural distinctions are, why they are unnatural, and whether such distinctions persist to the present day. By contrast, establish what some natural distinctions between men and women are and whether Wollstonecraft has taken them into consideration.

2. References are made throughout the piece to prostitution and to the debaucheries of men. Paragraph 7 specifically refers to the "wanton tricks" of prostitutes. What is Wollstonecraft's attitude toward men in regard to sexuality and their attitudes toward women—both the women of the brothels and the women with whom men live? Find passages in the piece that you can quote and analyze in an effort to examine her views.

3. In paragraph 2, Wollstonecraft complains that "the respect due only to talents and virtue" is instead being given to people on account of their property. Further, she says in paragraph 9 that riches are "destructive . . . to the human character." Determine carefully, by means of reference to and analysis of specific passages, just what Wollstonecraft means by such statements. Then, use your own anecdotes or "episodical observations" to take a stand on whether these are views you yourself can hold for our time. Are riches destructive to character? Is too much respect paid to those who possess property? If possible, use metaphor or allusion—literary or personal.

4. In paragraph 4, Wollstonecraft speaks of "men who can be gratified by the fawning fondness of spaniel-like affection" from their women. Search through the essay for other instances of similar views and analyze them carefully. Establish exactly what the men she describes want their women to be like. Have today's men changed very much in their expectations? Why? Why not? Use personal observations where possible in answering this question.

5. The question of what roles women ought to have in society is addressed in paragraphs 26, 27, and 28. What are those roles? Why are they defined in terms of work? Do you agree that they are, indeed, the roles that women should assume? Would you include more roles? Do women in our time have greater access to those roles? Consider what women actually did in Wollstonecraft's time and what they do today.

6. **CONNECTIONS**   Compare Wollstonecraft's views on the ways in which women are victims of prejudice with the views of Martin Luther King Jr. How much do women of Wollstonecraft's time have in common with the conditions of African Americans as described by King? What political issues are central to the efforts of both groups to achieve justice and equal opportunity? Might Wollstonecraft see herself in the same kind of struggle as King, or would she draw sharp distinctions?

7. **CONNECTIONS**   Consider Wollstonecraft's essay in relation to the Dalai Lama's "The Ethic of Compassion." What concerns do these thinkers have in common? Could this selection be considered an essay on ethics as well as an essay on feminism? Explain. Does Wollstonecraft seem to have issues of morality at the center of her discourse? What connection, if any, is there between Wollstonecraft's views on feminism and the Dalai Lama's views on ethics?

VIRGINIA WOOLF
Shakespeare's Sister

VIRGINIA WOOLF (1882–1941), one of the most gifted of the
modernist writers, was a prolific essayist and novelist in what
came to be known as the Bloomsbury group, named after a section of
London near the British Museum. Most members of the group were
writers, such as E. M. Forster, Lytton Strachey, and the critic Clive
Bell, and some were artists, such as Duncan Grant and Virginia
Woolf's sister, Vanessa Bell. The eminent economist John Maynard
Keynes was part of the group as well, along with a variety of other
accomplished intellectuals.

Virginia Woolf published some of the most important works of
the early twentieth century, including the novels *Jacob's Room* (1922),
Mrs. Dalloway (1925), *To the Lighthouse* (1927), *Orlando* (1928), and
The Waves (1931). Among her many volumes of nonfiction prose is
A Room of One's Own (1929). In this book Woolf speculates on what
life would have been like for an imaginary gifted sister of William
Shakespeare.

In discussing the imaginary Judith Shakespeare, Woolf examines
the circumstances common to women's lives during the Renaissance.
For example, women had little or no say in their future. Unlike their
male counterparts, they were not educated in grammar schools and
did not learn trades that would enable them to make a living for
themselves. Instead, they were expected to marry as soon as possible, even as young as thirteen or fourteen years of age, and begin
raising a family of their own. When they did marry, their husbands
were men selected by their parents; the wives essentially became the
property of those men. Under English law a married couple was regarded as one entity, and that entity was spoken for only by the man.
Similarly, the women of the period had few civil rights. As Woolf

From *A Room of One's Own*.

points out, the history books do not mention women very often, and when they do, it is usually to relate that wife beating was common and generally approved of in all classes of society.

As Woolf comments on the opportunities that women were denied during the Renaissance, she agrees with an unnamed bishop who said that no woman could have written Shakespeare's plays. Woolf explains that no woman could have had enough contact with the theater in those days to be received with anything but disdain and discourtesy. Women could not even act on stage in Shakespeare's time, much less write for it.

It would be all but impossible in a society of this sort to imagine a woman as a successful literary figure, much less as a popular playwright. After all, society excluded women, marginalizing them as insignificant—at least in the eyes of historians. Certainly women were mothers; as such, they bore the male children who went on to become accomplished and famous. However, without a trade or an education, women in Shakespeare's time were all but chattel slaves in a household.

In this setting, Woolf places a brilliant girl named Judith Shakespeare, a fictional character who, in Woolf's imaginative construction, had the same literary fire as her famous brother. How would she have tried to express herself? How would she have followed her talent? Woolf suggests the results would be depressing, and with good reason. No one would have listened to Judith; in all likelihood her life would have ended badly.

The women of Shakespeare's time mentioned in the history books are generally Elizabeths and Marys, queens and princesses whose power was inherent in their positions. Little is known, Woolf says, about the lives of ordinary middle-class women. In Woolf's time, historians were uninterested in such information. However, the feminist movement of the mid twentieth century promoted deeper research into women's society. As a result, many recent books have included detailed research into the lives of people in the Elizabethan period. Studying journals, day-books (including budgets and planning), and family records, modern historians have found much more information than English historian George Trevelyan (to whom Woolf refers in her essay) drew on. In fact, it is now known that women's lives were more varied than even Woolf implies, but women still had precious few opportunities compared to men of the period.

Woolf's Rhetoric

This selection is the third chapter from *A Room of One's Own*; thus, it begins with a sentence that implies continuity with an earlier section. The context for the essay's opening is as follows: a male dinner guest has said something insulting to women at a dinner party, and Woolf wishes she could come back with some hard fact to contradict the insult. However, she has no hard fact, so her strategy is to construct a situation that is as plausible and as accurate as her knowledge of history permits. Lacking fact, the novelist Virginia Woolf relies on imagination.

As it turned out, Woolf's portrait of Judith Shakespeare is so vivid that many readers actually believed William Shakespeare had such a sister. Judith Shakespeare did not exist, however. Her fictional character enables Woolf to speculate on how the life of any talented woman would have developed given the circumstances and limitations imposed on all women at the time. In the process, Woolf tries to reconstruct the world of Elizabethan England and place Judith in it.

Woolf goes about this act of imagination with extraordinary deliberateness. Her tone is cool and detached, almost as if she were a historian herself. She rarely reveals contempt for the opinions of men who are dismissive of women, such as the unnamed bishop. Yet, we catch an edgy tone when she discusses his views on women in literature. On the other hand, when she turns to Mr. Oscar Browning, a professor who believed the best women in Oxford were inferior to the worst men, we see another side of Woolf. She reveals that after making his high-minded pronouncements, Mr. Browning returned to his quarters for an assignation with an illiterate stable boy. This detail is meant to reveal the true intellectual level of Mr. Browning, as well as his attitude toward women.

Woolf makes careful use of simile in such statements as "for fiction, imaginative work that is, is not dropped like a pebble upon the ground, as science may be; fiction is like a spider's web, attached ever so lightly perhaps, but still attached to life at all four corners" (para. 2). Later, she shows a highly efficient use of language: "to write a work of genius is almost always a feat of prodigious difficulty.... Dogs will bark; people will interrupt; money must be made; health will break down" (para. 11). For a woman—who would not even have had a room of her own in an Elizabethan household—the impediments to creating "a work of genius" were insurmountable.

One reason for Woolf's controlled and cool tone is that she wrote with the knowledge that most men were very conservative on matters of feminism. In 1929, people would not read what she wrote if she became enraged on paper. They would turn the page and ignore her argument. Thus, her tone seems inviting and cautious, almost as if Woolf is portraying herself as conservative on women's issues and in agreement with men like the historian Trevelyan and the unnamed bishop. However, nothing could be further from the truth. Woolf's anger may seethe and rage beneath the surface, but she keeps the surface smooth enough for those who disagree with her to be lured on to read.

One of the interesting details of Woolf's style is her allusiveness. She alludes to the work of many writers — male writers such as John Keats, Alfred, Lord Tennyson, and Robert Burns, and women writers such as Jane Austen, Emily Brontë, and George Eliot. Woolf's range of reference is that of the highly literary person — which she was; yet the way in which she makes reference to other important writers is designed not to offend the reader. If the reader knows the references, then Woolf will communicate on a special shared level of understanding. If the reader does not know the references, there is nothing in Woolf's manner that makes it difficult for the reader to continue and understand her main points.

Woolf's rhetoric in this piece is singularly polite. She makes her points without rancor and alarm. They are detailed, specific, and in many ways irrefutable. What she feels she has done is nothing less than telling the truth.

PREREADING QUESTIONS: WHAT TO READ FOR

The following prereading questions may help you anticipate key issues in the discussion of Virginia Woolf's "Shakespeare's Sister." Keeping them in mind during your first reading of the selection should help focus your attention.

- What was the expected role of women in Shakespeare's time?
- By what means could Shakespeare's imaginary sister have become a dramatist?

Shakespeare's Sister

It was disappointing not to have brought back in the evening some important statement, some authentic fact. Women are poorer than men because — this or that. Perhaps now it would be better to give up seeking for the truth, and receiving on one's head an avalanche of opinion hot as lava, discolored as dish-water. It would be better to draw the curtains; to shut out distractions; to light the lamp; to narrow the enquiry and to ask the historian, who records not opinions

but facts, to describe under what conditions women lived, not throughout the ages, but in England, say in the time of Elizabeth.

For it is a perennial puzzle why no woman wrote a word of 2
that extraordinary literature when every other man, it seemed, was
capable of song or sonnet. What were the conditions in which
women lived, I asked myself; for fiction, imaginative work that is, is
not dropped like a pebble upon the ground, as science may be; fiction is like a spider's web, attached ever so lightly perhaps, but still
attached to life at all four corners. Often the attachment is scarcely
perceptible; Shakespeare's plays, for instance, seem to hang there
complete by themselves. But when the web is pulled askew, hooked
up at the edge, torn in the middle, one remembers that these webs
are not spun in midair by incorporeal creatures, but are the work of
suffering human beings, and are attached to grossly material things,
like health and money and the houses we live in.

I went, therefore, to the shelf where the histories stand and 3
took down one of the latest, Professor Trevelyan's[1] *History of England*.
Once more I looked up Women, found "position of," and turned to
the pages indicated. "Wife-beating," I read, "was a recognised right of
man, and was practised without shame by high as well as low. . . .
Similarly," the historian goes on, "the daughter who refused to marry
the gentleman of her parents' choice was liable to be locked up,
beaten and flung about the room, without any shock being inflicted
on public opinion. Marriage was not an affair of personal affection,
but of family avarice, particularly in the 'chivalrous' upper classes. . . .
Betrothal often took place while one or both of the parties was in the
cradle, and marriage when they were scarcely out of the nurses'
charge." That was about 1470, soon after Chaucer's time. The next
reference to the position of women is some two hundred years later,
in the time of the Stuarts. "It was still the exception for women of
the upper and middle class to choose their own husbands, and
when the husband had been assigned, he was lord and master, so far
at least as law and custom could make him. Yet even so," Professor
Trevelyan concludes, "neither Shakespeare's women nor those of authentic seventeenth-century memoirs, like the Verneys and the
Hutchinsons, seem wanting in personality and character." Certainly,
if we consider it, Cleopatra must have had a way with her; Lady Macbeth, one would suppose, had a will of her own; Rosalind, one
might conclude, was an attractive girl. Professor Trevelyan is speaking no more than the truth when he remarks that Shakespeare's
women do not seem wanting in personality and character. Not being

---

[1] **Trevelyan: George Macaulay (1876–1962)** One of England's great historians. [Woolf's note]

a historian, one might go even further and say that women have burnt like beacons in all the works of all the poets from the beginning of time—Clytemnestra, Antigone, Cleopatra, Lady Macbeth, Phèdre, Cressida, Rosalind, Desdemona, the Duchess of Malfi, among the dramatists; then among the prose writers: Millamant, Clarissa, Becky Sharp, Anna Karenina, Emma Bovary, Madame de Guermantes—the names flock to mind, nor do they recall women "lacking in personality and character." Indeed, if woman had no existence save in the fiction written by men, one would imagine her a person of the utmost importance; very various; heroic and mean; splendid and sordid; infinitely beautiful and hideous in the extreme; as great as a man, some think even greater.[2] But this is woman in fiction. In fact, as Professor Trevelyan points out, she was locked up, beaten and flung about the room.

A very queer, composite being thus emerges. Imaginatively she   4
is of the highest importance; practically she is completely insignificant. She pervades poetry from cover to cover; she is all but absent from history. She dominates the lives of kings and conquerors in fiction; in fact she was the slave of any boy whose parents forced a ring upon her finger. Some of the most inspired words, some of the most profound thoughts in literature fall from her lips; in real life she could hardly read, could scarcely spell, and was the property of her husband.

It was certainly an odd monster that one made up by reading the   5
historians first and the poets afterwards—a worm winged like an eagle; the spirit of life and beauty in a kitchen chopping up suet. But these monsters, however amusing to the imagination, have no existence in fact. What one must do to bring her to life was to think poetically and prosaically at one and the same moment, thus keeping in

---

[2] **even greater** "It remains a strange and almost inexplicable fact that in Athena's city, where women were kept in almost Oriental suppression as odalisques or drudges, the stage should yet have produced figures like Clytemnestra and Cassandra, Atossa and Antigone, Phèdre and Medea, and all the other heroines who dominate play after play of the 'misogynist' Euripides. But the paradox of this world where in real life a respectable woman could hardly show her face alone in the street, and yet on the stage a woman equals or surpasses a man, has never been satisfactorily explained. In modern tragedy the same predominance exists. At all events, a very cursory survey of Shakespeare's work (similarly with Webster, though not with Marlowe or Jonson) suffices to reveal how this dominance, this initiative of women, persists from Rosalind to Lady Macbeth. So too in Racine; six of his tragedies bear their heroines' names; and what male characters of his shall we set against Hermione and Andromaque, Bérénice and Roxane, Phèdre and Athalie? So again with Ibsen; what men shall we match with Solveig and Nora, Hedda and Hilda Wangel and Rebecca West?"—F. L. Lucas, *Tragedy*, pp. 114–15. [Woolf's note]

touch with fact—that she is Mrs. Martin, aged thirty-six, dressed in blue, wearing a black hat and brown shoes; but not losing sight of fiction either—that she is a vessel in which all sorts of spirits and forces are coursing and flashing perpetually. The moment, however, that one tries this method with the Elizabethan woman, one branch of illumination fails; one is held up by the scarcity of facts. One knows nothing detailed, nothing perfectly true and substantial about her. History scarcely mentions her. And I turned to Professor Trevelyan again to see what history meant to him. I found by looking at his chapter headings that it meant—

"The Manor Court and the Methods of Open-field Agriculture . . . 6 The Cistercians and Sheep-farming . . . The Crusades . . . The University . . . The House of Commons . . . The Hundred Years' War . . . The Wars of the Roses . . . The Renaissance Scholars . . . The Dissolution of the Monasteries . . . Agrarian and Religious Strife . . . The Origin of English Sea-power . . . The Armada . . ." and so on. Occasionally an individual woman is mentioned, an Elizabeth, or a Mary; a queen or a great lady. But by no possible means could middle-class women with nothing but brains and character at their command have taken part in any one of the great movements which, brought together, constitute the historian's view of the past. Nor shall we find her in any collection of anecdotes. Aubrey[3] hardly mentions her. She never writes her own life and scarcely keeps a diary; there are only a handful of her letters in existence. She left no plays or poems by which we can judge her. What one wants, I thought—and why does not some brilliant student at Newnham or Girton[4] supply it?— is a mass of information; at what age did she marry; how many children had she as a rule; what was her house like; had she a room to herself; did she do the cooking; would she be likely to have a servant? All these facts lie somewhere, presumably, in parish registers and account books; the life of the average Elizabethan woman must be scattered about somewhere, could one collect it and make a book of it. It would be ambitious beyond my daring, I thought, looking about the shelves for books that were not there, to suggest to the students of those famous colleges that they should rewrite history, though I own that it often seems a little queer as it is, unreal, lopsided; but why should they not add a supplement to history? calling it, of course, by some inconspicuous name so that women might

---

[3]**John Aubrey (1626–1697)** English antiquarian noted for his *Brief Lives*, biographical sketches of famous men.

[4]**Newnham and Girton** Two women's colleges founded at Cambridge in the 1870s. [Woolf's note] Newnham (1871) and Girton (1869) were the first women's colleges at Cambridge University.

figure there without impropriety? For one often catches a glimpse of them in the lives of the great, whisking away into the background, concealing, I sometimes think, a wink, a laugh, perhaps a tear. And, after all, we have lives enough of Jane Austen; it scarcely seems necessary to consider again the influence of the tragedies of Joanna Baillie upon the poetry of Edgar Allan Poe; as for myself, I should not mind if the homes and haunts of Mary Russell Mitford were closed to the public for a century at least. But what I find deplorable, I continued, looking about the bookshelves again, is that nothing is known about women before the eighteenth century. I have no model in my mind to turn about this way and that. Here am I asking why women did not write poetry in the Elizabethan age, and I am not sure how they were educated; whether they were taught to write; whether they had sitting-rooms to themselves; how many women had children before they were twenty-one; what, in short, they did from eight in the morning till eight at night. They had no money evidently; according to Professor Trevelyan they were married whether they liked it or not before they were out of the nursery, at fifteen or sixteen very likely. It would have been extremely odd, even upon this showing, had one of them suddenly written the plays of Shakespeare, I concluded, and I thought of that old gentleman, who is dead now, but was a bishop, I think, who declared that it was impossible for any woman, past, present, or to come, to have the genius of Shakespeare. He wrote to the papers about it. He also told a lady who applied to him for information that cats do not as a matter of fact go to heaven, though they have, he added, souls of a sort. How much thinking those old gentlemen used to save one! How the borders of ignorance shrank back at their approach! Cats do not go to heaven. Women cannot write the plays of Shakespeare.

Be that as it may, I could not help thinking, as I looked at the works of Shakespeare on the shelf, that the bishop was right at least in this; it would have been impossible, completely and entirely, for any woman to have written the plays of Shakespeare in the age of Shakespeare. Let me imagine, since facts are so hard to come by, what would have happened had Shakespeare had a wonderfully gifted sister, called Judith, let us say. Shakespeare himself went, very probably—his mother was an heiress—to the grammar school, where he may have learnt Latin—Ovid, Virgil and Horace—and the elements of grammar and logic. He was, it is well known, a wild boy who poached rabbits, perhaps shot a deer, and had, rather sooner than he should have done, to marry a woman in the neighborhood, who bore him a child rather quicker than was right. That escapade sent him to seek his fortune in London. He had, it seemed, a taste for the theatre; he began by holding horses at the stage door. Very soon he got work in the theatre, became a successful actor, and lived at the hub of the universe, meeting everybody, knowing everybody, practicing his art on the boards, exercising his wits in the streets, and even getting access to the palace of the queen. Meanwhile his extraordinarily gifted sister, let us suppose, remained at home. She was as adventurous, as imaginative, as agog to see the world as he was. But she was not sent to school. She had no chance of learning grammar and logic, let alone of reading Horace and Virgil. She picked up a book now and then, one of her brother's perhaps, and read a few pages. But then her parents came in and told her to mend the stockings or mind the stew and not moon about with books and papers. They would have spoken sharply but kindly, for they were substantial people who knew the conditions of life for a woman and loved their daughter—indeed, more likely than not she was the apple of her father's eye. Perhaps she scribbled some pages up in an apple loft on the sly, but was careful to hide them or set fire to them. Soon, however, before she was out of her teens, she was to be betrothed to the son of a neighboring wool-stapler. She cried out that marriage was hateful to her, and for that she was severely beaten by her father. Then he ceased to scold her. He begged her instead not to hurt him, not to shame him in this matter of her marriage. He would give her a chain of beads or a fine petticoat, he said; and there were tears in his eyes. How could she disobey him? How could she break his heart? The force of her own gift alone drove her to it. She made up a small parcel of her belongings, let herself down by a rope one summer's night and took the road to London. She was not seventeen. The birds that sang in the hedge were not more musical than she was. She had the quickest fancy, a gift like her brother's, for the tune of words. Like him, she had a taste for the theatre. She stood at the stage door; she wanted to act, she said. Men laughed in her face. The manager—a fat, loose-lipped man—guffawed. He bellowed something about poodles dancing and women acting—no woman, he said, could possibly be an actress. He hinted—you can imagine what. She could get no training in her craft. Could she even seek her dinner in a tavern or roam the streets at midnight? Yet her genius was for fiction and lusted to feed abundantly upon the lives of men and women and the study of their ways. At last—for she was very young, oddly like Shakespeare the poet in her face, with the same grey eyes and rounded brows—at last Nick Greene, the actor-manager took pity on her; she found herself with child by that gentleman and so—who shall measure the heat and violence of the poet's heart when caught and tangled in a woman's body?—killed

herself one winter's night and lies buried at some cross-roads where
the omnibuses now stop outside the Elephant and Castle.[5]

That, more or less, is how the story would run, I think, if a   8
woman in Shakespeare's day had had Shakespeare's genius. But for
my part, I agree with the deceased bishop, if such he was—it is un-
thinkable that any woman in Shakespeare's day should have had
Shakespeare's genius. For genius like Shakespeare's is not born among
laboring, uneducated, servile people. It was not born in England
among the Saxons and the Britons. It is not born today among the
working classes. How, then, could it have been born among women
whose work began, according to Professor Trevelyan, almost before
they were out of the nursery, who were forced to it by their parents
and held to it by all the power of law and custom? Yet genius of a sort
must have existed among women as it must have existed among the
working classes. Now and again an Emily Brontë or a Robert Burns[6]
blazes out and proves its presence. But certainly it never got itself on
to paper. When, however, one reads of a witch being ducked, of a
woman possessed by devils, of a wise woman selling herbs, or even
of a very remarkable man who had a mother, then, I think we are on
the track of a lost novelist, a suppressed poet, of some mute and in-
glorious Jane Austen, some Emily Brontë who dashed her brains out
on the moor or mopped and mowed about the highways crazed with
the torture that her gift had put her to. Indeed, I would venture to
guess that Anon, who wrote so many poems without signing them,
was often a woman. It was a woman Edward Fitzgerald,[7] I think, suggested who made the ballads and the folk-songs, crooning them to
her children, beguiling her spinning with them, or the length of the
winter's night.

This may be true or it may be false—who can say?—but what   9
is true in it, so it seemed to me, reviewing the story of Shakespeare's
sister as I had made it, is that any woman born with a great gift in
the sixteenth century would certainly have gone crazed, shot herself,
or ended her days in some lonely cottage outside the village, half
witch, half wizard, feared and mocked at. For it needs little skill in
psychology to be sure that a highly gifted girl who had tried to use
her gift for poetry would have been so thwarted and hindered by
other people, so tortured and pulled asunder by her own contrary

---

[5] **Elephant and Castle** A bus stop in London. The name came from a local pub.
[6] **Emily Brontë (1818–1848)** wrote *Wuthering Heights*; **Robert Burns
(1759–1796)** was a Scots poet; **Jane Austen (1775–1817)** wrote *Pride and Prejudice* and many other novels. All three wrote against very great odds.
[7] **Edward Fitzgerald (1809–1883)** British scholar, poet, and translator who
wrote *The Rubaiyat of Omar Khayyam*.

instincts, that she must have lost her health and sanity to a certainty. No girl could have walked to London and stood at a stage door and forced her way into the presence of actor-managers without doing herself a violence and suffering an anguish which may have been irrational — for chastity may be a fetish invented by certain societies for unknown reasons — but were none the less inevitable. Chastity had then, it has even now, a religious importance in a woman's life, and has so wrapped itself round with nerves and instincts that to cut it free and bring it to the light of day demands courage of the rarest. To have lived a free life in London in the sixteenth century would have meant for a woman who was poet and playwright a nervous stress and dilemma which might well have killed her. Had she survived, whatever she had written would have been twisted and deformed, issuing from a strained and morbid imagination. And undoubtedly, I thought, looking at the shelf where there are no plays by women, her work would have gone unsigned. That refuge she would have sought certainly. It was the relic of the sense of chastity that dictated anonymity to women even so late as the nineteenth century. Currer Bell, George Eliot, George Sand,[8] all the victims of inner strife as their writings prove, sought ineffectively to veil themselves by using the name of a man. Thus they did homage to the convention, which if not implanted by the other sex was liberally encouraged by them (the chief glory of a woman is not to be talked of, said Pericles, himself a much-talked-of man), that publicity in women is detestable. Anonymity runs in their blood. The desire to be veiled still possesses them. They are not even now as concerned about the health of their fame as men are, and, speaking generally, will pass a tombstone or a signpost without feeling an irresistible desire to cut their names on it, as Alf, Bert or Chas. must do in obedience to their instinct, which murmurs if it sees a fine woman go by, or even a dog, *Ce chien est à moi.*[9] And, of course, it may not be a dog, I thought, remembering Parliament Square, the Sieges Allee and other avenues; it may be a piece of land or a man with curly black hair. It is one of the great advantages of being a woman that one can pass even a very fine negress without wishing to make an Englishwoman of her.

That woman, then, who was born with a gift of poetry in the six-   10
teenth century, was an unhappy woman, a woman at strife against herself. All the conditions of her life, all her own instincts, were hostile to the state of mind which is needed to set free whatever is in the

---

[8] **Currer Bell (1816–1855), George Eliot (1819–1880), George Sand (1804–1876)** Masculine pen names for Charlotte Brontë, Mary Ann Evans, and Amandine-Aurore-Lucille Dudevant, three major novelists of the nineteenth century.
   [9] **Ce chien est à moi** That's my dog.

brain. But what is the state of mind that is most propitious to the act of creation, I asked. Can one come by any notion of the state that furthers and makes possible that strange activity? Here I opened the volume containing the Tragedies of Shakespeare. What was Shakespeare's state of mind, for instance, when he wrote *Lear* and *Antony and Cleopatra*? It was certainly the state of mind most favorable to poetry that there has ever existed. But Shakespeare himself said nothing about it. We only know casually and by chance that he "never blotted a line." Nothing indeed was ever said by the artist himself about his state of mind until the eighteenth century perhaps. Rousseau perhaps began it. At any rate, by the nineteenth century self-consciousness had developed so far that it was the habit for men of letters to describe their minds in confessions and autobiographies. Their lives also were written, and their letters were printed after their deaths. Thus, though we do not know what Shakespeare went through when he wrote *Lear*, we do know what Carlyle went through when he wrote the *French Revolution*; what Flaubert went through when he wrote *Madame Bovary;* what Keats[10] was going through when he tried to write poetry against the coming of death and the indifference of the world.

And one gathers from this enormous modern literature of confession and self-analysis that to write a work of genius is almost always a feat of prodigious difficulty. Everything is against the likelihood that it will come from the writer's mind whole and entire. Generally material circumstances are against it. Dogs will bark; people will interrupt; money must be made; health will break down. Further, accentuating all these difficulties and making them harder to bear is the world's notorious indifference. It does not ask people to write poems and novels and histories; it does not need them. It does not care whether Flaubert finds the right word or whether Carlyle scrupulously verifies this or that fact. Naturally, it will not pay for what it does not want. And so the writer, Keats, Flaubert, Carlyle, suffers, especially in the creative years of youth, every form of distraction and discouragement. A curse, a cry of agony, rises from those books of analysis and confession. "Mighty poets in their misery dead"—that is the burden of their song. If anything comes through in spite of all this, it is a miracle, and probably no book is born entire and uncrippled as it was conceived. 11

But for women, I thought, looking at the empty shelves, these difficulties were infinitely more formidable. In the first place, to have a room of her own, let alone a quiet room or a sound-proof 12

---

[10] **Thomas Carlyle (1795–1881), Gustave Flaubert (1821–1880), and John Keats (1795–1821)** Important nineteenth-century writers, all men.

room, was out of the question, unless her parents were exceptionally rich or very noble, even up to the beginning of the nineteenth century. Since her pin money, which depended on the good will of her father, was only enough to keep her clothed, she was debarred from such alleviations as came even to Keats or Tennyson or Carlyle, all poor men, from a walking tour, a little journey to France, from the separate lodging which, even if it were miserable enough, sheltered them from the claims and tyrannies of their families. Such material difficulties were formidable; but much worse were the immaterial. The indifference of the world which Keats and Flaubert and other men of genius have found so hard to bear was in her case not indifference but hostility. The world did not say to her as it said to them, Write if you choose; it makes no difference to me. The world said with a guffaw, Write? What's the good of your writing? Here the psychologists of Newnham and Girton might come to our help, I thought, looking again at the blank spaces on the shelves. For surely it is time that the effect of discouragement upon the mind of the artist should be measured, as I have seen a dairy company measure the effect of ordinary milk and Grade A milk upon the body of the rat. They set two rats in cages side by side, and of the two one was furtive, timid and small, and the other was glossy, bold and big. Now what food do we feed women as artists upon? I asked, remembering, I suppose, that dinner of prunes and custard. To answer that question I had only to open the evening paper and to read that Lord Birkenhead is of opinion—but really I am not going to trouble to copy our Lord Birkenhead's opinion upon the writing of women. What Dean Inge says I will leave in peace. The Harley Street specialist may be allowed to rouse the echoes of Harley Street with his vociferations without raising a hair on my head. I will quote, however, Mr. Oscar Browning, because Mr. Oscar Browning was a great figure in Cambridge at one time, and used to examine the students at Girton and Newnham. Mr. Oscar Browning was wont to declare "that the impression left on his mind, after looking over any set of examination papers, was that, irrespective of the marks he might give, the best woman was intellectually the inferior of the worst man." After saying that Mr. Browning went back to his rooms—and it is this sequel that endears him and makes him a human figure of some bulk and majesty—he went back to his rooms and found a stable-boy lying on the sofa—"a mere skeleton, his cheeks were cavernous and sallow, his teeth were black, and he did not appear to have the full use of his limbs. . . . 'That's Arthur' [said Mr. Browning]. 'He's a dear boy really and most high-minded.'" The two pictures always seem to me to complete each other. And happily in this age of biography the two pictures often do complete each other, so that we are able to interpret the opinions of great men not only by what they say, but by what they do.

But though this is possible now, such opinions coming from the   13
lips of important people must have been formidable enough even fifty years ago. Let us suppose that a father from the highest motives did not wish his daughter to leave home and become writer, painter or scholar. "See what Mr. Oscar Browning says," he would say; and there was not only Mr. Oscar Browning; there was the *Saturday Review*; there was Mr. Greg—the "essentials of a woman's being," said Mr. Greg emphatically, "are that *they are supported by, and they minister to, men*"—there was an enormous body of masculine opinion to the effect that nothing could be expected of women intellectually. Even if her father did not read out loud these opinions, any girl could read them for herself; and the reading, even in the nineteenth century, must have lowered her vitality, and told profoundly upon her work. There would always have been that assertion—you cannot do this, you are incapable of doing that—to protest against, to overcome. Probably for a novelist this germ is no longer of much effect; for there have been women novelists of merit. But for painters it must still have some sting in it; and for musicians, I imagine, is even now active and poisonous in the extreme. The woman composer stands where the actress stood in the time of Shakespeare. Nick Greene, I thought, remembering the story I had made about Shakespeare's sister, said that a woman acting put him in mind of a dog dancing. Johnson repeated the phrase two hundred years later of women preaching. And here, I said, opening a book about music, we have the very words used again in this year of grace, 1928, of women who try to write music. "Of Mlle. Germaine Tailleferre one can only repeat Dr. Johnson's dictum concerning a woman preacher, transposed into terms of music. 'Sir, a woman's composing is like a dog's walking on his hind legs. It is not done well, but you are surprised to find it done at all.'"[11] So accurately does history repeat itself.

Thus, I concluded, shutting Mr. Oscar Browning's life and push-   14
ing away the rest, it is fairly evident that even in the nineteenth century a woman was not encouraged to be an artist. On the contrary, she was snubbed, slapped, lectured and exhorted. Her mind must have been strained and her vitality lowered by the need of opposing this, of disproving that. For here again we come within range of that very interesting and obscure masculine complex which has had so much influence upon the woman's movement; that deep-seated desire, not so much that *she* shall be inferior as that *he* shall be superior,

---

[11] *A Survey of Contemporary Music*, Cecil Gray, p. 246. [Woolf's note]

which plants him wherever one looks, not only in front of the arts, but barring the way to politics too, even when the risk to himself seems infinitesimal and the suppliant humble and devoted. Even Lady Bessborough, I remembered, with all her passion for politics, must humbly bow herself and write to Lord Granville Leveson-Gower: ". . . notwithstanding all my violence in politics and talking so much on that subject, I perfectly agree with you that no woman has any business to meddle with that or any other serious business, farther than giving her opinion (if she is ask'd)." And so she goes on to spend her enthusiasm where it meets with no obstacle whatsoever upon that immensely important subject, Lord Granville's maiden speech in the House of Commons. The spectacle is certainly a strange one, I thought. The history of men's opposition to women's emancipation is more interesting perhaps than the story of that emancipation itself. An amusing book might be made of it if some young student at Girton or Newnham would collect examples and deduce a theory—but she would need thick gloves on her hands, and bars to protect her of solid gold.

But what is amusing now, I recollected, shutting Lady Bessbor- 15
ough, had to be taken in desperate earnest once. Opinions that one now pastes in a book labelled cock-a-doodle-dum and keeps for reading to select audiences on summer nights once drew tears, I can assure you. Among your grandmothers and great-grandmothers there were many that wept their eyes out. Florence Nightingale shrieked aloud in her agony.[12] Moreover, it is all very well for you, who have got yourselves to college and enjoy sitting-rooms—or is it only bed-sitting-rooms?—of your own to say that genius should disregard such opinions; that genius should be above caring what is said of it. Unfortunately, it is precisely the men or women of genius who mind most what is said of them. Remember Keats. Remember the words he had cut on his tombstone.[13] Think of Tennyson; think—but I need hardly multiply instances of the undeniable, if very unfortunate, fact that it is the nature of the artist to mind excessively what is said about him. Literature is strewn with the wreckage of men who have minded beyond reason the opinions of others.

And this susceptibility of theirs is doubly unfortunate, I thought, 16
returning again to my original enquiry into what state of mind is most propitious for creative work, because the mind of an artist, in order to achieve the prodigious effort of freeing whole and entire the work that is in him, must be incandescent, like Shakespeare's mind, I conjectured,

---

[12] *See Cassandra* by Florence Nightingale, printed in *The Cause*, by R. Strachey. [Woolf's note]

[13] **words . . . tombstone** "Here lies one whose name is writ on water." [Woolf's note]

looking at the book which lay open at *Antony and Cleopatra*. There must be no obstacle in it, no foreign matter unconsumed.

For though we say that we know nothing about Shakespeare's state   17
of mind, even as we say that, we are saying something about Shakespeare's state of mind. The reason perhaps why we know so little of Shakespeare—compared with Donne or Ben Jonson or Milton[14]—is that his grudges and spites and antipathies are hidden from us. We are not held up by some "revelation" which reminds us of the writer. All desire to protest, to preach, to proclaim an injury, to pay off a score, to make the world the witness of some hardship or grievance was fired out of him and consumed. Therefore his poetry flows from him free and unimpeded. If ever a human being got his work expressed completely, it was Shakespeare. If ever a mind was incandescent, unimpeded, I thought, turning again to the bookcase, it was Shakespeare's mind.

---

[14]**John Donne (1572–1631), Ben Jonson (1572/3–1637), John Milton (1608–1674)** Three of the most important seventeenth-century poets.

QUESTIONS FOR CRITICAL READING

1. How did Elizabethan gender roles limit opportunities in literature?
2. Why does Woolf begin by referring to an eminent historian?
3. Why does history treat sixteenth- and seventeenth-century women with so little notice?
4. What is Woolf's point regarding the behavior of Oscar Browning?
5. Why does Woolf worry over the relation of opinions to facts?
6. What is the difference between the way women are represented in history and the way they are depicted in fiction?
7. Why does Woolf have Judith Shakespeare become pregnant?

SUGGESTIONS FOR WRITING

1. Woolf says that a woman "born with a gift of poetry in the sixteenth century, was an unhappy woman, a woman at strife against herself" (para. 10). What does it mean for a woman to be "at strife against herself"? What are the characteristics of such a strife, and what are its implications for the woman? In what ways would she be aware of such inner strife?
2. Look up brief biographies of the women writers who took men's names. Woolf lists three together: Currer Bell, George Eliot, and George Sand.

What did they have in common? Why did they feel the need to use a man's name for their pseudonym? What did they do to avoid being stigmatized as women writers? Were they equally successful? Are they now considered feminist writers?

3. Despite the calmness of her tone, it is clear that Woolf feels very deeply about the issues that she discusses in this piece. In what ways can you justify this as a formative piece of feminist writing? What elements establish it as either feminist or not? If you feel it is not a feminist piece, explain why, and try to show what changes would help it to qualify as a feminist essay.

4. Read the book from which this essay comes, *A Room of One's Own*. The last chapter discusses androgyny, the quality of possessing characteristics of both sexes. Woolf argues that perhaps a writer should not be exclusively male or female in outlook, but should combine both. How effective is her argument in that chapter? How much of an impact did the book have on your own views of feminism?

5. Explain why it is so important for a woman to have "a room of one's own." Obviously, the use of the word *room* stands for much more than a simple room with four walls and a door. What is implied in the way Woolf uses this term? Do you think this point is still valid for women in the twenty-first century? Why are so many women in any age denied the right to have "a room of one's own"?

6. Woolf says that "even in the nineteenth century a woman was not encouraged to be an artist. On the contrary, she was snubbed, slapped, lectured and exhorted. Her mind must have been strained and her vitality lowered by the need of opposing this, of disproving that" (para. 14). Explain the implications of this statement, and decide whether it still describes the situation of many or most women. Use your personal experience where relevant, but consider the situations of any women you find interesting.

7. **CONNECTIONS** In what ways are Mary Wollstonecraft and Virginia Woolf in agreement about the waste of women's talents in any age? As you comment on this, consider, too, the ways in which these writers differ in their approach to discussing women and the ways in which women sometimes cooperate in accepting their own restrictions. Which of these writers is more obviously a modern feminist in your mind? Which of them is more convincing? Why?

8. **CONNECTIONS** Based on Woolf's attitudes in this essay, which of the male writers in this collection comes closest to supporting feminist views? Consider especially the work of Karl Marx, Martin Luther King Jr., Henry David Thoreau, and the Dalai Lama. Which of their views seems most sympathetic to the problems Woolf considers here?

9. **SEEING CONNECTIONS** Virginia Woolf appeared on the following *Time* magazine cover on April 12, 1937. That year Woolf and Wallis Simpson (1896–1986), an American divorcée whose marriage to Great Britain's King Edward VIII led to his abdication of the throne, were the only women to appear solo on *Time* covers.

How does the *Time* cover below compare with the portrait of Woolf on p. 760? The accompanying *Time* cover story, a review of Woolf's novel *The Years*, describes her this way: "She has no children. Careless of her clothes, her face, her greying hair, at 55 she is the picture of a sensitive, cloistered literary woman." How do you think Woolf would have reacted to this description? Why? What does *Time*'s choice of portrait and description tell you about how intellectual women such as Woolf were viewed in 1937?

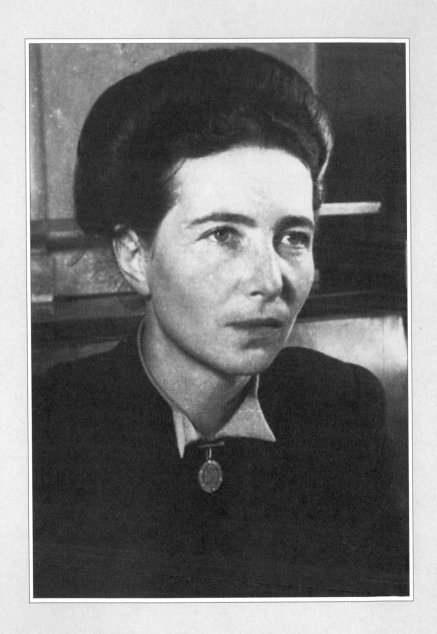

SIMONE DE BEAUVOIR
Woman: Myth and Reality

SIMONE DE BEAUVOIR (1908–1986) was one of the most important post–World War II French intellectuals. Her work was primarily philosophical, and she herself taught philosophy and lived for
a time with one of France's preeminent existentialist philosophers,
Jean-Paul Sartre (1905–1980). These two independent and brilliant
leftist thinkers represented the ideal couple to many intellectuals, although recent biographical studies have demonstrated that in their
relationship Beauvoir's ambitions were subjugated to those of Sartre.

Beauvoir prepared for a career as a teacher at the École Nor-
male Superieure and taught in Marseilles, Rouen, and Paris, all the
while writing novels, memoirs, and essays. Her best-known book is
Le Deuxième Sexe (1949), published in English in 1953 as *The Second Sex*, a book now regarded as a beacon for the modern feminist
movement. When Beauvoir began work on this book, French women
were not permitted to vote (they did not win suffrage until 1945).
In *The Second Sex* Beauvoir discusses how women are cast as the
Other, the alienated of society. She explores the implications of
defining women in relation to men—as *what men are not* rather
than as *what women are*, as a category in and of themselves.

According to Beauvoir, a person is not born a woman but makes
herself a woman. This suggestion implies, for Beauvoir, that the
individual is shaped and formed by social convention, especially
by conventions associated with gender. Certain conventions maintain a social fiction that pleases the "ruling caste," which in Beauvoir's view is exclusively masculine. She compares the myth of
the Eternal Feminine with a Platonic idea. For Plato, the reality of
the world is inferior to the pure ideas that exist in heaven. These
ideas are fixed and unaltered by experience. In that sense, Beauvoir

From *The Second Sex*. Translated and edited by H. M. Parshley.

regards the myth of the Eternal Feminine as an idea that does not change, even in the face of human experience that contradicts it.

Part of the idea of the Eternal Feminine involves the myth that women are mysterious and incomprehensible to men; they are completely unlike men and, therefore, the Other. Beauvoir complains that no amount of personal experience seems to shatter the myth of women's mystery. She also states that mysteriousness does not serve women well, nor does it serve men; nevertheless, the concept of mystery lingers. She explains that in the relationship of master to slave, it is always the slave who is mysterious and difficult to understand. The slave is always the Other. Through this logic Beauvoir leads us to understand that as long as the mystery of woman defines her, woman will always be in a subordinate relationship to men.

One important consequence of accepting the myth of woman is that men will fail to understand women as they are — as friends, as equals. Even worse, women who accept the myth will constantly distort their personalities in order to please the "master." Beauvoir asks, which is it that a woman loves: her husband or her marriage? Women who accept the myth will manipulate men for their own purposes by trading on that myth, but in the process they will lose their individual nature, surrendering it to some imagined "immanence." *Immanence* is one of the most frequently repeated words in the essay (see para. 5); by this term, Beauvoir usually means an imagined essential quality, associated here with a myth.

The problem is that the myth of the Eternal Feminine, however it is expressed, contradicts the essential nature of individuals. It is an archetype that cannot be altered even when we see individuals contradicting the archetype. When that happens, Beauvoir says, we assume the individual is aberrant in some way. Beauvoir encourages us to reject the myth of the Eternal Feminine and to accept the reality that presents itself before our eyes. Thus, Beauvoir does not subscribe to the Platonic view; instead she follows the Aristotelian view that prefers examination of a scientific sort, one that accepts perceived facts.

Beauvoir's Rhetoric

This essay makes a plea for equality between men and women on several levels. As society is structured, Beauvoir knows, the concept of equality is impossible. The social order, she tells us, is essentially patriarchal. As a result, women have a subordinate and restricted role that is maintained in part by the persistence of the myth of the Eternal Feminine. Therefore, the general structure of the essay is as an argument decrying the persistence of the myth and revealing the damage that it does to members of society, both men and women.

At the time she wrote this piece, Beauvoir was not known as a feminist. Indeed, in the late 1940s and early 1950s, few modern feminists were known in the United States or in France. Long before Beauvoir aligned herself with certain militant feminists in the 1970s, *The Second Sex* provided a rallying cry because it was a treatise that examined with great authority the representation of women in many different intellectual and cultural arenas. For that reason, the book became a memorable document of great political power. Its rhetoric is not patterned or self-conscious but simple and straightforward. The calm, reasonable, direct style enforces the author's persuasiveness.

Beauvoir's method in this piece is careful analysis of a circumstance that she defines at the outset: the myth of the Eternal Feminine. Once she has described and defined this myth—and in the process established its persistence—she analyzes its character and its implications. Her analysis of the myth's uses in society reveals how it guarantees a woman's subordination. Beauvoir also calls women to task for accepting a myth that ultimately imprisons them. She urges change, suggesting that certain basic transformations may make it possible for men and women to achieve a form of equality that preserves their respective masculinity and femininity without demanding that one become the Other.

Beauvoir has drawn criticism for the tone of her description of women's behavior. Writers such as the poet Stevie Smith have accused Beauvoir of standing aside from the mass of women as if she herself were in a separate category. Some readers and close friends felt that her relationship with Sartre, in which they saw her treated as an absolute equal intellectually, led her to develop a distorted view of the nature of women's subjection and gave her writing a cool, overly reserved, academic quality.

In fact, it is true that this piece is reserved. It is also true, however, that Beauvoir strikes at a given in the social order of mid-twentieth-century Europe and America. And it is true that she generally talks about women who are in a comfortable social class, women whom bell hooks would refer to as bourgeois and privileged. Nonetheless, Beauvoir maintains that as long as women are seen as mysterious and different in a male-dominated world, they will remain subordinate. The myths associated with women may be several, contradictory, and seemingly harmless, but Beauvoir insists they are ultimately damaging to women and to the relationship between the sexes.

One of the most distinctive qualities of *The Second Sex* is its learnedness. To avoid giving the impression that she is merely stating opinion, Beauvoir pauses occasionally to make references to important writers such as Auguste Comte, Søren Kierkegaard, André Gide, and Maurice Maeterlinck. Most of the writers she refers to are men, and most are long-standing philosophers and classic authors. By citing such authorities she reveals a capacious mind, one that is not ignorant of the role of male writers and the problems of a society dominated by males.

The power of the piece lies in its clarity and depth of thought. Beauvoir was a consummate intellectual in an environment that nurtured such types of thinkers, and what she has to say demands our attention and respect.

PREREADING QUESTIONS:
WHAT TO READ FOR

The following prereading questions may help you anticipate key issues in the discussion of Simone de Beauvoir's "Woman: Myth and Reality." Keeping them in mind during your first reading of the selection should help focus your attention.

- What is the myth of the Eternal Feminine?
- Why do men prefer the myth of the Eternal Feminine to the reality of women?
- How does men's power benefit from the myth(s) of women?

Woman: Myth and Reality

The myth of woman plays a considerable part in literature; but what is its importance in daily life? To what extent does it affect the customs and conduct of individuals? In replying to this question it will be necessary to state precisely the relations this myth bears to reality.

There are different kinds of myths. This one, the myth of woman, sublimating an immutable aspect of the human condition—namely, the "division" of humanity into two classes of individuals—is a static myth. It projects into the realm of Platonic ideas a reality that is directly experienced or is conceptualized on a basis of experience; in place of fact, value, significance, knowledge, empirical law, it substitutes a transcendental Idea, timeless, unchangeable, necessary. This idea is indisputable because it is beyond the given: it is endowed with absolute truth. Thus, as against the dispersed, contingent, and multiple existences of actual women, mythical thought opposes the Eternal Feminine, unique and changeless. If the definition provided for this concept is contradicted by the behavior of flesh-and-blood women, it is the latter who are wrong: we are told not that Femininity is a false entity, but that the women concerned are not feminine. The contrary facts of experience are impotent against the myth. In a way, however, its source is in experience. Thus it is quite true that woman is other than man, and this alterity[1] is directly felt in desire, the embrace, love; but the real relation is one of reciprocity; as such it gives rise to authentic drama. Through eroticism, love, friendship, and their alternatives, deception, hate, rivalry, the relation is a struggle between conscious beings each of whom wishes to be essential, it is the mutual recognition of free beings who confirm one another's freedom, it is the vague transition from aversion to participation. To pose Woman is to pose the absolute Other, without reciprocity, denying against all experience that she is a subject, a fellow human being.

In actuality, of course, women appear under various aspects; but each of the myths built up around the subject of woman is intended to sum her up *in toto*; each aspires to be unique. In consequence, a number of incompatible myths exist, and men tarry musing before the strange incoherencies manifested by the idea of Femininity. As every woman has a share in a majority of these archetypes—each of which lays claim to containing the sole Truth of woman—men of today also are moved again in the presence of their female companions to an astonishment like that of the old sophists who failed to understand how man could be blond and dark at the same time! Transition toward the absolute was indicated long ago in social phenomena: relations are easily congealed in classes, functions in types, just as relations, to the childish mentality, are fixed in things. Patriarchal society, for example, being centered upon the conservation of the patrimony, implies necessarily, along with those who own and transmit wealth, the existence of men and women who take property away from its owners and put it into circulation. The men—adventurers, swindlers, thieves, speculators—are generally repudiated by the group; the women, employing their erotic attraction, can induce young men and even fathers of families to scatter their patrimonies, without ceasing to be within the law. Some of these women appropriate their victims' fortunes or obtain legacies by using undue influence; this role being regarded as evil, those who play it are called "bad women." But the fact is that quite to the contrary they are able to appear in

---

[1] **alterity** Otherness.

some other setting—at home with their fathers, brothers, husbands, or lovers—as guardian angels; and the courtesan who "plucks" rich financiers is, for painters and writers, a generous patroness. It is easy to understand in actual experience the ambiguous personality of Aspasia or Mme de Pompadour.[2] But if woman is depicted as the Praying Mantis, the Mandrake, the Demon, then it is most confusing to find in woman also the Muse, the Goddess Mother, Beatrice.

As group symbols and social types are generally defined by means of antonyms in pairs, ambivalence will seem to be an intrinsic quality of the Eternal Feminine. The saintly mother has for correlative the cruel stepmother, the angelic young girl has the perverse virgin: thus it will be said sometimes that Mother equals Life, sometimes that Mother equals Death, that every virgin is pure spirit or flesh dedicated to the devil. 4

Evidently it is not reality that dictates to society or to individuals their choice between the two opposed basic categories; in every period, in each case, society and the individual decide in accordance with their needs. Very often they project into the myth adopted the institutions and values to which they adhere. Thus the paternalism that claims woman for hearth and home defines her as sentiment, inwardness, immanence. In fact every existent is at once immanence and transcendence; when one offers the existent no aim, or prevents him from attaining any, or robs him of his victory, then his transcendence falls vainly into the past—that is to say, falls back into immanence. This is the lot assigned to woman in the patriarchate; but it is in no way a vocation, any more than slavery is the vocation of the slave. The development of this mythology is to be clearly seen in Auguste Comte.[3] To identify Woman with Altruism is to guarantee to man absolute rights in her devotion, it is to impose on women a categorical imperative. 5

The myth must not be confused with the recognition of significance; significance is immanent in the object; it is revealed to the mind through a living experience; whereas the myth is a transcendent Idea that escapes the mental grasp entirely. When in *L'Age d'homme* Michel Leiris[4] describes his vision of the feminine organs, he tells us things of significance and elaborates no myth. Wonder at the feminine body, dislike for menstrual blood, come from perceptions of a concrete 6

---

[2]**Aspasia . . . Mme de Pompadour** Aspasia (5th century B.C.) was mistress to the great Greek statesman, Pericles; Mme. de Pompadour (1721–1764) was mistress to France's Louis XV. Both were powerful women and both were sometimes the object of popular scorn.

[3]**Auguste Comte (1798–1857)** Comte is credited with having founded the study of sociology.

[4]**Michel Leiris (1901–1990)** A popular French writer and art critic.

reality. There is nothing mythical in the experience that reveals the voluptuous qualities of feminine flesh, and it is not an excursion into myth if one attempts to describe them through comparisons with flowers or pebbles. But to say that Woman is Flesh, to say that the Flesh is Night and Death, or that it is the splendor of the Cosmos, is to abandon terrestrial truth and soar into an empty sky. For man also is flesh for woman; and woman is not merely a carnal object; and the flesh is clothed in special significance for each person and in each experience. And likewise it is quite true that woman—like man—is a being rooted in nature; she is more enslaved to the species than is the male, her animality is more manifest; but in her as in him the given traits are taken on through the fact of existence, she belongs also to the human realm. To assimilate her to Nature is simply to act from prejudice.

Few myths have been more advantageous to the ruling caste   7 than the myth of woman: it justifies all privileges and even authorizes their abuse. Men need not bother themselves with alleviating the pains and the burdens that physiologically are women's lot, since these are "intended by Nature"; men use them as a pretext for increasing the misery of the feminine lot still further, for instance by refusing to grant to woman any right to sexual pleasure, by making her work like a beast of burden.[5]

Of all these myths, none is more firmly anchored in masculine   8 hearts than that of the feminine "mystery." It has numerous advantages. And first of all it permits an easy explanation of all that appears inexplicable; the man who "does not understand" a woman is happy to substitute an objective resistance for a subjective deficiency of mind; instead of admitting his ignorance, he perceives the presence of a "mystery" outside himself: an alibi, indeed, that flatters laziness and vanity at once. A heart smitten with love thus avoids many disappointments: if the loved one's behavior is capricious, her remarks stupid, then the mystery serves to excuse it all. And finally, thanks again to the mystery, that negative relation is perpetuated which seemed to Kierkegaard[6] infinitely preferable to positive possession, in the company of a living enigma man remains alone—alone with his dreams, his hopes, his fears, his love, his vanity. This subjective game, which can go all the way from vice to mystical ecstasy, is for many a

---

[5] Cf. Balzac: *Physiology of Marriage*: "Pay no attention to her murmurs, her cries, her pains; *nature has made her for our use* and for bearing everything: children, sorrows, blows and pains inflicted by man. Do not accuse yourself of hardness. In all the codes of so-called civilized nations, man has written the laws that ranged woman's destiny under this bloody epigraph: '*Væ victis!* Woe to the weak!'" [Beauvoir's note]

[6] **Søren Kierkegaard (1813–1855)** A major Danish philosopher, often credited with having founded the school of philosophy known as existentialism, to which Beauvoir was sympathetic.

more attractive experience than an authentic relation with a human being. What foundations exist for such a profitable illusion?

Surely woman is, in a sense, mysterious, "mysterious as is all the world," according to Maeterlinck.[7] Each is *subject* only for himself; each can grasp in immanence only himself, alone: from this point of view the *other* is always a mystery. To men's eyes the opacity of the self-knowing self, of the *pour-soi*, is denser in the *other* who is feminine; men are unable to penetrate her special experience through any working of sympathy: they are condemned to ignorance of the quality of woman's erotic pleasure, the discomfort of menstruation, and the pains of childbirth. The truth is that there is mystery on both sides: as the *other* who is of masculine sex, every man, also, has within him a presence, an inner self impenetrable to woman; she in turn is in ignorance of the male's erotic feeling. But in accordance with the universal rule I have stated, the categories in which men think of the world are established *from their point of view, as absolute*: they misconceive reciprocity, here as everywhere. A mystery for man, woman is considered to be mysterious in essence.

To tell the truth, her situation makes woman very liable to such a view. Her physiological nature is very complex; she herself submits to it as to some rigmarole from outside; her body does not seem to her to be a clear expression of herself; within it she feels herself a stranger. Indeed, the bond that in every individual connects the physiological life and the psychic life—or better the relation existing between the contingence of an individual and the free spirit that assumes it—is the deepest enigma implied in the condition of being human, and this enigma is presented in its most disturbing form in woman.

But what is commonly referred to as the mystery is not the subjective solitude of the conscious self, nor the secret organic life. It is on the level of communication that the word has its true meaning: it is not a reduction to pure silence, to darkness, to absence; it implies a stammering presence that fails to make itself manifest and clear. To say that woman is mystery is to say, not that she is silent, but that her language is not understood; she is there, but hidden behind veils; she exists beyond these uncertain appearances. What is she? Angel, demon, one inspired, an actress? It may be supposed either that there are answers to these questions which are impossible to discover, or, rather, that no answer is adequate because a fundamental ambiguity marks the feminine being; and perhaps in her heart she is even for herself quite indefinable: a sphinx.

9

10

11

---

[7] **Maurice Maeterlinck (1862–1949)** A Belgian playwright whose *Pelleas and Melisande* (1892) was one of the greatest of the symbolist dramas of the late nineteenth century.

The fact is that she would be quite embarrassed to decide *what* 12 she *is*; but this not because the hidden truth is too vague to be discerned: it is because in this domain there is no truth. An existent *is* nothing other than what he does; the possible does not extend beyond the real, essence does not precede existence: in pure subjectivity, the human being *is not anything*. He is to be measured by his acts. Of a peasant woman one can say that she is a good or a bad worker, of an actress that she has or does not have talent; but if one considers a woman in her immanent presence, her inward self, one can say absolutely nothing about her, she falls short of having any qualifications. Now, in amorous or conjugal relations, in all relations where the woman is the vassal, the other, she is being dealt with in her immanence. It is noteworthy that the feminine comrade, colleague, and associate are without mystery; on the other hand, if the vassal is male, if, in the eyes of a man or a woman who is older, or richer, a young fellow, for example, plays the role of the inessential object, then he too becomes shrouded in mystery. And this uncovers for us a substructure under the feminine mystery which is economic in nature.

A sentiment cannot be supposed to *be* anything. "In the domain 13 of sentiments," writes Gide,[8] "the real is not distinguished from the imaginary. And if to imagine one loves is enough to be in love, then also to tell oneself that one imagines oneself to be in love when one is in love is enough to make one forthwith love a little less." Discrimination between the imaginary and the real can be made only through behavior. Since man occupies a privileged situation in this world, he is in a position to show his love actively; very often he supports the woman or at least helps her; in marrying her he gives her social standing; he makes her presents; his independent economic and social position allows him to take the initiative and think up contrivances: it was M. de Norpois who, when separated from Mme de Villeparisis, made twenty-four-hour trips to visit her. Very often the man is busy, the woman idle: he *gives* her the time he passes with her; she takes it: is it with pleasure, passionately, or only for amusement? Does she accept these benefits through love or through self-interest? Does she love her husband or her marriage? Of course, even the man's evidence is ambiguous: is such and such a gift granted through love or out of pity? But while normally a woman finds numerous advantages in her relations with a man, his relations with a woman are profitable to a man only in so far as he loves her. And so one can almost judge the degree of his affection by the total picture of his attitude.

---

[8] **André Gide (1869–1951)** Gide won the Nobel Prize for Literature in 1947. He was an influential French philosopher, writer, and art critic.

But a woman hardly has means for sounding her own heart; ac- 14
cording to her moods she will view her own sentiments in different
lights, and as she submits to them passively, one interpretation will
be no truer than another. In those rare instances in which she holds
the position of economic and social privilege, the mystery is reversed,
showing that it does not pertain to *one* sex rather than the other, but
to the situation. For a great many women the roads to transcendence
are blocked: because they *do* nothing, they fail to *make themselves*
anything. They wonder indefinitely what they *could have* become,
which sets them to asking about what they *are*. It is a vain question.
If man fails to discover that secret essence of femininity, it is simply
because it does not exist. Kept on the fringe of the world, woman
cannot be objectively defined through this world, and her mystery
conceals nothing but emptiness.

Furthermore, like all the oppressed, woman deliberately dissem- 15
bles her objective actuality; the slave, the servant, the indigent, all
who depend upon the caprices of a master, have learned to turn toward him a changeless smile or an enigmatic impassivity; their real
sentiments, their actual behavior, are carefully hidden. And moreover
woman is taught from adolescence to lie to men, to scheme, to be
wily. In speaking to them she wears an artificial expression on her
face; she is cautious, hypocritical, play-acting.

But the Feminine Mystery as recognized in mythical thought is a 16
more profound matter. In fact, it is immediately implied in the
mythology of the absolute Other. If it be admitted that the inessential
conscious being, too, is a clear subjectivity, capable of performing the
Cogito,[9] then it is also admitted that this being is in truth sovereign
and returns to being essential; in order that all reciprocity may appear quite impossible, it is necessary for the Other to be for itself an
other, for its very subjectivity to be affected by its otherness; this
consciousness which would be alienated as a consciousness, in its
pure immanent presence, would evidently be Mystery. It would be
Mystery in itself from the fact that it would be Mystery for itself; it
would be absolute Mystery.

In the same way it is true that, beyond the secrecy created by their 17
dissembling, there is mystery in the Black, the Yellow, in so far as they
are considered absolutely as the inessential Other. It should be noted
that the American citizen, who profoundly baffles the average European, is not, however, considered as being "mysterious": one states more
modestly that one does not understand him. And similarly woman
does not always "understand" man; but there is no such thing as a

---

[9] **Cogito** Reference to René Descartes (1596–1650), who "proved" his existence
with the Latin phrase, "Cogito, ergo sum"—I think, therefore I am.

masculine mystery. The point is that rich America, and the male, are on the Master side and that Mystery belongs to the slave.

To be sure, we can only muse in the twilight byways of bad faith upon the positive reality of the Mystery; like certain marginal hallucinations, it dissolves under the attempt to view it fixedly. Literature always fails in attempting to portray "mysterious" women; they can appear only at the beginning of a novel as strange, enigmatic figures; but unless the story remains unfinished they give up their secret in the end and they are then simply consistent and transparent persons. The heroes in Peter Cheyney's books, for example, never cease to be astonished at the unpredictable caprices of women: no one can ever guess how they will act, they upset all calculations. The fact is that once the springs of their action are revealed to the reader, they are seen to be very simple mechanisms: this woman was a spy, that one a thief; however clever the plot, there is always a key; and it could not be otherwise, had the author all the talent and imagination in the world. Mystery is never more than a mirage that vanishes as we draw near to look at it.

We can see now that the myth is in large part explained by its usefulness to man. The myth of woman is a luxury. It can appear only if man escapes from the urgent demands of his needs; the more relationships are concretely lived, the less they are idealized. The fellah of ancient Egypt, the Bedouin peasant, the artisan of the Middle Ages, the worker of today has in the requirements of work and poverty relations with his particular woman companion which are too definite for her to be embellished with an aura either auspicious or inauspicious. The epochs and the social classes that have been marked by the leisure to dream have been the ones to set up the images, black and white, of femininity. But along with luxury there was utility; these dreams were irresistibly guided by interests. Surely most of the myths had roots in the spontaneous attitude of man toward his own existence and toward the world around him. But going beyond experience toward the transcendent Idea was deliberately used by patriarchal society for purposes of self-justification; through the myths this society imposed its laws and customs upon individuals in a picturesque, effective manner; it is under a mythical form that the group-imperative is indoctrinated into each conscience. Through such intermediaries as religions, traditions, language, tales, songs, movies, the myths penetrate even into such existences as are most harshly enslaved to material realities. Here everyone can find sublimation of his drab experiences: deceived by the woman he loves, one declares that she is a Crazy Womb; another, obsessed by his impotence, calls her a Praying Mantis; still another enjoys his wife's company: behold, she is Harmony, Rest, the Good Earth! The taste for eternity at a bargain, for a pocket-sized absolute, which is shared by a majority of men, is satisfied by myths. The smallest emotion, a slight annoyance, becomes the reflection of a timeless Idea—an illusion agreeably flattering to the vanity.

The myth is one of those snares of false objectivity into which the 20 man who depends on ready-made valuations rushes headlong. Here again we have to do with the substitution of a set idol for actual experience and the free judgments it requires. For an authentic relation with an autonomous existent, the myth of Woman substitutes the fixed contemplation of a mirage. "Mirage! Mirage!" cries Laforgue.[10] "We should kill them since we cannot comprehend them; or better tranquilize them, instruct them, make them give up their taste for jewels, make them our genuinely equal comrades, our intimate friends, real associates here below, dress them differently, cut their hair short, say anything and everything to them." Man would have nothing to lose, quite the contrary, if he gave up disguising woman as a symbol. When dreams are official community affairs, clichés, they are poor and monotonous indeed beside the living reality; for the true dreamer, for the poet, woman is a more generous fount than is any down-at-heel marvel. The times that have most sincerely treasured women are not the period of feudal chivalry nor yet the gallant nineteenth century. They are the times—like the eighteenth century—when men have regarded women as fellow creatures; then it is that women seem truly romantic, as the reading of *Liaisons dangereuses*, *Le Rouge et le noir*, *Farewell to Arms*, is sufficient to show. The heroines of Laclos, Stendhal, Hemingway[11] are without mystery, and they are not the less engaging for that. To recognize in woman a human being is not to impoverish man's experience: this would lose none of its diversity, its richness, or its intensity if it were to occur between two subjectivities. To discard the myths is not to destroy all dramatic relation between the sexes, it is not to deny the significance authentically revealed to man through feminine reality; it is not to do away with poetry, love, adventure, happiness, dreaming. It is simply to ask that behavior, sentiment, passion be founded upon the truth.[12]

---

[10] **Jules Laforgue (1860–1887)** A French symbolist poet.

[11] **Pierre Choderlos de Laclos (1741–1803), Stendhal (1783–1842), Ernest Hemingway (1899–1961)** Laclos was a French novelist who wrote *Dangerous Liaisons* and *On the Education of Women*; Stendhal was the pen name of Marie-Henri Beyle, a French novelist who wrote *The Red and the Black* and *The Charterhouse of Parma*; Ernest Hemingway was an important twentieth-century American novelist who wrote *The Sun Also Rises* and *A Farewell to Arms*.

[12] Laforgue goes on to say regarding woman: "Since she has been left in slavery, idleness, without occupation or weapon other than her sex, she has over-developed this aspect and has become the Feminine. . . . We have permitted this hypertrophy; she is here in the world for our benefit. . . . Well! that is all wrong. . . . Up to now we have played with woman as if she were a doll. This has lasted altogether too long! . . ." [Beauvoir's note]

"Woman is lost. Where are the women? The women of today are   21
not women at all!" We have seen what these mysterious slogans mean.
In men's eyes—and for the legion of women who see through men's
eyes—it is not enough to have a woman's body nor to assume the female function as mistress or mother in order to be a "true woman." In
sexuality and maternity woman as subject can claim autonomy; but to
be a "true woman" she must accept herself as the Other. The men of
today show a certain duplicity of attitude which is painfully lacerating
to women; they are willing on the whole to accept woman as a fellow
being, an equal; but they still require her to remain the inessential. For
her these two destinies are incompatible; she hesitates between one
and the other without being exactly adapted to either, and from this
comes her lack of equilibrium. With man there is no break between
public and private life: the more he confirms his grasp on the world in
action and in work, the more virile he seems to be; human and vital
values are combined in him. Whereas woman's independent successes
are in contradiction with her femininity, since the "true woman" is required to make herself object, to be the Other.

It is quite possible that in this matter man's sensibility and sexuality   22
are being modified. A new æsthetics has already been born. If the fashion of flat chests and narrow hips—the boyish form—has had its brief
season, at least the overopulent ideal of past centuries has not returned.
The feminine body is asked to be flesh, but with discretion; it is to be
slender and not loaded with fat; muscular, supple, strong, it is bound to
suggest transcendence; it must not be pale like a too shaded hothouse
plant, but preferably tanned like a workman's torso from being bared
to the open sun. Woman's dress in becoming practical need not make
her appear sexless: on the contrary, short skirts made the most of legs
and thighs as never before. There is no reason why working should
take away woman's sex appeal.[13] It may be disturbing to contemplate
woman as at once a social personage and carnal prey: in a recent series
of drawings by Peynet (1948), we see a young man break his engage-
ment because he was seduced by the pretty mayoress who was getting
ready to officiate at his marriage. For a woman to hold some "man's
position" and be desirable at the same time has long been a subject for
more or less ribald joking; but gradually the impropriety and the irony
have become blunted, and it would seem that a new form of eroticism
is coming into being—perhaps it will give rise to new myths.

What is certain is that today it is very difficult for women to ac-   23
cept at the same time their status as autonomous individuals and

---

[13] A point that hardly needs to be made in America, where even cursory ac-
quaintance with any well-staffed business office will afford confirmatory evidence.
[Translator's note]

their womanly destiny; this is the source of the blundering and restlessness which sometimes cause them to be considered a "lost sex."
And no doubt it is more comfortable to submit to a blind enslave-
ment than to work for liberation: the dead, for that matter, are better
adapted to the earth than are the living. In all respects a return to the
past is no more possible than it is desirable. What must be hoped for
is that the men for their part will unreservedly accept the situation
that is coming into existence; only then will women be able to live in
that situation without anguish. Then Laforgue's prayer will be answered: "Ah, young women, when will you be our brothers, our
brothers in intimacy without ulterior thought of exploitation? When
shall we clasp hands truly?" Then Breton's "Mélusine, no longer
under the weight of the calamity let loose upon her by man alone,
Mélusine set free . . ." will regain "her place in humanity." Then she
will be a full human being, "when," to quote a letter of Rimbaud,[14]
"the infinite bondage of woman is broken, when she will live in and
for herself, man—hitherto detestable—having let her go free."

---

[14]**Arthur Rimbaud (1854–1891)** A French symbolist poet of great imaginative power.

QUESTIONS FOR CRITICAL READING

1. What do you understand to be the myth of the Eternal Feminine?
2. In what literary works or films have you seen the myth of woman illustrated?
3. What role does mystery play in the relationship of men to women?
4. Does a myth of the Eternal Masculine exist?
5. What are some of the contradictory aspects of myths about women?
6. What is the patrimony that Beauvoir refers to in paragraph 3, and how
   does it shape social experience?
7. Do you think people actually maintain the myth of the Eternal Feminine today?
8. What is Beauvoir's strongest argument for eliminating the myth of the
   Eternal Feminine?

SUGGESTIONS FOR WRITING

1. Beauvoir points out that whatever the myth of woman might be, it "is
   intended to sum her up in toto" (para. 3). Therefore, she says, there will
   be necessary contradictions in myths that disagree with each other.

Give some examples of what Beauvoir means, and show how they might affect the behavior of those who accept such myths. If possible, draw on experiences of your own to demonstrate how people who accept the myths behave.

2. Explain the very important concept that Beauvoir outlines in paragraph 3 concerning the role of patrimony in "patriarchal society." She refers to moneyed families that pass down their wealth to their sons and expect that those sons will in turn pass it to their own sons. The role of women in this system is obviously restricted. How does Beauvoir treat this issue? How important do you think it is? Why do you think the words *patrimony* and *matrimony* have such distinct meanings for men and women?

3. Beauvoir says, "group symbols and social types are generally defined by means of antonyms in pairs" (para. 4). What symbols can you define that exist in contradictory types? How do they work? What effect are they likely to have on people's behavior? One obvious contradiction is to see woman as either virgin or whore, but nothing in between. Do such contradictions exist in your own social circle? Do such contradictions surprise you? Has your social group made progress in dealing with social symbols of this type?

4. Beauvoir says again and again that reality and experience do not seem to affect the way people think about women. The myths, in other words, stand for reality and seem more powerful than reality. Do you agree with this assertion? Can you see evidence of that behavior at work in your own social experience? Do you know people who seem to ignore reality and prefer the myth?

5. Beauvoir says that woman's "animality is more manifest" than man's (para. 6). Examine this statement, and decide first what she means. Then decide if she is convincing. Take a stand yourself, and treat the issue with some thoroughness. Avoid oversimplifying your position; try to impart an understanding of the complexity of Beauvoir's statement.

6. Why has the "myth of woman" been advantageous for the "ruling caste"? Beauvoir says that no feminine myth "is more firmly anchored in masculine hearts than that of the feminine 'mystery'" (para. 8). How true is this statement? Why is belief in such a myth of advantage for men? How does it "justify all privileges" and authorize their "abuse" (para. 7)?

7. **CONNECTIONS** Bell hooks believes bourgeois white feminists are limited in their understanding of the role of black women in the feminist movement. How would hooks critique Beauvoir's essay, and how would Beauvoir defend her views? Consider their respective arguments, and offer an analysis that takes into account at least one major argumentative position from each author.

8. **CONNECTIONS** How would Mary Wollstonecraft, Virginia Woolf, or Carol Gilligan react to de Beauvoir's emphasis on the "mystery of woman"? What are their positions on the relationship of women to men? How, if at all, would they justify de Beauvoir's position? Do you think they would regard de Beauvoir's essay as forward looking or as old-fashioned; as helpful or harmful to the feminist movement? Why?

CAROL GILLIGAN
Woman's Place in Man's Life Cycle

CAROL GILLIGAN (b. 1936) is professor of education at Harvard University. She concentrates on issues in psychology and has made important contributions to theories concerning the ways in which women develop differently from men, from childhood to adulthood. In 1997, she received the Heinz Award in the Human Condition. Her work has involved various aspects of psychological development, but one important focus has been the development of the individual's moral nature. In talking about these issues, she has examined the work of some of the world's most important psychologists, such as Sigmund Freud (1856–1939), Jean Piaget (1896–1980), Erik Erikson (1902–1994), and her own teacher, Lawrence Kohlberg (1927–1987). As she demonstrates in her discussion, the work of these men in establishing parameters of social and moral development depended almost entirely on studying boys, not girls. Gilligan suggests that the differences in early development between boys and girls makes those observations of limited value.

Gilligan's book *In a Different Voice: Psychological Theory and Women's Development* (1982) was the result of many years of research on the ways in which women treat the relational aspects of life differently from men—in part because of the different ways in which girls and boys are raised. "Woman's Place in Man's Life Cycle" is the first chapter in that book; it establishes the need to account appropriately for women's development by examining how women are socialized in school and at home.

Some of the factors that appear to impede women's success, Gilligan finds, actually confer strength on them. For example, the nature of boys' games differs from that of girls' because boys accept competition—including the need for one party to lose while another

---

From *In a Different Voice: Psychological Theory and Women's Development*.

wins—as a natural course, provided the rules are followed carefully. Girls tend to treat rules as more elastic if they interfere with the pleasure of the games. This pattern, according to some male psychologists, tends to make it difficult for women to achieve success in later life. Gilligan, however, explains that this pattern actually helps women succeed on a deeper personal level in ways that men do not normally achieve, especially in mid-life when both sexes better understand the need for intimacy and closeness.

Gilligan's efforts to move psychologists away from using only male-based data for establishing norms of behavior and development seems like common sense. Why, then, did people not consider this previously? One reason is that when Gilligan was formulating her ideas in the 1970s, many feminists felt that establishing key differences between men and women would only fuel the controversy about whether women and men should be treated equally. If there were to be complete fairness in gender relations, they reasoned, the false distinctions that Mary Wollstonecraft and her twentieth-century counterparts felt were holding women back would only be accentuated. Fair treatment of the sexes, they thought, demanded that the sexes be considered as more alike than different.

Gilligan fought against this tide at some risk, but her psychological model eventually won out by helping to promote the view that Simone de Beauvoir supported: avoiding the judging of women by men's standards. In Beauvoir's view, men tend to judge women as the Other, or as not-men, rather than as women with their own natures and identities. Gilligan's efforts moved this discourse on gender to a new level by doing what seems natural and reasonable in retrospect: studying the way girls interact and seeing how that interaction is different from that of boys. As she points out in this piece, children have a very powerful gender sense by age three, and their development along gender lines begins no later than that.

Gilligan's work has pointed out the ways in which boys need to break away from their mothers early on in an effort to model themselves on their fathers or other masculine figures, thereby achieving independence. Girls, on the other hand, see themselves as more like their mothers. In girls' socialization there is greater emphasis on familial continuity, and as a result women develop a sense of connectedness, intimacy, and interdependence that men are less aware of because of their own individual needs.

In addition, by examining these qualities in girls, Gilligan finds that intimacy, concern for others, empathy, and a need for interdependence are not exclusively characteristics of women. Indeed, such qualities are essential to the human condition and have probably aided our biological survival. Although they are sometimes masked by social pressures in early child development, men possess these qualities as well. As one commentator observed, Gilligan "began by posing a deceptively simple question: What are we missing by not listening to half the population?" The answer was a great deal.

Gilligan's Rhetoric

By opening her essay with a reference to *The Cherry Orchard* by Anton Chekhov, Gilligan establishes herself as a literate analyst, taking the conversation from Chekhov's play and revealing its deeper significance. In a way, this is a model for psychoanalysis as well as a model for interpretation that would serve in any given study. Gilligan's conclusions about the distinctions in women's development actually arise from extensive interviews analyzed in similar ways. According to some critics, not everyone would come to the same conclusions that Gilligan reaches. But the point is that "reading" implies interpretation, and Gilligan's interpretation of the texts she gathered has convinced her that earlier psychologists were wrong in thinking that women had limited moral development compared to men.

"Woman's Place in Man's Life Cycle" has been praised as the foundation of Gilligan's argument in *In a Different Voice*. This opening chapter establishes not only her views but those of earlier academics as well. Therefore, the essay has the flavor of an academic study, revealing Gilligan's extensive reading and research while at the same time offering her the opportunity to analyze each important figure she treats. What this establishes rhetorically is thoroughness. Gilligan presents the authorities that are important to consider and thus offers us the opportunity to read them on our own.

Some of the authorities to which she refers are giants in the field: Freud, Piaget, and Erikson certainly, but also psychologist Bruno Bettelheim (1903–1990) and novelists Maxine Hong Kingston (b. 1940) and Virginia Woolf (1882–1941). Some are current researchers, such as Nancy Chodorow and Janet Lever, whose works Gilligan examines and then builds upon. This rhetorical method is basic to academic research and imparts to the reader a sense of completion. The early part of the essay reviews the current intellectual discussion on women's development and the differences in the ways in which women observe and analyze events, especially moral events. The latter part of the essay clarifies Gilligan's own position on these issues.

Gilligan worked with Lawrence Kohlberg, her teacher at Harvard. To the moral development of the child, Kohlberg applied a

theory of Jean Piaget concerning the stages of intellectual development of the child. Piaget conceived of three stages of development,
and so did Kohlberg, although he broke each stage into two sub-
stages. Kohlberg titled his three stages as follows: preconventional
(up to age nine); conventional (to age twenty); and postconven-
tional (age twenty and above, but possibly never achieved). He regarded the earliest stage of moral development as being dominated
by the avoidance of punishment. The second stage was dominated
by gaining approval and avoiding disapproval. The third stage involved recognizing the rights of others and establishing personal
moral values on the basis of a sense of justice. Some people,
Kohlberg felt, might never achieve the last stage of establishing
personal moral values.

In paragraph 39, Gilligan presents a man's response to one of
Kohlberg's interviews. In paragraph 40, she offers a response from a
woman in one of her own interviews to demonstrate some of the
gender differences that she has been discussing. This strategy permits the reader to participate in the study in a genuine way, because
the reader can validate Gilligan's views directly from the data.

Just as Gilligan opens the passage with a literary reference, she
closes it with another. This time she refers to the classical myth of
Demeter and Persephone, complete with a moral for the story. The
final paragraph of the essay, a careful analysis of the Persephone
myth, shows that the principles of female behavior are timeless.
Moreover, in the final paragraph Gilligan makes a plea that "the
continuing importance of attachment in the human life cycle" be
recognized for its potential to maintain life and to sustain a healthy
relationship between men and women.

PREREADING QUESTIONS: WHAT TO READ FOR

The following prereading questions may help you anticipate key issues
in the discussion of Carol Gilligan's "Woman's Place in Man's Life Cycle."
Keeping them in mind during your first reading of the selection should
help focus your attention.

- What are the differences between men and women in terms of the way
  they regard relationships?

- What is the result of basing theories of human development on studies
  that include only boys?

- How do boys and girls differ in their regard for rules?

Woman's Place in Man's Life Cycle

In the second act of *The Cherry Orchard*, Lopahin, a young mer- 1
chant, describes his life of hard work and success. Failing to convince Madame Ranevskaya to cut down the cherry orchard to save
her estate, he will go on in the next act to buy it himself. He is the
self-made man who, in purchasing the estate where his father and
grandfather were slaves, seeks to eradicate the "awkward, unhappy
life" of the past, replacing the cherry orchard with summer cottages
where coming generations "will see a new life." In elaborating this developmental vision, he reveals the image of man that underlies and
supports his activity: "At times when I can't go to sleep, I think: Lord,
thou gavest us immense forests, unbounded fields and the widest
horizons, and living in the midst of them we should indeed be
giants"—at which point, Madame Ranevskaya interrupts him, saying, "You feel the need for giants—They are good only in fairy tales,
anywhere else they only frighten us."

Conceptions of the human life cycle represent attempts to order 2
and make coherent the unfolding experiences and perceptions, the
changing wishes and realities of everyday life. But the nature of such
conceptions depends in part on the position of the observer. The
brief excerpt from Chekhov's play suggest that when the observer is
a woman, the perspective may be of a different sort. Different judgments of the image of man as giant imply different ideas about
human development, different ways of imagining the human condition, different notions of what is of value in life.

At a time when efforts are being made to eradicate discrimina- 3
tion between the sexes in the search for social equality and justice,
the differences between the sexes are being rediscovered in the social
sciences. This discovery occurs when theories formerly considered to
be sexually neutral in their scientific objectivity are found instead to
reflect a consistent observational and evaluative bias. Then the presumed neutrality of science, like that of language itself, gives way to
the recognition that the categories of knowledge are human constructions. The fascination with point of view that has informed the
fiction of the twentieth century and the corresponding recognition
of the relativity of judgment infuse our scientific understanding as
well when we begin to notice how accustomed we have become to
seeing life through men's eyes.

A recent discovery of this sort pertains to the apparently inno- 4
cent classic *The Elements of Style* by William Strunk and E. B. White.
A Supreme Court ruling on the subject of sex discrimination led one
teacher of English to notice that the elementary rules of English

usage were being taught through examples which counterposed the birth of Napoleon, the writings of Coleridge, and statements such as "He was an interesting talker. A man who had traveled all over the world and lived in half a dozen countries," with "Well, Susan, this is a fine mess you are in" or, less drastically, "He saw a woman, accompanied by two children, walking slowly down the road."

Psychological theorists have fallen as innocently as Strunk and   5 White into the same observational bias. Implicitly adopting the male life as the norm, they have tried to fashion women out of a masculine cloth. It all goes back, of course, to Adam and Eve—a story which shows, among other things, that if you make a woman out of a man, you are bound to get into trouble. In the life cycle, as in the Garden of Eden, the woman has been the deviant.

The penchant of developmental theorists to project a masculine   6 image, and one that appears frightening to women, goes back at least to Freud (1905), who built his theory of psychosexual development around the experiences of the male child that culminate in the Oedipus complex. In the 1920s, Freud struggled to resolve the contradictions posed for his theory by the differences in female anatomy and the different configuration of the young girl's early family relationships. After trying to fit women into his masculine conception, seeing them as envying that which they missed, he came instead to acknowledge, in the strength and persistence of women's pre-Oedipal attachments to their mothers, a developmental difference. He considered this difference in women's development to be responsible for what he saw as women's developmental failure.

Having tied the formation of the superego or conscience to castra-   7 tion anxiety, Freud considered women to be deprived by nature of the impetus for a clear-cut Oedipal resolution. Consequently, women's superego—the heir to the Oedipus complex—was compromised: it was never "so inexorable, so impersonal, so independent of its emotional origins as we require it to be in men." From this observation of difference, that "for women the level of what is ethically normal is different from what it is in men," Freud concluded that women "show less sense of justice than men, that they are less ready to submit to the great exigencies of life, that they are more often influenced in their judgements by feelings of affection or hostility" (1925, pp. 257–258).

Thus a problem in theory became cast as a problem in women's   8 development, and the problem in women's development was located in their experience of relationships. Nancy Chodorow (1974), attempting to account for "the reproduction within each generation of certain general and nearly universal differences that characterize masculine and feminine personality and roles," attributes these differences between the sexes not to anatomy but rather to "the fact that women, universally, are largely responsible for early child care." Because this early social environment differs for and is experienced differently by male and female children, basic sex differences recur in personality development. As a result, "in any given society, feminine personality comes to define itself in relation and connection to other people more than masculine personality does" (pp. 43–44).

In her analysis, Chodorow relies primarily on Robert Stoller's 9 studies which indicate that gender identity, the unchanging core of personality formation, is "with rare exception firmly and irreversibly established for both sexes by the time a child is around three." Given that for both sexes the primary caretaker in the first three years of life is typically female, the interpersonal dynamics of gender identity formation are different for boys and girls. Female identity formation takes place in a context of ongoing relationship since "mothers tend to experience their daughters as more like, and continuous with, themselves." Correspondingly, girls, in identifying themselves as female, experience themselves as like their mothers, thus fusing the experience of attachment with the process of identity formation. In contrast, "mothers experience their sons as a male opposite," and boys, in defining themselves as masculine, separate their mothers from themselves, thus curtailing "their primary love and sense of empathic tie." Consequently, male development entails a "more emphatic individuation and a more defensive firming of experienced ego boundaries." For boys, but not girls, "issues of differentiation have become intertwined with sexual issues" (1978, pp. 150, 166–167).

Writing against the masculine bias of psychoanalytic theory, 10 Chodorow argues that the existence of sex differences in the early experiences of individuation and relationship "does not mean that women have 'weaker' ego boundaries than men or are more prone to psychosis." It means instead that "girls emerge from this period with a basis for 'empathy' built into their primary definition of self in a way that boys do not." Chodorow thus replaces Freud's negative and derivative description of female psychology with a positive and direct account of her own: "Girls emerge with a stronger basis for experiencing another's needs or feelings as one's own (or of thinking that one is so experiencing another's needs and feelings). Furthermore, girls do not define themselves in terms of the denial of pre-Oedipal relational modes to the same extent as do boys. Therefore, regression to these modes tends not to feel as much a basic threat to their ego. From very early, then, because they are parented by a person of the same gender . . . girls come to experience themselves as less differentiated than boys, as more continuous with and related to the external object-world, and as differently oriented to their inner object-world as well" (p. 167).

Consequently, relationships, and particularly issues of depen- 11
dency, are experienced differently by women and men. For boys
and men, separation and individuation are critically tied to gender
identity since separation from the mother is essential for the development of masculinity. For girls and women, issues of femininity or
feminine identity do not depend on the achievement of separation
from the mother or on the progress of individuation. Since masculinity is defined through separation while femininity is defined
through attachment, male gender identity is threatened by intimacy
while female gender identity is threatened by separation. Thus males
tend to have difficulty with relationships, while females tend to have
problems with individuation. The quality of embeddedness in social
interaction and personal relationships that characterizes women's lives
in contrast to men's, however, becomes not only a descriptive difference but also a developmental liability when the milestones of childhood and adolescent development in the psychological literature are
markers of increasing separation. Women's failure to separate then
becomes by definition a failure to develop.

The sex differences in personality formation that Chodorow de- 12
scribes in early childhood appear during the middle childhood years
in studies of children's games. Children's games are considered by
George Herbert Mead (1934) and Jean Piaget (1932) as the crucible of
social development during the school years. In games, children learn
to take the role of the other and come to see themselves through another's eyes. In games, they learn respect for rules and come to understand the ways rules can be made and changed.

Janet Lever (1976), considering the peer group to be the agent 13
of socialization during the elementary school years and play to be a
major activity of socialization at that time, set out to discover whether
there are sex differences in the games that children play. Studying
181 fifth-grade, white, middle-class children, ages ten and eleven,
she observed the organization and structure of their playtime activities. She watched the children as they played at school during re-
cess and in physical education class, and in addition kept diaries
of their accounts as to how they spent their out-of-school time.
From this study, Lever reports sex differences: boys play out of doors
more often than girls do; boys play more often in large and age-
heterogeneous groups; they play competitive games more often, and
their games last longer than girls' games. The last is in some ways
the most interesting finding. Boys' games appeared to last longer not
only because they required a higher level of skill and were thus less
likely to become boring, but also because, when disputes arose in
the course of a game, boys were able to resolve the disputes more
effectively than girls: "During the course of this study, boys were
seen quarrelling all the time, but not once was a game terminated

because of a quarrel and no game was interrupted for more than seven minutes. In the gravest debates, the final word was always, to 'repeat the play,' generally followed by a chorus of 'cheater's proof'" (p. 482). In fact, it seemed that the boys enjoyed the legal debates as much as they did the game itself, and even marginal players of lesser size or skill participated equally in these recurrent squabbles. In contrast, the eruption of disputes among girls tended to end the game.

Thus Lever extends and corroborates the observations of Piaget   14 in his study of the rules of the game, where he finds boys becoming through childhood increasingly fascinated with the legal elaboration of rules and the development of fair procedures for adjudicating conflicts, a fascination that, he notes, does not hold for girls. Girls, Piaget observes, have a more "pragmatic" attitude toward rules, "regarding a rule as good as long as the game repaid it" (p. 83). Girls are more tolerant in their attitudes toward rules, more willing to make exceptions, and more easily reconciled to innovations. As a result, the legal sense, which Piaget considers essential to moral development, "is far less developed in little girls than in boys" (p. 77).

The bias that leads Piaget to equate male development with   15 child development also colors Lever's work. The assumption that shapes her discussion of results is that the male model is the better one since it fits the requirements for modern corporate success. In contrast, the sensitivity and care for the feelings of others that girls develop through their play have little market value and can even impede professional success. Lever implies that, given the realities of adult life, if a girl does not want to be left dependent on men, she will have to learn to play like a boy.

To Piaget's argument that children learn the respect for rules   16 necessary for moral development by playing rule-bound games, Lawrence Kohlberg (1969) adds that these lessons are most effectively learned through the opportunities for role-taking that arise in the course of resolving disputes. Consequently, the moral lessons inherent in girls' play appear to be fewer than in boys'. Traditional girls' games like jump rope and hopscotch are turn-taking games, where competition is indirect since one person's success does not necessarily signify another's failure. Consequently, disputes requiring adjudication are less likely to occur. In fact, most of the girls whom Lever interviewed claimed that when a quarrel broke out, they ended the game. Rather than elaborating a system of rules for resolving disputes, girls subordinated the continuation of the game to the continuation of relationships.

Lever concludes that from the games they play, boys learn   17 both the independence and the organizational skills necessary for coordinating the activities of large and diverse groups of people. By participating in controlled and socially approved competitive situations, they learn to deal with competition in a relatively forthright manner—to play with their enemies and to compete with their friends—all in accordance with the rules of the game. In contrast, girls' play tends to occur in smaller, more intimate groups, often the best-friend dyad, and in private places. This play replicates the social pattern of primary human relationships in that its organization is more cooperative. Thus, it points less, in Mead's terms, toward learning to take the role of "the generalized other," less toward the abstraction of human relationships. But it fosters the development of the empathy and sensitivity necessary for taking the role of "the particular other" and points more toward knowing the other as different from the self.

The sex differences in personality formation in early childhood   18 that Chodorow derives from her analysis of the mother-child relationship are thus extended by Lever's observations of sex differences in the play activities of middle childhood. Together these accounts suggest that boys and girls arrive at puberty with a different interpersonal orientation and a different range of social experiences. Yet, since adolescence is considered a crucial time for separation, the period of "the second individuation process" (Blos, 1967), female development has appeared most divergent and thus most problematic at this time.

"Puberty," Freud says, "which brings about so great an accession   19 of libido in boys, is marked in girls by a fresh wave of *repression*," necessary for the transformation of the young girl's "masculine sexuality" into the specifically feminine sexuality of her adulthood (1905, pp. 220–221). Freud posits this transformation on the girl's acknowledgment and acceptance of "the fact of her castration" (1931, p. 229). To the girl, Freud explains, puberty brings a new awareness of "the wound to her narcissism" and leads her to develop, "like a scar, a sense of inferiority" (1925, p. 253). Since in Erik Erikson's expansion of Freud's psychoanalytic account, adolescence is the time when development hinges on identity, the girl arrives at this juncture either psychologically at risk or with a different agenda.

The problem that female adolescence presents for theorists of   20 human development is apparent in Erikson's scheme. Erikson (1950) charts eight stages of psychosocial development, of which adolescence is the fifth. The task at this stage is to forge a coherent sense of self, to verify an identity that can span the discontinuity of puberty and make possible the adult capacity to love and work. The preparation for the successful resolution of the adolescent identity crisis is delineated in Erikson's description of the crises that characterize the preceding four stages. Although the initial crisis in infancy of "trust versus mistrust" anchors development in the experience of relationship, the task then clearly becomes one of individuation. Erikson's second stage centers on the crisis of "autonomy versus shame and doubt," which marks the walking child's emerging sense of separateness and agency. From there, development goes on through the crisis of "initiative versus guilt," successful resolution of which represents a further move in the direction of autonomy. Next, following the inevitable disappointment of the magical wishes of the Oedipal period, children realize that to compete with their parents, they must first join them and learn to do what they do so well. Thus in the middle childhood years, development turns on the crisis of "industry versus inferiority," as the demonstration of competence becomes critical to the child's developing self-esteem. This is the time when children strive to learn and master the technology of their culture, in order to recognize themselves and to be recognized by others as capable of becoming adults. Next comes adolescence, the celebration of the autonomous, initiating, industrious self through the forging of an identity based on an ideology that can support and justify adult commitments. But about whom is Erikson talking?

Once again it turns out to be the male child. For the female, Erikson (1968) says, the sequence is a bit different. She holds her identity in abeyance as she prepares to attract the man by whose name she will be known, by whose status she will be defined, the man who will rescue her from emptiness and loneliness by filling "the inner space." While for men, identity precedes intimacy and generativity in the optimal cycle of human separation and attachment, for women these tasks seem instead to be fused. Intimacy goes along with identity, as the female comes to know herself as she is known, through her relationships with others.   21

Yet despite Erikson's observation of sex differences, his chart of life-cycle stages remains unchanged: identity continues to precede intimacy as male experience continues to define his life-cycle conception. But in this male life cycle there is little preparation for the intimacy of the first adult stage. Only the initial stage of trust versus mistrust suggests the type of mutuality that Erikson means by intimacy and generativity and Freud means by genitality. The rest is separateness, with the result that development itself comes to be identified with separation, and attachments appear to be developmental impediments, as is repeatedly the case in the assessment of women.   22

Erikson's description of male identity as forged in relation to the world and of female identity as awakened in a relationship of intimacy with another person is hardly new. In the fairy tales that Bruno Bettelheim (1976) describes an identical portrayal appears. The dynamics of male adolescence are illustrated archetypically by   23 the conflict between father and son in "The Three Languages." Here a son, considered hopelessly stupid by his father, is given one last chance at education and sent for a year to study with a master. But when he returns, all he has learned is "what the dogs bark." After two further attempts of this sort, the father gives up in disgust and orders his servants to take the child into the forest and kill him. But the servants, those perpetual rescuers of disowned and abandoned children, take pity on the child and decide simply to leave him in the forest. From there, his wanderings take him to a land beset by furious dogs whose barking permits nobody to rest and who periodically devour one of the inhabitants. Now it turns out that our hero has learned just the right thing: he can talk with the dogs and is able to quiet them, thus restoring peace to the land. Since the other knowledge he acquires serves him equally well, he emerges triumphant from his adolescent confrontation with his father, a giant of the life-cycle conception.

In contrast, the dynamics of female adolescence are depicted   24
through the telling of a very different story. In the world of the fairy tale, the girl's first bleeding is followed by a period of intense passivity in which nothing seems to be happening. Yet in the deep sleeps of Snow White and Sleeping Beauty, Bettelheim sees that inner concentration which he considers to be the necessary counterpart to the activity of adventure. Since the adolescent heroines awake from their sleep, not to conquer the world, but to marry the prince, their identity is inwardly and interpersonally defined. For women, in Bettelheim's as in Erikson's account, identity and intimacy are intricately conjoined. The sex differences depicted in the world of fairy tales, like the fantasy of the woman warrior in Maxine Hong Kingston's (1977) recent autobiographical novel which echoes the old stories of Troilus and Cressida and Tancred and Chlorinda, indicate repeatedly that active adventure is a male activity, and that if a woman is to embark on such endeavors, she must at least dress like a man.

These observations about sex difference support the conclusion   25
reached by David McClelland (1975) that "sex role turns out to be one of the most important determinants of human behavior; psychologists have found sex differences in their studies from the moment they started doing empirical research." But since it is difficult to say "different" without saying "better" or "worse," since there is a tendency to construct a single scale of measurement, and since that scale has generally been derived from and standardized on the basis of men's interpretations of research data drawn predominantly or exclusively from studies of males, psychologists "have tended to regard male behavior as the 'norm' and female behavior as some kind of deviation from that norm" (p. 81). Thus, when women do not

conform to the standards of psychological expectation, the conclusion has generally been that something is wrong with the women.

What Matina Horner (1972) found to be wrong with women   26
was the anxiety they showed about competitive achievement. From the beginning, research on human motivation using the Thematic Apperception Test (TAT) was plagued by evidence of sex differences which appeared to confuse and complicate data analysis. The TAT presents for interpretation an ambiguous cue—a picture about which a story is to be written or a segment of a story that is to be completed. Such stories, in reflecting projective imagination, are considered by psychologists to reveal the ways in which people construe what they perceive, that is, the concepts and interpretations they bring to their experience and thus presumably the kind of sense that they make of their lives. Prior to Horner's work it was clear that women made a different kind of sense than men of situations of competitive achievement, that in some way they saw the situations differently or the situations aroused in them some different response.

On the basis of his studies of men, McClelland divided the con-   27
cept of achievement motivation into what appeared to be its two logical components, a motive to approach success ("hope success") and a motive to avoid failure ("fear failure"). From her studies of women, Horner identified as a third category the unlikely motivation to avoid success ("fear success"). Women appeared to have a problem with competitive achievement, and that problem seemed to emanate from a perceived conflict between femininity and success, the dilemma of the female adolescent who struggles to integrate her feminine aspirations and the identifications of her early childhood with the more masculine competence she has acquired at school. From her analysis of women's completions of a story that began, "after first term finals, Anne finds herself at the top of her medical school class," and from her observation of women's performance in competitive achievement situations, Horner reports that, "when success is likely or possible, threatened by the negative consequences they expect to follow success, young women become anxious and their positive achievement strivings become thwarted" (p. 171). She concludes that this fear "exists because for most women, the anticipation of success in competitive achievement activity, especially against men, produces anticipation of certain negative consequences, for example, threat of social rejection and loss of femininity" (1968, p. 125).

Such conflicts about success, however, may be viewed in a differ-   28
ent light. Georgia Sassen (1980) suggests that the conflicts expressed by the women might instead indicate "a heightened perception of the

'other side' of competitive success, that is, the great emotional costs at which success achieved through competition is often gained—an understanding which, though confused, indicates some underlying sense that something is rotten in the state in which success is defined as having better grades than everyone else" (p. 15). Sassen points out that Horner found success anxiety to be present in women only when achievement was directly competitive, that is, when one person's success was at the expense of another's failure.

In his elaboration of the identity crisis, Erikson (1968) cites the life of George Bernard Shaw to illustrate the young person's sense of being co-opted prematurely by success in a career he cannot wholeheartedly endorse. Shaw at seventy, reflecting upon his life, described his crisis at the age of twenty as having been caused not by the lack of success or the absence of recognition, but by too much of both: "I made good in spite of myself, and found, to my dismay, that Business, instead of expelling me as the worthless imposter I was, was fastening upon me with no intention of letting me go. Behold me, therefore, in my twentieth year, with a business training, in an occupation which I detested as cordially as any sane person lets himself detest anything he cannot escape from. In March 1876 I broke loose" (p. 143). At this point Shaw settled down to study and write as he pleased. Hardly interpreted as evidence of neurotic anxiety about achievement and competition, Shaw's refusal suggests to Erikson "the extraordinary workings of an extraordinary personality [coming] to the fore" (p. 144).

We might on these grounds begin to ask, not why women have conflicts about competitive success, but why men show such readiness to adopt and celebrate a rather narrow vision of success. Remembering Piaget's observation, corroborated by Lever, that boys in their games are more concerned with rules while girls are more concerned with relationships, often at the expense of the game itself—and given Chodorow's conclusion that men's social orientation is positional while women's is personal—we begin to understand why, when "Anne" becomes "John" in Horner's tale of competitive success and the story is completed by men, fear of success tends to disappear. John is considered to have played by the rules and won. He has the *right* to feel good about his success. Confirmed in the sense of his own identity as separate from those who, compared to him, are less competent, his positional sense of self is affirmed. For Anne, it is possible that the position she could obtain by being at the top of her medical school class may not, in fact, be what she wants.

"It is obvious," Virginia Woolf says, "that the values of women differ very often from the values which have been made by the other sex" (1929, p.76). Yet, she adds, "it is the masculine values that prevail."

As a result, women come to question the normality of their feelings and to alter their judgments in deference to the opinion of others. In the nineteenth century novels written by women, Woolf sees at work "a mind which was slightly pulled from the straight and made to alter its clear vision in deference to external authority." The same deference to the values and opinions of others can be seen in the judgments of twentieth century women. The difficulty women experience in finding or speaking publicly in their own voices emerges repeatedly in the form of qualification and self-doubt, but also in intimations of a divided judgment, a public assessment and private assessment which are fundamentally at odds.

Yet the deference and confusion that Woolf criticizes in women 32 derive from the values she sees as their strength. Women's deference is rooted not only in their social subordination but also in the substance of their moral concern. Sensitivity to the needs of others and the assumption of responsibility for taking care lead women to attend to voices other than their own and to include in their judgment other points of view. Women's moral weakness, manifest in an apparent diffusion and confusion of judgment, is thus inseparable from women's moral strength, an overriding concern with relationships and responsibilities. The reluctance to judge may itself be indicative of the care and concern for others that infuse the psychology of women's development and are responsible for what is generally seen as problematic in its nature.

Thus women not only define themselves in a context of human 33 relationship but also judge themselves in terms of their ability to care. Women's place in man's life cycle has been that of nurturer, caretaker, and helpmate, the weaver of those networks of relationships on which she in turn relies. But while women have thus taken care of men, men have, in their theories of psychological development, as in their economic arrangements, tended to assume or devalue that care. When the focus on individuation and individual achievement extends into adulthood and maturity is equated with personal autonomy, concern with relationships appears as a weakness of women rather than as a human strength (Miller, 1976).

The discrepancy between womanhood and adulthood is nowhere 34 more evident than in the studies on sex-role stereotypes reported by Broverman, Vogel, Broverman, Clarkson, and Rosenkrantz (1972). The repeated finding of these studies is that the qualities deemed necessary for adulthood—the capacity for autonomous thinking, clear decision-making, and responsible action—are those associated with masculinity and considered undesirable as attributes of the feminine self. The stereotypes suggest a splitting of love and work that relegates expressive capacities to women while placing instrumental

abilities in the masculine domain. Yet looked at from a different perspective, these stereotypes reflect a conception of adulthood that is
itself out of balance, favoring the separateness of the individual self
over connection to others, and leaning more toward an autonomous
life of work than toward the interdependence of love and care.

The discovery now being celebrated by men in mid-life of the im-   35
portance of intimacy, relationships, and care is something that women
have known from the beginning. However, because that knowledge in
women has been considered "intuitive" or "instinctive," a function of
anatomy coupled with destiny, psychologists have neglected to describe its development. In my research, I have found that women's
moral development centers on the elaboration of that knowledge
and thus delineates a critical line of psychological development in
the lives of both of the sexes. The subject of moral development not
only provides the final illustration of the reiterative pattern in the
observation and assessment of sex differences in the literature on
human development, but also indicates more particularly why the
nature and significance of women's development has been for so
long obscured and shrouded in mystery.

The criticism that Freud makes of women's sense of justice, see-   36
ing it as compromised in its refusal of blind impartiality, reappears
not only in the work of Piaget but also in that of Kohlberg. While in
Piaget's account (1932) of the moral judgment of the child, girls are
an aside, a curiosity to whom he devotes four brief entries in an
index that omits "boys" altogether because "the child" is assumed
to be male, in the research from which Kohlberg derives his theory,
females simply do not exist. Kohlberg's (1958, 1981) six stages that
describe the development of moral judgment from childhood to adulthood are based empirically on a study of eighty-four boys whose development Kohlberg has followed for a period of over twenty years.
Although Kohlberg claims universality for his stage sequence, those
groups not included in his original sample rarely reach his higher
stages (Edwards, 1975; Holstein, 1976; Simpson, 1974). Prominent among those who thus appear to be deficient in moral development when measured by Kohlberg's scale are women, whose
judgments seem to exemplify the third stage of his six-stage sequence. At this stage morality is conceived in interpersonal terms
and goodness is equated with helping and pleasing others. This
conception of goodness is considered by Kohlberg and Kramer
(1969) to be functional in the lives of mature women insofar as
their lives take place in the home. Kohlberg and Kramer imply that
only if women enter the traditional arena of male activity will they
recognize the inadequacy of this moral perspective and progress
like men toward higher stages where relationships are subordinated

to rules (stage four) and rules to universal principles of justice (stages five and six).

Yet herein lies a paradox, for the very traits that traditionally   37
have defined the "goodness" of women, their care for and sensitivity to the needs of others, are those that mark them as deficient in moral development. In this version of moral development, however, the conception of maturity is derived from the study of men's lives and reflects the importance of individuation in their development. Piaget (1970), challenging the common impression that a developmental theory is built like a pyramid from its base in infancy, points out that a conception of development instead hangs from its vertex of maturity, the point toward which progress is traced. Thus, a change in the definition of maturity does not simply alter the description of the highest stage but recasts the understanding of development, changing the entire account.

When one begins with the study of women and derives develop-   38
mental constructs from their lives, the outline of a moral conception different from that described by Freud, Piaget, or Kohlberg begins to emerge and informs a different description of development. In this conception, the moral problem arises from conflicting responsibilities rather than from competing rights and requires for its resolution a mode of thinking that is contextual and narrative rather than formal and abstract. This conception of morality as concerned with the activity of care centers moral development around the understanding of responsibility and relationships, just as the conception of morality as fairness ties moral development to the understanding of rights and rules.

This different construction of the moral problem by women   39
may be seen as the critical reason for their failure to develop within the constraints of Kohlberg's system. Regarding all constructions of responsibility as evidence of a conventional moral understanding, Kohlberg defines the highest stages of moral development as deriving from a reflective understanding of human rights. That the morality of rights differs from the morality of responsibility in its emphasis on separation rather than connection, in its consideration of the individual rather than the relationship as primary, is illustrated by two responses to interview questions about the nature of morality. The first comes from a twenty-five-year-old man, one of the participants in Kohlberg's study:

> [*What does the word morality mean to you?*] Nobody in the world knows the answer. I think it is recognizing the right of the individual, the rights of other individuals, not interfering with those rights. Act as fairly as you would have them treat you. I think it is basically to preserve the human being's right to existence. I think

that is the most important. Secondly, the human being's right to do as he pleases, again without interfering with somebody's else's rights.

[*How have your views on morality changed since the last interview?*] I think I am more aware of an individual's rights now. I used to be looking at it strictly from my point of view, just for me. Now I think I am more aware of what the individual has a right to.

Kohlberg (1973) cites this man's response as illustrative of the principled conception of human rights that exemplifies his fifth and sixth stages. Commenting on the response, Kohlberg says: "Moving to a perspective outside of that of his society, he identifies morality with justice (fairness, rights, the Golden Rule), with recognition of the rights of others as these are defined naturally or intrinsically. The human's being right to do as he pleases without interfering with somebody else's rights is a formula defining rights prior to social legislation" (pp. 29–30).

The second response comes from a woman who participated in   40
the rights and responsibilities study. She also was twenty-five and, at the time, a third-year law student:

[*Is there really some correct solution to moral problems, or is everybody's opinion equally right?*] No, I don't think everybody's opinion is equally right. I think that in some situations there may be opinions that are equally valid, and one could conscientiously adopt one of several courses of action. But there are other situations in which I think there are right and wrong answers, that sort of inhere in the nature of existence, of all individuals here who need to live with each other to live. We need to depend on each other, and hopefully it is not only a physical need but a need of fulfillment in ourselves, that a person's life is enriched by cooperating with other people and striving to live in harmony with everybody else, and to that end, there are right and wrong, there are things which promote that end and that move away from it, and in that way it is possible to choose in certain cases among different courses of action that obviously promote or harm that goal.

[*Is there a time in the past when you would have thought about these things differently?*] Oh, yeah, I think that I went through a time when I thought that things were pretty relative, that I can't tell you what to do and you can't tell me what to do, because you've got your conscience and I've got mine.

[*When was that?*] When I was in high school. I guess that it just sort of dawned on me that my own ideas changed, and because my own judgment changed, I felt I couldn't judge another person's judgment. But now I think even when it is only the person himself who is going to be affected, I say it is wrong to the extent it doesn't cohere with what I know about human nature and what

I know about you, and just from what I think is true about the operation of the universe, I could say I think you are making a mistake.

[*What led you to change, do you think?*] Just seeing more of life, just recognizing that there are an awful lot of things that are common among people. There are certain things that you come to learn promote a better life and better relationships and more personal fulfillment than other things that in general tend to do the opposite, and the things that promote these things, you would call morally right.

This response also represents a personal reconstruction of morality following a period of questioning and doubt, but the reconstruction of moral understanding is based not on the primacy and universality of individual rights, but rather on what she describes as a "very strong sense of being responsible to the world." Within this construction, the moral dilemma changes from how to exercise one's rights without interfering with the rights of others to how "to lead a moral life which includes obligations to myself and my family and people in general." The problem then becomes one of limiting responsibilities without abandoning moral concern. When asked to describe herself, this woman says that she values "having other people that I am tied to, and also having people that I am responsible to. I have a very strong sense of being responsible to the world, that I can't just live for my enjoyment, but just the fact of being in the world gives me an obligation to do what I can to make the world a better place to live in, no matter how small a scale that may be on." Thus while Kohlberg's subject worries about people interfering with each other's rights, this woman worries about "the possibility of omission, of your not helping others when you could help them."

The issue that this woman raises is addressed by Jane Loevinger's fifth "autonomous" stage of ego development, where autonomy, placed in a context of relationships, is defined as modulating an excessive sense of responsibility through the recognition that other people have responsibility for their own destiny. The autonomous stage in Loevinger's account (1970) witnesses a relinquishing of moral dichotomies and their replacement with "a feeling for the complexity and multifaceted character of real people and real situations" (p. 6). Whereas the rights conception of morality that informs Kohlberg's principled level (stages five and six) is geared to arriving at an objectively fair or just resolution to moral dilemmas upon which all rational persons could agree, the responsibility conception focuses instead on the limitations of any particular resolution and describes the conflicts that remain.

Thus it becomes clear why a morality of rights and noninterfer-   43
ence may appear frightening to women in its potential justification of
indifference and unconcern. At the same time, it becomes clear why,
from a male perspective, a morality of responsibility appears inconclu-
sive and diffuse, given its insistent contextual relativism. Women's
moral judgments thus elucidate the pattern observed in the description of the developmental differences between the sexes, but they also
provide an alternative conception of maturity by which these differences can be assessed and their implications traced. The psychology of
women that has consistently been described as distinctive in its
greater orientation toward relationships and interdependence implies
a more contextual mode of judgment and a different moral understanding. Given the differences in women's conceptions of self and
morality, women bring to the life cycle a different point of view and
order human experience in terms of different priorities.

The myth of Demeter and Persephone, which McClelland (1975)   44
cites as exemplifying the feminine attitude toward power, was associated with the Eleusinian Mysteries celebrated in ancient Greece for
over two thousand years. As told in the Homeric *Hymn to Demeter*, the
story of Persephone indicates the strengths of interdependence, building up resources and giving, that McClelland found in his research on
power motivation to characterize the mature feminine style. Although,
McClelland says, "it is fashionable to conclude that no one knows what
went on in the Mysteries, it is known that they were probably the most
important religious ceremonies, even partly on the historical record,
which were organized by and for women, especially at the onset before
men by means of the cult of Dionysos began to take them over." Thus
McClelland regards the myth as "a special presentation of feminine
psychology" (p. 96). It is, as well, a life-cycle story par excellence.

Persephone, the daughter of Demeter, while playing in a meadow   45
with her girlfriends, sees a beautiful narcissus which she runs to pick.
As she does so, the earth opens and she is snatched away by Hades,
who takes her to his underworld kingdom. Demeter, goddess of the
earth, so mourns the loss of her daughter that she refuses to allow anything to grow. The crops that sustain life on earth shrivel up, killing
men and animals alike, until Zeus takes pity on man's suffering and
persuades his brother to return Persephone to her mother. But before
she leaves, Persephone eats some pomegranate seeds, which ensures
that she will spend part of every year with Hades in the underworld.

The elusive mystery of women's development lies in its recogni-   46
tion of the continuing importance of attachment in the human life
cycle. Woman's place in man's life cycle is to protect this recognition
while the developmental litany intones the celebration of separation,
autonomy, individuation, and natural rights. The myth of Persephone

speaks directly to the distortion in this view by reminding us that narcissism leads to death, that the fertility of the earth is in some mysterious way tied to the continuation of the mother-daughter relationship, and that the life cycle itself arises from an alternation between the world of women and that of men. Only when life-cycle theorists divide their attention and begin to live with women as they have lived with men will their vision encompass the experience of both sexes and their theories become correspondingly more fertile.

SELECTED BIBLIOGRAPHY
FOR GILLIGAN'S "WOMAN'S PLACE
IN MAN'S LIFE CYCLE"

Carol Gilligan mentions a number of important authorities in psychology in "Woman's Place in Man's Life Cycle." Here are some of the books to which she refers:

Bruno Bettelheim. *The Uses of Enchantment.* New York: Knopf, 1976.

Nancy Chodorow. *The Reproduction of Mothering.* Berkeley: University of California Press, 1978.

Erik H. Erikson. *Childhood and Society.* New York: W. W. Norton, 1950.

Lawrence Kohlberg. *The Philosophy of Moral Development.* San Francisco: Harper and Row, 1981.

Janet Lever. "Sex Differences in the Games Children Play." *Social Problems* 23 (1976): 478–487.

Jane Loevinger and Ruth Wessler. *Measuring Ego Development.* San Francisco. Jossey-Bass, 1970.

David C. McClelland. *Power: The Inner Experience.* New York: Irvington, 1975.

George Herbert Mead. *Mind, Self, and Society.* Chicago: University of Chicago Press, 1934.

Jean Piaget. *The Moral Judgment of the Child* (1932). New York: The Free Press, 1965.

QUESTIONS FOR CRITICAL READING

1. Do you agree that men and women observe things differently?
2. What is the importance of Gilligan's observations about *The Elements of Style* (see para. 4)?
3. What does it mean that "developmental theorists . . . project a masculine image" (para. 6)?

4. Why did Freud think women "show less sense of justice than men" (para. 7)?
5. Do you agree that "mothers tend to experience their daughters as more like, and continuous with, themselves" (para. 9)?
6. Does your experience validate the conclusion that women express more empathy than men?
7. What differences do you see between the games boys play and the games girls play?

SUGGESTIONS FOR WRITING

1. Psychologists place great importance on the ways in which boys and girls play games. Judging from your own experience playing games as a child, can you validate that there is an important socializing difference in the games that boys and girls play and how they play them? Establish the values that you gained from the socialization that is implied in playing games. How much of what you learned in playing games still operates in your behavior?

2. One of the chief theories of psychologists concerns the link between boys and their mothers and girls and their mothers. One theory is that because mothers see their daughters as like themselves they tend to treat them as continuous with themselves, thus making it difficult for women later to break away. Boys, however, because of the gender distinction, find it easier as adults to break away and pursue successful careers. How true do you think this hypothesis is? Find examples to use in your argument.

3. Judging from your own experiences, what kinds of quarrels do boys have among themselves? How do they differ from the quarrels that girls have among themselves? What do the differences imply for the development of boys into men and girls into women? Try to be as specific as possible in recalling or describing quarrels of your own. You may wish to interview a member of the opposite sex to get a different perspective.

4. Read Sigmund Freud on the Oedipus complex and comment on his observations about the development of boys and girls. Is it clear that, as Gilligan suggests, he worked entirely from observation of the male gender and did not take into account differences in anatomy or in social development between boys and girls? What claims by Freud seem most unlikely to you?

5. The term *narcissism* is mentioned in the text (paras. 19, 46). Look up the term in a psychological dictionary or psychological handbook. What is narcissism? Why do we think of it as a problem? Look up the myth of Narcissus and see what has been said about it. Is narcissism more likely to be a problem of men or of women? What kind of problems does it produce in individuals?

6. Erik Erikson suggests that "the female comes to know herself as she is known, through her relationships with others" (para. 21). To what

extent do you think this is true? How differently does self-knowledge come to men? Do you feel there is a distinction between the ways in which men and women define themselves? Which sex is most affected by social identification, accepting the definitions of friends and acquaintances?

7. **CONNECTIONS**   Life is full of rules. Do you observe a distinction in the ways in which men and women regard rules? What are some of the rules by which you live? How do you regard them? Is it essential to learn how to abide by rules in order to be a fully moral person? Was Henry David Thoreau typical of the male who understands and respects the rules? Is his sense of justice typically male?

8. **CONNECTIONS**   Virginia Woolf addressed "Shakespeare's Sister" to an audience of young women in college. To what extent does her essay reflect the views that Gilligan develops in her essay? Would Woolf consider Gilligan to be a feminist? What aspects of Woolf's comments on Shakespeare's hypothetical sister do you think most support the views that Gilligan presents in her essay?

BELL HOOKS
The Significance of
Feminist Movement

BELL HOOKS (b. 1952) is the pen name of Gloria Jean Watkins, who was born in Hopkinsville, Kentucky, and received her B.A. at Stanford University and her Ph.D. from the University of California at Santa Cruz. She eventually took the name of her great-grandmother and prefers lower-case letters for her name as a way of taking the spotlight off herself as author and putting it on her works instead. Hooks began her first book at nineteen, and after eight years of research and writing she published *Ain't I a Woman: Black Women and Feminism* (1981) while she was still in graduate school. Her works have focused on black feminism, third world issues, and her own personal experiences. She is a memoirist as well as a keen social critic.

In 1994 hooks was named Distinguished Professor of English at City College, City University of New York. She is one of the most visible of America's black intellectuals but has steadfastly asserted, despite her own academic connections, that intellectual achievements are not limited to universities. Much of her work is devoted to analyzing popular culture, such as contemporary films and rap music. Among her works are *Talking Back: Thinking Feminist, Thinking Black* (1989); *Teaching to Transgress: Education as the Practice of Freedom* (1994); *Outlaw Culture: Resisting Representation* (1994); *Feminism Is for Everybody* (2000); and two personal memoirs, *Bone Black: Memoirs of a Girlhood* (1996) and *Wounds of Passion: The Writing Life* (1997).

The book from which the following essay is taken, *Feminist Theory: From Margin to Center*, was published first in 1984 and then in a new, revised edition in 2000. The selection included here is Chapter Three in that book. It addresses some of the problems

From *Feminist Theory: From Margin to Center*.

that the feminist movement in the United States faced at the beginning, when it seemed that feminists were attacking all men and focusing on male domination. Hooks believes, on the contrary, that it is not men themselves who are the problem so much as it is the values of the culture that helps support the kinds of oppression feminism tried to attack. Sexism, racism, classism, imperialism, and other forms of oppression are all connected, hooks tells us, and therefore the feminist movement must be seen in these contexts.

Hooks feels that the radical feminists of the 1960s and later were in many ways reactionaries, in that they were looking backward, limiting themselves by insisting that all men were oppressors and, as she states, "*enemies of all women*" (para. 1). That is a reactionary position because it does not offer a total analysis of the nature of oppression in general. In her essay, hooks tries to repair this gap.

She also feels that many early feminists assumed that their middle-class "bourgeois" views were universal. However, different groups in society saw the issues from different points of view, and as a result some feminists' efforts actually pushed people away who might have had a significant stake in the movement. For hooks this was especially true for women of color, whose personal life experiences were often different from those of privileged white women who saw themselves trapped in lives of limited opportunity.

Part of the problem seems to have been, hooks suggests, that women in the movement in the sixties were mainly concerned with expressing their own agenda, which was sometimes extremely radical. As hooks states, "Building a mass-based women's movement was never the central issue on their agenda" (para. 3). In other words, radical feminists failed to explain how all women—as well as men and society in general—would benefit from the social change.

In her analysis of the problems the movement faced, hooks disputes the assertion that "sexist oppression" was "the basis of all other oppressions" (para. 5). She feels that many Western cultural values work together to assist in the oppression of women as well as other groups, and that the movement is only part of a reaction to larger forms of oppression that exploit and limit people in society. As she states, "The primary contradiction in Western cultural thought is the belief that the superior should control the inferior" (para. 5). This is a profound observation and one that needs close examination.

Hooks's Rhetoric

One of the hallmarks of hooks's rhetoric is her use of fairly long paragraphs to analyze a specific point. In paragraph 6, for example, she considers the issue of how sexist oppression might be thought of as "of primary importance." Hooks does not feel that sexism is the root of all other oppression, but she does assign to it primary importance because it is a form of oppression that all of us see. Whether women are bourgeois or poor, part of a family or not, people see in everyday situations the ways in which women can be discriminated against for better jobs or important opportunities, or marginalized in institutions or organizations. By introducing the ways in which women are oppressed or exploited in the family, she makes us aware of what most people take for granted as the appropriate role for women. Men are the wage-earners who go out into the world and make the money that keeps the family together, while women remain home in a limited environment and take care of the children. Of course, today, many married women also work outside the home, but hooks would claim that their status is still limited by the assumptions most of us take for granted in a family.

In paragraph 7, hooks begins a pattern that marks much of the rest of the essay. She quotes other authorities liberally to help her expand and reinforce her view that for the feminist movement to succeed it must recognize the larger cultural issues that make sexism possible. In successive paragraphs, she analyzes the importance of families and what she calls "kinship structure" (para. 8) in order to clarify and deepen her argument. She considers the question of how "power struggles" (para. 8) in a family teach us the value and naturalness of domination and oppression.

She goes further in paragraph 9 and considers whether or not the feminist movement aims to disintegrate the family entirely. In this paragraph she begins to consider alternative views of the family, especially as understood by women of color, for whom the family is a source of dignity and support. She states that "many black women find the family the least oppressive institution" (para. 9). Her point earlier was that bourgeois white feminists found the family among the most oppressive institutions and therefore assumed that what was true for them was true for all women. For hooks, this is an essential error and has led to much misunderstanding of the feminist movement.

On the other hand, hooks is also aware that there are political implications to any analysis of the effect of the family on issues such as sexism. She becomes controversial when she declares that "the white supremacist, patriarchal state relies on the family to indoctrinate its members with values supportive of hierarchical control and coercive authority" (para. 11). She sees this reliance on the family as central to the position of the political right in the United States, which places a very heavy emphasis on the nuclear family and preserving its position as central in all political decisions.

**In this selection, hooks demonstrates how feminism is funda-
mentally a political movement and not just a reaction of a few privileged people to a difficult situation.**

PREREADING QUESTIONS:
WHAT TO READ FOR

The following prereading questions may help you anticipate key issues
in the discussion of bell hooks's "The Significance of Feminist Movement."
Keeping them in mind during your first reading of the selection should
help focus your attention.

- What does hooks see as the mistakes of the early feminists?

- What role does the family have in promoting sexism, according to
  hooks?

- What are the connections among sexism, racism, classism, and imperialism?

The Significance of
Feminist Movement

Contemporary feminist movement in the United States called   1
attention to the exploitation and oppression of women globally. This
was a major contribution to feminist struggle. In their eagerness to
highlight sexist injustice, women focused almost exclusively on the
ideology and practice of male domination. Unfortunately, this made
it appear that feminism was more a declaration of war between
the sexes than a political struggle to end sexist oppression, a struggle
that would imply change on the part of women and men. Underlying much white women's liberationist rhetoric was the implication
that men had nothing to gain by feminist movement, that its success
would make them losers. Militant white women were particularly
eager to make feminist movement privilege women over men. Their
anger, hostility, and rage was so intense that they were unable to resist turning the movement into a public forum for their attacks. Although they sometimes considered themselves "radical feminists,"
their responses were reactionary. Fundamentally, they argued *that
all men are the enemies of all women* and proposed as solutions to this

problem a utopian woman nation, separatist communities, and even the subjugation or extermination of all men. Their anger may have been a catalyst for individual liberatory resistance and change. It may have encouraged bonding with other women to raise consciousness. It did not strengthen public understanding of the significance of authentic feminist movement.

Sexist discrimination, exploitation, and oppression have created   2 the war between the sexes. Traditionally the battleground has been the home. In recent years, the battle ensues in any sphere, public or private, inhabited by women and men, girls and boys. The significance of feminist movement (when it is not co-opted by opportunistic, reactionary forces) is that it offers a new ideological meeting ground for the sexes, a space for criticism, struggle, and transformation. Feminist movement can end the war between the sexes. It can transform relationships so that the alienation, competition, and dehumanization that characterize human interaction can be replaced with feelings of intimacy, mutuality, and camaraderie.

Ironically, these positive implications of feminist movement were   3 often ignored by liberal organizers and participants. Since vocal bourgeois white women were insisting that women repudiate the role of servant to others, they were not interested in convincing men or even other women that feminist movement was important for everyone. Narcissistically, they focused solely on the primacy of feminism in their lives, universalizing their own experiences. Building a mass-based women's movement was never the central issue on their agenda. After many organizations were established, leaders expressed a desire for greater participant diversity; they wanted women to join who were not white, materially privileged, middle-class, or college-educated. It was never deemed necessary for feminist activists to explain to masses of women the significance of feminist movement. Believing their emphasis on social equality was a universal concern, they assumed the idea would carry its own appeal. Strategically, the failure to emphasize the necessity for mass-based movement, grassroots organizing, and sharing with everyone the positive significance of feminist movement helped marginalize feminism by making it appear relevant only to those women who joined organizations.

Recent critiques of feminist movement highlight these failures   4 without stressing the need for revision in strategy and focus. Although the theory and praxis of contemporary feminism with all its flaws and inadequacies has become well established, even institutionalized, we must try and change its direction if we are to build a feminist movement that is truly a struggle to end sexist oppression. In the interest of such a struggle we must, at the onset of our analysis, call attention to the positive, transformative impact the eradication of sexist oppression could have on all our lives.

Many contemporary feminist activists argue that eradicating sex- 5 ist oppression is important because it is the primary contradiction, the basis of all other oppressions. Racism, as well as class structure, is perceived as stemming from sexism. Implicit in this line of analysis is the assumption that the eradication of sexism, "the oldest oppression," "the primary contradiction," is necessary before attention can be focused on racism or classism. Suggesting a hierarchy of oppression exists, with sexism in first place, evokes a sense of competing concerns that is unnecessary. While we know that sex-role divisions existed in the earliest civilizations, not enough is known about these societies to conclusively document the assertion that women were exploited or oppressed. The earliest civilizations discovered so far have been in archaic black Africa, where presumably there was no race problem and no class society as we know it today. The sexism, racism, and classism that exist in the West may resemble systems of domination globally, but they are forms of oppression that have been primarily informed by Western philosophy. They can be best understood within a Western context, not via an evolutionary model of human development. Within our society, all forms of oppression are supported by traditional Western thinking. The primary contradiction in Western cultural thought is the belief that the superior should control the inferior. In *The Cultural Basis of Racism and Group Oppression*, philosopher John Hodge argues that Western religious and philosophical thought are the ideological basis of all forms of oppression in the United States.

Sexist oppression is of primary importance not because it is the 6 basis of all other oppression, but because it is the practice of domination most people experience, whether their role be that of discriminator or discriminated against, exploiter or exploited. It is the practice of domination most people are socialized to accept before they even know that other forms of group oppression exist. This does not mean that eradicating sexist oppression would eliminate other forms of oppression. Since all forms of oppression are linked in our society because they are supported by similar institutional and social structures, one system cannot be eradicated while the others remain intact. Challenging sexist oppression is a crucial step in the struggle to eliminate all forms of oppression.

Unlike other forms of oppression, most people witness and/or 7 experience the practice of sexist domination in family settings. We tend to witness and/or experience racism or classism as we encounter the larger society, the world outside the home. In his essay "Dualist Culture and Beyond," Hodge stresses that the family in our society, both traditionally and legally, "reflects the Dualist values of hierarchy and coercive authoritarian control," which are exemplified in parent-child and husband-wife relationships:

> It is in this form of the family where most children first learn the meaning and practice of hierarchical, authoritarian rule. Here is where they learn to accept group oppression against themselves as non-adults, and where they learn to accept male supremacy and the group oppression of women. Here is where they learn that it is the male's role to work in the community and control the economic life of the family and to mete out the physical and financial punishments and rewards, and the female's role to provide the emotional warmth associated with motherhood while under the economic rule of the male. Here is where the relationship of superordination-subordination, of superior-inferior, of master-slave is first learned and accepted as "natural."

Even in families where no male is present, children may learn to value dominating, authoritative rule via their relationship to mothers and other adults, as well as strict adherence to sexist-defined role patterns.

In most societies, family is an important kinship structure: a 8 common ground for people who are linked by blood ties, heredity, or emotive bonds; an environment of care and affirmation, especially for the very young and the very old, who may be unable to care for themselves; a space for communal sharing of resources. In our society, sexist oppression perverts and distorts the positive function of family. Family exists as a space wherein we are socialized from birth to accept and support forms of oppression. In his discussion of the cultural basis of domination, Hodge emphasizes the role of the family:

> The traditional Western family, with its authoritarian male rule and its authoritarian adult rule, is the major training ground which initially conditions us to accept group oppression as the natural order.

Even as we are loved and cared for in families, we are simultaneously taught that this love is not as important as having power to dominate others. Power struggles, coercive authoritarian rule, and brutal assertion of domination shape family life so that it is often the setting of intense suffering and pain. Naturally, individuals flee the family. Naturally, the family disintegrates.

Contemporary feminist analyses of family often implied that 9 successful feminist movement would either begin with or lead to the abolition of family. This suggestion was terribly threatening to many women, especially non-white women. (In their essay "Challenging

Imperial Feminism," Valerie Amos and Pratibha Parmar examine the way in which Euro-American feminist discussions of family are ethnocentric and alienate black women from feminist movement.) While there are white women activists who may experience family primarily as an oppressive institution (it may be the social structure wherein they have experienced grave abuse and exploitation), many black women find the family the least oppressive institution. Despite sexism in the context of family, we may experience dignity, self-worth, and a humanization that is not experienced in the outside world wherein we confront all forms of oppression. We know from our lived experiences that families are not just households composed of husband, wife, and children, or even blood relations; we also know that destructive patterns generated by belief in sexism abound in varied family structures. We wish to affirm the primacy of family life because we know that family ties are the only sustained support system for exploited and oppressed peoples. We wish to rid family life of the abusive dimensions created by sexist oppression without devaluing it.

Devaluation of family life in feminist discussion often reflects   10 the class nature of the movement. Individuals from privileged classes rely on a number of institutional and social structures to affirm and protect their interests. The bourgeois woman can repudiate family without believing that by so doing she relinquishes the possibility of relationship, care, protection. If all else fails, she can buy care. Since many bourgeois women active in feminist movement were raised in the modern nuclear household, they were particularly subjected to the perversion of family life created by sexist oppression; they may have had material privilege and no experience of abiding family love and care. Their devaluation of family life alienated many women from feminist movement. Ironically, feminism is the one radical political movement that focuses on transforming family relationships. Feminist movement to end sexist oppression affirms family life by its insistence that the purpose of family structure is not to reinforce patterns of domination in the interest of the state. By challenging Western philosophical beliefs that impress on our consciousness a concept of family life that is essentially destructive, feminism would liberate family so that it could be an affirming, positive kinship structure with no oppressive dimensions based on sex differentiation, sexual preference, etc.

Politically, the white supremacist, patriarchal state relies on the   11 family to indoctrinate its members with values supportive of hierarchical control and coercive authority. Therefore, the state has a vested interest in projecting the notion that feminist movement will destroy family life. Introducing a collection of essays, *Rethinking the Family: Some Feminist Questions*, sociologist Barrie Thorne makes the point that feminist critique of family life has been seized upon by New Right groups in their political campaigns:

> Of all the issues raised by feminists, those that bear on the family—among them, demands for abortion rights, and for legitimating an array of household and sexual arrangements, and challenges to men's authority, and women's economic dependence and exclusive responsibility for nurturing—have been the most controversial.

Feminist positions on the family that devalue its importance have been easily co-opted to serve the interests of the state. People are concerned that families are breaking down, that positive dimensions of family life are overshadowed by the aggression, humiliation, abuse, and violence that characterizes the interaction of family members. They must not be convinced that anti-feminism is the way to improve family life. Feminist activists need to affirm the importance of family as a kinship structure that can sustain and nourish people; to graphically address links between sexist oppression and family disintegration; and to give examples, both actual and visionary, of the way family life is and can be when unjust authoritarian rule is replaced with an ethic of communalism, shared responsibility, and mutuality. The movement to end sexist oppression is the only social-change movement that will strengthen and sustain family life in all households.

Within the present family structure, individuals learn to accept sexist oppression as "natural" and are primed to support other forms of oppression, including heterosexist domination. According to Hodge: 12

> The domination usually present within the family—of children by adults, and of female by male—are forms of group oppression which are easily translated into the "rightful" group oppression of other people defined by "race" (racism), by nationality (colonialism), by "religion," or by "other means."

Significantly, struggle to end sexist oppression that focuses on destroying the cultural basis for such domination strengthens other liberation struggles, Individuals who fight for the eradication of sexism without supporting struggles to end racism or classism undermine their own efforts. Individuals who fight for the eradication of racism or classism while supporting sexist oppression are helping to maintain the cultural basis of all forms of group oppression. While they may initiate successful reforms, their efforts will not lead to revolutionary change. Their ambivalent relationship to oppression in general is a contradiction that must be resolved, or they will daily undermine their own radical work.

Unfortunately, it is not merely the politically naive who demon- 13 strate a lack of awareness that forms of oppression are interrelated. Often brilliant political thinkers have had such blind spots. Men like Frantz Fanon, Albert Memmi, Paulo Freire, and Aimé Césaire,[1] whose works teach us much about the nature of colonization, racism, classism, and revolutionary struggle, often ignore issues of sexist oppression in their own writing. They speak against oppression but then define liberation in terms that suggest it is only oppressed "men" who need freedom. Frantz Fanon's important work *Black Skin, White Masks* draws a portrait of oppression in the first chapter that equates the colonizer with white men and the colonized with black men. Towards the end of the book, Fanon writes of the struggle to overcome alienation:

> The problem considered here is one of time. Those Negroes and white men will be disalienated who refuse to let themselves be sealed away in the materialized Tower of the Past. For many other Negroes, in other ways, disalienation will come into being through their refusal to accept the present definitive.
>
> I am a man, and what I have to recapture is the whole past of the world. I am not responsible solely for the revolt in Santo Domingo.
>
> Every time a man has contributed to the victory of the dignity of the spirit, every time a man has said no to an attempt to subjugate his fellows, I have felt solidarity with his act.

In Paulo Freire's book *Pedagogy of the Oppressed*, a text that has 14 helped many of us to develop political consciousness, there is a tendency to speak of people's liberation as male liberation:

> Liberation is thus a childbirth, and a painful one. The man who emerges is a new man, viable only as the oppressor-oppressed contradiction is superseded by the humanization of all men. Or to put it another way, the solution of this contradiction is borne in the labor which brings into the world this new man: no longer oppressor, no longer oppressed, but man in the process of achieving freedom.

(In a discussion with Freire on this issue, he supported wholeheartedly this criticism of his work and urged me to share this with readers.) The sexist language in these translated texts does not prevent feminist activists from identifying with or learning from the

---

[1] **Frantz Fanon (1925–1961), Albert Memmi (b. 1920), Paulo Freire (1921–1997), Aimé Césaire (b. 1913)** Prominent critics of colonialism and oppression.

message content. It diminishes without negating the value of the works. It also does support and perpetuate sexist oppression.

Support of sexist oppression in much political writing concerned 15 with revolutionary struggle as well as in the actions of men who advocate revolutionary politics undermines all liberation struggle. In many countries wherein people are engaged in liberation struggle, subordination of women by men is abandoned as the crisis situation compels men to accept and acknowledge women as comrades in struggle, e.g., Cuba, Angola, and Nicaragua. Often when the crisis period has passed, old sexist patterns emerge, antagonism develops, and political solidarity is weakened. It would strengthen and affirm the praxis of any liberation struggle if a commitment to eradicating sexist oppression were a foundation principle shaping all political work. Feminist movement should be of primary significance for all groups and individuals who desire an end to oppression. Many women who would like to participate fully in liberation struggles (the fight against imperialism, racism, classism) are drained of their energies because they are continually confronting and coping with sexist discrimination, exploitation, and oppression. In the interest of continued struggle, solidarity, and sincere commitment to eradicating all forms of domination, sexist oppression cannot continue to be ignored and dismissed by radical political activists.

An important stage in the development of political conscious- 16 ness is reached when individuals recognize the need to struggle against all forms of oppression. The fight against sexist oppression is of grave political significance—it is not for women only. Feminist movement is vital both in its power to liberate us from the terrible bonds of sexist oppression and in its potential to radicalize and renew other liberation struggles.

QUESTIONS FOR CRITICAL READING

1. What does hooks feel men have to gain from the feminist movement?
2. What did bourgeois white women assume were the normal demands of all women?
3. What are hooks's views on the structure of the family?
4. In what ways does hooks place special emphasis on the concept of the superior/inferior relationship in society?
5. What difference does hooks say exists between white and black feminists regarding the family?
6. Would the "movement to end sexist oppression . . . strengthen and sustain family life in all households" (para. 11), as hooks suggests?

SUGGESTIONS FOR WRITING

1. In paragraph 5 hooks talks about the question of primacy in terms of the importance of the feminist movement. Examine her argument in this paragraph and elsewhere in the essay. What do you feel is the most important aspect of this discussion? What do you see as the most important thing to consider when taking a position on the primacy of the feminist movement? How primary is it in the culture that you inhabit and understand?

2. If you are male, examine the fundamental principles of feminism as they have been outlined in this essay. Do you feel that in a society that advocated the kinds of changes feminists yearn for, you would be affected detrimentally? Or do you feel that you would benefit from such changes? Try to be specific by pointing to the areas in school and in life that would be altered by the implementation of feminist values.

3. If you are female, outline what you feel are the most important aspects of the feminist movement as hooks understands it. Then explain how they would benefit you or perhaps be detrimental to your lifestyle. What aspects of feminism do you find most difficult to accept, and what aspects are of genuine importance and value to you? How would your life change if hooks's feminist principles were put in place?

4. How accurate do you think hooks is in her analysis of the family as a means of promoting the values that lead to oppression and sexism? How could the family be structured in a way that might avoid promoting the negative values hooks describes? Does it seem that feminists are directly attacking the family as we know it? Explain.

5. Hooks states, "Within our society, all forms of oppression are supported by traditional Western thinking" (para. 5). What are hooks's primary reasons for holding this view? Do you accept her views or do you feel that she distorts traditional Western thinking? Is such a radical view warranted by what you have observed of both the family and Western thinking?

6. **CONNECTIONS**   In what ways do the selections by Mary Wollstonecraft and Virginia Woolf reveal the problems between women of different socioeconomic groups that hooks claims hurt the feminist movement? Do you find Wollstonecraft's or Woolf's brand of feminism class conscious? Do you think either woman would be open to the problems of black women? Would they be open to the problems of women of the servant classes of their own time? How might hooks critique their work?

7. **CONNECTIONS**   To what extent are Simone de Beauvoir's concerns about the myth of woman relevant to hooks's views in this essay? How does the act of mythicizing women—regardless of color—affect them negatively? To what extent does mythicizing women fit into the pattern of Western values hooks decries? Is it a source of sexism and a means of oppressing women? Explain.

WRITING ABOUT IDEAS
An Introduction to Rhetoric

Writing about ideas has several functions. First, it helps make our thinking available to others for examination. The writers whose works are presented in this book benefited from their first readers' examinations and at times revised their work considerably as a result of such criticism. Writing about ideas also helps us to refine what we think—even without criticism from others—because writing is a self-instructional experience. We learn by writing in part because writing clarifies our thinking. When we think silently, we construct phrases and then reflect on them; when we speak, we both utter these phrases and sort them out in order to give our audience a tidier version of our thoughts. But spoken thought is difficult to sustain because we cannot review or revise what we said an hour earlier. Writing has the advantage of permitting us to expand our ideas, to work them through completely, and possibly to revise in the light of later discoveries. It is by writing that we truly gain control over our ideas.

GENERATING TOPICS FOR WRITING

Filled with sophisticated discussions of important ideas, the selections in this volume endlessly stimulate our responses and our writing. Reading the works of great thinkers can also be chastening to the point of making us feel sometimes that they have said it all and there is no room for our own thoughts. However, the suggestions that follow will assist you in writing your response to the ideas of an important thinker.

Thinking Critically: Asking a Question. One of the most reliable ways to start writing is to ask a question and then to answer it. In many ways, that is what the writers in this book have done again and again. Melanie Klein asked whether what Freud said about female psychology was true. Adam Smith asked what the principles of accumulating wealth really were and proceeded to examine the economic system of his time in such detail that his views are still valued. He is associated with the capitalist system as firmly as Marx is with the communist system. John Kenneth Galbraith asked questions about why poverty existed in a prosperous nation such as the United States. John Rawls asked whether justice could be fair. Michio Kaku asked whether the theory of dark matter constituting 90 percent of the universe can be true. Such questioning is at the center of all critical thinking.

As a writer stimulated by other thinkers, you can use the same technique. For example, turn back to the Machiavelli excerpt annotated in "Evaluating Ideas: An Introduction to Critical Reading" (p. 5). All the annotations can easily be turned into questions. Any of the following questions, based on the annotations and our brief summary of the passage, could be the basis of an essay:

- Should a leader be armed?
- Is it true that an unarmed leader is despised?
- Will those leaders who are always good come to ruin among those who are not good?
- To remain in power, must a leader learn how not to be good?

One technique is to structure an essay around the answer to such a question. Another is to develop a series of questions and to answer each of them in various parts of an essay. Yet another technique is to use the question indirectly — by answering it, but not in an obvious way. In "Why the Rich Are Getting Richer and the Poor, Poorer," for example, Robert B. Reich answers a question we may not have asked. In the process he examines the nature of our current economy to see what it promises for different sectors of the population. His answer to the question concerns the shift in labor from manufacturing to information, revealing that what he calls "symbolic analysts" have the best opportunities in the future to amass wealth.

Many kinds of questions can be asked of a passage even as brief as the sample from Machiavelli. For one thing, we can limit ourselves to our annotations and go no further. But we also can reflect on larger issues and ask a series of questions that constitute a fuller inquiry. Out of that inquiry we can generate ideas for our own writing.

Two important ideas were isolated in our annotations. The first was that the prince must devote himself to war. In modern times, this implies that a president or other national leader must put matters of defense first — that a leader's knowledge, training, and concerns must revolve around warfare. Taking that idea in general, we can develop other questions that, stimulated by Machiavelli's selection, can be used to generate essays:

- Which modern leaders would Machiavelli support?
- Would Machiavelli approve of our current president?
- Do military personnel make the best leaders?
- Should our president have a military background?
- Could a modern state survive with no army or military weapons?
- What kind of a nation would we have if we did not stockpile nuclear weapons?

These questions derive from "The prince's profession should be war," the first idea that we isolated in the annotations. The next group of questions comes from the second idea, the issue of whether a leader can afford to be moral:

- Can virtues cause a leader to lose power?
- Is Machiavelli being cynical about morality, or is he being realistic (as he claims he is)? (We might also ask if Machiavelli uses the word *realistic* as a synonym for *cynical*.)
- Do most American leaders behave morally?
- Do most leaders believe that they should behave morally?
- Should our leaders be moral all the time?
- Which vices can we permit our leaders to have?
- Are there any vices we want our leaders to have?
- Which world leaders behave most morally? Are they the ones we most respect?
- Could a modern government govern well or at all if it were to behave morally in the face of immoral adversaries?

One reason for reading Machiavelli is to help us confront broad and serious questions. One reason for writing about these ideas is to help clarify our own positions on such important issues.

Using Suggestions for Writing. Every selection in this book is followed by a number of questions and a number of writing assignments. The questions are designed to help clarify the most important issues raised in the piece. Unlike the questions derived from annotation, their purpose is to stimulate a classroom discussion so that you can benefit from hearing others' thoughts on these issues. Naturally, subjects for essays can arise from such discussion, but the discussion is most important for refining and focusing your ideas. The writing assignments, on the other hand, are explicitly meant to provide a useful starting point for producing an essay of five hundred to one thousand words.

A sample suggestion for writing about Machiavelli follows:

> Machiavelli advises the prince to study history and reflect on the actions of great men. Do you support such advice? Machiavelli mentions a number of great leaders in his essay. Which leaders would you recommend a prince should study? How do you think Machiavelli would agree or disagree with your recommendations?

Like most of the suggestions for writing, this one can be approached in several ways. It can be broken down into three parts. The first question is whether it is useful to study, as Machiavelli does, the performance of past leaders. If you agree, then the second question asks you to name some leaders whose behavior you would recommend studying. If you do not agree, you can point to the performance of some past leaders and explain why their study would be pointless today. Finally, the third question asks how you think Machiavelli would agree or disagree with your choices.

To deal successfully with this suggestion for writing, you could begin by giving your reasons for recommending that a political leader study "the actions of great men." George Santayana once said, "Those who cannot remember the past are condemned to repeat it." That is, we study history in order not to have to live it over again. If you believe that a study of the past is important, the first part of an essay can answer the question of why such study could make a politician more successful.

The second part of the suggestion focuses on examples. In the sample from Machiavelli above, we omitted the examples, but in the complete essay they are very important for bringing Machiavelli's point home. Few things can convince as completely as examples, so the first thing to do is to choose several leaders to work with. If you have studied a world leader, such as Indira Gandhi, Winston Churchill, Franklin Delano Roosevelt, or Margaret Thatcher, you could use that figure as one of your examples. If you have not done so, then use the research library's sections on history and politics to find books or articles on one or two leaders and read them with an eye to establishing their usefulness for your argument. An Internet search can help you gather information efficiently. Consult the Internet resources created specially for this book at www.bedford stmartins.com/worldofideas. The central question you would seek to answer is how a specific world leader could benefit from studying the behavior and conduct of a modern leader.

The third part of the suggestion for writing—how Machiavelli would agree or disagree with you—is highly speculative. It invites you to look through the selection to find quotes or comments that indicate probable agreement or disagreement on Machiavelli's part. You can base your argument only on what Machiavelli says or implies, and this means that you will have to reread his essay to find evidence that will support your view.

In a sense, this part of the suggestion establishes a procedure for working with the writing assignments. Once you clarify the parts of the assignment and have some useful questions to guide you, and once you determine what research, if any, is necessary, the next step is to reread the selection to find the most appropriate information to help you write your own essay. One of the most important activities in learning how to write from these selections is to reread while paying close attention to the annotations that you've made in the margins of the essays. It is one way in which reading about significant ideas differs from reading for entertainment. Important ideas demand reflection and reconsideration. Rereading provides both.

DEVELOPING IDEAS IN WRITING

Every selection in this book—whether by Francis Bacon or Simone de Beauvoir, Frederick Douglass or Karl Marx—employs specific rhetorical techniques that help the author communicate important ideas. Each introduction identifies the special rhetorical techniques used by the writer, partly to introduce you to the way in which such techniques are used.

Rhetoric is a general term used to discuss effective writing techniques. For example, an interesting rhetorical technique that Machiavelli uses is illustration by example, usually to prove his points. Francis Bacon uses the technique of enumeration by partitioning his essay into four sections. Enumeration is especially useful when the writer wishes to be very clear or to cover a subject point by point, using each point to accumulate more authority in the discussion. Martin Luther King Jr. uses the technique of allusion, reminding the religious leaders who were his audience that St. Paul wrote similar letters to help early Christians better understand the nature of their faith. By alluding to the Bible and St. Paul, King effectively reminded his audience that they all were serving God.

A great many more rhetorical techniques may be found in these readings. Some of the techniques are familiar because many of us already use them, but we study them to understand their value and to use them more effectively. After all, rhetorical techniques make it possible for us to communicate the significance of important ideas. Many of the authors in this book would surely admit that the effect of their ideas actually depends on the way they are expressed, which is a way of saying that they depend on the rhetorical methods used to express them.

Methods of Development

Most of the rhetorical methods used in these essays are discussed in the introductions to the individual selections. Several represent exceptionally useful general techniques. These are methods of development and represent approaches to developing ideas that contribute to the fullness and completeness of an essay. You may think of them as techniques that can be applied to any idea in almost any situation. They can enlarge on the idea, clarify it, express it, and demonstrate its truth or effectiveness. Sometimes a technique may be direct, sometimes indirect. Sometimes it calls attention to itself, sometimes it works behind the scenes. Sometimes it is used alone, sometimes in conjunction with other methods. The most important techniques are explained and then illustrated with examples from the selections in the book.

Development by Definition.   Definition is essential for two purposes: to make certain that you have a clear grasp of your concepts and that you communicate a clear understanding to your reader. Definition goes far beyond the use of the dictionary in the manner of "According to Webster's, . . ." Such an approach is facile because complex ideas are not easily reduced to dictionary definitions. A more useful strategy is to offer an explanation followed by an example. Because some of the suggestions for writing that follow the selections require you to use definition as a means of writing about ideas, the following tips should be kept in mind:

- Definition can be used to develop a paragraph, a section, or an entire essay.
- It considers questions of function, purpose, circumstance, origin, and implications for different groups.
- Explanations and examples make all definitions more complete and effective.

Many of the selections are devoted almost entirely to the act of definition. For example, in "The Position of Poverty," John Kenneth Galbraith begins by defining the two kinds of poverty that he feels characterize the economic situation of the poor—case poverty and insular poverty. He defines case poverty in this paragraph:

> Case poverty is commonly and properly related to some characteristic of the individuals so afflicted. Nearly everyone else has mastered his environment; this proves that it is not intractable. But some quality peculiar to the individual or family involved— mental deficiency, bad health, inability to adapt to the discipline of industrial life, uncontrollable procreation, alcohol, discrimination involving a very limited minority, some educational handicap unrelated to community shortcoming, or perhaps a combination of several of these handicaps—has kept these individuals from participating in the general well-being. (para. 7)

When he begins defining insular poverty, however, he is unable to produce a neat single-paragraph definition. He first establishes that insular poverty describes a group of people alienated from the majority for any of many reasons. Next, he spends five paragraphs discussing what can produce such poverty—migration, racial prejudice, and lack of education. When working at the level of seriousness that characterizes his work, Galbraith shows us that definition works best when it employs full description and complex, detailed discussion.

An essay on the annotated selection from Machiavelli might define a number of key ideas. For example, to argue that Machiavelli is cynical in suggesting that his prince would not retain power if he acted morally, we would need to define what it means to be cynical and what moral behavior means in political terms. When we argue any point, it is important to spend time defining key ideas.

Martin Luther King Jr., in "Letter from Birmingham Jail," takes time to establish some key definitions so that he can speak forcefully to his audience:

> Let us consider a more concrete example of just and unjust laws. An unjust law is a code that a numerical or power majority group compels a minority group to obey but does not make binding on itself. This is *difference* made legal. By the same token, a just law is a code that a majority compels a minority to follow and that it is willing to follow itself. This is *sameness* made legal. (para. 17)

This is an adequate definition as far as it goes, but most serious ideas need more extensive definition than this passage gives us. And King does go further, providing what Machiavelli does in his essay: examples and explanations. Every full definition will profit from the extension of understanding that an explanation and example will provide. Consider this paragraph from King:

> Let me give another explanation. A law is unjust if it is inflicted on a minority that, as a result of being denied the right to vote, had

no part in enacting or devising the law. Who can say that the legislature of Alabama which set up that state's segregation laws was democratically elected? Throughout Alabama all sorts of devious methods are used to prevent Negroes from becoming registered voters, and there are some counties in which, even though Negroes constitute a majority of the population, not a single Negro is registered. Can any law enacted under such circumstances be considered democratically structured? (para. 18)

King makes us aware of the fact that definition is complex and capable of great subtlety. It is an approach that can be used to develop a paragraph or an essay.

Development by Comparison.   Comparison is a natural operation of the mind. We rarely talk for long about any topic without comparing it with something else. We are fascinated with comparisons between ourselves and others and come to know ourselves better as a result of such comparisons. Machiavelli, for example, compares the armed with the unarmed prince and shows us, by means of examples, the results of being unarmed.

Comparison usually includes the following:

- A definition of two or more elements to be compared (by example, explanation, description, or any combination of these),
- Discussion of shared qualities,
- Discussion of unique qualities,
- A clear reason for making the comparison.

Virginia Woolf's primary rhetorical strategy in "Shakespeare's Sister" is to invent a comparison between William Shakespeare and a fictional sister that he never had. Woolf's point is that if indeed Shakespeare had had a sister who was as brilliant and gifted as he was, she could not have become famous like her brother. The Elizabethan environment would have expected her to remain uneducated and to serve merely as a wife and mother. In the sixteenth century, men like William Shakespeare could go to London and make their fortune. Women, in comparison, were prisoners of social attitudes regarding their sex. As Woolf tells us,

He was, it is well known, a wild boy who poached rabbits, perhaps shot a deer, and had, rather sooner than he should have done, to marry a woman in the neighborhood, who bore him a child rather quicker than was right. That escapade sent him to seek his fortune in London. He had, it seemed, a taste for the theatre; he began by holding horses at the stage door. Very soon he got work in the theatre, became a successful actor, and lived at the hub of the universe, meeting everybody, knowing everybody, practicing his art on the boards, exercising his wits in the streets, and even getting access to the palace of the queen. Meanwhile his extraordinarily gifted sister, let us suppose, remained at home. She was as adventurous, as imaginative, as agog to see the world as he was. But she was not sent to school. She had no chance of learning grammar and logic, let alone of reading Horace and Virgil. She picked up a book now and then, one of her brother's perhaps, and read a few pages. But then her parents came in and told her to mend the stockings or mind the stew and not moon about with books and papers. (para. 7)

Woolf's comparison makes it clear that the social circumstances of the life of a woman in Shakespeare's time worked so much against her personal desires and ambitions that it would be all but impossible for her to achieve anything of distinction on the London stage — or in any other venue in which men dominated. Even though a woman was monarch in England, it was a man's world.

Development by Example.   Examples make abstract ideas concrete. When Machiavelli talks about looking at history to learn political lessons, he cites specific cases and brings them to the attention of his audience, the prince. Thomas Jefferson in the Declaration of Independence devotes most of his text to examples of the unacceptable behavior of the English king toward the colonies. Elizabeth Cady Stanton follows his lead and does the same, beginning her list of examples of gender discrimination with the assertion that "The history of mankind is a history of repeated injuries and usurpations on the part of man toward woman, having in direct object the establishment of an absolute tyranny over her. To prove this, let facts be submitted to a candid world" (para. 3). Then she lists the facts just as did Jefferson. Every selection in this book offers examples either to convince us of the truth of a proposition or to deepen our understanding of a statement.

Examples need to be chosen carefully because the burden of proof and of explanation and clarity often depends on them. When the sample suggestion given earlier for writing on Machiavelli's essay asks who among modern world leaders Machiavelli would approve, it is asking for carefully chosen examples. When doing research for an essay, it is important to be sure that your example or examples really suit your purposes.

Examples can be used in several ways. One is to do as Charles Darwin does and present a large number of examples that force readers to a given conclusion. This indirect method is sometimes time-consuming, but the weight of numerous examples can be effective. A second method, such as Machiavelli's, also can be effective.

By making a statement that is controversial or questionable and that can be tested by example, you can lead your audience to draw a reasonable conclusion.

When using examples, keep these points in mind:

- Choose a few strong examples that support your point.
- Be concrete and specific—naming names, citing events, and giving details where necessary.
- Develop each example as fully as possible, and point out its relevance to your position.

In some selections, such as Darwin's discussion of natural selection, the argument hinges entirely on examples, and Darwin cites one example after another. Stephen Jay Gould shows how a particular example, that of the parasitical ichneumon fly, causes certain philosophical difficulties for theologians studying biology and therefore for anyone who looks closely at nature. The ichneumon, which people find ugly, attacks caterpillars, which people find sympathetic. As Gould tells us, we tend to dislike the parasite and sympathize with its victim. But there is another side to this, a second theme:

> The second theme, ruthless efficiency of the parasites, leads to the opposite conclusion—grudging admiration for the victors. We learn of their skill in capturing dangerous hosts often many times larger than themselves. Caterpillars may be easy game, but the psammocharid wasps prefer spiders. They must insert their ovipositors in a safe and precise spot. Some leave a paralyzed spider in its own burrow. *Planiceps hirsutus*, for example, parasitizes a California trapdoor spider. It searches for spider tubes on sand dunes, then digs into nearby sand to disturb the spider's home and drive it out. When the spider emerges, the wasp attacks, paralyzes its victim, drags it back into its own tube, shuts and fastens the trapdoor, and deposits a single egg upon the spider's abdomen. Other psammocharids will drag a heavy spider back to a previously prepared cluster of clay or mud cells. Some amputate a spider's legs to make the passage easier. Others fly back over water, skimming a buoyant spider along the surface. (para. 13)

Gould's example demonstrates that there are two ways of thinking about the effectiveness of the parasitic psammocharid. The wasp does not always make its life easier by attacking defenseless prey; instead, it goes after big game spiders. Gould's description technique, emphasizing the wasp's risk of danger, forces readers to respect the daring and ingenuity of the parasite even if at first we would not think to do so.

Development by Analysis of Cause and Effect. People are interested in causes. We often ask what causes something, as if understanding the cause will somehow help us accept the result. Yet cause and effect can be subtle. With definition, comparison, and example, we can feel that the connections between a specific topic and our main points are reasonable. With cause and effect, however, we need to reason out the cause. Be warned that development by analysis of cause and effect requires you to pay close attention to the terms and situations you write about. Because it is easy to be wrong about causes and effects, their relationship must be examined thoughtfully. After an event has occurred, only a hypothesis about its cause may be possible. In the same sense, if no effect has been observed, only speculation about outcomes with various plans of action may be possible. In both cases, reasoning and imagination must be employed to establish a relationship between cause and effect.

The power of the rhetorical method of development through cause and effect is such that you will find it in every section of this book, in the work of virtually every author. Keep in mind these suggestions for using it to develop your own thinking:

- Clearly establish in your own mind the cause and the effect you wish to discuss.

- Develop a good line of reasoning that demonstrates the relationship between the cause and the effect.

- Be sure that the cause-effect relationship is real and not merely apparent.

In studying nature, scientists often examine effects in an effort to discover causes. Darwin, for instance, sees the comparable structure of the skeletons of many animals of different species and makes every effort to find the cause of such similarity. His answer is a theory: evolution. Another theorist, Michio Kaku, informs us that 90 percent of the universe is composed of dark matter: "Dark matter is a strange substance, unlike anything ever encountered before. It has weight but cannot be seen. In theory, if someone held a clump of dark matter in their hand, it would appear totally invisible. The existence of dark matter is not an academic question, because the ultimate fate of the universe, whether it will die in a fiery Big Crunch or fade away in a Cosmic Whimper of Big Chill, depends on its precise nature" (para. 6). Having said that, he goes on to explain the cause and effect equation:

> However, Ostriker and Peebles showed that the standard picture of a galaxy, based on our solar system, was unstable; by rights, the galaxy should fly apart. The gravitational pull of the stars was not enough to hold the galaxy together. They then showed that a galaxy can become stable if it is surrounded by a massive invisible halo that holds the galaxy together and if 90 percent of its mass was actually in the halo in the form of dark matter. (para. 18)

In this case, Kaku reveals that on the basis of the observed effect — that the universe does not fall apart even though it seems that it should — a theory must be constructed to explain the cause of its remaining held together. That theory produces the very puzzling concept of dark matter.

Everywhere in this collection authors rely on cause and effect to develop their thoughts. Thomas Jefferson establishes the relationship between abuses by the British and America's need to sever its colonial ties. Karl Marx establishes the capitalist economic system as the cause of the oppression of the workers who produce the wealth enjoyed by the rich. John Kenneth Galbraith is concerned with the causes of poverty, which he feels is an anomaly in modern society. Henry David Thoreau establishes the causes that demand civil disobedience as an effect. Bell hooks believes traditional Western values support the subordination of women and other forms of oppression.

Development by Analysis of Circumstances.   Everything we discuss exists as certain circumstances. Traditionally, the discussion of circumstances has had two parts. The first examines what is possible or impossible in a given situation. Whenever you try to convince your audience to take a specific course of action, it is helpful to show that given the circumstances, no other action is possible. If you disagree with a course of action that people may intend to follow because none other seems possible, however, you may have to demonstrate that another is indeed possible.

The second part of this method of development analyzes what has been done in the past: if something was done in the past, then it may be possible to do it again in the future. A historical survey of a situation often examines circumstances.

When using the method of analysis of circumstances to develop an idea, keep in mind the following tips:

- Clarify the question of possibility and impossibility.

- Review past circumstances so that future ones can be determined.

- Suggest a course of action based on an analysis of possibility and past circumstances.

- Establish the present circumstances, listing them if necessary. Be detailed, and concentrate on facts.

Martin Luther King Jr. examines the circumstances that led to his imprisonment and the writing of "Letter from Birmingham Jail." He explains that "racial injustice engulfs this community," and he reviews the "hard brutal facts of the case." His course of action is clearly stated and reviewed. He explains why some demonstrations were postponed and why his organization and others have been moderate in demands and actions. But he also examines the possibility of using nonviolent action to help change the inequitable social circumstances that existed in Birmingham. His examination of past action goes back to the Bible and the actions of the Apostle Paul. His examination of contemporary action is based on the facts of the situation, which he carefully enumerates. He concludes his letter by inviting the religious leaders to whom he addresses himself to join him in a righteous movement for social change.

Machiavelli is also interested in the question of possibility, because he is trying to encourage his ideal prince to follow a prescribed pattern of behavior. As he constantly reminds us, if the prince does not do so, it is possible that he will be deposed or killed. Taken as a whole, "The Qualities of the Prince" is a recitation of the circumstances that are necessary for success in politics. Machiavelli establishes this in a single paragraph:

> Therefore, it is not necessary for a prince to have all of the above-mentioned qualities, but it is very necessary for him to appear to have them. Furthermore, I shall be so bold as to assert this: that having them and practicing them at all times is harmful; and appearing to have them is useful; for instance, to seem merciful, faithful, humane, forthright, religious, and to be so; but his mind should be disposed in such a way that should it become necessary not to be so, he will be able and know how to change to the contrary. And it is essential to understand this: that a prince, and especially a new prince, cannot observe all those things by which men are considered good, for in order to maintain the state he is often obliged to act against his promise, against charity, against humanity, and against religion. And therefore, it is necessary that he have a mind ready to turn itself according to the way the winds of Fortune and the changeability of affairs require him; and, as I said above, as long as it is possible, he should not stray from the good, but he should know how to enter into evil when necessity commands. (para. 23)

This is the essential Machiavelli, the Machiavelli who is often thought of as a cynic. He advises his prince to be virtuous but says that it is not always possible to be so. Therefore, the prince must learn how not to be good when "necessity commands." The circumstances, he tells us, always determine whether it is possible to be virtuous. A charitable reading of this passage must conclude that his advice is at best amoral.

Many of the essays in this collection rely on an analysis of circumstances. Frederick Douglass examines the circumstances of slavery and freedom. When Karl Marx reviews the changes in economic history in *The Communist Manifesto*, he examines the circumstances under which labor functions:

> The feudal system of industry, under which industrial production was monopolized by closed guilds, now no longer sufficed for the growing wants of the new market. The manufacturing system took its place. The guild-masters were pushed on one side by the manufacturing middle-class: division of labor between the different corporate guilds vanished in the face of division of labor in each single workshop. (para. 14)

Robert B. Reich examines the circumstances of our contemporary economy. He determines, among other things, that the wages of in-person servers—bank tellers, retail salespeople, restaurant employees, and others—will continue to be low despite the great demand for such workers. Not only are these workers easily replaced, but automation has led to the elimination of jobs—including bank teller jobs made redundant by automatic tellers and by banking with personal computers and routine factory jobs replaced by automation. Under current circumstances, these workers will lose out to the "symbolic analysts" who know how to make their specialized knowledge work for them and who cannot be easily replaced.

Development by Analysis of Quotations. Not all the essays in this collection rely on quotations from other writers, but many do. "Letter from Birmingham Jail," for example, relies on quotations from the Bible. In that piece, Martin Luther King Jr. implies his analysis of the quotations because the religious leaders to whom he writes know the quotations well. By invoking the quotations, King gently chides the clergy, who ought to be aware of their relevance. In a variant on using quotations, Robert B. Reich relies on information taken from various government reports. He includes the information in his text and supplies numerous footnotes indicating the sources, which are usually authoritative and convincing.

When you use quotations, remember these pointers:

- Quote accurately, and avoid distorting the original context.
- Unless the quotation is absolutely self-evident, offer your own clarifying comments.
- To help your audience understand why you have chosen a specific quotation, establish its function in your essay.

The feminist bell hooks, in "The Significance of Feminist Movement," relies on several important quotations to bolster her argument. She quotes John Hodge to establish that the family is the place where children "first learn the meaning and practice of hierarchical, authoritarian rule" (para. 7). This is a central issue in her discussion, and she quotes Hodge liberally. She says of his book *The Cultural Basis of Racism and Group Oppression* that "the philosopher John Hodge argues that Western religious and philosophical thought are the ideological basis of all forms of oppression in the United States" (para. 5). Hodge, an established philosopher, becomes both a starting point for her discussion and a voice that both anticipates and verifies her own principles of argument. If you trust Hodge's authority, then you will trust hooks. Later, she quotes Paolo Freire, an innovative voice in education, showing that even he is unconsciously sexist in his writing, emphasizing the education of "the man" (para. 14) rather than the man *and* the woman. In other words, hooks demonstrates that the problem is almost universal. Hooks is an English professor; her method of textual analysis is accepted practice among scholars and helps her convince the reader of her argument.

In his examination of our tendency to anthropomorphize nature, Stephen Jay Gould uses quotations to show that there is a considerable literature on his subject. He quotes from J. H. Fabre, a French entomologist, to show how Fabre "humanized" caterpillars and demonstrated sympathy for the paralyzed victims of the parasitic wasps that fed off them. On the other hand, Gould points out that an equally interesting group of thinkers was impressed by the wasps' capacity to provide for their offspring. To support the viewpoint that admires the wasp, Gould quotes extensively from the writing of the Reverend William Kirby and other scientists, including Darwin (see paras.19–29). Although Gould interprets these paragraphs, they speak clearly for themselves and fit into his argument perfectly. He ends his essay with a quotation from Darwin about the relation of religion and evolution: "I feel most deeply that the whole subject is too profound for the human intellect. A dog might as well speculate on the mind of Newton. Let each man hope and believe what he can."

In your own writing you will find plenty of opportunity to cite passages from an author whose ideas have engaged your attention. In writing an essay in response to Machiavelli, Carl Jung, Carol Gilligan, or any other author in the book, you may find yourself quoting and commenting in some detail on specific lines or passages. This is especially true if you find yourself disagreeing with a point. Your first job, then, is to establish what you disagree with—and usually it helps to quote, which is essentially a way of producing evidence.

Finally, it must be noted that only a few aspects of the rhetorical methods used by the authors in this book have been discussed here. Rhetoric is a complex art that needs fuller study. But the points raised here are important because they are illustrated in many of the texts you will read, and by watching them at work you can begin to learn to use them yourself. By using them you will be able to achieve in your writing the fullness and purposiveness that mark mature prose.

A SAMPLE ESSAY

The following sample essay is based on the first several paragraphs of Machiavelli's "The Qualities of the Prince" that were annotated in "Evaluating Ideas: An Introduction to Critical Reading" (pp. 5–8). The essay is based on the annotations and the questions that were developed from them:

- Should a leader be armed?
- Is it true that an unarmed leader is despised?
- Will those leaders who are always good come to ruin among those who are not good?
- To remain in power, must a leader learn how not to be good?

Not all these questions are addressed in the essay, but they serve as a starting point and a focus for writing. The methods of development that are discussed above form the primary rhetorical techniques of the essay, and each method that is used is labeled in the margin. The sample essay does two things simultaneously: it attempts to clarify the meaning of Machiavelli's advice, and then it attempts to apply that advice to a contemporary circumstance. Naturally, the essay could have chosen to discuss only the Renaissance situation that Machiavelli described, but to do so would have required specialized knowledge of that period. In this sample essay the questions prompted by the annotations serve as the basis of the discussion.

The Qualities of the President

Introduction　　Machiavelli's essay, "The Qualities of the Prince," has a number of very worrisome points. The ones that worry me most have to do with the question of whether it is reasonable to expect a leader to behave virtuously. I think this is connected to the question of whether the leader should be armed. Machiavelli emphasizes that the prince must be armed or else face the possibility that someone will take over the government. When I think about how that advice applies to modern times, particularly in terms of how our president should behave, I find Machiavelli's position very different from my own.

Circumstance　　First, I want to discuss the question of being armed. That is where Machiavelli starts, and it is an important concern. In Machiavelli's time, the late fifteenth and early sixteenth centuries, it was common for men to walk in the streets of Florence wearing a rapier for protection. The possibility of robbery or even attack by rival political groups was great in those days. Even if he had a bodyguard, it was still important for a prince to know how to fight and to be able to defend himself. Machiavelli seems to be talking only about self-defense when he recommends that the prince be armed. In our time, sadly, it too is important to think about protecting the president and other leaders.

Examples   In recent years there have been many assassination attempts on world leaders, and our president, John F. Kennedy, was killed in Dallas in 1963. His brother Robert was killed when he was campaigning for the presidency in 1968. Also in 1968 Martin Luther King Jr. was killed in Memphis because of his beliefs in racial equality. In the 1980s Pope John Paul II was shot by a would-be assassin, as was President Ronald Reagan. They both lived, but Indira Gandhi, the leader of India, was shot and killed in 1984. This is a frightening record. Probably even Machiavelli would have been appalled. But would his solution--being armed--have helped? I do not think so.

Cause/Effect   For one thing, I cannot believe that if the pope had a gun he would have shot his would-be assassin, Ali Acga. The thought of it is almost silly. Martin Luther King Jr., who constantly preached the value of nonviolence, logically could not have shot at an assailant. How could John F. Kennedy have returned fire at a sniper? Robert Kennedy had bodyguards, and both President Reagan and Indira Gandhi were protected by armed guards. The presence of arms obviously does not produce the desired effect: security. The only thing that can produce that is to reduce the visibility of a leader. The president could speak on television or, when he must appear in public, use a bulletproof screen. The opportunities for would-be assassins can be reduced. But the thought of an American president carrying arms is unacceptable.

Comparison   The question of whether a president should be armed is to some extent symbolic. Our president stands for America, and if he were to appear in press conferences or state meetings wearing a gun, he would give a symbolic message to the world: look out, we're dangerous. Cuba's Fidel Castro usually appears in a military uniform with a gun, and when he spoke at the United Nations in 1960, he was the first, and I think the only, world leader to wear a pistol there. I have seen pictures of Benito Mussolini and Adolf Hitler appearing in public in military uniform, but never in a business suit. The same is true of Libyan leader Muammar al-Qaddafi and Iraq's Saddam Hussein. Today when a president or a head of state is armed there is often reason to worry. The current leaders of Russia usually wear suits, but Joseph Stalin always wore a military uniform. His rule in the Soviet Union was marked by the extermination of whole groups of people and the imprisonment of many more. We do not want an armed president.

Use of quotations   Yet Machiavelli plainly says, "among the other bad effects it causes, being disarmed makes you despised . . . for between an armed and an unarmed *also* man there is no comparison whatsoever" (para. 2). The problem with this statement is that it is more *Comparison* relevant to the sixteenth century than the twentieth. In our time the threat of assassination is so great that being armed would be no sure protection, as we have seen in the case of the assassination of President Sadat of Egypt, winner of the Nobel Peace Prize. On the other hand, the pope, like Martin Luther King Jr., would never have

appeared with a weapon, and yet it can hardly be
said they were despised. If anything, the world's
respect for them is enormous. America's president
also commands the world's respect, as does the prime
minister of Great Britain. Yet neither would ever
think of being armed. If what Machiavelli said was
true in the early 1500s, it is pretty clear that it
is not true today.

Definition   All this basically translates into a question of
whether a leader should be virtuous. I suppose the
definition of <u>virtuous</u> would differ with different
people, but I think of it as holding a moral
philosophy that you try to live by. No one is ever
completely virtuous, but I think a president ought
to try to be so. That means the president ought to
tell the truth, since that is one of the basic
virtues. The cardinal virtues--which were the same
in Machiavelli's time as in ours--are justice,
prudence, fortitude, and temperance. In a president,
the virtue of justice is absolutely a must, or else
what America stands for is lost. We definitely want
our president to be prudent, to use good judgment,
particularly in this nuclear age, when acts of
imprudence could get us blown up. Fortitude, the
ability to stand up for what is right, is a must for
our president. Temperance is also important; we do
not want a drunk for a president, nor do we want
anyone with excessive bad habits.

Conclusion   It seems to me that a president who was armed or
who emphasized arms in the way Machiavelli appears
to mean would be threatening injustice (the way
Stalin did) and implying intemperance, like many
armed world leaders. When I consider this issue, I
cannot think of any vice that our president ought to
possess at any time. Injustice, imprudence,
cowardice, and intemperance are, for me,
unacceptable. Maybe Machiavelli was thinking of
deception and lying as necessary evils, but they are

```
a form of injustice, and no competent president--no
president who was truly virtuous--would need them.
Prudence and fortitude are the two virtues most
essential for diplomacy. The president who has those
virtues will govern well and uphold our basic
values.
```

The range of this essay is controlled and expresses a viewpoint that is focused and coherent. This essay of about one thousand words illustrates each method of development discussed in the text and uses each one to further the argument. The writer disagrees with one of Machiavelli's positions and presents an argument based on personal opinion that is bolstered by example and by analysis of current political conditions as they compare with those of Machiavelli's time. A longer essay could have gone more deeply into issues raised in any single paragraph and could have studied more closely the views of a specific president, such as President Ronald Reagan, who opposed stricter gun control laws even after he was shot.

The range of the selections in this volume is great, constituting a significant introduction to important ideas in many areas. They are especially useful for stimulating our own thoughts and ideas. There is an infinite number of ways to approach a subject, but observing how writers apply rhetorical methods in their work is one way to begin our own development as writers. Careful analysis of each selection can guide our exploration of these writers, who encourage our learning and reward our study.

Acknowledgments

Hannah Arendt, "Total Domination." From *The Origins of Totalitarianism* by Hannah Arendt Copyright © 1973, 1968, 1966, 1958, 1951, 1948 by Hannah Arendt. Copyright renewed 2001, 1996, 1994, 1984 by Lotte Kohler. Copyright renewed 1979 by Mary McCarthy West. Copyright renewed 1976 by Hannah Arendt. Reprinted by permission of Harcourt, Inc.

Aristotle, "The Aim of Man." From *Nicomachean Ethics*, 1st ed., by Ostwald Martini, translator. Copyright © 1962. Reprinted by permission of Pearson Education, Inc., Upper Saddle River, NJ.

Simone de Beauvoir, "Women, Myth and Reality." From *The Second Sex* by Simone de Beauvoir, translated by H. M. Parshley. Copyright © 1952 and renewed 1980 by Alfred Knopf, a division of Random House, Inc. Used by permission of Alfred A. Knopf, a division of Random House, Inc.

Rachel Carson, "The Sunless Sea." From *The Sea Around Us* by Rachel Carson. Copyright © 1950, 1951, 1961 by Rachel L. Carson. Renewed 1979 by Roger Christie. Used by permission of Oxford University Press, Inc.

Stephen L. Carter, "The Separation of Church and State." From *The Culture of Disbelief: How American Law and Politics Trivialize Religious Devotion*. Copyright © 1993 by Stephen L. Carter.

Cicero, "The Defense of Injustice." From *On Government* by Cicero, translated by Michael Grant (Penguin Classics, 1993). Copyright © Michael Grant Publications Ltd. 1993. Reprinted with permission from Penguin Group (UK).

Sigmund Freud, "The Oedipus Complex." From *The Standard Edition of the Complete Psychological Works of Sigmund Freud*, Volume IV, pp. 122 ff. Copyright © 1953. A. W. Freud et al. Reprinted by permission of Sigmund Freud Copyrights, Literary & Copyright Agents.

Paulo Freire, "The Banking Concept of Education as an Instrument of Oppression." From *Pedagogy of the Oppressed* by Paulo Freire. Copyright © 1970, 1993 by Paulo Freire. Reprinted with the permission of The Continuum International Publishing Group.

John Kenneth Galbraith, "The Position of Poverty." Excerpt from *The Affluent Society*, 4th ed. Copyright © 1958, 1969, 1976, and 1984 by John Kenneth Galbraith. Reprinted by permission of Houghton Mifflin Company. All rights reserved.

Howard Gardner, "A Rounded Version: The Theory of Multiple Intelligences." From *Multiple Intelligences*. Copyright 1993 by Howard Gardner. Reprinted by permission of Basic Books, a member of Perseus Books, L.L.C.

Carol Gilligan, "Woman's Place in Man's Life Cycle." From *In A Different Voice: Psychological Theory and Women's Development* by Carol Gilligan. Copyright © 1982, 1993 by Carol Gilligan. Reprinted by permission of Harvard University Press.

Stephen Jay Gould, "Nonmoral Nature." From *Natural History*, February 1982, volume 9, #2. Copyright © 1982. Reprinted with the permission of Rhoda Shearer. "The Separation of Church and State."

Bell hooks, "Black Women: Shaping Feminist Theory." From *Feminist Theory From Margin to Center*, 2nd ed., by bell hooks. Copyright © 2000. Reprinted by permission of South End Press.

Carl Jung, "The Personal and the Collective Unconscious." From *Psyche and Symbol* by C. G. Jung. Copyright © 1991 Princeton University Press. Reprinted by permission of Princeton University Press.

Michio Kaku, "The Mystery of Dark Matter." From *Beyond Einstein: The Cosmic Quest for the Theory of the Universe* by Michio Kaku. Copyright © 1987, 1995 by Michio Kaku and Jennifer Trainer Thompson. Reprinted by permission of the Stuart Krichevsky Literary Agency, Inc.

John Maynard Keynes, "Social Consequences of Changes in the Value of Money." From *The Collected Writings of John Maynard Keynes,* vol. IX. Macmillan/St. Martin's Press.

Melanie Klein, "The Psychological Principles of Infant Analysis." From *Selected Melanie Klein,* edited by Juliet Mitchell (Free Press, Free Press). Copyright © Institute of Psychoanalysis, London, UK. Reprinted by Permission of The Free Press, an imprint of Simon & Schuster.

Martin Luther King Jr., "Letter from Birmingham Jail." Copyright 1963 by Martin Luther King Jr., copyright renewed 1991 by Coretta Scott King. Reprinted by arrangement with The Heirs to the Estate of Martin Luther King Jr., c/o Writers House Inc., as agent for the proprietor.

The Koran: N. J. Darwood, "Night Journey." From *The Koran,* translated by N. J. Darwood (Penguin classics 1956, Fifth revised ed. 1990). Copyright © N. J. Darwood 1956, 1959, 1966, 1968, 1974, 1990, 1993, 1997, 1999, 2003. Reprinted by permission of Penguin Books Ltd.

Dalai Lama and Alexander Norman, "The Ethic of Compassion." From *Ethics for the New Millennium* by Dalai Lama and Alexander Norman. Copyright © Tenzin Gyatso, His Holiness The Dalai Lama of Tibet, 1999. Used by permission of Riverhead Books, an imprint of Penguin Group (USA) Inc. and Gillon Aitken Associates.

Lao-tzu, from the *Tao-te Ching.* Excerpts as submitted from *Tao Te Ching* by Lao-tzu, A New English Version, with Foreword and Notes by Stephen Mitchell. Translation copyright © 1988 by Stephen Mitchell Reprinted by permission of HarperCollins Publishers, Inc.

Niccolò Machiavelli, excerpts from "The Prince," by Niccolò di Bernardo Machiavelli, Translated by Mark Musa and Peter Bondanella, from *The Portable Machiavelli,* edited by Peter Bondanella and Mark Musa, translated by Mark Musa and Peter Bondanella. Copyright © 1979 by Viking Penguin, Inc. Used by permission of Viking Penguin, and a division of Penguin Group (USA) Inc.

Michel de Montaigne, "Of the Education of Children." From *The Complete Works,* translated by Donald M. Franc. Copyright © 2003. Reprinted by permission of Everyman's Library.

Iris Murdoch, "Morality and Religion." From *Metaphysics as a Guide to Morals* by Iris Murdoch. Copyright © 1992 by Iris Murdoch. Published by Chatto & Windus. Used by permission of Penguin, a division of Penguin Group (USA) Inc. and The Random House Group Limited.

Friedrich Nietzsche, "Morality as Anti-Nature." From *The Portable Nietzsche* by Friedrich Nietzsche, edited by Walter Kaufmann, translated by Walter Kaufmann. Copyright © 1954 by The Viking Press, renewed © 1982 by Viking Penguin, Inc. Used by permission of Viking Penguin, a division of Penguin Group (USA) Inc.

Martha Nussbaum, "The Central Human Capabilities." From *Sex and Social Justice* by Martha Nussbaum. Copyright © 1999 by Martha Nussbaum. Used by permission of Oxford University Press, Inc.

John Rawls, "A Sense of Justice." From *A Theory of Justice* by John Rawls, pp. 362–367, Cambridge, Mass: The Belknap Press of Harvard University Press. Copyright © 1971, 1999 by the President and Fellows of Harvard College. Reprinted by permission of the publisher.

Robert Reich, "Why the Rich Are Getting Richer and the Poor, Poorer." From *The Work of Nations* by Robert Reich. Copyright © 1991 by Robert B. Reich. Reprinted by permission of Alfred A. Knopf, a division of Random House, Inc.

Jean-Jacques Rousseau, "The Origin of Civil Society." Translated by Gerard Hopkins, from *Social Contract: Essays by Locke, Hume and Rousseau* edited by Ernest Barker. Copyright © 1947. Reprinted with permission of Oxford University Press.

The Torah: "Moses and the Ten Commandments." From Exodus 19–23 in *New English Bible.* Copyright © Oxford University Press and Cambridge University Press 1961, 1970. Reprinted with permission of the publishers.

Virginia Woolf, "Shakespeare's Sister." From *A Room of One's Own* by Virginia Woolf. Copyright © 1929 by Harcourt, Inc. and renewed 1957 by Leonard Woolf. Reprinted by permission of the publisher.

INDEX OF
RHETORICAL TERMS

Where can you find more help?
At **bedfordstmartins.com**

We have a variety of online resources designed to help you with your most common writing concerns. At **bedfordstmartins.com**, you'll find advice from experts, models you can rely on, and exercises that will tell you right away how you're doing. And it's all free and available any hour of the day.

Need help with tricky grammar problems?
Exercise Central
bedfordstmartins.com/exercisecentral

Want to see what other papers for your course look like?
Model Documents Gallery
bedfordstmartins.com/modeldocs

Stuck somewhere in the research process? (Maybe at the beginning?)
The Bedford Research Room
bedfordstmartins.com/researchroom

Wondering whether a Web site is good enough to use in your paper?
Tutorial for Evaluating Online Sources
bedfordstmartins.com/onlinesourcestutorial

Having trouble figuring out how to cite a source?
Research and Documentation Online
bedfordstmartins.com/resdoc

Confused about plagiarism?
The St. Martin's Tutorial on Avoiding Plagiarism
bedfordstmartins.com/plagiarismtutorial

Want to learn more features of your word processor?
Using Your Word Processor
bedfordstmartins.com/wordprocessor

Trying to improve the look of your paper?
Using Your Word Processor to Design Documents
bedfordstmartins.com/docdesigntutorial

Need to create slides for a presentation?
Preparing Presentation Slides Tutorial
bedfordstmartins.com/presentationslidetutorial

Interested in creating a Web site?
Web Design Tutorial
bedfordstmartins.com/webdesigntutorial